The Mixed Methods Reader

This Reader is dedicated to the scholars advancing and participating in the growing mixed methods research community.

Vicki L. Plano Clark

John W. Creswell

Lincoln, Nebraska

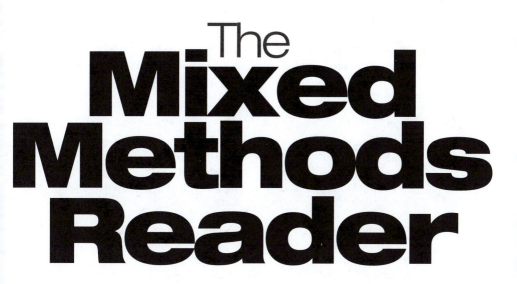

The Mixed Methods Reader

Vicki L. Plano Clark ■ John W. Creswell

University of Nebraska–Lincoln

SAGE Publications

Los Angeles • London • New Delhi • Singapore

For information:

Sage Publications, Inc.
2455 Teller Road
Thousand Oaks,
    California 91320
E-mail: order@sagepub.com

Sage Publications India Pvt. Ltd.
B 1/I 1 Mohan Cooperative
    Industrial Area
Mathura Road, New Delhi 110 044
India

Sage Publications Ltd.
1 Oliver's Yard
55 City Road
London EC1Y 1SP
United Kingdom

Sage Publications Asia-Pacific Pte. Ltd.
33 Pekin Street #02-01
Far East Square
Singapore 048763

Printed in the United States of America

Library of Congress Cataloging-in-Publication Data

The mixed methods reader/Vicki L. Plano Clark, John W. Creswell, editors.
    p. cm.
Includes bibliographical references and index.
ISBN 978-1-4129-5144-9 (cloth)
ISBN 978-1-4129-5145-6 (pbk.)
    1. Social sciences—Research—Methodology. I. Plano Clark, Vicki L.
II. Creswell, John W.

H62.M534 2008
300.72—dc22   2007023770

This book is printed on acid-free paper.

07   08   09   10   11   10 9 8 7 6 5 4 3 2 1

Acquisitions Editor:	Vicki Knight
Associate Editor:	Sean Connelly
Editorial Assistant:	Lauren Habib
Project Editor:	Astrid Virding
Copy Editor:	Pam Suwinsky
Typesetter:	C&M Digitals (P) Ltd.
Proofreader:	Joyce Li
Indexer:	Jean Casalegno
Cover Designer:	Candice Harman
Marketing Manager:	Stephanie Adams

Other Titles by the Editors

Designing and Conducting Mixed Methods Research
John W. Creswell and Vicki L. Plano Clark, ©2007

This text combines the latest thinking about mixed methods research designs with practical, step-by-step guidelines for the decisions that must be made in designing a mixed methods research study.

The Mixed Methods Reader and Designing and Conducting Mixed Methods Research (Bundle)
John W. Creswell and Vicki L. Plano Clark, ©2008

The perfect combination—a textbook and a reader on mixed methods by John W. Creswell and Vicki Plano L. Clark—is available as a bundle.

Qualitative Inquiry and Research Design: Choosing Among Five Approaches, Second Edition
John W. Creswell, ©2007

Creswell's bestselling text explores the philosophical underpinnings, history, and key elements of each of five qualitative inquiry approaches: narrative research, phenomenology, grounded theory, ethnography, and case study.

Research Design: Qualitative, Quantitative, and Mixed Methods Approaches, Second Edition (Look for the Third Edition in 2008)
John W. Creswell, ©2003

The bestselling **Research Design** offers a unique comparison of three key approaches to inquiry. This book is ideal for readers who seek assistance in designing a full research study or planning a proposal for a scholarly journal article, dissertation or thesis.

The Journal of Mixed Methods Research
Edited by John W. Creswell and Abbas Tashakkori
Managing Editor: Vicki L. Plano Clark

The *Journal of Mixed Methods Research* (*JMMR*) is an innovative, quarterly, international publication that focuses on empirical, methodological, and theoretical articles about mixed methods research across the social, behavioral, health, and human sciences.

For more information on these and other SAGE products visit www .sagepub.com.

Contents

List of Editors' Introduction Figures

Introduction

The field of mixed methods research has been established through the writings and practice of methodologists and researchers across research communities. As of January 2007, indicators of the growth of mixed methods research include the publication of a handbook (*Handbook of Mixed Methods in Social and Behavioral Research*; Tashakkori & Teddlie, 2003a); numerous textbooks (for example, Brewer & Hunter, 2005; Creswell & Plano Clark, 2007; Tashakkori & Teddlie, 1998); and a journal dedicated to its use (*Journal of Mixed Methods Research*). In addition, there have been countless journal articles discussing and applying mixed methods, along with Special Issues in diverse fields focusing on this approach, such as those from the *Annals of Family Medicine* (Stange, 2004), the *Journal of Research in Nursing* (Bishop, 2006), and *Research in the Schools* (Johnson, 2006). Mixed methods research has also been highlighted at recent professional conferences, such as sessions held by the Mixed Methods Research Special Interest Group (SIG) of the American Educational Research Association and the annual international Mixed Methods Conference held in Cambridge, England.

The multidisciplinary and international nature of the field of mixed methods research is an indication of its broad appeal. However, its multidisciplinary and international nature also presents a great challenge to researchers interested in learning more about mixed methods research. While more methodological books addressing mixed methods are becoming available, the important writings of this field are scattered across diverse disciplines (for example, evaluation, nursing, education, sociology) and reported in a wide range of publication outlets. Likewise, examples of high-quality mixed methods studies have appeared in journals spanning diverse disciplines and representing many different countries. While these resources are all currently available, they can be difficult to locate due to the lack of a common terminology (the term "mixed methods" has only been used widely since the publication of *The Handbook of Mixed Methods in Social and Behavioral Research*; Tashakkori & Teddlie, 2003a) and the need to examine diverse resources spread across many disciplines. Unfortunately, the scattered nature of the writings also detracts from viewing mixed methods as a field of inquiry with integrated writings and discussions. Researchers interested in developing a strong foundation in mixed methods research need to be aware of this larger literature base and need access to both foundational writings and exemplary published research studies.

Purpose of the *Reader*

In light of the dispersed nature of the mixed methods literature, the purpose of *The Mixed Methods Reader* is to organize and present a collection of key methodological mixed methods discussions and exemplar mixed methods research studies in one easy-to-access location. This integrative collection draws from the literature appearing across diverse research disciplines during the past thirty years. The very definition of mixed methods research has evolved during these years, and even today scholars vary as to what counts as mixed methods (Johnson, Onwuegbuzie, & Turner, 2007). Tashakkori and Creswell (2007) recently defined *mixed methods* as "research in which the investigator collects and analyzes data, integrates the findings, and draws inferences using both qualitative and quantitative approaches or methods in a single study or a program of inquiry" (p. 4). As such, we see mixed methods as a research design that incorporates both methodology and methods (Creswell & Plano Clark, 2007); aspects of both perspectives (that is, philosophical assumptions and implementation issues) are addressed in this volume.

The methodological selections discuss important questions associated with this approach to research. What are its philosophical foundations? What designs are available? How can mixed methods research be implemented and reported? What criticisms have been advanced? As such, these readings provide scholars with frameworks for discussing and designing mixed methods research. The selected exemplar research studies serve as applications of the methodological issues and provide scholars with models for conducting and reporting mixed methods research. Together, these readings present readers with a multidisciplinary look at the evolving field of mixed methods research.

Audience

The Mixed Methods Reader is intended primarily for graduate students, researchers, and methodologists interested in learning about different perspectives about and applications of mixed methods research. The readings have been selected and organized following the standard organization of methodological topics within the process of research. Therefore, the *Reader* can stand alone as an introduction to the methodology and application of mixed methods research or it can also be used in graduate courses to complement a standard mixed methods textbook. Using the *Reader* in tandem with another textbook provides the reader with both a consistent discussion of mixed methods research from a single perspective along with an introduction to other authors' ideas and viewpoints. The individual experienced with mixed methods as well as those new to the topic will find this compilation of readings useful to cite, to clarify understandings of topics, and to summarize the emerging body of literature.

Organization

The Mixed Methods Reader is divided into two parts: Part I: Methodological Selections and Part II: Exemplar Research Studies. Part I includes a collection of 14 foundational writings from the mixed methods research literature. These readings convey the overall development and evolution of mixed methods research and address essential topics for researchers new to the field of mixed methods research. These topics include its foundations; design types; implementation issues such as sampling, data analysis, and validity; rhetorical devices for reporting mixed methods studies; and critiques about the current thinking in the field.

We provide brief introductions at the beginnings of the methodological chapters in Part I. In each introduction, we note the general topic or problem addressed by the selection, and we include statements that point the reader toward the significant contributions that the selection makes to the mixed methods literature. These statements represent our own assessments and should not limit readers from drawing other significant points from their own reading of the selections. We also pose three discussion questions to accompany each chapter. These questions encourage the reader to apply, critique, and extend the selection's content. It is impossible to capture all important mixed methods writings or essential ideas related to mixed methods in a collection of 14 chapters. Therefore, each chapter introduction ends with references to additional readings that further extend the chapter's topic. In addition, readers should consider the references listed within the chapters to develop a comprehensive mixed methods reading list. In this way, readers are introduced to key methodological issues in Part I but can also develop a broader appreciation and awareness of the larger mixed methods literature.

Part II includes nine exemplar mixed methods research studies drawn from a range of disciplines and international scholars. The studies were intentionally selected to illustrate four major types of mixed methods designs found in the literature (Creswell & Plano Clark, 2007). As with the methodological chapters, we organize the exemplar research studies so that the reader can see a natural progression of the different approaches to conducting mixed methods research. Each chapter in Part II also includes an introduction that briefly summarizes the article and highlights our assessment of the significant features of the selected study. We also provide a visual diagram of the flow of activities for each of the research studies. These diagrams serve as overviews to help the readers understand how the studies were implemented and they are also examples of how readers may visually convey their own research studies.

The 23 selections are reproduced in the *Reader* as they originally appeared in print. Each selection's content and author information, therefore, represents information that was current at the time of first publication and may no longer be up to date.

Acknowledgments

We are indebted to many who played a role in the completion of this project. First and foremost we thank the authors of the selections, who have engaged us with their scholarly works. Without their insights, writings, and passion for this evolving field, there would not be a mixed methods literature base from which to assemble *The Mixed Methods Reader*. We also are grateful to our colleagues who help shape our work through our interactions and conversations, including Abbas Tashakkori and Nataliya V. Ivankova. We have also received much support from individuals in the Office of Qualitative and Mixed Methods Research at the University of Nebraska–Lincoln, including Amanda Garrett, Denise Green, and Ronald Shope. In addition, we thank the scholars who have participated in our mixed methods workshops and courses for sharing their questions and ideas with us.

Finally, we express our sincerest thanks for the assistance and guidance we have received from the personnel at Sage Publications. We thank our acquisitions editors, Lisa Cuevas Shaw and Vicki Knight, for their enthusiasm and support for this project as well as the editorial assistance of Sean Connelly, Karen Greene, and Astrid Virding. We also thank Pam Suwinsky for her careful copyediting and appreciate the thoughtful comments provided by six anonymous reviewers of the *Reader's* concept.

PART I

Methodological Selections

The field of mixed methods research has progressed beyond infancy into adolescence (Tashakkori & Teddlie, 2003a). As with any adolescent, interests have emerged in specific areas, angst has set in about identity, and peer groups (or stakeholder groups) are apparent. Certainly in the early 21st century mixed methods is a significant movement in research methodology in the United States and around the world. Major conferences are devoted to promoting it, several journals advance it, funding agencies support projects with it, and an extensive body of literature found in books, book chapters, and journal articles is advancing the field. In books alone, we have catalogued 12 different works that have emerged since 1988 and are specifically devoted to mixed methods research (Creswell & Tashakkori, 2007).

As editors of this collection of methodological selections, we hope to map the contours of this field of mixed methods research as found in the literature. Moreover, we want to identify key methodological articles that have made a contribution to the development of the field. Unfortunately, we have not had many guides for identifying this literature—authors have simply not turned their attention to this important step both for the novice and experienced researcher and for the advancement of the field. However, we can point to three sources that have been helpful in this quest. Certainly the *Handbook of Mixed Methods in Social and Behavioral Research* (Tashakkori & Teddlie, 2003a) was useful in determining the landscape of this literature. Within the *Handbook* is a chapter by Creswell, Tashakkori, Jensen, and Shapley (2003) that identifies the key topics in mixed methods and provides references to key readings. More recently, Greene (2006) grouped the issues and assumptions

1

of mixed methods social inquiry into four domains: philosophical assumptions and stances, inquiry logics, guidelines for practice, and sociopolitical commitments in science.

These have all been helpful in mapping the literature. To this we added our collective judgment and experiences. We have taught our mixed methods course at our institution for about ten years and we have used articles published in the 1970s to the present. We also identified articles in order to provide the perspectives of many writers. To this end, each selected scholar appears as first author only once. We sought articles that represent key developments in the history of mixed methods as well as the current thinking in the field. To indicate the breadth of the international and disciplinary involvement, we selected authors representing different nationalities and a wide variety of disciplines. The methodological selections include authors from the United States, United Kingdom, and Canada and individuals working in disciplines such as education, evaluation, management and organizational research, nursing, and sociology. We also paid attention to six reviewers' comments about this book and the types of articles that they recommended that we include.

Part I of this book includes a collection of 14 methodological writings spanning the mixed methods literature. They unfold in an order roughly approximating the process of research, beginning with broad philosophical ideas and ending with approaches to writing up the mixed methods report and critical perspectives about the entire process. As we introduce each selection, we highlight the significance of the selection for the development of the mixed methods body of literature. The first three chapters examine issues related to philosophical and theoretical perspectives about mixed methods research. Those engaged in mixed methods research can profit from learning about the history of the evolution of this field by noting how it shifted from the use of monomethods, to an integration of qualitative and quantitative methods, and finally to integrating the two strands throughout the process of research. This is a major insight provided by Tashakkori and Teddlie (1998) in Chapter 1. On a philosophical level, researchers want to know what philosophical foundation provides a rationale for mixed methods research. Morgan (2007) in Chapter 2 calls for pragmatism as the best philosophical foundation. As a counterpoint, Mertens (2003) argues in Chapter 3 for a different philosophical foundation, the use of a transformative-emancipatory perspective. Her link between this broad philosophical perspective and its use in each step of the process of research offers a novel approach to bridge the divide often found between philosophy and practice.

The next group of chapters represents discussions about mixed methods research designs. One helpful way to understand the designs is to learn about the early attempts to identify and discuss designs. Jick (1979), in Chapter 4, was ahead of his time in discussing the first type of design—the triangulation design—and how it might be practiced. Ten years later, Greene, Caracelli, and Graham (1989), in Chapter 5, extended the types of designs by focusing on the purpose for conducting mixed methods research and extensively reviewing published mixed methods studies in the field of evaluation. The types of designs they mentioned position their discussion as a classic in the field that is referred to by authors today. Despite these innovations in design, however, researchers still did not have a convenient way to describe these studies until Morse (1991), in Chapter 6, added a notation system for describing the types of designs. More recently, writers have identified a wide array of possibilities for the types of designs in mixed methods research. A review of the classification systems for types of designs and four criteria for choosing an appropriate design signaled an advance in our design thinking. This is found in Creswell, Plano Clark, Gutmann, and Hanson (2003) in Chapter 7.

A logical extension of the literature after identifying the types of designs is to inquire as to how they might be implemented in practice. Certainly procedures for sampling participants both in the quantitative and qualitative phases of research as well as in ways that will facilitate the implementation of mixed methods designs is important. Teddlie and Yu (2007) in Chapter 8 provide insight into this topic. Also, the topic of how to analyze data within a mixed methods context has not been given much attention. The key article by Caracelli and Greene (1993), in Chapter 9, specifies four data analysis strategies that can be used. One aspect of data analysis is the integration of quantitative and qualitative data. Although Greene, Caracelli, and Graham (1989; Chapter 5 in this volume) had identified five purposes for conducting mixed methods research, the discussion about designs raised new possibilities. Bryman (2006), in Chapter 10, identifies and discusses 16 reasons and thus expands our understanding as to why individuals conduct mixed methods research. Another procedural aspect—validity—cannot be overlooked because it is a centerpiece of inquiry for all researchers. However, the term *validity* is often associated with quantitative research, and we need a term that is "bilingual" and acceptable to both quantitative and qualitative researchers. Onwuegbuzie and Johnson (2006) in Chapter 11 suggest that we use the term *legitimation*, and they discuss multiple ways legitimation might be achieved in mixed methods studies. A final aspect of procedures in this form of inquiry is to address how mixed methods studies are composed and written up. Scant attention has been given to this topic, but Sandelowski (2003) addresses the topic in Chapter 12 and details the forms of writing strategies that help to shape the mixed methods research report.

Part I concludes with two chapters that serve as critiques of the current movement for mixed methods research. One issue that has surfaced is whether the mixed methods movement is dominated by quantitative researchers and, within this dominance, the role of qualitative research has been reduced to a supporting role. Nowhere is this more apparent than in experimental (or intervention) studies that contain a small qualitative component. Moreover, when qualitative research appears, it does not reflect the current trends toward interpretive research of multiple perspectives and a discourse with participants. Howe (2004) in Chapter 13 addresses these important issues in a critique of current mixed methods research. A second issue is whether mixed methods research is feasible given that quantitative and qualitative researchers tend to hold irreconcilable views of reality. The selection by Sale, Lohfeld, and Brazil (2002) in Chapter 14 first says that we cannot conduct mixed methods research because of this disparity in views of reality, and then lifts the ban by advancing a workable alternative.

This collection, therefore, presents our view of the contours of the field of mixed methods research. It also provides an introduction to its literature and provides an examination of its evolving literature and viewpoints.

1

The Evolution of Mixed Methods Research

Selection: Tashakkori, A., & Teddlie, C. (1998). Introduction to mixed method and mixed model studies in the social and behavioral sciences. In *Mixed methodology: Combining qualitative and quantitative approaches* (pp. 3–19). Thousand Oaks, CA: Sage.

Editors' Introduction

Discussions about the philosophical foundations of mixed methods research have permeated the mixed methods literature and represent essential background for mixed methods researchers. The role of philosophical foundations is important for all research (quantitative, qualitative, and mixed methods), but it has been a particularly contentious topic in the development of mixed methods. Therefore, this is a topic with which mixed methods researchers must have adequate familiarity in order to defend their research approach and to build rigorous designs from an understanding of the relevant philosophical foundations.

Abbas Tashakkori and Charles Teddlie, writing from backgrounds in social psychology and education, provide a good historical overview of the philosophical debates associated with mixed methods research as the opening chapter of their 1998 foundational textbook, *Mixed Methodology*. They present the key positions of the "paradigm wars," which argued against the viability of mixing paradigms and therefore, methods, and introduce the stance that pragmatism provides the best foundation for mixed methods. They also review the tenets of logical positivism, postpositivism, constructivism, and pragmatism and define important axioms that can be used to compare these major paradigms. The chapter concludes with a historical overview of the evolution of mixed methods from monomethod studies to studies that mix methods and on to those that mix throughout the different phases of research. This selection provides readers with the historical contexts of mixed methods research and an extensive collection of references representing the different stages of its development.

Discussion Questions and Applications

1. Describe your own personal stance on the six axioms discussed in the chapter. Which paradigm seems to provide the best fit to your beliefs?

2. In what ways could the different paradigms influence the way researchers conduct (or do not conduct) mixed methods research?

3. How prominent are discussions of paradigm within your discipline and what importance do the "debates" hold for those researchers considering mixing methods today?

Related References That Extend the Topic

Additional overview discussions of philosophical foundations for research include:

Creswell, J. W. (2003). *Research design: Qualitative, quantitative, and mixed methods approaches* (2nd ed.). Thousand Oaks, CA: Sage.

Guba, E. G., & Lincoln, Y. S. (2005). Paradigmatic controversies, contradictions, and emerging confluences. In N. K. Denzin & Y. S. Lincoln (Eds.), *The SAGE handbook of qualitative research* (3rd ed., pp. 191–215). Thousand Oaks, CA: Sage.

Introduction to Mixed Method and Mixed Model Studies in the Social and Behavioral Sciences

Abbas Tashakkori
Louisiana State University

Charles Teddlie
Louisiana State University

Paradigm Wars and Mixed Methodologies

Examples of the Wars

During the past three decades, several debates or "wars" (e.g., Datta, 1994; Gage, 1989; Guba & Lincoln, 1994; House, 1994; Rossi, 1994) have raged in the social and behavioral sciences regarding the superiority of one or the other of the two major social science paradigms or models. These two models are known alternately as the *positivist/empiricist* approach or the *constructivist/phenomenological* orientation (e.g., Cherryholmes, 1992; Guba & Lincoln, 1994).

Paradigms may be defined as the worldviews or belief systems that guide researchers (Guba & Lincoln, 1994). The importance currently attributed to

SOURCE: This chapter is reprinted from *Mixed Methodology: Combining Qualitative and Quantitative Approaches* (Tashakkori & Teddlie, 1998). Reprinted with permission of Sage Publications, Inc.

7

paradigms in the social and behavioral sciences derives from Kuhn's (1970) influential book titled *The Structure of Scientific Revolutions*. In this book, he argues that paradigms are the models that are imitated within any given field, and that competing paradigms may exist simultaneously, especially within immature sciences (Kneller, 1984; Kuhn, 1970).

The positivist paradigm underlies what are called *quantitative methods,* while the constructivist paradigm underlies *qualitative methods* (e.g., Guba & Lincoln, 1994; Howe, 1988; Lincoln & Guba, 1985). Therefore, the debate between these two paradigms has sometimes been called the qualitative-quantitative debate (e.g., Reichardt & Rallis, 1994). The abbreviations QUANs (for those preferring the quantitative point of view) and QUALs (for those preferring the qualitative point of view) have been used in describing participants in these debates or "wars" (e.g., Creswell 1994; Morse, 1991).

These *paradigm wars* have been fought across several "battlefields" concerning important conceptual issues, such as the "nature of reality" or the "possibility of causal linkages." No discipline in the social and behavioral sciences has avoided manifestations of these paradigm wars. Datta (1994) called the participants in such wars *wrestlers;* we prefer to use the term *warriors.*

"Warriors" from education include Lincoln and Guba (1985), who have contended that the tenets of positivism and the quantitative methodology that accompanies that paradigm have been discredited. These authors also contend that constructivism and qualitative methods are in ascendance. Smith and Heshusius (1986), also writing in the field of education, suggested "shutting down" the dialogue between the two camps, saying that their incompatibility made further dialogue unproductive. This point of view has been called the *incompatibility thesis.*

Likewise in psychology, the 1970s and 1980s witnessed important methodological debates between scholars such as Cronbach (1982) and Cook and Campbell (1979). These debates focused on the relative importance of internal validity (emphasizing *controlled settings,* which were considered sacrosanct by the positivists) and external validity (emphasizing *natural settings,* which were preferred by the constructivists). Gergen (1973) posed the question, "Is a science of social psychology possible?" challenging the tenets of positivism that underpinned that subarea of psychology, especially the possibility of making time- and context-free generalizations.

Similarly in anthropology, Gardner (1993) criticized Margaret Mead's anthropological work in Samoa for its overreliance on preconceived notions and naive acceptance of the reports of key informants. These responses are typical criticisms of the positivist camp toward the constructivists (or "naturalists").

A final example of these wars comes from the applied area of evaluation research. As noted by Datta (1994), the "dialogues" of three successive presidents of the American Evaluation Association (Fetterman, 1992; Lincoln, 1991; Sechrest, 1991) were very stringent in their defense of their own methodological positions and in their attack on the position of the "other side." Although such debate may have been inevitable, it became increasingly unproductive during the 1980s and early 1990s.

The End of the Paradigm Wars and the Emergence of Mixed Methods

There have been numerous attempts in the social and behavioral sciences to make peace between the two major paradigmatic positions. "Pacifists" have appeared who state that qualitative and quantitative methods are, indeed, compatible. In education and evaluation research (e.g., Howe, 1988; Reichardt & Rallis, 1994), authors have presented the compatibility thesis based on a different paradigm, which some have called *pragmatism.* Thus we may refer to the pacifists in the paradigm wars as *pragmatists.*

At this time, the paradigm debates have primary relevance within the history of social science philosophy because many active theorists and researchers have adopted the tenets of *paradigm relativism,* or the use of whatever philosophical and/or methodological approach works for the particular research problem under study (e.g., Howe, 1988; Reichardt & Rallis, 1994). Even some of the most noted warriors (i.e., Guba & Lincoln, 1994) have signaled an end to the wars, stating,

> The metaphor of paradigm wars described by Gage (1989) is undoubtedly overdrawn. Describing the discussions and altercations of the past decade or two as wars paints the matter as more confrontational than necessary. A resolution of paradigm differences can occur only when a new paradigm emerges that is more informed and sophisticated than any existing one. That is most likely to occur if and when proponents of these several points of view come together to discuss their differences. (p. 116)

Pragmatically oriented theorists and researchers now refer to "mixed methods" (or mixed methodology or methodological mixes), which contain elements of both the quantitative and qualitative approaches (e.g., Brewer & Hunter, 1989; Patton, 1990). For instance, Greene, Caracelli, and Graham (1989) presented 57 studies that employed mixed methods, and described the design characteristics of these mixed studies. Specific types of mixed methods will be discussed later in this chapter.

The Current State of Affairs

We accept the assumptions implicit within paradigm relativism and assume that the paradigm wars are over, having been superseded by the pragmatist orientation briefly described above. As noted by Brewer and Hunter (1989), most major areas of research in the social and behavioral sciences now use multiple methods as a matter of course: "Since the fifties, the social sciences have grown tremendously. And with that growth, there is now virtually no major problem-area that is studied exclusively within one method" (p. 22).

The detente in the paradigm wars has been positive for research development in many fields because most researchers now use whatever method is appropriate for their studies, instead of relying on one method exclusively. Nevertheless, pragmatists have often employed imprecise language in describing their methodologies, using some rather generic terms (e.g., *mixed methods*) to connote several different ways of conducting a study or a series of studies. Datta (1994) recently referred to what she called "mixed-up models" that derived from the "lack of a worldview, paradigm, or theory for mixed-model studies," concluding that "such a theory has yet to be fully articulated" (p. 59).

We don't pretend to present such a formal theory for mixed method and mixed model studies in this brief volume, but we do hope to offer some guidelines for more systematically conceptualizing such studies. Before introducing our taxonomy of mixed method and mixed model studies, however, we briefly describe some of the major issues related to the paradigm wars and their resolution in the next section of this chapter.

More Details Regarding the Paradigm Wars

The following section is intended for readers unfamiliar with the issues that were debated during the paradigm wars and how they were resolved to the satisfaction of much of the social scientific community. This brief historical review of the paradigm wars is not a treatise on the philosophy of science but is a "Cook's tour" through the paradigm wars and their aftermath. Those familiar with these issues may wish to skip this section.

The historical importance of these debates is partially illustrated by their longevity. Hammersley (1992) has noted that debates about quantitative and qualitative research actually have roots in the mid-nineteenth century and occurred in sociology in the 1920s and 1930s. Recent attention to the debate started with a revival of the fortunes of qualitative research methods in the 1960s in sociology and psychology, which had been dominated by quantitative methods (i.e., survey or experiment) throughout the 1940s and 1950s (Hammersley, 1992).

Although there are the two major opposing points of view, it is apparent that several philosophical orientations, or paradigms, have been posited and defended (e.g., Greene, 1994; Guba, 1990; Guba & Lincoln, 1994). We refer to four philosophical orientations: logical positivism, postpositivism, pragmatism, and constructivism (other variants of which are known as interpretivism, naturalism, and so on). We have chosen these orientations because they represent aspects of what we consider to be major stages in the paradigm debates: (a) the debunking of logical positivism after World War II, (b) the pervasiveness of the postpositivist position, (c) the ascendance of constructivism, followed by the paradigm wars, and (d) pragmatism and the compatibility thesis. Each of these stages is briefly described in the next four sections of this chapter.

The Debunking of Logical Positivism After World War II

Positivism (also called logical positivism) has origins dating back to nineteenth-century French philosopher August Comte. Positivism bases knowledge solely on observable facts and rejects speculation about "ultimate origins." Lincoln and Guba (1985) ascribed several "axioms" to positivism:

1. *Ontology* (nature of reality): Positivists believe that there is a single reality.

2. *Epistemology* (the relationship of the knower to the known): Positivists believe that the knower and the known are independent.

3. *Axiology* (role of values in inquiry): Positivists believe that inquiry is value-free.

4. *Generalizations:* Positivists believe that time- and context-free generalizations are possible.

5. *Causal linkages:* Positivists believe that there are real causes that are temporally precedent to or simultaneous with effects.

We will add a sixth distinction noted by many authors (e.g., Goetz & LeCompte, 1984; Patton, 1990):

6. *Deductive logic:* There is an emphasis on arguing from the general to the particular, or an emphasis on a priori hypotheses (or theory).

Logical positivism was discredited as a philosophy of science after World War II (e.g., Howe, 1988; Phillips, 1990; Reichardt & Rallis, 1994). Dissatisfaction with the axioms of positivism (especially with regard to ontology, epistemology, and axiology) became increasingly widespread throughout the social and behavioral sciences during the 1950s and 1960s, giving rise to *postpositivism.* As Guba and Lincoln (1994) have noted, postpositivism is the intellectual heir to positivism and has addressed several of the more widely discredited tenets of positivism.

The Pervasiveness of the Postpositivist Position

Landmark works of postpositivism (e.g., Hanson, 1958; Popper, 1959) appeared in the late 1950s, and they quickly gained widespread credibility throughout the social scientific community. Postpositivism was a reaction to the widely discredited axioms of positivism, and many of its tenets were in direct opposition to those of its predecessor.

While many QUANs continued to follow the tenets of positivism in the 1950s and 1960s, Reichardt and Rallis (1994) convincingly contended that some of the most influential quantitative methodologists of that period (e.g., Campbell & Stanley, 1966) were "unabashedly postpositivist" in their orientation. According to Reichardt and Rallis, these quantitative methodologists were postpositivists because their writings indicated that they agreed with the following tenets of that philosophy:

- *Value-ladenness of inquiry:* Research is influenced by the values of investigators.
- *Theory-ladenness of facts:* Research is influenced by the theory or hypotheses or framework that an investigator uses.
- *Nature of reality:* Our understanding of reality is constructed. (See Chapter 2 [Tashakkori & Teddlie, 1998] for a further discussion of these issues.)

These postpositivist tenets are currently shared by both qualitatively and quantitatively oriented researchers because they better reflect common understandings regarding both the "nature of reality" and the conduct of social and behavioral research in the second half of the twentieth century. Reichardt and Rallis (1994) concluded that postpositivism more accurately characterizes contemporary quantitative inquiry than does logical positivism, noting that there is a quantitatively oriented postpositivist camp that includes some of the best known quantitative researchers of the 1960s and 1970s.

For example, the experimental psychologist Rosenthal (1976) discussed at length what was called the experimenter effect: The way the experimenter looks, feels, or acts may unintentionally affect the results of a study. Cook and Campbell (1979), who were certainly quantitatively oriented, acknowledged experimenter bias as a threat to the validity of studies. This experimenter bias is a good example of a methodological flaw that might result in facts that are value- or theory-laden (basic tenets of postpositivism). Cook and Campbell (1979), in a discussion of causation in the social sciences, stated,

We share the postpositivists' belief that observations are theory-laden and that the construction of sophisticated scientific apparatus and procedures for data presentation often involve the explicit or implicit acceptance of well developed scientific theories, over and beyond the theory being tested. (p. 24)

Similarly, experimental social psychologists (e.g., Jones & Davis, 1966; Jones & Nisbett, 1972) explored and discussed dispositional attributions, which involve actor-observer differences in perception. They speculated on whether or not the testing of personality theory may be heavily influenced by the personal attributions (including values) of the researchers doing the work. Again, this is an example of researchers using traditional experimental methods and quantitative data who were actively exploring and discussing postpositivist tenets, such as the value-ladenness of facts.

Thus quantitative methodologists wrote about and provided empirical evidence for some of the tenets of postpositivism in the 1960–1980 time period. While these methodologists held assumptions associated with postpositivism, it is important to remember that they worked within a tradition that emphasized "methodological correctness" (Smith, 1994). When choices came down between the qualitative or quantitative orientations, these methodologists weighed in on the side of the experimental design, which characterizes traditional positivism. For example, Cook and Campbell (1979), in a spirited response to critics of their validity distinctions, concluded, "We assume that readers believe that causal inference is important and that experimentation is one of the most useful, if not *the* most useful, way of gaining knowledge about cause" (p. 91, italics in the original).

It is clear from a reading of this section of their well-known 1979 book that they prefer experimental (or quasi-experimental) work, value internal validity very highly, and believe that causal inferences are possible under certain heavily prescribed circumstances.

The Ascendance of Constructivism, Followed by the Paradigm Wars

The discrediting of positivism resulted in the increasing popularity of paradigms more "radical" than postpositivism. These paradigms have several names (constructivism, interpretivism, naturalism), with constructivism being the most popular. Theorists associated with these paradigms borrowed from postpositivism but then added dimensions of their own to the models (e.g., Denzin, 1992; Gergen, 1985; Goodman, 1984; Hammersley, 1989; LeCompte & Preissle, 1993; Schwandt, 1994). Some of these theorists were not content to see positivism, postpositivism, and their own philosophical orientation peacefully coexisting, believing that they had to argue for the superiority of their own paradigm to overcome the biases associated with the deeply embedded traditions of positivism and postpositivism. For example, Lincoln and Guba (1985) criticized one well-known quantitative methodologist for his attempts toward reconciliation of these points of view:

> Some scholars insist that postpositivism is nothing more than an overreaction, and that it is time for a rapprochement that realigns positivism with the relativism that characterizes postpositivism. One such writer is Donald T. Campbell, who suggests that it is time to move into a post-postpositivist era, in which positivism and postpositivism are married off and live happily ever after. (p. 32)

Lincoln and Guba then set up a series of contrasts between the positivist and naturalist (their version of constructivism) paradigms that made such a "marriage" between them impossible. Referring back to the five axioms of positivism described above, they posited the following five axioms of the naturalist paradigm.

1. *Ontology* (nature of reality): Naturalists believe that there are multiple, constructed realities.

2. *Epistemology* (the relationship of the knower to the known): Naturalists believe that the knower and the known are inseparable.

3. *Axiology* (the role of values in inquiry): Naturalists believe that inquiry is value-bound.

4. *Generalizations:* Naturalists believe that time- and context-free generalizations are not possible.

5. *Causal linkages:* Naturalists believe that it is impossible to distinguish causes from effects.

As indicated above, we will add a sixth distinction noted by many authors:

6. *Inductive logic:* There is an emphasis on arguing from the particular to the general, or an emphasis on "grounded" theory.

Given such black-and-white contrasts, it was inevitable that paradigm wars would break out between individuals convinced of what Smith (1994) has called the "paradigm purity" of their own position. For example, Guba (1987) stated that one paradigm precludes the other "just as surely as the belief in a round world precludes belief in a flat one" (p. 31). Guba and Lincoln (1990, 1994) have repeatedly emphasized the differences in ontology, epistemology, and axiology that exist among the paradigms, thus fueling the paradigm wars. Smith (1983) stated the incompatibility thesis as follows:

> One approach takes a subject-object position on the relationship to subject mat-ter; the other takes a subject-subject position. One separates facts and values, while the other sees them as inextricably mixed. One searches for laws, and the other seeks understanding. These positions do not seem compatible. (p. 12)

Paradigm "purists" have further posited the incompatibility thesis with regard to research methods: Compatibility between quantitative and quali-tative methods is impossible due to the incompatibility of the paradigms that underlie the methods. According to these theorists, researchers who try to combine the two methods are doomed to failure due to the inherent differ-ences in the philosophies underlying them.

Pragmatism and the Compatibility Thesis

Many influential researchers have stated that the differences between the two paradigms have been overdrawn, and that the schism is not as wide as has been portrayed by "purists." For example, House (1994) concluded that this dichotomization springs from a "misunderstanding of science," as he pointed out strengths and weaknesses of both the positivist and the construc-tivist traditions. House further contended that there "is no guaranteed methodological path to the promised land" (pp. 20–21).

There are a number of good reasons to declare detente in the paradigm wars. For example, writing within the evaluation discipline, Datta (1994) has given five convincing, practical reasons for "coexistence" between the two methodologies and their underlying paradigms:

- Both paradigms have, in fact, been used for years.
- Many evaluators and researchers have urged using both paradigms.
- Funding agencies have supported both paradigms.
- Both paradigms have influenced policy.
- So much has been taught by both paradigms.

On a philosophical level, pragmatists had to counter the incompatibility thesis of the paradigm warriors, which was predicated upon the link between epistemology and method. To counter this paradigm-method link, Howe (1988) posited the use of a different paradigm: pragmatism. Cherryholmes (1992) and Murphy (1990) have traced the roots of pragmatism to such American scholars as C. S. Peirce, William James, and John Dewey, with more contemporary theorists including W. V. O. Quine, Richard Rorty, and Donald Davidson. The philosophy has been identified almost exclusively with its place of origin (the United States), and European scholars have been somewhat disdainful of pragmatism due to its debunking of metaphysical concepts, such as truth (e.g., Nielsen, 1991; Rorty, 1990). Instead of searching for metaphysical truths, pragmatists consider truth to be "what works." Howe (1988) summarized this orientation as follows:

> After all, much of pragmatic philosophy (e.g., Davidson, 1973; Rorty, 1982; Wittgenstein, 1958) is *deconstructive*—an attempt to get philosophers to stop taking concepts such as "truth," "reality," and "conceptual scheme," turning them into superconcepts such as "Truth," "Reality," and "Conceptual Scheme," and generating insoluble pseudoproblems in the process. (p. 15, italics in the original)

A major tenet of Howe's concept of pragmatism was that quantitative and qualitative methods *are compatible*. Thus, because the paradigm says that these methods are compatible, investigators could make use of both of them in their research. Brewer and Hunter (1989) made essentially the same point:

> However, the pragmatism of employing multiple research methods to study the same general problem by posing different specific questions has some pragmatic implications for social theory. Rather than being wed to a particular theoretical style . . . and its most compatible method, one might instead combine methods that would encourage or even require integration of different theoretical perspectives to interpret the data. (p. 74)

Reichardt and Rallis (1994) have gone even further in their analysis of the compatibility of what they call "qualitative and quantitative inquiries." They contend that there are enough similarities in fundamental values between the QUANs and the QUALs to "form an enduring partnership" (Reichardt & Rallis, 1994, p. 85). These similarities in fundamental values include belief in the value-ladenness of inquiry, belief in the theory-ladenness of facts, belief that reality is multiple and constructed, belief in the fallibility of knowledge, and belief in the underdetermination of theory by fact.

The first three of these beliefs were discussed earlier in this chapter. Reichardt and Rallis (1994) contend that QUANs also believe (along with QUALs) that knowledge is fallible, quoting Cook and Campbell (1979): "We cannot prove a theory or other causal proposition" (Reichardt &

Rallis, 1994, p. 22). The authors further contend that the QUANs and QUALs agree with the *principle of the underdetermination of theory by fact,* that is, that "any given set of data can be explained by many theories" (Reichardt & Rallis, 1994, p. 88). Reichardt and Rallis also listed other shared ideologies in the field of evaluation between QUANs and QUALs concerning the importance of understanding and improving the human condition, the importance of communicating results to inform decisions, the belief "that the world is complex and stratified and often difficult to understand" (p. 89).

Thus it can be argued that there is a common set of beliefs that many social and behavioral scientists have that undergird a paradigm distinct from positivism or postpositivism or constructivism, which has been labeled pragmatism. This paradigm allows for the use of mixed methods in social and behavioral research.

The Evolution of Methodological Approaches in the Social and Behavioral Sciences

Thus there is growing agreement among many social and behavioral scientists concerning the basic assumptions that underlie the philosophical orientation of pragmatism. Now that these philosophical issues have been addressed, we can turn our attention to specific methodological issues associated with mixed method and mixed model studies.

A wide variety of writers from different disciplines (e.g., Blalock, 1978; Brewer & Hunter, 1989; Datta, 1994; Patton, 1990) have been calling for more coherence in our descriptions of the different methodologies that we now have at our disposal in the social and behavioral sciences. Brewer and Hunter (1989) have specifically called for a more integrated methodological approach, focusing on the need for individual researchers (and research teams) to combine methods in their investigations.

Part of that methodological integration involves having more precision in the language that we use to describe multiple methods. The novice researcher is faced with a bewildering array of names for the methods employed in the social and behavioral sciences: *monomethods* (quantitative and qualitative, plus all variants therein), multiple methods, *mixed methods,* multimethod research, *triangulation* of methods, methodological mixes, and so on. In this section, we will present a taxonomy of methodological approaches, including a brief review of the evolution of those methods.

The taxonomy of methodological approaches in the social and behavioral sciences is presented in Table 1.1. There are three broad categories: monomethods (dating from the emergence of the social sciences in the nineteenth century through the 1950s), mixed methods (emerging in the 1960s and becoming more common in the 1980s), and mixed model studies (emerging as a separate type in the 1990s but having earlier precursors).

General Stages in the Evolution of Methodological Approaches in the Social and Behavioral Sciences

We will argue in this section that there has been an evolution in the social and behavioral sciences from the use of monomethods to the use of what we call mixed model studies. There are three general points to be made in this discussion: (a) The evolution first involved the acceptance of the use of mixed methods, (b) the evolution then involved the application of the distinctions that emerged during the paradigm wars to all phases of the research process, and (c) this evolution has occurred during the past 30 years at an ever increasing pace.

The First Stage of the Evolution: From Monomethods to Mixed Methods

This involved going from the use of one basic scientific method only to the use of a variety of methods. Thus, in Table 1.1, this involved the movement from Period I to Period II. The paradigm wars and their denouement through pragmatism and the compatibility thesis resulted in this transition. The history of this process has been discussed in previous sections of this chapter. A more complete description of the different types of pure and mixed methods will be presented in Chapters 2 and 3 [Tashakkori & Teddlie, 1998].

The Second Stage of the Evolution: From Mixed Method to Mixed Model Studies

This involved moving from the consideration of distinctions in method alone to the consideration of distinctions in all phases of the research process. As indicated in Table 1.1, this involved the movement from Period II to Period III. While the emergence of multiple methods typically has been treated as a methodological issue only, the linking of epistemology to method during the paradigm wars made it necessary to consider how different orientations affect other phases of the research process (e.g., the framing of the problem, the design of the study, the analysis of the data, the interpretation of the data). As Howe (1988) concluded, "The quantitative-qualitative distinction is applied

Table 1.1   The Evolution of Methodological Approaches in the Social and Behavioral Sciences

---

Period I: The Monomethod or "Purist" Era
(circa the nineteenth century through 1950s)

  A. The Purely Quantitative Orientation
    1. Single Data Source (QUAN)
    2. Within One Paradigm/Model, Multiple Data Sources
      a. Sequential (QUAN/QUAN)
      b. Parallel/Simultaneous (QUAN + QUAN)

  B. The Purely Qualitative Orientation
    1. Single Data Source (QUAL)
    2. Within One Paradigm/Method, Multiple Data Sources
      a. Sequential (QUAL/QUAL)
      b. Parallel/Simultaneous (QUAL + QUAL)

Period II: The Emergence of Mixed Methods
(circa the 1960s to 1980s)

  A. Equivalent Status Designs (across both paradigms/methods)
    1. Sequential (i.e., two-phase sequential studies)
      a. QUAL/QUAN
      b. QUAN/QUAL
    2. Parallel/Simultaneous
      a. QUAL + QUAN
      b. QUAN + QUAL

  B. Dominant-Less Dominant Designs (across both paradigms/methods)
    1. Sequential
      a. QUAL/quan
      b. QUAN/qual
    2. Parallel/Simultaneous
      a. QUAL + quan
      b. QUAN + qual

  C. Designs With Multilevel Use of Approaches

Period III: The Emergence of Mixed Model Studies
(circa the 1990s)

  A. Single Application Within Stage of Study*
    1. Type of Inquiry—QUAL or QUAN
    2. Data Collection/Operations—QUAL or QUAN
    3. Analysis/Inferences—QUAL or QUAN

  B. Multiple Applications Within Stage of Study**
    1. Type of Inquiry—QUAL and/or QUAN
    2. Data Collection/Operations—QUAL and/or QUAN
    3. Analysis/Inferences—QUAL and/or QUAN

---

*There must be a mixing such that each approach appears in at least one stage of the study.

**There must be a mixing such that both approaches appear in at least one stage of the study.

at various levels: data, design and analysis, interpretation of results, and epistemological paradigm" (p. 15).

Creswell (1994) asked a basic question regarding this application of the paradigm-method link to other phases of the research process:

> The most efficient use of both paradigms would suggest another step toward combining designs: Can aspects of the design process other than methods—such as the introduction to a study, the literature and theory, the purpose statement, and research questions—also be drawn from different paradigms in a single study? (p. 176)

His answer was in the affirmative and he gave examples of how different paradigms or points of view could be applied to these phases of the research process.

Similarly, Brewer and Hunter (1989) applied their multimethod approach to all phases of the research process, not only to the measurement phase. Their phases included the formulation of the problem, the building and testing of theory, sampling, data collection/analysis, and reporting. They concluded,

> The decision to adopt a multimethod approach to measurement affects not only measurement but all stages of research. Indeed, multiple measurement is often introduced explicitly to solve problems at other stages of the research process. . . . These wider effects . . . of . . . multimethod tactics need to be examined in detail, including the new challenges that the use of multiple methods poses for data analysis, for writing and evaluating research articles for publication, and for doing research in an ethical manner. (Brewer & Hunter, 1989, p. 21)

In Chapter 3 [Tashakkori & Teddlie, 1998], we will explicitly apply the different philosophical approaches to several phases of a research project (determination of questions/hypotheses, data gathering and research operations, analyses, and inferences) using a taxonomy initially developed by Patton (1990). Indeed, this application will serve as the organizing framework for the remainder of this volume.

The Escalation of the Evolutionary Process

This evolutionary process toward the use of mixed method and mixed model studies has been occurring at an ever increasing pace during the past 30 years due to (a) the introduction of a variety of new methodological tools (both quantitative and qualitative), (b) the rapid development of new technologies (computer hardware and software) to access and use those methodological tools more easily, and (c) the increase in communication across the social and behavioral sciences.

A Taxonomy of Studies With Different Methodological Approaches

Three major types of studies are summarized in Table 1.1: monomethod studies, mixed method studies, and mixed model studies. Each of these basic types of studies is further divided into subcategories. In this section, we will provide brief definitions of these different methodological approaches; more detail with regard to their development and application will be forthcoming in Chapter 3 [Tashakkori & Teddlie, 1998].

Monomethod Studies

Monomethod studies are studies conducted by "purists" working exclusively within one of the predominant paradigms. Of course, the subdividing of the monomethod studies into the purely qualitative and the purely quantitative should come as no surprise to the reader. In Chapter 2 [Tashakkori & Teddlie, 1998], we will present examples of these pure designs, which are becoming increasingly rare in the social and behavioral sciences.

Mixed Method Studies

Mixed method studies are those that combine the qualitative and quantitative approaches into the research methodology of a single study or multiphased study. These methods are further subdivided into the five specific types of designs that are listed in Table 1.1.

All of the mixed method designs in Table 1.1 use triangulation techniques. These *triangulation techniques* evolved from the pioneer work of Campbell and Fiske (1959), who used more than one quantitative method to measure a psychological trait, a technique that they called the multimethod-multitrait matrix. Denzin (1978) described four different types of triangulation methods, including data triangulation, investigator triangulation, theory triangulation, and methodological triangulation. Methodological triangulation involves the use of both qualitative and quantitative methods and data to study the same phenomena within the same study or in different complementary studies. Patton (1990), in an influential book on evaluation methods, gave extensive examples of these four types of triangulation.

Creswell (1994) used the following distinctions in defining four of the mixed method designs that are presented in Table 1.1:

- *Sequential studies* (or what Creswell calls two-phase studies): The researcher first conducts a qualitative phase of a study and then a quantitative phase, or vice versa. The two phases are separate.

- *Parallel/simultaneous studies:* The researcher conducts the qualitative and quantitative phase at the same time.
- *Equivalent status designs:* The researcher conducts the study using both the quantitative and the qualitative approaches about equally to understand the phenomenon under study.
- *Dominant-less dominant studies:* The researcher conducts the study "within a single dominant paradigm with a small component of the overall study drawn from an alternative design" (Creswell, 1994, p. 177).

We have defined a fifth type of mixed method design, presented in Table 1.1:

- *Designs with multilevel use of approaches:* Researchers use different types of methods at different levels of data aggregation. For example, data could be analyzed quantitatively at the student level, qualitatively at the class level, quantitatively at the school level, and qualitatively at the district level.

Coincidentally, Miller and Crabtree (1994) presented a set of what they called "tools" for multimethod clinical research that closely resemble the types of studies that Creswell defined. They listed the following mixed method designs: *concurrent design* (analogous to parallel/simultaneous studies), *nested designs* (similar to dominant-less dominant studies), *sequential design* (analogous to sequential studies), and *combination design* (some combination of the above design options). Their work followed up on that of Stange and Zyzanski (1989), who were among the first to call for the integration of qualitative and quantitative research methods in clinical practice in the medical sciences.

Mixed Model Studies

The category that we designate as *mixed model studies* in Table 1.1 was defined as "mixed methodology designs" by Creswell (1994) who described them as follows: "This design represents the highest degree of mixing paradigms. . . . The researcher would mix aspects of the qualitative and quantitative paradigm at all or many . . . steps" (pp. 177–178).

Our definition of mixed model studies is somewhat different: *These are studies that are products of the pragmatist paradigm and that combine the qualitative and quantitative approaches within different phases of the research process.* There may be single applications within phases of the study, such as a quantitative (experimental) design, followed by qualitative data collection, followed by quantitative analysis after the data are converted. In this application, the qualitative data would be converted to numbers using the "quantitizing" technique described by Miles and Huberman (1994).

There could also be multiple applications within phases of the study, such as the following:

- A research design that calls for a field experiment and extensive ethnographic interviewing to occur simultaneously and in an integrated manner
- Data collection that includes closed-ended items with numerical responses as well as open-ended items on the same survey (e.g., Tashakkori, Aghajanian, & Mehryar, 1996)
- Data analysis that includes factor analysis of Likert scaled items from one portion of a survey, plus use of the constant comparative method (e.g., Glaser & Strauss, 1967; Lincoln & Guba, 1985) to analyze narrative responses to open-ended questions theoretically linked to the Likert scales

The remainder of this volume includes descriptions of several types (see Table 3.1 in Chapter 3 [Tashakkori & Teddlie, 1998]) of these mixed model studies and how to design them.

References

Blalock, H. M. (1978). Ordering diversity, *Society, 15*, 20–22.

Brewer, J. & Hunter, A. (1989), *Multimethod research: A synthesis of styles*. Newbury Park, CA: Sage.

Campbell, D., & Fiske, D. W. (1959). Convergent and discriminant validation by the multitrait-multimethod matrix. *Psychological Bulletin, 54*, 297–312.

Campbell, D.T., & Stanley, J. (1966). *Experimental and quasi-experimental design for research*. Chicago: Rand McNally.

Cherryholmes, C. H. (1992). Notes on pragmatism and scientific realism. *Educational Researcher, 21*, 13–17.

Cook, T. D., & Campbell, D. T. (1979). *Quasiexperimentation: Design and analysis issues for field settings*. Boston: Houghton Mifflin.

Creswell, J. W. (1994) *Research design: Qualitative and quantitative approaches*. Thousand Oaks, CA: Sage.

Cronbach, L. J. (1982). *Designing evaluations of educational and social programs*. San Francisco: Jossey-Bass.

Datta, L. (1994). Paradigm wars: A basis for peaceful coexistence and beyond. In C. S. Reichardt & S. F. Rallis (Eds.). *The qualitative-quantitative debate: New perspectives* (pp. 53–70). San Francisco: Jossey-Bass.

Davidson, D. (1973). On the very idea of a conceptual scheme. *Proceedings of the American Philosophical Association, 68*, 5–20.

Denzin, N. K. (1978). The logic of naturalistic inquiry. In N. K. Denzin (Ed.). *Sociological methods: A sourcebook*. New York: McGraw-Hill.

Denzin, N. K. (1992). *Symbolic interactionism and cultural studies*. Cambridge: Basil Blackwell.

Fetterman, D. M. (1992). In response to Lee Sechrest's 1991 AEA presidential address: "Roots: Back to our first generations," February 1991, 1–7. *Evaluation Practice, 13,* 171–172.

Gage, N. (1989). The paradigm wars and their aftermath: A "historical" sketch of research and teaching since 1989. *Educational Researcher, 18,* 4–10.

Gardner, M. (1993). The great Samoan hoax. *Skeptical Inquirer, 17,* 131–135.

Gergen, K. J. (1973). Social psychology as history. *Journal of Personality and Social Psychology, 26,* 309–320.

Gergen, K. J. (1985). The social constructionist movement in modern psychology. *American Psychologist, 40,* 266–275.

Glaser, B. G., & Strauss, A. L. (1967). *The discovery of grounded theory: Strategies for qualitative research.* Chicago: Aldine.

Goetz, J. P., & LeCompte, M. D. (1984). *Ethnography and qualitative design in educational research.* New York: Academic Press.

Goodman, N. (1984). *Of mind and other matters.* Cambridge, MA: Harvard University Press.

Greene, J. C. (1994). Qualitative program evaluation. In N. K. Denzin & Y. S. Lincoln (Eds.), *Handbook of qualitative research* (pp. 530–544). Thousand Oaks, CA: Sage.

Greene, J. C., Caracelli, V. J., & Graham, W. F. (1989). Toward a conceptual framework for mixed method evaluation designs. *Educational Evaluation and Policy Analysis, 11,* 255–274.

Guba E. G. (1987). What have we learned about naturalistic evaluation? *Evaluation Practice, 8,* 23–43.

Guba, E. G. (1990). *The paradigm dialog.* Newbury Park, CA: Sage.

Guba, E. G. & Lincoln, Y. S. (1990). *Fourth generation evaluation.* Newbury Park, CA: Sage.

Guba, E. G. & Lincoln, Y. S. (1994). Competing paradigms in qualitative research. In N. K. Denzin & Y. S. Lincoln (Eds.), *Handbook of qualitative research* (pp. 105–117). Thousand Oaks, CA: Sage.

Hammersley, M. (1989). *The dilemma of qualitative method: Herbert Blumer and the Chicago tradition.* London: Routledge Kegan Paul.

Hammersley, M. (1992). *What's wrong with ethnography.* London Routledge Kegan Paul.

Hanson, N. R. (1958). *Patterns of discovery: An inquiry into the conceptual foundations of science.* Cambridge: Cambridge University Press.

House, E. R. (1994). Integrating the quantitative and qualitative. In C. S. Reichardt & S. F. Rallis (Eds.), *The qualitative-quantitative debate: New perspectives* (pp. 13–22). San Francisco: Jossey-Bass.

Howe, K. R. (1988). Against the quantitative-qualitative incompatibility thesis or dogmas die hard. *Educational Researcher, 17,* 10–16.

Jones, E. E., & Davis, K. E. (1966). From acts to dispositions: The attribution process in person perception. In L. Berkowitz (Ed.), *Advances in experimental social psychology* (Vol. 2). New York: Freeman.

Jones, E. E., & Nisbett, R. F. (1972). The actor and the observer: Divergent perceptions of the causes of behavior. In E. E. Jones, D. E. Kanouse, H. H. Kelley, E. E. Nisbett, S. Valins, & B. Weiner (Eds.), *Attributions: Perceiving the causes of behavior.* Morristown, NJ: General Learning Press.

Kneller, G. F. (1984). *Movements of thought in modern education.* New York: John Wiley.

Kuhn, T. S. (1970). *The structure of scientific revolutions* (2nd ed.). Chicago: University of Chicago Press.

LeCompte, M. D., & Preissle, J., with Tesch, R. (1993). *Ethnography and qualitative design in educational research* (2nd ed.). New York: Academic Press.

Lincoln, Y. S. (1991). The arts and sciences of program evaluation. *Evaluation Practice, 12,* 1–7.

Lincoln, Y. S. & Guba, E. G. (1985). *Naturalistic inquiry.* Beverly Hills. CA: Sage.

Miles, M., & Huberman, M. (1994). *Qualitative data analysis: An expanded sourcebook* (2nd ed.). Thousand Oaks, CA: Sage.

Miller, W. L., & Crabtree, B. J. (1994). Clinical research. In N. K. Denzin & Y. S. Lincoln (Eds.), *Handbook of qualitative research* (pp. 340–352). Thousand Oaks, CA: Sage.

Morse, J. M. (1991). Approaches to qualitative-quantitative methodological triangulation. *Nursing Research, 40,* 120–123.

Murphy, J. P. (1990). *Pragmatism: From Peirce to Davidson.* Boulder, CO: Westview.

Nielsen, K. (1991). *After the demise of the tradition: Rorty, critical theory, and the fate of philosophy.* Boulder, CO: Westview.

Patton, M. Q. (1990). *Qualitative evaluation and research methods* (2nd ed.). Newbury Park, CA: Sage.

Phillips, D. C. (1990). Postpositivist science: Myths and realities. In E. Guba (Ed.), *The paradigm dialog.* Newbury Park, CA: Sage.

Popper, K. R. (1959). *The logic of scientific discovery.* New York: Basic Books.

Reichardt, C. S. & Rallis, S. F. (1994). Qualitative and quantitative inquiries are not incompatible: A call for a new partnership. In C. S. Reichardt & S. F. Rallis (Eds.), *The qualitative-quantitative debate: New perspectives* (pp. 85–92). San Francisco: Jossey-Bass.

Rorty, R. (1982). Pragmatism, relativism, and nationalism. In R. Rorty (Ed.), *Consequences of pragmatism* (pp. 160–175). Minneapolis: University of Minnesota Press.

Rorty, R. (1990). Introduction. In J. P. Murphy (Ed.), *Pragmatism: From Peirce to Davidson.* Boulder, CO: Westview.

Rosenthal, R. (1976). *Experimenter effects in behavioral research* (enlarged ed.). New York: Irvington.

Rossi, P. H. (1994). The war between the quals and quants: Is a lasting peace possible? In C. S. Reichardt & S. F. Rallis (Eds.), *The qualitative-quantitative debate: New perspectives* (pp. 23–36). San Francisco: Jossey-Bass.

Schwandt, T. A. (1994). Constructivist, interpretivist approaches to human inquiry. In N. K. Denzin & Y. S. Lincoln (Eds.), *Handbook of qualitative research* (pp. 118–137). Thousand Oaks, CA: Sage.

Sechrest, L. (1991). Roots: Back to our first generations. *Evaluation Practice, 13,* 1–7.

Smith, J. K. (1983). Quantitative versus qualitative research: An attempt to clarify the issue. *Educational Researcher, 12,* 6–13.

Smith, J. K., & Heshusius, I. (1986). Closing down the conservation: The end of the quantitative-qualitative debate among educational researchers. *Educational Researcher, 15,* 4–12.

Smith, M. L. (1994). Qualitative plus/versus quantitative: The last word. In C. S. Reichardt & S. F. Rallis (Eds.), *The qualitative-quantitative debate: New perspectives* (pp. 37–44). San Francisco: Jossey-Bass.

Stange, K. C., & Zyzanski, S. J. (1989). Integrating qualitative and quantitative research methods. *Family Medicine, 21*, 448–451.

Tashakkori, A., Aghajanian, A., Mehryar, A. H. (1996, July). *Consistency of Iranian adolescent behavioral intentions across two decades of change.* Paper presented at the 54th Annual Convention of the International Council of Psychologists, Banff. Alberta, Canada.

Wittgenstein, L. (1958). *The philosophical investigations* (2nd ed.). New York: Macmillan.

Abbas Tashakkori is Professor of Educational Research Methodology at Louisiana State University. He received his Ph.D. in social psychology from the University of North Carolina-Chapel Hill in 1979. He has served on the psychology faculties of the Shiraz University (Iran), Stetson University, and Louisiana State University. He has been a Post-doctoral Fellow of the Carolina Population Center at the University of North Carolina-Chapel Hill and a Visiting Scholar in the Department of Educational Administration at Texas A&M University. He has published numerous articles in national and international journals. His current scholarly work in progress include a coedited book titled *The Education of Hispanics in the US: Politics, Policies, and Outcomes.* Professors Tashakkori and Teddlie are currently planning the *Handbook of Mixed Model Research.*

Charles Teddlie is Professor of Educational Research Methodology at Louisiana State University. He received his Ph.D. in social psychology from the University of North Carolina-Chapel Hill in 1979 and thereafter served on the faculties of the University of New Orleans, the University of Newcastle-upon-Tyne (U.K.), and Louisiana State University. He has also served as Assistant Superintendent for Research and Development at the Louisiana Department of Education. He has published more than 70 chapters and articles and is the coauthor or coeditor of six books, including *Schools Make a Difference: Lessons Learned From a 10-year Study of School Effects* (1993), *Forty Years After the Brown Decision: Social and Cultural Implications of School Desegregation* (1997), and *The International Handbook of School Effectiveness Research* (in press). He has lectured on school effectiveness research and educational research methodology in the United Kingdom, the Republic of Ireland, the Netherlands, Norway, Russia, the Ukraine, and Belarus.

2

Pragmatism as a Philosophical Foundation for Mixed Methods Research

Selection: Morgan, D. L. (2007). Paradigms lost and pragmatism regained: Methodological implications of combining qualitative and quantitative methods. *Journal of Mixed Methods Research, 1*(1), 48–76.

Editors' Introduction

Tashakkori and Teddlie's chapter (Chapter 1 in this volume) reviewed the philosophically based discussions at the forefront of much of the mixed methods literature since the 1980s. Their use of terms such as *war* and *warriors* indicates the tenacity with which these discussions have raged. Although this discussion is ongoing in some venues (see Chapter 14 of this volume), many mixed methods scholars today have moved beyond questions of mixing paradigms to the search for a single paradigm as a foundation for mixed methods. For some, this foundation is pragmatism.

Sociologist David L. Morgan's (2007) article is a contemporary example of scholars' efforts to move to a critical examination of the implications of pragmatism and a pragmatic approach to research. In this thought-provoking work, Morgan begins by addressing the basic question of what is meant by the term paradigm, emphasizing the definition that paradigms are "systems of shared beliefs among a community of scholars." He then considers the recent renewal of attention to qualitative research as a means for understanding how combining qualitative and quantitative research could be lifted to a similar level of legitimacy. This legitimacy for qualitative research, he says, came from focusing on philosophical assumptions and separating methods from epistemology. For mixed methods researchers, pragmatism—emphasizing the utility of research—overcomes some of the difficulties seen in the evolution of qualitative research as well as preserving its strengths. Combining qualitative and quantitative research as a methodology with links to philosophy as well as methods provides an integrated methodology in the social sciences. In the end, Morgan provides a pragmatic definition for paradigm, illuminates how qualitative research grew through philosophical advocacy, and sketches the lessons learned from this history for encouraging efforts to replace the qualitative, metaphysical paradigm with a pragmatic approach.

Discussion Questions and Applications

1. What is your definition of *paradigm* and what role do you see it playing in mixed methods?

2. Describe how Morgan has changed the tenor of the discussion about paradigms and mixed methods research from the "wars" described by Tashakkori and Teddlie (Chapter 1).

3. What steps might help further establish the legitimacy of mixed methods in your discipline?

Related References That Extend the Topic

Examine the following references to learn more about pragmatism and mixed methods research:

Cherryholmes, C. H. (1992). Notes on pragmatism and scientific realism. *Educational Researcher, 21*(6), 13–17.

Johnson, R. B., & Onwuegbuzie, A. J. (2004). Mixed methods research: A research paradigm whose time has come. *Educational Researcher, 33*(7), 14–26.

Paradigms Lost and Pragmatism Regained

Methodological Implications of Combining Qualitative and Quantitative Methods

David L. Morgan
Portland State University, Oregon

This article examines several methodological issues associated with combining qualitative and quantitative methods by comparing the increasing interest in this topic with the earlier renewal of interest in qualitative research during the 1980s. The first section argues for the value of Kuhn's concept of paradigm shifts as a tool for examining changes in research fields such as social science research methodology. The next two sections consider the initial rise of the "metaphysical paradigm" that justified the renewed interest in qualitative research and the subsequent problems that have encouraged efforts to replace that paradigm. The final section of the paper advocates a "pragmatic approach" as a new guiding paradigm in social science research methods, both as a basis

SOURCE: This article is reprinted from *Journal of Mixed Methods Research,* Vol. 1, Issue 1, pp. 48–76, 2007. Reprinted with permission of Sage Publications, Inc.

Author's Note: This is an expanded version of a keynote address at the 2005 Conference on Mixed Methods in Health and Social Care, sponsored by the Homerton School of Health Studies, Cambridge. I would particularly like to thank the conference organizer, Tessa Muncey, for suggesting that I speak on "something controversial"—although my choice in that regard is entirely my own responsibility.

for supporting work that combines qualitative and quantitative methods and as a way to redirect our attention to methodological rather than metaphysical concerns.

Keywords: paradigms; pragmatism; research methodology

For the past two decades, much of the discussion in social science research methods has focused on the distinction between *Qualitative Research* and *Quantitative Research*. Note that I have capitalized these two terms to distinguish them from the more technical issues dealing with *qualitative* and *quantitative methods*. This also heightens the contrast between these two dominant approaches to social science research and the current alternative approach, which—depending on the language you prefer—either combines, integrates, or mixes qualitative and quantitative methods. This leads to the following question: To what extent is combining qualitative and quantitative methods simply about how we use *methods,* as opposed to raising basic issues about the nature of research *methodology* in the social sciences?

My answer to that question begins with an examination of the current state of social science research methodology and its history over roughly the past 25 years. My approach thus amounts to analyzing the recent history of social science research methodology through the interdisciplinary perspective known as "science studies" or "social studies of scientific knowledge" (Hess, 1997; Jasanoff, Markle, Peterson, & Pinch, 1995; Zammito, 2004). From this point of view, if we want to examine the issues raised by a new approach such as combining qualitative and quantitative methods, we must start by examining the "dominant paradigm." Hence, rather than assessing any new approach strictly on its own merits, the implications of that approach must be considered within an ongoing context where researchers have preexisting commitments to other systems of beliefs and practices. Within the science studies, the consensual set of beliefs and practices that guide a field is typically referred to as a "paradigm."

Paradigms have also become a central concept in social science research methodology, but often with a meaning that is rather different from the way that term is used in the field of science studies. To sort out the multiple meanings and uses of the word *paradigm,* the next section of this article summarizes the four most common versions of this term as it is found within the social sciences, as part of a brief overview of the sociology of science approach that will guide the article as whole. The second section will use that conceptual framework to review developments in social science research methodology as a field of studies over the past 25 years. The third section then considers the methodological issues raised by combining qualitative and quantitative methods and compares them to the currently dominant approach. Finally, the Conclusions section considers what it might mean to go beyond the recent interest in combining methods as a practical approach to research design and apply this shift in research practices to several key issues in social science research methodology.

Rather than treating this presentation as a mystery or suspense novel, where the reader has to search out clues to anticipate conclusions that the author reveals only at the end, let me give a quick preview of the key points that I will make in each of those sections. First, I will argue for a version of paradigms as systems of beliefs and practices that influence how researchers select both the questions they study and methods that they use to study them. In addition, I will contrast that version of paradigms to the currently widespread version in social science methodology, which emphasizes metaphysical issues related to the nature of reality and truth.

In the second section, I trace out the rise of this "metaphysical paradigm" in social science research methodology. In doing so, I will concentrate on the advocacy efforts of a set of researchers who promoted this view as a replacement for what they considered to be an outmoded "positivist paradigm." My summary of these events draws on typical "case study" techniques from science studies to make a case that the increasing acceptance of this metaphysical paradigm from the 1980s onward led to not only a widespread acceptance of qualitative methods but also a broader reconceptualization of methodological issues throughout the social sciences. In the third section, I contrast that metaphysical paradigm to basic beliefs and practices involved in combining qualitative and quantitative methods, and in the fourth section, I propose what I call a "pragmatic approach" as an alternative to the previous paradigm. Just as the debate between the positivist and metaphysical paradigms in the 1980s was about more than just research methods, a shift from the metaphysical paradigm to a pragmatic approach also raises much larger questions about how we do research in the social sciences. Finally, the Conclusions section outlines what I see as some of the most interesting and promising issues that a pragmatist approach would offer for future directions in social science research methodology.

This is obviously an ambitious and controversial agenda, and I must confess a certain hesitation in laying out these ideas because I have only minimal training in science studies and even less in the history of science as a specialized field. Hence, I want to be clear that what follows makes no attempt to be a *definitive* analysis of changes in the field of social science research methodology over the past several decades. Nor is it an exhaustive summary of the major historical events and documents in that period. Nonetheless, I hope that you, as an audience that includes many social science research methodologists, will find my account of past events credible and my suggestions for future directions worth considering.

Alternate Applications of the Paradigm Concept in Social Science Methodology

Thomas Kuhn's landmark book, *The Structure of Scientific Revolutions* (1962/ 1996), is directly responsible for the popularity of paradigms as a way to summarize researchers' beliefs about their efforts to create knowledge. A chief source of difficulty, however, is the great breadth of Kuhn's uses for his concept of paradigms, and one friendly critic (Masterman, 1970) claimed to have located more than 20 ways that Kuhn used the term his book. Kuhn (1970) responded to this lack of clarity about the meaning of paradigms by discussing this issue at length in a "Postscript" that he added to the later editions of his book (see Kuhn, 1974, for a similar set of arguments).

In hindsight, Kuhn wished that he had used a different term like *disciplinary matrix* to summarize the various forms of group commitments and consensus that we now associate with paradigms. He himself never actually adopted the term *disciplinary matrix,* however, and even though his later work (e.g., Kuhn, 2000) tended to avoid references to *paradigms,* that word and all its variant meanings is now a central concept in scholarly work. As a result, it is all too easy for social scientists to talk about "paradigms" and mean entirely different things. For example, after J. Patton (1982) spoke of the value of making "mind shifts back and forth between paradigms" (p. 190), Schwandt (1989) complained that it was unclear how "such an astonishing feat is to be accomplished" (p. 392). Yet J. Patton was referring to paradigms as frameworks for thinking about research design, measurement, analysis, and personal involvement (what I refer to below as "shared beliefs among members of a specialty area"), whereas Schwandt referred to paradigms as "worldviews" and beliefs about the nature of reality, knowledge, and values (a mixture of the two versions of paradigms I call "worldviews" and "epistemological stances").

I will review four basic versions of the paradigm concept, as shown in Table 2.1. All four versions treat paradigms as shared belief systems that influence the kinds of knowledge researchers seek and how they interpret the evidence they collect. What distinguishes the four versions is the level of generality of that belief system. Hence, the following descriptions move from the most general to the most specific versions of paradigms, along with a discussion of the relevance of each version for questions about combining qualitative and quantitative methods.

Table 2.1   Four Versions of Paradigms

	Paradigms as Worldviews	Paradigms as Epistemological Stances	Paradigms as Shared Beliefs in a Research Field	Paradigms as Model Examples
Defining characteristics	All-encompassing perspectives on the world	Ontology, epistemology, and methodology from philosophy of knowledge	Shared beliefs about the nature of questions and answers in a research field	Relies on specific exemplars of best or typical solutions to problems
Place in Kuhn's work	Implicit	Directly discussed but not favored	Directly discussed and favored	Directly discussed and favored
Place in social sciences	Common as nontechnical usage	Currently dominant version	Relatively uncommon	Largely absent
Advantages	Recognizes role of personal experience and culture in science	Relies on well-known elements from philosophy of knowledge	Can be studied by examining the work of actual researchers	Very explicit, concrete
Disadvantages	Too broad, little direct relevance to research	Broad approach to knowing, less direct connection to research	Usually describes smaller research groups, not whole disciplines	Very narrow, limited applications
Place in combining methods	Little explicit use	Major impact	Minor impact	Little explicit use

Paradigms as Worldviews

This broadest version treats paradigms as worldviews or all-encompassing ways of experiencing and thinking about the world, including beliefs about morals, values, and aesthetics. Although this was not one of the versions that Kuhn (1970) explicitly discussed in his Postscript chapter, it shows up quite frequently in the social sciences. For example, Rossman and Rallis's (2003)

text on qualitative methods highlighted "worldviews" and "shared understandings of reality" as synonyms for paradigms (p. 36), whereas Creswell
(1998) began his discussion of the concept by noting, "Qualitative researchers
approach their studies with a certain *paradigm or worldview*, a basic set of
assumptions that guide their inquiries" (p. 74). Similarly, Lincoln (1990)
described paradigms as alternative world views with such pervasive effects
that adopting a paradigm permeates every aspect of a research inquiry. As the
previous example of the disagreement between J. Patton (1982) and Schwandt
(1989) illustrates, problems arise if one simply stops at the broad sense of a
paradigm as a worldview, without carefully specifying the elements that are
contained within that worldview. It thus does little good to think of paradigms as worldviews that include virtually *everything* someone thinks or
believes; instead, it is important to clarify what is contained in a worldview,
which in this case would primarily focus on a person's thoughts about the
nature of research.

Making the connection between paradigms as worldviews and issues surrounding the combining of qualitative and quantitative methods points to
the many factors that go into decisions about what to study and how to do
such a study. For example, some researchers emphasize issues of social change
and justice, whereas others concentrate on testing or creating theories in
their specific fields. These kinds of preferences point to the influence of individual worldviews on the topics researchers choose to study and how they
choose to conduct that work. Such worldviews do little, however, to help us
understand issues such as why combining qualitative and quantitative methods has become both more popular and more controversial within social
science research over the past decade or so.

Paradigms as Epistemological Stances

The next version of paradigms treats the best known epistemological
stances (e.g., realism and constructivism) as distinctive belief systems that
influence how research questions are asked and answered and takes a nar-
rower approach by concentrating on one's worldviews about issues within
the philosophy of knowledge. This is one of the three major versions of the
paradigm concept that Kuhn discussed in his 1970 Postscript, and it is also
the most widespread version within social science research methodology.
This approach builds on the insight that research inherently involves epistemological issues about the nature of knowledge and knowing. In particular,
treating realism and constructivism as paradigms points to broad differences
in social scientists' assumptions about the nature of knowledge and the appropriate ways of producing such knowledge (e.g., Guba & Lincoln, 1994, 2005).

Once again, however, the breadth of this version of paradigms is also a limitation. Although paradigms as epistemological stances do draw attention to the deeper assumptions that researchers make, they tell us little about more substantive decisions such as what to study and how to do so.

With regard to combining qualitative and quantitative methods, paradigms as epistemological stances have had a major influence on discussions about whether this merger is possible, let alone desirable. This influential role in discussions about combining methods is not surprising, given the dominance of this version of paradigms in current social science research methodology more generally. Thus, Tashakkori and Teddlie (2003) relied on this version when they distinguished between approaches based on "paradigm incompatibility," which asserts that the conflict between Qualitative and Quantitative Research is so fundamental that it is impossible to combine them, and other approaches that claim it is possible to combine qualitative and quantitative methods without violating philosophical principles. Although Tashakkori and Teddlie did treat the paradigm incompatibility approach as "largely discredited" (p. 19), the mere fact that they organized much of their discussion around this approach continues to give it a life of its own. These issues will be a core topic in the next section of this article, but for now it is important to note that they are all based on a version of paradigms that emphasizes epistemological stances.

Paradigms as Shared Beliefs Among Members of a Specialty Area

At the next level of specificity is a version of paradigms as shared beliefs within a community of researchers who share a consensus about which questions are most meaningful and which procedures are most appropriate for answering those questions. This is the version of paradigms that Kuhn (1970, 1974) himself preferred, and it is the most common form in the fields that make up science studies, but it has received limited attention in discussions of social science methodology. When this version has appeared in the social sciences, it has typically been applied to whole disciplines, such as nursing (Newman, 1992) or sociology (Ritzer, 1975). Although Kuhn (1996) explicitly acknowledged that this version of paradigms could be applied to the broader assumptions that guide whole disciplines, he himself emphasized the more specific beliefs and practices shared within "research communities" consisting of "practitioners of a scientific specialty" with "perhaps one hundred members" who are "absorbed in the same technical literature" (pp. 177–178). Kuhn's emphasis on paradigms as governing "not a subject matter but a group of practitioners" (p. 180) has been a source of frustration for those who wish to characterize the paradigmatic assumptions of whole disciplines or the even the social sciences as a whole. Yet it has also served as a guiding insight for empirical work in science studies, which has concentrated on case studies of the changes in beliefs and practices that occur in specific subfields and the consequences that these smaller "paradigm shifts" may have for the larger fields in which those research specialties are embedded (e.g., Collins & Pinch, 1998).

With regard to combining qualitative and quantitative methods, this concept of paradigms as shared beliefs among a community of researchers has had considerably less impact than the epistemological stance version described above. Yet if we consider social science research methodology as the kind of specialty area that Kuhn described, then it makes sense to examine the shifts in our own beliefs and practices about how to do research. In particular, the past two decades have seen a rise in the legitimacy of Qualitative Research, which has been justified through an emphasis on the contrast between epistemological stances such as realism and constructivism. More recently, however, work on combining qualitative and quantitative methods has emphasized a largely pragmatist stance. These shifts within the field of social science research methodology, and their larger implications for social science research in general, are a central topic in this article.

Paradigms as Model Examples of Research

The final and most specific version of paradigms treats them as model examples that serve as "exemplars" for how research is done in a given field. This usage is most familiar in the form of "paradigmatic examples" that show newcomers how a field addresses its central issues. Although this version of paradigms was of special interest to Kuhn himself, it has received relatively little attention in subsequent work, and I have included it here largely for reasons of completeness. It does, however, have some relevance to the topic of combining qualitative and quantitative methods, simply because so many of the books and articles in this field rely on concrete examples to illustrate the broader principles they propose. This use of research projects as case studies that serve as paradigmatic examples is particularly common in descriptions of designs that combine multiple methods (e.g., Creswell, Plano Clark, Guttman, & Hanson, 2003; Morgan, 1998, 2006, in press). In addition, this version of paradigms is relevant to work that demonstrates the value of combining methods in a specific research area by summarizing noteworthy examples from that field (e.g., Hanson, Creswell, Plano Clark, Petska, & Creswell, 2005; Happ, Dabbs, Tate, Hricik, & Erlen, 2006; Neal, Hammer, & Morgan, 2006). That type of article is likely to become more common as this approach gains popularity.

Ultimately, it helps to think of these four increasingly specific versions of paradigms as nested within each other. The model examples researchers use to demonstrate the key content of their field reflect a set of shared beliefs about both the research questions they should ask and the methods they should use to answer them. Shared beliefs about research topics and methods are, in turn, based on epistemological stances that summarize researchers' assumptions about what can be known and how to go about such knowing. And at the broadest level, assumptions about the nature of knowledge and reality are an important component of each researcher's worldview.

This hierarchy from specificity to generality demonstrates that these four versions of the paradigm concept are not mutually exclusive. Nor is one of them right and the others wrong. Instead, the question is which version is most appropriate for any given purpose. In the present case, I will use the version of paradigms as "shared beliefs among the members of a specialty area." My reasons for relying on this version of paradigms matches the goal of examining shifts within the field of social science methodology and the broader effects of those changes on social science research in general. This goal is directly related to Kuhn's famous distinction between "normal science;" where researchers agree about which problems are worth pursuing and how to do so, versus "scientific revolutions" that call these assumptions into question.

The next two sections thus examine the recent history of paradigms in social science research methodology, including prolonged periods of agreement about both its central problems and the appropriate means for addressing those problems (i.e., "normal science"), as well as notable shifts in those shared assumptions (i.e., "paradigm changes" or "scientific revolutions"). Although the current presentation will concentrate on "social science research methodology" as a specific arena for debates about paradigms, I am also making the claim that specialty areas such as "theory" and "methods" occupy a privileged position within larger fields. Hence, I am assuming that paradigm shifts among theorists and methodologists often have impacts on a much wide range of researchers who draw on those core belief systems to guide their work on more substantive topics.

The Renewal of Qualitative Research and the Role of the "Metaphysical Paradigm"

It is easy to claim that one of if not *the* biggest shift within social science research from 1980 through 2000 was the renewed attention to Qualitative Research (e.g., Denzin & Lincoln, 1994). One of the clearest reflections of this trend is the tendency for major textbooks on research methods to provide increasingly even-handed coverage of both Qualitative and Quantitative

Research, which can be quite striking in the comparison of older and newer editions of the same text (e.g., Babbie, 1992, 1995, 2004). Of course, this is just the most recent shift in the relative balance between these two approaches during the history of the social sciences. After all, Qualitative Research is at least as old as Qualitative Research, and it has always maintained a dominant position in some fields such as social anthropology. Yet several studies on published articles (Platt, 1996) have noted a clear shift toward a reliance on quantitative methods in the post—World War II period. If we accept that this reliance on *quantitative methods* indicates the broader dominance of *Quantitative Research* from at least the 1960s until the 1980s, then the movement of Qualitative Research from a relatively marginal position to essential equality with Quantitative Research amounts to a clear shift in the historical pattern.

From a "history of science" or "science studies" perspective, this raises an obvious question: How did this transformation come about? My explanation is based on the analysis of this shift as a "paradigm change," based on the version of paradigms as a set of shared beliefs and practices among the members of a specialty area. In particular, I will portray these events as a paradigm change within social science research methodology as a field of studies. My analysis will emphasize the point that the increasing acceptance of Qualitative Research, like all major paradigm shifts, was the result of dedicated efforts by advocates for a particular point of view. Thus, the bulk of this section will portray the recent renewal of attention to Qualitative Research within the social sciences as a "case study" of paradigm change. This means that rather than following the call to "de-Kuhnify" the debate about Qualitative and Quantitative Research (Shadish, 1995b), my goal is to "re-Kuhnify" the debate by using a version of paradigms that is closer to what Kuhn himself expressed in his reconsideration of the concept (Kuhn, 1970, 1974).

Before presenting this summary, I want to note two crucial points. First, it is important to treat the claims of the various advocates in this account as something more than statements of facts. Following Kuhn, it is more useful to treat these historical events as a contest to influence beliefs, including beliefs about the nature of the past. For example, the claim that there was a "positivist paradigm" in the social sciences, let alone that it dominated social science research, is an interpretation of prior history rather than a statement about "facts." My second point is a recognition that an equally "reflexive" perspective also applies to my own account. Hence, I freely admit that what follows is not merely my personal interpretation of the events surrounding the renewed attention to Qualitative Research but also a deliberate effort to create a further paradigm change. In particular, I believe that the "metaphysical paradigm" I will describe below is now exhausted and should be replaced by a "pragmatic approach," which I will describe in the sections that follow this one.

The following description of what I am calling "The Shift from the Positivist to the Metaphysical Paradigm" is based on the key elements for paradigm change as described by Kuhn (1996):

- a clear characterization of an existing, "dominant paradigm,"
- an increasing sense of frustration with the problems in the existing paradigm,
- a clear characterization of a new paradigm, and
- agreement that the new paradigm resolves the problems in the existing paradigm.

Labeling Positivism as the Dominant Paradigm

When the renewed attention to Qualitative Research began to gain momentum in the late 1970s, there was no commonly agreed upon label for the dominant paradigm that characterized social science research methodology up to that point. As Kuhn's work (1996) demonstrates, this is hardly an unusual situation because researchers who are working within a long-standing paradigm (i.e., a period of "normal science") are often only implicitly aware of the beliefs and practices that guide their work. It is thus not unusual for an existing paradigm to lack both a well-known label and a clear characterization of its content—until that existing system is called into question by a set of challengers. In the present case, it was indeed the challengers who not only labeled the existing dominant approach as the "positivist paradigm" but also provided the initial summary of what was included in that paradigm.

Several commentators (e.g., Shadish, 1995a) have pointed out that this version of positivism has little to do with the formal movement in the philosophy of science that was known as "logical positivism." Instead, it largely served as a label that the advocates of Qualitative Research used to summarize the conventional approach to Quantitative Research, At this point, it is unclear when the advocates of Qualitative Research began emphasizing the term *positivism*, but it is worth noting that it corresponded to a larger use of "positivism" as a label to characterize what critics considered to be outmoded thinking a cross a range of academic disciplines. Eventually, those debates became a central element of what were known as the "science wars" in the 1990s (e.g., Labinger & Collins, 2001).

What mattered most about making the positivist paradigm the center of the debate, however, was that this framed the discussion around something more than the differences between "qualitative methods" versus "quantitative methods." From this perspective, arguments about which methods to use were merely mechanical or technical issues. *What was really at stake was the nature of research itself.* Furthermore, the advocates of Qualitative Research quite explicitly used Kuhn's own ideas about paradigm shifts to seek changes that were at the heart of social science methodology. By shifting the belief systems in this core specialty area, the advocates of Qualitative Research created an impact that spread across a wide range of disciplines.

This self-conscious use of paradigms was especially evident in the early statements within evaluation research, where M. Patton (1975) titled his first book an *Alternative Evaluation Research Paradigm* and Guba (1978) used a quote about paradigms from Kuhn in the opening of *Toward a Methodology of Naturalistic Inquiry in Educational Evaluation*. Later revisions and expansions of these two monographs became essential textbooks in the renewal of Qualitative Research (Guba & Lincoln, 1989; Lincoln & Guba, 1985; M. Patton, 1997, 2002). Although M. Patton and Guba ultimately parted ways on a great many issues, they did begin with an agreement that the larger debate was about a challenge to the "conventional wisdom" in social science research and not merely about methods. They deliberately chose the language of paradigms to make that point.

The Need for an Alternative to Positivism

Within the classic Kuhnian version of paradigms, the key threat to the existing beliefs and practices in a research field is the recognition of a series of "anomalies" that call the assumptions and findings of the existing paradigm into question. For Kuhn, anomalies were essentially empirical concerns that consisted of either failed predictions from the existing paradigm or new observations that were incompatible with that paradigm, and either of these sources could create an increasing sense of dissatisfaction with the dominant paradigm. Interestingly, the advocates of renewed attention to Qualitative Research did not use this classic emphasis on anomalies as the centerpiece of their attack on the positivist paradigm. There certainly were claims about the things that Quantitative Research could not accomplish, and which would be possible through Qualitative Research. Even so, the core of the debate was pitched at a much more abstract level, based on concerns from the philosophy of knowledge.

Questioning the dominant paradigm at the level of fundamental assumptions rather than focusing on empirical anomalies enhanced the legitimacy of Qualitative Research through a reinterpretation of basic methodological issues in the social sciences. On one hand, the critics problematized the previously unquestioned assumptions about the approach to research they referred to as positivism. On the other hand, they promised to address these problems by using concepts that they drew from a high-status source, the philosophy of knowledge. Like any good attempt to create a paradigm shift, this challenge not only summarized the problems with the dominant belief system but also provided what its proponents claimed was a superior alternative.

Creating an Alternative Paradigm

The best known approach to creating alternatives to positivism comes from the work of Egon Guba and Yvonna Lincoln, who developed a system for comparing different "paradigms" in social science research through a familiar trilogy of concepts from the philosophy of knowledge: ontology, epistemology, and methodology. Their early comparisons (Lincoln & Guba, 1985, 1988) were between positivism and a competing paradigm they called "naturalistic inquiry," which became better known as constructivism (and occasionally interpretivism). Guba and Lincoln explicitly referred to these approaches as two competing paradigms, in a sense that clearly falls within the "epistemological stance" version of paradigms. Ultimately, they expanded their system to consider other paradigms such as critical theory (Guba, 1990), post-positivism (Guba & Lincoln, 1994), and participatory research (Lincoln & Guba, 2000), but in each case, these comparisons were rooted in ontological issues, thus leading to my choice of the term *metaphysical paradigm* for this approach.

There are, of course, many different ways to draw boundaries within the field of philosophy as a whole, as well as within philosophy of knowledge as a subfield. In the version I follow here, metaphysics consists of issues related to the nature of reality and truth. As such, it both contains the field of ontology, which concentrates on the nature of reality, and makes a connection between ontology and epistemology through questions about the possibility of 'truth" in the form of "objective knowledge" about that reality. Hence, the idea of a metaphysical paradigm captures Guba and Lincoln's "top-down" approach, which started with ontological assumptions about the nature of reality, which in turn imposed constraints on any subsequent epistemological assumptions about the nature of knowledge. More specifically, their comparison of positivism and constructivism summarized how different assumptions about the nature of reality imposed limits on assumptions about the nature of knowledge and what could be known. These assumptions, in turn, limited the range of methodological assumptions about generating knowledge (with the understanding that this topic concerned general issues in producing knowledge, rather than mechanical concerns about the use of methods themselves). Even though Guba and Lincoln's framework nominally gave equal weight to ontology, epistemology, and methodology, its top-down orientation inevitably led to an emphasis on metaphysical questions about the nature of reality and the possibility of truth because these "higher order" assumptions imposed limits on every aspect of their system.

Although this tripartite linkage of ontology, epistemology, and methodology is the most common version of what I am calling the metaphysical paradigm, another philosophical concept, axiology, also appeared in some summaries of this paradigm (e.g., Creswell, 1998). Most references to axiology within the metaphysical paradigm associate it with the study of values, and Creswell's comparison of different traditions in Qualitative Research is a good example of using axiology as a way to consider values along with issues of ontology, epistemology, and methodology. The key problem here is that axiology is a poor fit with the emphasis on the *philosophy of knowledge* that Lincoln and Guba originated. In particular, when advocates of the metaphysical paradigm did consider axiology, they used this concept to address issues that traditionally fall within the branches of philosophy known as "ethics" and "aesthetics," rather than the philosophy of knowledge. Although the importance of both ethical issues and values more generally is undeniable in any consideration of social science research, there is no obvious basis for merging these topics with metaphysical concerns about the nature of reality or the possibility of objective truth. Hence, I will limit the version of the metaphysical paradigm that I describe to its three core concepts from the philosophy of knowledge, although I will return to the issue of axiology in the final section.

Another important aspect of the metaphysical paradigm was its reliance on another concept from Kuhn (1996): the "incommensurability" of paradigms. According to Kuhn, it could be difficult if not impossible to create a one-to-one correspondence between the ideas in two different paradigms. In his Postscript (1996, pp. 198–204), however, Kuhn noted that there could be considerable differences in the degree of "communication breakdown" that occurred during paradigm shifts. In the current case, the metaphysical paradigm took a strong stand on incommensurability, arguing that the radically different assumptions about the nature of reality and truth in paradigms like realism and constructivism made it impossible to translate or reinterpret research between these paradigms. Instead, researchers who chose to operate within one set of metaphysical assumptions inherently rejected the principles that guided researchers who operated within other paradigms.

In drawing out these key features of the metaphysical paradigm, I do not mean to imply that everyone who participated in the renewal of Qualitative Research relied on these assumptions. Although those who advocated for Qualitative Research often did make explicit references to the importance of paradigm differences, the key point for many researchers was not the specific metaphysical system that Guba and others provided. Rather, it was the creation and labeling of a set of alternatives to positivism, along with a justification for pursuing those alternatives instead of what was portrayed as an outdated approach to social science research.

The Metaphysical Paradigm as a Resolution to the Problems of Positivism

According to Kuhn's formulation of paradigm change, a new paradigm must both account for the successes of the previous paradigm at the same time that it opens opportunities within a community of scholars. The most obvious way that the metaphysical paradigm did this was to incorporate positivism as one of the options with a range of alternative "epistemological stances." Thus, positivism was not excluded from the realm of possibility in social science research. Instead, it was one of several possible sets of assumptions about the ontological, epistemological, and methodological issues that might stand behind any actual research project.

The major strength of this new system was that it reduced positivism to the status of just one among a series of competing "paradigms" in social science methodology. This is not the same as saying, however, that the majority of social science researchers shifted away from what the metaphysical paradigm called positivism, nor does it imply that larger numbers of practicing researchers shifted from Quantitative to Qualitative Research. Instead, I am asserting that the metaphysical paradigm succeeded in determining the terms for discussing the broad nature of social science research methodology. One way to evaluate this claim would be to examine the extent to which the metaphysical paradigm's emphasis on concepts from the philosophy knowledge has had an impact on the most recent textbooks on research methods. Incorporation into textbooks is one of the hallmarks that Kuhn suggested for a successful paradigm, and if discussions of ontology, epistemology, and methodology have become central elements in the instruction of the next generation of researchers, that would be clear evidence for the increasing dominance of the belief system associated with the metaphysical paradigm.

For many practicing researchers, however, the most important implication of this paradigm shift was to legitimatize alternative paradigms such as constructivism or critical theory. Most important, the ability to rely on these other belief systems justified both the pursuit of different kinds of research questions and the use of different kinds of methods to answer those questions. In addition, these researchers benefited from their association with lofty intellectual principles such as paradigms (in their descriptions of how scientific research developed) and the philosophy of knowledge (in their summary of the fundamental issues in the research process itself). Overall, the larger context provided by the metaphysical paradigm portrayed the renewed attention to Qualitative Research as much more than a new way to pursue the existing agenda in the social sciences; in addition, it offered the promise of rewriting that agenda.

This completes my account of the shift to the metaphysical paradigm as the belief system for thinking about methodological issues in social science research. By following the Kuhnian version of paradigms that treats them as systems of beliefs and practices among the members of a scholarly specialty, I am claiming that the rise of the metaphysical paradigm led to major changes in methodologists' thinking about both the kinds of problems that were most meaningful for their field as well as the means they preferred for answering those questions. Under this new paradigm, the key questions for research methodologists shifted toward a focus on differences in the underlying philosophical assumptions associated with different ways of doing research. Furthermore, the appropriate means for addressing these issues introduced concepts from the philosophy of knowledge that seldom appeared in earlier discussion of social science research. Seen in this light, the rise of the metaphysical paradigm did, indeed, do much more than justify Qualitative Research; it also changed much of the discourse that social science methodologists used to discuss the key issues in their field.

The Exhaustion of the Metaphysical Paradigm and the Need for a New Alternative

In this and the section that follow, I will continue my larger argument that we are currently in the midst of a new paradigm shift that will replace the metaphysical paradigm as a dominant belief system for discussing core issues in social science research methodology, just as it replaced positivism. I will make this point by following the same four key elements for paradigm change that I introduced at the beginning of the previous section. In particular, that section provided my characterization of the existing dominant paradigm, whereas this section will lay out the problems that have produced a sense of frustration with that paradigm. The following section will then describe what I call the "pragmatic approach" as the new alternative paradigm, showing how it can both resolve the problems caused by the metaphysical paradigm while also providing a new range of opportunities for scholars in the field of social science research methodology.

The current description of the problems with the metaphysical paradigm will, once again, follow a more Kuhnian approach by emphasizing a series of specific anomalies that methodologists have uncovered in their efforts to apply the metaphysical paradigm—as opposed to the previous effort to downplay anomalies in favor of importing external sources of legitimacy as a means of challenging the dominant paradigm. First, I will consider the problems with the ways that advocates of the metaphysical paradigm define and place boundaries around the different paradigms that are supposed to characterize social science research. Second, I will examine the problems associated with advocates of the metaphysical paradigm's preference for a strong version of incommensurability, which underlies their claims about the incompatibility of the research paradigms. Finally, I will focus on the extent to which metaphysical assumptions actually determine the key decisions that social science researchers make in the course of their work.

How Should We Define the Paradigms?

As the previous section noted, Guba and Lincoln's (e.g., Guba, 1978; Lincoln & Guba, 1985) system began by labeling and comparing only two paradigms, which generally came to be known as positivism and constructivism. In the later version of their work, however, this expanded to a list of five paradigms that also included critical theory, post-positivism, and participatory research (e.g., Guba & Lincoln, 2005). The existence of such a list obviously raises a question about what constitutes a paradigm within social science research methodology—and more important, who gets to define and label the paradigms that are included in that list.

Addressing this issue requires a shift from the conception of paradigms as epistemological stances to a version of paradigms that emphasizes the belief systems and practices within a field, which leads to questions about who defines and draws boundaries around groups of scholars who are working. This shift in attention often locates active campaigns to establish or undermine the legitimacy of competing groups and their belief systems. For example, in the present case, proponents of post-positivism such as Philips (1990) fought back against being lumped into the essentially pejorative category of positivism and eventually were given their own separate identity. From this point of view, the issue of whether a basic list should include 2 or 5 or 10 paradigms becomes a question about who is making the list and the purposes they are trying to accomplish by comparing a given set of paradigms.

These issues come up repeatedly in the evolving list of paradigms that Guba and Lincoln put forward. One persistent problem was their preferred contrast between constructivism and a version of "positivism" that looked far more like "naïve" or "crude" realism, rather than anything that was actually proposed by the logical positivists themselves (Shadish, 1995a). Yet it was easier for Guba and Lincoln to make their proconstructivist points by using a caricature of positivism, rather than dealing with the more serious and subtle challenges posed by realism, despite the importance of the realist position within social science research (e.g., Sayer, 2000). A similar problem occurs with Guba and Lincoln's portrayal of "post-positivism" as little more than a few minor changes in any attempt to repair a hopelessly broken paradigm. Once again, drawing such a narrow set of boundaries around post-positivism made it easier to ignore the robust and influential developments (e.g., Shadish, Cook, & Campbell, 2002) in an important area of social science research methodology. As a final example, the issue of who controls the list of "accepted" paradigms is particularly important for methodologists who are interested in combining qualitative and quantitative methods because nearly all the lists proposed within the metaphysical paradigm ignore pragmatism, even though it is the favored approach within that subfield (but see Creswell [2003] for one notable effort to include the metaphysical paradigms standard list to include pragmatism).

These examples point to a "political" or social-movement-based" account of who gets to define and draw boundaries around paradigms, whether this amounts to post-positivists pushing for a place on this list, only to be given second-class citizenship, or the continual exclusion of pragmatism as a member of the club. In this view, paradigms in social science research methodology are not abstract entities with timeless characteristics; instead, what counts as a paradigm and how the core content of a paradigm is portrayed involves a series of ongoing struggles between competing interest groups. Yet if the content of paradigms is subject to this level of human agency, then it makes little sense to claim that principles such as ontology, epistemology, and methodology are actually *defining* characteristics for such paradigms. This shift from a view of paradigms as enduring epistemological stances to dynamic systems of belief within a community of scholars calls into question the metaphysical paradigm's basic attempt to "impose order" on the practices in social science research through an externally defined, a priori system from the philosophy of knowledge. I will return to these larger issues elsewhere in this section, but the key point here is to emphasize the essential arbitrariness in the process of defining and placing boundaries around the set of paradigms that are the core of the metaphysical paradigm itself.

When Are Paradigms Incommensurate?

Aside from charges of favoritism or arbitrariness, the question of how to define paradigms is also closely connected to the claim that different research paradigms produce "incommensurable" kinds of knowledge. Because the metaphysical paradigm took a strong stance with regard to incommensurability, this meant that "accepting" any one of its paradigms required rejecting all the others, while also creating major communication barriers between the knowledge that was produced through each of these paradigms. This system might make sense if there were indeed clearly defined boundaries that separated paradigms into airtight categories, but this is highly unlikely in a world where paradigms are created through competition and cooperation among human researchers.

Given the previously discussed problems in defining and bounding paradigms, it is not surprising that Guba and Lincoln's own summaries (2005) showed considerable areas of overlap between paradigms such as positivism and post-positivism as well as constructivism and critical theory. This creates a troublesome dilemma, however, because allowing weak or permeable boundaries between paradigms raises questions about the extent to which incommensurability occurs, whereas an absolutist stance means that even "small differences" in paradigmatic assumptions produce serious problems with incommensurability. Guba and Lincoln (2005) proposed a compromise on this issue by accepting a degree of permeability across paradigms, as long as it does not involve key ontological assumptions. This choice is also likewise no surprise, given the top-down, ontology-driven nature of the metaphysical paradigm. Even so, this compromise is not only arbitrary but still does little to inform social science researchers about when issues of incommensurability do or do not apply in actual practice.

A different problem with the metaphysical paradigm's approach to incommensurability is that it ignores Kuhn's statements in the Postscript to the later editions of his book, where from 1970 on he explicitly rejected the claim "that proponents of incommensurable theories cannot communicate with each other at all" (1996, pp. 198–199). Instead, he emphasized that a process of *persuasion* was at the core of conflicts over paradigmatic beliefs but that such persuasion depended on a commonly agreed upon vocabulary to prevent the kind of "breakdown in communication" that he himself associated with the term *incommensurability* (1996, pp. 200–201). Thus, for Kuhn, there is nothing about the nature of paradigms (in the sense of shared beliefs among the members of a specialty area) that inherently prevents the followers of one such paradigm from understanding the claims of another. Rather, the essential question is how effectively the proponents of the two camps can communicate with each other.

In general, the metaphysical paradigm sidestepped this issue by concentrating on precisely the sorts of differences that were most likely to produce a breakdown in communication—metaphysical assumptions about the nature of reality and truth. Unfortunately, without any solid guidance on when incommensurability mattered and when it did not, the top-down nature of the system led all too easily to the conclusion that incompatibili-ties at the ontological level implied the further impossibility of communicat-ing about epistemological and methodological issues, and thus the inability to combine different methods or even compare the results from projects that originated in different metaphysical paradigms. Yet there is clearly a differ-ence between incommensurable assumptions about the nature of reality ver-sus communication about the similarities and differences in research findings among those who work in the same field. For example, Guba and Lincoln (2005) themselves have argued that it is possible to combine qualitative and quantitative methods, but others (e.g., Sale, Lohfeld, & Brazil, 2002) have continued to use the basic arguments from the metaphysical paradigm to deny the possibility of combining methods that are rooted in different para-digmatic assumptions.

To What Extent Do Metaphysical Assumptions Guide Our Research?

The issues just raised about combining methods bring us back to the basic question of how much impact metaphysical assumptions actually have on the key issues that occupy the field of social science research methodology. Questions about methods also bring us back to the rather odd "disconnect" between the philosophical discussions that define the metaphysical paradigm and the more practical issues associated with the renewed attention to Qualitative Research in general and qualitative methods in particular. Thus, one of the metaphysical paradigm's most serious anomalies was that it never directly addressed one of the central issues it raised: What is the relationship between metaphysical beliefs and research practices?

Some of the key works in the metaphysical paradigm (e.g., Lincoln & Guba, 1985) were a mixture of theoretical discussions about the nature of social science research as a knowledge-producing enterprise and explicit guidance about how to do such research within the constructivist framework. Outside of "how-to" advice about constructivism, however, the metaphysi-cal paradigm was mostly absorbed with abstract discussions about the philo-sophical assumptions behind the paradigms that it defined, with correspondingly little attention to how those choices influenced the practical decisions being made by actual researchers. Interestingly, Guba and Lincoln (1994) alluded to this issue in a footnote to their chapter in the first edition of the *Handbook on Qualitative Research:*

It is unlikely that a practitioner of any paradigm would agree that our sum-maries closely describe what he or she thinks or does. Workaday scientists rarely have either the time or the inclination to assess what they do in philosophical terms. We do contend, however, that these descriptions [of paradigms] are apt as broad brush strokes, if not always at the individual level. (p. 117)

However, that relatively balanced assessment of the role of paradigms contrasts sharply with the prescriptive tones of their final sentence from that same chapter:

Paradigm issues are crucial; no inquirer, we maintain, ought to go about the business of inquiry without being clear about just what paradigm informs and guides his or her approach. (p. 116)

This combination of strong demands for self-conscious allegiance to one particular paradigm but less advice about how that should play out in the practices of "workaday" researchers created ongoing difficulties for the metaphysical paradigm. Many of these difficulties arose because the chief proponents of the metaphysical paradigm were well-known qualitative researchers and self-avowed constructivists. This led to the widespread assumption that everything about the metaphysical paradigm promoted the use of qualitative methods. Yet as noted above, Guba and Lincoln were never completely opposed to the use of quantitative methods—even within their own favored form of naturalistic inquiry (e.g., Lincoln & Guba, 1985, 1988). Although any approval of quantitative methods in their work is rare and typically occurs only in passing, Guba and Lincoln (1988) did provide at least one example of how a survey might be used within naturalistic inquiry. Just as important, Guba and Lincoln (2005) and other strong supporters of the metaphysical paradigm (e.g., Smith & Heshusius, 1986) explicitly stated that they had no objection to combining *methods,* as long as there was no attempt to combine *paradigms*—or, at least, as long as there was no attempt to combine elements of constructivism and positivism.

Probably the simplest summary of Guba and Lincoln's position on the relationship between paradigms and methods was that although they themselves were strongly in favor of qualitative methods, there was nothing about the metaphysical paradigm itself that was *inherently* opposed to quantitative methods. From their point of view, the most important aspects of paradigm allegiances were ontological commitments, not the mundane use of research methods. Rather than coming down completely on one side or the other of the methods divide, almost all the proponents of the metaphysical paradigm insisted instead that the research question should determine the choice of the research method. Interestingly, they never associated this particular position with what they labeled *positivism,* thus making this one central element of the previous "conventional wisdom" that was maintained within the meta-physical paradigm. Yet if it is the research question that is supposed to determine the actual procedures in any given project, then how is that advice related to the requirement to work within one and only one of the paradigms on the list supplied by the metaphysical paradigm?

Following Kuhn, this is exactly the sort of anomaly that creates problems when a paradigm gets challenged. Yet these anomalies often do not come to the forefront until such a challenge occurs. In the current case, it was the increasing interest in combining qualitative and quantitative methods that led to calls for greater clarity about the linkage between philosophical commitments at the so-called paradigm level and practical procedures at the level of data collection and analysis. As not only practicing researchers but also more and more research methodologists pointed to the value of combining qualitative and quantitative methods across a wide variety of research problems, this raised troubling questions about the extent to which metaphysical assumptions actually do guide our work. In particular, if the metaphysical paradigm was supposed to guide work within the field of social science research methodology, then should not those insights translate into practical guidance for how to make decisions about actual research?

This completes my presentation on the serious anomalies that have arisen with the metaphysical paradigm, which may be summarized as follows:

1. Despite the metaphysical paradigm's emphasis on ontology, epistemology, and methodology as the defining characteristics of paradigms in social science research, the actual process of creating these paradigms and drawing boundaries is based on events that occur well outside the philosophy of knowledge.

2. Despite the metaphysical paradigm's insistence that different paradigms create "incommensurable" kinds of knowledge, the attempt to use this strong version of incommensurability repeatedly fails at every level except for debates about the nature of reality and truth.

3. Despite the metaphysical paradigm's claim that methodological problems in the social sciences could be addressed through an ontology-driven version of the philosophy of knowledge, this belief system remains disconnected from practical decisions about the actual conduct of research.

Considering all three of these anomalies, there is an undeniable irony in the contrast between Kuhn's own approach to paradigms versus that of the self-avowed constructivists who created the metaphysical paradigm. For Kuhn, it was the beliefs and practices of the researchers that defined a paradigm, and incommensurability emphasized processes of communication and persuasion about the actual work within a specialty area. This stands in direct contrast with not only the definition of paradigms through standards from the philosophy of knowledge but also the strong claims of incommensurability based on these external standards. Ultimately, this placed the constructivists who created the metaphysical paradigm in the paradoxical position of advocating ontology, epistemology, and methodology as an "objective standard" for comparing belief systems within social science research methodology.

Perhaps the ultimate irony, however, can be found in the close match between the history of these events and Kuhn's own preferred version of the paradigm concept, which emphasized human engagement in changing the beliefs and practices that govern research fields. Seen from this perspective, the methodologists who created and promoted the metaphysical paradigm initially benefited by borrowing much of their system from an "authoritative" source such as the philosophy of knowledge. In addition, borrowing Kuhn's concepts of paradigm and incommensurability linked them to the "intellectual capital" associated with those ideas. As Kuhn would have predicted, however, anomalies accumulated over time as social science methodologists put this belief system into practice within their field. In the present case, these anomalies are especially troubling because they consistently point to problems that originate in the metaphysical paradigm's borrowings from both Kuhn and the philosophy of science, thus calling into question the foundational assumptions on which that paradigm stands. Kuhn would also predict, however, that paradigms seldom fall simply because of their own anomalies. Instead, change arises from new alternatives that promise to address those anomalies.

An Alternative: The "Pragmatic Approach" to Methodology in the Social Sciences

This section begins by taking on the requirement that an alternative to the dominant paradigm must be able to resolve the anomalies in the existing system. Next, it considers the equally important task of demonstrating that the new paradigm also retains many of the virtues of the previous system. Finally, it presents the range of new options that a shift to a pragmatic approach offers to social science methodologists. Before doing so, however, I want to clarify one preliminary point.

In labeling my proposed alternative to what I have been calling the metaphysical paradigm, I have carefully chosen to avoid using the word *paradigm* in the name. Of course, I do consider the "pragmatic approach" to be a direct challenge to the "metaphysical paradigm," but I also want to sort out the confusions around the concept of paradigm as it was used in the previous system. In particular, my commitment to a Kuhnian view of paradigms as systems of shared beliefs among a community of scholars gives me a strong motive for moving away from the "epistemological stance" version of paradigms that was at the core of the metaphysical paradigm. Indeed, I might have preferred avoiding the "P-word" in my labeling of that earlier approach, if it were not for that system's own heavy and self-conscious reliance on paradigms as a defining element of their approach to social science methodology. Now, however, I believe it is time to return the term *paradigm* to the fields of the history of science and science studies, where it has served as such a useful analytic tool. Of course, the fact that this article is itself an exercise in the history and study of science means that I will continue to refer to paradigms, but I will do my best to restrict my usage to the self-imposed limits I just described.

Addressing the Anomalies in the Metaphysical Paradigm

The previous section identified three basic anomalies in the metaphysical paradigm: how to define paradigms, whether those paradigms were incommensurate, and the extent to which metaphysical assumptions actually guide research in the social sciences. Starting with issues related to defining paradigms, if the previous system ran into trouble by concentrating on ontological assumptions about the nature of reality to distinguish different approaches to social science methodology, then what does the pragmatic approach have to offer as an alternative? Drawing on the core tenets of pragmatism, I propose to concentrate instead on concepts such as "lines of action" (from William James and George Herbert Mead) and "warranted assertions" (from John Dewey), along with a general emphasis on "workability" (from both James and Dewey). There are, of course, many variations within pragmatism as a philosophical system (for useful introductions, see De Waal, 2005; Rescher, 2000), and I certainly do not claim to be an expert in that area. Hence, my preference is to stay close to the central ideas of those who had the most influence on the social sciences—John Dewey, William James, and George Herbert Mead.

Within that tradition, the task of understanding social science research methodology is no different from understanding any other kind of human endeavor. In particular, deciding on a site for a vacation, selecting a method for a research project, or developing a framework for talking about the decisions that researchers make all amount to what Dewey would call "inquiries," which we undertake to assess either the workability of any potential line of action or the bases for what we claim as warranted assertions. In comparison to the metaphysical paradigm, this means giving up on the assumption that there is some external system that will explain our beliefs to us. Fortunately, there is an alternative close at hand, because we can follow Kuhn's advice and treat our field as composed of groups of scholars who share a consensus about which questions are most important to study and which methods are most appropriate for conducting those studies. Although I would not go so far as to identify Kuhn himself as a traditional pragmatist, I believe that applying his approach to our own field would be considerably more useful than the stance advocated by the metaphysical paradigm—and to say that something is truly "useful" is high praise indeed from a pragmatist perspective.

I am thus claiming that there is a fundamental similarity between saying that members of a specialty area share a consensus about which questions are worth asking and which methods are most appropriate for answering them and saying that they share a consensus about the bases for warranted assertions about the workability of different lines of action. At a practical level, researchers in the field of science studies have created a number of empirical approaches for identifying groups of researchers who share these kinds of paradigmatic interests, including cocitation analysis (Small & Griffith, 1974; White & McCain, 1998). As an example, those tools should be able to locate a group of methodologists who share an interest in different ways of combining qualitative and quantitative methods, and I personally believe that a further investigation within that subfield would currently identify a fascination with typologies as a preferred means for addressing that issue.

Turning to the anomalies associated with the metaphysical paradigm's reliance on a strong version of incommensurability, a pragmatic approach would deny that there is any a priori basis for determining the limits on meaningful communication between researchers who pursue different approaches to their field. Instead, a pragmatic approach would place its emphasis on *shared meanings* and *joint action*. In other words, to what extent are two people (or two research fields) satisfied that they understand each other, and to what extent can they demonstrate the success of that shared meaning by working together on common projects? Here again, the essential emphasis is on actual behavior ("lines of action"), the beliefs that stand behind those behaviors ("warranted assertions"), and the consequences that are likely to follow from different behaviors ("workability").

This approach also makes a useful connection to Kuhn's (1970) revised account of incommensurability in his Postscript, with its emphasis on communication and persuasion. Issues of language and meaning are essential to pragmatism, along with an emphasis on the actual interactions that humans use to negotiate these issues. It would be foolhardy to claim that every person on earth could eventually arrive at a perfect understanding of every other person on earth, but for pragmatism the key issues are, first, how much shared understanding can be accomplished, and then, what kinds of shared lines of behavior are possible from those mutual understandings. This is a far cry from a strong version of incommensurability that peremptorily denies the possibility of meaningful communication across externally defined boundaries. For example, if a realist and a constructivist share an intellectual exchange on a conference panel and the audience applauds in response, that is more than enough to convince a pragmatist that something other than complete incommensurability has happened.

Finally, the anomalies associated with the essential role that research questions rather than metaphysical assumptions play is little more than a restatement of the pragmatist approach itself. In fact, this quintessentially pragmatic approach has always been at the foundation of social science's approach to questions about how to connect "theory" and "methods" in our research—what M. Patton (1988, 2002) called a "paradigm of choices." Finding this kind of continuity between the principles that have guided our previous work and the key tenets of a "new" paradigm is reassuring, to say the least. Even so, there remains the larger task of sifting through the work done under the previous paradigm to locate the useful accomplishments that need to be maintained within the new belief system. Sheer newness is not a virtue, however, and it is important to sift through the accomplishments of previous paradigms to locate the useful elements that need to be maintained.

Retaining the Valuable
Contributions of the Previous Paradigm

In this section, I want to address two contributions from the metaphysical paradigm that I think are especially important to retain and build upon: the importance of epistemological issues within social science research methodology and the need to recognize the central place of worldviews in our work as researchers. Fortunately, I believe the pragmatic approach I am advocating has considerable strengths to offer in building on these prior accomplishments.

My first choice for a valuable contribution from the metaphysical paradigm is its success in shifting discussions about social science research beyond the mostly mechanical concerns that previously dominated this field. Methodology is indeed about more than just methods. To advance that part of our ongoing conversation about bigger issues in social science methodology, I would like to raise the question of why pragmatism was consistently omitted from the list of approaches considered in the metaphysical paradigm.

Actually, there is a relatively straightforward explanation for this exclusion because most pragmatists take a much broader approach to the metaphysical issue. For example, James had an essentially agnostic view toward metaphysics as a whole, whereas Dewey created a revised version of metaphysics that focused on the experience of actions in the world, rather than the existence of either a world outside those experiences or experiences outside such a world. This contrasts sharply with the metaphysical paradigm's emphasis on the nature of reality and possibility of objective truth. Instead, one of the defining features of pragmatism would be an emphasis on "what difference it makes" to believe one thing versus another or to act one way rather than another. Hence, descriptions of pragmatism do not fit easily into a system that it is organized around the essential assumptions of the foundation of the metaphysical paradigm.

Within the philosophy of knowledge, the possibility of separating the more metaphysical aspects of ontology from epistemological and methodological issues is a widely accepted option, and even those approaches that do emphasize the connections between ontology and epistemology often treat them as "loosely coupled" (Giere, 1999; Hacking, 1983, 2000; Zammito, 2004). Thus, what I am calling the pragmatist approach does not ignore the relevance of epistemology and other concepts from the philosophy of knowledge. It does, however, reject the top-down privileging of ontological assumptions in the metaphysical paradigm as simply too narrow an approach to issues in the philosophy of knowledge.

The value of maintaining our attention to epistemological issues in social science research methodology can easily be preserved with a pragmatic approach; however, I would argue that we do need to be more restrained in this regard. The pragmatic approach that I am advocating would concentrate on methodology as an area that connects issues at the abstract level of epistemology and the mechanical level of actual methods. There is thus little reason why *purely* epistemological issues should be of major interest to social science research methodologists—that is the province of philosophers. Yet the "top-down" approach that characterized the metaphysical paradigm had a strong tendency not only to privilege epistemology over methods but also to emphasize ontological issues above all others. In contrast, a pragmatic approach would treat issues related to research itself as the principal "line of action" that methodologists should study, with equal attention to both the epistemological and technical "warrants" that influence how we conduct our research. In particular, I believe that we need to devote equal attention to studying both the connection between methodology and epistemology and the connection between methodology and methods. Furthermore, we need to use our study of methodology to connect issues in epistemology with issues in research design, rather than separating our thoughts about the nature of knowledge from our efforts to produce it. Figure 2.1 illustrates this relationship.

The second aspect of the metaphysical paradigm that the pragmatic approach should not merely retain but build upon is the attention to how our worldviews influence the research that we do. At several points, I have summarized the essential elements of Kuhn's concept of paradigms as a set of shared beliefs among the members of a specialty area about both which questions are most important and which methods are most appropriate for answering those questions. But research questions are not inherently "important," and methods are not automatically "appropriate." Instead, it is we ourselves who make the choices about what is important and what is appropriate, and those choices inevitably involve aspects of our personal history, social background and cultural assumptions. Furthermore, I do not believe for one moment that the participants in any research field ever represent a random assortment with regard to personal history, social background, and cultural assumptions. So we need to continue the reflexive outlook toward what we choose to study and how we choose to do so.

It is important to note that these aspects of our worldviews as researchers involve essentially ethical and moral issues. In addition, recall that some versions of the metaphysical paradigm went beyond the typical emphasis on ontology, epistemology, and methodology to include ethical and moral concerns under the heading of axiology. Earlier, I argued that this inclusion of axiology was too great a departure from the core emphasis on the philosophy on knowledge that was the defining feature of most work within the metaphysical paradigm. In contrast, questions about the connection between

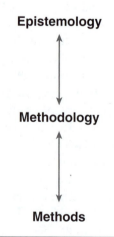

Figure 2.1   Placing Methodology at the Center

ethics and epistemology were a long-standing concern for pragmatists such as James, Dewey, and Mead. In particular, it is not the abstract pursuit of knowledge through "inquiry" that is central to a pragmatic approach, but rather the attempt to gain knowledge in the pursuit of desired ends. Fortunately, the long-standing and central role that ethical issues have played within the field of pragmatism not only reinforces this continuity with the concerns raised by the metaphysical paradigm but also provides a more direct connection to those issues, in contrast to the less direct connection between axiology and the core elements from the philosophy of knowledge.

This attention to the ethical aspects of both the lines of action that people follow and the means they choose to attain them is not, however, the sort of crude pragmatism that simply claims "the ends justify the means." Fortunately, Dewey, James, and Mead all provided useful role models in this regard through their key roles in the original American "Progressive Movement" (Mills, 1969). Each of these scholars was aware of how their own values shaped their research goals, and they each used their writings to further their preferred political agendas. Whether one agrees or disagrees with those values and politics, the more important point is that a pragmatic approach reminds us that our values and our politics are always a part of who we are and how we act. In the end, these aspects of our worldviews are at least as important as our beliefs about metaphysical issues, and a pragmatic approach would redirect our attention to investigating the factors that have the most impact on what we choose to study and how we choose to do so.

New Opportunities Offered by the Pragmatic Approach

Pragmatism is certainly not new to the social sciences, and there are several good reviews of pragmatism, both as a general belief system for the social sciences (e.g., Maxcy, 2003) and as a specific justification for combining qualitative and quantitative methods (Johnson & Onwuegbuzie, 2006). My goal in this section is to add to that existing work by suggesting several ways that pragmatism provides new options for addressing methodological issues in the social sciences. Table 2.2 provides a simple summary of the framework I propose. The columns represent the main comparative distinctions in the table, contrasting a pragmatic approach with the two most common methodological stances in the social sciences, Qualitative and Quantitative Research. The rows make these comparisons in terms of three choices that are central to both the kinds of purposes we pursue and the kinds of procedures we use in that pursuit. The table is thus self-consciously organized around key issues in social science research methodology, rather than the metaphysical paradigm's emphasis on abstract issues in the philosophy of knowledge.

In proposing Table 2.2 as an organizing framework for understanding what the pragmatic approach can offer social science methodology, I must acknowledge a distinct debt to Michael Patton, whose earliest work (1975) divides the differences between Qualitative and Quantitative Research along similar lines, and whose recent work (2002) also seeks a "third way" to address these divisions. In contrast to M. Patton, however, I have reduced the number of rows in my table to the smallest set of key issues that can capture the essential difference between these approaches. This reframing of the key issues also leads me to a rather different summary of what pragmatism has to offer.

Starting with the top row, the distinction between induction and deduction shows up in almost every methods textbook as one of the key features that distinguishes Qualitative and Quantitative Research. Such a sharp separation between these two ways of connecting theory and data is undoubtedly useful for teaching beginning students about the most basic options in making decisions about the kind of research they will do. Yet any experienced researcher knows that the actual process of moving between theory and data never operates in only one direction. Outside of introductory textbooks, the only time that we pretend that research can be either purely inductive or deductive is when we write up our work for publication. During the actual design, collection, and analysis of data, however, it is impossible to operate in either an exclusively theory- or data-driven fashion. Try to imagine acting in the real world for as long as 5 minutes while operating in either a strictly theory-driven, deductive mode or a data-driven, inductive mode—I certainly would not want to be on the same road as anyone who had such a fatally limited approach to driving a vehicle!

The pragmatic approach is to rely on a version of *abductive* reasoning that moves back and forth between induction and deduction—first converting observations into theories and then assessing those theories through

Table 2.2   A Pragmatic Alternative to the Key Issues in Social Science Research Methodology

	Qualitative Approach	Quantitative Approach	Pragmatic Approach
Connection of theory and data	Induction	Deduction	Abduction
Relationship to research process	Subjectivity	Objectivity	Intersubjectivity
Inference from data	Context	Generality	Transferability

action. I must note, however, that my particular version of abduction goes somewhat beyond its traditional use within pragmatism, where it is often treated solely as using theories to account for observations, and thus as an aspect of inductive inferences. From a pragmatic point of view, however, the only way to assess those inferences is through action. Hence, one of the most common uses of abduction in pragmatic reasoning is to further a process of inquiry that evaluates the results of prior inductions through their ability to predict the workability of future lines of behavior.

This particular version of the abductive process is quite familiar to researchers who combine qualitative and quantitative methods in a sequential fashion (Ivankova, Creswell, & Stick, 2006; Morgan, 1998, 2006, in press), where the inductive results from a qualitative approach can serve as inputs to the deductive goals of a quantitative approach, and vice versa. This movement back and forth between different approaches to theory and data does not have to be limited to combinations of methods within a single project. A far more interesting option is to explore the potential for working back and forth between the kinds of knowledge we have already produced under the separate banners of Qualitative and Quantitative Research. What if Quantitative Researchers paid more attention to the incredible range of hypotheses that Qualitative Researchers have "generated" for them? And what if Qualitative Researchers spent more time exploring the range of phenomena that Quantitative Researchers have sought to define and test? Rather than each camp dismissing the others' work as based on wholly incompatible assumptions, our goal would be to search for useful points of connection. These are the kinds of opportunities that a pragmatic approach to social science research has to offer.

Table 2.2 also argues that the usual forced dichotomy between subjective and objective is an equally artificial summary of the relationship between the researcher and the research process. Thus, although one often hears arguments about the impossibility of "complete objectivity," it is just as hard to imagine what "complete subjectivity" would be. Once again, it is only for teaching purposes that we can discuss the possibility of being either completely subjective or objective. Any practicing researcher has to work back and forth between various frames of reference, and the classic pragmatic emphasis on an *intersubjective* approach captures this duality. Inevitably, we need to achieve a sufficient degree of mutual understanding with not only the people who participate in our research but also the colleagues who read and review the products of our research. Thus, this dimension represents the emphasis on processes of communication and shared meaning that are central to any pragmatic approach.

Intersubjectivity also represents the pragmatic response to issues of incommensurability. In a pragmatic approach, there is no problem with asserting both that there is a single "real world" and that all individuals have their own unique interpretations of that world. Rather than treating incommensurability as an all-or-nothing barrier between mutual understanding, pragmatists treat issues of intersubjectivity as a key element of social life. In particular, the pragmatist emphasis on creating knowledge through lines of action points to the kinds of "joint actions" or "projects" that different people or groups can accomplish together. From a methodological point of view, this suggests a "reflexive" orientation where we pay more attention to the social processes that produce both consensus and conflict within our field by asking the following questions: Which aspects of our beliefs about research are in contention and which are widely shared, and how do issues make the transition back and forth between these statuses?

The final dualism that Table 2.2 seeks to transcend is the distinction between knowledge that is either specific and context-dependent or universal and generalized. In this case, the pragmatic approach once again rejects the need to choose between a pair of extremes where research results are either completely specific to a particular context or an instance of some more generalized set of principles. I do not believe it is possible for research results to be either so unique that they have no implications whatsoever for other actors in other settings or so generalized that they apply in every possible historical and cultural setting. From a pragmatic approach, an important question is the extent to which we can take the things that we learn with one type of method in one specific setting and make the most appropriate use of that knowledge in other circumstances. Once again, this involves a process of working back and forth, in this case between specific results and their more general implications.

I have borrowed the idea of *transferability* of research results from Lincoln and Guba, who treated the question of whether the things learned in one context can be applied in another as an "empirical" issue (1985, p. 297). In other words, we cannot simply assume that our methods and our approach to research makes our results either context-bound or generalizable; instead, we need to investigate the factors that affect whether the knowledge we gain can be transferred to other settings. The classic example is assessing whether the results from one particular program evaluation have implications for the use of similar programs in other contexts. This advocacy of transferability thus arises from a solidly pragmatic focus on what people can do with the knowledge they produce and not on abstract arguments about the possibility or impossibility of generalizability. Instead, we always need to ask how much of our existing knowledge might be usable in a new set of circumstances, as well as what our warrant is for making any such claims.

Overall, I believe that an emphasis on abduction, intersubjectivity, and transferability creates a range of new opportunities for thinking about classic methodological issues in the social sciences. At the same time, I want to avoid being misinterpreted as claiming that there is no value in the distinctions between induction and deduction, subjectivity and objectivity, or context and generality. These concepts do have their uses for comparing different approaches to social science research. In particular, I find it helpful to think of Qualitative Research as research that emphasizes an inductive–subjective–contextual approach, whereas Quantitative Research emphasizes a deductive–objective–generalizing approach. Where we encounter problems is by treating these broad tendencies as absolute, defining characteristics for these two different approaches, and these problems become even worse when we deny the possibility of working back and forth between the two extremes. Fortunately, the pragmatic approach offers an effective alternative through its emphasis on the abductive–intersubjective–transferable aspects of our research.

Conclusions

One of the major goals of this article was to examine the recent renewal of attention to Qualitative Research in an effort to understand how combining qualitative and quantitative methods could be lifted to a similar level of legitimacy. My primary "tool" for this analysis was a version of the paradigm concept that both emphasized shared beliefs within a community of researchers and encouraged investigating changes within any field as an active social process. I will thus conclude by focusing on two lessons that can be learned from my reading of this recent history, with an emphasis on the practical implications of those lessons for those of us who are currently engaged in creating a further paradigm shift.

One important lesson from the successful advocacy for renewed attention to Qualitative Research was the value of separating mechanical issues related to qualitative methods per se from a larger set of questions about why we do the kind of research that we do. I believe that there is considerable value in maintaining that distinction. For those who wish to promote the combining of qualitative and quantitative methods, this points to the importance of treating this approach as more than just a mechanically superior way to answer research questions. Although we need to avoid the metaphysical excesses of the previous paradigm, we also need to acknowledge and pursue the epistemological implications of our broader approach to social science research. Fortunately, a pragmatic approach not only supports the kinds of research methods that we advocate but also provides a basis for reorienting the field of social science research methodology in the directions that we favor. The great strength of this pragmatic approach to social science research methodology is its emphasis on the connection between epistemological concerns about the nature of the knowledge that we produce and technical concerns about the methods that we use to generate that knowledge. This moves beyond technical questions about mixing or combining methods and puts us in a position to argue for a properly *integrated methodology* for the social sciences.

The final lesson I want to draw is that merely offering better ways to answer existing questions is not enough to create major changes in a dominant belief system. Thus, despite the problems that resulted from an excessively metaphysical approach to social science methodology, it is also important to recall the initial excitement that greeted those ideas. New paradigms offer new ways to think about the world—new questions to ask and new ways to pursue them. This is the essential nature of paradigms as "worldviews," and those of us who value the possibilities that come from combining qualitative and quantitative methods need to promote a worldview that encourages others to share our beliefs. One part of that work involves inspiring others about the practical value of research designs that combine different methods. Another part involves linking those practical strengths to larger methodological issues in ways that create a sense of excitement about the directions in which our field is headed, and that is the ultimate goal of this article.

References

Babbie, E. (1992). *The practice of social research* (6th ed.). Belmont, NJ: Wadsworth.

Babbie, E. (1995). *The practice of social research* (7th ed.). Belmont, NJ: Wadsworth.

Babbie, E. (2004). *The practice of social* research (10th ed.). Belmont, NJ: Wadsworth.

Collins, H., & Pinch, T. (1998). *The golem: What you should know about science.* Cambridge, UK: Cambridge University Press.

Creswell, J. (1998). *Qualitative inquiry and research design: Choosing among five traditions.* Thousand Oaks, CA: Sage.

Creswell, J. (2003). *Research design: Qualitative, quantitative, and mixed methods approaches* (2nd ed.). Thousand Oaks, CA: Sage.

Creswell, J. W., Plano Clark, V. L., Guttman. M., & Hanson, W. (2003). Advanced mixed methods research designs. In A. Tashakkori & C. Teddlie (Eds.), *Handbook of mixed methods in social & behavioral research* (pp. 209–240). Thousand Oaks, CA: Sage.

Denzin, N., & Lincoln, Y. (1994). Introduction: Entering the field of qualitative research. In N. Denzin & Y, Lincoln (Eds.), *Handbook of qualitative research* (pp. 1–17). Thousand Oaks, CA: Sage.

De Waal, C, (2005). *On pragmatism.* Belmont, NJ: Wadsworth.

Giere, R. (1999). *Science without laws*. Chicago: University of Chicago Press.

Guba, E. (1978). *Toward a methodology of naturalistic inquiry in educational evaluation*. Los Angeles: Center for the Study of Evaluation, University of California, Los Angeles.

Guba, E. (1990). *The paradigm dialog*. Newbury Park, CA: Sage.

Guba, E., & Lincoln, Y. (1989). *Fourth generation evaluation*. Newbury Park, CA: Sage.

Guba. E., & Lincoln, Y. (1994). Competing paradigms in qualitative research. In N. Denzin & Y. Lincoln (Eds.), *Handbook of qualitative research* (pp. 105–177). Thousand Oaks, CA: Sage.

Guba, E., & Lincoln, Y. (2005). Paradigmatic controversies, contradictions, and emerging confluences. In N. Denzin & Y. Lincoln (Eds.), *Handbook of qualitative research* (3rd ed., pp. 191–215). Thousand Oaks, CA: Sage.

Hacking, I. (1983). *Representing and intervening: Introductory topics in the philosophy of natural science*. New York: Cambridge University Press.

Hacking, I. (2000). *The social construction of what?* Cambridge, MA: Harvard University Press.

Hanson, W., Creswell J., Plano Clark, V., Petska, K., & Creswell, J. (2005). Mixed-methods research designs in counseling psychology. *Journal of Counseling Psychology, 52*(2), 224–235.

Happ, M., Dabbs, A., Tate, J., Hricik, A., & Erlen, J. (2006). Exemplars of mixed methods data combination and analysis. *Nursing Research, 55*(2), 43–49.

Hess, D. (1997). *Science studies: An advanced introduction*. New York: New York University Press.

Ivankova, N., Creswell, J., & Stick, S. (2006). Using mixed methods in sequential explanatory design: From theory to practice. *Field Methods, 18*(3), 3–20.

Jasanoff, S., Markle, G., Peterson, J., & Pinch, T. (1995). *Handbook of science and technology studies*. Thousand Oaks, CA: Sage.

Johnson, B., & Onwuegbuzie, A. (2006). Mixed methods research: A research paradigm whose time has come. *Educational Researcher, 33*(7), 14–26.

Kuhn, T. (1970). Postscript—1969. In T. Kuhn, *The structure of scientific revolutions* (2nd ed., pp. 174–210). Chicago: University of Chicago Press.

Kuhn, T. (1974). *The essential tension: Selected studies in scientific tradition and change*. Chicago: University of Chicago Press.

Kuhn, T. (1996). *The structure of scientific revolutions* (3rd ed.). Chicago: University of Chicago Press. (Original work published 1962)

Kuhn, T. (2000). *The road since structure*. Chicago: University of Chicago Press.

Labinger, J., & Collins, H. (Eds.). (2001). *The one culture: A conversation about science*. Chicago: University of Chicago Press.

Lincoln, Y. (1990). The making of a constructivist: A remembrance of transformations past. In E. Guba (Ed.), *The paradigm dialog* (pp. 67–87). Newbury Park, CA: Sage.

Lincoln, Y., & Guba, E. (1985). *Naturalistic inquiry*. Beverly Hills, CA: Sage.

Lincoln, Y., & Guba, E. (1988). Do inquiry paradigms imply inquiry methodologies? In D. Fetterman (Ed.), *Qualitative approaches to evaluation in educational research* (pp. 89–115). Newbury Park, CA: Sage.

Lincoln, Y., & Guba, E. (2000). Paradigmatic controversies, contradictions, and emerging confluences, In N. Denzin & Y. Lincoln (Eds.), *Handbook of qualitative research* (2nd ed., pp. 163–189). Thousand Oaks, CA: Sage.

Masterman, M. (1970). The nature of paradigms. In I. Lakatos & A. Musgrave (Eds.), *Criticism and the growth of knowledge.* New York: Cambridge University Press.

Maxcy, S. (2003). Pragmatic threads in mixed methods research in the social sciences: The search for multiple modes of inquiry and the end of the philosophy of formalism. In A. Tashakorri & C. Teddlie (Eds.), *Handbook of mixed methods in social & behavioral research* (pp. 51–90). Thousand Oaks, CA: Sage.

Mills, C. (1969). *Sociology and pragmatism: The higher learning in America.* New York: Oxford University Press.

Morgan, D. (1998). Practical strategies for combining qualitative and quantitative methods: Applications to health research. *Qualitative Health Research, 8*(3), 362–376.

Morgan, D. (2006). Connected contributions as a motivation combining qualitative and quantitative methods. In L. Curry, R. Shield, & T. Wetle (Eds.), *Applying qualitative and mixed methods in aging and public health research.* Washington, DC: American Public Health Association.

Morgan, D. (in press). *Integrating qualitative and quantitative methods.* Thousand Oaks, CA: Sage.

Neal, M., Hammer, L., & Morgan, D. (2006). Using mixed methods in research related to work and family. In M. Pitt-Cassouphes, E. Kossek, & S. Sweet (Eds.), *The work and family handbook: Multidisciplinary perspectives and approaches.* Mahwah, NJ: Lawrence Erlbaum.

Newman, M. (1992). Prevailing paradigms in nursing. *Nursing Outlook, 10*(1). 10–13, 32.

Patton, J. (1982). *Practical evaluation.* Beverly Hills, CA: Sage.

Patton, M. (1975). *Alternative evaluation research paradigm.* Grand Forks: University of North Dakota Press.

Patton, M. (1988). Paradigms and pragmatism. In D. Fetterman (Ed.), *Qualitative approaches to evaluation in educational research* (pp. 116–137). Newbury Park, CA: Sage.

Patton, M. (1997). *Utilization focused evaluation: The new century text* (3rd ed.). Thousand Oaks, CA: Sage.

Patton, M. (2002). *Qualitative methods and evaluation* (3rd ed.). Thousand Oaks, CA: Sage.

Philips D. (1990). Positivistic science: Myths and realities. In E. Guba (Ed.), *The paradigm dialog* (pp. 31–45). Newbury Park, CA: Sage.

Platt, J. (1996). A *history of sociological research methods in America, 1920–1960.* New York: Cambridge University Press.

Rescher, N. (2000). *Realistic pragmatism: An introduction to pragmatic philosophy.* Albany: State University of New York Press.

Ritzer, G. (1975). *Sociology: A multiple paradigm science.* Boston: Allyn & Bacon.

Rossman, G., & Rallis, S. (2003). *Learning in the field: An introduction to qualitative research* (2nd ed.). Thousand Oaks, CA: Sage.

Sale, J., Lohfeld, L., & Brazil, K. (2002). Revisiting the quantitative-qualitative debate: Implications for mixed methods. *Quality & Quantity, 36*(1), 43–53.

Sayer, .A. (2000). *Realism and social science.* Thousand Oaks, CA: Sage.

Schwandt, T. (1989). Solutions to the paradigm controversy: Coping with uncertainty. *Journal of Contemporary Ethnography, 17*(4), 379–407.

Shadish, W. (1995a). Philosophy of science and the quantitative-qualitative debates: Thirteen common errors. *Evaluation and Program Planning, 18*(1), 63–75.

Shadish, W. (1995b). The quantitative-qualitative debates: "DeKuhnifying" the conceptual context. *Evaluation and Program Planning, 18*(1), 47–49.

Shadish, W., Cook, T., & Campbell, D. (2002). *Experimental and quasi-experimental designs for causal inference.* Boston: Houghton Mifflin.

Small, H., & Griffith, B. (1974). The structure of scientific literatures, I: Identifying and graphing specialties. *Science Studies, 4*(1), 17–40.

Smith J., & Heshusius, L. (1986). Closing down the conversation: The end of the quantitative-qualitative debate among educational inquirers. *Educational Leadership, 15*(12), 4–12.

Tashakkori, A., & Teddlie, C. (2003). Major issues and controversies in the use of mixed methods in the social and behavioral sciences. In A. Tashakorri & C. Teddlie (Eds.), *Handbook of mixed methods in social & behavioral research* (pp. 3–50). Thousand Oaks, CA: Sage.

White, H., & McCain, K. (1998). Visualizing a discipline: An author co-citation analysis of information science, 1972–1995. *Journal of the American Society for Information Science, 49*(4), 327–355.

Zammito, J. (2004). *A nice derangement of epistemes: Post-positivism in the study of science from Quine to Latour.* Chicago: University of Chicago Press.

3

The Transformative-Emancipatory Perspective as a Philosophical Foundation for Mixed Methods Research

Selection: Mertens, D. M. (2003). Mixed methods and the politics of human research: The transformative-emancipatory perspective. In A. Tashakkori & C. Teddlie (Eds.), *Handbook of mixed methods in social and behavioral research* (pp. 135–164). Thousand Oaks, CA: Sage.

Editors' Introduction

While much of the mixed methods community now accepts pragmatism as the best philosophical basis for mixed methods research (Tashakkori & Teddlie, 2003b), other positions have also been advanced. For example, Greene and Caracelli (1997, 2003) discuss a dialectical perspective for mixing methods. They argue that researchers can use multiple paradigms and that such explicit use can lead to a better understanding of a topic through the tensions and contested arguments that emerge when conducting mixed methods.

Donna M. Mertens (2003) also advances an alternative to pragmatism in the present chapter. Drawing extensively from her work as an educator and evaluator, Mertens describes how a transformative-emancipatory perspective can provide a philosophical foundation for mixed methods. Her work and the many included illustrative examples are based on diverse writings, such as those by feminists, disability scholars, and critical theory scholars. Adding to the overall paradigm conversation, Mertens discusses the ontological, epistemological, and methodological stances that form the basis of the transformative-emancipatory perspective and argues for the important role of social justice values in research. In this chapter, Mertens insightfully bridges philosophy with practice when she relates the transformative-emancipatory perspective to the process of conducting research, such as defining the problem, selecting the design, collecting and analyzing data, and using the results.

Discussion Questions and Applications

1. Consider the study by Messer, Steckler, and Dignan (Chapter 19 in this volume). What features of this study are consistent with a transformative-emancipatory perspective? What else might the researchers have done?

2. Tashakkori and Teddlie (2003b) suggest that the transformative-emancipatory perspective might be better conceptualized as a purpose for research instead of a philosophical foundation of research. How do you react to this?

3. In what ways are pragmatism and the transformative-emancipatory perspective similar to and different from each other?

Related References That Extend the Topic

Examine the following references to read alternative perspectives about the foundations for mixed methods:

Greene, J. C., & Caracelli, V. J. (Eds.). (1997). *Advances in mixed-method evaluation: The challenges and benefits of integrating diverse paradigms* (New Directions for Evaluation, No. 74). San Francisco: Jossey-Bass.

Oakley, A. (1998). Gender, methodology and people's ways of knowing: Some problems with feminism and the paradigm debate in social science. *Sociology, 32*(4), 707–731.

Mixed Methods and the Politics of Human Research

The Transformative-Emancipatory Perspective

Donna M. Mertens
Gallaudet University

Researchers in social and behavioral sciences work within and as part of human society and thus are confronted with the full complexity of that society including issues of pluralism and social justice. Historically, research methods texts did not concern themselves with the politics of human research and social justice. However, changing conditions outside and inside of the research world have brought increased attention to the need to address these issues in such work. In society at large, trends in demographics and increased social pluralism increase the importance of recognizing cultural differences and injustice based on those cultural differences. Inside the world of research, the emergence of scholars from diverse ethnic/racial groups, people with disabilities, and feminists has contributed to the conversation by explicating a paradigmatic view of research known as the transformative-emancipatory paradigm. More broadly, the research community has increased its recognition of the importance of the role of values in research. These themes are explored in this chapter to illustrate the potential importance, underlying philosophical

SOURCE: This chapter is reprinted from *Handbook of Mixed Methods in Social and Behavioral Research* (Tashakkori & Teddlie, 2003). Reprinted with permission of Sage Publications, Inc.

assumptions, and methodological implications of the transformative-emancipatory paradigm within the discussion of mixed methods in research.

Demographic Trends and Social Justice

The increase in diverse ethnic/racial groups in the United States has tipped the balance such that those who were termed minority groups in the past are now in the majority in several urban areas, and the projection is that by the year 2020, 70% of all beginning first-grade students will be from non-White groups (Booth, 2000; U.S. Bureau of the Census, 2000). The presence of people with disabilities is also increasing in the United States such that current population estimates indicate that more than 50 million citizens have disabilities (McNeil, 1997), thus suggesting that most research study samples will include people with disabilities even if their disabilities are invisible to the researcher.

The relationship between knowledge about diversity within communities and implications for social justice and equity for diverse groups provides another layer of understanding for researchers. For example, more than 45% of Hispanic youths ages 18 to 24 years are high school dropouts as compared with only 18% of White youths. The dropout rate for Black youths is about 26% (U.S. Bureau of the Census, 1997). Graduation rates have improved for students with disabilities following the passage of the Americans With Disabilities Act and the Individuals With Disabilities Act and its amendments (Horn & Berktold, 1999). However, students with disabilities, especially students with learning disabilities, leave secondary school with dim prospects. They tend to be undereducated and underemployed. Yet if students with disabilities graduate from 4-year colleges and get jobs, their income level is as competitive as that of their nondisabled peers. Worldwide, increased schooling is associated with increased literacy and employment and with decreased poverty and infant mortality (Grant, 1993).

Hill Collins (2000) described the challenges facing U.S. Black women as follows: "Despite differences of age, sexual orientation, social class, region, and religion, U.S. Black women encounter societal practices that restrict us to inferior housing, neighborhoods, schools, jobs, and public treatment" (p. 25). Stanfield (1999) acknowledged the lower economic, employment, and educational opportunities available to many people of color while at the same time cautioning researchers to be mindful of a tendency to "negatively romanticize people of color" (p. 421). The consequence may be studying only negative questions about Black experiences and not asking questions that might shed a more positive light on Black people.

Scholarly Roots of the Transformative-Emancipatory Paradigm

Despite Descartes's attempt to separate science and values during the Age of Enlightenment, current philosophers of science have recognized that science, while an empirically based tradition, is also influenced by values. Thus, scientists cannot ignore the powerful influence of values.

> What counts for or against a claim or theory is how it is integrated in a larger theory or set of theories, and how well these interconnected claims and theories collectively predict, explain, and integrate the firings of our sensory receptors. All of this seems to invite, or at least allow, the inclusion of value claims, or value laden claims, within science. (J. Nelson, 1996, p. 65)

House and Howe (1999) examined tensions between the notion of value-free science and value recognition in social research by raising the questions of values in terms of whose values, which values, and the role of the researcher within the context of values. While Teddlie and Tashakkori argue (Chapter 1, this volume [Tashakkori & Teddlie, 2003]) that pragmatism represents an alternative paradigm that underlies the choice of mixed methods, House and Howe (1999) view the use of practicality as the value basis for a researcher's choices as unsatisfactory in that practicality by itself does not answer the question "Practical for what?" Writing within the context of program evaluation, they stated, "Something could be practical for bad ends. Using practicality as the primary criterion . . . means evaluators (researchers) may serve whatever ends clients or policy makers endorse. Evaluation should be premised on higher social goals than being useful to those in power" (p. 36). Furthermore, the researcher has an important role in documenting the goals and values of programs and policies and in critically examining the goals and values of the interventions under investigation. House and Howe concluded their argument by asserting that subjectivities are important; social arrangements are irremediably interest laden, power laden, and value laden; and the goal of research and evaluation should be a more just and democratic society. Thus, there is an explicit recognition of an important value that should be part of social and behavioral research and evaluation.

Several groups have extended the thinking concerning the place of values in research, including feminists, members of diverse ethnic/racial groups, and people with disabilities. Feminist philosophers of science recognize that there are two kinds of evidence for individual theories, research projects, methodologies, and claims (L. Nelson, 1996). One of these is observation (data), and the other is a body of accepted methods, standards, and theory. L. Nelson

(1996) contended that both of these kinds of evidence are social in nature and are thus influenced by the values of the scientist and the scientific community. Feminist epistemologists hold that it is a mistake to ask for value-free science (Tuana, 1996). Rather, it is important for good science to focus attention on the dynamics of gender and oppression in the theories and methods of science.

Feminist Scholars

Feminist views on research take many different forms, but all are premised on the knowledge of women's oppression and the vision of social justice for women through research as one of a range of strategies (Olesen, 2000; Ribbens & Edwards, 1998; Truman, Mertens, & Humphries, 2000). Feminists have made a unique contribution by exposing the centrality of male power in the social construction of knowledge. They have also challenged some of the fundamental binaries of traditional approaches such as objectivity and distance from the participants and hierarchies among researchers and the researched. Yet Black and Third World women (e.g., Bhavnani, 1991; Hill Collins, 2000; Mohanty, 1991) and lesbian and disabled feminists (e.g., Dockery, 2000; Mertens, 2000b) have criticized the "White," able-bodied, heterosexual feminist movement as not adequately representing their viewpoints. Hill Collins (2000) argued that human solidarity and social justice are the values that underlie transformative-emancipatory research. However, she also recognized the need to take into account the uniqueness of the Black women's experience when she stated,

> While U.S. Black women's experiences resemble others, such experiences remain unique. The importance of Black women's leadership in producing Black feminist thought does not mean that others cannot participate. It does mean that the primary responsibility for defining one's own reality lies with the people who live that reality, who actually have those experiences. (p. 35)

Stanfield (1999) discussed the implications of living in a racist society that is dominated by White supremacy so pervasive that no one can escape its touch in terms of socialization, including social and behavioral scientists. He defined racialism as "attitudes and actions of stereotyping, exclusive practices, and the creation and maintenance of unequal access to resources, education, gainful employment markets, investment capital, the polity, and natural resources" (p. 420). He contrasted racialism with racism, which is a more blatant or covert bigotry against racialized out-groups in attitudes and/or behavior. Racialism is more insidious in some ways as it may masquerade as a more benign effort on the part of researchers to study Black people, but with inappropriate processes or pursuing overly negative questions. Researchers need to be cognizant of the historical background of people of color, the racialist nature of society, and the impact of these forces on their choice of methods and the substance of the questions they investigate. Contemporary conventions of social science research on people of color commonly are based on assumptions of individual or cultural deficits in the Black community and discourage empowerment epistemologies, theories, methods, and intervention strategies.

Disability Scholars

People with disabilities have been viewed through various lenses throughout history. Gill (1999) described the moral model and the medical model of disability (Longmore, 1994). The moral model suggests that the disability results as a punishment for sin or as a means of inspiring or redeeming others. The medical model sees the disability as a problem or a measurable defect located in the individual that needs a cure or alleviation that can be provided by medical experts. In the disability community, Seelman (1998) described a shift away from the medical model that essentially focused on the impairment as a sickness and the role of the professional in treating this malady. Gill (1999) recognized a more progressive stance in the rehabilitation model where the goal is to help the individual regain as much normal independent functioning as possible.

Seelman (1998) described a new paradigm of service and opportunities that shifts the location of the problem from within the individual to the environmental response to the disability. This paradigm that evolved from the efforts of scholars, activists with disabilities, and their non-disabled allies departs from these former models in terms of its definition of disability problems, the scope of potential solutions, and the values underlying both the definition of the problems and solutions (Gill, 1999). The new paradigm frames disability from the perspective of a social, cultural minority group such that disability is defined as a dimension of human difference and not a defect (Gill, 1999; Mertens, 1998, 2000b). Within this paradigm, the category of disability is recognized as being socially constructed such that its meaning is derived from society's response to individuals who deviate from cultural standards. Furthermore, disability is viewed as one dimension of human difference. According to Gill (1999), the goal for people with disabilities is not to eradicate their sickness but instead to celebrate their distinctness, pursue their equal place in American society, and acknowledge that their differentness is not defective but rather valuable.

Critical Theory

Critical theory has contributed to the understanding of oppression and discrimination primarily on the basis of socioeconomic status and class (Humphries, Mertens, & Truman, 2000; Kellner 1997; Kincheloe & McLaren, 2000). Critical theorists share concerns with feminists, people of diverse ethnic/cultural backgrounds, and people with disabilities in terms of power differentials and a search for a more egalitarian and democratic social order. With a specific focus on the political nature of institutions, critical theorists analyze power interests and how research can be used to either challenge or support the status quo. While current critical theorists have expressed an understanding that there are multiple forms of power, including race, gender, and sexual orientation, there is still a core belief that economic factors can never be separated from other axes of oppression (Kincheloe & McLaren, 2000).

Paradigmatic Assumptions of the Transformative-Emancipatory Paradigm

A Paradigm is a conceptual model of a person's worldview, complete with the assumptions that are associated with that view. Three major paradigms are operating in the research community today. The positivist-postpositivist paradigm is associated with traditional research approaches such as experimental or quasi-experimental designs and causal comparative and correlational research approaches. The interpretive-constructivist paradigm is associated with many qualitative approaches to research such as ethnography, case studies, and phenomenological investigations. The third is the transformative-emancipatory paradigm, which is described as follows:

> Transformative scholars assume that knowledge is not neutral but is influenced by human interests, that all knowledge reflects the power and social relationships within society, and that an important purpose of knowledge construction is to help people improve society (Banks, 1993, 1995). Transformative theory is used as an umbrella term that encompasses paradigmatic perspectives such as emancipatory (Lather, 1992; Mertens, 1998), anti-discriminatory (Humphries & Truman, 1994; Truman, Mertens, & Humphries, 2000), participatory (Reason, 1994; DeKoning & Martin, 1996; Whitmore, 1998), and Freirian approaches (McLaren & Lankshear, 1994) and is exemplified in the writings of feminists (Alcoff & Potter, 1993; Fine, 1992; Hill Collins, 2000; Reinharz, 1992), racial/ethnic minorities (Stanfield, 1999; Stanfield & Dennis, 1993; Madison, 1992), people with disabilities (Gill, 1999; Oliver, 1992; Mertens & McLaughlin, 1995), and people who work on behalf of marginalized groups. (Mertens, 1999, p. 4)

The transformative paradigm is characterized as placing central importance on the lives and experiences of marginalized groups such as women, ethnic/racial minorities, members of the gay and lesbian communities, people with disabilities, and those who are poor. The researcher who works within this paradigm consciously analyzes asymmetric power relationships, seeks ways to link the results of social inquiry to action, and links the results of the inquiry to wider questions of social inequity and social justice (Mertens, 1998; Mertens, Farley, Madison, & Singleton, 1994; Truman et al., 2000).

According to researchers, there are three defining questions that determine our worldview (Guba & Lincoln, 1994; Mertens, 1998). The ontological question asks, "What is the nature of reality and, by extension, truth?" The epistemological question asks, "What is the nature of knowledge and the relationship between the knower and the would-be known?" The methodological question asks, "How can the knower go about obtaining the desired knowledge and understanding?" Each question is answered differently by scholars who align themselves with the three respective paradigms. After a brief explanation of how these three questions are answered for each of the three major paradigms, a more in-depth explanation is provided for the transformative-emancipatory paradigm and accompanying implications for the use of mixed methods research approaches within that context.

Ontology

The postpositivist paradigm's ontological view holds that there is one reality—one truth—that can be known within a certain level of probability (Mertens, 1998). The interpretive-constructivists have argued for the recognition of multiple socially constructed realities. One simple example is that many fairy tales end with the phrase "They all lived happily ever after." But as can be seen in the tale of Little Red Riding Hood, it depends on whose viewpoint is being used to tell the story. Do you think that if the wolf told the story, he would end it that way? This is not meant to imply that a postpositivist scholar would reach such an overly simplistic conclusion that everyone lived happily ever after. However, there might be a tendency to focus on a reductive assessment of how happy the characters were at the end, expressed in quantitative terms with plus or minus some degree of error. Because the interpretive-constructivist scholars would tend to focus on a credible description of the multiplicity of viewpoints (the wolf, Little Red Riding Hood, and the grandmother), these researchers have been subjected to the criticism that they are mired in absolute relativism such that no one perspective is any truer than any other perspective.

The transformative-emancipatory ontological assumption holds that there are diversities of viewpoints with regard to many social realities but that those viewpoints need to be placed within political, cultural, historical, and economic value systems to understand the basis for the differences. And then, researchers need to struggle with revealing those multiple constructions as well as with making the decisions about privileging one perspective over another.

For example, there are many concepts that are socially constructed, including what are appropriate gender roles. Clearly, there are diverse opinions as to how to define this concept, ranging from a submissive compliant doormat to a self-determined empowered woman who can think clearly and act decisively when the situation requires it. In investigating gender roles, the transformative-emancipatory researcher would ask, "When we as a society teach girls to be passive and subservient, what are the consequences of that in terms of their physical safety, earnings, and mental health?" While this question could be asked by researchers from all paradigms, it would be inescapable and of central importance for the transformative-emancipatory researcher.

Epistemology

In epistemological terms, the issue of objectivity is salient, along with implications for the nature of the relationship between the researcher and the researched (Mertens, 1998). In the postpositivist paradigm, objectivity is considered to be paramount and is thought to be achieved by observing from a somewhat distant and dispassionate standpoint. In the interpretive-constructivist paradigm, interaction between the researcher and the participants is felt to be essential as they struggle together to make their values explicit and create the knowledge that will be the results of the study.

In transformative terms, objectivity is valued in the sense of providing a balanced and complete view of the program processes and effects such that bias is not interjected because of a lack of understanding of key viewpoints. However, to obtain this depth of understanding, it is necessary for the researcher to be involved in the communities affected by the service, program, or policy to a significant degree. This epistemological assumption underscores the importance of an interactive link between the researcher and the participants, with sensitivity given to the impact of social and historical factors in the relationship between the researcher and the participants as well as the impact of those variables on the construction of knowledge.

Feminists have rejected the "view from nowhere" conception of objectivity and suggested that an alternative notion of objectivity might be more appropriate (Harding, 1993; Mertens, 1999; Tuana, 1996). One common tenet is that objectivity be redefined as the reduction of bias because of adequate representation of diverse groups to ensure objectivity. This requires a closeness in terms of interactions between the researchers and members of diverse groups. As Tuana (1996) wrote from the feminist perspective,

> It should be no surprise that it is feminist philosophers of science and episte-mologists who are vociferously rejecting the Cartesian model of the isolated knowing subject and replacing it with models that emphasize the centrality of our relationships with others to the process of knowing. (p. 31)

And Stanfield (1999) pragmatically asked, "How ethical is it to view one-self as an authority in the study of the racialized oppressed, when one has had marginal or no contact with or real interest in the lives of the people involved?" (p. 429).

Methodological Assumptions

Finally, in methodological terms, the postpositivist paradigm is character-ized as using primarily quantitative methods that are interventionist and decontextualized (Mertens, 1998). The interpretive-constructivist paradigm is characterized as using primarily qualitative methods in a hermeneutical and dialectical manner. The transformative paradigm might involve quanti-tative, qualitative, or mixed methods, but the community affected by the research would be involved to some degree in the methodological and pro-grammatic decisions. Mixed methods designs that use both quantitative and qualitative methods can be used in any paradigm; however, the underlying assumptions determine which paradigm is operationalized.

These philosophical assumptions provide the foundation for guiding methodology for transformative research. The research is conducted with involvement of all relevant communities, especially the least advantaged. The research conclusions are data based, but the data are generated from an inclusive list of persons affected by the research, with special efforts to include those who have been traditionally underrepresented. It does not exclude those who have been traditionally included in the research process, that is, the decision makers, program administrators and staff, and funding agency representatives. It does explicitly recognize that certain voices have been absent, misrepresented, or marginalized and that inclusion of these voices is necessary for a rigorous research study. Conclusions are based on the collection, analysis, and interpretation of inclusive data and are not for-gone conclusions. Qualitative, quantitative, or mixed methods can be used; however, contextual and historical factors must be described, with special sensitivity given to issues of power that can influence the achievement of social justice and avoidance of oppression.

Implications of the Transformative-Emancipatory Paradigm for Mixed Methods Research

The most fundamental principle of the transformative-emancipatory paradigm in terms of methodology is that it has a pervasive influence throughout the research process. This section contains explanations of the implications of recognition and implementation of paradigmatic assumptions from the transformative-emancipatory paradigm, with examples of implications drawn from a variety of studies. The following aspects of a mixed methods research design are discussed and illustrated: (a) defining the problem and searching the literature; (b) identifying the research design; (c) identifying data sources and selecting participants; (d) identifying or constructing data collection instruments and methods; and (e) analyzing, interpreting, and reporting results.

Defining the Problem and Searching the Literature

Who researchers talk to, what literature they read, and whose opinions are given privilege in the formulation of the research problem and approach have an impact on their ability to address an issue that has relevance to the least advantaged populations and to accurately represent the diverse voices of research participants. Conducting a literature review is typically considered one of the first steps for researchers to begin formulating a research question (Mertens, 1998). Researchers can direct the literature search to be inclusive of quantitative, qualitative, and mixed methods approaches. They can also deliberately search for literature that addresses the concerns of diverse groups and issues of discrimination and oppression. However, they should be aware of at least three biases in traditional mainstream literature sources. First, quantitative research continues to dominate most journals in the social and behavioral sciences, either because of choice of the researchers or because of the gatekeepers who decide which articles will be published. Second, it is uncommon to find articles that directly address issues of discrimination and oppression within the context of research variables. Third, published literature represents an elite perspective that may well be different from that found in the streets and communities where the less powerful groups live.

Literature reviews are excellent ways to gather information related to the historical and contextual issues of importance to the population of concern. Buchanan's (1999) historical study, *Illusions of Equality,* provides an example of both the benefits of literature for gaining historical perspective and the limitations of this approach with respect to marginalized groups. Buchanan conducted a historical study of the working lives of deaf men and women in the United States from the mid-19th century to the establishment of an industrial-based working class during World War II. Using both quantitative and qualitative data, he explained the varied factors within the deaf community and U.S. society at large that have alternatively restrained and advanced the fortunes of deaf workers. Because his study was primarily based on organized state and national associations, he acknowledged that it focused on the most highly educated and professionally successful White males. The study was not centered on deaf women, deaf individuals of color, or marginally schooled and employed deaf adults because they are not generally represented in official documents.

Meadow-Orlans (2002) presented a picture of the complex terrain in the area of deafness research by explaining the impact of social change and conflict in that context. She reviewed quantitative and qualitative research in the area of sign language and achievement, and she traced its impact to policy changes in educational practices with deaf children. While Meadow-Orlans chronicled positive changes, she also noted that bitter skirmishes and conflicts have accompanied nearly every positive change. For example, a contemporary controversy emanates from the emerging use of cochlear implants to improve hearing. The medical community and some hearing parents describe the cochlear implant as a modern miracle of biotechnology (Lane, 1993). Yet many members of the deaf community (those who consider themselves to be culturally deaf) object to the surgical procedures as the "work of the devil" that the medical community is using to try to stamp out their cultural community. Any researcher who wants to work in a marginalized community should carefully explore the historical background and be well-versed in the historical and cultural conflicts, such as those described in this paragraph for the deaf community, that can affect the research process.

Thus, a literature review is an important step in formulating the research problem and questions, but it is not sufficient to define the problem adequately. Scholars in the field of participatory research have long recognized the importance of allowing the problem definition to arise from the community of concern (Kemmis & McTaggart, 2000; Whitmore, 1998). In keeping with the transformative-emancipatory paradigm, a problem can be defined through a synergistic relationship with the important participants, with a special sensitivity to issues of power. Stanfield (1999) criticized research questions and approaches that function at a distance from the populations under study. He wrote, "In many research areas, research can be done in the comforts of the library, computer lab, or Internet. Correspondingly, it has become increasingly easy to do research on human beings without talking to a single person representative of a population or community" (p. 418). He described researchers who are reluctant to venture out into a poor non-White neighborhood to have conversations with people representative of those in their impersonal secondary data sets.

Stanfield (1999) recommended that investigators who are specializing in research on the poor and/or on people of color spend quality time with the people about whom they claim professional authority. They may find that many of their academic ideas about the population on which they are supposedly authoritative are irrelevant, obsolete, or popular (but biased) "folk wisdoms." Stanfield called for "relevance validity" and defined that as "data that fit the realities of the people it supposedly represents" (p. 419). Steps toward achieving the definition of a problem by spending quality time with people may require the researcher to apply a mixed methods approach in the definition of the problem. Observation, interviewing, review of demographic and other statistical data, and sometimes preliminary surveys are mixed methods strategies that can be brought to problem definition.

Spending quality time with the population of concern can ameliorate several biases, specifically (a) building trust, (b) using an appropriate theoretical framework, (c) developing balanced questions, and (d) developing questions that might lead to transformative answers.

Building Trust. Stanfield (1999) claimed that researchers who do research without firsthand contact tend to view those studied as commodities or objects, while those who are studied in such circumstances tend to view the researcher as an exploiter who is only interested in extracting data and then disappearing. Cohen-Mitchell's (2000) study of an economic development program for disabled women in El Salvador illustrated the strategy of using firsthand quality contact time with the women in the study as a way to set a research agenda that was geared toward social change. By focusing her research design on the women's social reality, Cohen-Mitchell was able to create research questions that were geared toward documenting the impact of the women on creating development programs that would potentially affect their lives. She wrote,

> Before I could begin with interviews, it was necessary to build an environment of trust and confidence with the women I would be inviting to work on a collaborative research effort for the next five months. . . . Since people were constantly streaming in and out of the office and the ceramics workshop, my presence there and willingness to engage in spontaneous conversation was important. This allowed the women to sound me out and decide for themselves whether or not I was someone they felt comfortable inviting into their lives. (p. 150)

Theoretical Framework. As discussed in the introductory section of this chapter, various theoretical frameworks have been used to explain the poor academic performance or social conditions in the lives of women, people of color, people with disabilities, and other marginalized groups. The medical model of disability has been used to frame research in terms of how to "fix" the problem in disabled persons. Theoretical frameworks used with people of color have either blamed the individuals (genetic inferiority) or blamed the culture. Such deficit models lead to framing the problem of poverty and underachievement of children in poor urban or rural schools in terms of social deficiency or cultural deficits rather than in terms of the marginal resources of their schools and the racialized politics of local, state, and federal governments (Mertens, 1998, 1999; Stanfield, 1999; Villegas, 1991). The transformative paradigm frames gender, race/ethnicity, disability, sexual orientation, and other bases of diversity from the perspective of a social, cultural minority group such that the defining characteristic is viewed as a dimension of human difference and not a defect (Gill, 1999; Mertens, 1998, 2000b). Within this paradigm, the category of diversity is recognized as being socially constructed such that its meaning is derived from society's response to individuals who deviate from cultural standards.

For example, Cohen-Mitchell (2000) rejected the deficit model that had shaped previous economic development research on women with disabilities in El Salvador and other countries. Instead of focusing on a preset agenda of rehabilitation and vocational skill training, she engaged in dialogue with the women to determine their own views of themselves as disabled women and the need to reframe that perception according to their own needs, desires, and possibilities.

Balanced Questions. Stanfield (1999) indicated that researchers are socialized to ask negative questions about Black experiences, ignoring questions that might shed a more positive light on Black people. He wrote,

> For instance, while we may ask community residents about the needs of their community, we rarely ask questions about strengths. In some quarters, perhaps including evaluation, this is changing. But the focus of many interventions on social problems sustains the tendency to focus on negatives. While we may ask questions about why Black youth or adults get into trouble with the law, we rarely try to find the good kids and grown-ups with sterling moral characters and ask them how and why is it they maintain their impeccable moral characters in high risk environments. (pp. 421–422)

Thus, Stanfield recommended that researchers balance their research questions so as to be inclusive of both positive and negative aspects of the phenomena under study.

Social Transformation. To follow this strand of thinking to the next step, if a transformative theoretical framework guides the study and balanced questions are asked, then what is the nature of the questions that will facilitate a link between the study's findings and social transformation? How can the questions be molded to get at what is needed for social transformation? The overall research questions need to be framed to acknowledge that it is not the individual's psychological, physical, or cultural deficits that are the focus of the questions. Rather, the focus should be on structural frameworks of authority and relations of power in institutions and communities.

This is the perspective adopted by Bowen and Bok (1998) in *The Shape of the River*, a study of how race-sensitive admissions policies work and their effects on students of different races. They asked questions such as the following:

- How much do race-sensitive admissions increase the likelihood that Blacks will be admitted to selective universities?
- How well do Black students perform academically in comparison to their White classmates, and what success do they have in their subsequent careers?
- How actively do Black graduates participate in civic and community affairs?
- How do graduates of selective universities perceive the contribution of having been part of a diverse study body to their capacity to live and work with people of other races?

The authors concluded by asking what the effect of terminating such race-sensitive policies would be on the lives of both Black and White people and on the communities in which they live. Thus, they framed their questions on the broader structural frameworks of authority in the institutions that have the power to influence national policy on this issue.

Identifying the Research Design

Traditional quantitative approaches to research include experimental, quasi-experimental, causal comparative, correlational, and surveys. Qualitative approaches include focus groups, case studies, ethnographic research, and participatory models of research. Within the assumptions associated with the transformative-emancipatory perspective, several of these approaches could be combined in a mixed methods design. However, several ethical issues associated with different design choices arise from this perspective.

Truman (2000) addressed several ethical issues that arose in an emancipatory study of safe sex and health issues among the gay community in Manchester, England. She selected a mixed methods design, combining qualitative and quantitative methods, based on the needs of her client (an activist group of gay men) and her own emancipatory philosophical beliefs. The client wanted her to conduct a needs assessment that the group could then use to approach funding agencies to support a program of materials distribution on the topic of safe sex. She described the decision to adopt a quantitative design as follows: "The group believed that a large-scale quantitative survey for gay and bisexual men would provide the 'factual evidence' for this need. Thus, a quasi-positivist framework for the conduct of the study was required to meet this criteria" (p. 30). However, she understood that a purely quantitative approach would not sufficiently capture the complexity of the problem. Therefore, she enlisted the help of members of the gay community to provide a qualitative review of the instrument as a part of the pilot-testing.

Bowen and Bok (1998) chose a complex quantitative-qualitative design to study the long-term consequences of considering race in college and university admissions. They chose a causal comparative quantitative design that allowed comparisons to be made between the academic performance of more than 80,000 Black and White college students who were included in the *College and Beyond* database. The database contains information from students who had matriculated at 28 academically selective colleges and universities during the fall of 1951, the fall of 1976, and the fall of 1989. The study was designed to allow comparisons of Black-White differences as well as differences in subgroups of students based on gender, low-high Scholastic Aptitude Test (SAT) scores, college majors, and level of terminal degree (bachelor's degree or graduate education). Further quantitative comparisons were designed into the study through the use of a comparison group of students who did not attend the selective colleges and universities in the *College and Beyond* database. To supplement the quantitative data and aid in the interpretation of the results, they included a qualitative component that involved follow-up interviews with a subsample of the larger sample. The interviews were designed to be "free-flowing rather than structured" (p. 301). The comments from the interviews were carefully described as not being intended for scientific analysis, but they seemed to be useful to illustrate trends identified in the empirical analysis or to offer possible explanations for the findings.

Delk and Weidekamp (2000) used a mixed methods design to determine the effects of the Shared Reading Project, a program designed to provide hearing parents and caregivers with visually based strategies to read books to their deaf and hard-of-hearing children. It targets the families of deaf and hard-of-hearing children from birth through 8 years of age. David Schleper, Jane Fernandes, and Doreen Higa first began the Shared Reading Project at the Hawai'i Center for the Deaf and the Blind in 1993. Subsequently, the program was implemented at the Kendall Demonstration Elementary School on the Gallaudet University campus. During 1997–1998, the project was expanded to include five other sites: an urban center school for the deaf, a residential school with satellite programs in a rural state, an urban public school program, and two not-for-profit organizations serving families with deaf and hard-of-hearing children in urban and rural areas.

Hopson, Lucas, and Peterson (2000) chose a mixed methods design to examine the effects of a community-based HIV/AIDS prevention and intervention program based on an inclusive participatory philosophy. Their beliefs led them to emphasize the importance of listening to what program people said about their understandings and valuing what the disease meant to those who were infected with and affected by the disease. A sociolinguistic framework allowed the researchers to explore the meanings of those infected with and affected by the disease during the early stages of the study so as to design more appropriate data collection strategies and interventions. They supported their choice of a mixed methods design as follows: "When language meanings of program beneficiaries reveal how they align or perceive themselves in the context of HIV/AIDS, evaluation and program planners might use this to structure more valid instruments or design interventions that are appropriate and meaningful" (p. 31).

One of the most serious criticisms raised by many feminists and other ethicists in terms of research designs refers to the use of control groups in experimental studies (Mertens, 1998). An ethical problem emerges with the use of control groups in that the experimental group receives the treatment but the control group does not. Feminists raise the following question: Is it ethical to deny "treatment" to one group on a random basis? Many times, school or social agency policies prevent the random assignment of people to conditions, and thus a true experimental design is not possible.

The major professional associations in the human sciences, such as the American Educational Research Association, the American Psychological Association, and the American Evaluation Association, all have ethical guidelines that are designed to protect the welfare of human participants in research. Nevertheless, controversies arise in the use of random assignment in blind clinical trials to test the effectiveness of new drugs (Stephens, 2000). Drug companies are turning to Third World countries more and more to test new drugs because, compared with the United States, the restrictions are not as stringent, costs are lower, and the patients they need for the testing are plentiful and more naive (Flaherty, Nelson, & Stephens, 2000). While some researchers support the use of placebos (inert dummy medicines) to be given to the control group, the *Declaration of Helsinki* (an international medical document on ethics in research) was revised to state that "experimental therapies always should be tested against 'best current' treatments" and that "placebos should be used only when no treatment exists" (Okie, 2000, p. A3).

While all researchers recognize the need to protect human participants, the transformative-emancipatory researchers have raised additional ethical issues related to design choices and have suggested alternative approaches. Consideration can be given to designs that do not involve denial of treatment such as time-series designs, use of a known alternative treatment, comparison with an extant group whose members have similar characteristics but who are not in a position to access the intervention, or comparison with a larger statistical base in terms of known levels of incidence (Mertens & McLaughlin, 1995). For example, in the Shared Reading Project, plans for comparison groups might include young deaf children of deaf parents because their literacy has typically been higher than that of deaf children of hearing parents.

Identifying Data Sources and Selecting Participants

Many issues arise within the context of identifying data sources and selecting participants, including the following questions. Who is in the target group? What are the implications of different choices for labeling the target group? What are the implications of diversity within the target group? What can be done to improve the inclusiveness of the sample to increase the probability that traditionally marginalized groups are adequately and accurately represented?

Members of the Target Group. Inherent in the choice to work within the transformative-emancipatory paradigm is the need to define groups based on the characteristics that are associated with greater discrimination and oppression. In simplistic terms, these could be listed as race/ethnicity, sex/gender, disability, sexual orientation, and economic status. However, researchers must delve into these categories in such a way that they can meaningfully select people who are representative of diverse groups to be included in their studies. This is not a simple task.

Take race and ethnicity as examples. Race is defined as "a biological grouping within the human species with shared physical characteristics and genetic material" (Walsh, Smith, Morales, & Sechrest, 2000, pp. 1–3). Ethnicity is defined as "an individual's identification as a member of a social group with a common background, usually racial, national, tribal, religious, or linguistic" (pp. 1–3). Choices for identifying someone's race or ethnicity such as self-identification, third-party identification, and use of a government protocol such as the census categories are problematic. Even the use of the category "multiracial" is problematic in that it might include those of German-Irish descent as well as those of Hispanic-African descent.

Typically, transformative-emancipatory researchers are interested in studying those characteristics thought to be associated with acts of prejudice and discrimination, such as racial phenotypes (e.g., skin color, facial features), rather than establishing a genetic link between a particular race and a societal impact. Walsh et al. (2000) acknowledged that the race variable is used as a proxy for other variables that are known or believed to correlate with race.

However, they recommended that researchers be explicit about which variables they believe have a substantial causal role in their studies and then be explicit about those and measure them more directly. Writing within the context of mental health research, they provided a list of possible ecological variables that might be asserted as possible influences on mental health service use and outcomes such as level of acculturation or availability of coping strategies, comfort with ethnic and cultural differences, communication and language skills, age-related issues, attitudes toward mental health and illness, education and literacy, group identification, gender-related issues, and support networks.

Rather than relying on a simplistic categorization of race/ethnicity as explanatory variables, researchers should strive to identify those variables that are theoretically linked to program use and impact. For example, in mental health research, they should consider including variables such as perceived stigma of mental disorder, availability of other mental health services, insurance status, social class, beliefs about treatment efficacy, and trust in providers (Walsh et al., 2000). A further discussion of how overly simplistic reliance on racial categories as explanatory variables can be is provided later in the subsection on analyzing, interpreting, and using research findings (Agar, 2000).

Impact of Labeling Target Groups. Two research studies have struggled with strategies for operationalizing their sample definitions in the context of youths who are homeless or labeled "at risk" in ways that did not put the young people at greater risk because of negative connotations associated with the sample definition (Madison, 2000; Rheaume & Roy, 2000). Rheaume and Roy (2000) studied street youths from diverse cultural groups of recent immigrants to Canada who were residents of community-supported housing. The authors began with the concept that they were studying street kids but changed their focus in midstream when they realized that they were studying youths in serious trouble, perhaps suffering from family problems. Once they reframed the definition as troubled youths who had sought community support voluntarily, the social construction of the categories influenced the research design in many other ways. The focus of the intervention shifted to identifying legal interventions that could be used to place the youths in safer housing and identifying social services that could help to reintegrate the youths with their families.

Madison (2000) also challenged the label used to identify participants as "at-risk" youths in developing and evaluating social programs. In a study of a statewide youth program, she reported that *at-risk youth* was used as a label for low-income African American, Latino, and Asian youths and thus served as a stereotypical sociopolitical label. Madison argued,

The term *at-risk youth* was coined to inter-changeably describe both the problem and the youth. Some use the term primarily to describe a category of young people who are a problem to society. This language not only provides social group identity to this category of youth, but the contextual meaning of the language stigmatizes the youth as undesirable rather than the social situation responsible for placing them at risk. (p. 20)

The at-risk label led to negative self-images on the part of the youths and blaming of parents who were struggling economically and were thus unavailable to their children. She recommended reframing the definition of the program participants in terms of youths who were growing up without adults to guide and nurture them through the critical adolescent development stage. Thus, the focus of interventions could change to the provision of a safe environment to engage youths in productive activities supervised by adults during the nonschool hours. And the study addressed the broader policy implications for addressing the educational inequities and structural unemployment that create the economic deprivation that contributes to the parents' inability to be available to their children.

Diversity Within the Target Population. One of the major contributions that has come from transformative scholars is exploration of the myth of homogeneity, that is, that all members of a minority group share the same characteristics (Stanfield, 1993, 1999). As Seelman (1999) noted about the demographics within the disability community, there is great diversity within the 20% of the national population who have disabilities. The diversity includes not only severity and types of disabilities but also functional limitations, limitations in performance of activities and instrumental activities of daily living, use of assistive devices, and receipt of certain benefits associated with disabilities. Demographic variations are also important. Women have higher rates of severe disabilities than do men (9.7% vs. 7.7%), while men have slightly higher rates of nonsevere disabilities. Considering both sex and race, Black women have the highest rate of severe disabilities (14.3%), followed by Black men (12.6%). Rates of severe disabilities for men and women who are American Indian, Eskimo, or Aleut are nearly as high; persons who are American Indian have the highest rates of nonsevere disabilities. Researchers who undertake research with these populations need to be knowledgeable about the diversity within the community.

In preparing a sample design for a study of court accessibility for deaf and hard-of-hearing people in the United States, Mertens (2000a) worked with an advisory board that included people who preferred a variety of communication modes and represented different aspects of the judicial system. The sample design was constructed to represent the diversity of communication modes in the deaf and hard-of-hearing communities, including highly educated deaf users of American Sign Language (ASL); deaf adults with limited education and reading skills, some of whom communicated with sign language, gestures, and pantomime; deaf/blind adults who used interpreters at close range; highly educated hard-of-hearing adults who used personal assistive listening devices; deaf adults who used Mexican Sign Language (MSL); and deaf adults who relied on oral communication (reading lips and print English). In addition to the diversity in terms of communication preference, the groups were selected to be diverse in terms of gender, race/ethnicity, and status with the court (e.g., juror, witness, victim).

The Canadian Research Institute for the Advancement of Women (1996) suggested that researchers consider the following questions to guide them in determining whether they have been inclusive in their sampling strategies:

- Are we including people from both genders and diverse abilities, ages, classes, cultures, ethnicities, families, incomes, languages, races, disabilities, and sexualities?
- What barriers are we erecting to exclude a diversity of people?
- Have we chosen the appropriate data collection strategies for diverse groups, including providing for preferred modes of communication?

Thus, the transformative-emancipatory perspective prods the researcher to go beyond consideration of sample size to examine the barriers that might be impeding the full inclusion of diverse groups.

Identifying or Constructing Data Collection Instruments and Methods

The combination of both quantitative and qualitative data collection methods is not unusual. For example, the Shared Reading Project collected both quantitative and qualitative data—a mixed methods approach—to address its evaluation questions. The questions that call for a quantitative analysis included wording such as "To what extent . . . ?" and "Did they read more?" The qualitative data consisted of about 50 interviews with site coordinators, parents, and their tutors. They were designed to obtain information about the processes that were successful or unsuccessful in the project.

Scholars working within the transformative-emancipatory paradigm have raised the following issues-related choices about data collection strategies: (a) consideration of how the data collection process and outcomes will benefit the community being studied; (b) credibility of the research findings to that community; (c) the appropriateness of communication methods, knowledge about those methods, and resources to support and willingness to engage in effective communication methods; (d) knowledge about response tendencies within the community and sensitivity to culturally appropriate ways to ask questions; and (e) tying the collection of data to transformation either by influencing the design of the treatment intervention or by providing avenues for participation in the social change process. This section examines these issues.

Benefits and Credibility. Truman (2000) demonstrated her commitment to ensure that research money was spent within the gay community in a study of gay and bisexual men's needs for information about safe sex practices. She did not hire interviewers from within the university where she was employed, as is typically done. Rather, she recruited interviewers from within the gay community to undertake face-to-face interviews. She described the benefits of this choice of data collection methods as follows:

> Apart from the direct benefits of receiving payment for their work, our interviewers received training and experience of research work, thus enhancing their skills. . . . From the gay community's perspective, it was involvement in the research that was important since involvement could contribute to the greater good. (p. 32)

The choice of this data collection strategy highlights two aspects of transformative-emancipatory work. First, there were benefits to members of the community of concern in terms of payment for services and enhancement of research skills. Second, the credibility of the study was enhanced for the participants when they saw that the study was being done "with" them rather than "on" them.

Involving members of marginalized groups can be one strategy that will lead to better data collection instruments (Chelimsky, 1998; Oliver, 1992). Oliver (1992) identified questions from the Office of Population Census and Surveys in Great Britain that represented a "blame the victim" theory, including those suggesting that it was the people's fault that they could not open a door by themselves, communicate with others, or attend the school of their choice. He suggested that questions written from a transformative perspective would ask about the aspects of the social and physical environment that were serving as barriers to full access or personal freedom rather than locating the problem of disability within the individual.

Cohen-Mitchell (2000) started with interview questions about the problems experienced by disabled women in El Salvador. However, she reported that when women were asked directly about the problems they faced as disabled women in El Salvador, many of them were unable to answer. Cohen-Mitchell changed her introductory question by asking the women to describe their disabilities and then to explain their lives in relation to them. By using this sequence of questions, she was able to obtain data about what had gone right for the women as well as some of the broader problems they had experienced.

Chelimsky (1998) described one study in which the evaluators at the U.S. General Accounting Office used such a strategy that involved surveying disabled people before conducting a survey to determine the effectiveness of the Americans With Disabilities Act:

> We used their responses in constructing both the design and the survey instruments, recognizing—based on what we had learned from them—the need to ask probing questions of business owners and operators not just about observable barriers, but also about invisible ones, such as whether a blind person with a guide dog might be refused entry to a cafe or restaurant. (USGAO/ PEMD, 1993, cited in Chelimsky, 1998, p. 47)

This practice of basing questions on the lives of those with personal insights and experience about the problems is in keeping with the tenets of transformative theory.

Appropriate Communication Strategies. Another consideration in data collection strategies, particularly with diverse groups, is arranging for appropriate communication to occur. With the court access project mentioned previously (Mertens, 2000a), different configurations of technical support were needed to facilitate effective communication. For example, in the group in which the individuals had a low level of language functioning, the staff included hearing and deaf co-moderators; an ASL interpreter who signed for the hearing moderator and voiced for the deaf participants; a deaf relay interpreter who translated the ASL signing into a combination of signs, pantomime, and gestures for one individual whose language functioning was too low to understand a pure ASL presentation; and a deaf-blind interpreter who signed into the hands of one visually impaired woman in the group. In addition, a court reporter observed the group and entered the comments of everyone into a written transcript that ran as real-time captions across two television screens that were strategically situated in the room.

In the focus group in which the participants used MSL, the communication loop consisted of a hearing focus group moderator who voiced in English; his words were translated into ASL by a hearing interpreter and the hearing interpreter's signs were interpreted into MSL by a deaf interpreter who knew both ASL and MSL. This process was reversed for the focus group moderator to understand what the participants were saying.

One obvious challenge in trying to start off thought from marginalized lives as Harding (1993) suggests is the need for in-depth knowledge of how to facilitate that participation for these cultural groups, access to resources to cover the expense of providing for meaningful participation, and patience to handle the added complexity of ensuring that those with the least power can meaningfully participate in the provision of data. The staff and the focus group moderator expressed frustration about the communication; it seemed slow and difficult to control. One could guess that the reaction of court personnel to this type of communication system might be similar. This, in itself, was a valuable insight that was shared with court system personnel to elucidate the potential for cultural conflicts emanating from different expectations concerning language use.

Data collection strategies for the Shared Reading Project were modified to accommodate both quantitative and qualitative data collection in light of the needs of hearing and deaf participants (Delk & Weidekamp, 2000). On-site videotaping, however, would be difficult to arrange and expensive to analyze. After much discussion, the Shared Reading Project staff and evaluators decided on a different strategy for the tutor interviews after recognizing the special needs of diverse audiences. For example, the evaluators originally intended to conduct end-of-year interviews with tutors by phone using a telecommunications device for the deaf. This strategy was based on the assumption that all of the tutors hired by the expansion sites would be fluent in English as well as in ASL, so that an English-based interview would not be an impediment to clear communication. Several of the site coordinators reported, however, that some of the tutors they hired were strong ASL users and had excellent interpersonal skills with parents but were less fluent in English. One of the deaf site coordinators strongly recommended that the tutor interviews be conducted face-to-face using sign language. The Shared Reading Project staff concurred and also recommended that these interviews be conducted by a deaf interviewer and that they be audiotaped given that the evaluators wanted to have a verbatim record.

A deaf interviewer fluent in ASL was trained and traveled with an interpreter to each of the sites to interview the sample of tutors, as recommended by the site coordinators. Each interview was audiotaped, using an interpreter to voice into the tape recorder for both the interviewer and the interviewee. In this way, each interview was conducted in a manner conducive to clear and direct communication, and a verbal record of the interview was obtained for analysis.

Lee (1999) raised interesting issues concerning the validity of data collected in research with people with mental health disabilities. She contrasted her experience in asking about satisfaction with health services for people who have private insurance and transportation with that for people whose access to housing, rent subsidies, and medications necessary for life and perhaps sanity comes from one agency that is within reach by public transportation and Medicaid. She suggested that the chances are very good that people's responses will be influenced if they have already learned to settle for less when it comes to medical care or if they are unwilling to risk criticizing the programs of those who hold so much power in their hands, no matter how much the respondents are assured of anonymity. English (1997) suggested that people who are dependent on mental health services feel the threat of potential sanctions and that this has an influence on their cooperation with researchers. Mayberg (1997) reported that people with serious mental illnesses who are hospitalized do not feel they have a choice and thus will tend to report the data that they believe the researcher wants to hear.

Cultural Sensitivity. Agar (2000) identified a number of pitfalls that occurred when cultural sensitivity in the data collection process was not sufficiently present. He described the difficulties that community health workers experienced in a study of a tuberculosis (TB) screening project in an inner-city urban area. The study included both quantitative and qualitative components in the data collection plan. However, interviewers were instructed to stand at the door and speak from a standard protocol. The questions involved areas such as income, prison, drug and alcohol use, and sexual practices that were seen as too personal and intimate by most of the respondents. Some of the answers called for time line estimates that simply did not map onto the way respondents thought about their activities. Agar wrote,

> People were often suspicious—some slammed the door—and they wondered why they had to be interviewed when they had no interest in being tested. And, finally, the neighborhood selected for community screening is a serious crack area. Needless to say, crack houses and crack users are not known for their predisposition to discuss income and hours per day spent at work with community health workers. (p. 98)

Agar concluded that the data collection problem emanated from a contradiction between the scientific requirement for acquiring the data in a certain way and the communicative norms of the situation in which the interviewing was done.

Ryen (2000) provided yet another, somewhat amusing example of the results of asking culturally insensitive questions. A Norwegian researcher in Tanzania asked a local man for directions. He phrased his question as follows: "Is this the way to Arusha?" The man answered "yes." The Norwegian drove many miles before he realized that he was indeed heading in the wrong direction. This story illustrates the importance of understanding cultural codes. The European man viewed the Tanzanian as stupid and untrustworthy. However, the Tanzanian man was answering the question in accordance with local norms. He was showing politeness toward the European by avoiding opposing the guest. The way the question was worded left the Tanzanian man with no options. The European could have learned the correct direction by rewording his question as follows: "Which way is Arusha?"

Integrating Data Collection and Social Action. A final point in data collection relates to integration of the data collection strategies with the transformative goals of the research. Hopson et al. (2000) addressed this issue in their study in the HIV/ AIDS community where they conducted 75 ethnographic interviews as well as used 40 semistructured questionnaires about respondents' sociodemographics, daily routines, drug use profiles, knowledge of HIV/AIDS risks, and drug and sexual sociobehavioral characteristics. In addition, 35 participants completed open-ended interviews that explored themes related to perceptions and meanings assigned to HIV/AIDS, how the disease was affecting them and their support systems, and other discourse and attitudes surrounding the disease. Hopson et al. analyzed these data to be used as a basis for developing interventions and preventions that were relevant to the predominantly African American context.

Another aspect of transformative emancipatory data collection involves designing the data collection that opens up avenues for participation in the social change process. In the study of court access for deaf and hard-of-hearing persons (Mertens, 2000a), the data collection strategies were designed with an eye toward facilitating transformative change. As part of the training programs for judges and other court personnel, deaf and hard-of-hearing people and their advocates were invited to attend the training workshops with representatives of the court systems in their state. The final session of the workshop involved small groups from each state working together to complete an action plan so that state-level teams could assess their current status in terms of court accessibility and make plans for future actions. Each item on the action plan form was the topic of a plenary session prior to the planning session so that the participants would have the most up-to-date information available on the topics to use in their planning discussions. The idea of planning together as a team with court personnel and representatives of the deaf and hard-of-hearing communities was emphasized repeatedly. Through the action plan process, participants were asked to reflect on actions that were not limited to appropriate use of interpreters and technology but also included legislation and attitudes as they influence achievement of equal justice.

Analyzing, Interpreting, Reporting, and Using Results

Typically, qualitative data are used to help explain quantitative results, as illustrated in three studies reviewed in this section (Agar, 2000; Bowen & Bok, 1998; Delk & Weidenkamp, 2000). However, this is not the only use of the findings, and other issues arise in analysis, interpretation, reporting, and using results from the transformative-emancipatory paradigm, including (a) raising hypotheses concerning the dynamics that underlie the quantitative results, (b) conducting subgroup analyses to look at the differential impact on diverse groups in the study, (c) improving understanding of the results from the perspective of power relationships, and (d) reporting the results in such a way as to facilitate social change.

Raising Hypotheses Concerning Dynamics. The analysis choices for the Bowen and Bok (1998) study of race-based college admissions was largely quantitative. They presented tabulations, cross-tabulations, and bar charts and other figures. They used statistical techniques such as multivariate regression to disentangle the many forces that jointly affect student performance in college, receipt of advanced degrees, and later-life outcomes. In addition, they used the qualitative comments from a subgroup of students to illuminate the findings and interpretations. For example, based on a regression analysis that controlled for other student and institutional characteristics, they reported that the typical Black *College and Beyond* graduate earns more than do most holders of bachelor's degrees in the United States. They hypothesized that graduation from an elite university might open doors that help Black graduates to overcome negative stereotypes that might otherwise restrict their earnings potential. They supported this hypothesis with a quotation from one of the qualitative interviews in which the respondent reported,

> "I worked in the corporate auditor's office through some Yale [University] connection and got to see the workings of a corporation from an inside—and interesting—position as opposed to doing some sort of scut work. . . . It wasn't that any of these people knew me. They knew the association I belonged to at Yale—one of the secret societies. . . . I earned my way and got the job. But it was these connections that got me the introduction." (p. 131)

Subgroup Analyses. The Shared Reading Project evaluation resulted in a complex multilevel data set. The quantitative analysis was used to answer questions such as "To what extent . . . ?" and "Did they read more?" For these questions, descriptive and inferential statistics were calculated using the SPSS program. The characteristics of the children, families, and tutors were tabulated and reported as numbers and percentages to describe the different groups of stakeholders participating in the evaluation. For example, the evaluators found that 87% of the participating deaf and hard-of-hearing children belonged to one or more of the traditionally underserved groups. The average age of these children was between 4 and 5 years.

Another measure of reading frequency was the number of times families shared books during their participation in the Shared Reading Project, which parents recorded on the "family reading records." Book-sharing events were tabulated by week for each family, and average reading rates were computed for each week of the project. The families reported that they shared books an average of five times a week while participating in the project.

These data were also subjected to repeated-measures analysis of variance to determine whether there was a statistically significant increase in the number of book-sharing events during the project. Surprisingly, this analysis showed that as soon as the tutors started working with the families, parents and other family members started sharing books frequently with their children and continued doing so until the end of the tutoring sessions. This analysis did not reveal anything, however, about how the families were sharing books, only that they were sitting down with the books together and doing something.

Here is where the qualitative data collected through in-person, on-site interviews helped to explain what was happening. Parents described how they began to improve their sign language, how they gained confidence, how they began to understand better the questions their children were asking about the books, and how they learned to use more facial and body expressions to make the stories more interesting to their children. The interviews with the parents, tutors, and site coordinators also revealed that, while many of the parents increased their book-sharing abilities during the 20-week intervention, they still had more to learn and still struggled with different aspects of the story-reading process. Many of the parents asked their tutors and site coordinators if they could continue with the Shared Reading Project the following year.

Comparison of the mean number of book-sharing events for different groups yielded other interesting results. There was no significant difference in the average number of book-sharing events per week for children who were or were not members of traditionally underserved groups. This indicated that children who have not traditionally had access to the same educational services as other children were being read to just as often as children who have traditionally had more access to educational services—a good example of a negative statistical result that has a positive interpretation.

Elucidating Power Relationships. Agar (2000) was hired to conduct a qualitative follow-up to a quantitative study that suggested that a TB screening program in an urban community had not been successful. He found that interviews with the community health workers provided data that, in their view, the program had been successful. He also explored reasons why the partnership between the university medical professionals and the community church representatives had failed. The ethnographic data from the community health workers revealed that they viewed the TB screening project as an opportunity to show that they cared about the people in the program even if the people did not choose to have the TB screening procedure. The workers knew that the program clients were people who often suffer from multiple life problems, including racism, violence, poverty, dysfunctional families, drug and alcohol abuse, and other health problems. From their point of view, the workers were successful if they could demonstrate that they cared about the clients in relation to any of the these problems, and they did not view the clients' lack of interest in TB screening as a failure. Agar concluded that the medical model offered too narrow a definition of success by focusing only on the numerical count of how many people participated in TB screening when in fact the people in the community faced many complex problems and TB was not necessarily the most salient issue for them.

Another interesting finding based on the ethnographic portion of the study related to the breakdown in the relationship between the White university researcher and the Black minister who initiated the project in the community. The university researcher was frustrated by her inability to bridge the differences between the medical culture and the community. She concluded that "the country may not be ready for successful black/white partnerships because of the magnitude and subtlety of the difference" (Agar, 2000, p. 103). The minister framed the problem as one of inequitable power relations and control of resources in that the control stayed in the hands of the university representative. A third person was interviewed who was also a minister but who worked for the university as a liaison to the community. He suggested that the problem reflected a history of distrust between the community and the university as well as clashes between two strong personalities with divergent interests. Agar cautioned against an overly simplistic interpretation of the dissolution of this relationship based solely on Black-White differences. His collection of additional qualitative data supported the hypothesis that the relationship foundered because of strong personalities, changing directions, control over resources and process, and the church-science divide. In addition, historical relationships between the university and the community had to be considered. He concluded, "The demographics of race clearly define the context of the program, but the way those demographics played out locally link them to more general issues of organizational process" (p. 109).

Brown (2000) raised interesting issues related to power relationships in terms of male-female contributions in focus groups by using both quantitative and qualitative analysis of the transcripts. She counted the number of contributions made by men and women in focus groups during time that was structured by the moderator (i.e., the moderator went around the group asking each person to respond) and during unstructured time (i.e., anyone could speak as he or she wanted). During the structured time, Brown found that the men and women made an equal number of contributions based on number of lines in the transcript attributed to each subgroup. During the unstructured time, the balance shifted to 60% of the comments being made by men and 40% being made by women. However, Brown also looked at the length of the responses for males and females. This revealed that the majority of minimal responses and supportive one-word lines were made by women, thus inflating the actual quantitative contribution of the women in the counts.

To determine who contributed more content, Brown (2000) conducted a qualitative analysis of strategies for taking the floor and topic raising. She reported,

> The overriding themes that emerged from the data show that men and women used language in quite different ways to take the floor. Men were very assertive: when they desired the floor, they often took it through interruption. Men regularly used verbal means for taking the floor, which simply meant that they began to speak and state their fact or opinion. Women, on the contrary, typically used nonverbal means of obtaining the floor. They made signals—raising a hand, raising eyebrows, and so on—as a means of conveying a desire to speak. Afterward they patiently waited for the moderator to call on them to speak. (p. 63)

Brown also reported that men introduced new topics and women tended to play a supportive role, building on the topics that men raised. When women did raise topics, either they were ignored or the men reintroduced the topics and took credit for them by claiming the ideas as their own.

From this quantitative and qualitative analysis, Brown (2000) concluded that men contributed more concrete data to the focus group study. She suggested that researchers' recognition and understanding that language differences exist between the sexes is crucial to the reliability and validity of a good research study. Differences may exist in contributions to content based on other characteristics as well. Moderators of focus groups must be assertive to ensure that specific voices are not silenced. If the study warrants, it might be best to use homogeneous groups based on salient characteristics such as race/ethnicity, sex, and disability.

Reporting Research to Facilitate Action. Mienczakowski (2000) described a way of presenting results from a research study that would facilitate the use of the information for the purpose of social change. Having conducted ethno-graphic studies of alcohol detoxification centers and psychiatric settings that serve people with schizophrenia, Mienczakowski sought ways to present the information that would go beyond the typically small audiences for academic reports. He developed critical ethno-dramas based on each study that con-sisted of two-act, full-length performance pieces. He wrote, "The guiding prin-ciple leading this critical theory-based ethnographic approach is to attempt to accurately give voice to groups of health consumers who otherwise consider themselves to be disempowered or disenfranchised in some way" (p. 129).

The ethno-dramas are performed for health professionals, students in health-related training programs, and the general public. Following each performance, the researcher conducts a discussion forum in which the audi-ence questions and debates the representations made on stage with the actors, the health care provider and consumer informants, and the project writers and directors. By these means, the data in the productions continue to evolve and integrate diverse reactions to the portrayals of alcohol depen-dency and schizophrenia. Throughout the process, the audience's percep-tions of people served by mental health programs and their understandings of people with these two diseases are challenged and expanded. "Critical ethno-drama seeks to emancipate audiences and informants from stereotyp-ical and oppressive understandings of illness, and in so doing [to] free infor-mants from the historified perceptions of their health constraints" (p. 133).

Despite the fact that Mienczakowski's (2000) data were qualitative, the approach he used for the reporting of the information could be adapted to a mixed methods research study as well. Audience members are provided with the transcripts of the plays as well as with health education materials relevant to the topic. Researchers could consider including relevant statistics portrayed in graphics that could communicate the quantitative results as well. The important principle is the portrayal of valid data that represents the voices of the disempowered, as well as the professionals who serve them, in such a way that it engages the audience in discussions of strategies for change.

Conclusions: Summary, Optimism, and Concerns

Changing conditions inside and outside of the research community have brought increased attention to the need to address the politics of human research and issues of social justice. Trends in demographics that have resulted in increased social pluralism and scholarly writers from the transformative-emancipatory paradigm have addressed the importance of the role of values in research. Teddlie and Tashakkori argue in this handbook (Chapter 1 [Tashakkori & Teddlie, 2003]) that pragmatics provides a potential underlying paradigm that supports the choice of mixed methods. Transformative-emancipatory researchers suggest caution on basing methodological choices solely on pragmatics. The value of pragmatics that drives the desire to adopt a mixed methods stance in research is seen as inadequate and unexamined because it does not answer the question "Practical for whom and to what end?" (House & Howe, 1999). Transformative-emancipatory scholars recommend the adoption of an explicit goal for research to serve the ends of creating a more just and democratic society that permeates the entire research process, from the problem formulation to the drawing of conclusions and the use of the results (Mertens, 1998).

The transformative-emancipatory paradigm places central importance on the lives and experiences of those who suffer oppression and discrimination, whatever the basis of that is—be it sex, race/ethnicity, disability, sexual orientation, or socioeconomic status. Researchers working within this paradigm are consciously aware of power differentials in the research context, and they search for ways to ameliorate the effects of oppression and discrimination by linking their research activities to social action and wider questions of social inequity and social justice. Ontologically, reality is described within a historical, political, cultural, and economic context. Epistemologically, interaction between the researchers and the participants is essential and requires a level of trust and understanding to accurately represent viewpoints of all groups fairly. Methodologically, mixed methods offer avenues to address the issues of diverse groups appropriately.

In defining the research problem, a literature search can be used to establish the boundaries of published knowledge about an issue. However, this is seldom sufficient because of biases inherent in the nature of literature that is published. In addition, the research problem requires spending time with members of the population of interest to build trust. Methods that might supplement literature review include observation, interviewing, reviewing demographic and other statistical data, and sometimes using preliminary surveys. The reader should also be aware of prevailing theoretical frameworks that have depicted members of marginalized groups or their cultures as deficient. Questions can ask about positive and negative experiences in a study and can be linked to policy or social actions that can lead to societal transformation.

A mixed methods research design framed within the transformative-emancipatory paradigm might include the use of both qualitative and quantitative methods for the purpose of capturing the complexity of a situation, raising hypotheses about the reasons why a result is found, or providing insights into the development of more valid data collection instruments or program interventions. One ethical concern that has been raised by this approach is the choice of denying treatment to a group so as to have a true experimental design. Options include comparing the new treatment to the best known treatment, using a time-series design, making comparisons with an extant group with similar characteristics, and using a larger statistical base in terms of known levels of incidence.

Many issues have been raised with regard to the sample identification and selection in the transformative-emancipatory literature. Of particular importance is the beginning step of specifying who is in the target group along with the use of a theoretical framework that delineates the variable thought to be associated with the outcomes of interest. Caution is necessary to avoid labeling groups in such a way that it negatively affects both their self-concepts and the development of appropriate interventions. In addition, the diversity within groups must be acknowledged, whether that be in terms of severity of disability or experience with the relevant institution such as the courts. Steps must be taken to ensure that the diversity within groups is attended to by means of how individuals are invited and the support that is given to them once they have agreed to participate in the study.

Data collection issues include consideration of how the data collection process and outcomes will benefit the community being studied in terms of opportunities to contribute to the collection of more valid data as well as in terms of increasing the skills and expertise of members of the targeted community in the research process itself. Such steps can lead to an increase in the credibility of the results of the study for members of that community. However, demands are placed on researchers to achieve appropriate communication methods and resources to support the use of more complex communication strategies. As always, cultural sensitivity will mean the difference between quality data and inaccurate or irrelevant findings. Finally, the link between data collection and social change can be built into the data collection process itself by including mechanisms for the marginalized groups to influence plans for future actions based on the study's outcomes, influencing the development of additional data collection instruments or interventions, and providing information to policymaking bodies.

The ways in which data are analyzed, interpreted, reported, and used are also influenced by the transformative-emancipatory paradigm. The qualitative data can be used to test hypotheses concerning how certain dynamics affect the results that are evidenced in the quantitative data. Subgroup analyses can indicate when differential outcomes are indicative of more or less success with various sub-populations. One very interesting use is to examine the dynamics within the research study itself to determine the effects of different value systems and power relationships on the study's outcomes and the relationships among the participants in the study. This is particularly important in cross-cultural studies that pose challenges both in terms of the social problem being addressed and in terms of the relationships among the researchers and participants. Reporting results should also follow the personal and political tendencies seen in the other parts of the research study. Engaging the readers in a way that presents the results such that the full human impact is felt and understood is a challenge. Yet strategies such as ethno-drama provide such a mechanism for addressing complex social problems in this way (Mienczakowski, 2000). To increase use of research findings, the researchers need to be aware of the networks of relationships that must be established and nurtured. Finding ways to really listen and understand is a big challenge. However, it will mean more credible information that can be used to inform policies that are needed to address the inequities in the world. The social conditions and the politics within the research community can work to either impede or foster further developments of mixed methods approaches based on the transformative-emancipatory paradigm.

References

Agar, M. (2000). Border lessons: Linguistic "rich points" and evaluative understanding. In R. Hopson (Ed.), *How and why language matters in evaluation* (New Directions in Evaluation, No. 86, pp. 93–110). San Francisco: Jossey-Bass.

Alcoff, L., & Potter, E. (Eds.). (1993). *Feminist epistemologies.* New York: Routledge.

Banks, J. A. (1993). The canon debate, knowledge construction, and multicultural education. *Educational Researcher, 22*(5), 4–14.

Banks, J. A. (1995). The historical reconstruction of knowledge about race: Implications for transformative teaching. *Educational Researcher, 24*(2), 15–25.

Bhavnani, K. K. (1991). What's power got to do with it? Empowerment and social research. In I. Parker & J. Shotter (Eds.), *Deconstructing social psychology.* London: Routledge.

Booth, W. (2000, August 31). California minorities are now the majority. *Washington Post,* p. A1.

Bowen, W., & Bok, D. (1998). *The shape of the river: Long-term consequences of considering race in college and university admissions.* Princeton, NJ: Princeton University Press.

Brown, C. L. (2000). Sociolinguistic dynamics of gender in focus groups. In R. Hopson (Ed.), *How and why language matters in evaluation* (New Directions in Evaluation, No. 86, pp. 55–68). San Francisco: Jossey-Bass.

Buchanan, R. M. (1999). *Illusions of equality: Deaf Americans in school and factory, 1850–1950.* Washington, DC: Gallaudet University Press.

Canadian Research Institute for the Advancement of Women. (1996). *Feminist research ethics: A process.* Ottawa, Ontario: Author.

Chelimsky, E. (1998). The role of experience in formulating theories of evaluation practice. *American Journal of Evaluation, 19*(1), 35–56.

Cohen-Mitchell, J. B. (2000). Disabled women in El Salvador reframing themselves: An economic development program for women. In C. Truman, D. M. Mertens, & B. Humphries (Eds.), *Research and inequality* (pp. 143–176). London: Taylor & Francis.

DeKoning, K., & Martin, M. (Eds.). (1996). *Participatory research in health*. London: Zed Books.

Delk, L., & Weidekamp, L. (2000). *Shared Reading Project evaluation*. Washington, DC: Gallaudet University, Laurent Clerc National Deaf Education Center.

Dockery, G. (2000). Participatory research: Whose roles, whose responsibilities? In C. Truman, D. M. Mertens, & B. Humphries (Eds.), *Research and inequality* (pp. 95–110). London: Taylor & Francis.

English, B. (1997). Conducting ethical evaluations with disadvantaged and minority target groups. *Evaluation Practice, 18*(1), 49–54.

Fine, M. (Ed.). (1992). *Disruptive voices*. Ann Arbor: University of Michigan Press.

Flaherty, M. P., Nelson, D., & Stephens, J. (2000, December 18). The Body Hunters: Overwhelming the watchdogs. *Washington Post,* pp. Al, A16–A17.

Gill, C. (1999). Invisible ubiquity: The surprising relevance of disability issues in evaluation. *American Journal of Evaluation, 20*(2), 279–287.

Grant, J. P. (1993). *The state of the world's children: 1993*. New York: Oxford University Press.

Guba, E. G., & Lincoln, Y. S. (1994). Competing paradigms in qualitative research. In N. K. Denzin & Y. S. Lincoln (Eds.), *The handbook of qualitative research* (pp. 105–117). Thousand Oaks, CA: Sage.

Harding, S. (1993). Rethinking standpoint epistemology: What is strong objectivity? In L. Alcoff & E. Potter (Eds.), *Feminist epistemologies* (pp. 49–82). New York: Routledge.

Hill Collins, P. (2000). *Black feminist thought: Knowledge, consciousness, and the politics of empowerment*. New York: Routledge.

Hopson, R. K., Lucas, K. J., & Peterson, J. A. (2000). HIV/AIDS talk: Implications for prevention, intervention, and evaluation. In R. Hopson (Ed.), *How and why language matters in evaluation* (New Directions in Evaluation, No. 86, pp. 29–42). San Francisco: Jossey-Bass.

Horn, L., & Berktold, J. (1999). *Students with disabilities in post-secondary education: A profile of preparation, participation, and outcomes* (NCES 1999–187). Washington, DC: U.S. Department of Education, National Center for Education Statistics.

House, E. R., & Howe, K. R. (1999). *Values in evaluation and social research*. Thousand Oaks, CA: Sage.

Humphries, B., Mertens, D. M., & Truman, C. (2000). Arguments for an "emancipatory" research paradigm. In C. Truman, D. M. Mertens, & B. Humphries (Eds.), *Research and inequality* (pp. 3–23). London: Taylor & Francis.

Humphries, B., & Truman, C. (Eds.). (1994). *Re-thinking social research*. Aldershot, UK: Avebury.

Kellner, D. (1997). Critical theory and cultural studies: The missed articulation. In M. McGuigan (Ed.), *Cultural methodologies* (pp. 12–41). Thousand Oaks, CA: Sage.

Kemmis, S., & McTaggart. R. (2000). Participatory action research. In N. K. Denim & Y. S. Lincoln (Eds.), *Handbook of qualitative research* (2nd ed., pp. 567–606). Thousand Oaks, CA: Sage.

Kincheloe, J. L., & McLaren, P. (2000). Rethinking critical theory and qualitative research. In N. K. Denzin & Y. S. Lincoln (Eds.), *Handbook of qualitative research* (2nd ed., pp. 279–314). Thousand Oaks, CA: Sage.

Lane, H. (1993). Cochlear implants: Their cultural and historical meaning. In J. V. Van Cleave (Ed.), *Deaf history unveiled: Interpretations from the new scholarship* (pp. 272–291). Washington, DC: Gallaudet University Press.

Lather, P. (1992). Critical frames in educational research: Feminist and post-structural perspectives. *Theory Into Practice, 31*(2), 1–13.

Lee, B. (1999). The implications of diversity and disability for evaluation practice: Commentary on Gill. *American Journal of Evaluation, 20,* 289–293.

Longmore, P. K. (1994, August). *History of people with disabilities.* Keynote presentation of the Leadership Development Institute for Post-Secondary Students With Disabilities, Minneapolis.

Madison, A. M. (1992). *Minority issues in program evaluation* (New Directions for Program Evaluation, Vol. 53). San Francisco: Jossey-Bass.

Madison, A. M. (2000). Language in defining social problems and in evaluating social programs. In R. Hopson (Ed.), *How and why language matters in evaluation* (New Directions in Evaluation, No. 86, pp. 17–28). San Francisco: Jossey-Bass.

Mayberg, 5. (1997, April). *The future for quality in managed care.* Paper presented at Outcomes Conference, Tampa, FL.

McLaren, P. L., & Lankshear, C. (Eds.). (1994). *Politics of liberation.* New York: Routledge.

McNeil, J. M. (1997, August). Americans with disabilities: 1994–95. *Current Population Reports,* pp. 61–70.

Meadow-Orlans, K. (2002). Social change and conflict: Context for research on deafness. In M. D. Clark, M. Marschark, & M. Karchmer (Eds.), *Context, cognition, and deafness* (pp. 161–178). Washington, DC: Gallaudet University Press.

Mertens, D. M. (1998). *Research methods in education and psychology: Integrating diversity with quantitative and qualitative approaches.* Thousand Oaks, CA: Sage.

Mertens, D. M. (1999). Inclusive evaluation: Implications of transformative theory for evaluation. *American Journal of Evaluation, 20*(1), 1–14.

Mertens, D. M. (2000a). Deaf and hard of hearing people in court: Using an emancipatory perspective to determine their needs. In C. Truman, D. M. Mertens, & B. Humphries (Eds.), *Research and inequality* (pp. 111–125). London: Taylor & Francis.

Mertens, D. M. (2000b, January). *Researching disability and diversity: Merging paradigms.* Paper presented at the meeting of the National Institute for Disability and Rehabilitative Research, Washington, DC.

Mertens, D. M., Farley, J., Madison, A. M., & Singleton, P. (1994). Diverse voices in evaluation practice: Feminists, minorities, and persons with disabilities. *Evaluation Practice, 15*(2), 123–129.

Mertens, D. M., & McLaughlin, J. (1995). *Research methods in special education.* Thousand Oaks, CA: Sage.

Mienczakowski, J. (2000). Ethnography in the form of theatre with emancipatory intentions. In C. Truman, D. M. Mertens, & B. Humphries (Eds.), *Research and inequality* (pp. 126–142). London: Taylor & Francis.

Mohanty, C. T. (1991). Cartographies of struggle: Third World women and the politics of feminism. In C. T. Mohanty, A. Russo, & L. Torres (Eds.), *Third World women and the politics of feminism.* Bloomington: Indiana University Press.

Nelson, J. (1996). The last dogma of empiricism? In L. H. Nelson & J. Nelson (Eds.), *Feminism, science, and the philosophy of science* (pp. 59–78). Boston: Kluwer Academic.

Nelson, L. H. (1996). Empiricism without dogmas. In L H. Nelson & J. Nelson (Eds.), *Feminism, science, and the philosophy of science* (pp. 95–120). Boston: Kluwer Academic.

Okie, S. (2000, November 24). Health officials debate ethics of placebo use. *Washington Post,* p. A3.

Olesen, V. (2000). Feminisms and qualitative research at and into the millennium. In N. K. Denzin & Y. S. Lincoln (Eds.), *Handbook of qualitative research* (2nd ed., pp. 215–256). Thousand Oaks, CA: Sage.

Oliver, M. (1992). Changing the social relations of research production? *Disability, Handicap, & Society, 7*(2), 101–114.

Reason, P. (Ed.). (1994). *Participation in human inquiry.* London: Sage.

Reinharz, S. (1992). *Feminist methods in social research.* New York: Oxford University Press.

Rheaume, J., & Roy, S. (2000). Defining without discriminating? Ethnicity and social problems—The case of street youth in Canada. In C. Truman, D. M. Mertens, & B. Humphries (Eds.), *Research and inequality* (pp. 236–247). London: Taylor & Francis.

Ribbens, J., & Edwards, R. (Eds.). (1998). *Feminist dilemmas in qualitative research.* Thousand Oaks, CA: Sage.

Ryen, A. (2000). Colonial methodology? Methodological challenges to cross-cultural projects collecting data by structured interviews. In C. Truman, D. M. Mertens, & B. Humphries (Eds.), *Research and inequality* (pp. 220–235). London: Taylor & Francis.

Seelman, K. (1998, March). *Change and challenge: The integration of the new paradigm of disability into research and practice.* Paper presented at the National Council on Rehabilitation Education Conference, Vancouver, WA.

Seelman, K. (1999). *Testimony to the Commission on Advancement of Women and Minorities in Science, Engineering, and Technology.* Washington, DC: National Institute on Disability and Rehabilitation Research.

Stanfield, J. H., II (1993). Methodological reflections: An introduction. In J. H. Stanfield & R. Dennis (Eds.), *Race and ethnicity in research methods* (pp. 3–15). Newbury Park, CA: Sage.

Stanfield, J. H., II (1999). Slipping through the front door: Relevant social scientific evaluation in the people-of-color century. *American Journal of Evaluation, 20,* 415–432.

Stanfield, J. H., & Dennis, R. (Eds.). (1993). *Race and ethnicity in research methods.* Newbury Park, CA: Sage.

Stephens, J. (2000, December 17). The Body Hunters: As drug testing spreads, profits and lives hang in balance. *Washington Post,* p. Al.

Tuana, N. (1996). Revaluing science: Starting from the practices of women. In L. H. Nelson & J. Nelson (Eds.), *Feminism, science, and the philosophy of science* (pp. 17–35). Boston: Kluwer Academic.

Truman, C. (2000). New social movements and social research. In C. Truman, D. M. Mertens, & B. Humphries (Eds.), *Research and inequality* (pp. 24–36). London: Taylor & Francis.

Truman, C., Mertens, D. M., & Humphries, B. (Eds.). (2000). *Research and inequality*. London: Taylor & Francis.

U.S. Bureau of the Census. (1997). *Statistical abstracts of the United States, 1997.* Washington, DC: Government Printing Office.

U.S. Bureau of the Census. (2000). *Resident population estimates of the United States* (NP-T5-C). Washington, DC: Government Printing Office.

Villegas, A. M. (1991). *Culturally responsive pedagogy for the 1990's and beyond.* Princeton, NJ: Educational Testing Service.

Walsh, M., Smith, R., Morales, A., & Sechrest, L. (2000). *Ecocultural research: A mental health researcher's guide to the study of race, ethnicity, and culture.* Cambridge, MA: Human Services Research Institute.

Whitmore, E. (Ed.). (1998). *Framing participatory evaluation.* San Francisco: Jossey-Bass.

Donna M. Mertens is Professor in the Department of Educational Foundations and Research at Gallaudet University. She teaches research methods, program evaluation, and educational psychology to deaf and hearing students at the undergraduate and graduate levels. She is a past president and current board member of the American Evaluation Association, providing leadership for its Building Diversity Initiative and International Committee. She has authored or edited several books, including *Parent Experiences With Young Deaf or Hard of Hearing Children* (2002, with Kay Meadow Orlans and Marilyn Sass Lehrer), *Research and Inequality* (2000, with Carole Truman and Beth Humphries), *Research Methods in Education and Psychology: Integrating Diversity* (Sage, 1998), and *Research Methods in Special Education* (Sage, 1995, with John McLaughlin). She has also published in journals such as the *American Journal of Evaluation, American Annals of the Deaf,* and *Educational Evaluation and Policy Analysis.*

4

Triangulation as the First
Mixed Methods Design

Selection: Jick, T. D. (1979). Mixing qualitative and quantitative methods: Triangulation in action. *Administrative Science Quarterly, 24,* 602–611.

Editors' Introduction

While many scholars debated the philosophical bases of mixing qualitative and quantitative methods during the 1970s and 1980s, other scholars considered how the two types of data could be meaningfully combined within research studies. An often-cited discussion arguing for mixing methods from this time period is Todd D. Jick's article from 1979. This article has served a central role in the evolution of mixed methods research since that time.

The main premise of Jick's article is that quantitative and qualitative methods should be mixed for purposes of triangulation because the individual strengths of one method offset the other method's weaknesses. Therefore, the goal of this approach is generally to seek convergence between the different methods. He states that this combination can lead to greater confidence in results, the use of creative methods, better understandings when divergent findings are explained, a synthesis of theories, and critical tests of competing theories. This idea of counterbalanced strengths and weaknesses has been the historical argument for mixed methods research for the past 25 years.

Jick also outlined many challenges associated with mixed methods triangulation, such as the need to reconcile divergent results, difficulty of replicating complex studies, using each method in a significant way, matching the approach to the overall research purpose, and managing constraints like the required amount of time. Jick's article represents an important turning point in mixed methods research in that he discussed combining or integrating quantitative and qualitative methods rather than merely collecting two different sets of data without conscious integration.

Discussion Questions and Applications

1. List some specific ways in which the strengths of qualitative methods may compensate for the weaknesses associated with quantitative methods (or vice versa).

2. Is the offsetting strengths and weaknesses argument a useful reason for conducting mixed methods research? Can you think of other reasons?

3. If triangulation means that three reference points are being intersected, what are the three points in mixed methods research?

Related References That Extend the Topic

See the following references as additional examples of researchers discussing ways to combine quantitative and qualitative data in the 1970s:

Sieber, S. D. (1973). The integration of fieldwork and survey methods. *American Journal of Sociology, 78,* 1335–1359.

Reichardt, C. S., & Cook, T. D. (1979). Beyond qualitative versus quantitative methods. In T. D. Cook & C. S. Reichardt (Eds.), *Qualitative and quantitative methods in evaluation research* (pp. 7–32). Beverly Hills, CA: Sage.

Mixing Qualitative and Quantitative Methods

Triangulation in Action

Todd D. Jick
Cornell University

There is a distinct tradition in the literature on social science research methods that advocates the use of multiple methods. This form of research strategy is usually described as one of convergent methodology, multimethod/multitrait (Campbell and Fiske, 1959), convergent validation or, what has been called "triangulation" (Webb et al., 1966). These various notions share the conception that qualitative and quantitative methods should be viewed as complementary rather than as rival camps. In fact, most textbooks underscore the desirability of mixing methods given the strengths and weaknesses found in single method designs.

Yet those who most strongly advocate triangulation (e.g., Webb et al., 1966; Smith, 1975; Denzin, 1978) fail to indicate how this prescribed triangulation is actually performed and accomplished. Graduate training usually prepares us to use one method or another as appropriate and preferred, but not to combine methods effectively. And even those who use multiple methods do not generally explain their "technique" in sufficient detail to indicate exactly how convergent data are collected and interpreted.

SOURCE: Jick, T. D. (1979). Mixing qualitative and quantitative methods: Triangulation in action. *Administrative Science Quarterly, 24,* 602–611. Reprinted with permission of Cornell University.

Author's Note: I am indebted to Dafna Izraeli for helpful comments and criticisms of an earlier version of this paper.

What Is Triangulation?

Triangulation is broadly defined by Denzin (1978: 291) as "the combination of methodologies in the study of the same phenomenon." The triangulation metaphor is from navigation and military strategy that use multiple reference points to locate an object's exact position (Smith, 1975: 273). Given basic principles of geometry, multiple viewpoints allow for greater accuracy. Similarly, organizational researchers can improve the accuracy of their judgments by collecting different kinds of data bearing on the same phenomenon.

In the social sciences, the use of triangulation can be traced back to Campbell and Fiske[1] (1959) who developed the idea of "multiple operationism." They argued that more than one method should be used in the validation process to ensure that the variance reflected that of the trait and not of the method. Thus, the convergence or agreement between two methods " . . . enhances our belief that the results are valid and not a methodological artifact" (Bouchard, 1976: 268).

This kind of triangulation is labeled by Denzin (1978: 302) as the "between (or across) methods" type, and represents the most popular use of triangulation. It is largely a vehicle for cross validation when two or more distinct methods are found to be congruent and yield comparable data. For organizational researchers, this would involve the use of multiple methods to examine the same dimension of a research problem. For example, the effectiveness of a leader may be studied by interviewing the leader, observing his or her behavior, and evaluating performance records. The focus always remains that of the leader's effectiveness but the mode of data collection varies. Multiple and independent measures, if they reach the same conclusions, provide a more certain portrayal of the leadership phenomenon.

Triangulation can have other meanings and uses as well. There is the "within-method" kind (Denzin 1978: 301) which uses multiple techniques within a given method to collect and interpret data. For quantitative methods such as survey research, this can take the form of multiple scales or indices focused on the same construct. For qualitative methods such as participant observation, this can be reflected in "multiple comparison groups" (Glaser and Strauss, 1965: 7) to develop more confidence in the emergent theory. In short, "within-method" triangulation essentially involves cross-checking for internal consistency or reliability while "between-method" triangulation tests the degree of external validity.

Blending and integrating a variety of data and methods, as triangulation demands, may be seen on a continuum that ranges from simple to complex designs (Figure 4.1). Scaling, that is, the quantification of qualitative measures, would be at the simple end. Smith (1975: 273) concluded that scaling is only a "primitive triangulatory device." It does not effectively force a mix of independent methods, neither does it reflect fundamentally diverse observations nor varieties of triangulated data. Another primitive form of triangulation often found in organizational research is the parenthetical, even somewhat patronizing, use of field observations to strengthen statistical results. For example, a hypothetical study of job satisfaction among employees might revolve around a significant chi-square result demonstrating deep discontent. To support the results, it might be noted that a strike occurred earlier that year. But, we are likely not informed about the intensity, dynamics, meaning, and aftermath of the strike. Thus, important qualitative data had been insufficiently integrated with quantitative findings.

		Convergent	Holistic (or Contextual)
Scaling	Reliability	Validation	Description

Simple Design			Complex Design

Figure 4.1   A Continuum of Triangulation Design

A somewhat more sophisticated triangulation design, already discussed, would be the "within-methods" strategy for testing reliability. The limitations of this approach lie in the use of only one method. As Denzin noted (1978: 301–02), "observers delude themselves into believing that five different variations of the same method generate five distinct varieties of triangulated data. But the flaws that arise using one method remain. . . ." Next in the continuum is the conventional form, the "between methods" approach designed for convergent validation. The use of complementary methods is generally thought to lead to more valid results, as noted. It is currently the archetype of triangulation strategies.

Triangulation, however, can be something other than scaling, reliability, and convergent validation. It can also capture a more complete, *holistic,* and contextual portrayal of the unit(s) under study. That is, beyond the analysis of overlapping variance, the use of multiple measures may also uncover some unique variance which otherwise may have been neglected by single methods. It is here that qualitative methods, in particular, can play an especially prominent role by eliciting data and suggesting conclusions to which other methods would be blind. Elements of the context are illuminated. In this sense, triangulation may be used not only to examine the same phenomenon from multiple perspectives but also to enrich our understanding by allowing for new or deeper dimensions to emerge.

In all the various triangulation designs one basic assumption is buried. The effectiveness of triangulation rests on the premise that the weaknesses in each single method will be compensated by the counter-balancing strengths of another. That is, it is assumed that multiple and independent measures do not share the same weaknesses or potential for bias (Rohner, 1977: 134). Although it has always been observed that each method has assets and liabilities, triangulation purports to exploit the assets and neutralize, rather than compound, the liabilities.

Perhaps the most prevalent attempts to use triangulation have been reflected in efforts to integrate fieldwork and survey methods. The viability and necessity of such linkages have been advocated by various social scientists (e.g., Vidich and Shapiro, 1955; Reiss, 1968; McCall and Simmons, 1969; Spindler, 1970; Diesing, 1971; Sieber, 1973). They all argue that quantitative methods can make important contributions to fieldwork, and vice versa.

Thus, researchers using qualitative methodology are encouraged to systematize observations, to utilize sampling techniques, and to develop quantifiable schemes for coding complex data sets. As Vidich and Shapiro (1955: 31) wrote, "Without the survey data, the observer could only make reasonable guesses about his area of ignorance in the effort to reduce bias." Survey research may also contribute to greater confidence in the generalizability of results.

Conversely, quantitative-oriented researchers are encouraged to exploit "the potentialities of social observation" (Reiss, 1968: 360). Among other assets, field methods can contribute to survey analysis with respect to the validation of results, the interpretation of statistical relationships, and the clarification of puzzling findings (Sieber, 1973: 1345). Thus, informants can be utilized during the course of quantitative research (Campbell, 1955) and "holistic interpretation" (i.e., context variables) can be used to shed light on quantitative data (Diesing, 1971: 171). More implicitly, the very selection of a research site is typically a function of qualitative data as is the process of building and pretesting a survey instrument.

Diesing (1971: 5) boldly concluded that the variety of combinations is so great that survey research and fieldwork are better viewed as two ends of a continuum rather than as two distinct kinds of methods. Yet, research designs that extensively integrate both fieldwork (e.g., participant observation) and survey research are rare. Moreover, journals tend to specialize by methodology thus encouraging purity of method.

Fortunately, there are some exceptions to be found. Some particularly good examples of combining methods include LaPiere's (1934) seminal investigation of the relationship between attitudes and behavior, Reiss' study of police and citizen transactions (1968: 355), Sales' (1973) study of authoritarianism, Van Maanen's (1975) data on police socialization, and the studies described in, or modeled after, Webb et al. (1966). Furthermore, it is probable that the triangulation approach is embedded in many doctoral theses that, when packaged into articles, tend to highlight only the quantitative methods. Thus the triangulation model is not new. However, this model of research and its advantages have not been appreciated. In this respect, it would be helpful to articulate and describe its usage.

An Illustration of How Triangulation Works

The triangulation strategy was used in a study I conducted on the effects of a merger on employees (Jick, 1979). Early interviews suggested that employees were intensely anxious in this state of flux, especially concerning their job security. One focus of the research was to document and examine the sources and symptoms of anxiety, the individuals experiencing it and its impact on the functioning of the newly merging organization.

How have anxiety and its dynamics in an organization been measured? Marshall and Cooper (1979: 86) noted, for example, that there is no one generally agreed way of measuring stress manifestations. On the basis of past research, there are several alternative techniques one could use: (a) Ask the person directly, (b) Ask the person indirectly (e.g., projective tests), (c) Ask someone who interacts with the person, and (d) Observe systematically the person's behavior or (e) Measure physiological symptoms. Predictably, each of these strategies has both strengths and weaknesses. Most of the limitations revolve around the likelihood of high demand characteristics and considerable obstacles in the measurement process.

Given high demand characteristics in the study of anxiety and the potential pitfalls in each method, the most appropriate research strategy was deemed to be triangulation. No single method was sufficient and thus a design evolved that utilized a combination of methods. Data were collected over a period of 14 months which incorporated multiple viewpoints and approaches: both feelings and behaviors, direct and indirect reports, obtrusive and unobtrusive observation. Methods were wide-ranging enough to tap a variety of anxiety dimensions.

The research "package" used in the investigation of the dynamics of anxiety and job insecurity included many standard features. Surveys were distributed to a random sample of employees. They contained a combination of standard and new indices related to stresses and strains. To complement these data, a subsample was selected for the purposes of semistructured, probing interviews. The survey also contained items related to the symptoms of anxiety as well as projective measures. These were developed to be indirect, nonthreatening techniques. In addition to self-reports, interviews were conducted with supervisors and coworkers to record their observations of employees' anxiety.

Another set of methods, somewhat less conventional, proved to be especially fruitful. Predominantly qualitative in nature, they were based on unobtrusive and nonparticipant observation as well as archival materials. For example, one of the merging organizations housed an archives library, which contained a variety of files, books, and organization memorabilia from its 100-year history. It also contained a comprehensive set of newspaper clippings that cited the organization and the merger, as well as a broad variety of internal memos to employees. This was indeed a rich data source.

The development of unobtrusive measures tends to be far more unorthodox and innovative than most research methods. Perhaps the most instructive unobtrusive measure in this case was a kind of anxiety "thermometer." The idea emerged because of certain fortuitous circumstances in that a further research opportunity was found in the archives. The archivist mentioned that employees were frequently using the files. When asked why, he said that they came to compare recent news reports and memos (regarding the organization's future) with past pronouncements. Since recent information tended to be ambiguous, if not contradictory, the files provided an opportunity to review materials systematically. Most employees were apparently seeking information to relieve their anxiety about the uncertain shape of things to come.

Hence these visits to the archives were treated as expressions of employee anxiety, a thermometer of anxiety level in the organization. The search for information seemed to represent an attempt to reduce uncertainty. It was hypothesized that the more people who visited the archives to use the files, the higher the anxiety level. Thus emerged an effort to track the pattern of visits. The archivist consented to record the number of archive users along with some supplementary data on the visitors such as age, work location, and the amount of time spent at the files.

The pattern of archive usage was then compared with data culled from ongoing interviews, the cross-sectional survey, and other unobtrusive techniques. These other measures also tracked anxiety-related behavior, as for example, (a) archival data on turnover and absenteeism trends and (b) a content analysis of rumors, news stories, and hospital events reflecting to the flow of "shocks" to which employees were subjected.

It should be underscored that the quantitative results were used largely to supplement the qualitative data, rather than the reverse which is far more common in organizational research. The surveys became more meaningful when interpreted in light of critical qualitative information just as other statistics were most useful when compared with content analyses or interview results. Triangulation, in this respect, can lead to a prominent role for qualitative evidence (just as it also should assure a continuing role for quantitative data).

Putting It All Together: Is There Convergence?

These various techniques and instruments generated a rather rich and comprehensive picture of anxiety and job insecurity (Greenhalgh and Jick, 1979; Jick, 1979). Self-reports, interviews, and coworker observations reflected a range of perceptions—some qualitatively described while others quantitatively represented. In turn, behavioral and objective data collected through archival sources and unobtrusive measures complemented the other data.

It is a delicate exercise to decide whether or not results have converged. In theory, a multiple confirmation of findings may appear routine. If there is congruence, it presumably is apparent. In practice, though, there are few guidelines for systematically ordering eclectic data in order to determine congruence or validity. For example, should all components of a multimethod approach be weighted equally, that is, is all the evidence equally useful? If not, then it is not clear on what basis the data should be weighted, aside from personal preference. Given the differing nature of multimethod results, the determination is likely to be subjective. While statistical tests can be applied to a particular method, there are no formal tests to discriminate between methods to judge their applicability. The concept of "significant differences" when applied to qualitatively judged differences does not readily compare with the statistical tests which also demonstrate "significant differences."

The various methods together produced largely consistent and convergent results. Archival and interview data indicated a strong relation between high turnover rates and job insecurity/anxiety while survey data showed a parallel relation between expressed propensity to leave and job insecurity.[2] These findings were formed on the basis of telephone interviews with employees who quit, personal interviews with their former supervisors, significant correlations found in survey data with a large random sample of employees, and the clear pattern seen between lay-off rumors reported in news stories and turnover statistics. Not only were the within-methods comparisons consistent, but there was also consistency in between-methods comparisons. Thus, the sociometric charting results of archive visits were congruent with the expressed anxiety reported in surveys and interviews. Both sets of results confirmed which events tended to be most anxiety producing and under what conditions anxiety was reduced. Thus, different measures of the same construct were shown to yield similar results (Phillips, 1971: 19).

There were also some surprises and discrepancies in the multimethod results which led to unexpected findings. When different measures yield dissimilar results, they demand that the researcher reconcile the differences somehow. In fact, divergence can often turn out to be an opportunity for enriching the explanation.

For example, in my study, those most stressed (according to surveys of self-reports) were least likely to visit the archive's news files (according to sociometric data), *contrary* to what was hypothesized. That is, while the survey showed that the group reporting the most anxiety were the least educated and least professionally mobile in terms of job skills, these low-skilled employees were underrepresented at the archive's library. One method produced results which predicted manifestations of anxiety but a second method failed to confirm the prediction. However, further interviews and observations—still other qualitative methods—helped to reconcile the disagreement by suggesting that the poorly educated employees tended to rely more on oral communication (e.g., close informal grapevines) than written documents. This interpretation resulted then from the divergent findings based on sociometric data, nonparticipant observations at work and outside work, and open-ended interviewing.

In seeking explanations for divergent results, the researcher may uncover unexpected results or unseen contextual factors. In one instance, interview data helped to suggest a relation between job insecurity/anxiety and certain attitudinal symptoms. Survey results, however, indicated that while employees at the site of the central organization were less insecure in their jobs than employees at the satellite site the magnitude of symptoms was the reverse. That is, the "victors" reported more symptoms than the "vanquished." But further interviewing and an analysis of field notes showed that the more severe symptoms reflected unique sources of anxiety at the central organization. Fieldwork and survey results were thus compatible as a variety of previously unconsidered contextual factors were brought to light.

The process of compiling research material based on multimethods is useful whether there is convergence or not. Where there is convergence, confidence in the results grows considerably. Findings are no longer attributable to a method artifact. However, where divergent results emerge, alternative, and likely more complex, explanations are generated. In my investigation of anxiety, triangulation allowed for more confident interpretations, for both testing and developing hypotheses, and for more unpredicted and context-related findings.

Overall, the triangulating investigator is left to search for a logical pattern in mixed-method results. His or her claim to validity rests on a judgment, or as Weiss (1968: 349) calls it, "a capacity to organize materials within a plausible framework." One begins to view the researcher as builder and creator, piecing together many pieces of a complex puzzle into a coherent whole. It is in this respect that the firsthand knowledge drawn from qualitative methods can become critical. While one can rely on certain scientific conventions (e.g., scaling, control groups, etc.) for maximizing the credibility of one's findings, the researcher using triangulation is likely to rely still more on a "feel" of the situation. This intuition and firsthand knowledge drawn from the multiple vantage points is centrally reflected in the interpretation process. Glaser and Strauss' (1965: 8) observation about fieldworkers summarizes this point of how triangulated investigations seem to be crystallized:

> The fieldworker knows that he knows, not only because he's been there in the field and because of his careful verifications of hypotheses, but because "in his bones" he feels the worth of his final analysis.

The "Quality" in Triangulation

Triangulation provides researchers with several important opportunities. First it allows researchers to be more confident of their results. This is the overall strength of the multimethod design. Triangulation can play many other constructive roles as well. It can stimulate the creation of inventive methods, new ways of capturing a problem to balance with conventional data-collection methods. In my study, this was illustrated by the development of an anxiety "thermometer," which unobtrusively measured changes in anxiety level.

Triangulation may also help to uncover the deviant or off-quadrant dimension of a phenomenon. Different viewpoints are likely to produce some elements which do not fit a theory or model. Thus, old theories are refashioned or new theories developed. Moreover, as was pointed out, divergent results from multimethods can lead to an enriched explanation of the research problem.

The use of multimethods can also lead to a synthesis or integration of theories. In this sense, methodological triangulation closely parallels theoretical triangulation (Denzin, 1978: 295); that is, efforts to bring diverse theories to bear on a common problem (e.g., LeVine and Campbell, 1972; Marris, 1975). Finally, triangulation may also serve as the critical test, by virtue of its comprehensiveness, for competing theories.

A thread linking all of these benefits is the important part played by qualitative methods in triangulation. The researcher is likely to sustain a profitable closeness to the situation which allows greater sensitivity to the multiple sources of data. Qualitative data and analysis function as the glue that cements the interpretation of multimethod results. In one respect, qualitative data are used as the critical counterpoint to quantitative methods. In another respect, the analysis benefits from the perceptions drawn from personal experiences and firsthand observations. Thus enters the artful researcher who uses the qualitative data to enrich and brighten the portrait. Finally, the convergent approach utilizes qualitative methods to illuminate "behavior in context" (Cronbach, 1975) where situational factors play a prominent role. In sum, triangulation, which prominently involves qualitative methods, can potentially generate what anthropologists call "holistic work" or "thick description." As Weiss concluded, "Qualitative data are apt to be superior to quantitative data in density of information, vividness, and clarity of meaning—characteristics more important in holistic work, than precision and reproducibility" (1968: 344–345).

The triangulation strategy is not without some shortcomings. First of all, replication is exceedingly difficult. Replication has been largely absent from most organizational research, but it is usually considered to be a necessary step in scientific progress. Replicating a mixed-methods package, including idiosyncratic techniques, is a nearly impossible task and not likely to become a popular exercise. Qualitative methods, in particular, are problematic to replicate. Second, while it may be rather obvious, multimethods are of no use with the "wrong" question. If the research is not clearly focused theoretically or conceptually, all the methods in the world will not produce a satisfactory outcome. Similarly, triangulation should not be used to legitimate a dominant, personally preferred method. That is, if either quantitative or qualitative methods become mere window dressing for the other, then the design is inadequate or biased. Each method should be represented in a significant way. This does however raise the question of whether the various instruments may be viewed as equally sensitive to the phenomenon being studied. One method may, in fact, be stronger or more appropriate but this needs to be carefully justified and made explicit. Otherwise, the purpose of triangulation is subverted.

Triangulation is a strategy that may not be suitable for all research purposes. Various constraints (e.g., time costs) may prevent its effective use. Nevertheless, triangulation has vital strengths and encourages productive research. It heightens qualitative methods to their deserved prominence and, at the same time, demonstrates that quantitative methods can and should be utilized in complementary fashion. Above all, triangulation demands creativity from its user—ingenuity in collecting data and insightful interpretation of data. It responds to a foreboding observation suggested by one sociologist (Phillips, 1971: 175):

> We simply cannot afford to continue to engage in the same kinds of sterile, unproductive, unimaginative investigations which have long characterized most . . . research.

In this sense, triangulation is not an end in itself and not simply a fine-tuning of our research instruments. Rather, it can stimulate us to better define and analyze problems in organizational research.

Notes

1. Webb et al. (1963: 3) list other sources from the 1950s, but Campbell and Fiske's article is most often cited elsewhere in the literature.
2. For specific results and data tables, see Jick (1979).

References

Becker, Howard S., and Blanche Geer 1957 "Participant observation and interviewing: A comparison." *Human Organization, 16*: 28–32.

Bouchard, Thomas J., Jr. 1976 "Unobtrusive measures: An inventory of uses." *Sociological Methods and Research, 4*: 267–300.

Campbell, Donald T. 1955 "The informant in quantitative research." *American Journal of Sociology, 60*: 339–342.

Campbell, Donald T., and D. W. Fiske 1959 "Convergent and discriminant validation by the multitrait-multimethod matrix." *Psychological Bulletin, 56*: 81–105.

Cronbach, Lee J. 1975 "Beyond the two disciplines of scientific psychology." *American Psychologist, 30*: 116–127.

Denzin, Norman K. *1978 The Research Act,* 2d ed. New York: McGraw-Hill.

Diesing, Paul 1971 *Patterns of Discovery in the Social Sciences.* Chicago: Aldine-Atherton.

Glaser, Barney G., and Anselm L. Strauss 1965 "Discovery of substantive theory: A basic strategy underlying qualitative research." *American Behavioral Scientist, 8*: 5–12.

Greenhalgh, Leonard, and Todd D. Jick 1979 "The relationship between job security and turnover and its differential effects on employee quality level." Paper presented to Academy of Management conference, Atlanta, Georgia.

Jick, Todd D. 1979 Process and Impacts of a Merger: Individual and Organizational Perspectives. Doctoral dissertation, New York State School of Industrial and Labor Relations, Cornell University.

LaPiere, R. T. 1934 "Attitudes vs. actions." *Social Forces, 13*: 230–237.

LeVine, R. A., and D. T. Campbell 1972 *Ethnocentrism, Theories of Conflict, Ethnic Attitudes, and Group Behavior.* New York: Wiley.

Marris, Peter 1975 *Loss and Change.* Garden City: Anchor Books-Doubleday.

Marshall, Judi, and Cary Cooper 1979 "Work experiences of middle and senior managers: The pressures and satisfactions." *Management International Review, 19*: 81–96.

McCall, George J., and J. L. Simmons, eds. 1969 *Issues in Participant Observation: A Text and Reader.* Reading, MA: Addison-Wesley.

Phillips, Derek L. 1971 *Knowledge from What?: Theories and Methods in Social Research.* Chicago: Rand McNally.

Reiss, Albert J. 1968 "Stuff and nonsense about social surveys and observation." In Howard Becker, Blanche Geer, David Riesman, and Robert Weiss (eds.), *Institutions and the Person*: 351–367. Chicago: Aldine.

Rohner, Ronald P. 1977 "Advantages of the comparative method of anthropology." *Behavior Science Research, 12*: 117–144.

Sales, Stephen M. 1973 "Threat as a factor in authoritarianism: An analysis of archival data." *Journal of Personality and Social Psychology, 28*: 44–57.

Sieber, Sam D. 1973 "The integration of fieldwork and survey methods." *American Journal of Sociology, 78*: 1335–1359.

Smith, H. W. 1975 *Strategies of Social Research: The Methodological Imagination.* Englewood Cliffs, NJ: Prentice Hall.

Spindler, George D., ed. 1970 *Being an Anthropologist.* New York: Holt, Rinehart and Winston.

Van Maanen, John 1975 "Police socialization: A longitudinal examination of job attitudes in an urban police department." *Administrative Science Quarterly, 20*: 207–228.

Vidich, Arthur J., and Gilbert Shapiro 1955 "A comparison of participant observation and survey data." *American Sociological Review, 20*: 28–33.

Webb, Eugene J., Donald T. Campbell, Richard D. Schwartz, and Lee Sechrest 1966 *Unobtrusive Measures: Nonreactive Research in the Social Sciences.* Chicago: Rand McNally.

Weiss, Robert S. 1968 "Issues in holistic research." In Howard S. Becker, Blanche Geer, David Riesman, and Robert Weiss (eds.), *Institutions and the Person*: 342–350. Chicago: Aldine.

5

Identifying the Purposes for Mixed Methods Designs

Selection: Greene, J. C., Caracelli, V. J., & Graham, W. F. (1989). Toward a conceptual framework for mixed-method evaluation designs. *Educational Evaluation and Policy Analysis, 11*(3), 255–274.

Editors' Introduction

Jennifer C. Greene, Valerie J. Caracelli, and Wendy F. Graham (1989) published the following examination of mixed methods designs from the perspective of the program evaluation literature. Many mixed methods scholars view this article as one of the classic works that initiated the mixed methods field as we know it today. Therefore, it is a key background reading for all scholars interested in mixed methods research.

Greene, Caracelli, and Graham's article stands out in three different ways. One, they were the first to advance a typology of five mixed methods designs (triangulation, complementarity, development, initiation, and expansion) in mixed methods research. This typology provides researchers with a set of common purposes for using a combined approach within a research or evaluative study. Two, they apply this typology to a collection of 57 empirical mixed methods studies published within the field of evaluation. These studies serve as exemplars of this typology and provide evidence that scholars have been combining quantitative and qualitative approaches for some time now. Finally, the authors analyze each study for seven design characteristics and examine how these characteristics are applied to address the different design purposes. Many scholars today still refer to these design types and identify these characteristics as important features when discussing mixed methods research or reporting studies that used mixed methods approaches.

Discussion Questions and Applications

1. Consider a mixed methods study such as reported by Donovan et al. (Chapter 17 in this volume) or Way, Stauber, Nakkula, and London (Chapter 20). Apply Greene et al.'s typology to classify the design and design characteristics used in the study.

2. Consider the five designs that make up this typology. Are they clearly differentiated from each other or do you find overlap among some of the purposes and characteristics?

3. How did this article extend the reasons for mixing methods beyond Jick's (Chapter 4) discussion?

Related References That Extend the Topic

Examples of other early mixed methods design classifications include:

Morgan, D. L. (1998). Practical strategies for combining qualitative and quantitative methods: Applications to health research. *Qualitative Health Research, 8*(3), 362–376.

Steckler, A., McLeroy, K. R., Goodman, R. M., Bird, S. T., & McCormick, L. (1992). Toward integrating qualitative and quantitative methods: An introduction. *Health Education Quarterly, 19*(1), 1–8.

Toward a Conceptual Framework for Mixed-Method Evaluation Designs

Jennifer C. Greene
Cornell University

Valerie J. Caracelli
Cornell University

Wendy F. Graham
Cornell University

In recent years evaluators of educational and social programs have expanded their methodological repertoire with designs that include the use of both qualitative and quantitative methods. Such practice, however, needs to be grounded in a theory that can meaningfully guide the design and implementation of mixed-method evaluations. In this study, a mixed-method conceptual framework was developed from the theoretical literature and then refined through an analysis of 57 empirical mixed-method evaluations. Five purposes for mixed-method

SOURCE: This article is reprinted from *Educational Evaluation and Policy Analysis*, Vol. 11, Issue 3, pp. 255–274, 1989. Reprinted with permission of the American Educational Research Association.

An earlier version of this paper was presented as a panel at the 1988 Annual Meeting of the American Evaluation Association in New Orleans. The authors are indebted to Melvin Mark for his insightful and constructive comments on the work presented herein, both at the conference and in subsequent personal communications (Mark, 1988).

evaluations are identified in this conceptual framework: triangulation, complementarity, development, initiation, and expansion. For each of the five purposes, a recommended design is also presented in terms of seven relevant design characteristics. These design elements encompass issues about methods, the phenomena under investigation, paradigmatic framework, and criteria for implementation. In the empirical review, common misuse of the term triangulation was apparent in evaluations that stated such a purpose but did not employ an appropriate design. In addition, relatively few evaluations in this review integrated the different method types at the level of data analysis. Strategies for integrated data analysis are among the issues identified as priorities for further mixed-method work.

The inevitable organizational, political, and interpersonal challenges of program evaluation mandate the use of multiple tools from evaluators' full methodological repertoire (Cook, 1985; Mathison, 1988). In recent years, this repertoire has been considerably expanded with the acceptance of qualitative methods as appropriate, legitimate, and even preferred for a wide range of evaluation settings and problems. Concomitantly, evaluators have expressed renewed interest in mixed-method evaluation designs employing both quantitative and qualitative methods (e.g., Cook & Reichardt, 1979; Madey, 1982; Rossman & Wilson, 1985; Smith & Louis, 1982). However, the territory of mixed-method designs remains largely uncharted. Of particular need is a clear differentiation of alternative purposes for mixing qualitative and quantitative methods and of alternative designs, analysis strategies, and contexts appropriate for each purpose (Greene & McClintock, 1985). For example, in current practice, quite different mixed-method designs are advocated and used in varied evaluation contexts for the common proclaimed purpose of *triangulation*. Such practice muddles the concept of triangulation as originally construed and remains insensitive to other possible benefits of mixed-method designs (Mathison, 1988). Further, just as careful planning and defensible rationales accompany the design and implementation of evaluation case studies, ethnographies, surveys, and quasi-experiments, so must similar thoughtfulness be given to the design and implementation of mixed-method studies.

Toward these ends, the present study contributes to the development of a conceptual framework, thus enabling more thoughtful and defensible mixed-method evaluative inquiry. In this study, we defined mixed-method designs as those that include at least one quantitative method (designed to collect numbers) and one qualitative method (designed to collect words), where neither type of method is inherently linked to any particular inquiry paradigm.

Through an analytic review of first theoretical and then empirical literature on mixed-method inquiry, this study generated valuable information on mixed-method *purposes* and *design characteristics*. Review procedures and findings for these two components of our mixed-method conceptual framework thus constitute the focus of the present discussion. Relatively little information was garnered relevant to other components of this framework, including the differential *utilization* of quantitative and qualitative information, *data analysis strategies* and *contexts* appropriate for mixed-method inquiries, as well as mixed-method *project management* and *resource* issues. These concerns are briefly discussed at the conclusion of the present article as issues warranting further work.

Theoretical Base

This study on mixed-method evaluation inquiry was grounded in an initial review of four theoretical starting points, selected for their conceptual attention to one or more of the key issues represented in our mixed-method conceptual framework.

Triangulation. (See Campbell & Fiske, 1959; Denzin, 1978; Webb, Campbell, Schwartz, & Sechrest, 1966; see also Mathison, 1988, for an excellent discussion of triangulation from these same sources.) From its classic sources, triangulation refers to the designed use of multiple methods, with offsetting or counteracting biases, in investigations of the same phenomenon in order to strengthen the validity of inquiry results. The core premise of triangulation as a design strategy is that all methods have inherent biases and limitations, so use of only one method to assess a given phenomenon will inevitably yield biased and limited results. However, when two or more methods that have offsetting biases are used to assess a given phenomenon, and the results of these methods converge or corroborate one another, then the validity of inquiry findings is enhanced. As noted by Greene and McClintock (1985), this triangulation argument requires that the two or more methods be intentionally used to assess the same conceptual phenomenon, be therefore implemented simultaneously, and, to preserve their counteracting biases, also be implemented independently.

Multiplism. (See Cook, 1985; Mark & Shotland, 1987; Shotland & Mark, 1987.) Thomas Cook's critical multiplism acknowledges the decreased authority of social science theory and data in a postpositivist world and then seeks to reaffirm and strengthen the validity of, and thereby users' confidence in, empirical work by extending the basic logic of triangulation to all aspects of the inquiry process.

The fundamental postulate of multiplism is that when it is not clear which of several options for question generation or method choice is "correct," all of them should be selected so as to "triangulate" on the most useful or the most likely to be true. . . . Multiplism aims to foster truth by establishing correspondences across many different, but conceptually related, ways of posing a question and by ruling out whether any obtained correspondences are artifacts of any epiphenomena of value, substantive theory, or method choice that may have been inadvertently incorporated into individual tests. (Cook, 1985, pp. 38 and 46)

Congruent with the basic logic of triangulation, Cook's multiplism emphasizes enhanced validity via convergence of results from multiple methods, theoretical orientations, and political or value perspectives. Cook also acknowledges that the results of multiple methods may serve more complementary than convergent purposes, as when different methods are used for different components of a multitask study. Elaborating on this point, Mark and Shotland (1987) offer three different purposes for multiple-method designs: (a) triangulation, which seeks convergence of findings; (b) bracketing, which seeks a range of estimates on the correct answer (or triangulation with a confidence interval); and (c) complementarity, in which different methods are used to assess different study components or phenomena, to assess the plausibility of identified threats to validity, or to enhance the interpretability of assessments of a single phenomenon—for example, via broader content coverage or alternate levels of analysis.

Mixing methods and paradigms. (See Guba & Lincoln, 1984; Kidder & Fine, 1987; Reichardt & Cook, 1979; Rossman & Wilson, 1985; Smith, 1983; Smith & Heshusius, 1986.) This set of references was selected primarily for their common discussion of the following design issue: Are mixed-method evaluation designs, in which the qualitative and quantitative methods *are* linked to contrasting inquiry paradigms, meaningful, sensible, and useful? Rossman and Wilson (1985) outline a continuum of three stances on this issue: the purists, the situationalists, and the pragmatists.

The purists (including Guba & Lincoln, 1984; Smith, 1983; and Smith & Heshusius, 1986) answer with an unequivocal "no" to the issue posed. They argue that the attributes of a paradigm form a "synergistic set" that cannot be meaningfully segmented or divided up. Moreover, different paradigms typically embody incompatible assumptions about the nature of the world and what is important to know, for example, realist versus relativist ontologies. So, mixed-method evaluation designs, in which the qualitative and quantitative methods are conceptualized and implemented within different paradigms (characteristically, interpretive and postpositivist paradigms, respectively), are neither possible nor sensible.

In contrast, Reichardt and Cook (1979) argue pragmatically that paradigm attributes are logically independent and therefore can be mixed and matched, in conjunction with methods choices, to achieve the combination most appropriate for a given inquiry problem. The practical demands of the problem are primary; inquirer flexibility and adaptiveness are needed to determine what will work best for a given problem. Or, in the pragmatic view of Miles and Huberman (1984), epistemological purity does not get research done.

The middle-ground situationalist position, articulated by Kidder and Fine (1987), retains the paradigmatic integrity stance of the purists but also argues, like the pragmatists, that our understanding of a given inquiry problem can be significantly enhanced by exploring convergences in stories generated from alternate paradigms. Congruent with Cook's proposal for aggressive meta-analyses, Kidder and Fine suggest that such explorations occur across studies, in particular, across quantitative (postpositivist) and qualitative (interpretivist) studies. This strategy may yield "stories that converge" or discrepancies that invoke fresh perspectives and new, more illuminating explanations.

In a similar vein, Rossman and Wilson (1985) sought their own middle ground on this issue of mixing paradigms by outlining three functions for mixed methodology: (a) corroboration, as in establishing convergence; (b) elaboration, as in providing richness and detail; and (c) initiation, which "prompts new interpretations, suggests areas for further exploration, or recasts the entire research question. Initiation brings with it fresh insight and a feeling of the creative leap. . . . Rather than seeking confirmatory evidence, this [initiation] design searches for the provocative" (Rossman & Wilson, 1985, pp. 637 and 633).

Mixed-method design strategies. (See Greene, 1987; Greene & McClintock, 1985; Knapp, 1979; Madey, 1982; Mark & Shotland, 1987; Maxwell, Bashook, & Sandlow, 1986; Sieber, 1973; Trend, 1979.) This more diverse set of references was reviewed primarily for additional ideas on alternative mixed-method purposes and on design characteristics that may differentiate among these purposes. Building on the work of Greene and McClintock (1985), Greene's (1987) synthesis of these ideas with those represented in the other three theoretical starting points served as a key foundation for the present conceptual work (and is thus incorporated within our later presentation of findings).

Empirical Review

Believing that sound conceptual work requires an interplay of theory and practice, we next conducted a comprehensive review of a purposive sample of 57 mixed-method evaluation studies. Our review guide included all of the components of our mixed-method conceptual framework (purpose, design characteristics, utilization, data analysis, contexts, management, and resources), with directed emphasis from the theoretical starting points on the first two.[1] The sample was purposive in that we aimed to identify studies in which the mixed-method aspect of the design was prominent and thus in concert with our research objectives. The search was limited to studies reported from 1980 to 1988. We also sought a broad representation of different approaches to evaluation, different kinds of evaluands, and different types of evaluation documents. Our final sample, which included 18 published evaluation studies, 17 evaluation reports, and 22 evaluation papers, met all of our sampling criteria except representation across evaluands. Compared with other data bases employed during sampling, ERIC yielded many more appropriate studies; hence, our sample tilted toward mixed-method evaluations conducted on educational programs.

Our reviews of these selected literatures on the theory and practice of mixed-method evaluation yielded most importantly a set of five different mixed-method purposes and seven relevant design characteristics. These results are presented in the following two sections.

Results for Mixed-Method Purposes

Theory. The five mixed-method purposes generated from our theoretical review are presented in Table 5.1 and briefly elaborated below.

A mixed-method design with a *triangulation* intent seeks convergence in the classic sense of triangulation. The use of both a qualitative interview and a quantitative questionnaire to assess program participants' educational aspirations illustrates this triangulation intent. In conjunction with this intent, Shotland and Mark (1987) caution that different methods may be biased in the same direction or, in fact, may be asking different questions. Variations within this triangulation purpose include Campbell and Fiske's (1959) advocacy of multiple methods to evaluate discriminant as well as convergent validity, and Mark and Shotland's (1987) idea of using multiple methods to bracket rather than converge on the correct answer. This idea of triangulation with a confidence interval is drawn from Reichardt and Gollob (1987).

In a *complementarity* mixed-method study, qualitative and quantitative methods are used to measure overlapping but also different facets of a phenomenon, yielding an enriched, elaborated understanding of that phenomenon. This differs from the triangulation intent in that the logic of convergence requires that the different methods assess the same conceptual phenomenon. The complementarity intent can be illustrated by the use of a qualitative interview to measure the nature and level of program participants' educational

Table 5.1   Purposes for Mixed-Method Evaluation Designs

Purpose	Rationale	Key theoretical sources
TRIANGULATION seeks convergence, corroboration, correspondence of results from the different methods.	To increase the validity of constructs and inquiry results by counteracting or maximizing the heterogeneity of irrelevant sources of variance attributable especially to inherent method bias but also to inquirer bias, bias of substantive theory, biases of inquiry context.	Campbell & Fiske, 1959 Cook, 1985 Denzin, 1978 Shotland & Mark, 1987 Webb et al., 1966
COMPLEMENTARITY seeks elaboration, enhancement, illustration, clarification of the results from one method with the results from the other method.	To increase the interpretability, meaningfulness, and validity of constructs and inquiry results by both capitalizing on inherent method strengths and counteracting inherent biases in methods and other sources.	Greene, 1987 Greene & McClintock, 1985 Mark & Shotland, 1987 Rossman & Wilson, 1985
DEVELOPMENT seeks to use the results from one method to help develop or inform the other method, where development is broadly construed to include sampling and implementation, as well as measurement decisions.	To increase the validity of constructs and inquiry results by capitalizing on inherent method strengths.	Madey, 1982 Sieber, 1973
INITIATION seeks the discovery of paradox and contradiction, new perspectives of frameworks, the recasting of questions or results from one method with questions or results from the other method.	To increase the breadth and depth of inquiry results and interpretations by analyzing them from the different perspectives of different methods and paradigms.	Kidder & Fine, 1987 Rossman & Wilson, 1985
EXPANSION seeks to extend the breadth and range of inquiry by using different methods for different inquiry components.	To increase the scope of inquiry by selecting the methods most appropriate for multiple inquiry components.	Madey, 1982 Mark & Shotland, 1987 Sieber, 1973

aspirations, as well as *influences* on these aspirations, combined with a quantitative questionnaire to measure the nature, level, and *perceived ranking within peer group* of participants' educational aspirations. The two measures in this example are assessing similar, as well as different, aspects of the aspirations phenomenon. One variation within this complementarity intent is the use of different methods to assess different levels of a phenomenon (Mark & Shotland, 1987), which we characterized with the analogy of peeling the layers of an onion.

Sieber (1973) and Madey (1982), for sociological and evaluation contexts, respectively, provide many creative examples of mixing methods for *development* purposes. All involve the sequential use of qualitative and quantitative methods, where the first method is used to help inform the development of the second. For example, a quantitative survey of program participants' educational aspirations could be used to identify a purposive sample for more in-depth interviews about these aspirations.

For a given mixed-method study, *initiation* as the discovery of paradox and fresh perspectives may well emerge rather than constitute a planned intent. However, in complex studies, as well as across studies, both consistencies and discrepancies in qualitative compared with quantitative findings can be intentionally analyzed for fresh insights invoked by means of contradiction and paradox.

A mixed-method study with an *expansion* intent is a "multitask" study in Cook's (1985) multiplism framework or a study that aims for scope and breadth by including multiple components. In evaluation contexts, this mixed-method expansion purpose is commonly illustrated by the use of qualitative methods to assess program processes and by quantitative methods to assess program outcomes.

Practice. Our empirical review results substantially confirmed this conceptualization of mixed-method purposes. For all studies with a discernible rationale for mixing methods, this rationale matched one or more of these five purposes. Hence, we offer this set of purposes as representing both the practice and potential of mixed-method evaluation strategies (see also Smith, 1986) and as progress toward a common parlance for conceptualizing and describing mixed-method rationales in program evaluation.[2]

In the empirical review, mixed-method purposes were tabulated both according to the study authors' statement of purpose and by our definitions. As shown in Table 5.2, the authors' stated primary or secondary purpose for using a mixed-method design was often triangulation (23%) or expansion (26%). However, in a similar proportion of evaluations, no purpose for the mixed-method design was stated or could be readily inferred. By our definitions, four fifths of the primary purposes and one half of the 70 total purposes were either complementarity (not triangulation) or expansion.

Table 5.2 Empirical Review: Crosstabulation of Mixed-Method Purposes as Stated and by Our Definition

	By our definition										Totals			
	Triangulation		*Complementarity*		*Development*		*Initiation*		*Expansion*		*P*		*s*	
Authors' statement	P	s	P	s	P	s	P	s	P	s	No.	%	s	% all
Triangulation	3	2	5	2	2			1	1		11	19	5	23
Complementarity			8	2							8	14	2	14
Development					5	1					5	9	1	9
Initiation							1	1			1	2	1	3
Expansion									16	2	16	28	2	26
Not stated			5	1			1	1	10		16	28	2	26
Totals	3 (5%)	2	18 (32%)	5	7 (12%)	1	2 (4%)	3	27 (47%)	2	57		13	
% all	7%	7%	33%		11%		7%		41%					

NOTE: P = primary purpose; s = secondary purpose.

The more interesting finding in Table 5.2 is the backward **Z** pattern formed by this cross-tabulation. The diagonal represents agreement between the authors' statements and our definitions of mixed-method purposes. For example, five of the empirical studies reviewed had a primary or secondary purpose of triangulation (upper left cell) according to both determinations. When there was such agreement about purpose, the authors were usually very explicit in their stated rationale for the particular mixed-method design chosen. For example, in an evaluation of a physical education project, "the data were examined . . . and presented employing the processes of triangulation and corroboration in order to arrive at valid and reliable statements" (Moody, 1982, Abstract). Additional illustrations of this diagonal, or instances of our mixed-method purposes in evaluation practice, follow.

> The evaluation instruments were designed to give overlapping [complementarity] and cross checking [triangulation] assessments of the perceptions of those involved. (Peters, Marshall, & Shaw, 1986, p. 16)

> Overall, the methodologies used confirmed that any paper-and-pencil instrument ought to be supplemented by qualitative methods. This would enrich and provide depth to the statistical data obtained. (Martin, 1987, pp. 14–15) [complementarity]

> Quantitative methods can establish the degree to which perceptions are shared, but uncovering the perceptions themselves must be [first] done naturalistically. (Gray & Costello, 1987, p. 12) [development]

> Qualitative in addition to quantitative methods were included so the evaluation could "tell the full story." (Hall, 1981, p. 127) [expansion]

> The whole is greater than the sum of the parts when qualitative and quantitative approaches and methods are combined. (Smith, 1986, p. 37) [initiation]

The horizontal lines forming the top and bottom of the backward **Z** show disagreement between the authors' stated intentions for the mixed-method design and our determination of purposes. This discrepancy is of one of two types: Either the authors stated triangulation as the purpose for the mixed-method design when it was not, or the authors did not state a purpose when we were able to identify one. The latter discrepancy is difficult to illustrate because of the absence of a stated purpose by the authors. An excerpt from Moran (1987) illustrates the first discrepancy. This evaluator stated triangulation as the purpose for the mixed-method design, when we identified primary and secondary purposes of development and initiation, respectively.

Some researchers maintain that a two-tiered methodology is not really a *triangulation*. Greene and McClintock (1985) contend that . . ."a nonindependent, sequential mixed-method strategy loses the capacity for triangulation. In this strategy, the methods are deliberately interactive, not independent, and they are applied singly over time so that they may or may not be measuring the same phenomenon." Given the dynamic nature of the public service, it is difficult to discern how any evaluation routine could meet the[se] criticisms. . . . The idea behind an interactive sequential methodology is not to measure the same phenomenon at the same time, but *to use the findings of one methodology to inform the issues to be addressed in the subsequent evaluation*. Under this construct, qualitative data are employed to ensure that the quantitative study is current. Quantitative data in turn are used to *reformulate the issues* for the qualitative study. (Moran, 1987, pp. 623–624, emphases added)

Results for Mixed-Method Design Characteristics

The seven characteristics of mixed-method designs presented in Table 5.3 represent an integration of results from our theoretical and empirical reviews. Although the empirical review did not alter the initial set of theoretically-derived design characteristics,[3] it did serve to refine and clarify our conceptualization of each. Nonetheless, we do not consider this set of mixed-method design characteristics to be exhaustive, but rather we anticipate future refinements and additions. Brief descriptions of the seven mixed-method design characteristics generated in this study follow. Empirical results for these design characteristics are presented in the next section, differentiated by primary mixed-method purpose.

Methods. The methods characteristic represents the degree to which the qualitative and quantitative methods selected for a given study are similar to or different from one another in form, assumptions, strengths, and limitations or biases (as argued by Campbell & Fiske, 1959). A scaled questionnaire and structured interview would be considered similar, whereas an achievement test and open-ended interview would be considered different. Mid-range positions can occur when the methods share some characteristics, especially biases, but not others, as in the combined use of a quantitative written questionnaire and a qualitative critical incident (also written) diary.

Phenomena. The term *phenomena* refers to the degree to which the qualitative and quantitative methods are intended to assess totally different phenomena or exactly the same phenomenon. When different methods are implemented to assess different phenomena, the methods are usually responding to different questions. To illustrate, quantitative measures like standardized achievement tests are often used to assess the degree of success of an educational program,

Table 5.3   Mixed-Method Design Characteristics

Characteristic	Refinement						Key
Methods	Similar					Different	
Phenomena	Different	A	B	C	D	Same	A = totally different phenomena B = dissimilar but related phenomena C = overlapping phenomena or different facets, dimensions of a single phenomenon D = exactly the same phenomenon
Paradigms	Different	A	B	C	D	Same	A = all qualitative methods in one paradigm, all quantitative methods in another B = all qualitative or quantitative methods in one paradigm, most of the other methods in another C = most methods of both types in one paradigm, a few methods of one or both types in another D = all methods in the same paradigm
Status	Unequal					Equal	
Implementation: Independence	Interactive					Independent	
Implementation: Timing	Sequential	A	B	C	D (E)	Simultaneous	A = sequential: different methods implemented sequentially B = bracketed: one method implemented before and after the other C = concurrent: one method implemented within the time frame spanned by implementation of the other D = simultaneous: different methods implemented simultaneously E = not applicable: one method represents the use of existing data
Study	> One study					One study	

and qualitative measures such as interviews and observations are used to understand how and why a program is successful or unsuccessful.

Mid-range phenomena positions occur when qualitative and quantitative methods overlap in their intent, yet also capitalize on the strengths of one or both methods to secure additional information. For example, Smith and Robbins (1984) used quantitative surveys to provide a detailed picture of the nature, causes, and consequences of parental involvement in four different federal programs. A qualitative site review, which included interviews, observations, and document analysis, was intended to secure similar information on parental involvement, as well as additional information about the effects of parental involvement in varied program settings (e.g., rural vs. urban).

Paradigms. The design characteristic labeled *paradigms* refers to the degree to which the different method types are implemented within the same or different paradigms. We recognize that any given pair of quantitative and qualitative methods either is or is not implemented within the same paradigm, rendering this design characteristic dichotomous. Evaluation practice, however, commonly includes multiple methods of both types. Thus, the ratings in Table 5.3 are intended to be holistic, representing the degree to which the whole set of methods is conceptualized, designed, and implemented within the same or different epistemological frameworks. Assessments of this design element should be made independently of the relative number and status of qualitative versus quantitative methods.

Status. This characteristic represents the degree to which a study's qualitative and quantitative methods have equally important or central roles vis-à-vis the study's overall objectives. In contrast to paradigms, the status design characteristic should directly reflect the relative weight and influence of the qualitative and quantitative methods with respect to their frequency and their centrality to study objectives.

Implementation: Independence. The degree to which the qualitative and quantitative methods are conceptualized, designed, and implemented interactively or independently can be viewed on a continuum. Sometimes a study includes both components, representing a mid-range position. For example, in part of Louis's (1981) study, mixed-method implementation was independent: Standardized data collection by central project staff occurred simultaneously with the development of 42 miniethnographies by field staff, who worked without knowledge of the central staff's emerging findings. Part of Louis's study was also interactive: During analysis and interpretation, every individual who contributed as a major author or analyst to the study was familiar with all data available.

Implementation: Timing. Although we represent this characteristic as a continuum, we again recognize that a given pair of methods is typically implemented concurrently or sequentially, not in between. Yet, a short quantitative method could be paired with a longer qualitative method, or pre-post tests could be implemented before and after participant observation (illustrating, from Table 5.3, "concurrent" and "bracketed" timing, respectively). Variation on this design element also arises from the use of multiple methods within a mixed set. With reflection we refined this characteristic by dividing it into categories (see Table 5.3) that could be assessed for a whole set of mixed methods or, as appropriate, for each pair of methods.

Study. The final design characteristic labeled *study* is essentially categorical. The empirical research either encompassed one study or more than one study. Although our own review yielded little variation on this design characteristic (all but four evaluations represented a single study), it remains an important consideration for continued discussion of mixed-method designs (Cook, 1985; Kidder & Fine, 1987).

Mixed-Method Purposes × Design Characteristics: Recommended Designs

To review, the long-range goal of this study is the development of a conceptual framework that could inform and guide the practice of mixed-method inquiry. Such guidance would include a description of the kind of design (and analysis, context, etc.) most appropriate for a given mixed-method purpose. For this reason, we analyzed the empirical review results on mixed-method design characteristics separately for studies grouped by *our* definition of primary purpose. This analysis is presented in Figure 5.1.

Each row of Figure 5.1 represents one of our five mixed-method purposes; each column presents a single design characteristic and the scale by which it was rated. The five points in these scales correspond to the following ratings of these design elements which we viewed as continua during our empirical review: at either end (1 and 5), near either end (2 and 4), near the middle (3). Each cell entry in Figure 5.1 thus displays the distribution of our ratings on a single design characteristic for a given mixed-method purpose. For example, the graph in the upper left-hand cell shows that the qualitative and quantitative methods were rated *different* (a score of 5) in all three evaluations with a triangulation purpose.

Incorporating these empirical review results on design characteristics, this section heuristically presents a recommended design for each of the identified mixed-method purposes. There are three caveats to keep in mind as these recommendations are presented. First, the importance of these seven characteristics to mixed-method designs is generally supported by our empirical review. Nonetheless, we have greater confidence in our definitions of

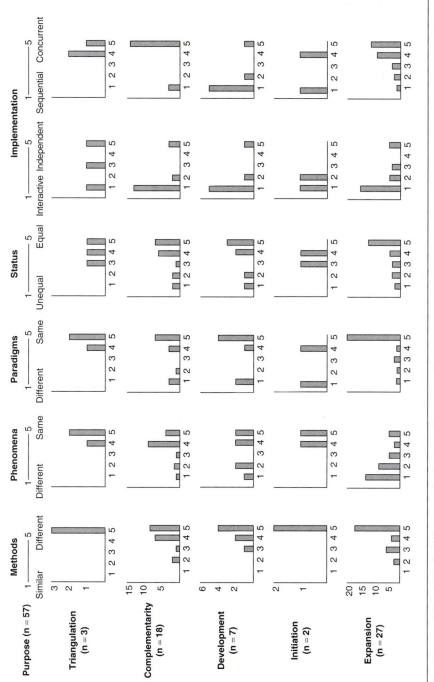

Figure 5.1 Mixed-Method Purposes by Design Characteristics

NOTE: Study not reported because only four evaluations included more than one study. In a few studies, some design elements could not be rated because of missing information.

mixed-method purposes and consider elements of mixed-method design choice an open area of investigation. Second, mixed-method strategies are often guided by more than one purpose. Thus, designs will not appear as pristine on these characteristics in practice as we have set them forth here. Third, we acknowledge that some departures from these recommended designs can be readily defended. Mark (1988), for example, suggested that for a triangulation design, the different methods need not be implemented simultaneously if the phenomenon of interest is stable over time. In short, we present these recommended designs to underscore the importance of design element choice in mixed-method frameworks, but we present them as working ideas rather than prescriptive models.

Figure 5.2 profiles our five recommended mixed-method designs. In this figure, each letter represents a different mixed-method purpose. Individual letters denote a recommended position on a design characteristic for a particular purpose. Letters with bars indicate that the recommended position can range somewhat. The omission of a letter means that a *specific* position on a characteristic is not warranted.

Triangulation (T) design. The combined use of quantitative and qualitative methods for the purpose of triangulation dominates current discussions about mixed-method rationales. Yet, as indicated by our empirical review (see Table 5.2), methodological triangulation in its classic sense is actually quite rare in mixed-method practice. Our recommended triangulation design is based on the logic of convergence embedded in the classic conceptualization of triangulation.

This logic requires that the quantitative and qualitative methods be different from one another with respect to their inherent strengths and limitations/biases and that both method types be used to assess the same phenomenon. Methods that are biased in the same direction or that ask/answer different questions can undermine the triangulation logic and result in spurious inferences (Shotland & Mark, 1987). Relatedly, the methods need to be conceptualized, designed, and implemented within the same paradigmatic framework (Greene & McClintock, 1985; Kidder & Fine, 1987). Strong between-methods triangulation is also enhanced when the status of the different methods—that is, their relative weight and influence—is equal and when the quantitative and qualitative study components are implemented independently and simultaneously. Across mixed-method purposes, the recommended independent implementation of the different methods is unique to triangulation.

Complementarity (C) design. One apparently common purpose for combining qualitative and quantitative methods is to use the results from one method to elaborate, enhance, or illustrate the results from the other. The recommended

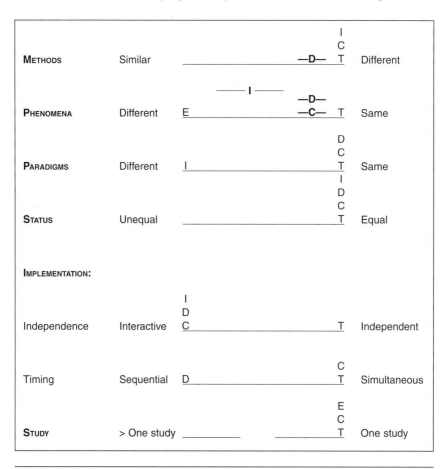

Figure 5.2   Recommended mixed-method designs

NOTE: T = triangulation; C = complementarity; D = development; I = initiation; E = expansion.

complementarity design depicted in Figure 5.2 is similar to the triangulation design, with the exception of the phenomena and implementation-independence characteristics. The phenomena characteristic has a slight range, indicating that the quantitative and qualitative methods should be used to examine overlapping phenomena or different facets of a single phenomenon. In complementarity designs, the paradigmatic framework for both types of methods should also be similar, and in interpretability is best enhanced when the methods are implemented simultaneously and interactively within a single study.

In our empirical review there were 18 mixed-method evaluations implemented for the primary purpose of complementarity. A comparison of the design characteristics of these 18 studies (see Figure 5.1) with our recommended complementarity design yields considerable congruence. On each design characteristic with the exception of status, approximately three fourths of these mixed-method studies were judged to be at or close to our recommended position. Somewhat more variability was evident for status. This congruence of theory with practice supports and encourages both.

Development (D) design. The salient feature of our recommended development design is the sequential timing of the implementation of the different methods. One method is implemented first, and the results are used to help select the sample, develop the instrument, or inform the analysis for the other method. By definition, then, implementation is also interactive, and the different methods are used to assess the same or similar phenomena, conceptualized within the same paradigm. We further maintain that strong development designs use dissimilar methods of equal status. Mixed-method studies with a development intent can occur within a single study or across studies, conducted sequentially to capitalize on the benefits derived from each method type.

Like the theory-to-practice comparison for complementarity, the design characteristics of the seven empirical mixed-method studies conducted for purposes of development (see Figure 5.1) were quite congruent with this recommended design. The designs of five or six of these studies were at or close to the recommended position on all characteristics except phenomena. Surprisingly, for this design element, three studies used mixed methods to assess different rather than similar phenomena. An interesting variation was found in one study that implemented the different methods simultaneously rather than sequentially (Bower, Anderson, & Thompson, 1986). In this case, a small "prefatory naturalistic study" provided a descriptive base of information, which was then used for three successively larger "waves" of data collection, each of which included both quantitative and qualitative measures.

Gray and Costello (1987) stretch our conceptions about this design by advocating mixing methods, as well as paradigms for development purposes. Their main argument is that the use of naturalistic qualitative methods to assess *context* first does not preclude the use of positivist quantitative methods for other purposes later in the study. Gray and Costello's work also supports our call for a more thorough understanding of the contexts appropriate for various mixed-method purposes and of the influence that contextual factors may have on mixed-method designs.

Initiation (I) design. In a mixed-method study with an initiation intent, the major aim of combining qualitative and quantitative methods is to uncover paradox and contradiction. Jick (1983) discussed similar purposes in outlining his "holistic triangulation" design. Rossman and Wilson (1985) demonstrated that iterative use of both method types can intentionally seek areas of nonconvergence in order to "initiate interpretations and conclusions, suggest areas for further analysis, or recast the entire research question" (p. 633).

Nonetheless, purposeful initiation may well be rare in practice. One excellent example of a more emergent initiation design from our empirical review is Louis's (1981) evaluation of the Research and Development Utilization program (RDU). This eight-million-dollar demonstration project was funded by NIE (National Institute for Education) between 1976 and 1979 to promote the adoption of new curricula and staff development materials in 300 local schools. Louis discusses key features and examples of the "cyclical interaction" model developed during the course of this evaluation, including the following:

1. Purposive sampling of particular cases was combined with random sampling for survey or other structured data collection in order to maximize both discovery and generalizability.

2. An iterative approach to instrumentation for both field data collection and more standardized instruments was achieved through ongoing interaction between qualitative and quantitative analyses.

3. Analysis began with the first data collection and occurred at periodic intervals throughout the project. The same staff engaged in simultaneous analysis of both qualitative and quantitative data. Testing and verification of both types of data sources increased reliability and validity.

A second example of a more emergent initiation design is Maxwell et al.'s (1986) evaluation of the use of "medical care evaluation committees" in physician education. In this unusual study, ethnographic methods were employed within an experimental framework. Initiation features were evident in the authors' comments regarding the advantages of the ethnographic approach: "It allowed us to discover aspects of the committees' educational functioning that we had not anticipated and would have missed had we relied on quantitative methods" (p. 138). Specifically, the qualitative data prompted a recasting of how medical care evaluation committees influenced physicians' performance. In the original hypothesis, committee participation was expected to directly increase a physician's knowledge and thereby enhance his/her performance. The data indicated, however, that committee participation served to increase the physician's confidence to apply knowledge he/she already had, and this enhanced confidence underlay performance changes.

Drawing in part on these empirical examples, our recommended design for a mixed-method evaluation with an initiation intent incorporates two distinctive features. First, the phenomena investigated with initiation-oriented mixed methods could cover a broad range. Second, to maximize the possibility of unlikely findings, mixing paradigms in this design is acceptable and even encouraged. This advocacy of mixed epistemological frameworks is congruent with Cook's (1985) call for multiple theoretical and value frameworks in applied social inquiry.

Expansion (E) design. In our empirical review, the most frequently cited mixed-method purpose was expansion. This suggests that many evaluators are mixing methods primarily to extend the scope, breadth, and range of inquiry by using different methods for different inquiry components. Typically, in the empirical studies reviewed, quantitative methods were used to assess program outcomes, and qualitative measures to assess implementation. Figure 5.2 recommends only two elements for a mixed-method expansion design. The empirical work would be encompassed within a single study, and, unique to expansion designs, the phenomena investigated would be distinct. Our sample of mixed-method expansion designs is fairly congruent with these recommendations (see Figure 5.1).

The decision to "expand" an evaluation to include both process and product components is undoubtedly motivated by the desire to produce a more comprehensive evaluation. However, in many of the evaluations of this genre that we reviewed, there was a paramedic quality to the qualitative component. That is, qualitative data often appeared in the emergency room of report writing as a life-saving device to resuscitate what was either a failed program or a failed evaluation. Problematic programs or evaluations with insufficient (quantitative) controls or statistical power were discussed in terms of (qualitative) participant experiences, implementation impediments, and recommendations for program improvement.

What is at issue here is how qualitative and quantitative methods in an expansion design can be mixed meaningfully and effectively. Even in the stronger expansion studies reviewed, the qualitative and quantitative methods were kept separate throughout most phases of the inquiry. The term *parallel design* (Louis, 1981) may appear more appropriate. Yet, we prefer the term *expansion* because we believe it more accurately reflects the "multitask" intent of such studies in Cook's multiplism framework.[4] We also believe that mixed-method expansion studies have not yet tested the limits of their potential. For example, in a higher order expansion design, a more integrated use of methods could be achieved by employing combinations of qualitative and quantitative methods to assess both implementation and outcomes. Such a study may well incorporate elements of triangulation and complementarity into its design, becoming, in effect, a multipurpose study. Or a higher order expansion design could use a mix of different methods, each creatively designed to assess conceptual strands that span or link program implementation and outcomes. The major benefit of such higher order designs would be strengthened inferences. In contrast, our review suggested that the current normative expansion design keeps the different methods separated and thus does not realize such benefits.

In summary, Figure 5.3 presents a funnel array of recommended design options for the various mixed-method purposes. This array indicates that design options are relatively constrained and narrow for some mixed-method purposes but more flexible and wider for others. The order from most to least constrained design options for mixed-method purpose is as follows: triangulation, complementarity, development, initiation, and expansion.

Results for Mixed-Method Data Analyses

Our empirical review also assessed the nature and degree of qualitative and quantitative integration attained by the studies reviewed during their data analysis and interpretation/reporting stages. The results were grouped in four categories: (a) no integration—both analyses and interpretation were conducted separately; (b) analyses were conducted separately, but some integration occurred during interpretation; (c) integration occurred during both analyses and interpretation; and (d) analyses not reported. A crosstabulation of these analysis results with mixed-method purposes is shown in Table 5.4. These results reveal that although nearly equal numbers of the studies reviewed attained some degree of qualitative and quantitative integration as did not (23 and 25, respectively), only 5 studies achieved such integration during the analysis process itself. The results further suggest that relatively low levels of integration may characterize studies with an expansion intent, and perhaps relatively high levels may accompany studies with an initiation intent.

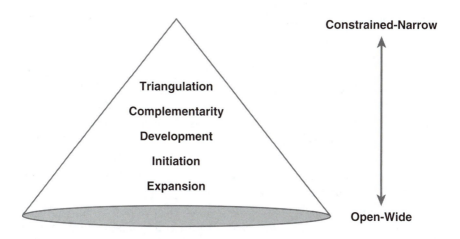

Figure 5.3   Flexibility of Design Options for Mixed-Method Purposes

Toward Further Development of Mixed-Method Theory and Practice

In this analysis of selected theoretical and empirical literature, we have begun to chart the territory of mixed-method evaluation designs. Our focus has been on clearly differentiating alternative purposes for mixing qualitative and quantitative methods. Design characteristics relevant to mixed-method strategies and appropriate for specific purposes were also explored. In addition to further refinement of these mixed-method purposes and design elements, we believe several other issues within our overall conceptual framework represent high priorities for future work. These issues include the relationship of mixed-method strategies to evaluation purpose, continuing paradigm questions, procedures for mixed data analysis, utilization, and relevant contextual factors.

With respect to the first issue, we surmised that important distinctions in mixed-method purposes and designs might arise with different evaluation intents—that is, formative versus summative or process versus product. An analysis of our own sample of empirical studies (which included 11 process studies, 12 product studies, and 30 evaluations with both process and product components) yielded no marked differences in mixed-method purpose. Nonetheless, the relationship between evaluation purposes and mixed-method strategies is an important area for further research.

To the probable dismay of purists, in this study we sidestepped the knotty paradigmatic issues involved in mixed-method inquiry. Yet, a comprehensive mixed-method framework must eventually address whether it is appropriate to mix paradigms when mixing methods. Our own thinking to date suggests that the notion of mixing paradigms is problematic for designs with triangulation or complementarity purposes, acceptable but still problematic for designs with a development or expansion intent, and actively encouraged for designs with an initiation intent.

Future research also need to address the issue of data analysis strategies for mixed-method evaluations. In our empirical review, only five studies integrated qualitative and quantitative data during the analysis process. The creative and promising strategies used by these evaluators are reported more fully in a separate article (Caracelli, Greene, & Graham, 1989). In 18 additional studies that we reviewed, some measure of integration of the different data sets was attained during interpretation and reporting. Typically, in these studies, qualitative data were brought in to support or explain quantitative findings, to flesh out conclusions, or to make recommendations. However, when data mismatches occurred, there was little discussion in any of

Table 5.4 Crosstabulation of Mixed-Method Analyses and Purposes

Analysis category	Purpose					Totals	
	Triangulation	Complementarity	Development	Initiation	Expansion	No.	%
No integration		6	2		17	25	44
Integration during interpretation	3	8	2		5	18	32
Integration during analysis and interpretation		1	1	2	1	5	9
Not reported		3	2		4	9	16

these studies about these discrepancies, nor were there efforts to resolve them. Both Trend (1979) and Jick (1983) discuss the importance and the challenge of reconciling nonconvergent findings. "When different methods yield dissimilar results, they demand that the researcher reconcile the differences somehow. In fact, divergence can often turn out to be an opportunity for enriching the explanation" (Jick, 1983, p. 143). Shotland and Mark (1987) also underscore the importance of the "empirical puzzles" (Cook, 1985) that arise when results do not converge, and they call for a more systematic exploration of the possible causes of such inconsistent results.

An additional important area of inquiry concerns utilization specifically as it relates to mixed-method strategies. The fundamental issue here is this: In what common and different ways is quantitative and qualitative information used? And what implications do these utilization processes have for mixed-method approaches to evaluation? Further, attention to contextual factors keeps us mindful of an important question: Is the problem guiding our choice of methods, or vice versa?

These identified areas of future mixed-method inquiry—the role of evaluation purpose, paradigm issues, data analysis strategies, and utilization—as well as others of particular interest to other inquirers, are fundamental to the inherent aim of the research presented herein. Careful planning and defensible rationales must accompany the design and implementation of mixed-methods evaluations. This goal can be achieved only with a more comprehensive theory to guide use of mixed methods in evaluation practice.

Notes

1. In order to be able to describe current mixed-method practice, we also extracted from each selected study a description of the evaluand and of the evaluation approach, purpose (e.g., formative or summative), time frame, and qualitative and quantitative methods used. This descriptive information and reference list for our sample of mixed-method evaluation practice is available from the authors upon request, as are the complete details of our sampling and review procedures.

2. Seven of the empirical studies reviewed cited as a secondary rationale the inclusion of either qualitative or, more commonly, quantitative methods, not for methodological or theoretical reasons, but rather in anticipation of study audiences' known preferences or needs for this form of information. This political *responsiveness* intent for mixing methods can be viewed, in part, as a tactical maneuver to increase the utilization of evaluation results. However, in contrast

to the other mixed-method purposes, a responsiveness intent is unlikely to invoke any significant effort at integration, either at the level of methods, or, more importantly, with respect to the inferences drawn (Mark, 1988). For this reason, we view responsiveness as conceptually different from the other five mixed-method purposes.

3. An eighth design characteristic identified from the theoretical literature was deleted during the pilot testing of the empirical review guide. From Cook (1985) and Shotland and Mark (1987), this characteristic was the following: Are the criteria used to decide which phenomena to assess with multiple methods (i.e., what to make multiple) derived from theory (substantive or methodological) or from the context? Though deleted as a design element, this concern was retained in the descriptive section of the empirical review guide.

4. Alternatively, Mark (1988) suggested that expansion be viewed, in conjunction with complementarity and triangulation, as a continuum of mixed-method purposes. This continuum is essentially our phenomena design characteristic, representing the use of different methods to assess different, related, similar, or the same phenomena.

References

Bower, J. C., Anderson, B. N., & Thompson, B. (1986, April). *Triangulation in the evaluation of school system interventions*. Paper presented at the annual meeting of the American Educational Research Association, San Francisco.

Campbell, D. T., & Fiske, D. W. (1959). Convergent and discriminant validation by the multitrait—multimethod matrix. *Psychological Bulletin, 56*, 81–105.

Caracelli, V. J., Greene, J. C., & Graham, W. F. (1989). *Mixed-method data analysis: Strategies and issues*. Manuscript in preparation.

Cook, T. D. (1985). Postpositivist critical multiplism. In R. L. Shotland & M. M. Mark (Eds.), *Social science and social policy* (pp. 21–62). Beverly Hills, CA: Sage.

Cook, T. D., & Reichardt, C. S. (Eds.). (1979). *Qualitative and quantitative methods in evaluation research*. Beverly Hills, CA: Sage.

Denzin, N. K. (1978). *The research act: An introduction to sociological methods* (chap. 10). New York: McGraw-Hill.

Gray, P., & Costello, M. (1987, October). *Context as determinant of methodology in multi-client service organizations*. Paper presented at the annual meeting of the American Evaluation Association, Boston.

Greene, J. C. (1987). *Uses and misuses of mixed-method evaluation designs*. Proposal for the 1988 annual meeting of the American Education Research Association, New Orleans.

Greene, J. C., & McClintock, C. (1985). Triangulation in evaluation: Design and analysis issues. *Evaluation Review, 9*, 523–545.

Guba, E. G., & Lincoln, Y. S. (1984). *Do inquiry paradigms imply inquiry methodologies?* Copyrighted manuscript.

Hall, J. N. (1981). *Evaluation and comparison: Social learning curriculum and instrumental enrichment. Final report* (Contract No. G008001869, U.S. Department of Education). Nashville, TN: George Peabody College for Teachers. (ERIC Document Reproduction Service No. ED 244 484).

Jick, T. D. (1983). Mixing qualitative and quantitative methods: Triangulation in action. In J. VanMaanen (Ed.), *Qualitative methodology* (pp. 135–148). Beverly Hills, CA: Sage.

Kidder, L. H., & Fine, M. (1987). Qualitative and quantitative methods: When stories converge. In M. M. Mark & R. L. Shotland (Eds.), *Multiple methods in program evaluation: New Directions for Program Evaluation 35* (pp. 57–75). San Francisco: Jossey-Bass.

Knapp, M.S. (1979). Ethnographic contributions to evaluation research. In T. D. Cook & C. S. Reichardt (Eds.), *Qualitative and quantitative methods in evaluation research* (pp. 118–139). Beverly Hills, CA: Sage.

Louis, K. S. (1981, April). *Policy researcher as sleuth: New approaches to integrating qualitative and quantitative methods.* Paper presented at the annual meeting of the American Educational Research Association, Los Angeles. (ERIC Document Reproduction Service No. ED 207–256)

Madey, D. L. (1982). Some benefits of integrating qualitative and quantitative methods in program evaluation, with illustrations. *Educational Evaluation and Policy Analysis, 4,* 223–236.

Mark, M. M. (1988, October). *Discussant remarks on "Toward a theory of mixed-method evaluation designs."* Panel presented at the annual meeting of the American Evaluation Association, New Orleans.

Mark, M. M., & Shotland, R. L. (1987). Alternative models for the use of multiple methods. In M. M. Mark & R. L. Shotland (Eds.). *Multiple methods in program evaluation: New Directions for Program Evaluation 35* (pp. 95–100). San Francisco: Jossey-Bass.

Martin, G. O. (1987, October). *The use of qualitative and quantitative evaluation methods for program evaluation. The California International Studies Project: A case study.* Paper presented at the annual meeting of the American Evaluation Association, Boston.

Mathison, S. (1988). Why triangulate? *Educational Researcher, 17*(2), 13–17.

Maxwell, J. A., Bashook, P. G., & Sandlow, C. J. (1986). Combining ethnographic and experimental methods in educational evaluation. In D. M. Fetterman & M. A. Pitman (Eds.), *Educational evaluation: Ethnography in theory, practice, and politics* (pp. 121–143). Beverly Hills, CA: Sage.

Miles, M. B., & Huberman, A. M. (1984). *Qualitative data analysis: A sourcebook of new methods.* Beverly Hills, CA: Sage.

Moody, P. R. (1982). *Pitt Meadows physical education project: Evaluation of an implementation project* (Report No. 82:13). Vancouver: Educational Research Institute of British Columbia. (ERIC Document Reproduction Service No. ED 222 564)

Moran, T. K. (1987). Research and managerial strategies for integrating evaluation research into agency decision making. *Evaluation Review, 11*, 612–630.

Peters, M., Marshall, J., & Shaw, R. (1986). The development and trials of a decision making model: An evaluation. *Evaluation Review, 10*, 5–27.

Reichardt, C. S., & Cook, T. D. (1979). Beyond qualitative *versus* quantitative methods. In T. D. Cook & C. S. Reichardt (Eds.), *Qualitative and quantitative methods in evaluation research* (pp. 7–32). Beverly Hills, CA: Sage.

Reichardt, C. S., & Gollob, H. F. (1987). Taking uncertainty into account when estimating effects. In M. M. Mark & R. L. Shotland (Eds.), *Multiple methods in program evaluation: New Directions for Program Evaluation 35* (pp. 7–22). San Francisco: Jossey-Bass.

Rossman, G. B., & Wilson, B. L. (1985). Numbers and words: Combining quantitative and qualitative methods in a single large-scale evaluation study. *Evaluation Review, 9*, 627–643.

Shotland, R. L., & Mark, M. M. (1987). Improving inferences from multiple methods. In M. M. Mark & R. L. Shotland (Eds.). *Multiple methods in program evaluation: New Directions for Program Evaluation 35* (pp. 77–94). San Francisco: Jossey-Bass.

Sieber, S. D. (1973). The integration of field work and survey methods. *American Journal of Sociology, 78*, 1335–1359.

Smith, A. G., & Louis, K. S. (Eds.). (1982). Multimethod policy research: Issues and applications [Special issue]. *American Behavioral Scientist, 26*.

Smith, A. G., & Robbins, A. E. (1984). Multi-method policy research: A case study of structure and flexibility. In D. M. Fetterman (Ed.), *Ethnography in educational evaluation* (pp. 115–130). Beverly Hills, CA: Sage.

Smith, J. K. (1983). Quantitative versus qualitative: An attempt to clarify the issue. *Educational Researcher, 12*, 6–13.

Smith, J. K., & Heshusius, L. (1986). Closing down the conversation: The end of the quantitative-qualitative debate. *Educational Researcher, 15*(1), 4–12.

Smith, M. L. (1986). The whole is greater: Combining qualitative and quantitative approaches in evaluation studies. In D. D. Williams (Ed.), *Naturalistic evaluation: New Directions for Program Evaluation 30* (pp. 37–54). San Francisco: Jossey-Bass.

Trend, M. J. (1979). On the reconciliation of qualitative and quantitative analyses: A case study. In T. D. Cook & C. S. Reichardt (Eds.), *Qualitative and quantitative methods in evaluation research* (pp. 68–86). Beverly Hills, CA: Sage.

Webb, E. J., Campbell, D. T., Schwartz, R. D., & Sechrest, L. (1966). *Unobtrusive measures* (chap. 1). Chicago: Rand McNally.

Jennifer C. Greene, Associate Professor, Human Service Studies, Cornell University, N136B Martha Van Rensselear Hall, Ithaca, NY 14853. *Specializations*: program evaluation, applied social research methodology.

Valerie J. Caracelli, Social Science Analyst, General Government Division, U.S. General Accounting Office, 441 G St., N.W., Washington, DC 20548. *Specializations*: mixed-methods evaluation research; adolescent and adult development.

Wendy F. Graham, Director of Planning and Information Systems, Cornell University, College of Human Ecology, Martha Van Renselear Hall, Ithaca, NY 14853. *Specializations*: program evaluation, educational administration, survey research methods.

6

A Notation System for
Mixed Methods Designs

Selection: Morse, J. M. (1991). Approaches to qualitative-quantitative methodological triangulation. *Nursing Research, 40,* 120–123.

Editors' Introduction

Janice M. Morse, a renowned nursing researcher and qualitative researcher, wrote the following article in 1991 and, in doing so, advanced the thinking about types of mixed methods research designs and established a notation system for describing procedures in mixed methods research that has had a lasting impact on the field.

Using the terminology of the day, she discusses "methodological triangulation," which she defines as the use of at least two methods, usually qualitative and quantitative, to address the same research problem. She took an important step forward by describing two different procedures that mixed methods researchers might use. They might conduct triangulation by (1) using the qualitative and quantitative methods simultaneously or (2) using one method sequentially to plan for the next. No one had emphasized the time dimension for classifying mixed methods designs before Morse's conceptualization. She also states that one method needs to provide the theoretical drive for the study, and thus the methods cannot be equal in importance. In this way, either the quantitative or the qualitative method could be given priority.

These ideas provide the basis for her notation system for mixed methods procedures that has been used by mixed methods writers ever since. This notation includes using (1) the shorthand of "qual" and "quan," (2) uppercase letters (QUAL or QUAN) to indicate the prioritized method, and (3) plus signs (+) to indicate simultaneous methods and arrows (→) to indicate sequential methods. Therefore, Morse added to our knowledge of types of research designs and sketched out a notation system that can usefully describe the procedures in a study.

Discussion Questions and Applications

1. Consider a mixed methods study such as reported by Luzzo (Chapter 15 in this volume) or Richter (Chapter 23 in this volume). Using Morse's system, indicate the notation that describes each study's theoretical drive and timing.

2. To what extent do you agree with Morse's statement that "the qualitative and quantitative aspects of a research project cannot be equally weighted"?

3. How would you identify whether the theoretical drive is quantitative or qualitative in a mixed methods study?

Related References That Extend the Topic

Additional discussions of notations and diagrams to visually depict mixed methods studies include:

Ivankova, N. V., Creswell, J. W., & Stick, S. (2006). Using mixed-methods sequential explanatory design: From theory to practice. *Field Methods, 18*(1), 3–20.
Tashakkori, A., & Teddlie, C. (2003). The past and future of mixed methods research: From data triangulation to mixed model designs. In A. Tashakkori & C. Teddlie (Eds.), *Handbook of mixed methods in social and behavioral research* (pp. 671–701). Thousand Oaks, CA: Sage.

Approaches to Qualitative-Quantitative Methodological Triangulation

Janice M. Morse
University of Alberta

Recently, there has been discussion in nursing journals regarding the appropriateness, advantages, and disadvantages of methodological triangulation.[1] The issue that has prompted the most interest is combining qualitative and quantitative methods within the same project. Some authors have published examples on how this was accomplished within a particular project, identifying the issues involved with such strategies (Imle & Atwood, 1988; Knafl, Pettengill, Bevis, & Kirchhoff, 1988; Murphy, 1989; Tripp-Reimer, 1985). Others have identified unresolved issues (Clarke & Yaros, 1988; Duffy, 1987a, 1987b; Phillips, 1988a, 1988b) or noted that guidelines for the use of methodological triangulation are lacking (Mitchell, 1986). In particular, Mitchell (1986) notes five areas of concern: the difficulty of merging numeric and textual data; the interpretation of divergent results obtained from the use of qualitative and quantitative methods; the lack of delineation of concepts and the merging of concepts; the weighing of information from

SOURCE: This article is reprinted with permission from Morse, J. M. (1991). Approaches to qualitative-quantitative methodological triangulation. *Nursing Research*, Vol. 40, Issue 2, 120–123.

The author wishes to thank Sally Hutchinson, PhD, FAAN, University of Florida, Kathryn May, DNSc, FAAN, Vanderbilt University, and Brenda Munroe, PhD. and the doctoral students at the University of Alberta for their comments on earlier drafts of this article. The research was supported in part by a Research Scholar Award from MRC/NIIRDP.

different data sources; and the difficulty in ascertaining the contribution of each method when assimilating the results. The purpose of this article is to explore the principles underlying the use of methodological triangulation when combining qualitative and quantitative methods. These principles are related to consistency between the purpose of research, the research question, the method used, the selection of sample, and the interpretation of results.

Methodological Triangulation: Methodological triangulation is the use of at least two methods, usually qualitative and quantitative, to address the same research problem. When a single research method is inadequate, triangulation is used to ensure that the most comprehensive approach is taken to solve a research problem. A less common use of triangulation is to ensure validity of the instruments used (Knafl & Breitmayer, 1989). However, this approach should be used cautiously, since an instrument should be tested prior to implementation or its validity established during a pilot stage.

Methodological triangulation can be classified as simultaneous or sequential (Field & Morse, 1985). *Simultaneous triangulation* is the use of the qualitative and quantitative methods at the same time. In this case, there is limited interaction between the two datasets during the data collection, but the findings complement one another at the end of the study. *Sequential triangulation* is used if the results of one method are essential for planning the next method. The qualitative method is completed before the quantitative method is implemented or vice versa.

The first step in qualitative-quantitative triangulation is to determine if the research problem is primarily qualitative or quantitative. Characteristics of a qualitative research problem are: (a) the concept is "immature," due to a conspicuous lack of theory and previous research; (b) a notion that the available theory may be inaccurate, inappropriate, incorrect, or biased; (c) a need exists to explore and describe the phenomena and to develop theory; or (d) the nature of the phenomenon may not be suited to quantitative measures (see Field & Morse, 1985).

If a research problem is primarily quantitative, the above characteristics are not applicable. The researcher can locate substantial and relevant literature on the topic, create a theoretical framework, and identify testable hypotheses. In this case, the research design is comparative or correlational (i.e., Level II) or experimental or quasi-experimental (i.e., Level III) (Brink & Wood, 1989).

Thus, in methodological triangulation, the key issue is whether the theory that drives the research (May, 1989) is developed *inductively* from the research per se or used *deductively* as in quantitative inquiry.

This differentiation results in several types of methodological triangulation. If the research is driven by an inductive process and the theory developed qualitatively and complemented by quantitative methods, the notation QUAL+quan is used to indicate simultaneous triangulation. If the project is deductive, driven by an a priori theoretical framework, quantitative methods take precedence and may be complemented by qualitative methods. In this case, the notation QUAN+qual is used. Sequential triangulation is indicated by QUAL→quan with an inductive project, that is, when the theoretical drive is inductive and uses a qualitative foundation. When the notation QUAN→qual is used, it indicates a deductive approach. That is, when following the completion of the quantitative step, a qualitative method is used to examine outliers or to explore unexpected findings. Note that the theoretical drive does *not* refer to the valuing of the qualitative or quantitative paradigm (Myers & Haase, 1989), the amount of effort required nor the amount of time spent answering each qualitative or quantitative question.

The following cases are examples of simultaneous triangulation:

QUAL+quan

What is it like to be a relative of a patient in the ICU? This is clearly a qualitative problem, and the methods of ethnography or grounded theory may be used to describe the experience of anxious, waiting relatives. From the inception of the project, we can quite safely assume that the relative will be anxious. But how anxious? Clearly, it would strengthen our description of the sample if we could administer a standardized anxiety scale and include a description of the levels of anxiety that relatives may be experiencing.

QUAN+qual

The conceptual framework of this study predicts that the sicker the child, the greater the spatial distance between the parents and the child; and the greater the spatial distance between the parents and the child, the greater the child's anxiety. How do we measure spatial distance in this situation? One way would be to do participant observation at randomly selected intervals: an other way would be to use video cameras to observe the distance between the parents and their child. From these observations an ordinal scale is developed: close (touching range), midway (from arms reach to the end of the bed), and distant (beyond the end of the bed). Hypotheses related to parental spatial distance and severity of illness of the child can then be tested.

The following cases are examples of sequential triangulation:

QUAL→quan

A qualitative study on the responses of adolescents to menarche provided many insights into adolescent behavior and their affective response to menstruation at this time. But what were the normative attitudes of adolescent girls towards menarche? The domains from the content analysis were used to construct a Likert scale, and the items were derived directly from the qualitative data. Quantitative methods of ensuring reliability and validity were used, and the Likert scale was administered to a randomly selected sample.

QUAN→qual

A large infant feeding survey of a Third World country produced the unexpected finding that there was no difference in the incidence of infantile diarrhea in infants from homes with or without refrigeration. Qualitative interviews with a sample of residents from homes with refrigerators revealed that infant formula bottles were not kept in the refrigerator. Refrigerators were used for making and storing ice, which was sold to supplement the family income.

From the above examples, it is obvious that the qualitative and quantitative aspects of a research project cannot be equally weighted; rather, a project must be either theoretically driven by the qualitative methods incorporating a complementary quantitative component, or theoretically driven by the quantitative method, incorporating a complementary qualitative component. The important point is that each method must be complete in itself; that is, all methods used must meet appropriate criteria for rigor. If qualitative interviews are conducted, then they must he conducted as if this method stands alone. The interviews should be continued until saturation is reached, and the content analysis conducted inductively, rather than forcing the data into some preconceived categories to fit the quantitative study or to prove a point. Further, this standard enables each component to be published independently. This may be particularly important to an investigator using sequential triangulation in a project extending over several years.

Implementing Methodological Triangulation: Given the fact that methods need to be used independently within a single project, the real issue in triangulation is not incompatibility between the different assumptions of the two paradigms as many researchers have argued (see Duffy, 1987b; Phillips, 1988a). It is not the incompatibility of contrasting philosophical issues from static and dynamic realities, objective and subjective perspectives, inductive and deductive approaches, or holistic and particular views. Nor is it the infeasible merging of textual and numerical data or of simultaneously considering the antagonistic approaches of acausality and causality. Blending or merging of the data does not occur in the process of analysis but in the fitting of the results from each study into a cohesive and coherent outcome or theory, or confirming or revising existing theory. This is achieved by being aware of and adhering to the rules and assumptions inherent in each method related to the selection of the sample, the purpose of the method, and the contribution of the results to the overall research plan.

Combining Samples: The greatest threat to validity is the use of inadequate or inappropriate samples. Perhaps for reasons of convenience, investigators are tempted to use the same subjects for both qualitative and quantitative methods, even though it is clearly inappropriate to interchange these samples. For instance, quantitative research is based on the assumption that large, randomly selected samples will be used so that the sample will be representative of the population. Adequacy of the sample is determined statistically (using *n* or sample size) and appropriateness is determined by the representativeness of the sample to the total population. In qualitative research, appropriateness is ascertained by how well the sample can represent the phenomena of interest (i.e., to what extent the participants have experienced the phenomena and can articulate their experiences), and the sample is deemed adequate when saturation of data is reached (Morse, 1987). Yet, in light of the overall purpose of the research, there is no reason (other than that of convenience), to use the same subjects for both samples. Clearly, when incorporating quantitative methods into a qualitative study, the qualitative sample is apt to be inadequate for quantitative purposes. The lack of representativeness of the purposefully selected qualitative sample is inappropriate and threatens validity. The sample selection for the qualitative and quantitative components of sequential (QUAL→quan) or simultaneous (QUAL+quan) triangulation must be independent. As the qualitative sample is inappropriate and inadequate, the investigator has no choice but to draw a quantitative sample from the population. However, when quantitative methods are being used to add further information about the qualitative sample (QUAL+quan), exceptions may be made if norms or a normal comparison group are available for interpreting the findings. In the example of the anxious relatives in the waiting room, the anxiety scale scores would be interpreted within the norms available for the anxiety scale (see Table 6.1).

A subsample of the larger quantitative sample may be used for the qualitative component of QUAN+qual or QUAL→quan triangulation, but those subjects included or incidents observed in the qualitative portion must be selected according to the criteria for "good" participants rather than randomly selected. That is, the subjects selected from the quantitative sample should be the most experienced and articulate, and the observations chosen should be considered the best examples of the situation.

Combining Results: Mitchell's (1986) problem of weighing the results of each component are resolved if findings are interpreted within the context of present knowledge. As such, each component should fit like pieces of a puzzle. This type of interpretation is not accomplished using a mathematical formula to weigh the findings from each method; rather, it is an informed thought process, involving judgment, wisdom, creativity, and insight and includes the privilege of creating or modifying theory. It is an exciting part of every research

Table 6.1   Limitations and Resolutions for Each Type of Methodological Triangulation

Approach	Type	Purpose	Limitations	Resolution
QUAL+quan	Simultaneous	enrich description of sample	Qualitative sample	Utilize normative data for comparison of results
QUAL→quan	Sequential	test emerging H_0; determine distribution of phenomena in population	Qualitative sample	Draw adequate random sample from same population
QUAN+qual	Simultaneous	to describe part of phenomena that cannot be quantified	Quantitative sample	Select appropriate theoretical sample from random sample
QUAN→qual	Sequential	to examine unexpected results	Quantitative sample	Select appropriate theoretical sample from random sample

project, and when triangulating different methods, it can be especially exciting. If contradictory results occur from triangulating qualitative and quantitative methods, then one set of findings is invalid and/or the end result of the total study inadequate, incomplete, or inaccurate. If the study is deductively driven, the theoretical framework may be incorrect.

Methodological triangulation is not a term that is applied to ethnography, when the research method includes the use of semi-structured interviews, some level of participant observation, the use of records, and perhaps, the administration of questionnaires. It is the combination of such techniques that constitute ethnography and that make ethnography, ethnography. It is not a matter of blending or "integrating guidelines from both qualitative and quantitative texts" (Knafl et al., 1988), but rather, the use of appropriate strategies for maintaining validity for each method. QUAN+qual methodological triangulation is not merely the "addition of narrative and linguistic data" to an experimental design (Clarke & Yaros, 1988), unless interview data are collected and analyzed with adherence to the assumptions and principles of the qualitative method (see Haase & Myers, 1988; May, 1989, pp. 205–206). Similarly, incorporating one or two open-ended questions into a quantitative survey, does not make the study qualitative.

Conversely, the use of quantitative data in a qualitative study, such as frequency data to enhance description, does not constitute a quantitative study. Methodological triangulation is not a technique to be used for reasons of researchers' speed and convenience (see Knafl et al., 1988, p. 31). Properly done, it probably has the reverse short-term effect, greatly increasing the work involved in a project and increasing the duration of a project. But the long-term gains achieved from such thorough groundwork are immeasurable.

Simultaneous methodological triangulation is not a technique of concurrent validation. Although the same strategies may be used, they are implemented in a study for different reasons. The purpose of concurrent validation is to ascertain whether the results of two methods measuring the same concept are equivalent. The purpose of simultaneous triangulation is to obtain different but complementary data on the same topic, rather than to replicate results.

Methodological triangulation is not a matter of "maximizing the strengths and minimizing the weakness of each" (Knafl et al., 1988). If not approached cautiously, the end result may be to enhance the weakness of each method and invalidate the entire research project. Rather, methodological triangulation is a method of obtaining complementary findings that strengthen research results and contribute to theory and knowledge development.

Some of the controversy on methodological triangulation has focused on the issue of "qualitative versus quantitative research." This controversy advocates combining methods "as long as there is consistency with the 'theoretical researcher'" (Clarke & Yaro, 1988; Phillips, 1988b). Researchers who purport to subscribe to the philosophical underpinnings of only one research approach have lost sight of the fact that research methodologies are merely tools, instruments to be used to facilitate understanding. Smart researchers are versatile and have a balanced and extensive repertoire of methods at their disposal.

References

Brink, P. J., & Wood M. J. (1989). *Advanced design in nursing research.* Newbury Park, CA: Sage.

Clarke, P. N., & Yaros, P. S. (1988). Transitions to new methodologies in nursing science [Commentary]. *Nursing Science Quarterly, 1*(4), 147–149.

Duffy. M. (1987a). Methodological triangulation: A vehicle for merging quantitative and qualitative research methods. *Image: Journal for Nursing Scholarship, 19,* 130–133.

Duffy. M. E. (1987b). Quantitative and qualitative research: Antagonistic or complementary? *Nursing and Health Care, 8,* 356–357.

Field, P. A., & Morse, J. M. (1985). *Qualitative nursing research: The application of qualitative approaches.* Rockville, MD: Aspen.

Haase, J. E., & Myers, S. T. (1988). Reconciling paradigm assumptions of qualitative and quantitative research. *Western Journal of Nursing Research, 10,* 128–137.

Imle, M. A., & Atwood J. R (1988). Retaining qualitative validity while gaining quantitative reliability and validity: Development of the Transition to Parenthood Concerns Scale. *Advances in Nursing Science, 11,* 61–75.

Knafi, K. A., & Breitmayer, B. J. (1989). Triangulation in qualitative research: Issues of conceptual clarity and purpose. In J. M. Morse (Ed.), *Qualitative nursing research: A contemporary dialogue* (pp. 209–220). Rockville, MD: Aspen.

Knafi, K. A., Pettengili, M. M., Bevis, M. E., & Kirchhoff, K. (1988). Blending qualitative and quantitative approaches to instrument development and data collection. *Journal of Professional Nursing, 4,* 30–37.

May, K. A. (1989). Dialogue: On triangulation. In J. M. Morse (Ed.), *Qualitative nursing research. A contemporary dialogue* (pp. 205–206). Rockville, MD: Aspen.

Mitchell, E. S. (1986). Multiple triangulation: A methodology for nursing science. *Advances in Nursing Science, 8*(3), 18–26.

Morse, J. M. (1987). Qualitative and quantitative research: Strategies for sampling. In P. Chinn (Ed.), *Nursing Research: Methodological Issues* (pp. 181–193). Rockville, MD: Aspen.

Murphy, S. A (1989). Multiple triangulation: Applications in a program of research. *Nursing Research, 38,* 294–298.

Phillips, J. R (1988a). Research blenders. *Nursing Science Quarterly, 1,* 4–5.

Phillips, J. R. (1988b). Diggers of deeper holes [Response]. *Nursing Science Quarterly, 1,* 147–151.

Tripp-Reimer T. (1985). Combining qualitative and quantitative methodologies. In M. M. Leinenger (Ed.), *Qualitative research methods in nursing* (pp. 179–194). Orlando, FL: Grune & Stratton.

Note

1. In addition to methodological triangulation, Knafl & Breitmayer (1989) discuss investigator, data source, unit of analysis, and theoretical triangulation, and the reader is referred to this source for a discussion on the role and purpose of other types of triangulation.

Janice M. Morse, RN, PhD (Nursing), PhD (Anthropology), is a professor and MRC/NHRDP Research Scholar in the faculty of nursing and is adjunct professor in the department of family studies at the University of Alberta. She is associate clinical nurse researcher at the University of Alberta Hospitals and is adjunct professor in the department of nursing at the University of Northern Arizona.

7

An Expanded Typology for Classifying Mixed Methods Research Into Designs

Selection: Creswell, J. W., Plano Clark, V. L., Gutmann, M. L., & Hanson, W. E. (2003). Advanced mixed methods research designs. In A. Tashakkori & C. Teddlie (Eds.), *Handbook of mixed methods in social and behavioral research* (pp. 209–240). Thousand Oaks, CA: Sage.

Editors' Introduction

Research designs are important because they provide road maps for how to rigorously conduct studies to best meet certain objectives. As illustrated in Chapters 4–6 of this volume, mixed methods scholars have devoted much attention to the issue of classifying mixed methods research designs. John W. Creswell, Vicki L. Plano Clark, Michelle Gutmann, and William E. Hanson represent educational backgrounds, including educational psychology and counseling psychology. They expanded the typology for classifying mixed methods research in their 2003 chapter.

Creswell et al. begin their discussion by presenting a historical perspective to the design classification typologies appearing in the mixed methods literature. They summarize the important typologies published before 2003 in a table that lists the authors, designs within the typology, and disciplinary field from which the typology has emerged. Creswell et al. then add to this ongoing discussion by describing a parsimonious set of mixed methods designs that builds from these earlier works. They distill four criteria that are implicit within all mixed methods designs, including the phase of research in which "mixing" occurs (integration) and the use of a theoretical lens (for example, feminist research). These additional criteria make explicit new design characteristics that had not been emphasized in other discussions. They then present a set of six major designs found in the mixed methods literature using these criteria. Finally, the authors discuss the relationship of paradigms to designs and suggest that different paradigms may provide the foundation for different mixed methods designs.

Discussion Questions and Applications

1. Consider a mixed methods study such as reported by Victor, Ross, and Axford (Chapter 18 in this volume) or Milton, Watkins, Studdard, and Burch (Chapter 22 in this volume). Determine how Creswell et al.'s design criteria were implemented and the study's overall design.

2. How would you identify if a mixed methods study used a theoretical perspective?

3. Compare and contrast Creswell et al.'s typology with those presented in Chapters 5 and 6. What advantages and/or disadvantages do you find with each?

Related References That Extend the Topic

Other recent mixed methods design typologies can be found in:

Creswell, J. W., & Plano Clark, V. L. (2007). *Designing and conducting mixed methods research*. Thousand Oaks, CA: Sage.

Tashakkori, A., & Teddlie, C. (2003). The past and future of mixed methods research: From data triangulation to mixed model designs. In A. Tashakkori & C. Teddlie (Eds.), *Handbook of mixed methods in social and behavioral research* (pp. 671–701). Thousand Oaks, CA: Sage.

Advanced Mixed Methods
Research Designs

John W. Creswell
University of Nebraska–Lincoln

Vicki L. Plano Clark
University of Nebraska–Lincoln

Michelle L. Gutmann
University of Nebraska–Lincoln

William E. Hanson
University of Nebraska–Lincoln

O ne approach to learning about mixed methods research designs is to begin with a mixed methods study and explore the features that characterize it as mixed methods research. Although many such studies are available in the literature, we begin here with a study in education exploring the factors associated with parental savings for postsecondary education, a topic to which many people can relate. Hossler and Vesper (1993) conducted a study examining the factors associated with parental savings for children attending higher education campuses. Using longitudinal data collected from students and parents over a 3-year period, the authors examined factors most strongly associated with parental savings for postsecondary education. Their results indicated that parental support, educational expectations, and

SOURCE: This chapter is reprinted from *Handbook of Mixed Methods in Social and Behavioral Research* (Tashakkori & Teddlie, 2003). Reprinted with permission of Sage Publications, Inc.

knowledge of college costs were important factors. Most important for our purposes, the authors collected information from parents and students on 182 surveys and from 56 interviews.

To examine this study from a mixed methods perspective, we would like to draw attention to the following:

- The authors collected "mixed" forms of data, including quantitative survey data and qualitative open-ended interview data.
- The authors titled the study "An Exploratory Study of the Factors Associated With Parental Savings for Postsecondary Education," containing words suggestive of both quantitative and qualitative approaches. The word *exploratory* is often associated with qualitative research, while the word *factors* implies the use of variables in quantitative research.
- The authors advanced a purpose statement that included a rationale for mixing methods: "The interviews permitted us to look for emerging themes from both the survey and from previous interview data, which could then be explored in more depth in subsequent interviews" (p. 146).
- The authors reported two separate data analyses: first the quantitative results of the survey, followed by the findings from the qualitative interviews. An examination of these two sections shows that the quantitative analysis is discussed more extensively than the qualitative analysis.
- The authors ended the article with a discussion that compared the quantitative statistical results with the qualitative thematic findings.

Based on these features, we see the authors mixing quantitative and qualitative research in this study—mixed methods research. More specifically, with information from recent literature on mixed methods research designs, the "type" of mixed methods design used by Hossler and Vesper (1993) in their study might be called a "concurrent triangulation method design," indicating a triangulation of data collection, separate data analysis, and the integration of databases at the interpretation or discussion stage of the report. Furthermore, their design gave priority to quantitative research.

To give their study a mixed methods name and to identify the characteristics of the design may not have affected whether it was accepted for publication or whether it was given enhanced status in the social science community. However, being able to identify the characteristics of the study that make it mixed methods and giving the design a specific name conveys to readers the rigors of their study. It also provides guidance to others who merge quantitative and qualitative data into a single study. If they were presenting it to journal editors, faculty committees, or funding agencies, the labeling of the design and an identification of its characteristics helps reviewers to decide the criteria and the personnel most qualified to review the study. If Hossler and Vesper (1993) had created a visual representation or figure of their procedures, it would have enhanced the study's readability to audiences not used to seeing complex and interrelated data collection and analysis procedures.

Like many other studies of its kind, the Hossler and Vesper (1993) study falls into a category of research called mixed methods designs. Although these studies are frequently reported in the literature, they are seldom discussed as a separate research design. However, with an increasing number of authors writing about mixed methods research as a separate design, it is now time to seriously consider it as a distinct design in the social sciences. To do this calls for a review of disparate literature about mixed methods research designs found in journals across the social sciences as well as in chapters, books, and conference papers.

This chapter presents a synthesis of recent literature about mixed methods research as a separate design. It creates an analysis of the discussion today and its historical roots over the past 20 years. It then reviews four criteria that have emerged during the past few years that provide guidance for a researcher trying to identify the type of mixed methods design to use in a particular study. From these criteria emerge six core designs under which many types of design currently being discussed can be subsumed. We then review three issues in implementing the designs: the use of paradigm perspectives, the data analysis procedures used with each design, and the use of expanded visualizations and procedures. We end by returning to the Hossler and Vesper (1993) study to review how it might be presented and understood as a mixed methods design.

Mixed Methods Research as a Separate Design

There are a number of arguments for why mixed methods research might be considered a separate research design in the social sciences. By design, we mean a procedure for collecting, analyzing, and reporting research such as that found in the time-honored designs of quantitative experiments and surveys and in the qualitative approaches of ethnographies, grounded theory studies, and case studies. These arguments take several forms. Authors have increasingly recognized the advantages of mixing both quantitative and qualitative data collection in a single study. Numerous mixed methods studies have been reported in the scholarly journals for social scientists to see and use as models for their own studies. In addition, authors have delineated more carefully a definition for mixed methods research, although consensus has been slow to develop for a single definition recognized by all inquirers.

Finally, method and methodological authors who write about mixed methods research have identified procedures that point toward critical design elements such as a visual model of procedures, a notation system, the explication of types of designs, and specific criteria useful in deciding what type of design to employ in a given study.

A Recognition of Advantages

The collection and combination of both quantitative and qualitative data in research has been influenced by several factors. Unquestionably, both quantitative and qualitative data are increasingly available for use in studying social science research problems. Also, because all methods of data collection have limitations, the use of multiple methods can neutralize or cancel out some of the disadvantages of certain methods (e.g., the detail of qualitative data can provide insights not available through general quantitative surveys) (Jick, 1979). Thus, there is wide consensus that mixing different types of methods can strengthen a study (Greene & Caracelli, 1997). Qualitative research has become an accepted legitimate form of inquiry in the social sciences, and researchers of all methodological persuasions recognize its value in obtaining detailed contextualized information. Also, because social phenomena are so complex, different kinds of methods are needed to best understand these complexities (Greene & Caracelli, 1997).

Published Mixed Methods Studies

Given these advantages, authors writing about mixed methods research have frequently analyzed published mixed methods studies in terms of their procedures. For example, Greene, Caracelli, and Graham (1989) reviewed 57 evaluation studies so as to develop a classification scheme of types of designs based on purpose and design characteristics. Creswell, Goodchild, and Turner (1996) discussed 19 mixed methods studies about postsecondary education and illustrated steps in the studies. The "box feature" was used extensively in Tashakkori and Teddlie's (1998) book to illustrate examples of mixed methods research projects. In fact, a review of the many procedural discussions about mixed methods research [see Datta's (1994) review of 18 methodological discussions about mixed methods research from 1959 to 1992] shows references to published studies across the social science disciplines.

The Issue of Definition

Finding these published studies, however, requires some creative searching of the literature. The actual terms used to denote a mixed methods study vary considerably in the procedural discussions of this design. Writers have referred to it as multitrait-multimethod research (Campbell & Fiske, 1959), integrating qualitative and quantitative approaches (Glik, Parker, Muligande, & Hategikamana, 1986–1987; Steckler, McLeroy, Goodman, Bird, & McCormick, 1992), interrelating qualitative and quantitative data (Fielding & Fielding, 1986), methodological triangulation (Morse, 1991), multimethodological research (Hugentobler, Israel, & Schurman, 1992), multimethod designs and linking qualitative and quantitative data (Miles & Huberman, 1994), combining qualitative and quantitative research (Bryman, 1988; Creswell, 1994; Swanson-Kauffman, 1986), mixed model studies (Datta, 1994), and mixed methods research (Caracelli & Greene, 1993; Greene et al., 1989; Rossman & Wilson, 1991). Central to all of these terms is the idea of combining or integrating different methods. The term *mixed methods* is perhaps most appropriate, although one; of the authors of this chapter has used others (Creswell, 1994; Creswell et al., 1996; Creswell & Miller, 1997). Mixing provides an umbrella term to cover the multifaceted procedures of combining, integrating, linking, and employing multi-methods.

To argue for mixed methods research as a specific research design requires not only an accepted term but also a common definition. Building on earlier definitions of mixed methods research (Fielding & Fielding, 1986; Greene et al., 1989), a mixed methods research design at its simplest level involves mixing both qualitative and quantitative methods of data collection and analysis in a single study (Creswell, 1999). A more elaborate definition would specify the nature of data collection (e.g., whether data are gathered concurrently or sequentially), the priority each form of data receives in the research report (e.g., equal or unequal), and the place in the research process in which "mixing" of the data occurs such as in the data collection, analysis, or interpretation phase of inquiry. Combining all of these features into a single definition suggests the following definition:

> A *mixed methods study* involves the collection or analysis of both quantitative and/or qualitative data in a single study in which the data are collected concurrently or sequentially, are given a priority, and involve the integration of the data at one or more stages in the process of research.

This definition, although a reasonable beginning point for considering mixed methods research designs, masks several additional questions that are developed further in this chapter. For example, this definition does not account for multiple studies within a sustained program of inquiry in which researchers may mix methods at different phases of the research. It also creates an artificial distinction between quantitative and qualitative methods of data collection that may not be as firmly in place as people think (see

Johnson and Turner's detailed discussion about types of data in Chapter 11 of this volume [Tashakkori & Teddlie, 2003]). Furthermore, it does not account for a theoretical framework that may drive the research and create a larger vision in which the study may be posed.

The Trend Toward Procedural Guidelines

The history of mixed methods research has been adequately traced elsewhere (see Creswell, 2002; Datta, 1994; Tashakkori & Teddlie, 1998). Central to this discussion is the development of procedural guidelines that argue for viewing mixed methods research as a separate design. The evolution of procedural guidelines for mixed methods studies is seen in the creation of visual models, a notation system, and the specification of types of designs.

Visual Models. Procedures for conducting a mixed methods study first emerged from discussions in which authors described the flow of activities typically used by researchers when they conducted this type of study. For example, Sieber (1973) suggested the combination of in-depth case studies with surveys, creating a "new style of research" and the "integration" of research techniques within a single study (p. 1337). Patton (1990) identified several forms of research as "mixed forms" such as experimental designs, qualitative data and content analysis or experimental designs, qualitative data, and statistical data. Soon, writers began to draw procedures graphically and create figures that displayed the overall flow of research activities. A good example of these visuals is found in health education research. As shown in Figure 7.1, Steckler et al. (1992) provided four alternative procedures for collecting both quantitative and qualitative research and gave a brief rationale for the reason for combining methods. These models show both quantitative and qualitative methods (actually data collection) and use arrows to indicate the sequence of activities in the mixed methods study. Models 2 and 3 are similar except that the procedures begin with qualitative data in Model 2 and with quantitative data in Model 3.

Notation System. Models such as these provide a useful way for readers to understand the basic procedures used in mixed methods studies. Implied in these models is also the idea that a notation system exists to explain the procedures. In 1991, Morse, a nursing researcher, developed a notation system that has become widely used by researchers designing mixed methods studies (see also Morse's notation system as she discusses types of designs in Chapter 7 of this volume [Tashakkori & Teddlie, 2003]). As shown in Figure 7.2, Morse discussed several types of mixed methods studies and illustrated them with a plus (+) sign to denote the simultaneous collection of quantitative and

Model 1. Qualitative methods are used to help develop quantitative measures and instruments.

Model 2. Quantitative methods are used to embellish a primarily qualitative study.

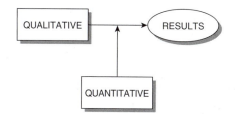

Model 3. Qualitative methods are used to help explain quantitative findings.

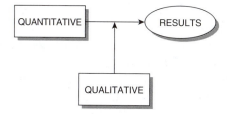

Model 4. Qualitative and quantitative methods are used equally and in parallel.

Figure 7.1   Example of Visual Presentation of Procedures

SOURCE: Steckler, McLeroy, Goodman, Bird, and McCormick (1992).

qualitative data, an arrow (→) to designate that one form of data collection followed another, uppercase letters to suggest major emphasis (e.g., QUAN, QUAL) on the form of data collection, and lowercase letters to imply less emphasis (e.g., quan, qual). It is also noteworthy that the terms *quantitative* and *qualitative* were now shortened to *quan* and *qual,* respectively, implying that both approaches to research are legitimate and of equal stature.

Types of Designs. As is apparent in Morse's (1991) notation system, she provided names for her approaches such as *simultaneous* and *sequential.* Terms such as these, and a few more, have now become types or variants of mixed

Approach	Type
QUAL + quan	Simultaneous
QUAL → quan	Sequential
QUAN + qual	Simultaneous
QUAN → qual	Sequential

Figure 7.2   Examples of Types of Designs Using Morse's (1991) Notation System

methods designs. As shown in Table 7.1, authors from diverse discipline fields, such as evaluation, nursing, public health, and education, have identified the types of designs that they believe capture the array of possibilities. A brief review of eight studies shown in the table indicates that Morse's simultaneous and sequential labels continue to be used routinely. However, new terms have also emerged such as a mixed methods study that is based on *initiation* or *development* (Greene et al., 1989), on *complementary* designs (Morgan, 1998), or on *mixed model* designs (Tashakkori & Teddlie, 1998). Unquestionably, authors have yet to reach consensus on the types of designs that exist, the names for them, or how they might be represented visually.

Criteria Implicit in the Designs

Although the variants of designs may be baffling, to distinguish among them is useful in choosing one to use for a study. To accomplish this requires examining the design's fundamental assumptions, a line of thinking already used by Morgan (1998). If one could understand the assumptions implicit within the designs, then a researcher could configure a procedure that best meets the needs of the problem and that includes the collection of both quantitative and qualitative data. Morgan identified two core assumptions: that the designs varied in terms of a sequence of collecting quantitative and qualitative data and that they varied in terms of the priority or weight given to each form of data. Other assumptions can be added as well. Tashakkori and Teddlie (1998) suggested that the design contain an integration of the data in different phases such as in the statement of the research questions, the data collection, the data analysis, and the interpretation of the results. Finally, in the recent writings of Greene and Caracelli (1997), we find that some mixed methods writers include a transformational value- or action-oriented dimension to their study. Thus, we have another assumption that needs to

Table 7.1   Classifications of Mixed Methods Designs

Author	Mixed Methods Designs	Discipline/Field
Greene, Caracelli, & Graham (1989)	Initiation Expansion Development Complementary Triangulation	Evaluation
Patton (1990)	Experimental design, qualitative data, and content analysis Experimental design, qualitative data, and statistical analysis Naturalistic inquiry, qualitative data, and statistical analysis Naturalistic inquiry, quantitative data, and statistical analysis	Evaluation
Morse (1991)	Simultaneous triangulation QUAL + quan QUAN + qual Sequential triangulation QUAL → quan QUAN → qual	Nursing
Steckler, McLeroy, Goodman, Bird, & McCormick (1992)	Model 1: qualitative methods to develop quantitative measures Model 2: quantitative methods to embellish qualitative findings Model 3: qualitative methods to explain quantitative findings Model 4: qualitative and quantitative methods used equally and parallel	Public health education
Greene & Caracelli (1997)	Component designs Triangulation Complementary Expansion Integrated designs Iterative Embedded or nested Holistic Transformative	Evaluation
Morgan (1998)	Complementary designs Qualitative preliminary Quantitative preliminary Qualitative follow-up Quantitative follow-up	Health research

(Continued)

Table 7.1 (Continued)

Author	Mixed Methods Designs	Discipline/Field

Tashakkori & Teddlie (1998)	Mixed method designs
	Equivalent status (sequential or parallel)
	Dominant-less dominant (sequential or parallel)
	Multilevel use
	Mixed model designs
	    I: Confirmatory/Qual Data/Statistical analysis and inference
	    II: Confirmatory/Qual Data/Qualitative inferences
	    III: Exploratory/Quant Data/Statistical analysis and inference
	    IV: Exploratory/Qual Data/Statistical analysis and inference
	    V: Confirmatory/Quant Data/Qualitative inferences
	    VI: Exploratory/Quant Data/Qualitative inferences
	    VII: Parallel mixed model
	    VIII: Sequential mixed model
		Educational research

Creswell (1999)	Convergence model Sequential model Instrument-building model	Educational Policy

be included in the matrix for typing and identifying forms of mixed methods designs. Four factors, as illustrated in Figure 7.3, help researchers to determine the type of mixed methods design for their study: the implementation of data collection, the priority given to quantitative or qualitative research, the stage in the research process at which integration of quantitative and qualitative research occurs, and the potential use of a transformational value- or action-oriented perspective in their study.

Implementation of Data Collection

Implementation refers to the sequence the researcher uses to collect both quantitative and qualitative data. Several authors have discussed this procedure

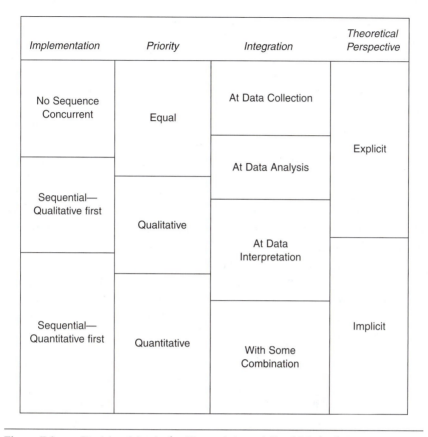

Implementation	Priority	Integration	Theoretical Perspective
No Sequence Concurrent	Equal	At Data Collection	Explicit
Sequential— Qualitative first	Qualitative	At Data Analysis	
		At Data Interpretation	
Sequential— Quantitative first	Quantitative	With Some Combination	Implicit

Figure 7.3   Decision Matrix for Determining a Mixed Methods Design

in mixed methods research (Greene et al., 1989; Morgan, 1998; Morse, 1991). The options for implementation of the data collection consist of gathering the information at the same time (i.e., concurrently) or introducing the information in phases over a period of time (i.e., sequentially). When the data are introduced in phases, either the qualitative or the quantitative approach may be gathered first, but the sequence relates to the objectives being sought by the researcher in the mixed methods study. When qualitative data collection precedes quantitative data collection, the intent is to first explore the problem under study and then follow up on this exploration with quantitative data that are amenable to studying a large sample so that results might be inferred to a population. Alternatively, when quantitative data precede qualitative data, the intent is to explore with a large sample first to test variables and then to explore in more depth with a few cases during the qualitative phase. In concurrently gathering both forms of data at the same time, the researcher seeks to compare both forms of data to search for congruent findings (e.g., how the themes identified in the qualitative data collection compare with the statistical results in the quantitative analysis).

The choice of implementation strategy has several consequences for the form of the final written report. When two phases of data collection exist, the researcher typically reports the data collection process in two phases. The report may also include an analysis of each phase of data separately and the integration of information in the discussion or conclusion section of a study. The implementation approach also raises an issue about iterative phases of a design where a researcher may cycle back and forth between quantitative and qualitative data collection. For instance, the research may begin with a qualitative phase of interviewing, followed by a quantitative phase of survey instrument design and testing with a sample, and continued on with a third qualitative phase of exploring outlier cases that emerge from the quantitative survey. The implementation decision also calls for clearly identifying the core reasons for collecting both forms of data in the first place and understanding the important interrelationship between the quantitative and qualitative phases in data collection. These reasons need to be clearly articulated in any mixed methods written report.

Priority

A less obvious issue, and one more difficult to make a decision about, is the priority given to quantitative and qualitative research in the mixed methods study (Morgan, 1998). Unlike the frame of reference of data collection in the implementation decision, here the focus is on the priority given to quantitative or qualitative research as it occurs throughout the data collection process. This process might be described as including how the study is introduced, the use of literature, the statement of the purpose of the study and the research questions, the data collection, the data analysis, and the interpretation of the findings or results (Creswell, 2002). The mixed methods researcher can give equal priority to both quantitative and qualitative research, emphasize qualitative more, or emphasize quantitative more. This emphasis may result from practical constraints of data collection, the need to understand one form of data before proceeding to the next, or the audience preference for either quantitative or qualitative research. In most cases, the decision probably rests on the comfort level of the researcher with one approach as opposed to the other.

Operationalizing the decision to give equal or unequal emphasis to quantitative or qualitative research translates is problematic. For instance, the study may begin with essentially a quantitative orientation with a focus on variables, specific research questions or hypotheses, and an extensive discussion of the literature that informs the questions. Another study might convey a different priority through the length of discussions such as the inclusion of extensive discussions about the qualitative data collection with minimal information about the quantitative instruments used in the study. A project might be seen by readers as providing more depth for one method than for the other such as assessed by the number of pages given to quantitative research (e.g., as in the Hossler & Vesper [1993] article). A graduate student may of necessity delimit the study by including a substantive quantitative analysis and a limited qualitative data collection, a model referred to as the dominant-less dominant model (Creswell, 1994). A final example is that the published article provides equal emphasis on both quantitative and qualitative research as judged by separate sections of approximately equal length and treatment. Unquestionably, in each of these examples, researchers and readers make an interpretation of what constitutes priority, a judgment that may differ from one inquirer to another. On a practical level, however, we can see these different priorities in published mixed methods studies, and researchers need to make informed decisions about the weight or attention given to quantitative and qualitative research during all phases of their research.

Stage of Integration

Of the mixed methods design writers, it has been Tashakkori and Teddlie (1998) and Greene et al. (1989) who have emphasized the importance of considering the stage of the research process at which integration of quantitative and qualitative data collection takes place. Integration can be defined as the combination of quantitative and qualitative research within a given stage of inquiry. For example, integration might occur within the research questions (e.g., both quantitative and qualitative questions are presented), within data collection (e.g., open-ended questions on a structured instrument), within data analysis (e.g., transforming qualitative themes into quantitative items or scales), or in interpretation (e.g., examining the quantitative and qualitative results for convergence of findings). The decision that needs to be made relates to a clear understanding of the sequential model of the research process and approaches typically taken by both quantitative and qualitative researchers at each stage. (As a contrast, see the interactive model as advanced by Maxwell and Loomis in Chapter 9 of this volume [Tashakkori & Teddlie, 2003].)

Examine Table 7.2, which presents four stages in the process of research and approaches researchers take in both the quantitative and qualitative areas. In quantitative research, investigators ask questions that try to confirm hypotheses or research questions, with a focus on assessing the relationship or association among variables or testing a treatment variable. These questions or hypotheses are assessed using instruments, observations, or documents that yield numerical data. These data are, in turn, analyzed descriptively or inferentially so as to generate interpretations that are generalizable to a population. Alternatively, in qualitative research, the inquiry is more exploratory, with a strong emphasis on description and with a thematic focus on understanding a central phenomenon. Open-ended data collection helps to address questions of this kind through procedures such as interviews, observations, documents, and audiovisual materials. Researchers analyze these databases for a rich description of the phenomenon as well as for themes to develop a detailed rendering of the complexity of the phenomenon, leading to new questions and personal interpretations made by the inquirers. Although both the quantitative and qualitative processes described here are oversimplifications of the actual steps taken by researchers, they serve as a baseline of information to discuss where integration might take place in a mixed methods study.

During the phases of problem/question specification, data collection, data analysis, and interpretation, it is possible for the mixed methods researcher

Table 7.2   Stages Integration and Quantitative and Qualitative Approaches

	Research Problems/Data Questions	Data Collection/ Method	Data Analysis/ Procedure	Data Interpretation
Quantitative	Confirmatory Outcome based	Instruments Observations Documents Score oriented Closed-ended process Predetermined hypotheses	Descriptive statistics Inferential statistics	Generalization Prediction based Interpretation of theory
Qualitative	Exploratory Process based Descriptive Phenomenon of interest	Interviews Documents Observations Audiovisual Participant-determined process Open-ended process Text/image oriented	Description Identify themes/ categories Look for interconnectedness among categories/ themes (vertically and horizontally)	Particularization (contextualizing) Larger sense-making Personal interpretation Asking questions

to integrate components of both quantitative and qualitative research. Unquestionably, the most typical case is the integration of the two forms of research at the data analysis and interpretation stages after quantitative data (e.g., scores on instruments) and qualitative data (e.g., participant observations of a setting) have been collected. For example, after collecting both forms of data, the analysis process might begin by transforming the qualitative data into numerical scores (e.g., themes or codes are counted for frequencies) so that they can be compared with quantitative scores. In another study, the analysis might proceed separately for both quantitative and qualitative data, and then the information might be compared in the interpretation (or discussion) stage of the research (see, e.g., Hossler & Vesper, 1993). Less frequently found in mixed methods studies is the integration at data collection. A good example of integration at this stage is the use of a few open-ended questions on a quantitative survey instrument. In this approach, both quantitative and qualitative data are collected and integrated in a single instrument of data collection. It is also possible for integration to occur earlier in the process of research such as in the problem/question stage. In some studies, the researcher might set forth both quantitative and qualitative questions in which the intent is to both test some relationships among variables and explore some general questions. This approach is seen in studies where a concurrent form of data collection exists and the researcher is interested in triangulating (Mathison, 1988) data from different sources as a major intent of the research. Finally, it should be noted that integration can occur at multiple stages. Data from a survey that contains both quantitative and qualitative data might be integrated in the analysis stage by transforming the qualitative data into scores so that the information can be easily compared with the quantitative scores.

Deciding on the stage or stages to integrate depends on the purpose of the research, the ease with which the integration can occur (e.g., data collection integration is easier and cleaner than data analysis integration), the researcher's understanding of the stages of research, and the intent or purpose of a particular study. What clouds this decision is the permeability of the categories displayed in Table 7.2. Data collection is a good case in point. What constitutes quantitative or qualitative data collection is open to debate; indeed, LeCompte and Schensul (1999), and many ethnographers, consider both quantitative and qualitative data collection as options for field data. A similar concern might be raised about the fine distinctions being made between quantitative and qualitative research problems and questions. Many inquirers actually go back and forth between confirming and exploring in any given study, although qualitative inquirers refrain from specifying variables in their questions and attempt to keep the study as open as possible to best learn from participants. Despite these potential issues that need to be considered, the mixed methods researcher needs to design a study with a clear understanding of the stage or stages at which the data will be integrated and the form this integration will take.

Theoretical Perspectives

One question raised by qualitative researchers in the social sciences, especially during the 1990s (Creswell, 2002), is that all inquiry is theoretically driven by assumptions that researchers bring to their studies. At an informal level, the theoretical perspective reflects researchers' personal stances toward the topics they are studying, a stance based on personal history, experience, culture, gender, and class perspectives. At a more formal level, social science researchers bring to their inquiries a formal lens by which they view their topics, including gendered perspectives (e.g., feminist theory), cultural perspectives (e.g., racial/ethnic theory), lifestyle orientation (e.g., queer theory), critical theory perspectives, and class and social status views.

Only recently have these theoretical perspectives been discussed in the mixed methods research design literature. As recently as 1997, Greene and Caracelli discussed the use of a theoretical lens in mixed methods research. They called such a lens the use of transformative designs that "give primacy to the value-based and action-oriented dimensions of different inquiry traditions" (p. 24). Greene and Caracelli (1997) further explicated the nature of transformative designs when they wrote,

> Designs are transformative in that they offer opportunities for reconfiguring the dialog across ideological differences and, thus, have the potential to restructure the evaluation context. . . . Diverse methods most importantly serve to include a broader set of interests in the resulting knowledge claims and to strengthen the likely effectiveness of action solutions. (p. 24)

The commonality across transformative studies is ideological, such that no matter what the domain of inquiry, the ultimate goal of the study is to advocate for change. The transformative element of the research can either be experienced by the participants as they participate in the research or follow the study's completion when the research spawns changes in action, policy, or ideology. Transformative designs are found in evaluative research as well as in health care. Issues as diverse as class, race, gender, feminist scholarship, and postmodernist thinking often inform transformative designs. To illustrate how this design might work, a researcher might examine the inequity that exists in an organization's salary structure that marginalizes women in the organization. The issue of inequity frames the study, and the inquirer proceeds to first gather survey data measuring equity issues in the organization. This initial quantitative phase is then followed by a qualitative phase in which several in-depth cases studies are developed to explore in more detail the quantitative results. These case studies might examine the issue of inequality from the standpoint of managers, middle managers, and workers on an assembly line. In the end, the researcher is interested in bringing about change in the salary structure and in using the research as evidence for needed change and to advocate for change. Also, through the research, the dialogue among organizational members is "transformed" to focus on issues of inequity.

The use of a theoretical lens may be explicit or implicit within a mixed methods study. Those espousing transformative model encourage researchers to make the lens explicit in the study, although Greene and Caracelli (1997) were not specific about how this might be done. However, examining the use of a theoretical or an ideological lens within other studies, we can see that it often informs the purpose and questions being asked. These purposes may be to promote equity and justice for policies and practices so as to create a personal, social, institutional, and/or organizational impact (as addressed by Newman, Ridenour, Newman, & DeMarco in Chapter 6 of this volume [Tashakkori & Teddlie, 2003]) or to address specific questions related to oppression, domination, alienation, and inequality. A transformative model would also indicate the participants who will be studied (e.g., women, the marginalized, certain groups that are culturally and ethnically diverse), how the data collection will proceed (e.g., typically collaboratively so as not to marginalize the study participants further), and the conclusion of the study for advocacy and change to improve society or the lives of the individuals being studied. In summary, the nature of transformative mixed research methodology is such that in both perspective and outcomes, it is dedicated to promoting change at levels ranging from the personal to the political. Furthermore, it is possible to conduct any quantitative, qualitative, or mixed methods study with a transformative or advocacy purpose.

Six Major Designs

The four criteria—implementation, priority, integration, and theoretical perspective—can be useful in specifying six different types of major designs that a researcher might employ. This short list of designs might not be as inclusive of types as those identified by other writers (see the types introduced in Table 7.1), but arguably, all variants of designs might be subsumed within these six types. Moreover, by identifying a small number of generic types, it can be suggested that the mixed methods researcher has the flexibility to choose and innovate within the types to fit a particular research situation. These six types build on the four decision criteria and integrate them into specific designs with a label that we believe captures the variants of the design. An overview of the types of designs by the four criteria is seen in Table 7.3. For each design, we identify its major characteristics, examples of variants on the design, and strengths and weaknesses in implementing it. In addition, a visual presentation is made for each design type and annotated with specific steps to be undertaken in the process of research. The visuals are shown in Figures 7.4 and 7.5.

Sequential Explanatory Design

The sequential explanatory design is the most straightforward of the six major mixed methods designs. It is characterized by the collection and analysis of quantitative data followed by the collection and analysis of qualitative data. Priority is typically given to the quantitative data, and the two methods are integrated during the interpretation phase of the study. The steps of this design are pictured in Figure 7.4a. The implementation of this design may or may not be guided by a specific theoretical perspective.

The purpose of the sequential explanatory design is typically to use qualitative results to assist in explaining and interpreting the findings of a primarily quantitative study. It can be especially useful when unexpected results arise from a quantitative study (Morse, 1991). In this case, the qualitative data collection that follows can be used to examine these surprising results in more detail. In an important variation of this design, the qualitative data collection and analysis is given the priority. In this case, the initial quantitative phase of the study may be used to characterize individuals along certain traits of interest related to the research question. These quantitative results can then be used to guide the purposeful sampling of participants for a primarily qualitative study.

The straightforward nature of this design is one of its main strengths. It is easy to implement because the steps fall into clear separate stages. In addition, this design feature makes it easy to describe and report. In fact, this design can be reported in two distinct phases with a final discussion that brings the results together. The sequential explanatory design is also useful when a quantitative researcher wants to further explore quantitative findings. Furthermore, the implementation of qualitative data collection and analysis within this design framework can be comfortable for quantitative researchers, and therefore it can provide an effective introduction to qualitative research methods to researchers unfamiliar with the techniques. The main weakness of

Table 7.3   Types of Designs by Four Criteria

Design Type	Implementation	Priority	Stage of Integration	Theoretical Perspective
Sequential explanatory	Quantitative followed by qualitative	Usually quantitative; can be qualitative or equal	Interpretation phase	May be present
Sequential exploratory	Qualitative followed by quantitative	Usually qualitative; can be quantitative or equal	Interpretation phase	May be present
Sequential transformative	Either quantitative followed by qualitative or qualitative followed by quantitative	Quantitative, qualitative or equal	Interpretation phase	Definitely present (i.e., conceptual framework, advocacy, empowerment)
Concurrent triangulation	Concurrent collection of quantitative and qualitative data	Preferably equal; can be quantitative or qualitative	Interpretation phase or analysis phase	May be present
Concurrent nested	Concurrent collection of quantitative and qualitative data	Quantitative or qualitative	Analysis phase	May be present
Concurrent transformative	Concurrent collection of quantitative and qualitative data	Quantitative, qualitative, or equal	Usually analysis phase; can be during interpretation phase	Definitely present (i.e., conceptual framework advocacy, empowerment)

this design is the length of time involved in data collection to complete the two separate phases. This is especially a drawback if the two phases are given equal priority. Therefore, a sequential explanatory design giving equal priority to both qualitative and quantitative methods may be a more applicable approach for a research program than for a single study.

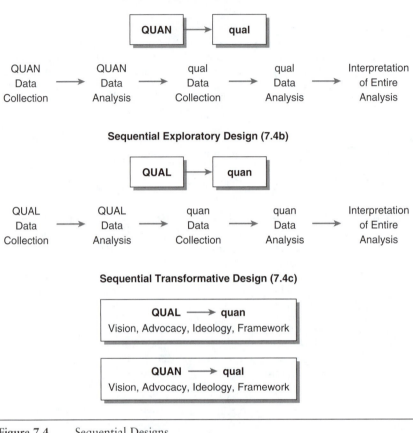

Figure 7.4   Sequential Designs
(a) Sequential Explanatory Design
(b) Sequential Exploratory Design
(c) Sequential Transformative Design

Sequential Exploratory Design

The sequential exploratory design has many features similar to the sequential explanatory design. It is conducted in two phases, with the priority generally given to the first phase, and it may or may not be implemented within a prescribed theoretical perspective (see Figure 7.4b). In contrast to the sequential explanatory design, this design is characterized by an initial phase of qualitative data collection and analysis followed by a phase of quantitative data collection and analysis. Therefore, the priority is given to the qualitative aspect of the study. The findings of these two phases are then integrated during the interpretation phase (see Figure 7.4b).

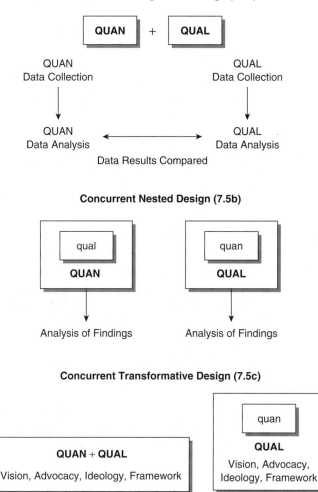

Figure 7.5 Concurrent Designs
(a) Concurrent Triangulation Design
(b) Concurrent Nested Design
(c) Concurrent Transformative Design

At the most basic level, the purpose of this design is to use quantitative data and results to assist in the interpretation of qualitative findings. Unlike the sequential explanatory design, which is better suited to explaining and interpreting relationships, the primary focus of this design is to explore a phenomenon. Morgan (1998) suggested that this design is appropriate to use when testing elements of an emergent theory resulting from the qualitative phase and that it can also be used to generalize qualitative findings to different samples. Similarly, Morse (1991) indicated that one purpose for selecting this design would be to determine the distribution of a phenomenon within a chosen population. Finally, the sequential exploratory design is often discussed as the design used when a researcher develops and tests an instrument (see, e.g., Creswell, 1999). One possible variation on this design is to give the priority to the second quantitative phase. Such a design might be undertaken when a researcher intends to conduct a primarily quantitative study, but it needs to begin with initial qualitative data collection so as to identify or narrow the focus of the possible variables. In addition, it is possible to give equal weight to the quantitative and qualitative phases, but such an approach may be too demanding for a single study due to time constraints, resource limitations, and the limitations of a researcher's experience.

The sequential exploratory design has many of the same advantages as the sequential explanatory design. Its two-phase approach makes it easy to implement and straightforward to describe and report. It is useful to a researcher who wants to explore a phenomenon but also wants to expand on the qualitative findings. This design is especially advantageous when a researcher is building a new instrument. In addition, this design could make a largely qualitative study more palatable to a quantitatively oriented adviser, committee, or research community that may be unfamiliar with the naturalistic tradition.

As with the sequential explanatory design, the sequential exploratory design also requires a substantial length of time to complete both data collection phases, which can be a drawback for some research situations. In addition, the researcher may find it difficult to build from the qualitative analysis to the subsequent quantitative data collection.

Sequential Transformative Design

As with the previously described sequential designs, the transformative sequential design has two distinct data collection phases, one following the other (see Figure 7.4c). However, in this design, either method may be used first, and the priority may be given to either the quantitative or the qualitative phase (or even to both if sufficient resources are available). In addition, the results of the two phases are integrated together during the interpretation phase. Unlike the sequential exploratory and explanatory designs, the sequential transformative design definitely has a theoretical perspective present to guide the study. The aim of this theoretical perspective, whether it be a conceptual framework, a specific ideology, or advocacy, is more important in guiding the study than the use of methods alone.

The purpose of a sequential transformative design is to employ the methods that will best serve the theoretical perspective of the researcher. By using two phases, a sequential transformative researcher may be able to give voice to diverse perspectives, to better advocate for participants, or to better understand a phenomenon or process that is changing as a result of being studied. The variations of this design would be best described by the diverse range of possible theoretical perspectives instead of the range of possible methodological choices.

The sequential transformative design shares the same methodological strengths and weaknesses as the other two sequential mixed methods designs. Its use of distinct phases facilitates its implementation, description, and sharing of results, although it also requires the time to complete two data collection phases. More important, this design places mixed methods research within a transformative frame-work. Therefore, this design may be more appealing and acceptable to those researchers already using a transformative framework within one distinct methodology such as qualitative research. It will also include the strengths typically found when using a theoretical perspective in other research traditions. Unfortunately, because to date little has been written on this design, one weakness is that there is little guidance on how to use the transformative vision to guide the methods. Likewise, it may be unclear how to move from the analysis of the first phase to the data collection of the second phase.

Concurrent Triangulation Design

The concurrent triangulation design is probably the most familiar of the six major mixed methods designs (see Figure 7.5a). It is selected as the design when a researcher uses two different methods in an attempt to confirm, cross-validate, or corroborate findings within a single study (Greene et al., 1989; Morgan, 1998; Steckler et al., 1992). This design generally uses separate quantitative and qualitative methods as a means to offset the weaknesses inherent within one method with the strengths of the other method. In this case, the quantitative data collection and qualitative data collection are concurrent, happening during one phase of the research study. Ideally, the priority would be equal between the two methods, but in practical application, the priority may be given to either the quantitative or the qualitative approach. This design usually integrates the results of the two methods during the interpretation phase. This interpretation either may note the convergence of the findings as a way to strengthen the knowledge claims of the study or must explain any lack of convergence that may result.

This traditional mixed methods design is advantageous because it is familiar to most researchers and can result in well-validated and substantiated findings. In addition, the concurrent data collection results in a shorter data collection time period as compared with that of the sequential designs. This design also has a number of limitations. It requires great effort and expertise to adequately study a phenomenon with two separate methods. It can also be difficult to compare the results of two analyses using data of different forms. In addition, it may be unclear to a researcher how to resolve discrepancies that arise in the results.

Other variations of this design also exist. For example, it would be possible for a researcher to integrate the two methods earlier in the research process such as during the analysis phase. This would require the transformation of the data from a quantitative to a qualitative form or from a qualitative to a quantitative form. While such transformations have been discussed in the literature (see, e.g., Caracelli & Greene, 1993; Tashakkori & Teddlie, 1998), there is still limited guidance for how to conduct and analyze such transformations in practice.

Concurrent Nested Design

Like the concurrent triangulation design, the concurrent nested design can be identified by its use of one data collection phase during which quantitative and qualitative data both are collected simultaneously (see Figure 7.5b). Unlike the traditional triangulation design, a nested design has a predominant method that guides the project. Given less priority, a method (quantitative or qualitative) is embedded, or nested, within the predominant method (qualitative or quantitative). This nesting may mean that the embedded method addresses a question different from that addressed by the dominant method or that the embedded method seeks information from different levels [the analogy to hierarchical analysis in quantitative research is helpful in conceptualizing these levels (see Tashakkori & Teddlie, 1998)]. The data collected from the two methods are mixed during the analysis phase of the project. This design may or may not have a guiding theoretical perspective.

The concurrent nested design may be used to serve a variety of purposes. Often, this design is used so that a researcher may gain broader perspectives from using the different methods as opposed to using the predominant method alone. For example, Morse (1991) noted that a primarily qualitative design could embed some quantitative data to enrich the description of the sample participants. Likewise, she described how qualitative data could be used to describe an aspect of a quantitative study that cannot be quantified. In addition, a concurrent nested design may be employed when a researcher chooses to use different methods to study different groups or levels within a design. For example, if an organization is being studied, then employees could be studied quantitatively, managers could be interviewed qualitatively, entire divisions could be analyzed with quantitative data, and so forth. Tashakkori and Teddlie (1998) described this approach as a multilevel design. Finally, one method could be used within a framework of the other method such as if a researcher designed and conducted an experiment but used case study methodology to study each of the treatment conditions.

This mixed methods design has many strengths. A researcher is able to simultaneously collect the data during one data collection phase. It provides a study with the advantages of both quantitative and qualitative data. In addition, by using the two different methods in this fashion, a researcher can gain perspectives from the different types of data or from different levels within the study. There are also limitations to consider when choosing this design. The data need to be transformed in some way so that they can be integrated within the analysis phase of the research. There has been little written to date to guide a researcher through this process. In addition, there is little advice to be found for how a researcher should resolve discrepancies that occur between the two types of data. Because the two methods are unequal in their priority, this design also results in unequal evidence within a study, and this may be a disadvantage when interpreting the final results.

Concurrent Transformative Design

As with the sequential transformative design, the concurrent transformative design is guided by the researcher's use of a specific theoretical perspective (see Figure 7.5c). This perspective can be based on ideologies such as critical theory, advocacy, participatory research, and a conceptual or theoretical framework. This perspective is reflected in the purpose or research questions of the study (see Newman et al., Chapter 6, this volume [Tashakkori & Teddlie, 2003]). It is the driving force behind all methodological choices such as defining the problem; identifying the design and data sources; and analyzing, interpreting, and reporting results throughout the research process (see Mertens, Chapter 5, this volume [Tashakkori & Teddlie, 2003]). The choice of a concurrent design (whether it is triangulation or a nested design) is made to facilitate this perspective. For example, the design may be nested so that diverse participants are given a voice in the change process of an organization that is studied primarily quantitatively. It may involve a triangulation of both quantitative and qualitative data to best converge information so as to provide evidence for an inequality of policies in an organization.

Thus, the concurrent transformative design may take on the design features of either a triangulation or nested design. That is, the two types of data are collected at the same time during one data collection phase and may have equal or unequal priority. The integration of these different data would most often occur during the analysis phase, although integration during the interpretation phase would be a possible variation. Because the concurrent transformative design shares common features with the triangulation and nested designs it also shares their specific strengths and weaknesses. However, this design also has the added advantage of positioning mixed methods research within a transformative framework, and this may make it especially appealing to those qualitative or quantitative researchers already using a transformative framework to guide their inquiry.

Issues in Implementing Designs

Although there are several discussions currently under way among those writing about mixed design applications, issues related to implementation fall into three categories: whether the design needs to be lodged within a paradigm perspective; how data analysis varies by design and the use of computer programs that handle both quantitative and qualitative data; and the placement of design procedures within a study, especially the elaboration of visual presentations of the procedures.

Paradigms and Designs

Substantial discussion has taken place in the mixed methods literature about the "compatibility" of quantitative and qualitative research and whether paradigms of research and methods can be mixed. For example, can a qualitative philosophical perspective, such as the existence of multiple realities, be combined with a quantitative study that uses a closed-ended survey to gather data and restrict the perspectives of the participants? The linking of paradigms and methods has been referred to as the "paradigm debate" (Cook & Reichardt, 1979; Reichardt & Rallis, 1994). Although this debate has largely subsided due to the use of multiple methods regardless of paradigm perspective, the discussion helped to raise the issue of whether philosophical perspectives should be explicitly stated and acknowledged in mixed methods studies. More specifically to the point of this chapter is this question: Should a philosophical position be embraced by the author of a mixed methods study, and will this position vary by types of design? Several authors (e.g., Patton, 1990; Rossman & Wilson, 1985; Tashakkori & Teddlie, 1998) have suggested that pragmatism is the foundation for these designs. This philosophy, drawn from Deweyan ideas and most recently articulated by Cherryholmes (1992), maintains that researchers should be concerned with applications, with what works, and with solutions to problems. In light of this, the authors have called for the use of both quantitative and qualitative methods to best understand research problems.

However, as applied to the six designs advanced in this chapter, a single philosophical framework does not work with all designs. If one takes the perspective that the mixed methods researcher should be explicit about the paradigm or philosophy behind his or her design, then a number of philosophical perspectives can enter into the study. Today, multiple paradigms exist for our inquiries such as positivism, postpositivism, interpretivism, and participatory/ advocacy perspectives (Denzin & Lincoln, 2000). In a sequential explanatory design, strongly based on quantitative research, the paradigm stated may be postpositivist, while in a sequential exploratory design, with the lead taken by qualitative research, the paradigm may be more interpretive or participatory/ advocacy oriented. A triangulation design may use several paradigms as a framework for the study. A transformative design may employ qualitative, quantitative, or mixed methods so long as the ideological lens of advocacy or participation is a central element in shaping the purpose, the questions, the collaborative nature of data collection and analysis, and the interpreting and report of results (see Mertens's chapter in this volume [Chapter 5, Tashakkori & Teddlie, 2003]). While Greene and Caracelli (1997) recommended that researchers employing mixed methods research be explicit about their paradigms, we can now extend this suggestion to a consideration of what paradigm is best given the choice of a design for the mixed methods study.

Data Analysis and Designs

Approaches to data analysis also need to be sensitive to the design being implemented in a mixed methods study. Different analysis approaches have been suggested for integrating quantitative and qualitative data that explore how the information might be transformed or analyzed for outlier cases (Caracelli & Greene, 1993). Further approaches to analyzing data are also found in Tashakkori and Teddlie (1998), Creswell (2002), and Onwuegbuzie and Teddlie's chapter in this volume (Chapter 13 [Tashakkori & Teddlie, 2003]). When the six types of designs are considered, we see in the sequential designs that the data analysis typically proceeds independently for both the quantitative and qualitative phases. The researcher relies on standard data analysis approaches (e.g., descriptive and inferential analysis of quantitative data, coding and thematic analysis of qualitative data). Alternatively, in the concurrent designs, the analysis requires some data transformation so as to integrate and compare dissimilar databases (e.g., quantitative scales are compared with qualitative themes, qualitative themes are converted into scores). Other options exist as well, as seen in Table 7.4, which shows the relationship among data analysis approaches as well as a description of each approach and its relationship to each of the six designs.

Table 7.4   Type of Mixed Methods Design and Data Analysis/Interpretation Procedures

Type of Mixed Methods Design	Examples of Analytic Procedures
Concurrent (triangulation, nested, transformative)	• Quantify qualitative data: Code qualitative data, assign numbers to codes, and record the number of times codes appear as numeric data. Descriptively analyze quantitative data for frequency of occurrence. Compare the two data sets. • Qualifying quantitative data: Factor-analyze the quantitative data from questionnaires. These factors then become themes. Compare these themes to themes analyzed from qualitative data. • Comparing results: Directly compare the results from qualitative data collection to the results from quantitative data collection. Support statistical trends by qualitative themes or vice versa. • Consolidating data: Combine qualitative and quantitative data to form new variables. Compare original quantitative variables to qualitative themes to form new quantitative variables. (Caracelli & Greene, 1993) • Examining multilevels: Conduct a survey at the student level. Gather qualitative data through interviews at the class level. Survey the entire school at the school level. Collect qualitative data at the district level. Information from each level builds to the next level. (Tashakkori & Teddlie, 1998)
Sequential (explanatory, exploratory, transformative)	• Following up on outliers or extreme cases: Gather quantitative data and identify outlier or residual cases. Collect qualitative data to explore the characteristics of these cases. (Caracelli & Greene, 1993) • Explaining results: Conduct a quantitative survey to identify how two or more groups compare on a variable. Follow up with qualitative interviews to explore the reasons why these differences were found. • Using a typology: Conduct a quantitative survey, and develop factors through a factor analysis. Use these factors as a typology to identify themes in qualitative data such as observations and interviews. (Caracelli & Greene, 1993) • Locating an instrument: Collect qualitative data and identify themes. Use these themes as a basis for locating instruments that use parallel concepts to the qualitative themes.

Type of Mixed Methods Design	*Examples of Analytic Procedures*
	• Developing an instrument: Obtain themes and specific statements from individuals that support the themes. During the next phase, use these themes and statements to create scales and items in a questionnaire. Alternatively, look for existing instruments that can be modified to fit the themes and statements found in the qualitative exploratory phase of the study. After developing the instrument, test it out with a sample of a population.
	• Forming categorical data: Site-level characteristics (e.g., different ethnic groups) gathered in an ethnography during the first phase of a study become a categorical variable during a second-phase correlational or regression study. (Caracelli & Greene, 1993)
	• Using extreme qualitative cases: Qualitative data cases that are extreme in a comparative analysis are followed by quantitative surveys during a second. (Caracelli & Greene, 1993)

SOURCE: Adapted from Creswell (2002).

A related issue is whether a computer program should be used in mixed methods research and what programs are amenable to the analysis of both quantitative and qualitative data (see Bazeley's discussion of computer data analysis in Chapter 14 of this volume [Tashakkori & Teddlie, 2003]). Several qualitative data analysis programs allow for the import and export of quantitative data in table, formats (Creswell & Maietta, 2002). Programs such as ETHNOGRAPH 5, HyperRESEARCH 2.5, Classic NUD.IST Versions 4 and 5, NVIVO, ATLAS.ti, and WinMAX allow the user to move to and from quantitative and spreadsheet packages with direct links into document identification numbers. For example, it is now possible to create a numerical SPSS file at the same time that a text file is being developed and to merge the data using qualitative software computer packages.

Procedures and Designs

With the discussion of mixed methods research designs have emerged additional questions about how researchers should conceptualize and present their discussions about designs and how they can articulate them so that proposal reviewers, editorial board reviewers, and conference attendees can easily understand the procedures involved in the mixed methods discussions. With the complex features often found in these designs, it is not surprising that writers have presented figures in their studies that portray the general flow of procedures such as those advanced by Steckler et al. (1992) and shown in Figure 7.1. But such visualizations do not go far enough. Added to these visual models can also be the procedures employed by the researcher, so that readers see the visual picture and learn about the accompanying procedures involved in each step. Thus, the discussion in the mixed methods literature about visual models (see Steckler et al., 1992) and the steps in the research process (as discussed by Creswell, 1999) can be combined.

Such a combination of ideas in a single figure is illustrated in Figure 7.6. In this figure, we see a two-phase mixed methods study. There are three levels introduced in the visualization of procedures. First, readers find the phases to be organized into qualitative research followed by quantitative research for each year of the project. Then, the more general procedures of data collection and analysis are presented in the circles and boxes on the left and, finally, the more specific procedures are identified on the right. Arrows help readers to see how the two phases are integrated into a sequential process of research. Although Figure 7.6 is only for the sequential exploratory model in our designs, one can extrapolate the basic design features to the other design possibilities and emerge with visualizations of designs that are both useful and clear to readers and reviewers of mixed methods studies.

Returning to the Hossler and Vesper Mixed Methods Study

The Hossler and Vesper (1993) study that began our discussion can now be advanced in a visual diagram and assessed in terms of the four criteria and the six types of designs. As mentioned earlier, we can now see the Hossler and Vesper study as a concurrent triangulation design with priority given to quantitative research. The study began with quantitative questions (i.e., "To what extent are parents saving for postsecondary education? What factors are associated with parental savings? Do certain kinds of information appear to influence parental savings?" [p. 141]), but the data were collected concurrently in the form of surveys and interviews. The authors then analyzed the survey data separately from the interview data. Their intent was to triangulate the findings, which readers will find in the discussion section. They did not use a theoretical framework to frame the study, and they did not provide a visualization their research procedures. It they had incorporated this, visualization, then it might have looked like the representation shown in Figure 7.7, where there are simultaneous quantitative and qualitative data collection and analysis and an interpretation in which they converged the data. If the data were presented in a "box text" diagram as shown in Box 7.1, as is used by writers of mixed methods research designs

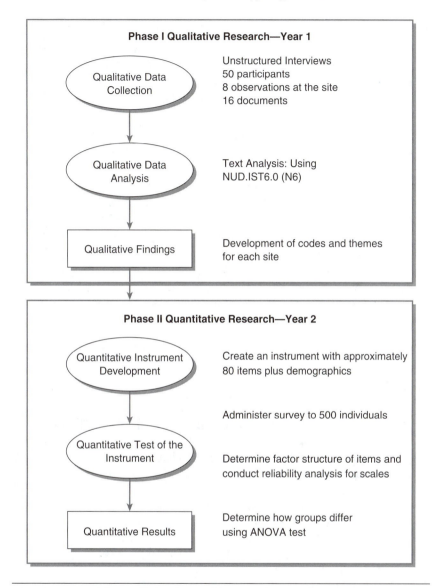

Figure 7.6   Elaborated Visualization for Mixed Methods Procedures

(e.g., see Tashakkori & Teddlie, 1998), then the essential information about the study that marks it as a mixed methods project could be illustrated through information about the methodology, aspects about the participants and data collection, the data analysis, and the discussion. Further information could be supplied about the four decision criteria made by the researchers.

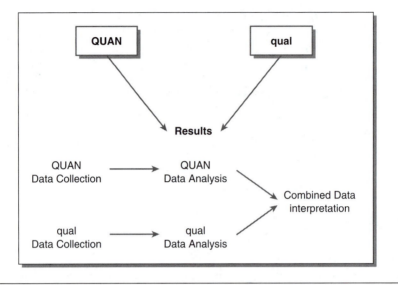

Figure 7.7   Proposed Visualization of the Concurrent Triangulation Design
Used in Hossler and Vesper (1993)

Box 7.1   Summary of the Hossler and Vesper Study

Hossler, D., & Vesper, N. (1993). An exploratory study of the factors associated with parental saving for postsecondary education. *Journal of Higher Education, 64*(2), 140–165.

This article provides an example of how qualitative and quantitative methods can be combined in educational research. As the title of the article suggests, two methodologies are used, and rationales for the use of each method are provided to readers. The primary goal of the research is to add information to the dearth of extant research in this area.

The principal methodology of this study was quantitative with a strong qualitative complement. Student and parent data garnered from a longitudinal study involving multiple surveys over a 3-year time line served as the basis for logistic regression that was used to identify the specific factors most strongly associated with parental saving for post-secondary education. Additional insights into the phenomenon of interest were gained from interviews of a small subsample of students and parents who were interviewed five times during the 3-year duration of the study. Interviews were used both to explore emerging themes in greater detail and to triangulate findings.

Components of data collection:

A total of 182 students and parents participated.

All participants completed surveys 10 times over a 4-year span.

A total of 56 students and their parents from eight high schools in the sample participated in interviews four times each year while the students were in their junior and senior years in high school.

Development of both the surveys and the interview protocols was an iterative process.

Data analysis:

Quantitative data were statistically analyzed via logistic regression, with significant discussion of coding of independent and dependent variables.

Qualitative data were analyzed via thematic analysis, with data being unitized and categorized.

Discussion and inferences:

Both quantitative and qualitative results were discussed jointly in the discussion section of the article. Significant factors identified by the logistic regression were corroborated with the theme that had emerged from the interviews. Areas of overlap between the analyses were discussed, although there was little mention of any inconsistencies in the data.

Triangulating the results from the survey and interview data allowed the authors to posit a model of parental saving.

Priority: QUANTITATIVE

Sequence: qual + QUAN simultaneously

Integration: data collection, data analysis, and inference stages

Transformative: not present

Strengths: Combining methods of data collection and analysis allowed for the construction of more sensitive survey instruments as well as a better and broader understanding of the phenomenon of interest. Directions for intervention and policy development were identified and discussed.

Weaknesses: It was difficult to separate the quantitative and qualitative components in the discussion section. Implementing a mixed method design would be difficult if contradictory quantitative and qualitative data were found.

This review of the Hossler and Vesper study highlights how discussions about mixed methods designs need to consider the underlying decisions that go into selecting a design; the type of design being used; and issues related to paradigms, data analysis, and the delineation of procedures using visuals.

Undoubtedly, more issues will emerge about designing mixed methods studies, and a periodic assessment needs to provide an ongoing synthesis of the literature. In this way, we can continue to explore the methodology of mixed methods research and present additional guidelines for both novice and experienced researchers as they continue to develop, write, and publish these studies.

References

Bryman, A. (1988). *Quantity and quality in social science research*. London: Routledge.

Campbell, D., & Fiske, D. (1959). Convergent and discriminant validation by the multitrait-multimethod matrix. *Psychological Bulletin, 56*, 81–105.

Caracelli, V. J., & Greene, J. C. (1993). Data analysis strategies for mixed-method evaluation designs, *Educational Evaluation and Policy Analysis, 15*(2), 195–207.

Cherryholmes, C. H, (1992, August-September). Notes on pragmatism and scientific realism. *Educational Researcher, 21*, 13–17.

Cook, T. D., & Reichardt, C. S. (Eds.). (1979). *Qualitative and quantitative methods in evaluation research*. Beverly Hills, CA: Sage.

Creswell, J. W. (1994). *Research design: Qualitative and quantitative approaches*. Thousand Oaks, CA: Sage.

Creswell, J. W. (1999). Mixed method research: Introduction and application. In T. Cijek (Ed.), *Handbook of educational policy* (pp. 455–472). San Diego, CA: Academic Press.

Creswell, J. W. (2002). *Educational research: Planning, conducting, and evaluating quantitative and qualitative approaches to research*. Upper Saddle River, NJ: Merrill/Pearson Education.

Creswell, J. W., Goodchild, L., & Turner, P. (1996). Integrated qualitative and quantitative research: Epistemology, history, and designs. In J. Smart (Ed.), *Higher education: Handbook of theory and research* (Vol. 11, pp. 90–136). New York: Agathon Press.

Creswell, J. W., & Maietta, R. C. (2002). Qualitative research. In N. J. Salkind (Ed.), *Handbook of social research* (2nd ed., pp. 143–184). Thousand Oaks, CA: Sage.

Creswell, J. W., & Miller, G. A. (1997). Research methodologies and the doctoral process. In L. Goodchild, K. E. Green, E. L. Katz, & R. C. Kluever (Eds.), *Rethinking the dissertation process: Tackling personal and institutional obstacles* (New Directions for Higher Education, No. 99, pp. 33–46). San Francisco: Jossey-Bass.

Datta, L. (1994). Paradigm wars: A basis for peaceful coexistence and beyond. In C. S. Reichardt & S. F. Rallis (Eds.), *The qualitative-quantitative debate: New perspectives* (New Directions for Program Evaluation, No. 61, pp. 53–70). San Francisco: Jossey-Bass.

Denzin, N., & Lincoln, Y. S. (2000). *Handbook of qualitative research* (2nd ed.). Thousand Oaks, CA: Sage.

Fielding, N. G., & Fielding, J. L. (1986). *Linking data*. Newbury Park, CA: Sage.

Glik, D. C., Parker, K., Muligande, G., & Hategikamana, D. (1986–1987). Integrating qualitative and quantitative survey techniques. *International Quarterly of Community Health Education, 7*(3), 181–200.

Greene, J. C., & Caracelli, V. J. (Eds.). (1997). *Advances in mixed-method evaluation: The challenges and benefits of integrating diverse paradigms* (New Directions for Evaluation, No. 74). San Francisco: Jossey-Bass.

Greene, J. C., Caracelli, V. J., & Graham, W. F. (1989). Toward a conceptual framework for mixed-method evaluation designs. *Educational Evaluation and Policy Analysis, 11,* 255–274.

Hossler, D., & Vesper, N. (1993). An exploratory study of the factors associated with parental savings for postsecondary education. *Journal of Higher Education, 64*(2), 140–165.

Hugentobler, M. K., Israel, B. A., & Schurman, S. J. (1992). An action research approach to workplace health: Integrating methods. *Health Education Quarterly, 19*(1), 55–76.

Jick, T. D. (1979). Mixing qualitative and quantitative methods: Triangulation in action. *Administrative Science Quarterly, 24,* 602–611.

LeCompte, M. D., & Schensul, J. J. (1999). *Designing and conducting ethnographic research* (Ethnographer's Toolkit, No. 1). Walnut Creek, CA; AltaMira.

Mathison, S. (1988). Why triangulate? *Educational Researcher, 17*(2), 13–17.

Miles, M. B., & Huberman, A. M. (1994). *Qualitative data analysis* (2nd ed.). Thousand Oaks, CA; Sage.

Morgan, D. (1998). Practical strategies for combining qualitative and quantitative methods; Applications to health research. *Qualitative Health Research, 8,* 362–376.

Morse, J. M. (1991). Approaches to qualitative-quantitative methodological triangulation. *Nursing Research, 40,* 120–123.

Patton, M. Q. (1990). *Qualitative evaluation and research methods.* Newbury Park, CA: Sage.

Reichardt, C. S., & Rallis, S. E. (1994). The relationship between the qualitative and quantitative research traditions. In C. S. Reichardt & S. F. Rallis (Eds.), *The qualitative-quantitative debate: New perspectives* (New Directions for Program Evaluation, No. 61, pp. 5–11). San Francisco: Jossey-Bass.

Rossman, G. B., & Wilson, B. L. (1985). Number and words; Combining quantitative and qualitative methods in a single large-scale evaluation study. *Evaluation Review, 9,* 627–643.

Rossman, G. B., & Wilson, B. L. (1991). *Numbers and words revisited: Being "shamelessly eclectic."* Washington, DC: Office of Educational Research and Improvement. (ERIC Document Reproduction Service No. 337 235)

Sieber, S. D. (1973). The integration of field work and survey methods. *American Journal of Sociology, 78,* 1335–1359.

Steckler, A., McLeroy, K. R., Goodman, R. M., Bird, S. T., & McCormick, L. (1992). Toward integrating qualitative and quantitative methods: An introduction. *Health Education Quarterly, 19*(1), 1–8.

Swanson-Kauffman, K. M. (1986). A combined qualitative methodology for nursing research. *Advances in Nursing Science, 8*(3), 58–69.

Tashakkori, A., & Teddlie, C. (1998). *Mixed methodology: Combining qualitative and quantitative approaches* (Applied Social Research Methods, No. 46). Thousand Oaks, CA: Sage.

John W. Creswell (Ph.D., University of Iowa) is Professor of Educational Psychology in the Graduate Program of Quantitative and Qualitative Methods in Education at the University of Nebraska–Lincoln. He specializes in research methods and design, qualitative inquiry, and mixed methods research, and he has authored eight books and numerous chapters and journal articles. His most recent three books address quantitative and qualitative research design, qualitative inquiry, and educational research.

Michelle L. Gutmann (M.S., C.C.C.-S.L.P.) is a speech-language pathologist with 10 years of clinical experience in augmentative and alternative communication. Throughout this time, she has worked with both adults and children across a variety of settings. She is currently pursuing her doctorate in speech pathology and is interested in outcome measures and in-depth study of specific clinical populations.

William E. Hanson (Ph.D., Arizona State University, M.A., University of Minnesota) is Assistant Professor in the Department of Educational Psychology at the University of Nebraska–Lincoln. He teaches in the Counseling Psychology Program. He specializes in psychological assessment, psychotherapy process and outcome research, and counselor training/supervision.

Vicki L. Plano Clark (M.S., Michigan State University) is Laboratory Manager in the Department of Physics and Astronomy, as well as a doctoral candidate in quantitative and qualitative methods in education, at the University of Nebraska–Lincoln. In addition to her doctoral work, which emphasizes mixed methods research, she has focused on curriculum development that incorporates computer-based technologies into introductory physics teaching laboratory courses. She has been a co-principal investigator on three National Science Foundation grants as well as the leader of numerous faculty development workshops at regional and national professional society meetings.

8

Different Sampling Techniques for Mixed Methods Studies

Selection: Teddlie, C., & Yu, F. (2007). Mixed methods sampling: A typology with examples. *Journal of Mixed Methods Research, 1*(1), 77–100.

Editors' Introduction

Once a researcher has selected a specific mixed methods design, many issues still must be addressed during its implementation. One important question related to data collection is, What sampling strategy or strategies will be used to select participants for the quantitative and qualitative strands of the study? Charles Teddlie and Fen Yu introduce a typology of five approaches to mixed methods sampling in their 2007 article and thus provide insightful direction to help researchers answer this question on mixed methods sampling.

To understand mixed methods sampling, researchers must first have a solid understanding of traditional sampling strategies, including probability, purposive, and convenience sampling. Teddlie and Yu begin by reviewing the purposes and specific techniques associated with these different types of sampling. They then contrast probability and purposive sampling along dimensions such as the overall sampling purpose, sample size, and when the sample is selected. From these differences they advance a sampling contin-uum on which mixed sampling falls between purely purposive and purely prob-ability strategies, and they present characteristics of mixed methods sampling strategies. They posit that mixed methods sampling needs to be considered in terms of the trade-off researchers face between achieving representativeness and saturation. Teddlie and Yu conclude their article with a discussion of five different mixed methods sampling techniques and by suggesting eight guidelines that researchers should follow when developing their mixed methods sampling plans.

Discussion Questions and Applications

1. Consider a mixed methods study such as reported by Thøgersen-Ntoumani and Fox (Chapter 21 in this volume) or Richter (Chapter 23 in this volume). Describe the mixed methods sampling.

2. How might sampling decisions such as using the same or different individuals in the two strands be related to different types of mixed methods designs?

3. Consider how each of the mixed methods sampling strategies might be used in studies related to one research problem. How would the studies differ from each other?

Related References That Extend the Topic

For additional discussions about sampling and collecting data in mixed methods research see:

Johnson, B., & Turner, L. A. (2003). Data collection strategies in mixed methods research. In A. Tashakkori & C. Teddlie (Eds.), *Handbook of mixed methods in social and behavioral research* (pp. 297–319). Thousand Oaks, CA: Sage.

Kemper, E. A., Stringfield, S., & Teddlie, C. (2003). Mixed methods sampling strategies in social science research. In A. Tashakkori & C. Teddlie (Eds.), *Handbook of mixed methods in social and behavioral research* (pp. 273–296). Thousand Oaks, CA: Sage.

Mixed Methods Sampling

A Typology With Examples

Charles Teddlie
Louisiana State University, Baton Rouge

Fen Yu
Louisiana State University, Baton Rouge

This article presents a discussion of mixed methods (MM) sampling techniques. MM sampling involves combining well-established qualitative and quantitative techniques in creative ways to answer research questions posed by MM research designs. Several issues germane to MM sampling are presented including the differences between probability and purposive sampling and the probability-mixed-purposive sampling continuum. Four MM sampling prototypes are introduced: basic MM sampling strategies, sequential MM sampling, concurrent MM sampling, and multilevel MM sampling. Examples of each of these techniques are given as illustrations of how researchers actually generate MM samples. Finally, eight guidelines for MM sampling are presented.

Keywords: mixed methods sampling; mixed methods research; multilevel mixed methods sampling; representativeness/saturation trade-off

SOURCE: This article is reprinted from *Journal of Mixed Methods Research*, Vol. 1, Issue 1, pp. 77–100, 2007. Reprinted with permission of Sage Publications, Inc.

Authors' Note: This article is partially based on a paper presented at the 2006 annual meeting of the American Educational Research Association, San Francisco.

Taxonomy of Sampling Strategies in the Social and Behavioral Sciences

Although sampling procedures in the social and behavioral sciences are often divided into two groups (probability, purposive), there are actually four broad categories as illustrated in Figure 8.1. Probability, purposive, and convenience sampling are discussed briefly in the following sections to provide a background for mixed methods (MM) sampling strategies.

Probability sampling techniques are primarily used in quantitatively oriented studies and involve "selecting a relatively large number of units from a population, or from specific subgroups (strata) of a population, in a random manner where the probability of inclusion for every member of the population is determinable" (Tashakkori & Teddlie, 2003a, p. 713). Probability samples aim to achieve representativeness, which is the degree to which the sample accurately represents the entire population.

Purposive sampling techniques are primarily used in qualitative (QUAL) studies and may be defined as selecting units (e.g., individuals, groups of individuals, institutions) based on specific purposes associated with answering

---

I. **Probability Sampling**
   A. Random Sampling
   B. Stratified Sampling
   C. Cluster Sampling
   D. Sampling Using Multiple Probability Techniques

II. **Purposive Sampling**
   A. Sampling to Achieve Representativeness or Comparability
   B. Sampling Special or Unique Cases
   C. Sequential Sampling
   D. Sampling Using Multiple Purposive Techniques

III. **Convenience Sampling**
   A. Captive Sample
   B. Volunteer Sample

IV. **Mixed Methods Sampling**
   A. Basic Mixed Methods Sampling
   B. Sequential Mixed Methods Sampling
   C. Concurrent Mixed Methods Sampling
   D. Multilevel Mixed Methods Sampling
   E. Combination of Mixed Methods Sampling Strategies

Figure 8.1   Taxonomy of Sampling Techniques for the Social and Behavioral Sciences

a research study's questions. Maxwell (1997) further defined purposive sampling as a type of sampling in which, "particular settings, persons, or events are deliberately selected for the important information they can provide that cannot be gotten as well from other choices" (p. 87).

Convenience sampling involves drawing samples that are both easily accessible and willing to participate in a study. Two types of convenience samples are captive samples and volunteer samples. We do not discuss convenience samples in any detail in this article, which focuses on how probability and purposive samples can be used to generate MM samples.

MM sampling strategies involve the selection of units[1] or cases for a research study using both probability sampling (to increase external validity) and purposive sampling strategies (to increase transferability).[2] This fourth general sampling category has been discussed infrequently in the research literature (e.g., Collins, Onwuegbuzie, & Jiao, 2006; Kemper, Stringfield, & Teddlie, 2003), although numerous examples of it exist throughout the behavioral and social sciences.

The article is divided into four major sections: a description of probability sampling techniques, a discussion of purposive sampling techniques, general considerations concerning MM sampling, and guidelines for MM sampling. The third section on general considerations regarding MM sampling contains examples of various techniques, plus illustrations of how researchers actually generate MM samples.

Traditional Probability Sampling Techniques

An Introduction to Probability Sampling

There are three basic types of probability sampling, plus a category that involves multiple probability techniques:

- Random sampling—occurs when each sampling unit in a clearly defined population has an equal chance of being included in the sample.
- Stratified sampling—occurs when the researcher divides the population into subgroups (or strata) such that each unit belongs to a single stratum (e.g., low income, medium income, high income) and then selects units from those strata.
- Cluster sampling—occurs when the sampling unit is not an individual but a group (cluster) that occurs naturally in the population such as neighborhoods, hospitals, schools, or classrooms.
- Sampling using multiple probability techniques—involves the use of multiple quantitative (QUAN) techniques in the same study.

Probability sampling is based on underlying theoretical distributions of observations, or sampling distributions, the best known of which is the normal curve.

Random Sampling

Random sampling is perhaps the most well known of all sampling strategies. A simple random sample is one is which each unit (e.g., persons, cases) in the accessible population has an equal chance of being included in the sample, and the probability of a unit being selected is not affected by the selection of other units from the accessible population (i.e., the selections are made independently). Simple random sample selection may be accomplished in several ways including drawing names or numbers out of a box or using a computer program to generate a sample using random numbers that start with a "seeded" number based on the program's start time.

Stratified Sampling

If a researcher is interested in drawing a random sample, then she or he typically wants the sample to be representative of the population on some characteristic of interest (e.g., achievement scores). The situation becomes more complicated when the researcher wants various subgroups in the sample to also be representative. In such cases, the researcher uses stratified random sampling,[3] which combines stratified sampling with random sampling.

For example, assume that a researcher wanted a stratified random sample of males and females in a college freshman class. The researcher would first separate the entire population of the college class into two groups (or strata): one all male and one all female. The researcher would then independently select a random sample from each stratum (one random sample of males, one random sample of females).

Cluster Sampling

The third type of probability sampling, cluster sampling, occurs when the researcher wants to generate a more efficient probability sample in terms of monetary and/or time resources. Instead of sampling individual units, which might be geographically spread over great distances, the researcher samples groups (clusters) that occur naturally in the population, such as neighborhoods or schools or hospitals.

Sampling Using Multiple Probability Techniques

Researchers often use the three basic probability sampling techniques in conjunction with one another to generate more complex samples. For example, multiple cluster sampling is a technique that involves (a) a first stage of sampling in which the clusters are randomly selected and (b) a second stage of sampling in which the units of interest are sampled within the clusters. A common example of this from educational research occurs when schools (the clusters) are randomly selected and then teachers (the units of interest) in those schools are randomly sampled.

Traditional Purposive Sampling Techniques

An Introduction to Purposive Sampling

Purposive sampling techniques have also been referred to as nonprobability sampling or purposeful sampling or "qualitative sampling." As noted above, purposive sampling techniques involve selecting certain units or cases "based on a specific purpose rather than randomly" (Tashakkori & Teddlie, 2003a, p. 713). Several other authors (e.g., Kuzel, 1992; LeCompte & Preissle, 1993; Miles & Huberman, 1994; Patton, 2002) have also presented typologies of purposive sampling techniques.

As detailed in Figure 8.2, there are three broad categories of purposive sampling techniques (plus a category involving multiple purposive techniques), each of which encompass several specific types of strategies:

- Sampling to achieve representativeness or comparability—these techniques are used when the researcher wants to (a) select a purposive sample that represents a broader group of cases as closely as possible or (b) set up comparisons among different types of cases.
- Sampling special or unique cases—employed when the individual case itself, or a specific group of cases, is a major focus of the investigation (rather than an issue).
- Sequential sampling—uses the gradual selection principle of sampling when (a) the goal of the research project is the generation of theory (or broadly defined themes) or (b) the sample evolves of its own accord as data are being collected. Gradual selection may be defined as the sequential selection of units or cases based on their relevance to the research questions, not their representativeness (e.g., Flick, 1998).
- Sampling using multiple purposive techniques—involves the use of multiple QUAL techniques in the same study.

A. **Sampling to Achieve Representativeness or Comparability**
   1. Typical Case Sampling
   2. Extreme or Deviant Case Sampling (also known as Outlier Sampling)
   3. Intensity Sampling
   4. Maximum Variation Sampling
   5. Homogeneous Sampling
   6. Reputational Case Sampling

B. **Sampling Special or Unique Cases**
   7. Revelatory Case Sampling
   8. Critical Case Sampling
   9. Sampling Politically Important Cases
   10. Complete Collection (also known as Criterion Sampling)

C. **Sequential Sampling**
   11. Theoretical sampling (also known as Theory-Based Sampling)
   12. Confirming and Disconfirming Cases
   13. Opportunistic Sampling (also known as Emergent Sampling)
   14. Snowball Sampling (also known as Chain Sampling)

D. **Sampling Using Combinations of Purposive Techniques**

Figure 8.2   A Typology of Purposive Sampling Strategies

SOURCE: These techniques were taken from several sources, such as Kuzel (1992), LeCompte and Preissle (1993), Miles and Huberman (1994), and Patton (2002).

Sampling to Achieve Representativeness or Comparability

The first broad category of purposive sampling techniques involves two goals:

- sampling to find instances that are *representative* or *typical* of a particular type of case on a dimension of interest, and
- sampling to achieve comparability across different types of cases on a dimension of interest.

There are six types of purposive sampling procedures that are based on achieving representativeness or comparability: typical case sampling, extreme or deviant case sampling, intensity sampling, maximum variation sampling, homogeneous sampling, and reputational sampling. Although some of these purposive sampling techniques are aimed at generating representative cases, most are aimed at producing contrasting cases. Comparisons or contrasts are at the very core of QUAL data analysis strategies (e.g., Glaser & Strauss, 1967; Mason, 2002; Spradley, 1979, 1980), including the contrast principle and the constant comparative technique.

An example of this broad category of purposive sampling is extreme or deviant case sampling, which is also known as "outlier sampling" because it involves selecting cases near the "ends" of the distribution of cases of interest. It involves selecting those cases that are the most outstanding successes or failures related to some topic of interest. Such extreme successes or failures are expected to yield especially valuable information about the topic of interest.

Extreme or deviant cases provide interesting contrasts with other cases, thereby allowing for comparability across those cases. These comparisons require that the investigator first determine a dimension of interest, then visualize a distribution of cases or individuals or some other sampling unit on that dimension (which is the QUAL researcher's informal sampling frame), and then locate extreme cases in that distribution. (Sampling frames are formal or informal lists of units or cases from which the sample is drawn, and they are discussed in more detail later in this article.)

Sampling Special or Unique Cases

These sampling techniques include special or unique cases, which have long been a focus of QUAL research, especially in anthropology and sociology. Stake (1995) described an intrinsic case study as one in which the case itself is of primary importance, rather than some overall issue. There are four types of purposive sampling techniques that feature special or unique cases: revelatory case sampling, critical case sampling, sampling politically important cases, and complete collection.

An example of this broad category is revelatory case sampling, which involves identifying and gaining entrée to a single case representing a phenomenon that had previously been "inaccessible to scientific investigation" (Yin, 2003, p. 42). Such cases are rare and difficult to study, yet yield very valuable information about heretofore unstudied phenomena.

There are several examples of revelatory cases spread throughout the social and behavioral sciences. For example, Ward's (1986) *Them Children: A Study in Language Learning* derives its revelatory nature from its depiction of a unique environment, the "Rosepoint" community, which was a former sugar plantation that is now a poor, rural African American community near New Orleans. Ward described how the Rosepoint community provided a "total environment" for the families she studied (especially for the children) that is quite different from the mainstream United States.

Sequential Sampling

These techniques all involve the principle of gradual selection, which was defined earlier in this article. There are four types of purposive sampling techniques that involve sequential sampling:

- theoretical sampling,
- confirming and disconfirming cases,
- opportunistic sampling (also known as emergent sampling), and
- snowball sampling (also known as chain sampling).

An example from this broad category is theoretical sampling, in which the researcher examines particular instances of the phenomenon of interest so that she or he can define and elaborate on its various manifestations. The investigator samples people, institutions, documents, or wherever the theory leads the investigation.

"Awareness of dying" research provides an excellent example of theoretical sampling utilized by the originators of grounded theory (Glaser & Strauss, 1967). Glaser and Strauss's research took them to a variety of sites relevant to their emerging theory regarding different types of awareness of dying. Each site provided unique information that previous sites had not. These sites included premature baby services, neurological services with comatose patients, intensive care units, cancer wards, and emergency services. Glaser and Strauss followed the dictates of gradual selection to that site or case that would yield the most valuable information for the further refinement of the theory.

Sampling Using Multiple Purposive Techniques

Sampling using combinations of purposive techniques involves using two or more of those sampling strategies when selecting units or cases for a research study. Many QUAL studies reported in the literature utilize more than one purposive sampling technique due to the complexities of the issues being examined.

For example, Poorman (2002) presented an example of multiple purposive sampling techniques from the literature related to the abuse and oppression of women. In this study, Poorman used four different types of purposive sampling techniques (theory based, maximum variation, snowball, and homogeneous) in combination with one another in selecting the participants for a series of four focus groups.

General Considerations Concerning Mixed Methods Sampling

Differences Between Probability and Purposive Sampling

Table 8.1 presents comparisons between probability and purposive sampling strategies. There are a couple of similarities between purposive and

Table 8.1   Comparisons Between Purposive and Probability Sampling Techniques

Dimension of Contrast	Purposive Sampling	Probability Sampling
Other names	Purposeful sampling Nonprobability sampling Qualitative sampling	Scientific sampling Random sampling Quantitative sampling
Overall purpose of sampling	Designed to generate a sample that will address research questions	Designed to generate a sample that will address research questions
Issue of generalizability	Sometimes seeks a form of generalizability (transferability)	Seeks a form of generalizability (external validity)
Rationale for selecting cases/units	To address specific purposes related to research questions The researcher selects cases she or he can learn the most from	Representativeness The researcher selects cases that are collectively representative of the population
Sample size	Typically small (usually 30 cases or less)	Large enough to establish representativeness (usually at least 50 units)
Depth/breadth of information per case/unit	Focus on depth of information generated by the cases	Focus on breadth of information generated by the sampling units
When the sample is selected	Before the study begins, during the study, or both	Before the study begins
How selection is made	Utilizes expert judgment	Often based on application of mathematical formulas
Sampling frame	Informal sampling frame somewhat larger than sample	Formal sampling frame typically much larger than sample
Form of data generated	Focus on narrative data Numeric data can also be generated	Focus on numeric data Narrative data can also be generated

probability sampling: They both are designed to provide a sample that will answer the research questions under investigation, and they both are concerned with issues of generalizability to an external context or population (i.e., transferability or external validity).

On the other hand, the remainder of Table 8.1 presents a series of dichoto-mous differences between the characteristics of purposive and probability sam-pling. For example, a purposive sample is typically designed to pick a small number of cases that will yield the most information about a particular phe-nomenon, whereas a probability sample is planned to select a large number of cases that are collectively representative of the population of interest. There is a classic methodological trade-off involved in the sample size difference between the two techniques: Purposive sampling leads to greater depth of information from a smaller number of carefully selected cases, whereas prob-ability sampling leads to greater breadth of information from a larger number of units selected to be representative of the population (e.g., Patton, 2002).

Another basic difference between the two types of sampling concerns the use of sampling frames, which were defined earlier in this article. As Miles and Huberman (1994) noted, "Just thinking in sampling-frame terms is good for your study's health" (p. 33). Probability sampling frames are usu-ally formally laid out and represent a distribution with a large number of observations. Purposive sampling frames, on the other hand, are typically informal ones based on the expert judgment of the researcher or some avail-able resource identified by the researcher. In purposive sampling, a sampling frame is "a resource from which you can select your smaller sample" (Mason, 2002, p. 140). (See Table 8.1 for more differences between proba-bility and purposive sampling.)

The Purposive-Mixed-Probability Sampling Continuum

The dichotomy between probability and purposive becomes a continuum when MM sampling is added as a third type of sampling strategy technique. Many of the dichotomies presented in Table 8.1 are better understood as continua with purposive sampling techniques on one end, MM sampling strategies in the middle, and probability sampling techniques on the other end. The "Purposive-Mixed-Probability Sampling Continuum" in Figure 8.3 illustrates this continuum.

Characteristics of Mixed Methods Sampling Strategies

Table 8.2 presents the characteristics of MM sampling strategies, which are combinations of (or intermediate points between) the probability and purposive sampling positions. The information from Table 8.2 could be inserted into Table 8.1 between the columns describing purposive and prob-ability sampling, but we have chosen to present it separately here so that we can focus on the particular characteristics of MM sampling.

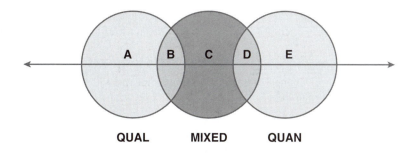

QUAL   **MIXED**   **QUAN**

Figure 8.3   Purposive-Mixed-Probability Sampling Continuum

SOURCE: Teddlie (2005).

NOTE: Zone A consists of totally qualitative (QUAL) research with purposive sampling, whereas Zone E consists of totally quantitative (QUAN) research with probability sampling. Zone B represents primarily QUAL research, with some QUAN components. Zone D represents primarily QUAN research, with some QUAL components. Zone C represents totally integrated mixed methods (MM) research and sampling. The arrow represents the purposive-mixed-probability sampling continuum. Movement toward the middle of the continuum indicates a greater integration of research methods and sampling. Movement away from the center (and toward either end) indicates that research methods and sampling (QUAN and QUAL) are more separated or distinct.

MM sampling strategies may employ all the probability and purposive techniques discussed earlier in this article. Indeed, the researcher's ability to creatively combine these techniques in answering a study's questions is one of the defining characteristics of MM research.[4]

The strand of a research design is an important construct that we use when describing MM sampling procedures. This term was defined in Tashakkori and Teddlie (2003b) as a phase of a study that includes three stages: the conceptualization stage, the experiential stage (methodological/analytical), and the inferential stage. These strands are typically either QUAN or QUAL, although transformation from one type to another can occur during the course of a study. A QUAL strand of a research study is a strand that is QUAL in all three stages, whereas a QUAN strand of a research study is a strand that is QUAN in all three stages.

The MM researcher sometimes chooses procedures that focus on generating representative samples, especially when addressing a QUAN strand of a study. On the other hand, when addressing a QUAL strand of a study, the MM researcher typically utilizes sampling techniques that yield information rich cases. Combining the two orientations allows the MM researcher to generate complementary databases that include information that has both depth and breadth regarding the phenomenon under study.

Table 8.2   Characteristics of Mixed Methods Sampling Strategies

Dimension of Contrast	*Mixed Methods Sampling*
Overall purpose of sampling	Designed to generate a sample that will address research questions.
Issue of generalizability	For some strands of a research design, there is a focus on external validity issues. For other strands, the focus is on transferability issues.
Number of techniques	All those employed by both probability and purposive sampling.
Rationale for selecting cases/units	For some strands of a research design, there is a focus on representativeness. For other strands, the focus is on seeking out information rich cases.
Sample size	There are multiple samples in the study. Samples vary in size dependent on the research strand and question from a small number of cases to a large number of units of analysis.
Depth/breadth of information per case/unit	Focus on both depth and breadth of information across the research strands.
When the sample is selected	Most sampling decisions are made before the study starts, but QUAL-oriented questions may lead to the emergence of other samples during the study.
How selection is made	There is a focus on expert judgment across the sampling decisions, especially because they interrelate with one another. Some QUAN-oriented strands may require application of mathematical sampling formulae.
Sampling frame	Both formal and informal frames are used.
Form of data generated	Both numeric and narrative data are typically generated. Occasionally, mixed methods sampling strategies may yield only narrative or only numeric data.

NOTE: QUAL qualitative; QUAN quantitative

There are typically multiple samples in an MM study, and these samples may vary in size (dependent on the research strand and question) from a small number of cases to a large number of units. Using an educational example, one might purposively select four schools for a study, then give surveys to all 100 teachers in those schools, then conduct six focus groups of students, followed by interviewing 60 randomly selected students.

Both numeric and narrative data are typically generated from MM samples, but occasionally MM sampling strategies may yield only narrative or only numeric data. Hence, it is important to present a brief discussion of the relationship between sampling techniques and the generation of different types of data.

Table 8.3 presents a theoretical matrix that crosses type of sampling technique (probability, purposive, mixed) by type of data generated by the study (QUAN only, QUAL only, mixed).[5] This 3 × 3 matrix illustrates that certain types of sampling techniques are theoretically more frequently associated with certain types of data: probability samples with QUAN data (Cell 1), purposive samples with QUAL data (Cell 5), and mixed samples with mixed data (Cell 9). The diagonal cells (1, 5, and 9) represent the most frequently occurring combination of sampling techniques and types of data generated. Despite these general tendencies, there are other situations where sampling techniques occasionally (Cells 3, 6, 7, and 8) or rarely (Cells 2 and 4) are associated with studies that generate different types of data.

The Representativeness/Saturation Trade-Off

Researchers often have to make sampling decisions based on available resources (e.g., time, money). Researchers conducting MM research sometimes make a compromise between the requirements of the QUAN and

Table 8.3   Theoretical Matrix Crossing Type of Sampling Technique by Type of Data Generated

Type of Sampling Technique	Generation of Quantitative Data Only	Generation of Qualitative Data Only	Generation of Both Qualitative and Quantitative Data
Probability sampling techniques	Happens often (Cell 1)	Happens rarely (Cell 2)	Happens occasionally (Cell 3)
Purposive sampling techniques	Happens rarely (Cell 4)	Happens often (Cell 5)	Happens occasionally (Cell 6)
Mixed methods sampling strategies	Happens occasionally (Cell 7)	Happens occasionally (Cell 8)	Happens often (Cell 9)

SOURCE: Kemper, Stringfield, and Teddlie (2003, p. 285).

QUAL samples in their study, which we call the representativeness/saturation trade-off. This trade-off means that the more emphasis that is placed on the representativeness of the QUAN sample, the less emphasis there is that can be placed on the saturation of the QUAL sample, and vice versa.

As noted earlier in this article, the aim of sampling in QUAN research is to achieve representativeness. That is, the researcher wants the sample to reflect the characteristics of the population of interest, and typically this requires a sample of a certain size relative to the population (e.g., Wunsch, 1986).

An important sample size issue in QUAL research involves saturation of information (e.g., Glaser & Strauss, 1967; Strauss & Corbin, 1998).[6] For example, in focus group studies the new information gained from conducting another session typically decreases as more sessions are held. Krueger and Casey (2000) expressed this guideline as follows:

> The rule of thumb is, plan three or four focus groups with any one type of participant. Once you have conducted these, determine if you have reached saturation. *Saturation* is a term used to describe the point when you have heard the range of ideas and aren't getting new information. If you were still getting new information after three or four groups, you would conduct more groups. (p. 26)

Figure 8.4 presents an illustration of this representativeness/saturation trade-off. In this example, a student conducting her dissertation research with limited resources had to compromise between the requirements of (a) the representatives of her survey sample and (b) the saturation of information gained from her interview study.

Types of Mixed Methods Sampling Strategies

We now turn our attention to descriptions of different types of MM sampling strategies with examples. We have defined MM sampling as involving the selection of units of analysis for a MM study through both probability and purposive sampling strategies. There is not a large literature on MM sampling strategies per se at this time, so we reviewed the scant literature devoted to the topic (e.g., Collins et al., 2006;[7] Kemper et al., 2003) and then searched for additional examples throughout the social and behavioral sciences. This literature search was often frustrating due to the lack of details presented by many authors with regard to sample selection.

There is no widely accepted typology of MM sampling strategies. In generating the provisional typology for this article, we faced the general issue of nomenclature in MM research (e.g., Teddlie & Tashakkori, 2003). One of

Aaron (2005) was interested in studying the leadership characteristics of the directors of programs in radiologic technology. She had both quantitatively and qualitatively oriented research questions. The QUAN questions were answered using an online survey administered to all radiologic program directors. The QUAL questions were answered using a telephone interview with a small sample of directors whose responses to the online survey indicated that they differed on two important dimensions [type of program administered (baccalaureate, associate, certificate) and type of leadership style (transformational, transactional)], resulting in six cells. Aaron wanted the survey study to have a representative sample and the interview study to result in "saturated" QUAL data.

Of the 590 program directors that were sent surveys, 284 responded for a 48% response rate. Extrapolating from the samples and population sizes (Wunsch, 1986), it appears that Aaron could be confident that her sample reflected the population within plus or minus 5%.

There were no clearly established standards for how large the interview sample should be to generate trustworthy results. Aaron selected 12 program directors to be interviewees based on her intuitions, plus the expert advice of her dissertation committee. This number also allowed her to select a stratified purposive sample (see description later in this chapter) in which program type and leadership style were the strata. She selected two interviewees for each of the six cells, resulting in 12 program directors and then (undeterred by superstition) selected a 13th interviewee whom she felt was a particularly information rich case (extreme or deviant case sampling).

If Aaron had attempted to increase the sample size of her survey data to reflect the population within plus or minus 1%, she would have had to send out at least one more round of surveys to all who had not already participated, thereby decreasing the time she had left to select and interact with the participants in the interview study. On the other hand, if she had increased the sample size of the interview study to 24, she would have had to reduce the amount of time and resources that she invested in the survey study. Her sampling choices appeared to meet the requirements for representativeness of QUAN sources and saturation of QUAL sources.

Figure 8.4   Example of the Representativeness/Saturation Rule

the major decisions that mixed methodologists have to make concerning nomenclature is whether to

- utilize a bilingual nomenclature that employs both the QUAL and the QUAN terms for basic issues such as research designs, validity and trustworthiness, sampling, and so forth;
- create a new language for mixed methodology that gives a common name for the existing sets of QUAL and QUAN terms; or
- combine the first two options by presenting new MM terms that are integrated with well-known QUAL/QUAN terms in the definition of the overall sampling strategy.

Sampling in the social and behavioral sciences has so many well-defined and specified QUAL and QUAN techniques, with commonly understood names, that it would be foolhardy to try to develop a new terminology. On the other hand, the literature indicates that mixed methodologists have combined probability and purposive sampling techniques in certain unique prescribed manners to meet the specification of popular MM designs (e.g., concurrent, sequential designs). In such cases, it seems reasonable to overlay the probability and purposive sampling terms with MM metaterms that encompass the totality of the sampling techniques used in the research projects.

The following is our provisional typology of MM sampling strategies:

- basic MM sampling strategies,
- sequential MM sampling,
- concurrent MM sampling,
- multilevel MM sampling, and
- sampling using multiple MM sampling strategies.

The "backgrounds" of the techniques presented in our typology are interesting. The basic MM sampling strategies discussed in the following section (i.e., stratified purposive sampling, purposive random sampling) are typically discussed as types of purposive sampling techniques (e.g., Patton, 2002), yet by definition they also include a component of probability sampling (stratified, random). These basic MM techniques may be used to generate narrative data only in QUAL oriented research (Cell 8 in Table 8.3) or to generate MM data (Cell 9 in Table 8.3).

Sequential and concurrent MM sampling follow from the well-known design types described by several authors (e.g., Creswell, Plano Clark, Gutmann, & Hanson, 2003; Johnson & Onwuegbuzie, 2004). Sequential MM sampling involves the selection of units of analysis for an MM study through the sequential use of probability and purposive sampling strategies (QUAN-QUAL), or vice versa (QUAL-QUAN). Sequential QUAN-QUAL sampling is the most common technique that we have encountered in our exploration of the MM literature, as described by Kemper et al. (2003):

> In sequential mixed models studies, information from the first sample (typically derived from a probability sampling procedure) is often required to draw the second sample (typically derived from a purposive sampling procedure). (p. 284)

Detailed examples of concurrent MM sampling are more difficult to find in the existing literature, at least from our review of it. Concurrent MM sampling involves the selection of units of analysis for an MM study through the simultaneous use of both probability and purposive sampling. One type of sampling procedure does not set the stage for the other in concurrent MM sampling studies; instead, both probability and purposive sampling procedures are used at the same time.

Multilevel MM sampling is a general sampling strategy in which probability and purposive sampling techniques are used at different levels of the study (Tashakkori & Teddlie, 2003a, p. 712).[8] This sampling strategy is common in contexts or settings in which different units of analysis are "nested" within one another, such as schools, hospitals, and various types of bureaucracies.

Basic Mixed Methods Sampling Strategies

One well-known basic MM sampling strategy is stratified purposive sampling (quota sampling). The stratified nature of this sampling procedure is characteristic of probability sampling, whereas the small number of cases typically generated through it is characteristic of purposive sampling. In this technique, the researcher first divides the group of interest into strata (e.g., above average, average, below average students) and then selects a small number of cases to study intensively within each strata based on purposive sampling techniques. This allows the researcher to discover and describe in detail characteristics that are similar or different across the strata or subgroups. Patton (2002) described this technique as selecting "samples within samples."

An example of stratified purposive sampling comes from Kemper and Teddlie (2000), who in one phase of a multiphase study generated six strata based on two dimensions (three levels of community type crossed by two levels of implementation of innovation). Their final sample had only six schools in it (one purposively selected school per stratum): one "typical" urban, one "typical" suburban, one "typical" rural, one "better" urban, one "better" suburban, and one "better" rural. This sampling scheme allowed the researchers to discuss the differences between "typical" and "better" schools at program implementation across a variety of community types. What differentiated a pair of schools in one strata or context (e.g., urban) could be quite different from what differentiated a pair of schools in another (e.g., rural).

Purposive random sampling involves taking a random sample of a small number of units from a much larger target population (Kemper et al., 2003). Kalafat and Illback (1999) presented an example of purposive random sampling in their evaluation of a large statewide program that used a school-based family support system to enhance the educational experiences of at-risk students. There were almost 600 statewide sites in this program, and a statistically valid sample would have required in-depth descriptions of more than 200 cases (Wunsch, 1986), which was well beyond the resources allocated to the evaluation. In an early stage of the study before the intervention began, the researchers utilized a purposive random sampling approach to select 12 cases from the overall target population. The researchers then closely followed these cases throughout the life of the project. This purposive random sample of a small number of cases from a much larger target population added credibility to the evaluation by generating QUAL, process-oriented results to complement the large-scale QUAN-oriented research that also took place.

Sequential Mixed Methods Sampling

There are examples of QUAN-QUAL and QUAL-QUAN MM sampling procedures throughout the social and behavioral sciences. Typically, the methodology and results from the first strand inform the methodology employed in the second strand.[9] In our examination of the literature, we found more examples of QUAN-QUAL studies in which the methodology and/or results from the QUAN strand influenced the methodology subsequently employed in the QUAL strand. In many of these cases, the final sample used in the QUAN strand was then used as the sampling frame for the subsequent QUAL strand. In these studies, the QUAL strand used a subsample of the QUAN sample.

One example of QUAN-QUAL mixed methods sampling comes from the work of Hancock, Calnan, and Manley (1999) in a study of perceptions and experiences of residents concerning dental service in the United Kingdom. In the QUAN portion of the study, the researchers conducted a postal survey that involved both cluster and random sampling: (a) The researchers selected 13 wards out of 365 in a county in southern England using cluster sampling, and (b) they randomly selected 1 out of every 28 residents in those wards resulting in an accessible population of 2,747 individuals, from which they received 1,506 responses (55%). The researchers could be confident that their sample reflected the accessible population within plus or minus 5% (Wunsch, 1986).

The questionnaires included five items measuring satisfaction with dental care (DentSat scores). The researchers next selected their sample for the QUAL strand of the study using intensity and homogeneous sampling: (a) 20 individuals were selected who had high DentSat scores through intensity sampling, (b) 20 individuals were selected who had low DentSat scores through intensity sampling, and (c) 10 individuals were selected who had not received dental care in the past 5 years, but also who did not have full dentures, using homogeneous sampling. In this study, the information generated through the QUAN strand was necessary to select participants with particular characteristics for the QUAL strand.

An example of a QUAL-QUAN sampling procedure comes from the work of Nieto, Mendez, and Carrasquilla (1999) in a study of malaria control in Colombia. The study was conducted in the area of Colombia where the incidence of the disease is the highest. In the QUAL strand of the study, the research team asked leaders from five urban districts to select individuals for participation in focus groups. The focus groups were formed using the following criteria: (a) The participants should belong to one of the local community organizations; (b) they should represent different geographical and age groups; (c) they should recognize the community's leadership and be fully committed to the community; and (d) the groups should be as homogeneous as possible with regard to educational level and socioeconomic and cultural status, which involved face-to-face interviews.

The five focus groups met for three sessions each and discussed a wide range of issues related to health problems in general and malaria in particular. The groups ranged in size from 15 to 18 members, and subgroups were formed during the sessions to encourage greater participation in the process. The focus group results were then used by the research team to design the QUAN survey, which was subsequently given to a large sample of households. The research team used stratified random sampling, with three geographical zones constituting the strata. The total sample for the QUAN strand was 1,380 households, each of which was visited by a member of the researcher team.

The QUAL and QUAN data gathered through the overall MM sampling strategy was very comparable in terms of the participants' knowledge of symptoms, perceptions of the causes of malaria transmission, and prevention practices. The QUAN strand of this study could not have been conducted without the information initially gleaned from the QUAL strand.

Concurrent Mixed Methods Sampling

We analyzed numerous MM articles while writing this article, but the lack of details regarding sampling in many of them precluded their inclusion in this article. In particular, very few articles that we analyzed included a concurrent MM design with an explicit discussion of both the purposive and probability sampling techniques that were used to generate it. Concurrent MM designs allow researchers to triangulate the results from the separate QUAN and QUAL components of their research, thereby allowing them to "confirm, cross-validate, or corroborate findings within a singe study" (Creswell et al., 2003, p. 229).

Nevertheless, we were successful in locating a few articles that enhanced our understanding of how researchers actually combine probability and purposive sampling in their concurrent MM studies. We have delineated two basic overall concurrent MM sampling procedures, but we are certain that there are others. These two basic procedures are as follows:

1. Concurrent MM sampling in which probability sampling techniques are used to generate data for the QUAN strand and purposive sampling techniques are used to generate data for the QUAL strand. *These sampling procedures occur independently.*

2. Concurrent MM sampling utilizing *a single sample generated through the joint use of probability and purposive techniques* to generate data for both the QUAN and QUAL strands of a MM study. This occurs, for example, when a sample of participants, selected through the joint application of probability and purposive techniques, responds to a MM survey that contains both closed-ended and open-ended questions.

Lasserre-Cortez (2006) presented a study that is an example of the first type of concurrent MM sampling procedure in which a probability sample addresses the QUAN strand and a purposive sample addresses the QUAL strand independently. The goals of the Lasserre-Cortez study were twofold:

- She wanted to test some QUAN research hypotheses regarding the differences in the characteristic of teachers and schools participating in professional action research collaboratives (PARCs) as opposed to matched control schools, and
- she wanted to answer QUAL research questions about the manner in which school climate affects teacher effectiveness in PARC schools.

Lasserre-Cortez (2006) drew two different samples, a probability sample to answer the QUAN research hypotheses and a purposive sample to answer the QUAL research questions. The probability sample involved a multiple cluster sample of schools participating in PARC programs and a set of control schools, which were matched to the PARC schools with regard to socioeconomic status of students and community type. A total of 165 schools (approximately half being PARC schools and half being control schools) were selected, and three teachers were then randomly selected within each school to complete school climate surveys.

The purposive sample involved 8 schools (4 PARC schools matched with 4 control schools) from the larger, 165-school sample. These 8 schools were chosen using maximum variation sampling, a purposive technique "that documents diverse variations and identifies common patterns" (Miles & Huberman, 1994, p. 28). The two selection variables were schoolwide achievement on a state test and community type (urban, rural). This purposive sampling process resulted in four types of schools: urban-high achievement, urban-low achievement, rural-high achievement, and rural-low achievement.

Lasserre-Cortez (2006) used two very different sampling procedures (one probability, one purposive) to separately answer her QUAN hypotheses and QUAL questions. The only point of commonality between the two samples was that the purposively drawn sample was a subset of the probability drawn sample. The data were collected concurrently and triangulated in the final phases of the data analysis.

Parasnis, Samar, and Fischer (2005) presented a study that is an example of the second type of concurrent MM sampling procedure: the single sample servicing the requirements of both the QUAL and QUAN strands. Their study was conducted on a college campus where there were a relatively large number of deaf students (around 1,200). Selected students were sent surveys that included both closed-ended and open-ended items; therefore, data for the QUAN and QUAL strands were gathered simultaneously. The analysis of data from each strand informed the analysis of the other.

The MM sampling procedure included both purposive and probability sampling techniques. First, all the individuals in the overall sample were deaf college students, which is an example of homogeneous sampling. The research team had separate sampling procedures for selecting racial/ethnic minority deaf students and for selecting Caucasian deaf students. There were a relatively large number of Caucasian deaf students on the campus, and a randomly selected number of them were sent surveys through regular mail and e-mail. Because there were a much smaller number of racial/ethnic minority deaf students, the purposive sampling technique known as complete collection (criterion sampling) was used. In this technique, all members of a population of interest are selected who meet some special criterion, in this case being a deaf racial/ethnic minority student on a certain college campus.

Altogether, the research team distributed 500 surveys and received a total of 189 responses, 32 of which were eliminated because they were foreign students. Of the remaining 157 respondents, 81 were from racial/ethnic minority groups (African Americans, Asians, Hispanics), and 76 were Caucasians. The combination of purposive (complete collection) and probability (random) sampling techniques in this concurrent MM study yielded a sample that allowed interesting comparisons between the two racial subgroups on a variety of issues, such as their perception of the social psychological climate on campus and the availability of role models.

Multilevel Mixed Methods Sampling

Multilevel MM sampling strategies are very common in research examining organizations in which different units of analysis are "nested within one another." In studies of these nested organizations, researchers are often interested in answering questions related to two or more levels or units of analysis.

Multilevel MM sampling from K–12 educational settings often involve the following five levels: state school systems, school districts, schools, teachers or classrooms, and students. Figure 8.5 presents an illustration of the structure of the sampling decisions required in studies conducted in K–12 settings. The resultant overall sampling strategy quite often requires multiple sampling techniques, each of which is employed to address one of more of the research questions.

Many educational research studies focus on the school and teacher levels because those are the levels that most directly impact students' learning (e.g., Reynolds & Teddlie, 2000; Rosenshine & Stevens, 1986). Figure 8.6 contains an example of a school/teacher effectiveness study that involved a multilevel

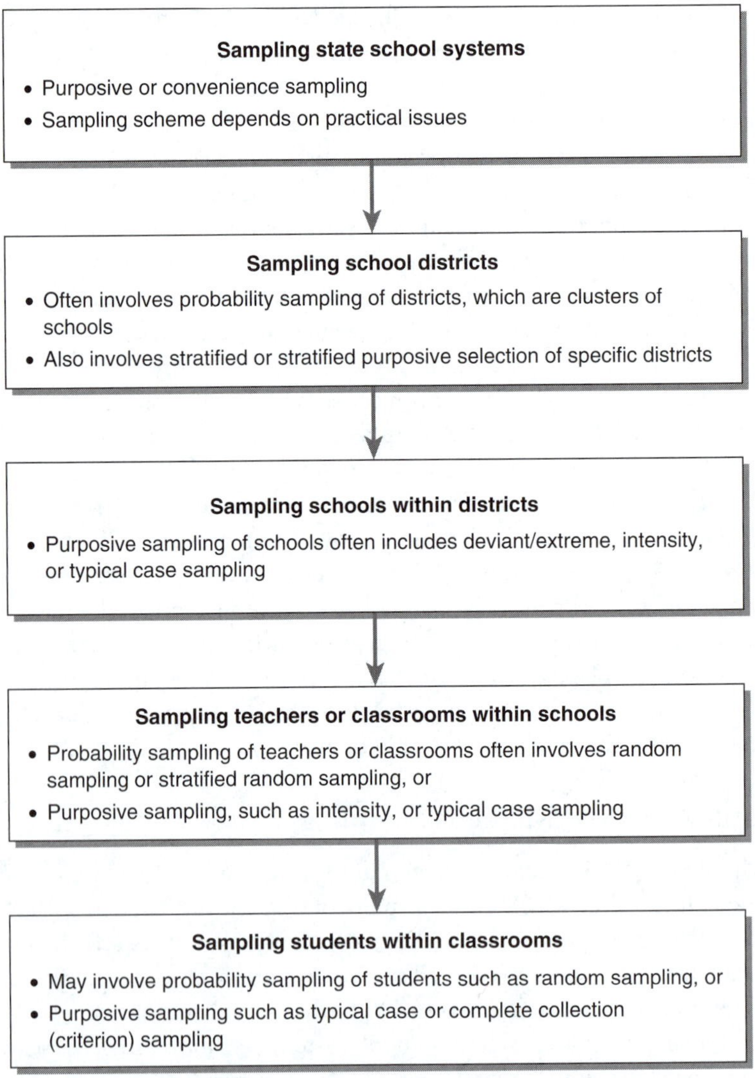

Sampling state school systems

- Purposive or convenience sampling
- Sampling scheme depends on practical issues

Sampling school districts

- Often involves probability sampling of districts, which are clusters of schools
- Also involves stratified or stratified purposive selection of specific districts

Sampling schools within districts

- Purposive sampling of schools often includes deviant/extreme, intensity, or typical case sampling

Sampling teachers or classrooms within schools

- Probability sampling of teachers or classrooms often involves random sampling or stratified random sampling, or
- Purposive sampling, such as intensity, or typical case sampling

Sampling students within classrooms

- May involve probability sampling of students such as random sampling, or
- Purposive sampling such as typical case or complete collection (criterion) sampling

Figure 8.5   Illustration of Multilevel Mixed Methods Sampling in K–12 Educational Settings

MM sampling strategy, with purposive sampling at the school level and probability sampling at the classroom level. Altogether, this example involves eight sampling techniques at five levels.

Teddlie and Stringfield (1993) described the following five levels of sampling in two phases of the Louisiana School Effectiveness Study:

1. Twelve school systems were selected based on maximum variation sampling so that a wide range of district conditions were included. An additional school district was included because of pressures to include it from a stakeholder group, thereby introducing sampling politically important cases. A district is a cluster of schools, and cluster sampling is a probability technique.

2. Pairs of school were selected within districts. Each pair of schools included one school that was more effective and one that was less effective, based on their students' scores on standardized tests. Intensity sampling was used in selecting these pairs of more effective or less effective schools, such that the schools were above average or below average, but not extremely so. The schools in each pair were matched on other important dimensions. Among the potential pairs of schools, three pairs were selected to be from rural areas, three from suburban areas, and three from urban areas. This is an example of stratified purposive sampling.

3. The third grade at each school was selected for closer examination. The selection procedure for grade level was homogeneous sampling, used to reduce variation across schools and to simplify data analyses. Other grade levels were also used to gather the classroom observation data, but the student and parental level data were gathered at the third grade level.

4. Classrooms for observation were selected using stratified random sampling such that all grades were selected and classes were randomly selected within grade level.

5. Student test and attitudinal data and parent attitudinal data were collected at the third grade only, and involved criterion or complete collection of information on all third graders and their parents. Of course there was some missing data, but this was kept to a minimum by administering the student tests and questionnaires during regularly scheduled class periods.

Figure 8.6   An Example of "Nested" Mixed Methods Sampling Strategies: The Louisiana School Effectiveness Study, Phases III–V

A Final Note on Mixed Methods Sampling Strategies

This section of the article has presented a provisional typology of MM sampling strategies, based on our review of studies using MM sampling throughout the social and behavioral sciences. This typology is, in fact, a simplified version of the range of MM sampling strategies that actually exist.

For instance, concurrent and sequential MM sampling procedures are based on design types, and those design types are based on strands (QUAL and QUAN). These strands as described by Tashakkori and Teddlie (2003b) did not take into consideration multiple units of analysis because that would have further complicated the already complex design typology that they presented. The

Methods-Strands Matrix presented by Tashakori and Teddlie (2003b) implicitly limited each QUAN or QUAL research strand to one level of analysis.

Multilevel MM sampling, on the other hand, is based on multiple levels of analysis, not strands, and explicitly indicates that there is more than one unit of analysis per strand. A logical question arises: How are multilevel MM sampling designs combined with concurrent and sequential MM designs? What happens when researchers combine sequential MM sampling with multilevel MM sampling or combine concurrent MM sampling with multilevel MM sampling? This type of complex sampling involves combinations of multiple strands of a research study with multiple levels of sampling within strands.

The Louisiana School Effectiveness Study described in Figure 8.6 actually included two concurrent strands (one QUAL, one QUAN) along with the following two major research questions of the study:

- Would the eight matched pairs of more effective and less effective schools remain differentially effective over time, or would some schools increase or decrease in effectiveness status over time? The major QUAN data used to answer this question were achievement scores and indices of student socioeconomic status.
- What are the processes whereby schools remained the same or changed over time with regard to how well they educated their students? The major QUAL data used to answer this question were classroom- and school-level observations and interviews with students, teachers, and principals.

Both the QUAN and QUAL strands of the Louisiana School Effectiveness Study used the same multilevel MM sampling strategy presented in Figure 8.6 (same school systems, same pairs of schools, same grade level for closer examination, same classrooms for observations) because the QUAL and QUAN questions were so tightly linked. Other research situations with more diverse QUAL and QUAN strands will require multilevel MM strategies that are quite different from one another.

Guidelines for Mixed Methods Sampling

The following section borrows from guidelines presented by other authors (e.g., Curtis, Gesler, Smith, & Washburn, 2000; Kemper et al., 2003; Miles & Huberman, 1994), plus consideration of important issues discussed in this article. These are general guidelines that researchers should consider when putting together a sampling procedure for a MM study.

1. *The sampling strategy should stem logically from the research questions and hypotheses that are being addressed by the study.* In most MM studies, this will involve both probability and purposive techniques, but there are some cases where either probability sampling (see Cell 3 in Table 8.3) or purposive sampling (see Cell 6 in Table 8.3) alone is appropriate. The researcher typically asks two basic questions:

  a. Will the purposive sampling strategy lead to the collection of data focused on the QUAL questions under investigation?

  b. Will the probability sampling strategy lead to the collection of data focused on the QUAN hypotheses or questions under investigation?

2. *Researchers should be sure to follow the assumptions of the probability and purposive sampling techniques that they are using.* In several of the MM studies that we have analyzed, the researchers started out with established probability and purposive techniques but violated the assumptions of one or the other during the course of the study. This is particularly the case with the probability sampling component because failure to recruit properly or attrition can lead to a convenience sample.

3. *The sampling strategy should generate thorough QUAL and QUAN databases on the research questions under study.* This guideline relates to the representativeness/saturation trade-off discussed earlier in this article.

  a. Is the overall sampling strategy sufficiently focused to allow researchers to actually gather the data necessary to answer the research questions?

  b. Will the purposive sampling techniques utilized in the study generate "saturated" information on the QUAL research questions?

  c. Will the probability sampling techniques utilized in the study generate a representative sample related to the QUAN research questions?

4. *The sampling strategy should allow the researchers to draw clear inferences from both the QUAL and QUAN data.* This guideline refers to the researchers' ability to "get it right" with regard to explaining what happened in their study or what they learned from their study. Sampling decisions are important here because if you do not have a good sample of the phenomena of interest, then your inferences related to the research questions will lack clarity or be inadequate.

  a. From the QUAL design perspective, this guideline refers to the credibility of the inferences.

  b. From the QUAN design perspective, this guideline refers to the internal validity of the inferences.

5. *The sampling strategy must be ethical.* There are very important ethical considerations in MM research. Specific issues related to sampling

include informed consent to participate in the study, whether participants can actually give informed consent to participate, the potential benefits and risks to the participants, the need for absolute assurances that any promised confidentiality can be maintained, and the right to withdraw from the study at any time.

6. *The sampling strategy should be feasible and efficient.* Kemper et al. (2003) noted that "sampling issues are inherently practical" (p. 273).

    a. The feasibility or practicality of a MM sampling strategy involves several issues. Do the researchers have the time and money to complete the sampling strategy? Do the researchers actually have access to all of the data sources? Is the selected sampling strategy congruent with the abilities of the researchers?

    b. The efficiency of a MM sampling strategy involves techniques for focusing the finite energies of the research team on the central research questions.

7. *The sampling strategy should allow the research team to transfer or generalize the conclusions of their study to other individuals, groups, contexts, and so forth if that is a purpose of the MM research.* This guideline refers to the external validity and transferability issues that were discussed throughout this article. It should be noted that not all MM studies are intended to be transferred or generalized.

    a. From the QUAL design perspective, this guideline indicates that the researchers should know a lot of information about the characteristics of "*both* sending and receiving contexts" (Lincoln & Guba, 1985, p. 297). Thus, when purposive sampling decisions are made, the researchers should know the characteristics of the study sample (sending context) and the characteristics of other contexts to which they want to transfer their study results (receiving contexts).

    b. From the QUAN design perspective, this guideline indicates that the researchers would want to increase the representativeness of the study sample as much as possible. Techniques to accomplish this include increasing sample size, using methods to ensure that that all subjects have an equal probability of participating, and so forth.

8. *The researchers should describe their sampling strategy in enough detail so that other investigators can understand what they actually did and perhaps use those strategies (or variants thereof) in future studies.* The literature related to MM sampling strategies is in its infancy, and more detailed descriptions of those strategies in the literature will help guide other investigators in drawing complex samples

Creativity and flexibility in the practical design of MM sampling schemes are crucial to the success of the research study. The success of a MM research project in answering a variety of questions is a function, to a large degree, of the combination of sampling strategies that are employed. In conclusion, it is important to remember that "in research, sampling is destiny" (Kemper et al., 2003, p. 275).

Notes

1. There are three general types of units that can be sampled: cases (e.g., individuals, institutions), materials, and other elements in the social situation. The mixed methodologist should consider all three data sources in drawing her sample.

2. External validity refers to the generalizability of results from a quantitative (QUAN) study to other populations, settings, times, and so forth. Transferability refers to the generalizability of results from one specific sending context in a qualitative (QUAL) study to another specific receiving context (e.g., Lincoln & Guba, 1985; Tashakkori & Teddlie, 1998).

3. Stratified sampling may be both a probability sampling technique and a purposeful sampling technique. The use of stratified sampling as a purposive technique is discussed later in this article under the topic of basic mixed methods (MM) sampling strategies (stratified purposeful sampling or quota sampling).

4. Combining QUAN and QUAL techniques often involves collaborative work between experts with different backgrounds (e.g., psychologists and anthropologists). Shulha and Wilson (2003) described examples of such collaborative mixed methods research.

5. We use the term *theoretical* because the matrix is *not* based on empirical research examining the frequency of sampling techniques by type of data generated. Common sense dictates that the diagonal cells (1, 5, and 9) in Table 8.3 represent the most frequently occurring combinations of sampling techniques and types of data generated. The information contained in the other cells is based on informed speculation.

6. Other important factors in determining the QUAL sample size include the generation of a variation of ranges, the creation of comparisons among relevant groups, and representativeness.

7. Collins, Onwuegbuzie, and Jiao (2006) presented their own typology of mixed methods sampling designs. They then analyzed a sample of mixed methods studies from electronic databases and calculated the prevalence rate for the designs in their typology.

8. Multilevel MM sampling is different from concurrent MM sampling, although they can both be used in studies that combine MM sampling strategies. Concurrent MM sampling requires at least two strands and typically focuses on just one level or unit of analysis. On the other hand, multilevel MM sampling may be employed within just one strand of a MM study and requires at least two levels or units of analysis.

9. MM studies may involve more than two strands (e.g., QUAN-QUAL-QUAN), but the discussion in this article is limited to two strands for the sake of simplicity.

References

Aaron, L. S. (2005). *Responsibilities and leadership styles of radiologic technology program directors: Implications for leadership development.* Unpublished doctoral dissertation, Louisiana State University, Baton Rouge.

Collins, K. M. T., Onwuegbuzie, A. J., & Jiao, Q. G. (2006, April). *Prevalence of mixed methods sampling designs in social science research and beyond.* Paper presented at the meeting of the American Educational Research Association, San Francisco.

Creswell, J. W., Plano Clark, V. L., Gutmann, M., & Hanson, W. (2003). Advanced mixed methods research designs. In A. Tashakkori & C. Teddlie (Eds.), *Handbook of mixed methods in social & behavioral research* (pp. 209–240). Thousand Oaks, CA: Sage.

Curtis, S., Gesler, W., Smith, G., & Washburn, S. (2000). Approaches to sampling and case selection in qualitative research: Examples in the geography of health. *Social Science and Medicine, 50*(2), 1001–1014.

Flick, U. (1998). *An introduction to qualitative research.* Thousand Oaks, CA: Sage.

Glaser, B. G., & Strauss, A. L. (1967). *The discovery of grounded theory: Strategies for qualitative research.* Chicago: Aldine.

Hancock, M., Calnan, M., & Manley, G. (1999). Private or NHS dental service care in the United Kingdom? A study of public perceptions and experiences. *Journal of Public Health Medicine, 21*(4), 415–420.

Johnson, R. B., & Onwuegbuzie, A. J. (2004). Mixed methods research: A research paradigm whose time has come. *Educational Researcher, 33*(7), 14–26.

Kalafat, J., & Illback, R. J. (1999). *Evaluation of Kentucky's school based family resource and youth services centers: Part I.* Louisville, KY: REACH of Louisville.

Kemper, E., Stringfield. S., & Teddlie, C. (2003). Mixed methods sampling strategies in social science research. In A. Tashakkori & C. Teddlie (Eds.), *Handbook of mixed methods in social & behavioral research* (pp. 273–296). Thousand Oaks, CA: Sage.

Kemper, E., & Teddlie, C. (2000) Mandated site based management in Texas: Exploring implementation in urban high schools. *Teaching and Change, 7,* 172–200.

Krueger, R. A., & Casey, M. A. (2000). *Focus groups: A practical guide for applied research* (3rd ed.). Thousand Oaks, CA: Sage.

Kuzel, A. J. (1992). Sampling in qualitative inquiry. In B. F. Crabtree & W. L. Miller (Eds.), *Doing qualitative research* (pp. 31–44). Newbury Park, CA: Sage.

Lasserre-Cortez, S. (2006). *A mixed methods examination of professional development through whole faculty study groups.* Unpublished doctoral dissertation, Louisiana State University, Baton Rouge.

LeCompte, M. D., & Preissle, J. (1993). *Ethnography and qualitative design in educational research* (2nd ed.). New York: Academic Press.

Lincoln, Y. S., & Guba, E. G. (1985). *Naturalistic inquiry.* Beverly Hills, CA: Sage.

Mason, J. (2002). *Qualitative researching* (2nd ed.). London: Sage.

Maxwell, J. (1997). Designing a qualitative study. In L. Bickman & D. J. Rog (Eds.) *Handbook of applied social research methods* (pp. 69–100). Thousand Oaks, CA: Sage.

Miles, M., & Huberman, M. (1994). *Qualitative data analysis: An expanded sourcebook* (2nd ed.). Thousand Oaks, CA: Sage.

Nieto, T., Mendez, F., & Carrasquilla, G. (1999). Knowledge, beliefs and practices relevant for malaria control in an endemic urban area of the Colombian Pacific. *Social Science and Medicine, 49*, 601–609.

Parasnis, I., Samar, V. J., & Fischer, S. D. (2005). Deaf college students' attitudes toward racial/ethnic diversity, campus climate, and role models. *American Annals of the Deaf, 150*(1), 47–58.

Patton, M. Q. (2002). *Qualitative research and evaluation methods* (3rd ed.). Thousand Oaks, CA: Sage.

Poorman, P. B. (2002). Perceptions of thriving by women who have experienced abuse or status-related oppression. *Psychology of Women Quarterly, 26*(1), 51–62.

Reynolds, D., & Teddlie, C. (2000). The processes of school effectiveness. In C. Teddlie & D. Reynolds (Eds.), *The international handbook of school effectiveness research* (pp. 134–159). London: Falmer.

Rosenshine, B., & Stevens, R. (1986). Teaching functions. In M. Wittrock (Ed.), *Third handbook of research on teaching*. New York: Macmillan.

Shulha, L., & Wilson, R. (2003). Collaborative mixed methods research. In A. Tashakkori & C. Teddlie (Eds.), *Handbook of mixed methods in social & behavioral research* (pp. 639–670). Thousand Oaks, CA: Sage.

Spradley, J. P. (1979). *The ethnographic interview.* New York: Holt, Rinehart & Winston.

Spradley, J. P. (1980). *Participant observation.* New York: Holt, Rinehart & Winston.

Stake, R. E. (1995). *The art of case study research.* Thousand Oaks, CA: Sage.

Strauss, A., & Corbin, J. (1998). *Basics of qualitative research: Techniques and procedures for developing grounded theory* (2nd ed.). Thousand Oaks, CA: Sage.

Tashakkori, A., and Teddlie, C. (1998). *Mixed methodology: Combining the qualitative and quantitative approaches.* Thousand Oaks, CA: Sage.

Tashakkori, A., & Teddlie, C. (Eds.). (2003a). *Handbook of mixed methods in social & behavioral research.* Thousand Oaks, CA: Sage.

Tashakkori, A., & Teddlie, C. (2003b). The past and future of mixed methods research: From data triangulation to mixed model designs. In A. Tashakkori & C. Teddlie (Eds.), *Handbook of mixed methods in social & behavioral research* (pp. 671–702). Thousand Oaks, CA: Sage.

Teddlie, C. (2005). Methodological issues related to causal studies of leadership: A mixed methods perspective from the USA. *Educational Management Administration & Leadership, 33*(2), 211–217.

Teddlie, C., & Stringfield, S. (1993). *Schools make a difference: Lessons learned from a 10-year study of school effects.* New York: Teachers College Press.

Teddlie, C., & Tashakkori, A. (2003). Major issues and controversies in the use of mixed methods in the social and behavioral sciences. In A. Tashakkori &

C. Teddlie (Eds.), *Handbook of mixed methods in social & behavioral research* (pp. 3–50). Thousand Oaks, CA: Sage.

Ward, M. (1986). *Them children: A study in language learning* (Reprint ed.). Long Grove, IL: Waveland.

Wunsch, D. R. (1986). Survey research: Determining sample size and representative response. *Business Education Forum, 40*(5), 31–34.

Yin, R. K. (2003). *Case study research: Design and methods* (3rd ed.). Thousand Oaks, CA: Sage.

9

Data Analysis Strategies in Mixed Methods Research

Selection: Caracelli, V. J., & Greene, J. C. (1993). Data analysis strategies for mixed-method evaluation designs. *Educational Evaluation and Policy Analysis, 15*(2), 195–207.

Editors' Introduction

In 1989, Greene et al. analyzed 57 mixed methods evaluation studies in terms of their use of mixed methods designs to address five different purposes (see Chapter 5 in this volume). From this analysis they found that only a few of the examined studies meaningfully integrated the qualitative and quantitative data during data analysis. Thus, evaluators Valerie J. Caracelli and Jennifer C. Greene continued their study of mixed methods in their 1993 article by specifically examining the strategies used by program evaluators who successfully integrated their two data sets during the data analysis stage. In this way, the authors brought focused attention to the data analysis stage in conducting mixed methods research.

Caracelli and Greene identify four distinct analytical strategies for integrating quantitative and qualitative data. First, researchers may choose data transformation, where one type of data is converted into the other type so that they can be analyzed together. Second, researchers may develop a typology from the analysis of one type of data and then use that typology to analyze the other type. A third option is to use extreme case analysis by identifying extreme cases in one data set and then examining those cases further with the other data type.

Fourth, researchers may consolidate or merge findings from both data sets to create new variables used in further analyses. Caracelli and Greene advance our understanding of different possible integrative data analysis strategies and provide examples of each from their review of published mixed methods studies.

Discussion Questions and Applications

1. Consider a mixed methods study that integrated the quantitative and qualitative data during analysis such as reported by Idler, Hudson, and Leventhal (Chapter 16 in this volume). Describe the mixed methods data analysis.

2. Do certain analytic strategies seem more appropriate for certain types of mixed methods designs? How might data analysis differ if the overall design is concurrent or sequential?

3. Consider a mixed methods study that you would like to conduct and develop a plan for how you will analyze the data.

Related References That Extend the Topic

For additional discussions about analyzing data in mixed methods research see:

Onwuegbuzie, A. J., & Teddlie, C. (2003). A framework for analyzing data in mixed methods research. In A. Tashakkori & C. Teddlie (Eds.), *Handbook of mixed methods in social and behavioral research* (pp. 351–383). Thousand Oaks, CA: Sage.

Tashakkori, A., & Teddlie, C. (1998). Alternatives to traditional data analytic strategies. In *Mixed methodology: Combining qualitative and quantitative approaches* (pp. 112–136). Thousand Oaks, CA: Sage.

Data Analysis Strategies for Mixed-Method Evaluation Designs

Valerie J. Caracelli
U.S. General Accounting Office

Jennifer C. Greene
Cornell University

Four integrative data analysis strategies for mixed-method evaluation designs are derived from and illustrated by empirical practice: data transformation, typology development, extreme case analysis, and data consolidation/merging. The appropriateness of these strategies for different kinds of mixed-method intents is then discussed. Where appropriate, such integrative strategies are encouraged as ways to realize the full potential of mixed-methodological approaches.

A formal acknowledgment of the increasing practice of using multiple methods in program evaluation appeared in the 1984 *Evaluation Studies Review Annual:*

> The challenge is to mix the best parts of multiple methods to accomplish our evaluation tasks. Thus far there are more calls for the use of multiple methods than actual examples of how this can be accomplished successfully. Nonetheless, this important shift in thinking is a necessary precondition for the development

SOURCE: This article is reprinted from *Educational Evaluation and Policy Analysis*, Vol. 15, Issue 2, pp. 195–207, 1993. Reprinted with permission of the American Educational Research Association.

of new models. Consequently, we anticipate that some very creative multiple method models will begin to appear in the [next] few years. (Connor, Altman, & Jackson, 1984, p. 17)

Since this time, a burgeoning literature has developed around issues pertinent to the use of multiple methods in evaluation and applied research, including triangulation (Mathison, 1988), multiplism (Cook, 1985; Mark & Shotland, 1987; Shadish, Cook, & Houts, 1986; Shotland & Mark, 1987), mixing methods and paradigms (Guba, 1990; Kidder & Fine, 1987; Rossman & Wilson, 1985; Smith & Heshusius, 1986), and mixed-method typologies (Greene & McClintock, 1985; Mark & Shotland, 1987; Maxwell, Bashook, & Sandlow, 1986). Each of these works builds on and extends the classic theoretical literature that underlies interest in multiple research strategies (Campbell & Fiske, 1959; Denzin, 1978; Reichardt & Cook, 1979; Webb, Campbell, Schwartz, & Sechrest, 1966). Only recently, however, has the challenge of developing new models for mixed-method evaluation designs—which fall under the umbrella of multiple methods—been addressed.

Mixed-Method Evaluation Designs in Theory and Practice

Greene, Caracelli, and Graham (1989) reviewed much of the theoretical literature just cited, as well as a purposive sample of 57 mixed-method evaluation studies, in order to begin developing a conceptual framework for mixed-method evaluation designs. In that work, mixed-method designs are defined as including at least one quantitative method (designed to collect numbers) and one qualitative method (designed to collect words), where neither type of method is inherently linked to a particular inquiry paradigm or philosophy.[1] Greene et al. concentrated this conceptual work on clearly differentiating alternative *purposes* for combining qualitative and quantitative methods in program evaluation and on identifying *elements of design choice* related to mixed methodology.[2]

Greene et al. (1989) identified five purposes for mixed-method evaluations, grounded both in the theoretical literature and in evaluation practice as represented by the 57 empirical studies reviewed: triangulation, complementarity, development, initiation, and expansion. In the classic sense, *triangulation* seeks convergence, corroboration, and correspondence of results across the different method types (Campbell & Fiske, 1959; Cook, 1985; Denzin, 1978; Shotland & Mark, 1987; Webb et al., 1966). A *complementarity* purpose is indicated when qualitative and quantitative methods are used to measure overlapping, but distinct facets of the phenomenon under investigation. Results from one method type are intended to enhance, illustrate, or clarify results from the other (Greene & McClintock, 1985; Mark & Shotland, 1987; Rossman & Wilson, 1985). In *development* designs the different method types are used sequentially. The intent, based on the work of Sieber (1973) and Madey (1982), is to use the results of one method to help develop or inform the other method. Development is broadly construed to include sampling and implementation, as well as measurement decisions. Rossman and Wilson (1985) demonstrate that the iterative use of both method types can intentionally seek the discovery of paradox and contradiction. Such *initiation* designs are meant to be provocative through the recasting of questions or results from one method type with questions or results from the contrasting method type. Finally, combining methods for purposes of *expansion* occurs when inquirers extend the breadth and range of inquiry by casting the method types for different inquiry components. In evaluation, quantitative methods frequently play the leading role in assessing program outcomes, while qualitative methods are chosen for the supporting role of examining program processes.

For each of the five purposes a recommended design was also elaborated in terms of seven design elements identified as relevant to mixed methodology. These elements encompass characteristics of methods, the phenomena under investigation, paradigmatic framework, relative status of the different methods, and criteria for implementation.

Greene et al. (1989) further grouped the mixed-method data analysis and interpretation/reporting approaches used in the 57 evaluations reviewed into four categories: (a) no integration, analyses and interpretation of qualitative and quantitative data conducted separately; (b) analyses separate but some integration during interpretation; (c) integration during both analyses and interpretation; and (d) analysis procedures not reported. These findings were crosstabulated by mixed-method purpose.

The results showed that the authors of the majority of empirical studies reviewed either did not report how they conducted their data analyses ($n = 9$) or kept both analysis and interpretation of the two data types separate ($n = 25$). This was especially true for studies that combined methods for the purpose of expansion. When data types were integrated, it was most often at the level of interpretation ($n = 18$) and much more rarely during the analysis process itself ($n = 5$). The paucity of instances of meaningful integration of qualitative and quantitative data at the analysis stage was perplexing given the intentional mixed-method design of these studies.

We believe that a comprehensive conceptual framework for mixed-method evaluations must consider planning for data analysis as a task concomitant with planning the design of a program evaluation. Hence, the present discussion focuses on elaborating the mixed-method analytic strategies used in the handful of evaluations reviewed that did, effectively and at times creatively, integrate quantitative and qualitative data during data analysis, interpretation, and reporting (Hall, Hord, & Griffin, 1980; Louis, 1981; Schermerhorn, Williams, & Dickison, 1982; Talmage & Rasher, 1981). Four major strategies were gleaned from this review: data transformation, typology development, extreme case analysis, and data consolidation/merging. Although these strategies are not new, per se, it is useful to view these analytical techniques in the context of a mixed-method framework. We believe that a closer look at these studies, supplemented by other examples, can contribute to a rudimentary repertoire of promising analytic strategies for mixed-method evaluations. These strategies are defined in Table 9.1 and further elaborated in the ensuing discussion.

Integrative Strategies for Mixed-Method Data Analysis

Data Transformation

One means by which qualitative and quantitative data can be integrated during analysis is to transform one data type into the other to allow for statistical or thematic analysis of both data types together.

Larner, Nagy, and Halpern (1987) used this integrative data analysis strategy in their implementation evaluation study in which different methods were used to assess different aspects of program implementation (an expansion purpose). These investigators studied the Rural Alabama Pregnancy and Infant Heath Program (part of the Ford Foundation's Child Survival/Fair Start initiative) in order to determine which factors most importantly affected a client's level of participation in this home visiting program. A quantitative measure was used by the home visitor to assess the level of a mother's participation with respect to nine central aspects of a home visit; for example, how often does the mother ask questions about the lesson? How often does she share personal problems? In addition, home visitors classified the type of relationship they shared with the client as social worker, teacher, or friend. Interviews with clients were also conducted to assess client demographics and two indicators of client social support.[3]

Qualitative data from the interview were transformed into numeric ratings so that all variables could be included in the study's main analyses investigating which specific client characteristics were related to their level of participation in the program. A stepwise multiple regression was performed,

Table 9.1   Analytical Strategies for the Integration of Qualitative and Quantitative Data

1. Data Transformation—The conversion or transformation of one data type into the other so that both can be analyzed together: • Qualitative data are numerically coded and included with quantitative data in statistical analyses. • Quantitative data are transformed into narrative and included with qualitative data in thematic or pattern analysis. 2. Typology Development—The analysis of one data type yields a typology (or set of substantive categories) that is then used as a framework applied in analyzing the contrasting data type. Examples: • A set of conceptual dimensions resulting from a factor analysis of quantitative data is incorporated into the categorical analysis of qualitative data (i.e., category development and coding). • A respondent or site-level typology resulting from analysis of qualitative data forms a "group" explanatory variable for statistical analyses of quantitative data (e.g., ANOVA, regression analysis) or, as another possibility, is combined with other quantitative explanatory variables for the statistical analysis of qualitative (categorical) data (e.g., logit analysis).	3. Extreme Case Analysis—"Extreme cases" identified from the analysis of one data type and pursued via (additional data collection and) analysis of data of the other type, with the intent of testing and refining the initial explanation for the extreme cases. Examples: • Extreme cases in the form of high residuals from a regression analysis of quantitative data are pursued via (collection and) analysis of qualitative data, the results of which are used to refine the original explanatory model. • Extreme cases identified from constant comparative analysis of qualitative data are further examined via analysis of quantitative data, the results of which are used to refine the original interpretation. 4. Data Consolidation/Merging—The joint review of both data types to create new or consolidated variables or data sets, which can be expressed in either quantitative or qualitative form. These consolidated variables or data sets are the typically used in further analyses: • Qualitative and quantitative data are jointly reviewed and consolidated into numerical codes or narrative for purposes of further analysis.

yielding an overall R^2 of .67. Among the significant predictors, one was the home visitors' perceptions of their role as a friend to the client. From these results, relationship-building became one of the essential components of the home visitor training program.

Thus, in this example, the conjoint analysis of qualitative and quantitative data provided an enriched understanding of factors affecting a client's program participation and served to redirect the home visitor training program to incorporate these significant factors.

Typology Development

In the typology development mixed-method analysis strategy, the analysis of one data type considers the homogeneity within and heterogeneity between subgroupings of data on some dimension of interest, yielding a set of substantive categories or typology. This typology is then incorporated into the analysis of the contrasting data type.

Hall, Hord, and Griffin (1980), using a mixed-method design primarily for development purposes, illustrate the use of this strategy. The authors present results from a 3-year longitudinal study of the implementation of a science curriculum innovation for grades 3–6 in the Jefferson County School District, a large suburban system in Colorado. Both quantitative and qualitative methods were used to determine the factors that influenced teacher change in relation to the new curriculum. The intention was to integrate both types of data at the level of analysis in order to provide "more powerful insights about the change process than either could have produced alone" (p. 3).

The Concerns-Based Adoption Model (Hall, Wallace, & Dossett, 1973) served as a framework for the study. This model assumes that change is carried out by individuals and emphasizes two dimensions that are central to understanding the adoption and implementation of a curriculum innovation: Stages of Concern About the Innovation (SoC) and Levels of Use of the Innovation (LoU). In the curriculum evaluation, existing quantitative measures from this theoretical adoption model were used to classify teachers on these two dimensions. In addition, 41 volumes of ethnographic reports were compiled by a full-time ethnographer located on-site to assess implementation during the first 2 years of the curriculum innovation. District and research staff also contributed observational data and document reviews. Minicase studies were developed from this qualitative data base for nine schools that were representative of the varied phases of implementation across the school district.

The following data analysis strategy was used to achieve integration. A typology of the nine schools was created by placing them in one of three groups based on their SoC profiles. These three groupings represented management-concerned schools, impact-concerned schools, and schools concerned with both management and impact of the innovation. Analysis of the qualitative case study data then concentrated on searching for commonalities within these types of schools, as well as differences among them. Attention was focused on discerning factors (e.g., activities of district and school staff) that affected change among teachers. It was found that the principal's level of support for the innovation and his or her activities as a change facilitator were the main factors influencing the schools' SoC classification.

Thus, the integrated analysis yielded important factors explaining variation in teacher concern for and use of the new science curriculum. Although the primary purpose for using a mixed-method strategy in this evaluation was clearly in line with our definition of development, the actual strategies employed to combine qualitative and quantitative data added hypothesis-generating and initiation components to this evaluation.

A reverse sequence in this integrative analysis strategy can also be used. Patton (1980) discusses the development of emergent typologies from qualitative data. Implementing this procedure, Caracelli (1988) reviewed interview transcripts of adult reentry women in Fordham University's EXCEL program to create a typology of women representing differences in career goal focus. Women with focused career goals and women with unfocused career goals were then contrasted on data derived from quantitative measures, such as GPA, self-esteem, personality variables, and college satisfaction. The comprehensive portraits of these reentry women that resulted from combining qualitative and quantitative data sources through typology development had implications for program planning. The integrated analysis provided evidence that advisory and counseling needs differed for women depending upon their career goal focus.

In an important mixed-method paper, Rossman and Wilson (1985) illustrate a variation of the typology development analytic strategy, appropriate when the mixed-method purpose is triangulation (which they label *corroboration*). As required for this purpose, analyses of the different data types are conducted independently and then compared for convergence at the level of conclusions and interpretations. Rossman and Wilson's examples are drawn from a large-scale, 3-year evaluation of regional educational service agencies (RESAs). A qualitative review of documents indicated that the RESAs could be categorized as primarily oriented toward either assistance or enforcement activities. Quantitative surveys were then used to probe employees of each agency on the extent to which their work activities emphasized assistance and enforcement. Bivariate plots of mean agency scores from the survey data revealed two clusters that matched the qualitative categorization of RESAs into primarily assistance or enforcement roles for promoting educational reform. The quantitative results were therefore used in a triangulation framework to corroborate the qualitative typology.

These examples suggest that the typology development analysis strategy may be appropriately used for a variety of mixed-method purposes and contexts.

Although not illustrated by these examples, one important feature of this strategy is its potential for iteration. A typology could be created from one data type and applied to an analysis of the other data type, the results of which could, in turn, be used to refine and elaborate the typology. This enriched typology could then be reapplied in further analyses of either data type, and so forth, further explicating the initial analyses. Iteration is also a potential feature of the next analysis strategy.

Extreme Case Analysis

A third empirically derived strategy for mixed-method data analysis involves the identification and further analysis of extreme cases. Such cases are identified through analysis of one data type and then further investigated through (additional data collection and) analysis of the other data type. An enhanced understanding of these cases contributes to clarification and refinement of inquiry interpretations.

Rossman and Wilson (1985) also illustrate this analytic strategy from their RESA evaluation, again for the mixed-method purpose of triangulation or corroboration. Data from a survey of local school administrators were used to identify RESAs at both extremes of a continuum of "perceived usefulness." These RESAs were then investigated more intensively through qualitative case studies, the results of which were used to corroborate the survey findings.

In a variation of extreme case analysis, Fry, Chantavanich, and Chantavanich (1981) conducted three mixed-method cross-cultural studies in Thailand. These studies led the authors to espouse the technique of ethnographic residual analysis which, as an integrated analysis strategy, is closely aligned with our identified design purpose of initiation. In the context of cross-cultural educational research, the authors propose the technique in order to obtain "new ideas, insights, hypotheses, and understandings" (p. 153) and "a deeper and better understanding of the complex interrelationships among educational inputs, educational processes, and educational outcomes" (p. 155).

With this approach a school's expected effectiveness is specified by quantitative indicators, such as students' cognitive and noncognitive abilities, values, and attitudes. Then a school's expected effectiveness is compared with its actual effectiveness through multiple regression techniques that incorporate explanatory factors such as the socioeconomic background of students, school financial resources per person, and the teacher-student ratio. Anomalies in terms of schools that have either unusually high or unusually low quality, relative to their educational inputs, are then examined ethnographically to try to ascertain qualitative factors accounting for statistical deviance and unexplained error variance.

Ethnographic investigators, who are blind to the quantitative findings, are sent to these "extreme case" schools to study their educational process. The ethnographic analysis is specifically expected to generate insights that foster the development of new concepts or categories. For example, differences in teaching methods, principal characteristics, or community support for education may be factors important in assessments of school effectiveness. Finally, these ethnographic variables are incorporated back into the regression model in an effort to increase the explanatory power of the model, and thus the depth of conceptual understanding.

As a mixed-method integrated analysis strategy, ethnographic residual analysis has the potential for recasting or elaborating the theory that directs the initial analysis. It can be viewed as a mixed-method counterpart to the use of negative case analysis by participant observers (Kidder, 1981). Both negative case analysis and ethnographic residual analysis systematically search for cases that may provide disconfirming evidence for the hypothesis under investigation, leading to refinements of the hypothesis.

Data Consolidation/Merging

Our final mixed-method analysis strategy, data consolidation or merging, involves the more sophisticated, joint use of both data types to create new or consolidated variables or data sets. These consolidated data types can be expressed in either quantitative or qualitative form, and would be appropriately used in further analysis. As illustrated by the following studies, this data analysis strategy may be especially suitable for mixed-method designs with initiation intents (i.e., the use of mixed methods to uncover fresh insights or new perspectives). The more extensive examples offered for this strategy are intended to underscore its unique reliance on multiple, varied sets of data.

Talmage and Rasher's (1981) approach for merging qualitative and quantitative data at the level of analysis is explicitly linked to our mixed-method purpose of initiation. Their work demonstrated how the integration of both types of data could generate new variables, extending the scope of their data base to address elusive evaluation problems in a school setting. This formative evaluation assessed in 11 urban schools the Model Builders Project (MBP), a 3-year arts-in-the-schools program, and the factors that influenced implementation and program effects.

The authors summarize their dialectic approach to integrating both types of data in terms of a "spiral effect." In the first year of the evaluation, quantitative data were gathered in the form of self-report questionnaires, structured interviews, and structured classroom observations. The quasi-experimental design permitted comparisons among MBP participants, nonparticipants at MBP sites, and two comparison schools on students' perceptions of their classroom learning environment, degree of program implementation, art-related activities, and course evaluations. No program effects were discerned. Nevertheless, the evaluators "felt" there was a program impact that was escaping traditional instrumentation, and so they shifted the methodological thrust of the evaluation.

During the second and third years, mini-case studies were completed to examine the implementation and impact of the program within and across sites. Using semistructured, open-ended observation and interview instruments, trained data collectors gathered data from a wide range of sources, including administrators, teachers, artists/instructors, school support personnel, students, and parents. As the case studies were prepared, it was evident that much of the qualitative data had quantifiable aspects that not only were relevant to the case study but also could serve to augment the first-year quantitative data base. Thus, patterns within the qualitative data were transformed into quantitative form through categorization and ratings.

However, the quantitative data base was not augmented solely with the *addition* of transformed qualitative data. Rather, some new variables were created through a merging of both qualitative and quantitative data. The authors note that in addition to the two data forms providing [supplementary and] supportive information, a spiral effect was occurring; each type of information, when combined, displayed a dynamic interconnectedness. The integration was leading to a synthesis that produced a new variable (p. 9).

The example given by the authors focused on the creation of the variable "principal support." Qualitative data from principal interviews and quantitative data from teacher and artist/instructor questionnaires were both assessed in order to determine a quantifiable rating that would capture the level of "principal support" (1 = minimal to 4 = extensive) for the MBP project. This *merged-data* variable was found to be significantly correlated with the extent of implementation ($r = .74$, $p < .01$), thereby furnishing critical information that was not apparent from the independent analyses of either quantitative or qualitative data alone.

Schermerhorn, Williams, and Dickison (1982) provide a further example of this data consolidation and merging analysis strategy in their multi-purpose,[4] mixed-method evaluation of Project COMPAS. Project COMPAS (Consortium for Operating and Managing Programs for the Advancement of Skills) represented a cooperative effort among seven community colleges to develop cognitive skills programs for entry-level freshman. Again, initiation clements are evident in the authors' reflections on their analysis process:

> The reconciliation of the two data sets is thus more a task *of weaving together* the influences resulting from each set than of confirming one inference with

supportive evidence from a second perspective [as in triangulation]. In some instances a common theme is discerned, though for most concerns *only questions arise* as the two data sets are merged. (p. 95, italics added)

In other words, a recasting of questions concerning program impact for future evaluations of Project COMPAS was one important outcome of this study.

In this initial evaluation, the process of weaving together the qualitative and quantitative data sources resulted in the discovery of an important factor that had not been considered in the original evaluation design—the degree to which students were immersed in the program. To capture this phenomenon, an "immersion" variable was constructed using both quantitative and qualitative data sources. An important outcome of subsequent analyses was the finding that immersion contributed to or moderated program outcomes and the attendant recognition that measurement of the level of a student's immersion in the program would need to be refined and included in future assessments of project impacts.

Louis (1981, 1982) describes an interactive analytic model, again with clear links to initiation intents. Louis's model is explicitly focused on integrating the data obtained from different instruments, respondents, and observers. The model evolved during a multisite longitudinal evaluation of the Research and Development Utilization Program (RDU). This $8 million demonstration project was funded by the National Institute of Education between 1976 and 1979 to promote the adoption and implementation of new curriculum and staff development materials in 300 local schools.

A variety of data collection methods were used throughout the project, including mini-ethnographies based on interviews, observations, and document analysis; case study writers' surveys; standardized site-visit field reports; "event-triggered" reports monitoring a school's progress through the project; and formal principal and teacher surveys. Site-level data were thus rich and diverse; however, no more than 20% of the sites had a complete data set, which seriously constrained cross-site analysis possibilities. To overcome this constraint, these evaluators created a transformed and consolidated site-level data set via the development and application of a "consolidated coding form" (CCF). The form constituted 240 dichotomous or Likert scale items, which were scored by senior staff members who had visited at least four of the sites and were involved in an intensive 2-day session in which common interpretations for consolidated coding were reached. Included on the CCF were variables that could not be readily obtained through traditional survey methods, for example, quality of the decision-making process and patterns of influence of different actors over decisions at various stages in the change process. Moreover, the consolidated database reflected the holistic knowledge the site-visit team brought to the cases, as well as the reliability of standardized data, integrated both within and across sites.

The level of integration of qualitative and quantitative data achieved in the RDU evaluation is captured in the following summary statement:

> Can a database composed of numbers that is entirely dependent on the itera-tive, holistic judgments of experienced site field teams be described as only quantitative? While the analysis procedures used to manipulate the data are sta-tistical, the data itself, and any interpretation of results, is totally conditioned by its origins. On the other hand, as we approach any given analysis using case materials rather than quantified data, it has become genuinely impossible not to embed that activity in our knowledge of the descriptive statistics and correla-tional relationships that were available to us well before data collection had ended. (Louis, 1981, p. 21)

Louis cautions that this comprehensive, interactive approach to analytic integration requires constant attention by staff members who are skilled in both quantitative and qualitative data analysis techniques. Low rates of turnover among project staff, who are relatively free of paradigmatic prefer-ences, would also be essential to achieving the high level of integration that was obtained in this evaluation.

In these three examples of mixed-method inquiry, the data consolidation/merging analysis strategy was used effectively. Through data consolidation/merging, the authors of all three of these studies were able to create new vari-ables and conduct a more comprehensive analysis, which served to provoke insights and new perspectives on planned evaluation foci. The exigencies of multisite data coordination and analysis may have been the imperative behind the iterative nature of the analyses and maximal use of both data types. In Louis (1981, 1982) the development of a consolidated coding form provided a means by which a data base could be created from a plethora of sources that compensated for missing data, reflected the holistic knowledge of the site team, and ensured standardized data across sites. In both Talmage and Rasher (1981) and Schermerhorn, Williams, and Dickison (1982), new variables were constructed out of the joint use of both data types and were subsequently quantified for further analysis. It is certainly also possible to generate new themes or patterns from a merged analysis of quantitative and qualitative data and then use them in further qualitative analyses.

Discussion

This paper constitutes a continuing response to Connor et al.'s (1984) chal-lenge "to mix the best parts of multiple methods to accomplish our evaluation tasks." Under the umbrella of multiple methods, mixed-method evaluations now frequently dot the landscape of evaluation research. Our work is focused on providing a conceptual framework that can effectively guide mixed-method evaluation practice. Previously, we identified distinct mixed-method *purposes* and relevant *design elements*. The present discussion contributes an initial repertoire of four *data analysis strategies* appropriate for mixed-method studies. The critical defining characteristic of all four strategies is their integration of the different data sets during the analysis process itself. Some form of integration, we believe, constitutes the essence of a mixed-method approach.

As noted earlier, the data analysis strategies presented here are not, in and of themselves, new. It is common research practice, for example, to code numerically qualitative data for purposes of statistical analysis and to single out extreme cases or residuals for more intensive scrutiny. What is new, we believe, is the collection of these data analysis strategies within a mixed-method framework. This framework highlights the integrative potential of these strategies, and underscores their potential power not only to incorporate qualitative data into quantitative analyses, but also vice versa, and, even beyond, to spiral iteratively around the different data sets, adding depth of understanding with each cycle.

Yet, as noted, in our prior review of empirical studies mixed-method evaluation practice rarely incorporated an integrative analysis strategy. From this disjuncture, two questions arise: (a) When is an integrative analysis strategy appropriate, and (b) why is integrative analysis so rare in practice?

First, to the practical question of contextual appropriateness, we offer provisional guidelines that are linked to mixed-method purpose, for this remains the cornerstone of our conceptual framework. We suggest that, in general, integrative analytic strategies are appropriate when methods are mixed for purposes of initiation, expansion, or development, but less useful when triangulation is the mixed-method intent.

The studies reviewed in this article clearly illustrate the value of integrative analyses for initiating fresh insights and new perspectives that enhance conceptual understanding. The examples included initiation uses of three of the four analytic strategies discussed—typology development, extreme case analysis, and data consolidation/merging—suggesting a particularly strong match between initiation mixed-method designs and integrative data analysis strategies.

The Larner, Nagy, and Halpern (1987) evaluation of the rural Alabama home visitor health program provides an example of using data transformation as an analytic strategy in an expansion mixed-method design. In this study, qualitative data on program implementation were numerically coded and incorporated, along with quantitative implementation data, into a regression analysis predicting client program participation. Data transformation is perhaps the most obviously useful analysis strategy in expansion designs, where different methods are employed to increase the breadth and scope of the inquiry. Data transformation would enable analyses of the relationships between typically qualitative information on program processes and typically quantitative information on program outcomes. More effective use of this design, however, could be enabled by creative applications of other integrative data analysis strategies. For example, outcome data analyses could signal residuals or outliers or generate a typology useful for more intensive implementation analyses. Different data on different program components could even be consolidated or merged to capture dynamic patterns of program experiences. Expansion designs dominated our prior empirical review of mixed-method evaluation practice, composing nearly half the sample. Yet the potential power and benefits of such designs may well remain unfulfilled without more conscientious attention to integrative analyses.

A salient characteristic of development mixed-method designs is their *sequential* character, where the results of the first method are used to inform the development of the second (including instrumentation, sampling, and administration decisions). Two of the integrative analysis strategies described here are also sequential—typology development and extreme case analysis— and thus potentially strong analytic approaches for development designs. The Hall et al. (1980) evaluation of an innovative science curriculum illustrates the analytic value of typologies for mixed-method development studies. Specifically, a typology of schools created from the quantitative data usefully framed and focused the subsequent qualitative analysis in this study. And extreme case analysis can be viewed as a special case of the classic development design in which the results of the first method are used to select the samples for the second (Sieber, 1973). Because the different data types are processed simultaneously in the other two integrative analysis strategies, these are unlikely to support a mixed-method development design.

In evaluations where complementarity is the primary purpose for mixing methods, the decisions guiding separate versus integrative processing of the different data types are not as clear-cut. In part, this is due to the particularly wide contextual variability possible in the design of such studies. In complementarity designs, different methods are used to measure overlapping, but also distinct facets of a given phenomenon. The greater the overlap in the conceptualizations of the phenomenon guiding each method, the closer this design is to a triangulation design, for which we believe integrative analysis strategies are not generally useful. The less the overlap, the closer this design is to an expansion design, for which we believe integrative analysis strategies can offer strong support. The present review did not include an example of integrative analysis in a complementarity study. Logic nonetheless clearly suggests that there should be many cases where the joint analysis of data from methods implemented to develop an elaborated, enriched understanding of a phenomenon would serve well to do just that.

Finally, in contrast to our promotion of integrative analysis strategies for evaluations that mix methods for initiation, expansion, development, and complementarity purposes, the very concept of data integration is less meaningful when methods are mixed for purposes of triangulation. The underlying logic of triangulation requires independence of methods through data analysis and interpretation. Arguments for convergent validity of findings from different methods are stronger when such independence can be claimed. Hence, to integrate different data sets intentionally during data analysis is to undermine the potential power of a triangulation design.

To the second question of why integrative analyses in mixed-method evaluation practice are still a rarity, we offer two sets of speculations, one pertaining to the evolving contexts of program evaluation and the other to methodological stances within the field.[5] Contextually, funding has been reduced for large-scale, multisite evaluations that are conducive to thoughtful mixed-method designs and, as illustrated by the Louis (1981) study, invoke the need for integrative analyses. Smaller data sets from single sites may be more readily managed and understood without the felt need for coordination.

Methodologically, there are three recognized stances within the community of program evaluators that mitigate against meaningful integration in mixed-method practice. First, mixed-method designs are often inaccurately equated with the *in vogue* concept of triangulation. Integral to this concept is strong independence of the different methods used. So evaluators employing mixed-method designs who adopt the rubric of triangulation, even when theirs is not a triangulation design, may eschew or fail to even consider the potential of integrative strategies. Second, this is an era of dizzying pluralism in social inquiry approaches and justifications (see Guba, 1990). For many, this pluralism connotes a basic acceptance of diverse ways of knowing and diverse things worth knowing about, from propositional causal claims to experiential meaning and to critical sources of distortion in communications. In accepting diversity, however, many social inquirers have effectively retrenched, rejecting either the possibility or the desirability of integrative rapprochement among different kinds of knowledge claims. This kind of climate—where some are gathering with their own behind barricades, propelling philosophical and political salvos (Sechrest, 1992) over to the other side—is surely not very hospitable to the concept of integration. Yet, this challenge of paradigmatic integration remains important for future mixed-method development. Finally, in several currently popular evaluation approaches, integration is a sensible concept but not necessarily through data bases or analytic methods. These alternatives include interpretivist, qualitative approaches (from Stake, 1975, through Guba & Lincoln, 1989), in which integration and synthesis are intellectual tasks demanded of the individual evaluator; more openly ideological approaches like Schwandt's (1989), which calls for moral evaluation, and Sirotnik's and others' (Sirotnik, 1990), which call for an evaluation practice oriented around social justice in which integration becomes meaningful only in the service of some ideological aim.

In summary, we have identified four integrative data analysis strategies and provisionally argued for their value in many mixed-method evaluation designs. We believe that the intentional use of such strategies can significantly augment the power of these designs to advance conceptual understanding and insight. Clearly, further work is also needed. Concerted attention must be directed to the role of inquiry paradigms in integrative data analysis strategies and mixed-method inquiry more generally. How can contrasting epistemological assumptions and worldviews be integrated or reconciled within a mixed-method framework? From the present work, the data consolidation and merging approach emerged as a promising strategy for data integration yet perhaps also the strategy most vulnerable to abuse from conceptualization and measurement perspectives. For example, how, if at all, should different data types be weighted when consolidating or merging them (Cordray, 1986; Jick, 1983)? More examples of successful practice employing integrative data analysis strategies in mixed-method contexts are also needed; this work, in particular, relies on an iterative interplay of theory and practice.

In this pluralistic era in applied social inquiry, mixed-method approaches are likely to continue to increase in desirability and frequency. The power and added value of such designs can be realized only if mixed-method decisions are systematic and explicit. The integrative data analysis strategies presented here are offered as contributions toward that end.

Notes

The statements and opinions expressed in this article do not represent official policy of the General Accounting Office. The authors would like to extend grateful thanks to Leslie J. C. Riggin, Robert A. Johnson, and two anonymous reviewers for their constructive contributions to this manuscript.

1. The key distinction here is between methods that yield numerical data and those that yield narrative or other forms of data (see note 2). Although such different methods are often linked to different inquiry philosophies, these linkages do not inhere in the methods (Bednarz, 1983; Reichardt & Cook, 1979). In the Greene et al. mixed-method framework, this issue is addressed through the design element of inquiry paradigm, where the paradigm guiding each method type is delineated.

2. As envisioned, the full conceptual framework also includes broader issues related to evaluation context, purpose (e.g., formative, summative, critical), audience, and intended uses. Work on the conceptual framework to date has concentrated on mixing qualitative and quantitative inquiry methods. While this emphasis matches current practice, it is not intended to exclude the emerging importance of methods reflecting critical perspectives or perspectives drawn from the humanities.

3. The classification of measures as quantitative or qualitative by a third party is sometimes a matter of judgment. For the Lamer et al. study, a personal communication with the principal author revealed that the quantitative rating scale was derived from qualitative focus groups conducted with the home visitor staff. With this procedure, ratings would reflect the experiential nature of client-staff relationships as perceived by the home visitors. The interviews, which assessed demographics and social support, could actually be considered more quantitative than the rating scale.

4. The authors' stated primary purpose for using a mixed-method design was complementarity. We inferred, however, that a development purpose evolved from the study design and that both initiation and expansion purposes emerged during the analysis phase. In Greene et al. (1989) over a fifth ($n = 13$) of the evaluations were rated for both primary and secondary mixed-method purposes.

5. We are indebted to an anonymous reviewer for many of these ideas.

References

Bednarz, D. (1983). *Quantity and quality in evaluation research: A divergent view.* Revised version of paper presented at the Joint Meeting of the Evaluation Network and the Evaluation Research Society, Chicago.

Campbell, D. T., & Fiske, D. W. (1959). Convergent and discriminant validation by the multitrait-multimethod matrix. *Psychological Bulletin, 56,* 81–105.

Caracelli, V. J. (1988). *Adult women in college. Stability and change in identity and personality.* Unpublished doctoral dissertation, Cornell University, Ithaca, NY.

Connor, R. F., Altman, D. G., & Jackson, C. (1984). 1984: A brave new world for evaluation. In R. F. Connor, D. G. Altman, & C. Jackson (Eds.), *Evaluation Studies Review Annual: Vol. 9* (pp. 13–22). Beverly Hills, CA: Sage.

Cook, T. D. (1985). Postpositivist critical multiplism. In R. L. Shotland & M. M. Mark (Eds.), *Social science and social policy* (pp. 21–62). Beverly Hills, CA: Sage.

Cordray, D. S. (1986). Quasi-experimental analyses: A mixture of methods and judgment. In W. M. K. Trochim (Ed.), *Advances in quasi-experimental design and analysis. New Directions for Program Evaluation 31* (pp. 9–27). San Francisco: Jossey-Bass.

Denzin, N. K. (1978). *The research act: An introduction to sociological methods* (chap. 10). New York: McGraw-Hill.

Fry, G., Chantavanich, S., & Chantavanich, A. (1981). Merging quantitative and qualitative research techniques: Toward a new research paradigm. *Anthropology and Educational Quarterly, 12,* 145–158.

Greene, J. C., Caracelli, V. J., & Graham, W. F. (1989). Toward a conceptual framework for mixed-method evaluation designs. *Educational Evaluation and Policy Analysis, 11,* 255–274.

Greene, J. C., & McClintock, C. (1985). Triangulation in evaluation: Design and analysis issues. *Evaluation Review, 9,* 523–545.

Guba, E. G. (1990). *The paradigm dialog.* Newbury Park, CA: Sage.

Guba, E. G., & Lincoln, Y. S. (1989). *Fourth generation evaluation.* Newbury Park, CA: Sage.

Hall, G., Hord, S. M., & Griffin, T. H. (1980, April). *Implementation at the school building level: The development and analysis of nine mini-case studies.* Paper presented at the Annual Meeting of the American Educational Research Association, Boston. (ERIC Document Reproduction Service No. ED 207 170)

Hall, G. E., Wallace, R. C., & Dossett, W. A. (1973). *A developmental conceptualization of the adoption process within educational institutions.* Austin, TX: The University of Texas, Austin, Research and Development Center for Teacher Education.

Jick, T. D. (1983). Mixing qualitative and quantitative methods: Triangulation in action. In J. Van Maanen (Ed.), *Qualitative methodology* (pp. 135–148). Beverly Hills, CA: Sage.

Kidder, L. H. (1981). *Selltiz, Wrightsman and Cook's research methods in social relations* (4th ed.). New York: Holt, Rinehart & Winston.

Kidder, L. H., & Fine, M. (1987). Qualitative and quantitative methods: When stories converge. In M. M. Mark & R. L. Shotland (Eds.), *Multiple methods in program evaluation. New Directions for Program Evaluation 35* (pp. 57–75). San Francisco: Jossey-Bass.

Larner, M., Nagy, C., & Halpern, R. (1987, October). *Inside the black box: Understanding home visiting programs.* Paper presented at the annual meeting of the American Public Health Association, New Orleans.

Louis, K. S. (1981, April). *Policy researcher as sleuth: New approaches to integrating qualitative and quantitative methods.* Paper presented at the Annual Meeting of the American Educational Research Association, Los Angeles. (ERIC Document Reproduction Service No. ED 207 256)

Louis, K. S. (1982). Sociologist as sleuth: Integrating methods in the RDU study. *American Behavioral Scientist, 26*(1), 101–120.

Madey, D. L. (1982). Some benefits of integrating qualitative and quantitative methods in program evaluation, with illustrations. *Educational Evaluation and Policy Analysis, 4,* 223–236.

Mark, M. M., & Shotland, R. L. (1987). Alternative models for the use of multiple methods. In M. M. Mark & R. L. Shotland (Eds.), *Multiple methods in program evaluation. New Directions for Program Evaluation 35* (pp. 95–100). San Francisco: Jossey-Bass.

Mathison, S. (1988). Why triangulate? *Educational Researcher, 17*(2), 13–17.

Maxwell, J. A., Bashook, P. G., & Sandlow, C. J. (1986). Combining ethnographic and experimental methods in educational evaluation. In D. M. Fetterman & M. A. Pitman(Eds.), *Educational evaluation: Ethnography in theory, practice, and politics* (pp. 121–143). Beverly Hills, CA: Sage.

Patton, M. Q. (1980). *Qualitative evaluation models*. Beverly Hills, CA: Sage.

Reichardt, C. S., & Cook, T. D. (1979). Beyond qualitative *versus* quantitative methods. In T. D. Cook & C. S. Reichardt (Eds.), *Qualitative and quantitative methods in evaluation research* (pp. 7–32). Beverly Hills, CA: Sage.

Rossman, G. B., & Wilson, B. L. (1985). Numbers and words: Combining quantitative and qualitative methods in a single large-scale evaluation study. *Evaluation Review, 9,* 627–643.

Schermerhorn, L. L., Williams, L., & Dickison, A. (Eds.). (1982). *Project COMPAS [Consortium for operating and managing programs for the advancement of skills]: A design for change.* East Peoria, IL: Illinois Central College. (ERIC Document Reproduction Service No. ED 219 100)

Schwandt, T. A. (1989). Recapturing moral discourse in evaluation. *Educational Researcher, 18*(8), 11–16.

Sechrest, L. (1992). Roots: Back to our first generations. AEA 1991 presidential address. *Evaluation Practice, 13*(1), 1–7.

Shadish, W. R., Jr., Cook, T. D., & Houts, A. C. (1986). Quasi-experimentation in a critical multiplist mode. In W. M. K. Trochim (Ed.), *Advances in quasi-experimental design and analysis. New Directions for Program Evaluation 31,* (pp. 29–46). San Francisco: Jossey-Bass.

Shotland, R. L., & Mark, M. M. (1987). Improving inferences from multiple methods. In M. M. Mark & R. L. Shotland (Eds.), *Multiple methods in program evaluation. New Directions for Program Evaluation 35* (pp. 77–94). San Francisco: Jossey-Bass.

Sieber, S. D. (1973). The integration of field work and survey methods. *American Journal of Sociology, 78,* 1335–1359.

Sirotnik, K. A. (Ed.). (1990). *Evaluation and social justice. New Directions for Program Evaluation 45.* San Francisco: Jossey-Bass.

Smith, J. K., & Heshusius, L. (1986). Closing down the conversation: The end of the quantitative-qualitative debate. *Educational Researcher, 15*(1), 4–12.

Stake, R. E. (1975). *Evaluating the arts in education: A responsive approach.* Columbus, OH: Merrill.

Talmage, H., & Rasher, S. P. (1981, April). *Quantifying qualitative data: The best of both worlds.* Paper presented at the Annual Meeting of the American Educational Research Association, Los Angeles. (ERIC Document Reproduction Service No. 204 396)

Webb, E. J., Campbell, D. T., Schwartz, R. D., & Sechrest, L. (1966). *Unobtrusive measures* (chap. 1). Chicago: Rand McNally.

Valerie J. Caracelli, Senior Social Science Analyst, U.S. General Accounting Office, Program Evaluation and Methodology Division, 441 G St., NW, Washington, DC 20548. *Specializations:* multiple methods evaluation research, applied social science research methods.

Jennifier C. Greene, Associate Professor of Human Service Studies, Department of Human Service Studies, N136B MVR Hall, Cornell University, Ithaca, NY 14853. *Specializations:* evaluation theory and practice, participatory inquiry.

10

Expanding the Reasons for Conducting Mixed Methods Research

Selection: Bryman, A. (2006). Integrating quantitative and qualitative research: How is it done? *Qualitative Research, 6*(1), 97–113.

Editors' Introduction

Mixed methods scholars agree that integrating or mixing the quantitative and qualitative components of a mixed methods study is an essential aspect of mixed methods research. Despite its importance, authors writing about mixed methods have noted the lack of good integration within many published mixed methods studies. Working from a background in management and organizational research, Alan Bryman (2006, 2007) has devoted recent attention to the issue of mixed methods integration, including the following selection that examined reasons that researchers integrate quantitative and qualitative research.

Mixed methods researchers need to carefully consider both why they are integrating quantitative and qualitative research in their studies and how they are going to accomplish this integration in practice. A central element of Bryman's (2006) discussion is his comprehensive list of 16 reasons for integrating qualitative and quantitative research, building on the Greene et al. typology (1989; Chapter 5 in this volume) of five purposes. Further, an important insight he added is that the reasons may change during a study as researchers gain new understandings.

Bryman applied his list of reasons to analyze a sample of mixed methods studies from four social science disciplines, and his review of published studies conveys which reasons are currently more common. He advises researchers to clearly articulate their rationale for combining the two methods and how the mixing was done in practice. An additional feature of interest is his detailed description of how he located published mixed methods studies in the literature, which suggests useful search strategies for other scholars looking for examples of mixed methods research in their own disciplines.

Discussion Questions and Applications

1. Consider a published mixed methods study (such as from Part II) or one that you would like to conduct. What is (are) the reason(s) for integrating quantitative and qualitative research?

2. How should researchers choose which integration rationale is appropriate for their studies?

3. How do the rationales for integrating and methods of integrating in practice relate to the major types of mixed methods designs? Do certain rationales call for specific designs?

Related References That Extend the Topic

Discussions of integrating in mixed methods research include:

Bryman, A. (2007). Barriers to integrating quantitative and qualitative research. *Journal of Mixed Methods Research, 1*(1), 8–22.

Erzberger, C., & Kelle, U. (2003). Making inferences in mixed methods: The rules of integration. In A. Tashakkori & C. Teddlie (Eds.), *Handbook of mixed methods in social and behavioral research* (pp. 457–488). Thousand Oaks, CA: Sage.

Integrating Quantitative and Qualitative Research

How Is It Done?

Alan Bryman
University of Leicester

ABSTRACT: *This article seeks to move beyond typologies of the ways in which quantitative and qualitative research are integrated to an examination of the ways that they are combined in practice. The article is based on a content analysis of 232 social science articles in which the two were combined. An examination of the research methods and research designs employed suggests that on the quantitative side structured interview and questionnaire research within a cross-sectional design tends to predominate, while on the qualitative side the semi-structured interview within a cross-sectional design tends to predominate. An examination of the rationales that are given for employing a mixed-methods research approach and the ways it is used in practice indicates that the two do not always correspond. The implications of this finding for how we think about mixed-methods research are outlined.*

Keywords: qualitative research, quantitative research, mixed-methods research, multi-strategy research, typologies

There can be little doubt that research that involves the integration of quantitative and qualitative research has become increasingly common in recent years. While some writers express unease about the 'whatever works'

SOURCE: This article is reprinted from *Qualitative Research*, Vol. 6, Issue 1, pp. 97–113, 2006. Reprinted with permission of Sage Publications.

position that underpins it (e.g. Buchanan, 1992; Pawson and Tilly, 1997), so far as research practice is concerned, combining quantitative and qualitative research has become unexceptional and unremarkable in recent years. Indeed, for some writers it has come to be seen as a distinctive research approach in its own right that warrants comparison with each of quantitative and qualitative research. In this sense, we end up with three distinct approaches to research quantitative; qualitative; and what is variously called multi-methods (Brannen, 1992), multi-strategy (Bryman, 2004), mixed methods (Creswell, 2003; Tashakkori and Teddlie, 2003), or mixed methodology (Tashakkori and Teddlie, 1998) research. In the field of evaluation research, and indeed in several other applied fields, the case for a multi-strategy research approach seems to have acquired especially strong support (Tashakkori and Teddlie, 2003).

Typologies of Mixed-Methods Research

The discussion of the integration of quantitative and qualitative research has increasingly been taken over by a formalized approach which is especially apparent in the discussion and proliferation of typologies of integration. This has been a particular emphasis among North American contributors to the field. Creswell et al. (2003) argue that giving types of mixed-methods research names has certain advantages. It conveys a sense of the rigour of the research and provides guidance to others about what researchers intend to do or have done (for example, funding bodies and journal editors). To that extent, the typologies of mixed-methods or multi-strategy research can be helpful to researchers and writers in clarifying the nature of their intentions or of their accomplishments.

However, the variety and range of typologies has reached the point where these exercises have become almost too refined, bearing in mind that the range of concrete examples of multi-strategy research is not great. Indeed, most of the typologies have been constructed in largely theoretical terms and have not been apparently influenced in a systematic way by examples of multi-strategy research. To a large extent, they are exercises in logically possible types of integration, rather than being built up out of examples.

However, the dimensions out of which the typologies are constructed are instructive, in that they draw attention to the different aspects of multi-strategy research:

1. Are the quantitative and qualitative data collected simultaneously or sequentially? (Morgan, 1998; Morse, 1991).

2. Which has priority—the quantitative or the qualitative data? (Morgan, 1998; Morse, 1991).

3. What is the function of the integration—for example, triangulation, explanation, or exploration? (Creswell, 2003; Creswell et al., 2003; Greene et al., 1989).

4. At what stage(s) in the research process does multi-strategy research occur? (Tashakkori and Teddlie, 1998). It may be at stages of research question formulation, data collection, data analysis, or data interpretation.

5. Is there more than one data strand? (Tashakkori and Teddlie, 2003). With a multi-strand study, there is more than one research method and hence source of data. With a mono-strand study, there is one research method and hence one source of data. However, whether a mono-strand study can genuinely be regarded as a form of mixing methods is debatable.

A further issue with the use of these typologies is that they imply some forward commitment to a type of design, much like a decision to employ an experimental research design entails a commitment to uncovering data of a particular type. However, as some authors observe (e.g. Erzberger and Kelle, 2003), the outcomes of multi-strategy research are not always predictable. While a decision about design issues may be made in advance and for good reasons, when the data are generated, surprising findings or unrealized potential in the data may suggest unanticipated consequences of combining them.

What Do We Know About Mixing Quantitative and Qualitative Research?

The exercise of specifying typologies co-exists with unease among some authors about what we actually know about the ways in which quantitative and qualitative research are combined in practice. For example, it has been suggested that there are relatively few guidelines about 'how, when and why different research methods might be combined' (Bryman, 1988: 155). Maxwell has suggested that 'the theoretical debate about combining methods has prevented us from seeing the different ways in which researchers are *actually* combining methods' (Maxwell, 1990: 507, cited in Maxwell and Loomis, 2003: 251). He and Loomis have argued further that:

> Uncovering the actual integration of qualitative and quantitative approaches in any particular study is a considerably more complex undertaking than simply classifying the study into a particular category on the basis of a few broad dimensions or characteristics. (Maxwell and Loomis, 2003: 256)

Remarks such as these suggest that the formalization of approaches to multi-strategy research through typologies has moved too far ahead of a systematic appreciation of how quantitative and qualitative research are combined in practice. The writers who adopt a formalized strategy use many examples to illustrate their 'types' but we have relatively little understanding of the prevalence of different combinations, though there are some exceptions to this statement (e.g. Greene et al., 1989; Niglas, 2004).

An Investigation of Articles Combining Quantitative and Qualitative Research

With these kinds of consideration in mind, an investigation was undertaken of the ways that quantitative and qualitative research are combined in published journal articles. The findings reported in this article derive from only one phase of this research project, albeit a major component of it—namely, a content analysis of articles based on multi-strategy research. Journal articles do not encapsulate all possible contexts in which projects reporting multi-strategy research might be found. Conference papers and books are other possible sites. However, journal articles are a major form of reporting findings and have the advantage that, in most cases, the peer review process provides a quality control mechanism. By contrast, conference papers and books are sometimes not peer reviewed.

The approach to gleaning a sample was to search the Social Sciences Citation Index (SSCI) for articles in which relevant key words or phrases such as 'quantitative' and 'qualitative', or 'multi(-)method', or 'mixed method', or 'triangulation' appeared in the title, key words, or abstract. This means that the sample comprises articles which to some degree foreground the fact that the study is based on both quantitative and qualitative research. Searches using other kinds of key words, such as 'survey' and 'ethnography/ic', produce a far larger sample of articles than could be dealt with within the purview of this investigation. In conducting the search, the emphasis was on uncovering articles in five fields: sociology; social psychology; human, social and cultural geography; management and organizational behaviour; and media and cultural studies. The analysis was restricted to the 10-year period of 1994–2003. The fact that the findings are based on a large corpus of articles suggests that the sample is unlikely to be overly atypical, although claims of representativeness would be impossible to sustain. Judgments about whether articles fell within the purview of the investigation, in terms of whether they could be regarded as deriving from the five fields, were made on the basis of the journal title or information supplied in abstracts. In this way, a total of 232 articles was generated and content analyzed.

What was and was not an example of the combination of quantitative and qualitative research was occasionally problematic. The most notable of these occasions had to do with cases in which the researcher claimed to have used a qualitative approach or to be using qualitative data, but in fact the 'qualitative data' were based on a quantitative analysis of unstructured data—for example, of responses to open questions. Articles in which this occurred and where such data were the only source of the qualitative component were not included in the sample, because it is very debatable whether they can be regarded as indicative of a qualitative approach. This kind of quantification of qualitative data is more properly regarded as indicative of a quantitative research approach. Indeed, in some articles that were included in the sample, this kind of process was depicted by authors as indicative of a quantitative research approach rather than a qualitative one. There is clearly some confusion concerning whether the quantification of qualitative, unstructured data is indicative of a quantitative or a qualitative research approach. For the purposes of sample selection, it was taken to be the former, regardless of authors' claims. However, this was not a very common occurrence; although a log was not kept of these cases, they number no more than five or six articles.

The sample is likely to be biased in the sense that by no means all authors of articles reporting multi-strategy research foreground the fact that the findings reported derive from a combination of quantitative and qualitative research, or do not do so in terms of the key words that drove the online search strategy. An alternative search strategy is to select a sample of journals and to search for articles exhibiting multi-strategy research. This tactic was employed by Niglas (2004) in her investigation of multi-strategy research in education. Her sample of 145 articles derived from 1156 articles in 15 journals. This is a very good way of generating a sample but, in the context of a study that is meant to cover five fields of study, it is difficult to implement and also results in a lot of redundancy because a large number of articles have to be read in order to establish whether they are based on both quantitative and qualitative research (only 12.5 percent of articles read for Niglas's study were relevant to the main focus of her investigation). Moreover, foregrounding that a study is based on multi-strategy research is interesting because it implies that the fact that the different sources of data were employed is important and significant to the author(s) concerned. Since a major focus of the research was the kinds of purposes to which multi-strategy research is put, the online search strategy that was used for the study reported here was very relevant, because we might anticipate that researchers who choose to emphasize this aspect of their studies will have given greater consideration to the issues involved in combining quantitative and qualitative research. In this sense, the articles from which the findings derive constitute a purposive sample. A further issue that suggests some advantages to the sampling approach taken for this article is that it allows articles in a wide variety of journals to be uncovered. Thus, while it is certainly possible to trawl through sociology journals for instances of multi-strategy research articles in sociology, such a process risks neglecting many relevant sociology articles appearing in specialist journals.

Several writers have pointed out that quantitative and qualitative research can be combined at different stages of the research process: formulation of research questions; sampling; data collection; and data analysis. Articles for this study were chosen in terms of data collection and data analysis and then content analyzed in relation to these aspects of the research process. Issues of sampling did materialize in the study, as the findings below will indicate. Data collection and analysis were emphasized because these are arguably defining features of quantitative and qualitative research. Moreover, multi-strategy research articles nearly always entail the collection and analysis of both quantitative and qualitative data (Niglas, 2004).

Background Findings

First, a small number of background features of the articles analyzed thus far will be mentioned. When the primary discipline of each article is examined, we find that the major contributing discipline is sociology with 36 percent of all articles. This is followed by social psychology (27%); management and organizational behavior (23%); geography (8%); and media and cultural studies (7%). These findings strongly suggest that multi-strategy research is more commonly practised in some disciplines than others.

A further interesting background characteristic is the nation of the institutional affiliation of the author or first author of each article. North America is the major contributor with 49 percent of all articles; the UK comes second with 27 percent; followed by Europe and Australia (8% and 7%); Middle East (4%); with Asia, Africa and Latin America contributing 3 percent between them. These figures are obviously significantly affected by the fact that only English language publications were sought and read.

Research Methods and Research Designs Used

The first issue to be addressed in this article is: what research methods and research designs were employed in the articles? Each article was coded in terms of the research methods that were employed. Some of the research methods are perhaps better thought of as methods of data analysis, but they are frequently portrayed as research methods because of their distinctive approaches to sampling or capturing data (for example, content analysis, discourse analysis and conversation analysis). Table 10.1 presents the main methods used. The analysis presented derives from a multiple response analysis using SPSS.

A striking feature is that a small number of methods account for the vast majority of all methods employed. Survey methods and qualitative interviews account for the vast majority of methods employed in the articles. If we aggregate self-administered questionnaire, structured interview and questionnaire/ structured interview (a category used when it was unclear how survey instruments were administered), 82.4 percent of all articles coded used a survey instrument. If we aggregate semi-structured interview and unstructured interview, we find that data for 71.1 percent of articles derived from either of these two ways of conducting qualitative interviews. Further, 57.3 percent of all articles are based on a combination of a survey instrument and qualitative interviewing. In other words, one combination of research methods predominates in this data set—that is, one in which data are collected by either structured interview or questionnaire on the quantitative side along with either a semi-structured or unstructured interview on the qualitative side.

A further feature is that with 6.5 percent of articles, the quantitative data derive from an individual qualitative or focus group interview and that, in 20.7 percent of articles, the qualitative data derive from open questions in a structured interview or self-administered questionnaire. In the former case, the quantitative data derive from a research instrument associated with *qualitative*

Table 10.1   Research Methods Employed

	Number of articles using
Self-administered questionnaire	121
Structured interview	52
Structured observation	3
Content analysis	18
Quantification of qualitative interview questions	15
Questionnaire/structured interview	18
Semi-structured interview	159
Participant observation/ethnography	14
Unstructured interview	6
Qualitative analysis of documents	28
Answers to open questions in questionnaire	48
Focus groups	33
Language-based analysis	5
Other method	55

data collection while, in the second case, the qualitative data derive from a research instrument associated with *quantitative* data collection. In other words, for around 27 percent of articles, the collection of quantitative and qualitative data was *not* based on the administration of separate research instruments.

This finding is interesting because some methodologists might argue that a combination of quantitative and qualitative data based on the administration of one research instrument does not represent a true integration of quantitative and qualitative research because one will tend to be subordinate to the other. Thus, when multi-strategy research derives from the administration of a semi-structured interview, some of whose questions are quantified, an argument might be levelled that this does not represent a genuine form of quantitative research since the data have not been gathered in line with its underlying principles. Similarly, it might be argued that asking a small number of open questions in the course of a structured interview does not really provide an instance of multi-strategy research because the qualitative data have been collected in the course of administering a research instrument that has been devised in terms of survey principles. Moreover, such a situation requires a modification of approach to answering questions on the part of respondents in the course of responding to a research instrument. However, articles adopting an approach in which quantitative and qualitative data derived from the same research instrument were included.

When we turn to research designs, the aim of the analysis was to code articles in terms of the design employed for the quantitative data and the design employed for the qualitative data. In a small number of cases (4), because of the complexity of the data, a third research design was coded. Table 10.2 presents the data on this aspect of the investigation using a classification that follows Bryman's (2004) categorization of research designs. In this classification, a study is treated as a case study if it involves just a single case. If it was a multiple case study, involving two or more cases, it was treated as a comparative design. Again, the analysis derived from a multiple response analysis using SPSS.

As one might expect from the findings in Table 10.2, the bulk of the studies employed a cross-sectional design for the collection of both the quantitative and the qualitative data. Experimental and quasi-experimental designs barely figure in the findings. Employing a cross-sectional design for the collection of both quantitative and qualitative data is by far the most common design combination (62.9% of all articles). When we put the data relating to research methods and research designs together, we find that 41.8 percent of all articles included both a survey instrument and personal qualitative interviewing within a cross-sectional design for the collection of both sets of data.

Table 10.2   Research Designs Employed

	Number of articles using
Cross-sectional design 1	169
Cross-sectional design 2	148
Case study 1	24
Case study 2	16
Longitudinal 1	28
Longitudinal 2	19
Experimental 1 (includes quasi-experimental)	9
Experimental 2 (includes quasi-experimental)	5
Comparative 1 (includes multiple case study)	30
Comparative 2 (includes multiple case study)	19

Sometimes, although rarely, this format will have been accompanied by other sources of data.

Justifications for Combining Quantitative and Qualitative Research

A major focus of the content analysis was on the rationales proffered for combining quantitative and qualitative research. This aspect of the investigation was approached in several ways. First, the rationale given by authors for combining the two approaches to data collection and/or analysis was coded. For this exercise, the reasons that were given before the findings were presented were typically examined. Then, the ways in which quantitative and qualitative research were actually combined were coded. In doing so, the coding reflected authors' reflections on what they felt had been gleaned from combining quantitative and qualitative research, and any ways in which the two were combined which were not reflected in authors' accounts. The purpose of discriminating between these two ways of thinking about the justification for multi-strategy research was that authors' accounts of why they intended to combine quantitative and qualitative research might differ from how they actually combined them in practice. If a difference was sometimes found between the two accounts (that is, between the rationale and practice), this would be interesting because the scientific paper is often perceived among sociologists of science as an *ex post facto* reconstruction that rationalizes and injects coherence into the different elements of the research process (e.g. Gilbert and Mulkay, 1984).

In coding the justifications for combining quantitative and qualitative research, two different schemes were employed. First, the influential scheme devised in the context of evaluation research by Greene et al. (1989) was used. This scheme isolates five justifications for combining quantitative and qualitative research:

1. *Triangulation:* convergence, corroboration, correspondence or results from different methods. In coding triangulation, the emphasis was placed on seeking corroboration between quantitative and qualitative data.

2. *Complementarity:* 'seeks elaboration, enhancement, illustration, clarification of the results from one method with the results from another' (Greene et al., 1989: 259).

3. *Development:* 'seeks to use the results from one method to help develop or inform the other method, where development is broadly construed to include sampling and implementation, as well as measurement decisions' (Greene et al., 1989: 259).

4. *Initiation:* 'seeks the discovery of paradox and contradiction, new perspectives of [sic] frameworks, the recasting of questions or results from one method with questions or results from the other method' (Greene et al., 1989: 259).

5. *Expansion:* 'seeks to extend the breadth and range of enquiry by using different methods for different inquiry components' (Greene et al., 1989: 259).

This scheme has been quite influential and was employed by Niglas (2004) in her examination of education research articles. In their analysis of evaluation research articles, Greene et al. (1989) coded each article in terms of a primary and a secondary rationale, a procedure that was also employed by Niglas (2004). An advantage of the Greene et al. scheme is its parsimony, in that it boils down the possible reasons for conducting multi-strategy research to just five reasons, although the authors' analysis revealed that initiation was uncommon. A disadvantage is that it only allows two rationales to be coded (primary and secondary). Accordingly, a more detailed but considerably less parsimonious scheme was devised. It was based on an extensive review of the kinds of reasons that are frequently given in both methodological writings and research articles for combining quantitative and qualitative research. The scheme provided for the following rationales:

a) *Triangulation* or greater validity—refers to the traditional view that quantitative and qualitative research might be combined to triangulate findings in order that they may be mutually corroborated. If the term was used as a synonym for integrating quantitative and qualitative research, it was not coded as triangulation.

b) *Offset*—refers to the suggestion that the research methods associated with both quantitative and qualitative research have their own strengths and weaknesses so that combining them allows the researcher to offset their weaknesses to draw on the strengths of both.

c) *Completeness*—refers to the notion that the researcher can bring together a more comprehensive account of the area of enquiry in which he or she is interested if both quantitative and qualitative research are employed.

d) *Process*—quantitative research provides an account of structures in social life but qualitative research provides sense of process.

e) *Different research questions*—this is the argument that quantitative and qualitative research can each answer different research questions but this item was coded only if authors explicitly stated that they were doing this.

f) *Explanation*—one is used to help explain findings generated by the other.

g) *Unexpected results*—refers to the suggestion that quantitative and qualitative research can be fruitfully combined when one generates surprising results that can be understood by employing the other.

h) *Instrument development*—refers to contexts in which qualitative research is employed to develop questionnaire and scale items—for example, so that better wording or more comprehensive closed answers can be generated.

i) *Sampling*—refers to situations in which one approach is used to facilitate the sampling of respondents or cases.

j) *Credibility*—refers to suggestions that employing both approaches enhances the integrity of findings.

k) *Context*—refers to cases in which the combination is rationalized in terms of qualitative research providing contextual understanding coupled with either generalizable, externally valid findings or broad relationships among variables uncovered through a survey.

l) *Illustration*—refers to the use of qualitative data to illustrate quantitative findings, often referred to as putting 'meat on the bones' of 'dry' quantitative findings.

m) *Utility* or improving the usefulness of findings—refers to a suggestion, which is more likely to be prominent among articles with an applied focus, that combining the two approaches will be more useful to practitioners and others.

n) *Confirm and discover*—this entails using qualitative data to generate hypotheses and using quantitative research to test them within a single project.

o) *Diversity of views*—this includes two slightly different rationales—namely, combining researchers' and participants' perspectives through quantitative and qualitative research respectively, and uncovering relationships between variables through quantitative research while also revealing meanings among research participants through qualitative research.

p) *Enhancement* or building upon quantitative/qualitative findings—this entails a reference to making more of or augmenting either quantitative or qualitative findings by gathering data using a qualitative or quantitative research approach.

q) *Other/unclear.*
r) *Not stated.*

This classification includes a larger number of categories than other schemes and as such is meant to capture in finer detail the range of reasons that are given for conducting multi-strategy research. There are clearly symmetries between the Greene et al. scheme and the more fine-grained approach just outlined. For example, 'development of a research instrument' and 'for sampling/case study selection reasons' correspond to 'development', while 'to enhance or build upon quantitative/qualitative findings' corresponds to 'complementarity'.

Table 10.3 shows the distribution of articles in terms of just the primary rationale using the Greene et al. scheme (see column for 'Rationale'). In just over a quarter of all articles, no rationale was provided. Complementarity and expansion were the most frequently cited primary rationales with 29 percent and 25 percent of all articles mentioning each of them as a primary rationale. Triangulation and development were less commonly mentioned, while initiation was extremely uncommon. The latter was also the case in Greene et al. (1989) but was even more the case in the data reported here. Turning to the actual uses of the integration of quantitative and qualitative research, Table 10.3 (column for 'Practice') provides the primary use in terms of the Greene et al. scheme. All the frequencies are greater because the category of 'not stated' virtually disappears. Most striking is that nearly half of all articles can be subsumed into the complementarity category. In terms of the Greene et al. scheme, this is by far the most prominent primary approach to the integration of quantitative and qualitative research.

When the data for the 'practice' column in Table 10.3 using the Greene et al. scheme are contrasted with comparable data from Greene et al. (1989) and Niglas (2004), we find that the pattern is closer to Niglas's examination of educational articles than to that of Greene et al. Similarly to Niglas,

Table 10.3   Uses of Multi-Strategy Research—Greene et al. Scheme

Category	Rationale	%	Practice
Triangulation	7.8		12.5
Complementarity	28.9		44.8
Development	10.3		8.6
Initiation	0.4		1.3
Expansion	25.4		31.5
Not stated	27.2		1.3

NOTE: All percentages are based on 232 cases

complementarity is the most common use of multi-strategy research, followed by expansion. In the examination of evaluation research articles by Greene et al., it was the other way around in that expansion was more common that complementarity. In the case of all three studies, then, these two uses of multi-strategy research were the most common forms. 'Development' as a use occurs with noticeably greater frequency in educational articles than in the present study and that of Greene et al. These findings suggest that there are slightly different uses being made of multi-strategy research when we compare general social research (present study), evaluation research and educational research, though the differences are not great.

When the articles are examined in terms of the more detailed scheme devised for the research, the rationale for nearly one-third of all articles could be coded in terms of 'enhancement' (see Table 10.4, 'Rationale' column). Quite large numbers of articles appeared under the categories: 'completeness' (13%), 'triangulation' (12.5%), and 'sampling' (13.4%). A sizeable number could not be coded in terms of any category because no rationale could be discerned.

When the articles are examined in terms of practice and compared with rationales, there are some fairly striking differences (see Table 10.4). For

Table 10.4   Uses of Multi-Strategy Research—Alternative Scheme

Category	Rationale Number of articles		Practice (% of all 232 cases)	
Triangulation	29	(12.5)	80	(34.5)
Offset	7	(3)	4	(1.7)
Completeness	31	(13)	67	(28.9)
Process	5	(2.2)	6	(2.6)
Different research questions	13	(5.6)	10	(4.3)
Explanation	13	(5.6)	32	(13.8)
Unexpected results	0		2	(0.9)
Instrument development	18	(7.8)	21	(9.1)
Sampling	31	(13.4)	43	(18.5)
Credibility	2	(0.9)	5	(2.2)
Context	8	(3.4)	10	(4.3)
Illustration	4	(1.7)	53	(22.8)
Utility	2	(0.9)	2	(0.9)
Confirm and discover	9	(3.9)	15	(6.5)
Diversity of views	26	(11.2)	35	(15.1)
Enhancement	73	(31.5)	121	(52.2)
Other/unclear	8	(3.4)	14	(6.1)
Not stated	62	(26.7)	1	(0.4)

example, 'triangulation' and 'illustration' are considerably more likely to occur as practice than as a rationale. 'Unexpected results' unsurprisingly did not appear as a rationale but was relevant to a small number of cases (2) when practice was examined.

Comparing the rationale and practice columns in both Tables 10.3 and 10.4 suggests an interesting possibility—namely, that when multi-strategy research is employed—practice does not always tally with the reasons given for using the approach, if indeed reasons are given at all. Nor should it be assumed that all articles that appear in terms of a rationale will also be subsumed in that category in terms of use. For example, we should not assume that all the 26 articles coded in terms of 'diversity of views' will necessarily be included in the 35 articles that were coded in terms of this category when practice was the focus of attention.

In order to explore this issue, a contingency table analysis was undertaken relating rationale and practice having created a multiple response variable for each of these. The resulting table is extremely ungainly, so only highlights will be mentioned. Of the 29 articles that cited triangulation as a rationale, 19 used it in this way. In other words, one-third of all articles intending to use multi-strategy research for triangulation did not actually use multi-strategy research in this way or at least did not report doing so. Just as interestingly, we can look at this the other way around. Thus, 80 articles employed a triangulation approach, but for just 19 of these articles was triangulation a rationale. In other words, three-quarters of all articles reporting the triangulation of research findings provided other rationales for the use of multi-strategy research. What this seems to suggest is that, although triangulation may not always be a rationale for combining quantitative and qualitative research, when faced with the two (or in a small number of cases more than two) sets of data, some researchers find it hard to resist making allusions to the symmetry or otherwise between their findings.

Taking another example, 'completeness' was a rationale for 31 articles and most (83.9%) used it in this way. However, when practice is examined, completeness could be ascribed to 67 articles. Thus, 71.1 percent of all articles using completeness did not specify it as a rationale at the outset. 'Enhancement' provides a further example. Seventy-three articles specified this as a rationale, although over one-quarter of articles citing it as a rationale did not employ it in this way. More striking is that 121 articles employed the approach meaning that over one-half (56.2%) of articles using enhancement in practice had not specified it as a rationale. 'Diversity of views' was a rationale for 26 articles though quite a large percentage (30.8%) did not use it this way. Thirty-five articles employed a diversity of views approach to integrating quantitative and qualitative research, but nearly half (48.6%) did not specify this as a rationale. Among the 62 articles that appear in Table 10.4 as 'not stated', the most common uses were enhancement (45 articles), triangulation (14), illustration (15) and completeness (10).

What these findings suggest is that there is quite often a mismatch between the rationale for the combined use of quantitative and qualitative research and how it is used in practice. Multi-strategy research is something of a moveable feast. For several of the rationales, there is no evidence from the articles that quantitative and qualitative research are combined in the way that the rationale would lead one to suspect. This is not always the case. In particular, when 'instrument development' and 'sampling' are the rationales, they are nearly always used in this way. Only one article was found claiming 'instrument development' as a rationale and only one article claiming 'sampling' as a rationale, but they did not report combining quantitative and qualitative research in these ways.

Discussion

There are several possible ways of looking at these findings, but two will be the focus of attention for this discussion. First, it may be that they reflect a tendency for the rationales for using multi-strategy research not to be thought through sufficiently. This would explain why the rationales and uses of multi-strategy research are not always aligned. One of the striking findings of this research has been that in the case of only 10 articles was there a clear indication that quantitative and qualitative research had each been designed to answer specific and different research questions. In these 10 cases, there was a clear indication that the quantitative and the qualitative research were each geared to answering distinct research questions. Of course, a much larger number of articles specified research questions, though an impression gleaned from the examination of the articles is that these were not specified as commonly as textbooks might lead us to expect. This was not a dimension of the coding for the content analysis but, in the course of reading the articles, the relative *in*frequency of specified research questions was striking. In the field of organization studies, it has been found that only around one-fifth of articles discuss the relationship between research topics and the overall design of investigations (Grunow, 1995), so the relative lack of attention to research questions may be a reflection of this tendency which may have some generalizability beyond the confines of that discipline.

A second way of looking at these findings is to suggest that multi-strategy research provides such a wealth of data that researchers discover uses of the ensuing findings that they had not anticipated. It has been pointed out by some writers, for example, that triangulation may be an unanticipated consequence of conducting multi-strategy research (Deacon et al., 1998; Smith, 1986). This may arise when multi-strategy research is conducted for a reason other than triangulation but, in the course of interpreting the data, an inconsistency between the quantitative and qualitative findings is revealed. Similarly, a researcher may employ multi-strategy research with a purpose like 'diversity of views' in mind, but find that the qualitative evidence helps to explain some of the relationships uncovered through an analysis of survey data.

It is likely that there are elements of both these explanations (and probably others) which contribute to the moveable feast phenomenon. The first points to the possibility that the grounds on which multi-strategy research is undertaken have not been sufficiently articulated in the methodological literature, resulting in a lack of certainty about its uses. The second explanation is somewhat less negative in its connotations in implying that multi-strategy research frequently brings more to researchers' understanding than they anticipate at the outset. Indeed, it could be argued that, if the latter is the case, perhaps it ought to be acknowledged. There would then be little or no point in wasting time and energy on enunciating principles for the contexts in which combining quantitative and qualitative research is and is not appropriate! However, it also has to be acknowledged that, unless there is some rationale for the use of multi-strategy research, there is the possibility of data redundancy, whereby some data are generated which are highly unlikely to shed light on the topic of interest. This would entail not just a waste of research resources but also a waste of participants' time.

Conclusion

These results imply that there is indeed a case for encouraging researchers to be explicit about the grounds on which multi-strategy research is conducted but to recognize that, at the same time, the outcomes may not be predictable. This is, of course, a feature of much research. Qualitative research is often depicted as a research strategy whose emphasis on a relatively open-ended approach to the research process frequently produces surprises, changes of direction and new insights. However, quantitative research is by no means a mechanical application of neutral tools that results in no new insights. In quantitative data analysis, the imaginative application of techniques can result in new understandings. If the two are conducted in tandem, the potential—and perhaps the likelihood—of unanticipated outcomes is multiplied. More generally, however, the research reported here strongly suggests that there is considerable value in examining both the rationales that are given for combining quantitative and qualitative research and the ways in which they are combined in practice. Such a distinction implies that methodological writings concerned with the grounds for combining the two approaches need to recognize that there may be a disjuncture between the two when concrete examples of research are examined.

Acknowledgements

I wish to thank the referees of this article for their constructive comments. I also wish to thank the Economic and Social Research Council for funding the research project 'Integrating quantitative and qualitative research: prospects and limits' (Award number H333250003) which made possible the research on which this article is based.

References

Brannen, J. (1992) 'Combining Qualitative and Quantitative Approaches: An Overview', in J. Brannen (ed.) *Mixing Methods: Qualitative and Quantitative Research*, pp. 3–37. Aldershot: Avebury.

Bryman, A. (1988) *Quantity and Quality in Social Research*. London: Unwin Hyman.

Bryman, A. (2004) *Social Research Methods* (2nd edition). Oxford: Oxford University Press.

Buchanan, D. R. (1992) 'An Uneasy Alliance: Combining Qualitative and Quantitative Research', *Health Education Quarterly* 19(1): 117–35.

Creswell, J. W. (2003) *Research Design: Qualitative, Quantitative, and Mixed Methods Approaches* (2nd edition). Thousand Oaks, CA: Sage.

Creswell, J. W., Plano Clark, V. L., Gutmann, M. L. and Hanson, W. E. (2003) 'Advanced Mixed Methods Research Designs', in A. Tashakkori and C. Teddlie (eds.) *Handbook of Mixed Methods in Social and Behavioral Research*. Thousand Oaks, CA: Sage.

Deacon, D., Bryman, A. and Fenton, N. (1998) 'Collision or Collusion? A Discussion of the Unplanned Triangulation of Quantitative and Qualitative Research Methods'. *International Journal of Social Research Methodology* 1: 47–63.

Erzberger, C. and Kelle, U. (2003) 'Making Inferences in Mixed Methods: The Rules of Integration', in A. Tashakkori and C. Teddlie (eds.) *Handbook of Mixed Methods in Social and Behavioral Research,* pp. 457–90. Thousand Oaks, CA: Sage.

Gilbert, G. N. and Mulkay, M. (1984) *Opening Pandora's Box: A Sociological Analysis of Scientists' Discourse.* Cambridge: Cambridge University Press.

Greene, J. C., Caracelli, V. J. and Graham, W. F. (1989) 'Toward a Conceptual Framework for Mixed-method Evaluation Designs', *Educational Evaluation and Policy Analysis* 11(3): 255–74.

Grunow, D. (1995) 'The Research Design in Organization Studies: Problems and Prospects', *Organization Science* 6(1): 93–103.

Maxwell, J. A. (1990) 'Response to "Campbell's Retrospective and a Constructionist's Perspective"', *Harvard Educational Review* 60: 504–8.

Maxwell, J. A. and Loomis, D. M. (2003) 'Mixed Methods Design: An Alternative Approach', in A. Tashakkori and C. Teddlie (eds.) *Handbook of Mixed Methods in Social and Behavioral Research*, pp. 209–40. Thousand Oaks, CA: Sage.

Morgan, D. L. (1998) 'Practical Strategies for Combining Qualitative and Quantitative Methods: Applications for Health Research', *Qualitative Health Research* 8: 362–76.

Morse, J. M. (1991) 'Approaches to Qualitative-Quantitative Methodological Triangulation', *Nursing Research* 40(2): 120–3.

Niglas, K. (2004) *The Combined Use of Qualitative and Quantitative Methods in Educational Research*. Tallinn, Estonia: Tallinn Pedagogical University Dissertation on Social Sciences.

Pawson, R. and Tilly, N. (1997) *Realistic Evaluation*. London: Sage.

Smith, M. L. (1986) 'The Whole Is Greater: Combining Qualitative and Quantitative Approaches in Evaluation Studies', in D. D. Williams (ed.) *Naturalistic Evaluation*, pp. 37–54. San Francisco, CA: Jossey-Bass.

Tashakkori, A. and Teddlie, C. (1998) *Mixed Methodology: Combining Qualitative and Quantitative Approaches*. Thousand Oaks, CA: Sage.

Tashakkori, A. and Teddlie, C. (2003) *Handbook of Mixed Methods in Social and Behavioral Research*. Thousand Oaks, CA: Sage.

Alan Bryman is Professor of Organisational and Social Research, Management Centre, University of Leicester.

Address: Management Centre, Ken Edwards Building, University of Leicester, University Road, Leicester LE1 7RH, UK. [email: a.bryman@le.ac.uk]

11

Types of Legitimation (Validity) in Mixed Methods Research

Selection: Onwuegbuzie, A. J., & Johnson, R. B. (2006). The validity issue in mixed research. *Research in the Schools, 13*(1), 48–63.

Editors' Introduction

The treatment of validity in mixed methods research is challenging because the researcher combines both quantitative and qualitative research, each with its own forms (or emerging forms) of validity. How should a mixed methods researcher view validity? Two experienced methodological education writers in mixed methods, Anthony Onwuegbuzie and Burke Johnson (2006), address this issue.

Onwuegbuzie and Johnson begin by reviewing the forms of validity in quantitative research and in qualitative research. They build from the suggestion that when discussing mixed research, it is better to use a "bilingual nomenclature." They consequently advance the term *legitimation*, a term, they contend, that is more acceptable to both quantitative and qualitative researchers than the term *validity*. Legitimation means that researchers draw inferences in a mixed methods study that are credible, trustworthy, dependable, transferable, and/or confirmable. Based on this definition, the authors suggest nine types of legitimation in mixed research: integrating samples, reconciling insider-outsider views, minimizing weaknesses when combining methods, using the appropriate sequence of methods, scrutinizing data conversion approaches, using a continuum rather than dualisms of paradigms, seeking a third viewpoint that is neither pure quantitative or qualitative, employing multiple validities based on qualitative and quantitative approaches, and political legitimation, in which the inferences have value for stakeholders. The use of the term *legitimation* and these nine types of legitimation provide new perspectives and a language for looking at "validity" in mixed methods research.

Discussion Questions and Applications

1. How do Onwuegbuzie and Johnson's conceptualization of the forms of quantitative and qualitative validity in Figures 11.1 and 11.3 fit with your understanding of the forms of validity?

2. How would you compare and contrast their use of the term *legitimation* and criteria for evaluating a mixed methods study? Are they the same or different concepts?

3. Consider the criteria used in forming the nine types of legitimation in mixed research. Which ones do you feel are most legitimate in mixed methods studies in your field?

Related References That Extend the Topic

For additional discussions of validity issues see:

Maxwell, J. A. (1992). Understanding validity in qualitative research. *Harvard Educational Review, 62,* 279–299.

Tashakkori, A., & Teddlie, C. (2006, April). *Validity issues in mixed methods research: Calling for an integrative framework.* Paper presented at the annual meeting of the American Educational Research Association, San Francisco.

The Validity Issue in Mixed Research

Anthony J. Onwuegbuzie
University of South Florida

R. Burke Johnson
University of South Alabama

In quantitative research, the importance of validity has been long accepted. In qualitative research, discussions of validity have been more contentious and different typologies and terms have been produced. In mixed methods research, wherein quantitative and qualitative approaches are combined, discussions about "validity" issues are in their infancy. We argue that because mixed research involves combining complementary strengths and nonoverlapping weaknesses of quantitative and qualitative research, assessing the validity of findings is particularly complex; we call this the problem of integration. We recommend that validity in mixed research be termed legitimation in order to use a bilingual nomenclature. Tashakkori and Teddlie's (2003, 2006) evaluation criteria frameworks involving the concept of inference quality are summarized. Although providing a framework for assessing legitimation in mixed research always will be incomplete, it is important to address several legitimation types that come to the fore as a result of combining inferences from the quantitative and qualitative components of the study into the formation of meta-inferences. Nine types of legitimation are described here in order to continue this emerging and important dialogue among researchers and methodologists.

SOURCE: This article is reprinted with permission from *Research in the Schools*, Vol. 13, Issue 1, pp. 48–63. Copyright © 2006. Mid-South Educational Research Association.

We are grateful to Dr. Abbas Tashakkori for his constructive feedback on earlier versions of this manuscript.

This paper is focused on validity in mixed methods research or what we refer to more broadly as *mixed research*. However, to understand the validity issue (i.e., quality) in mixed research, a brief review of some related discussions in quantitative and qualitative research will be helpful for orientation. Because these issues have been discussed elsewhere in great detail, we provide only brief summaries of those literatures, but first we want to make a few introductory comments about our general approach to research validity or quality.

We try to take a "middle of the road" position, seeing some truth and insight to be gained from multiple perspectives. Our approach is only one among many, and we recommend that readers examine additional perspectives as more work is carried out in this emerging area in mixed methods research as well as in the more traditional areas of qualitative and quantitative research quality. The "validity" issue, at least as we use the term, is not about singular truths, and it certainly is not limited to quantitative measurement; rather, by validity we mean that a research study, its parts, the conclusions drawn, and the applications based on it can be of high or low quality, or somewhere in between. Research needs to be defensible to the research and practice communities for whom research is produced and used. The arbiters of research quality will be the research stakeholders, which means that the quality or validity issue can have subjective, intersubjective, and objective components and influences. At the same time, research is something about which we can "rationally" speak, and usually, after considering our external and our internal or epistemic standards, we can meaningfully assert that some research is of higher quality for certain purposes than is other research (Longino, 1990). Anthropology, sociology, and psychology teach us that communities, cultures, and various kinds of groupings (including communities of researchers) have some *shared* norms, practices, values, and beliefs.

We aim our sense of justification at the research community that sees many advantages to *sometimes* using both qualitative and quantitative research in their single or highly related sets of research studies. One of the exciting results of much mixed research is that in a single study practical questions can be addressed, different perspectives can be examined, and if well documented, practitioners can obtain some sense of what might be useful in their local situations. We do not want to *oversell* mixed research, however; the evidence will be in the results. If mixed research produces useful results over time, as well as useful theory, then progress will have been made. We agree with Kurt Lewin's statement that "There is nothing so practical as a good theory" (Lewin, 1952, p. 169), and we hope that all researchers, including mixed researchers, will attempt to produce *good* theories and other research works.

Validity in Quantitative Research

In quantitative research, discussions of "validity" have been common and the importance of validity has been long accepted, and this is well documented in the literature. Building on the seminal works of Campbell and Stanley (Campbell, 1957; Campbell & Stanley, 1963), and many others, Onwuegbuzie (2003) presented 50 different threats to internal and external validity that might occur at the research design/data collection, data analysis, and/or data interpretation stages of the quantitative research process. These threats are presented in Figure 11.1, in what was later called the *Quantitative Legitimation Model*. As illustrated in Figure 11.1, Onwuegbuzie identified 22 threats to internal validity and 12 threats to external validity at the research design/data collection stage of the quantitative research process. At the data analysis stage, 21 and 5 threats to internal validity and external validity were conceptualized, respectively. Finally, at the data interpretation stage, 7 and 3 threats to internal validity and external validity were identified, respectively. In Figure 11.2, Onwuegbuzie, Daniel, and Collins' (in press) have presented a schematic representation of instrument score validity, which also is provided here for review by interested readers.

Another very important work in validity in quantitative research is found in Shadish, Cook, and Campbell (2001). These authors continue to build on Campbell's earlier work and classify research validity into four major types: statistical conclusion validity, internal validity, construct validity, and external validity. Other selected seminal works showing the historical development of validity in quantitative research are summarized in the following references: American Educational Research Association, American Psychological Association, and National Council on Measurement in Education (1999), Bracht and Glass (1968), Campbell (1957), Campbell and Stanley (1963), Cook and Campbell (1979), Messick (1989, 1995), and Smith and Glass (1987).

Validity in Qualitative Research

In the qualitative research paradigm, a primary focus is for researchers to capture authentically the lived experiences of people. As noted by Denzin and Lincoln (2005), "Such experience, it is argued, is created in the social text written by the researcher. This is the representational problem. It confronts the inescapable problem of representation, but does so within a framework that makes the direct link between experience and text problematic" (p. 19).[2] Denzin and Lincoln (2005) also argue for "a serious rethinking of such terms as *validity, generalizability,* and *reliability,* terms already retheorized in postpositivist . . . , constructivist-naturalistic . . . , feminist . . . ,

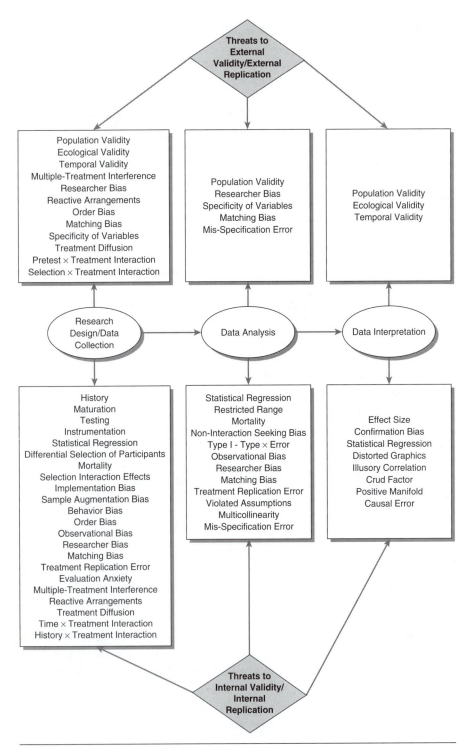

Figure 11.1   Threats to Internal and External Validity

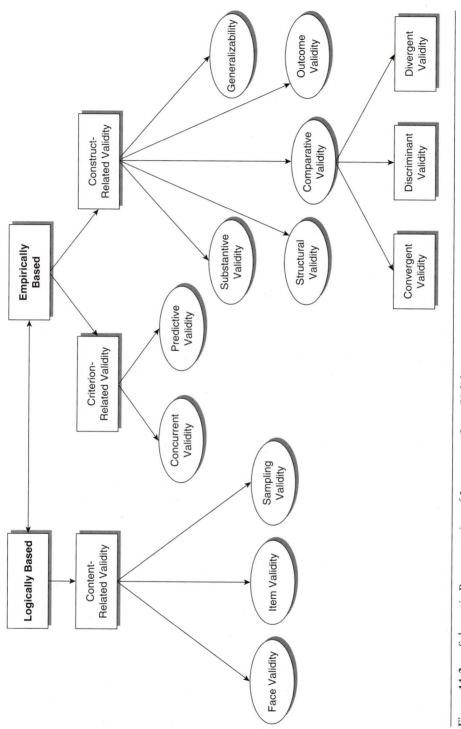

Figure 11.2   Schematic Representation of Instrument Score Validity

interpretive . . . , poststructural . . . , and critical . . . discourses. This problem asks, 'How are qualitative studies to be evaluated in the contemporary, post-structural moment?'" (pp. 19–20).[3, 4] Part of their solution to the "validity issue" has been to reconceptualize traditional quantitative validity concepts and to use labels that are more acceptable to qualitative researchers (Lincoln & Guba, 1985, 1990). One set of criteria (Lincoln & Guba, 1985) includes the following types: credibility (replacement for quantitative concept of internal validity), transferability (replacement for quantitative concept of external validity), dependability (replacement for quantitative concept of reliability), and confirmability (replacement for quantitative concept of objectivity).

Another useful classification for validity in qualitative research was provided by Maxwell (1992), who identified the following five types of validity in qualitative research: descriptive validity (i.e., factual accuracy of the account as documented by the researcher), interpretive validity (i.e., the extent to which an interpretation of the account represents an understanding of the perspective of the underlying group and the meanings attached to the members' words and actions), theoretical validity (i.e., the degree to which a theoretical explanation developed from research findings is consistent with the data), evaluative validity (i.e., the extent to which an evaluation framework can be applied to the objects of study, as opposed to a descriptive, interpretive, or explanatory one), and generalizability (i.e., the extent to which a researcher can generalize the account of a particular situation, context, or population to other individuals, times, settings, or context). With regard to the last validity type, Maxwell differentiates internal generalizability from external generalizability, with the former referring to the generalizability of a conclusion within the underlying setting or group, and the latter pertaining to generalizability beyond the group, setting, time, or context. According to Maxwell, internal generalizability is typically more important to qualitative researchers than is external generalizability (see also, Maxwell, 2005).

Onwuegbuzie and Leech (in press-a) conceptualized what they called the *Qualitative Legitimation Model*, which contains 29 elements of legitimation for qualitative research at the following three recursive stages of the research process: research design/data collection, data analysis, and data interpretation.[1] As illustrated in Figure 11.3, the following threats to internal credibility are viewed as pertinent to qualitative research: ironic legitimation, paralogical legitimation, rhizomatic legitimation, voluptuous (i.e., embodied) legitimation, descriptive validity, structural corroboration, theoretical validity, observational bias, researcher bias, reactivity, confirmation bias, illusory correlation, causal error, and effect size. Also in this model, the following threats to external credibility were identified as being pertinent to qualitative research: catalytic validity, communicative validity, action validity, investigation

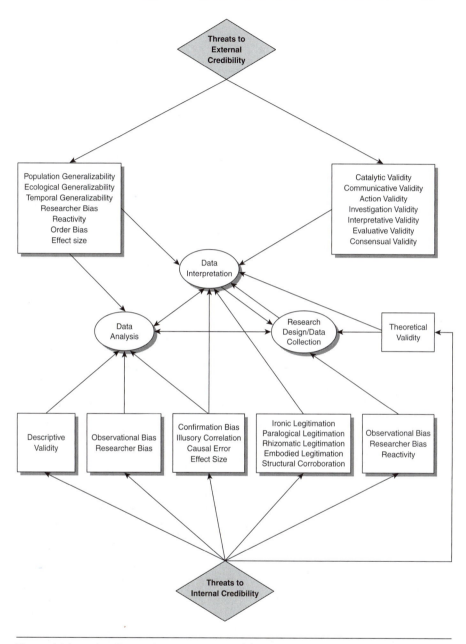

Figure 11.3   Qualitative Legitimation Model

validity, interpretive validity, evaluative validity, consensual validity, population generalizability, ecological generalizability, temporal generalizability, researcher bias, reactivity, order bias, and effect size.

Because of the association with the quantitative conceptualization of the research process, the term validity has generally been replaced by the term trustworthiness within qualitative research. The vast and important literature on trustworthiness is exemplified and discussed in the following references from the qualitative research literature: Creswell (1998), Glaser and Strauss (1967), Kvale (1995), Lather (1986, 1993), Lincoln and Guba (1985, 1990), Longino (1995), Maxwell (1992, 1996), Miles and Huberman (1984, 1994), Onwuegbuzie and Leech (in press-a), Schwandt (2001), Strauss and Corbin (1998), and Wolcott (1990).

Validity in Mixed Research

Mixed research involves the mixing of quantitative and qualitative methods or paradigm characteristics into research studies (Johnson & Onwuegbuzie, 2004; Onwuegbuzie & Johnson, 2004; Tashakkori & Teddlie, 1998, 2003). According to the *fundamental principle of mixed research,* it often should involve the combining of quantitative and qualitative methods, approaches, and concepts that have complementary strengths and nonoverlapping weaknesses (Brewer & Hunter, 1989; Johnson & Turner, 2003). This principle is meant to be viewed broadly; *it is not limited to triangulation or corroboration.* The words "complementary strengths" are meant to include all of the strengths of qualitative and quantitative research. Therefore, the principle can be used for the five traditional purposes of mixed research identified by Greene, Caracelli, and Graham (1989). By "complementary strengths" we are implying a putting together of different approaches, methods, and strategies in multiple and creative ways.

Mixed research still is plagued by the problems of representation, integration, and legitimation (Onwuegbuzie, in press). The *problem of representation* refers to the difficulty in capturing (i.e., representing) lived experiences using text in general and words and numbers in particular. The *problem of legitimation* refers to the difficulty in obtaining findings and/or making inferences that are credible, trustworthy, dependable, transferable, and/or confirmable. Indeed, in many instances, these problems are exacerbated in mixed research because both the quantitative and qualitative components of studies bring into the setting their own problems of representation and legitimation, likely yielding either an additive or a multiplicative threat—hence the *problem of integration.*

Mixed research can be conceptualized as combining quantitative or qualitative research in a concurrent, sequential, conversion (Tashakkori & Teddlie, 2003; Teddlie & Tashakkori, 2006), parallel (Onwuegbuzie & Leech, 2004a), or fully mixed (Leech & Onwuegbuzie, 2005; Teddlie & Tashakkori, 2006) manner. Quantitative and qualitative approaches can be combined in these ways whether the study represents primary research (Johnson & Onwuegbuzie, 2004; Teddlie & Tashakkori, 2006) or a mixed synthesis of the extant literature (i.e., integrating the findings from both quantitative and qualitative studies in a shared area of empirical research; Sandelowski, Voils, & Barroso, 2006). Further, quantitative and qualitative approaches can be combined in these ways regardless of which approach has priority in the study (cf. Creswell, Shope, Plano Clark, & Green, 2006). In basic concurrent mixed designs, the following three conditions hold: (a) both the quantitative and qualitative data are collected separately at approximately the same point in time, (b) neither the quantitative nor qualitative data analysis builds on the other during the data analysis stage, and (c) the results from each type of analysis are not consolidated at the data interpretation stage, until *both* sets of data have been collected and analyzed separately, and (d) after collection and interpretation of data from the quantitative and qualitative components, a meta-inference is drawn which integrates the inferences made from the separate quantitative and qualitative data and findings.

In basic sequential mixed designs, data collected and analyzed from one phase of the study (i.e., quantitative/qualitative data) are used to inform the other phase of the investigation (i.e., qualitative/quantitative data). Here, the data analysis begins *before* all the data are collected. At the highest level of integration, referred to as sequential mixed model studies, "multiple approaches to data collection, analysis, and inference are employed in a sequence of phases. Each phase, by itself, may use a mixed approach and provide conceptual and/or methodological grounds for the next one in the chain" (Tashakkori & Teddlie, 1998, pp. 149–150). Sequential mixed designs also can be applied when conducting what Chen (1990, 2006) conceptualizes as theory-driven evaluations, via the following two strategies: (a) switch strategy (e.g., first applying qualitative methods to illuminate program theory of stakeholders and then use quantitative methods to assess the program theory) and (b) contextual overlaying strategy (e.g., utilizing qualitative approaches to collect contextual information for facilitating the interpretation of quantitative data or reconciling findings).

Conversion mixed designs involve data transformation wherein one data form is converted into the other and then subsequently analyzed (Teddlie & Tashakkori, 2006). That is, the other data type evolves from the original data type either by converting the data from quantitative to qualitative or from qualitative to quantitative. Moreover, conversion occurs via techniques such as quantitizing data (i.e., transforming the qualitative data to a numerical form; Tashakkori & Teddlie, 1998) or qualitizing data (i.e., converting quantitative data into data that can be analyzed qualitatively; Tashakkori & Teddlie, 1998). Both data types are analyzed/re-analyzed, and inferences are made based on both sets of analyses.

In parallel mixed designs, the data are collected and analyzed separately. In this respect it is similar to concurrent designs. However, while inferences are made in concurrent designs on both sources of data in an integrated manner, in parallel mixed designs, each data source leads to its own set of inferences, and no attempt is made to reach what Tashakkori and Teddlie (2003) refer to as a "meta-inference" (p. 686), in which both sets of inferences are combined into a coherent whole. Such designs lead either to (a) two separate reports that would be presented or published separately or (b) two separate write-ups that are presented in two distinct sections of the same report. Whereas some researchers do not consider these designs as representing mixed research (e.g., Yin, 2006) but rather quasi-mixed designs (e.g., Teddlie & Tashakkori, 2006), other researchers do (e.g., Onwuegbuzie & Leech, 2004a). Given the formative stage of mixed research, we see, as does Greene (2006), these current disagreements as being good for the field as it continues to develop through hard conceptual and empirical work.

Fully mixed research designs (Leech & Onwuegbuzie, 2005), also known as fully integrated mixed research designs (Tashakkori & Teddlie, 2003; Teddlie & Tashakkori, 2006), involve mixing quantitative and qualitative approaches in an interactive way at all stages of the investigation (i.e., research objective, type of data/operations, type of analysis/inference; Onwuegbuzie & Johnson, 2004) such that at each stage, one approach (e.g., quantitative) influences the formulation of the other approach (e.g., qualitative). We agree with Teddlie and Tashakkori (2006) that fully mixed (and nearly fully mixed designs) are attractive because of the multiple points of integration.

Because of the complexity involved in combining qualitative and quantitative studies either in a concurrent, sequential, conversion, parallel, or fully mixed manner, mixed research gives rise to what we call the problem of integration. Surrounding this problem is the extent to which combining quantitative and qualitative approaches can address each of Greene et al. (1989) five empirically derived, general purposes of mixed-methodological research studies: (a) triangulation (i.e., seeking convergence and corroboration of findings from different methods that study the same phenomenon); (b) complementarity (i.e., seeking elaboration, illustration, enhancement, and clarification of the findings from one method with results from the other method); (c) development (i.e., using the findings from one method to help inform the other method); (d) initiation (i.e., discovering paradoxes and contradictions that lead to a re-framing of the research question); and (e) expansion (i.e., seeking to expand the breadth and range of inquiry by using different inquiry components). More generally, the problem of integration pertains to the extent to which combining quantitative and qualitative research techniques addresses one or more of Collins, Onwuegbuzie, and Sutton's (2006) four rationales for mixing or combining qualitative and quantitative approaches: participant enrichment (i.e., mixing quantitative and qualitative techniques to optimize the sample using techniques that include recruiting participants, engaging in activities such as Institutional Review Board debriefings, and ensuring that each participant selected is appropriate for inclusion), instrument fidelity (e.g., assessing the appropriateness and/or utility of existing instruments; creating new instruments; performance of human instruments), treatment integrity (i.e., assessing fidelity of intervention), and significance enhancement (e.g., facilitating thickness and richness of data; augmenting interpretation and usefulness of findings).

The problem of integration motivates us to ask questions such as the following: Is it misleading to triangulate, consolidate, or compare quantitative findings and inferences stemming from a large random sample on equal grounds with qualitative data arising from a small purposive sample? How much weight should be placed on quantitative data compared to qualitative data? Are quantitatively confirmed findings more important than findings that emerge during a qualitative study component? When findings conflict, what is one to conclude?

Before discussing the issue of integration more carefully, we will point out that we do not believe that the goal of mixed research is to replace either quantitative or qualitative research. Rather, the goal of this third type of research is to utilize the strengths of two or more approaches by combining them in one study, and by attempting to minimize the weaknesses of approaches in mixed designs. Philosophically, mixed research generally follows philosophical and methodological pragmatism (with a very broad and inclusive ontological realism where virtually everything a qualitative or quantitative researcher deems to be real can be considered, in some sense, to be real, including subjective realism, intersubjective realism, and objective realism). (See Johnson & Onwuegbuzie, 2004 for more discussion on the role of pragmatism in mixed research, and Sanders, 1997 for more discussion about inclusive ontology.) By pragmatism, we mean to search for workable solutions through the practice of research (e.g., follow the fundamental principle of mixed research, including the use of designs and criteria that are situation and context appropriate) to help answer questions that we value and to provide workable improvements in our world (i.e., help in bringing about desired outcomes). Our pragmatism includes a healthy dose of pluralism by which we mean that it is not logically contradictory to claim that quantitative and qualitative research are both useful, even if, at times, they appear to be contradictory; perhaps what is seen as contradictory are different perspectives that are complementary and enable one to more fully to see his or her world. Further, different standards of quality will be useful for different people in different contexts (see Patton's, 2002, five different sets of criteria for judging the quality of qualitative research), which is reasonable as long as one makes these standards clear to avoid arguments based on equivocation (which can produce misunderstandings based on nothing more than different meanings of terms being used by different people because they "talk past" one another). Clarity of language use is especially important when people from different communities are the interlocutors. Arguments about values can be healthy, and at this time more discussion among qualitative, quantitative, and mixed researchers about values needs to take place in order to understand better each other. Different researchers have different values and beliefs about research approaches for addressing important questions, and this diversity when put together is not a problem; we see it as a *potential strength* of research and practice, especially when simple and clear solutions are not readily forthcoming. In short, diversity of this sort is not a problem needing to be fixed by someone. Our pragmatism also is eclectic, by which we are referring to the inclusion of multiple quantitative and qualitative techniques in one's briefcase and then selecting combinations of assumptions, methods, and designs that best fit one's research questions of interest.

In every mixed research study researchers must deal with the problems of representation, legitimation, and integration but discussions about validity issues that characterize these problems are still in relative infancy. Developing justified inferences is at the center of many problems in mixed research. In fact, Teddlie and Tashakkori (2003) and Tashakkori and Teddlie (2003) identified drawing inferences as one of the six unresolved issues and controversies in mixed research. The purpose of the remainder of this paper is to contribute to the present dialogue about validity (trustworthy or defensibility or quality) issues in mixed research. We will discuss the following three unresolved and, at times, contentious issues in the domain of validity in mixed research:

(a) Labels for criteria for assessing mixed research studies;
(b) conceptualization of legitimation in mixed research studies; and
(c) identifying some types of legitimation for mixed research.

Label for Criteria for Assessing Mixed Research Studies

As noted by Teddlie and Tashakkori (2003), a primary decision that confronts the field of mixed research is what to call the concept of validity in mixed research. Although the term "validity" is routinely used in quantitative research, this term is disliked by many qualitative researchers. In fact, as noted by Schwandt (2001), some qualitative researchers object to the concept of validity based on their rejection of the correspondence theory of truth. They argue that because validity is the test of this correspondence, validity does not exist because there simply is no single reality, with truth being partially arbitrary as individuals interact with their worlds. These researchers also believe in *fallabilism* (i.e., all procedures for establishing legitimation represent "fallible means of making a case for a plausible and credible account"; Schwandt, 2001, pp. 268–269). Some qualitative researchers, although they believe that some validities are useful, contend that validity is always relative to a particular context, situation, language system, or worldview (Schwandt, 2001). These researchers refer to *contextualization* (i.e., legitimation represents the standards set by a particular community at a specific time and place). Some qualitative researchers refute any relationship between validity and objectivism, the latter of which is viewed as foundational. These researchers are referred to as representing *strong or radical relativism* (i.e., no single account can be judged as being superior to any other). Some qualitative researchers (i.e., postmodernists) view the concept of validity (and the word) as representing a debunked modernist perspective that champions universal rationality, rules, order, logic, and the like. Thus, we conclude that use of the word *validity* in mixed research can be counterproductive.

One attractive solution to this problem is for mixed researchers to use an alternative word that is more acceptable to both quantitative and qualitative researchers. This solution involves what Teddlie and Tashakkori (2003) refer to as "using a bilingual nomenclature" (p. 12). In this respect, a possible term that might be acceptable to both quantitative and qualitative investigators is *legitimation*. This would be consistent with its use in the Onwuegbuzie (2003) *Quantitative Legitimation Model* and the Onwuegbuzie and Leech (in press-a) *Qualitative Legitimation Model* presented in Figures 11.1 and 11.3. That is not to suggest that quantitative researchers should refrain from using the term validity or that qualitative researchers should cease using terms such as trustworthiness, credibility, plausibility, and dependability. It only is to suggest that in the context of discussing the overall criteria for assessment of mixed research studies, we recommend that the term legitimation, or a similarly descriptive and inclusive term, be used.

Conceptualization of Legitimation in Mixed Research Studies

In one of the very few essays written on the topic of validity or quality criteria in mixed research, Teddlie and Tashakkori (2003) stated that mixed methods researchers "should adopt a common nomenclature transcending the separate QUAL and QUAN orientations when the described processes (QUAL and QUAN) are highly similar and when appropriate terminology exists" (p. 12). Because inferences are made in research studies regardless of whether the associated interpretation is inductive or deductive in nature, these authors contended that the concept of "inference" transcends quantitative and qualitative research and they recommended that *inference quality* be used as the mixed research term for validity. This use has much merit, and we attempt to build on it below.

Teddlie and Tashakkori (2003) conceptualized inference quality as being associated with the following two research components: design quality and interpretive rigor. Design quality refers to the standards used for the evaluation of the methodological rigor of the mixed research study, whereas interpretive rigor pertains to the standards for evaluating the validity of conclusions. Teddlie and Tashakkori also presented the term *inference transferability* to denote the generalizability of the findings (for both quantitative and qualitative research), which comprises population transferability (i.e., transferability to other individuals, groups, or entities), ecological transferability (i.e., transferability to other contexts or settings), temporal transferability (i.e., transferability to other time periods), and operational transferability (i.e., transferability to other methods of measuring behaviors). Teddlie and Tashakkori appropriately differentiated data quality from inference quality. What also is appealing about Teddlie and Tashakkori's conceptualization of inference quality is their identification of the following four (non-exhaustive and not mutually exclusive) criteria for evaluation: (a) within-design consistency (i.e., "consistency of the procedures/design of study and from which the inference emerged"; p. 40); (b) conceptual consistency (i.e., "degree to which the inferences are consistent with each other and with the known state of knowledge and theory"; "consistency of inferences with each other within a study [cross-inference consistency]"; and "consistency of inference with current state of knowledge and theory [theoretical consistency]"; p. 40); (c) interpretive agreement (or consistency) (i.e., "consistency of interpretations across people"; p. 40); and (d) interpretive distinctiveness (i.e., the "degree to which the inferences are distinctively different from other possible interpretations of the results and rival explanations are ruled out," p. 40).

Building on the work of Teddlie and Tashakkori (2003), Tashakkori and Teddlie (2006) proposed an integrative model of quality that also comprises design quality and interpretive rigor. According to their model, design quality comprises (a) within-design consistency (as defined earlier), (b) design suitability (i.e., whether the methods of the study are appropriate for addressing the research question(s); and the design is consistent with the research question), (c) design fidelity (i.e., whether the procedures are implemented with quality and rigor; the methods are capable of capturing meaning, associations, or effects; and the components of the design such as sampling and data collection procedures, are implemented adequately); and (d) analytic adequacy (i.e., whether the data analysis techniques are appropriate for addressing the research question(s)). Interpretive rigor consists of (a) interpretive agreement (as defined earlier), (b) interpretive distinctiveness (as defined earlier), (c) interpretive consistency (i.e., whether the inferences closely follow the relevant findings in terms of type, intensity, and scope; and the multiple inferences made on the basis of the findings are consistent with each other), (c) theoretical consistency (i.e., whether the inferences are consistent with theory and the state of knowledge in the field), and integrative efficacy (i.e., whether the meta-inference adequately incorporates the inferences stemming from quantitative and qualitative phases of the study).

Teddlie and Tashakkori's (2003) and Tashakkori and Teddlie's (2006) conceptualizations present inference as an outcome. However, as appealing and useful as their conceptualization is, we believe it needs some elaboration and extension. We see useful extensions of their model in two ways. First, we view legitimation as a process, not just an outcome. Indeed, we believe that legitimation checks should occur at each stage of the mixed research process. Thus, the Quantitative Legitimation Model and Quantitative Legitimation Model, shown earlier, can be used for assessing legitimation of the quantitative and qualitative components of the study, respectively. While, clearly, making inferences is a vital part of the research process, giving inference quality primary emphasis could give the false impression that one does not have to scrutinize as carefully some of the other steps of the research process. Also, it is not clear yet what role the validity types presented in this paper (and in the selected references) will play in the evaluation process. Moreover, legitimation in mixed research should be seen as a continuous process rather than as a fixed attribute of a specific research study. Mixed research tends to be iterative and interactive (Onwuegbuzie & Johnson, 2004) such that, in a sense, *inference closure* (i.e., being able to make definitive statements about the quality of inferences made) might never be fully reached within a particular study or even over a series of systematically linked studies. We look forward to future dialogue about these issues as we all try to advance the field forward.

Some Types of Legitimation for Mixed Research

As noted earlier, the problems of representation and integration in mixed research suggest the need to identify specific legitimation issues that are not associated with monomethod designs. However, these legitimation issues are not addressed fully in Teddlie and Tashakkori's (2003) and Tashakkori and Teddlie's (2006) inference quality frameworks, nor do these issues appear to have been addressed, to date, in any other framework. Thus, we now will outline a new typology of legitimation types in mixed research for consideration, dialog, and refinement. Our typology currently is in its infancy, and it contains nine legitimation types. These legitimation types are summarized in Table 11.1. Each of these types of legitimation is discussed next.

Sample integration legitimation. This legitimation type applies to situations in which a researcher wants to make statistical generalizations from the sample

Table 11.1   Typology of Mixed Methods Legitimation Types

Legitimation Type	Description
Sample Integration	The extent to which the relationship between the quantitative and qualitative sampling designs yields quality meta-inferences.
Inside-Outside	The extent to which the researcher accurately presents and appropriately utilizes the insider's view and the observer's views for purposes such as description and explanation.
Weakness Minimization	The extent to which the weakness from one approach is compensated by the strengths from the other approach.
Sequential	The extent to which one has minimized the potential problem wherein the meta-inferences could be affected by reversing the sequence of the quantitative and qualitative phases.
Conversion	The extent to which the quantitizing or qualitizing yields quality meta-inferences.
Paradigmatic mixing	The extent to which the researcher's epistemological, ontological, axialogical, methodological, and rhetorical beliefs that underlie the quantitative and qualitative approaches are successfully (a) combined or (b) blended into a usable package.
Commensurability	The extent to which the meta-inferences made reflect a mixed worldview based on the cognitive process of Gestalt switching and integration.
Multiple Validities	The extent to which addressing legitimation of the quantitative and qualitative components of the study result from the use of quantitative, qualitative, *and* mixed validity types, yielding high quality meta-inferences.
Political	The extent to which the consumers of mixed methods research value the meta-inferences stemming from *both* the quantitative and qualitative components of a study.

participants to a larger target population. Unless exactly the same individuals or groups are involved in both the qualitative and quantitative components of a study, constructing meta-inferences by pulling together the inferences from the qualitative and quantitative phases can be problematic. For example, a researcher might conduct a concurrent design in which inferences made from quantitative data yielded by a large random sample were integrated (i.e., into a meta-inference) with inferences made from qualitative data arising from a smaller subset of this sample or from an entirely different group of people. However, if this meta-inference was generalized to the underlying population from which the large random sample was selected, it may not be justified for this inference to include inferences from the qualitative component, especially if the associated subsample is very small or if it forms a separate group of people. That is, because of the unrepresentative sample from the qualitative phase, the ensuing meta-inference might be poor (statistically speaking), which, in turn, would affect statistical generalizability (i.e., population transferability). To the degree to which the qualitative participants are similar a quantitative random sample, the problem will be reduced.

Both the inference quality and generalizability are even poorer if the quantitative sample is nonrandom, as is the case in the vast majority of empirical research studies (Onwuegbuzie & Leech, 2004b), and/or small. Even if the qualitative sample represented a random subset of the quantitative sample, as might be the case in a sequential mixed design, the meta-inference quality might still be poor. As such, when the researcher's goal is to make a statistical generalization we would urge caution in considering Teddlie and Tashakkori's (2003) contention that "in evaluating the quality of inferences in mixed research, the issue of dominance or priority of one methodological approach (e.g., QUAL-quan, qual-QUAN) over another is not very important" (p. 41). Specifically, the use of a dominant-less dominant design is more likely to lead to the combining of a strong inference (dominant phase) with a weak inference (less dominant design). If the inferences stemming from the quantitative and qualitative phases were consistent, then the meta-inference quality likely would be higher. However, a mixed methods researcher should not assume that this will always be the case. Regardless, criteria are needed to be developed to identify the range of conditions under which combining inferences from the qualitative and quantitative components of a study leads to meta-inference quality. Indeed, as noted by Collins, Onwuegbuzie, and Jiao (in press) and Onwuegbuzie and Collins (in press), the relationship between the quantitative and qualitative sampling designs (i.e., sampling scheme, sample size) is crucial to assessing meta-inference quality. Additional considerations regarding sample quality also should be considered when examining this type of legitimation. For example, in a qualitative sample, sometimes saturation is a useful criterion with regard to the conclusions (Guest, Bunce, & Johnson, 2006; Onwuegbuzie & Leech, 2005, in press-b; Strauss & Corbin, 1998; Teddlie & Yu, 2006). Sometimes theoretical generalizations can be made even in the absence of statistical sampling methods; for example, Yin (1994) has demonstrated this with some of the classic sociological community studies conducted in the twentieth century. In sum, it is essential that the way individuals and groups are selected be considered, and that additional consideration be made on how to combine legitimately different sets of people for use in making quality meta-inferences.

Inside-outside legitimation. As noted by Currall and Towler (2003), "etic refers to the trained observer's analysis of 'raw' data, whereas emic refers to how those data are interpreted by an 'insider' to the system or organization (Pike, 1967)" (p. 522). In other words, the *emic viewpoint* is the viewpoint of the group member, the insider. The *etic viewpoint* is that of the "objective" outsider looking at and studying the group. One can even speak of emic terms (language used by the group members) and etic terms (the language used by the outsider researcher) (Johnson & Christensen, 2004). Along the same lines as sample integration legitimation, when making meta-inferences by combining inferences from the qualitative and quantitative phases of a study, there are times when researchers should assess insider-outsider legitimation. This refers to the degree to which the researcher accurately presents and utilizes the insider's view *and* the observer's view. The ability to do this can be compromised when a researcher is ethnocentric or, on the other hand, when a researcher becomes so involved with the group that he or she "goes native."

A strategy for obtaining a justified etic viewpoint is for the researcher to use peer review; that is, the research can have another (disinterested and trained in social research) outsider/researcher examine the interpretations being made, the conceptualizations, and the relationship between the data and the conclusions. An important strategy for obtaining a justified insider viewpoint is member checking or participant review (i.e., have group members or participants assess the researcher's interpretations). A strategy for obtaining a justified meta-inference typically will be for everyone on the research team as well as some researchers outside of the team and participants inside the group under study to review the data and integration. In other words, the researcher should seek insider-outsider legitimation for the qualitative part of a study, for the quantitative part, and when the parts are put together or integrated (e.g., by maintaining a well informed and balanced perspective when collecting, analyzing, and interpreting what the whole set of qualitative and quantitative data mean). One might be able to make the case that quantitative research often seeks the objective outsider view, that qualitative research often seeks the insider's view, and that mixed research seeks to balance fully these two viewpoints.

Weakness minimization legitimation. Mixed research is in the optimal position for maximizing this form of legitimation simply because the researcher is able systematically to design a study that combines two or more methods. The key, however, is that the researcher must consciously and carefully assess the extent to which the weakness from one approach can be compensated by the strengths from the other approach and then plan and design the study to fulfill this potential; the researcher also must use this knowledge when combining, weighting, and interpreting the results. We refer to this process as *weakness minimization legitimation*. The greater the extent that the weakness from one approach is compensated by the strengths from the other approach, the more likely that combining a weak inference with a strong inference will lead to a superior or high quality meta-inference.

Sequential legitimation. When a sequential mixed research design is used, it is possible that the meta-inference that arises is solely or largely the effect of the sequencing itself. For example, if the results and interpretations would have been different if the order the quantitative and qualitative phases originally presented had been reversed, then this would indicate that the sequencing itself was a threat to legitimation. One method of assessing this is by changing the sequential design to a multiple wave design, in which the quantitative and qualitative data collection and data analysis phases oscillate multiple times (Sandelowski, 2003).

Conversion legitimation. All inferences or meta-inferences that are made after qualitizing and/or quantitizing the data must be scrutinized. The extent to which these data conversion techniques lead to interpretable data and high inference quality is called conversion legitimation. For example, a popularized way of quantitizing data is by counting. Obtaining counts of the themes present in qualitative data can prevent researchers from over-weighting or under-weighting emergent themes (Sandelowski, 2001). Also, qualitative researchers can sometimes obtain more meaning by obtaining counts of observations in addition to their narrative descriptions (Johnson & Christensen, 2004; Onwuegbuzie & Leech, 2004a; Onwuegbuzie & Teddlie, 2003; Sandelowski, 2001) because counting can provide additional useful information about how often or how many or how much. However, counting is not appropriate for some types of qualitative data and contexts. As noted by Sandelowski (2001), researchers should avoid the problems associated with verbal counting, misleading counting, over-counting, and acontextual counting. Such problems would affect the meta-inference quality. Similarly, a common method of qualitizing data is via narrative profile formation (i.e., modal profiles, average profiles, holistic profiles, comparative profiles, normative profiles). Such profiles involve constructing narrative descriptions from quantitative data. However, these descriptions can represent an over-generalization of the observed numeric data. Further, it is possible that a profile that emerges from qualitizing (e.g., via average profiles) yields a representation of people that is unrealistic.

Paradigmatic mixing legitimation. Combining quantitative and qualitative approaches is sometimes considered to be tenuous because of competing dualisms: epistemological (e.g., objectivist vs. subjectivist), ontological (e.g., single reality vs. multiple reality), axiological (e.g., value free vs. value-bound), methodological (e.g., deductive logic vs. inductive logic), and rhetorical (e.g., formal vs. informal writing style) beliefs. One solution is to use both viewpoints in a study (e.g., have a pure qualitative part and a pure quantitative part each based on the pure assumptions), and then attempt to make meaning from consideration of the two pure components of the study. Another solution is to think in terms of continua rather than dualisms and then take more moderate positions on each continuum: ontological (recognition of multiple affordances, levels of analysis, and disciplinary perspectives about what is studied; recognizing subjective, intersubjective, and objective types of reality; recognizing internal reality, external reality, and most importantly the interaction between the two), epistemological (intersubjective approach to knowledge generation), axiological (distinguishing between internal and external values, admitting and describing the value ladeness of the research; stating one's use of values in setting standards, determining what outcomes are to be valued, interpreting the data, making recommendations, and making explicit how one judged one's own study), and rhetorical (e.g., use of formal and informal writing styles using both impersonal and personal voices). When making meta-inferences, there are times when a researcher should evaluate the extent to which her or his epistemological, ontological, axiological, methodological, and rhetorical beliefs that underlie the quantitative and qualitative approaches are treated as separate *but* complementary or are used in less extreme forms and treated as being compatible. Legitimation comes from the researcher making the use of paradigm assumptions explicit and conducting research that fits with the stated assumptions.

Commensurability legitimation. This type of legitimation is based on a *rejection* of Kuhn's and Quine's (and others') concept of incommensurability of findings, theories, language, and worldviews. In order to meet this type of legitimation, the mixed researcher must learn to make Gestalt switches from qualitative lens to a quantitative lens, going back and forth, again and again. We believe this is possible through cognitive and empathy training. (If one believes this is not possible, then one can ignore "commensurability legitimation.") Through an iterative process, a third viewpoint is created, a viewpoint that is informed by, is separate from, and goes beyond what is provided by either a pure qualitative viewpoint or a pure quantitative viewpoint. To the extent that the researcher is able to negotiate cognitively this important Gestalt switch, the meta-inferences will provide a more fully mixed worldview;

it will go beyond the provision of both traditional viewpoints by offering a third, well-informed viewpoint based on consideration of both qualitative and quantitative thinking. This argument takes seriously what has been called the *compatibility thesis* (Howe, 1988; Reichardt & Rallis, 1994).

Multiple validities legitimation. This legitimation type, which is pertinent in virtually every mixed research study, refers to the extent to which all relevant research strategies are utilized and the research can be considered high on the multiple relevant "validities." For example, when addressing legitimation of the quantitative component, the relevant quantitative validities are addressed and achieved; when addressing legitimation of the qualitative component, the relevant qualitative "validities" are addressed and achieved; and during integration and to allow strong meta-inferences, the relevant mixed legitimation types are addressed and achieved. Relatedly, one should ask to what extent is the whole (i.e., meta-inference quality) greater than the sum of its parts (i.e., inferences arising from each component)?

Political legitimation. Onwuegbuzie (in press) has identified four challenges that researchers face when undertaking mixed methods research. One of these challenges is the challenge of politics. This challenge refers to power and value tensions that come to the fore as a result of combining quantitative and qualitative approaches. These tensions include any value or ideologically based conflicts that occur when different researchers are used for the quantitative and qualitative phases of a study, as well as differences in perspectives about contradictions and paradoxes that arise when the quantitative and qualitative findings are compared and contrasted. The challenge of politics also includes the difficulty in persuading the consumers of mixed methods research, including stakeholders and policymakers, to value the meta-inferences stemming from *both* the quantitative and qualitative components of a study. In traditional quantitative research, decision making and power over the research process is fully in the hands of the centralized researcher in a top down manner. In postmodern qualitative research, much power is placed in the research participants themselves, and the researcher takes the role of collaborator and facilitator. In mixed research, the researcher or research team sometimes will take multiple roles; consequently, mixed researchers will need to deal with issues surrounding multiple or distributed power in the planning, conduct, and the use of research (Fetterman, 2000). A strategy for achieving this form of legitimation is to advocate pluralism of perspectives and to strive to generate practical theory or results that consumers naturally will value because the results answer important questions and help provide workable solutions.

Summary and Conclusions

The purpose of this paper has been to contribute to the present dialogue about validity issues in mixed research. We first overviewed the ways validity is viewed and defined in quantitative and qualitative research, and we pointed out that there has been a problem of legitimation in both of these paradigms. Second, we contended that there is also a *problem of representation* and *problem of legitimation* in mixed research. We argued that because mixed research involves combining complementary strengths and nonoverlapping weaknesses of quantitative and qualitative research methods, assessing the validity of findings can be particularly complex—yielding a *problem of integration*. We recommended that validity in mixed research be termed legitimation in order to use a bilingual nomenclature that can be used by both quantitative and qualitative researchers. We briefly summarized Teddlie and Tashakkori's (2003) and Tashakkori and Teddlie's (2006) interesting, emerging evaluation criteria frameworks involving the concept of inference quality. We identified nine new types of legitimation that come to the fore as a result of combining inferences from the quantitative and qualitative components of a mixed research study to form meta-inferences. These nine types of legitimation were sample integration legitimation, insider-outsider legitimation, weakness minimization legitimation, sequential legitimation, conversion legitimation, paradigmatic mixing legitimation, commensurability legitimation, multiple validities legitimation, and political legitimation. These types of legitimation need to be studied more closely in order to determine when and how they operate and how they can be maximized or made to occur. Mixed methods researchers should keep in mind that legitimation represents a process that is analytical, social, aesthetic, emic, etic, political, and ethical, and which must involve the community of quantitative and qualitative scholars alike who are committed to addressing the multiple problems that can occur in mixed research. This is the only way that the promise of mixed research can be realized in research practice.

References

American Educational Research Association, American Psychological Association, & National Council on Measurement in Education (1999). *Standards for educational and psychological testing* (rev. ed.). Washington, DC: American Educational Research Association.

Bracht, G. H., & Glass, G. V. (1968). The external validity of experiments. *American Educational Research Journal, 5*, 437–474.

Brewer, J., & Hunter, A. (1989). *Multimethod research: A synthesis of styles.* Newbury Park, CA: Sage.

Campbell, D. T. (1957). Factors relevant to the validity of experiments in social settings. *Psychological Bulletin, 54,* 297–312.

Campbell, D. T., & Stanley, J. C. (1963). *Experimental and quasi-experimental designs for research.* Chicago: Rand McNally.

Chen, H. T. (1990). *Theory-driven evaluations.* Newbury Park, CA: Sage.

Chen, H. T. (2006). A theory-driven evaluation perspective on mixed methods research. *Research in the Schools, 13*(1), 75–83.

Collins, K. M. T., Onwuegbuzie, A. J., & Jiao, Q. G. (in press). Prevalence of mixed methods sampling designs in social science research. *Evaluation and Research in Education.*

Collins, K. M. T., Onwuegbuzie, A. J., & Sutton, I. L. (2006). A model incorporating the rationale and purpose for conducting mixed methods research in special education and beyond. *Learning Disabilities: A Contemporary Journal, 4,* 67–100.

Cook, T. D., & Campbell, D. T. (1979). *Quasi-experimentation: Design and analysis issues for field settings.* Chicago: Rand McNally.

Creswell, J. W. (1998). *Qualitative inquiry and research design: Choosing among five traditions.* Thousand Oaks, CA: Sage.

Creswell, J. W., Shope, R., Plano Clark, V. L., & Green, D. O. (2006). How interpretive qualitative research extends mixed methods research. *Research in the Schools, 13*(1), 1–11.

Currall, S. C., & Towler, A. J. (2003). Research methods in management and organizational research: Toward integration of qualitative and quantitative techniques. In A. Tashakkori & C. Teddlie (Eds.), *Handbook of mixed methods in social and behavioral research* (pp. 513–526). Thousand Oaks, CA: Sage.

Denzin, N. K., & Lincoln, Y. S. (2005). The discipline and practice of qualitative research. In N. K. Denzin & Y. S. Lincoln (Eds.), *Handbook of qualitative research* (3rd ed., pp. 1–32). Thousand Oaks, CA: Sage.

Fetterman, D. M. (2000). *Empowerment evaluation.* Newbury Park, CA: Sage.

Glaser, B. G., & Strauss, A. L. (1967). *The discovery of grounded theory: Strategies for qualitative research.* Chicago: Aldine.

Greene, J. C. (2006). Toward a methodology of mixed methods social inquiry. *Research in the Schools, 13*(1), 93–98.

Greene, J. C., Caracelli, V. J., & Graham, W. F. (1989). Toward a conceptual framework for mixed-method evaluation designs. *Educational Evaluation and Policy Analysis, 11,* 255–274.

Guest, G., Bunce, A., & Johnson, L. (2006). How many interviews are enough? An experiment with data saturation and variability. *Field Methods, 18*(1), 59–82.

Howe, K. R. (1988). Against the quantitative-qualitative incompatibility thesis or dogmas die hard. *Educational Researcher, 17*(8), 10–16.

Johnson, B., & Christensen, L. (2004). *Educational research: Quantitative, qualitative, and mixed approaches* (2nd ed.). Needham Heights, MA: Allyn & Bacon.

Johnson, R. B., & Onwuegbuzie, A. J. (2004). Mixed methods research: A research paradigm whose time has come. *Educational Researcher, 33*(7), 14–26.

Johnson, B., & Turner, L. A. (2003). Data collection strategies in mixed methods research. In A. Tashakkori and C. Teddlie (Eds.), *Handbook of mixed methods in social and behavioral research* (pp. 297–319). Thousand Oaks, CA: Sage.

Kvale, S. (1995). The social construction of validity. *Qualitative Inquiry, 1,* 19–40.

Lather, P. (1986). Issues of validity in openly ideological research: Between a rock and a soft place. *Interchange, 17,* 63–84.

Lather, P. (1993). Fertile obsession: Validity after poststructuralism. *Sociological Quarterly, 34,* 673–693.

Leech, N. L., & Onwuegbuzie, A. J. (2005, April). *A typology of mixed methods research designs.* Invited James E. McLean Outstanding Paper presented at the annual meeting of the American Educational Research Association, Montreal, Canada.

Lewin, K. (1952). *Field theory in social science: Selected theoretical papers by Kurt Lewin.* London: Tavistock.

Lincoln, Y. S., & Guba, E. G. (1985). *Naturalistic inquiry.* Beverly Hills, CA: Sage.

Lincoln, Y. S., & Guba, E. G. (1990). Judging the quality of case study reports. *International Journal of Qualitative Studies in Education, 3,* 53–59.

Longino, H. (1990). *Science as social knowledge: Values and objectivity in scientific inquiry.* Princeton, NJ: Princeton University Press.

Longino, H. (1995). Gender, politics, and the theoretical virtues. *Synthese, 104,* 383–397.

Maxwell, J. A. (1992). Understanding and validity in qualitative research. *Harvard Educational Review, 62,* 279–299.

Maxwell, J. A. (1996). *Qualitative research design.* Newbury Park, CA: Sage.

Maxwell, J. A. (2005). *Qualitative research design: An interactive approach* (2nd ed.). Newbury Park, CA: Sage.

Messick, S. (1989). Validity. In R. L. Linn (Ed.), *Educational measurement* (3rd ed., pp. 13–103). Old Tappan, NJ: Macmillan.

Messick, S. (1995). Validity of psychological assessment: Validation of inferences from persons' responses and performances as scientific inquiry into score meaning. *American Psychologist, 50,* 741–749.

Miles, M. B., & Huberman, A. M. (1984). *Qualitative data analysis: A sourcebook of new methods.* Beverly Hills, CA: Sage.

Miles, M., & Huberman, A. M. (1994). *Qualitative data analysis: An expanded sourcebook* (2nd ed.). Thousand Oaks, CA: Sage.

Onwuegbuzie, A. J. (2003). Expanding the framework of internal and external validity in quantitative research. *Research in the Schools, 10*(1), 71–90.

Onwuegbuzie, A. J. (in press). Mixed methods research in sociology and beyond. In G. Ritzer (Ed.), *Encyclopedia of sociology.* Cambridge, MA: Blackwell Publishers.

Onwuegbuzie, A. J., & Collins, K. M. T. (in press). A typology of mixed methods sampling designs in social science research. *The Qualitative Report.*

Onwuegbuzie, A. J., Daniel, L. G., & Collins, K. M. T. (in press). A meta-validation model for assessing the score-validity of student teaching evaluations. *Quality & Quantity: International Journal of Methodology.*

Onwuegbuzie, A. J., & Johnson, R. B. (2004). Mixed method and mixed model research. In B. Johnson & L. Christensen, *Educational research: Quantitative, qualitative, and mixed approaches* (pp. 408–431). Boston, MA: Allyn and Bacon.

Onwuegbuzie, A. J., & Leech, N. L. (2004a). Enhancing the interpretation of "significant" findings: The role of mixed methods research. *The Qualitative Report*, 9(4), 770–792. Retrieved April 19, 2005, from http://www.nova.edu/ssss/ QR/QR9-4/Onwuegbuzie.pdf

Onwuegbuzie, A. J., & Leech, N. L. (2004b). Post-hoc power: A concept whose time has come. *Understanding Statistics*, 3, 151–180.

Onwuegbuzie, A. J., & Leech, N. L. (2005). The role of sampling in qualitative research. *Academic Exchange Quarterly*, 9, 280–284.

Onwuegbuzie, A. J., & Leech, N. L. (in press-a). Validity and qualitative research: An oxymoron? *Quality & Quantity: International Journal of Methodology*.

Onwuegbuzie, A. J., & Leech, N. L. (in press-b). A call for qualitative power analyses: Considerations in qualitative research. *Quality & Quantity: International Journal of Methodology*.

Onwuegbuzie, A. J., & Teddlie, C. (2003). A framework for analyzing data in mixed methods research. In A. Tashakkori & C. Teddlie (Eds.), *Handbook of mixed methods in social and behavioral research* (pp. 351–383). Thousand Oaks, CA: Sage.

Patton, M. Q. (2002). *Qualitative research and evaluation methods*. Thousand Oaks, CA: Sage.

Pike, K. L. (1967). *Language in relation to a unified theory of the structure of human behavior*. The Hague, Netherlands: Mouton.

Reichardt, S. S., & Rallis, S. F. (1994). Qualitative and quantitative inquiries are not incompatible: a call for a new partnership. In C. S. Reichardt & S. F. Rallis (Eds.), *The qualitative-quantitative debate: New perspectives* (pp. 85–91). San Francisco, CA: Jossey-Bass.

Sandelowski, M. (2001). Real qualitative researchers don't count: The use of numbers in qualitative research. *Research in Nursing & Health*, 24, 230–240.

Sandelowski, M. (2003). Tables or tableaux? The challenges of writing and reading mixed methods studies. In A. Tashakkori & C. Teddlie (Eds.), *Handbook of mixed methods in social and behavioral research* (pp. 321–350). Thousand Oaks, CA: Sage.

Sandelowski, M., Voils, C. I., & Barroso, J. (2006). Defining and designing mixed research synthesis studies. *Research in the Schools*, 13(1), 29–40.

Sanders, J. T. (1997). An ontology of affordances. *Ecological Psychology*, 9(1), 97–112.

Schwandt, T. A. (2001). *Dictionary of qualitative inquiry* (2nd ed.). Thousand Oaks, CA: Sage.

Shadish, W. R., Cook, T. D., & Campbell, D. T. (2001). *Experimental and quasi-experimental designs for generalized causal inference*. Boston: Houghton Mifflin.

Smith, M. L., & Glass, G. V. (1987). *Research and evaluation in education and the social sciences*. Englewood Cliffs, NJ: Prentice Hall.

Strauss, A., & Corbin, J. (1998). *Basics of qualitative research: Techniques and procedures for developing grounded theory*. Thousand Oaks, CA: Sage.

Tashakkori, A., & Teddlie, C. (1998). *Mixed methodology: Combining qualitative and quantitative approaches*. Applied Social Research Methods Series (Vol. 46). Thousand Oaks, CA: Sage.

Tashakkori, A., & Teddlie, C. (2003). The past and future of mixed methods research: From data triangulation to mixed model designs. In A. Tashakkori & C. Teddlie (Eds.), *Handbook of mixed methods in social and behavioral research* (pp. 671–701). Thousand Oaks, CA: Sage.

Tashakkori, A., & Teddlie, C. (2006, April). *Validity issues in mixed methods research: Calling for an integrative framework.* Paper presented at the annual meeting of the American Educational Research Association, San Francisco, CA.

Teddlie, C., & Tashakkori, A. (2003). Major issues and controversies in the use of mixed methods in the social and behavioral sciences. In A. Tashakkori & C. Teddlie (Eds.), *Handbook of mixed methods in social and behavioral research* (pp. 3–50). Thousand Oaks, CA: Sage.

Teddlie, C., & Tashakkori, A. (2006). A general typology of research designs featuring mixed methods. *Research in the Schools, 13*(1), 12–28.

Teddlie, C., & Yu, F. (2006, April). *Mixed methods sampling procedures: Some prototypes with examples.* Paper presented at the annual meeting of the American Educational Research Association, San Francisco, CA.

Wolcott, H. F. (1990). On seeking—and rejecting—validity in qualitative research. In E. W. Eisner & A. Peshkin (Eds.), *Qualitative inquiry in education: The continuing debate* (pp. 121–152). New York: Columbia University, Teachers College Press.

Yin, R. K. (1994). *Case study research: Design and methods.* Thousand Oaks, CA: Sage.

Yin, R. K. (2006). Mixed methods research: Are the methods genuinely integrated or merely parallel? *Research in the Schools, 13*(1), 41–47.

Notes

1. Onwuegbuzie and Leech (2006) note that, unlike the case for quantitative research, in qualitative research, the research design/data collection, data analysis, and data interpretation stages are iterative. That is, in qualitative studies, the research design/data collection, data analysis, and data interpretation stages are recursive, and, thus, non-linear in nature.

2. Denzin and Lincoln (2000) refer to this as the *crisis of representation.*

3. Denzin and Lincoln (2000) refer to this as the *crisis of legitimation.*

4. According to Denzin and Lincoln (2000), there is also a *crisis of praxis* in qualitative research. This crisis asks, "Is it possible to effect change in the world if society is only and always a text?" (p. 17).

Correspondence should be addressed to Anthony J. Onwuegbuzie, Dept. of Educational Measurement and Research, College of Education, University of South Florida, 4202 East Fowler Ave., EDU 162, Tampa, Florida 33620.

Email: tonyonwuegbuzie@aol.com

12

Powerful Rhetorical Devices Used in Writing Mixed Methods Research

Selection: Sandelowski, M. (2003). Tables or tableaux? The challenges of writing and reading mixed methods studies. In A. Tashakkori & C. Teddlie (Eds.), *Handbook of mixed methods in social and behavioral research* (pp. 321–350). Thousand Oaks, CA: Sage.

Editors' Introduction

The challenges of conducting mixed methods research do not end with analyzing the data and validating findings. Researchers also face the challenge of deciding how to present and report the study in a way that is convincing and publishable. Margarete Sandelowski is a nursing researcher who has written extensively about qualitative and mixed methods research. In this 2003 chapter, she is one of the first to discuss issues pertinent to researchers as they craft rhetorical representations of their mixed methods studies.

Sandelowski begins with a careful examination of the language of mixed methods research, including scholars' inconsistent use of the terms *qualitative, quantitative, mixing,* and *triangulation*. She describes the potential conflict between traditional quantitative and qualitative reporting structures and their consequences for developing persuasive mixed methods reports. She suggests that the rhetoric of mixed methods studies can be enhanced with careful use of writing devices such as numbers, quotes, visual displays that link quantitative and qualitative data, and aesthetic "mixed metaphors." She also ties different writing styles to the use of different mixed methods designs. Her discussion concludes with an appeal to mixed methods researchers to be mindful of the larger rhetorical issues when crafting their study reports and to develop convincing descriptions of their studies through the respectful use of terms and writing structures that match the context of the study and intended audiences.

Discussion Questions and Applications

1. Locate a mixed methods study report and examine its rhetorical structure. In what ways did the author(s) craft (or not craft) a convincing mixed methods study?

2. Examine the studies in Part II of this volume and note the types of visual displays used. Did you find examples that link quantitative and qualitative data sets?

3. Consider your own mixed methods study. What rhetorical decisions and devices will you employ to craft a convincing argument based on your study's priority, design, and intended audiences?

Related References That Extend the Topic

For a discussion of how to write and organize mixed methods studies see:

Creswell, J. W., & Plano Clark, V. L. (2007). Writing and evaluating mixed methods research. In *Designing and conducting mixed methods research* (pp. 151–166). Thousand Oaks, CA: Sage.

For a critique of the language of mixed methods and how mixed methods is written see:

Freshwater, D. (2007). Reading mixed methods research: Contexts for criticism. *Journal of Mixed Methods Research, 1*(2), 134–146.

Tables or Tableaux?

The Challenges of Writing and Reading Mixed Methods Studies

Margarete Sandelowski
University of North Carolina at Chapel Hill

M ixed methods studies present researchers with many challenges. Not the least of these challenges, and the subject of this chapter, is how to present mixed methods studies for mixed audiences of researchers.[1] Mixed methods studies engender a "crisis of representation" (Denzin & Lincoln, 2000, p. 16) all their own as they mandate that researchers/writers communicate across entrenched divides often separating writers from readers, in general, and qualitative from quantitative writers and readers, in particular.

A major—and arguably the most important—criterion in evaluating the merits of a study lies in the ability of writers to persuade readers of its merits in their research reports. Aesthetic criteria, including the sense of rightness and comfort readers experience, is crucial to the judgments they make about the validity or trustworthiness of a study (Eisner, 1985). Indeed, a judgment of trustworthiness is as much—or even more—a judgment about attractiveness and appeal as it is about objectivity or truth. But qualitative and quantitative readers have different ideas about what is appealing (Golden-Biddle & Locke, 1993). They often belong to different "interpretive communities" of writers and readers (Fish, 1980) whose members vary in their access and attunement to, knowledge and acceptance of, and participation with, for example, references and allusions in a text, the varied uses of

SOURCE: This chapter is reprinted from *Handbook of Mixed Methods in Social and Behavioral Research* (Tashakkori & Teddlie, 2003). Reprinted with permission of Sage Publications, Inc.

words and numbers, and various genres or conventions of writing, Qualitative and quantitative readers bring different reading backgrounds, experiences, and expectations to research reports and thus interact with these texts differently, Mixed methods studies, which entail the active engagement of highly diverse communities of qualitative and quantitative writers and readers, thus call into question which appeals will produce the most convincing texts. The production of convincing mixed methods studies lies, in large part, in how well the needs and expectations of readers representing this mix of interpretive communities have been met.

Yet, mixed methods studies are often themselves employed as appeals to validity, that is, as overcoming the shortcomings of single method studies, in general, and of quantitative and especially qualitative studies, in particular. Researchers may emphasize the quantitative research in their mixed methods studies to authorize their use of qualitative research to readers deemed likely to view qualitative work as weak scholarship. John (1992) proposed that psychologists use statistics, in large part, to confer the "epistemic authority" (p. 146) of science on psychology, a field in which the claim to science is contested. As he observed, the power of statistics lies as much in their ability to engender a "sense of conviction" (p. 147) in their "evidentiary value" (p. 144) as to provide actual evidence about a target phenomenon. In a similar but contrasting vein, researchers may emphasize the qualitative research in their mixed methods studies to authorize their use of quantitative research to readers deemed likely to view quantitative work as thin scholarship.

In this chapter, I draw from literatures on mixed methods and qualitative research, and on aesthetic modes of knowing, *rhetoric* and *representation* in science, and reader response theories (Beach, 1993) to describe the challenges of writing and reading mixed methods studies. I present mixed methods study not only as a challenge to rhetoric but also as a kind of rhetoric itself.

Words and Worlds

The most important challenge to writing and reading mixed methods studies lies in the various and even bewildering uses of the words *qualitative, quantitative, mixed methods,* and *triangulation* in methodological literature about, and reports of the findings of, mixed methods studies. The phrases *mixed methods studies* and *triangulated studies* are commonly used to refer to the use of both qualitative and quantitative approaches to inquiry within the confines of a single study. Yet in the writings about and reports of mixed methods studies, including the chapters in this handbook [Tashakkori & Teddlie, 2003], there are no uniform presentations of (a) what distinguishes qualitative from quantitative research, (b) what qualitative and quantitative entities are mixed, (c) what kind of mixing is involved, and (d) why these entities are mixed are all. The consequence of this lack of uniformity is a confusing state of affairs for readers whereby mixes are claimed for studies having no mixes, for entities that cannot be mixed, and/or to resolve methodological problems that cannot be resolved by mixing.

Qualitative and Quantitative

Qualitative and *quantitative* are words that are used in a variety of ways to refer to an even wider variety of research entities, including (a) paradigms, or overarching worldviews or perspectives for inquiry, such as neo-positivism, social constructionism, and feminism; (b) kinds of data such as stories, self-reports, numbers, accounts, fieldnotes, and photographs; (c) kinds of research methods such as grounded theory and experiments; and (d) kinds of research techniques for sampling, data collection, and analysis such as random and theoretical sampling, questionnaires and in-depth interviewing, and multiple regression and qualitative content analysis. The words *qualitative* and *quantitative* are typically used to present research paradigms, methods, and/or techniques as one or the other. Mixed methods studies imply difference, as they entail the combination of entities—qualitative and quantitative—that are viewed as different from, albeit compatible with, each other.

Yet, also clear from the vast literature on the subject is that qualitative research is not an entity clearly distinguishable from quantitative research; rather, it is many things to many people. Although it seems "rhetorically unavoidable" to compare qualitative and quantitative research (Becker, 1996, p. 53), there is no consistent manner in which such comparisons are made. For some scholars, qualitative and quantitative research differ in kind, constituting entities as different from each other as cats and dogs, while for others, they differ only in degree. While some scholars emphasize and even celebrate the differences between qualitative and quantitative research, others minimize and even trivialize them. Schwandt (2000) proposed that qualitative inquiry is more appropriately viewed as a "reformist movement" (p. 189), or an "arena for social scientific criticism" (p. 190), than as any particular kind of inquiry. He suggested that qualitative research is "home" for a wide variety of scholars who appear to share very little except their general distaste for and distrust of "mainstream" (usually conceived as quantitative) research (p. 190). Indeed, these scholars are often seriously at odds with each other. Although the term *qualitative research* does manage to convey a shared "feeling tone" (Sapir, 1951, p. 308), what it signifies beyond that feeling varies with the reader and writer of qualitative research.

Accordingly, communicating the mix in mixed methods studies is complicated if only because studies might not actually include ingredients perceived by writers and/or readers as different, that is, as qualitative as opposed to quantitative. The appeal to difference fails here, thereby undermining the claim to having conducted a mixed methods study. For example, although they have been depicted as mixed methods studies, projects involving the addition of one or two open-ended questions at the end of a standardized questionnaire, a simple frequency count of topics raised by respondents in interviews, or a count of the numbers of theoretical categories created and the numbers of persons falling into those categories can hardly be considered examples of mixing qualitative with quantitative research. There are writers and readers who use the word *qualitative* as a synonym for any verbal data collected from human participants (including standardized instruments) or for any study that is not quantitative. Because mixed methods study has become somewhat of a fad, claiming to having conducted a mixed methods study becomes a way to be methodologically fashionable. Mixed methods study is used here as a rhetorical appeal not only to methodological fashion but also to methodological expertise and ecumenicism.

Adding to the confusion concerning whether anything at all is mixed in studies presented as mixed methods studies is that entities commonly conceived as qualitative, such as focus groups, are often actually implemented quantitatively. If *qualitative* refers not simply to verbal data but rather to an overarching interpretivist, hermeneutic, constructionist, or participatory perspective (Heron & Reason, 1997; Schwandt, 2000) concerning how inquiry should be conducted, there is arguably nothing qualitative about focus groups that are conducted like surveys, with highly structured interview guides allowing participants little freedom to structure responses that are, in turn, analyzed using descriptive statistics. There is nothing mixed in a purportedly mixed methods study that combines a survey tool with a focus group that is itself conducted and analyzed like a survey. Indeed, such a study is more accurately conceived as a multimethod study in which two or more like (quantitative or quantitatively informed) entities are used. A study comprised largely of focus groups treated like surveys, even if data are analyzed verbally as opposed to statistically, is at best (and depending on point of view) a *non*quantitative or *non*qualitative study.

The Mix in Mixed Methods Studies

In addition to the lack of uniformity in presenting qualitative versus quantitative research, which calls into question whether anything has been mixed at all, is the lack of clarity concerning what qualitative and quantitative entities have been mixed and the kind of mixing involved. Writers have variously depicted mixed methods studies as mixes, mergers, blends, integrations, reconciliations, or other combinations of qualitative and quantitative paradigms, methods, or techniques. In these presentations, mergers are claimed for entities that are not exclusively either qualitative or quantitative (e.g., case studies, feminist inquiry) or are at different levels of inquiry (e.g., a hermeneutic *paradigm* and a fixed response *data collection tool*) and for entities that cannot be merged (e.g., realist and relativist paradigms of inquiry).

What better distinguishes research entities and researchers is not whether they are qualitative or quantitative per se (as both focus groups and surveys involve verbal data and will therefore be labeled by some writers and readers as qualitative, while data from both sources can be analyzed statistically) but rather the overall attitude toward and interpretive treatment of the data collected in those studies. Methods do not by themselves signal much about the nature of inquiry; rather, it is the distinctive execution and representation of these methods that signal key differences in inquiry. Whether any mix has occurred at all is determined by ascertaining, for example, whether the interviews conducted in a study that also involves the use of questionnaires are treated like those questionnaires or as, for example, narratives of the self. In the former instance, a qualitative-quantitative mix arguably cannot justifiably be claimed, while in the latter instance, it arguably can.

The focus group, the interview, and participant observation are good examples of entities depicted at the level of both methodology and method. While some writers use the terms *methodology* and *method* synonymously, others take great pains to distinguish between them, using the term *methodology* to refer to an over all approach to inquiry regularly linked to particular theoretical frameworks (e.g., grounded theory that is linked to symbolic interactionism and pragmatism) and using the term *method* as a synonym for the techniques for sampling, data collection, and data analysis with which methodologies (e.g., grounded theory) are implemented. Some writers present the focus group, the interview, and participant observation as data collection techniques used, for example, to execute grounded theory or ethnographic studies, while others present them as wholly defining their studies (i.e., *as* methodologies), designating the studies themselves as focus group, interview, or participant observation studies. Because of the different uses to which *method* and *methodology* are put, and because the same entity may be conceived as either a method or a methodology and differently executed, the determination of what has been mixed and whether any mix has occurred at all can be difficult to make.

The determination of whether anything has been mixed is further complicated because scholars arguing for and against mixes are frequently not talking about the same mixes or claim mixes of entities that cannot be mixed. The disagreements between so-called purists and "compatibilists"

(Skrtic, 1990, p. 128) over whether qualitative and quantitative research can be mixed are often not true disagreements at all; purists tend to emphasize the irreconcilability of paradigms, while compatibilists tend to emphasize the reconcilability of methods or techniques. In short, they all are ostensibly discussing the mixing of qualitative and quantitative research, but they are more often than not referring to mixes at different (paradigm, method, or technique) levels of research, conceiving the same entities differently as paradigms, methods, or techniques and/or describing different research entities as qualitative or quantitative. In addition, researchers often do not mean the same thing when they talk of any one study as a mixed methods study. To some researchers, the mixed methods study to which they are referring is one study in a program of research involving other studies (that may or may not be mixed), while to other researchers, it refers to the program of research itself. A program of research necessarily entails more than one study and may include a series of single method (qualitative and quantitative) studies, but it is debatable whether the term *mixed methods study* ought to be used to refer to such a program of research.

Moreover, paradigms, if defined as overarching worldviews and belief systems, cannot be mixed. Paradigms, by this definition, entail competing and often contradictory views concerning the nature of reality, the proper relationship between researcher and participant, the objectives and values of inquiry, and how value is to be judged. Although paradigms are uniformly linked to neither methods nor techniques (e.g., feminist inquiry is not exclusively qualitative, nor is neo-positivist inquiry exclusively quantitative), paradigms do influence the way in which any one method or technique will be executed. Grounded theory will be differently executed and thus presented depending on whether it is informed by tenets of neo-positivism or constructivism (Annells, 1996; Charmaz, 2000). The interview will be differently conducted, and the interview data will be differently treated and presented, depending on whether researchers view the interview as an index of some external reality, such as facts or feelings (Silverman, 2000, p. 823), or as a "technology of biographical construction" (Atkinson & Silverman, 1997, p. 306). The interpretive treatment of the interview will depend on whether researchers view interview data as comprising reports of events or as public, private, moral, or other accounts of those events (Radley & Billig, 1996; West, 1990). Treatment will also depend on whether researchers view interviewees as potentially biased informants or forgetful reporters of events or as narrators or impression managers of them (Riessman, 1990). In fact, the treatment of the interview will depend on whether researchers view interviewees as fixed participants/objects of study at all. Scholars have increasingly challenged the humanist notion of a stable and individual self on which academic inquiry has been largely based (Blumenthal, 1999; Gergen & Gergen, 2000).

Accordingly, although a program of research might comprise of a series of studies that together combine two or more paradigms for inquiry, any one research project—including any one mixed methods study—can be informed by only one paradigm or viewing position. As graphic artist M. C. Escher demonstrated in his 1947 work *High and Low*, the tiled diamond entity in this work cannot simultaneously be viewed as both a ceiling and a floor (Schattschneider, 1994). Moreover, like religious beliefs, different beliefs about inquiry may be tolerated, but they are not so easily changed or exchanged by any one researcher. Any one research study, no matter what the methods or techniques used, cannot simultaneously or sequentially be informed by, for example, a belief that valid results are enhanced by a dualist and detached relationship between researcher and participant and by the opposing belief that valid results are obtained only when a fully participative relationship exists.

An excellent example of a mixed methods study in which a qualitative method (narrative analysis based on Kleinman's explanatory models framework) was used within a neo-positivist framework is the Borkan, Quirk, and Sullivan (1991) study of the relationship between elders' narrative constructions of hip fracture and functional outcomes. Borkan and his colleagues transformed and reduced the narrative data they collected into two variables so as to ascertain whether they predicted functional outcomes. The process by which this transformation took place included several sequences of interrater reliability coding, a quantitatively informed procedure reflecting the belief that truth is replicable and will elicit consensus. By contrast, researchers operating in an interpretive paradigm will treat narratives as inherently dynamic and revisionist and therefore not reducible to fixed variables in a correlation matrix or amenable to mathematized reliability testing.

An excellent example of a mixed methods study in which a quantitative technique (Spearman correlation) was used in an ethnographic/narrative framework is the Cohen, Tripp-Reimer, Smith, Sorofman, and Lively (1994) study of patient and professional explanations of diabetes. Cohen and her colleagues correlated glycosylated hemoglobin levels with interview data obtained from patients and health care professionals. They transformed these data into congruence scores, where 0 symbolized agreement (or no disagreement), 1 symbolized minor disagreement, and 2 symbolized major disagreement. The Spearman correlation coefficient showed a positive but nonsignificant relationship between explanatory model congruence and normal hemoglobin A1c levels.

Apple Juice, Orange Juice, and Fruit Juice

Also vague from many presentations of mixed methods studies is the kind of mixing that occurred. In one kind of mixed methods study, qualitative and quantitative entities are in mixed company with each other, while in the other kind, they are actually blended.

In the first kind of mixed methods study, entities are associated with or linked to each other but retain their essential characters; metaphorically, apple juice and orange juice both are used, but they are never mixed together to produce a new kind of juice. An example of this kind of mix was the use of grounded theory and ethological observation in a study my colleagues and I conducted of the transition to parenthood of infertile couples (Sandelowski, Holditch-Davis, & Harris, 1992). We used grounded theory to describe the aspects of this transition amenable to grounded theory study, and we used ethological observation to describe those aspects amenable to ethological observation. Wolfer (1993) proposed that different aspects of reality lend themselves to different methods of inquiry. More precisely, although there is no uniform paradigm-method link, there is a method-reality link.

We used grounded theory to describe the process by which infertile couples pursued parenthood, and we used ethological observation to describe their interactions with the children they eventually parented. Both of these methods are compatible in that they are forms of naturalistic inquiry in which no a priori theoretical framework is imposed on target phenomena and no variables are manipulated. In a mixed company mixed methods study, inferences about a target phenomenon are drawn from the findings of both qualitative and quantitative data sets, each of which are separately analyzed using like-to-like techniques. That is, qualitative techniques are used to analyze qualitative data (in the case of grounded theory, constant comparison analysis), and quantitative techniques are used to analyze quantitative data (in the case of ethological observation, statistical pattern and trend analyses). Inferences may be presented in the form of theory or sets of propositions or working hypotheses that incorporate both sets of findings, for example, the proposal of a direct association between the ways couples pursued an option (identified only from the use of grounded theory) and the ways they interacted with their children (identified only from ethological observation).

In contrast to mixed company mixed methods studies are studies entailing actual blendings of two or more entities conceived as qualitative and quantitative into one entity, either qualitative or quantitative (i.e., where apple juice and orange juice are combined to create a new kind of fruit juice that is either more apple than orange, more orange than apple, or equally apple and orange). Tashakkori and Teddlie (1998) referred to the process of transforming qualitative/verbal data into quantitative/numerical data as "quantitizing" (p. 126), while Boyatzis (1998) referred to this process as "quantitative translation" (p. 129). In the transition to parenthood study, my colleagues and I transformed interview data into a display comparing the numbers of couples having and not having an amniocentesis with the number of physicians encouraging or not encouraging them to have the procedure. We then used Fisher's exact probability test, which showed a nonsignificant statistical relationship between physician encouragement and couples' decision to have an amniocentesis (Sandelowski, Harris, & Holditch-Davis, 1991).

By contrast, qualitizing is the process by which quantitative/numerical data are transformed into qualitative/verbal data. An example of this process is a study in which quantitative cluster techniques are used to identify groups of individuals distinguished from each other by their responses to a set of data collection tools. A grounded theory study is then mounted to further profile these groups theoretically—to validate that mutually distinctive groups have been identified and to explicate further the features of the individual members of these groups that make them more like each other than members of the other groups identified. The quantitatively derived clusters provide the basis for theoretical sampling and further typology development.

Yet, not all such transformations are appropriately called mixed methods studies. Rothert and her colleagues (1990) interviewed three women from each of the four groups of women they identified using quantitative cluster analysis techniques on the basis of these women's responses to eight scenarios about hormone replacement therapy. Yet as presented in the report of their study, these interviews did not constitute a fully realized qualitative study, with a clearly defined methodological approach and deliberately selected sampling, data collection, and data analysis plans. Although it is a valuable study, it is not a mixed methods study, nor did the researchers present it as one. Indeed, the interview portion of this study does not even appear in the report until the discussion section.

Similarly, although it can be called qualitizing when researchers verbally profile the participants in their studies, by designating them as largely hypertensive because 15 of 20 participants had systolic blood pressures greater than 140 or diastolic blood pressures greater than 90, this kind of qualitizing is common to all studies and not just mixed methods studies. Although it can be called quantitizing when researchers count the number of persons or events fitting into a category, such counting is inherent to the process of extracting meaning from verbal data. Meaning depends on number, just as number depends on meaning (Dey, 1993, p. 28). Moreover, most studies in the social and behavioral sciences, as well as in the practice disciplines, entail the use of more than one of something (e.g., investigators, participants, sites) for data collection. The mere use of more than one of some research entity in a study does not constitute a mixed methods study and might not even constitute a multimethod study.

Conflicting Purposes and Questionable Appeals

Another persistent problem in presenting mixed methods studies concerns the depiction of the reason for mixing methods. There are two large and conflicting purposes for combining studies: to achieve a fuller understanding of a target phenomenon and to verify one set of findings against the other. In the first instance, the goal is to achieve a kaleidoscopic or prismatic view of a target event; in the second instance, the goal is to converge on the one "true" view. In the first instance, the appeal is to comprehensive understanding; in the second, it is to validity. Arguably, only the latter purpose is appropriately referred to as triangulation, which is a process specifically aimed toward the realist goal of establishing convergent validity (Sandelowski, 1995b). Confusion arises when writers use the term *triangulated study* as if this designates a methodology itself, such as grounded theory or the randomized controlled trial, or when they use the word *triangulation* to designate the effort to ascertain multiple points of view about a target phenomenon, that is, the use of two or more investigators, sites, data sets, theories, or other research entities in a single study or the use of anything qualitative with anything quantitative. When any kind of research combination is designated as triangulation, there is no inquiry that is not triangulated. Having too much meaning, the word *triangulation* has no meaning at all. Yet the word is overused precisely because it has such diverse appeal—because mixing methods is itself a "claims making activity" (Aronson, 1984). Triangulation appears as a "neartalismanic method" (Miles & Huberman, 1994, p. 266) for democratizing inquiry and resolving conflicts between qualitative and quantitative inquiry.

Indeed, in another validation context, both mixed methods and specifically triangulated studies are depicted as necessary to offset the so-called weaknesses or limitations of single method studies. Yet methods have neither strengths nor weaknesses except in relation to particular perspectives toward and standards of inquiry. It is not a weakness or a limitation of any qualitative study that nomothetic generalizations cannot be drawn or that samples are not statistically representative, just as it is neither a weakness nor a limitation of any quantitative study that case-bound generalizations cannot be drawn or that samples are not information rich. Rather, it is the researcher who is weak or limited who chooses inquiry approaches for the wrong reasons, executes them in the wrong way, or apologizes for method characteristics that require no apology. A rhetorical device still too often used in presenting qualitative research is to apologize for its failings relative to quantitative research and then to defend why, despite its failings, qualitative research can still contribute to the research enterprise so well-exemplified by quantitative research. While quantitative research reports seem to require the demonstration of "modesty" (Shapin, 1984, p. 494) to offset the immodesty of their claims, qualitative research reports seem to require the demonstration of contrition to offset the weakness of their claims.

Yet, what is considered a failing in one world of inquiry is often considered an advantage in another—another reason why worlds of inquiry, or paradigms, cannot be mixed. For example, participatory action researchers emphasize the necessity for nonhierarchical and engaged relationships between inquirers and participants, and they often even avoid drawing any distinction at all between researchers and participants. By contrast, neo-positivist researchers emphasize the necessity for hierarchical and dispassionate relationships between researchers and participants so as to control bias. Accordingly, the presentation of mixed methods studies as a defense against purportedly invalid research, or to offset the alleged weaknesses of specific kinds of research approaches, is a rhetorical device that masks the assumption of a specific set of standards by which research is judged to be invalid or weak. Indeed, such defenses typically reproduce the view of qualitative research as weak and of quantitative research as strong (Blaikie, 1991).

Technologies of Persuasion

In addition to the complicated mix of words in mixed methods studies—and of the diverse worlds they represent and create—is the challenge that lies in the very representation of the research report itself or the "write-up" (Wolcott, 1990). In quantitative research, the write-up is typically conceived as the end product of a clearly defined and sequentially arranged process of inquiry, beginning with the identification of a research problem, and research questions or hypotheses, progressing through the selection of a sample and the collection of data, and ending with the analysis and interpretation of those data (Golden-Biddle & Locke, 1993; Gusfield, 1976). The write-up is here conceived as an objective description of the activities engaged in during each phase of this process and of what was found as a result of this process. The standardization of form evident in the familiar scientific report reflects and reinforces the realist ideals and objectivist values associated with neo-positivist inquiry. Written in the third-person passive voice, separating method from findings and findings from interpretation, and representing inquiry as occurring in a linear process and findings as truths that anyone following the same procedures will also find, these "author-evacuated" texts (Geertz, 1988, p. 141) reproduce the neo-positivist assumption of an external reality apprehensible and demonstrable by objective inquiry procedures. Standardization of form is also actively sought in the belief that form ought not to confound content. Language is viewed as a neutral medium of communication by which objective scientific practices are conveyed. Readers know what to expect in the conventional science write-up, and the fulfillment of this expectation alone constitutes a major criterion by which readers will evaluate the merits of the study findings. A write-up that fails to meet readers' expectations for the write-up will jeopardize the status of a study as scientific (McGill, 1990). In the case of science reporting, familiarity breeds contentment and novelty breeds contempt or, at the very least, suspicion.

In qualitative research, the write-up is conceived less as an end product of inquiry than as inquiry in the making. The familiar components of the research process—sampling, data collection, analysis, interpretation, and representation—are in recursive and iterative relationships with each other throughout the life of any study. Decisions concerning who or what to sample next, and the means and direction for future analysis, are directed by the analysis of data collected from persons or objects already sampled. Accordingly, the qualitative write-up as an end is not easily differentiated from writing as a means of inquiry (Richardson, 2000) because writing to report findings typically leads researchers to more writing to discern (or, in a more constructivist vein, to create) findings. The embodied act of putting words on a page or on a screen to present a study to an audience usually leads researchers to see things, or things missing, in their analysis that they had not seen before. Writing up qualitative research for publication is therefore indistinguishable from analysis and interpretation; to analyze and interpret is to write. Moreover, qualitative researchers, especially those most influenced by the postmodern emphasis on language and discourse (e.g., Clifford & Marcus, 1986), view language as itself a subject for interpretation; language is perceived less to reflect than to contribute to, create, or comprise reality. In addition, although quantitative research reports are supposed to be deliberately devoid of literary frills and of emotion in the service of reporting the "plain unvarnished truth" (Golden-Biddle & Locke, 1993, p. 597), the use of expressive language is generally highly prized among qualitative researchers.

Although there is a widely accepted genre for communicating the results of quantitative research—the "experimental" scientific report (Bazerman, 1988)—there is no one accepted genre for reporting the results of qualitative studies. "One narrative size does not fit all" (Tierney, 1995, p. 389) qualitative research. Indeed, qualitative researchers have eschewed standardization in all components of inquiry, opting for more reflexive and "confessional" (Van Maanen, 1988, chap. 4) "author-saturated" texts (Geertz, 1988, p. 141) and, to a lesser extent, for more literary, performance, and other experimental modes of presenting findings such as drama, poetry, autoethnography, and dance (Norris, 1997; Richardson, 2000). Qualitative researchers feel more acutely the lack of "innocence" in the research report (Van Maanen, 1995, p. 1). Among qualitative researchers, there is disagreement on the extent to which poetry or prose, and perspective/vision or polyphony/voice, ought to inform their writing practices (Norris, 1997; Richardson, 2000; Sandelowski, 1994a, 1995a; Schwalbe, 1995; Thorne, 1997; Tyler, 1986). Qualitative researchers have been especially concerned about writing reports, or telling "tales of the field" (Van Maanen, 1988), that communicate not only methodological rigor but also methodological flexibility and, even more important, a fidelity to and feeling for the persons and events studied. The crisis of representation for qualitative researchers involves the desires to "record" experience and to "create" it (Schwalbe, 1995, p. 395), to give voice to the voiceless and to give discourse its due (Saukko, 2000), to be truthful and to be evocative and even provocative, to be faithful and fair to the people in their studies and to be faithful and fair to the values and ideals of scholarly inquiry itself, and to create texts that are scientifically and/or ethnographically valid and that are stylish and significant. (For some ethnographers, ethnographic validity resides in being self-consciously scientific.) A consequence of these seemingly contradictory goals is that there is no one way for writers to encode and for readers to decode qualitative write-ups.

Artful Science

This problem of encoding/decoding is further complicated in mixed methods studies where qualitative research is combined with quantitative research that generally conforms to a familiar set of rules for scientific representation. Indeed, in the qualitative researcher's desire to create something both scientific and artistic lies one of the greatest challenges to writing and reading mixed methods studies: Qualitative research lies on the "fault line" between science and art (Sandelowski, 1994a, p. 48), as both scientific and artistic traditions have influenced the conceptualization conduct, and representation of qualitative research and as these tradition have been variously depicted as like and unlike each other. For example, Eisner (1981) emphasized differences between scientific and artistic representations in the areas of form, degree of license, and criteria for appraisal. He also viewed the "arts as paradigm cases of qualitative intelligence in action" and viewed qualitative research as evoking the "epistemic functions" of the arts (Eisner, 1991, pp. 6, 108). By contrast, Eisner (1985), in another publication, and others (e.g., Nisbet, 1976; Root-Bernstein, 1984) have emphasized the similarities between science and art in their purposes; uses of image, metaphor, and visual display; and aesthetic criteria for evaluation.

Most notable for the purposes of this chapter are discussions of the "aesthetic [as] both a subject matter and a criterion for appraising the processes used to create works of science as well as art" (Eisner, 1985, p. 27). Eisner (1985) argued that both scientists and artists "create forms through which the world is viewed" (p. 26). While artists create paintings, poems, and pottery, scientists create "taxonomies, theories, frameworks, [and] conceptual systems" (p. 26). The familiar research report and the novel both are modes of representing reality (Krieger, 1983) and "highly stylized art forms" (Krieger, 1991, p. 117). The American Psychological Association (APA, 1994) publication manual is both an official style and a "prescriptive rhetoric" (Bazerman, 1988, p. 275) for writing up the findings of scientific studies that codifies and embodies objectivist beliefs about inquiry. Here is a major reason why adherents to other than objectivist beliefs—often those conducting qualitative research—will find it hard to adhere to APA style, especially where it prescribes that results/analysis be separated from discussion/interpretation and where it proscribes ambiguity, reflexivity, and emotion. Content and form are inextricable as "formatting requirements," and "editing rules" for research write-ups constrain what can be communicated (Star, 1983, pp. 211–212). As Richardson (1990) summarized it, "*How* we are expected to write affects *what* we can write about" (p. 16, italics in original). How we are expected to write thereby affects what and how we know.

As Shapin (1984) argued, the "production of knowledge" cannot be separated from the "communication of knowledge" by which "communities" of responsive readers are created and come to accept a study as valid (p. 481). The APA (1994) publication manual is part of a "literary technology" used to make readers "virtual witnesses" to events they have not directly seen (p. 490). As Shapin conceived it, this technology produces in readers' minds an image of a research scene that "obviates the necessity for either its direct witness or its replication" (p. 491). Indeed, the technology used to accomplish virtual witnessing is no different from the technology used to "facilitate replication." The researcher/writer "deploys the same linguistic resources in order to encourage the physical replication of experiments [as] to trigger in the reader's mind a naturalistic image of the [research] scene" (p. 491). The correlation coefficient is such a linguistic resource, that is, a numerical representation of—and appeal to—stability and consensus to those communities of scholars that will find such appeals convincing. Statistics are rhetoric, that is, "literary . . . displays treated as dramatic presentations to a scientific community" (Gephart, 1988, p. 47). Writers do not find quantitative significance so much as they participate with willing readers to create it (Gephart, 1986). Such technologies contribute to the illusion created in readers' minds that write-ups of research, are reflections of reality (Shapin, 1984, p. 510).

In their influential ethnographic study *Laboratory Life,* Latour and Woolgar (1986) introduced the concept of "inscription," by which they emphasized the importance of writing not so much as a method of conveying information as a "material operation of creating order" (p. 245). As they described it, the work of science is the creation of inscriptions. What we understand to be science is wholly composed of these inscriptions or the simplifications (e.g., traces, charts, models, figures) that constitute representations of the "facts" of nature that scientists create in the process of seeking to discover them. According to Latour and Woolgar, scientists are even more "obsessed" with inscriptions than are novelists because "there is nothing but a wall of archives, labels, protocol books, figures, and papers . . . between scientists and chaos" (p. 245).

Indeed, scientific forms, like artistic ones, are judged by how well they reduce chaos. As Eisner (1985) observed, all forms are evaluated by the same aesthetic criteria, including coherence, attractiveness, and economy. Quantification and graphical displays are common ways to achieve coherence and economy in science texts (Law & Whittaker, 1988). Scientific theories are accepted because they are coherent, harmonious, and parsimonious. In short, although quantitatively oriented scientists may deny it (Lynch & Edgerton, 1988), aesthetic considerations are not confined to the arts or popular renderings of scientific findings. Rather, the aesthetic is itself a "mode of knowing" (Eisner, 1985) in science. Both scientific and artistic forms are judged by how well they confer order, make sense, and evoke sensory images of the inquiry process.

Moreover, scientific representations are no more objective or less subjective than are artistic ones, illuminating here is Root Bernstein's (1984) discussion of painting and scientific illustration. To counter the commonplace view that 10 painters painting the same scene will produce 10 different pictures, Root-Bernstein showed the *similarity* between two artists' resolutions of the problem of how to introduce motion into paintings. To counter the commonplace view that 10 scientists addressing the same problem will produce the same results, Root-Bernstein showed the *dissimilarity* in three graphic representations of the periodic system of elements. Root-Bernstein argued against the simplistic view that scientific representations index external and eternal truths, while artistic representations vary with the artists. Both scientists and artists working in the same tradition, with the same methods, and on the same problem will likely produce comparable forms. Scientists are no less a part of their graphic displays than artists are of their paintings. Artistic forms are as much "experiments in perception, applications of new rules, or theories . . . or concepts" (p. 113) as are scientific forms.

Art historians and social scientists have emphasized the identity between representations in science and art as stylized constructions for ordering and making sense (Gifford-Gonzalez, 1993; Law & Lynch, 1988; Nisbet, 1976; Stafford, 1991, 1994). Especially notable here are sociological and critical/cultural studies of scientific practices as exercises in rhetoric, representation, and "aesthetic judgments" (Lynch & Edgerton, 1988, p. 185). These studies suggest additional reasons why mixed methods studies present such challenges for writing and reading them in that self-consciously science oriented inquirers will likely deny the art and craft in their work, while artistically oriented inquirers will emphasize them.

Artful Astronomy

In their ethnographic study of the relationship between aesthetics and science in astronomy, Lynch and Edgerton (1988) sought to reveal the "craft of visual representation . . . hidden" (p. 186) in the practices of astronomy. Describing the reliance of modern astronomers on digital representation of data and digital image processing to detect and represent astronomical phenomena, Lynch and Edgerton demonstrated the extent to which "aesthetic considerations enter into the way astronomers compose, transform, and select images for various audiences and purposes" (p. 187). They also observed astronomers' tendency to deny the influence of the aesthetic except in creating "pretty pictures" (p. 191) of astronomical findings for popular audiences. These scientists maintained a distinction between aesthetics and science, associating "false color renderings" (p. 193) with "promotion and popularization" (p. 193) but not with "doing science" (p. 195). Even more significant for the purposes of this chapter, astronomers used a familiar "quantitative/qualitative distinction" to distinguish between the "real physical quantities . . . numerical measures" revealed and the "feeling" pretty pictures evoked (p. 194). Despite the fact that the maps and graphs intended to represent the quantitatively informed science of astronomy were no less "tailored" (p. 203) than the pretty pictures intended to promote astronomy to the public, the astronomers viewed the former as a way to show natural phenomena more accurately. These scientists used digital techniques to "clean up" their data, that is, to remove "cosmetic defects" from them (p. 206). They also used colors to show phenomena, differentiating between those colors that appealed to a public audience and those colors that served as "indices of . . . objective properties" (p. 200). And they adjusted their pictures to conform to the reality they wanted to show. As Lynch and Edgerton observed, digital image processing counters the commonplace notion that captions of pictures tell readers what is in the pictures; rather, "the features of a picture can be adjusted to fit a caption" (p. 202).

Lynch and Edgerton (1988) demonstrated the extent to which aesthetic considerations are the "very fabric of [the] realism" (p. 214) scientists wish to convey. As "committed realists," the astronomers they observed sought to "endow their compositions with naturalistic adequacy" (p. 214). The work of science, and of astronomy in particular, "of composing visible coherences, discriminating differences, consolidating entities, and establishing evident relations" was accomplished by crafting and configuring them (p. 212). Although careful to separate the "appeal" of their compositions from their "representational function" (p. 216), the astronomers nevertheless drew from "currently fashionable formats and color schemes" to "package their representations" to appeal to both scientific and lay audiences (p. 213).

Artful Anatomy

Typically conceived as a "stable science" (Moore & Clarke, 1995, p. 259), human anatomy has long been of interest to artists and historians and, more recently to a variety of social scientists and cultural critics precisely because it epitomizes the lack of stability in science and the critical role of representation in the creating of scientific knowledge. As these diverse scholars have variously demonstrated, our understanding of human anatomy is nearly wholly made up of highly stylized visual representations of the human body that reflect, reproduce, and reinforce prevailing conventions for illustration (e.g., successively peeling away the layers of the body, showing cut away sections of body parts) and cultural prescriptions concerning normality, gender, and race. Far from being a "science that has been done," anatomy is revealed to be a "contested domain" and "key site" for the (re)production of cultural norms (pp. 256–257). Anatomical inscriptions reproduce cultural prescriptions. Most important here, anatomy is revealed to be a "kind of writing practice" that makes the body "readable" (Waldby, 2000, p. 94). As Cartwright (1998) demonstrated in her "cultural anatomy" of the Visible Human Project (a digital image library of data representing a normal adult human male and female), the way phenomena are represented will determine how and even whether we understand them. Although the Visible Human Project is intended to make human anatomy more understandable, the images detail and segment parts so minutely and arbitrarily that they preclude easy recognition and categorization. Indeed, they require an a priori textbook understanding of anatomy. A cross section of data might provide information about hearts, breasts, and bones, but this manner of offering information does not correspond to the familiar way of dividing the body by systems or organs, and the wealth of detail offered may overwhelm viewers. In short, viewers/readers have to learn new ways to view/read the body to keep the body in view, and these new ways may conflict sharply with old ways of viewing/reading it. Anatomical knowledge is thus "medium dependent"

(Waldby, 2000, p. 90), changing when the medium is the printed book or cyberspace. Whether book based or virtual, anatomy does not "illustrate" bodies so much as it "demonstrates" them (p. 91). Anatomical displays are not representations of the body as it is; rather, the body we know at any one moment in time is a display. Representation is shown in these studies not to be opposed to reality but rather as constituting it.

Mixed Media for Mixed Methods Studies for Mixed Audiences

Crafting convincing write-ups of mixed methods studies entails understanding that the form in which findings are shown themselves constitute those findings, recognizing the research write-up as rhetoric, and the deliberate selection and mindful use of the most convincing rhetorical tools of the trade. Reading mixed methods studies, in turn, requires an understanding of these tools and of how they convince.

Mixed methods writers have to decide whether and how to use the familiar genre of the experimental report, the ethnographic conventions of the realist or reflexive tale, or any of an array of other formats for "impression management" (Bazerman, 1988, p. 202). They have to decide how best to delineate the temporal, analytical, and interpretive relationships between the qualitative and quantitative entities in their studies. They have to decide whether to use a separate but equal sequential format to present qualitative and quantitative procedures and findings or to use a format that weaves both sets of procedures and findings together. Writers have also to decide what writing templates will give their write-ups the structure, coherence, and rhythm they seek to convey (Sandelowski, 1998). For example, the form of the write-up may reproduce the order in which researchers implemented the various phases and techniques of a study and the order in which findings were found or, instead, may reproduce the temporal flow of a life event as participants experienced it. As shown in Figure 12.1, if researchers used a sequential design format, then they may choose the conventional experimental style to describe first the procedures used and the findings produced from the initial quantitative or qualitative portion of their study and then to describe the procedures and findings from the qualitative or quantitative portion that followed. Or they may choose more ethnographically inclined formats that emphasize narratives or cases or that organize findings by methodological coding families, such as the "6 Cs" conditional matrix associated with grounded theory ("Theoretical Coding Families," 1998), or by concepts derived from established theories. Writers will also have to consider

Mixed Methods/Design	Type	Writing Style	Temporal/Thematic Logic
Sequential design, with quantitative priority	QUAN > qual qual > QUAN	Experimental	Research time
Concurrent design, with quantitative priority	QUAN + qual		
Sequential design, with qualitative priority	QUAL > quan quan > QUAL	Experimental -or-	Research time
Concurrent design, with qualitative priority	QUAL + quan	Narrative Comparison of cases -Typical, deviant Perspectival/Polyvocal Conceptual	Subject/Event time -Quantitatively informed -Shared/Divergent themes Shared/Divergent views/voices -Sensitizing concepts -Theoretical framework -Coding families
Wave design	Quan wave 1 wave 2 wave 3 Qual ongoing fieldwork	Experimental -or-	Research time
Sandwich design	Qual > Quan > Qual Quan > Qual > Quan	Narrative -Flash forward -Flashback	Subject/Event time

Figure 12.1   Examples of Writing Templates for Different Mixed Methods Designs

SOURCE: The first two columns were constructed from information in Miles and Huberman (1994), Morgan (1998), and Tashakkori and Teddlie (1998).

the use of devices that have different appearances, functions, and/or values in qualitative and quantitative research. Among these are visual displays, numbers, and quotes.

Visual Displays

Visual displays (e.g., graphs, charts, tables, lists) are familiar features of research reports. Indeed, their very familiarity paradoxically contributes to their disappearance as themselves objects of study and as powerful rhetorical devices. Yet these displays function not only "manifestly" to reduce large quantities of data into forms that can be more readily apprehended by readers but also "latently" to persuade readers of the validity of findings (McGill, 1990, p. 141). They "imply equivalence between the scientific and the tabular" or graphic (p. 136). They are components of the literary technology of science not only because they evoke images of the research that has taken place but also because they themselves constitute a visual source of information. They are part of the "iconography" of science, offering "visual assistance" to the virtual witness (Shapin, 1984, pp. 491–492).

Visual displays entail a decision (albeit often an unconscious one) to organize information in a certain way. For example, writers choose whether to construct matrices (rows and columns), networks (nodes and links), or Venn diagrams (independent and overlapping circles); what to put in the spaces in their displays (e.g., quotes, paraphrases, abbreviations, numbers, arrows, symbolic figures); and/or what to emphasize in their displays (e.g., time in a time-ordered display, event in an event-ordered display, conditions in a conditional display) (Miles & Huberman, 1994). The very organization of this information shapes the findings and how readers read them. Quantitative research reports tend to be characterized by tables and graphs numerically profiling the demographic composition of the studied sample and showing the results of the statistical tests from which conclusions were drawn as well as by figures depicting—often in numerical form—a theoretical formulation of the relationship between variables (e.g., a path diagram). Qualitative research write-ups tend to emphasize verbal texts over visual displays. Grounded theory reports often include figures of theories; indeed, some writers of grounded theory reports believe that a grounded theory cannot be conveyed without using such figures. But these figures tend also to include words as opposed to numbers. The advent of computerized text management systems for managing qualitative data has also encouraged the use of visual displays of reordered verbal text in qualitative write-ups. Indeed, these systems can be seen as important new additions to the literary technology of persuasion because they permit qualitative researchers to have printouts of data—like their quantitative counterparts—with all the veneer of scientific objectivity that such inscriptions confer. Even the purportedly "soft" data of qualitative research can become "hard" if produced by hardware (Sandelowski 1995a).

Whether they are used in qualitative or quantitative research, tables, figures, and lists tend to fix in time and space the phenomena they portray. Visual displays give "material form" and "scientific visibility" to entities that were previously immaterial and invisible (Lynch, 1985). Their properties come to "embody' the realities they disclose (p. 43). Visual displays are "technologies of representation" that variously work by simplification, discrimination, and integration (Law & Whittaker 1988, p. 163). Their rhetorical effect is to create a sense of order out of chaos. In effect, they reduce the meaningfulness of information into fixed meanings: they make the potentially too meaningful more meaningless so as to establish meaning. Moreover, they rely on "discontinuity rather than continuity" (Goody, 1977, p. 81) as they remove texts from their contexts.

In these effects of displays lie reasons why qualitative researchers may avoid displays, while quantitative researchers value them. Qualitative researchers tend to want to create tableaux and graphic accounts of experience, not tables and graphs. But in these effects lies also a means for qualitative researchers to make their reports more appealing to readers wanting the boundaries, order, and "immutability" (Latour, 1988, p. 36) that such devices offer. Graphs, tables, and lists enlist readers toward a defined, linear, and/or schematic view of a set of facts or relations. In qualitative research, they can assist readers in focusing on key dimensions of a complex phenomenon that writers want to communicate. Moreover, because they convey a "sense of proximity to the data collected" by the writers (McGill, 1990, p. 130), such displays will appeal to qualitative researchers' desire to communicate that they were "there" in the field (Geertz, 1988, chap. 1).

The Breitmayer, Ayres, and Knafl (1993) analysis of their mixed methods study of family responses to a child's chronic illness shows an effective use of visual displays. Table 12.1 summarizes and clarifies the qualitative (semistructured interviews) and quantitative (structured instruments) data they collected, the family members from whom they collected these data, and the link between these data and aspects of the family management style they hoped to illuminate. Tables 12.2 and 12.3 show how mood data were analytically linked to interview data to achieve a fuller understanding of family relationships and to ascertain convergent validity. The responses displayed in Table 12.2 suggest that mood can be partly explained by whether parents perceive that there is family support in managing the child's illness. The responses shown in Table 12.3 visually supported the researchers' hypothesis that parents with high mood disturbance scores would describe more difficulty in accepting a child's illness than would those with low scores.

Numbers

Numbers have been something of a "litmus test" (Linnekin, 1987, p. 920) of inquiry, serving in part to differentiate scientifically oriented/quantitative from humanistically oriented/qualitative research (Chibnik, 1999). Indeed,

Table 12.1   Mapping Data Collection Techniques in a Mixed Methods Study

| | Domain of Interest Family Management Style | | | |
Data Source	Definition of Situation	Management Behaviors	Sociocultural Context	Impact
Semistructured interviews				
Parent	X	X	X	X
Ill child	X	X	X	X
Sibling	X	X	X	X
Structured instruments				
Parent			FFFS	FFFS
				POMS
Ill child	CATIS			CBCL
				SPPC
				FSI
Sibling				CBCL
				SPPC

SOURCE: Breitmayer, Ayers, and Knafl (1993, p. 238). Used by permission of the authors and Sigma Theta Tau International.

NOTE: FFFS = Feetham Family Functioning Survey; POMS = Profile of Mood States; CATIS = Child Attitude Toward Illness Scale; CBCL = Child Behavior Checklist; FSI = Functional Status Instrument; SPPC = Self-Perception Profile for Children.

Table 12.2   Linking Instrument Scores and Quotes for Fuller Description

Profile of Mood State	Response to Interview Question on Effect of Illness on Family Relations
High mood disturbance mother	"I suppose in a way it kind of pulled us apart because it's so stressful and everything."
High mood disturbance father	"I would say in this family anything tragic pulls us together."
Low mood disturbance mother	"Probably pulled us closer."
Low mood disturbance father	"I think if anything it brought our family closer together. . . . Before, everyone went their separate ways."

SOURCE: Adapted and excerpted from Breitmayer, Ayres, and Knafl (1993, p. 240). Used by permission of the authors and Sigma Theta Tau International.

Table 12.3   Linking Instrument Scores and Quotes for Convergent Validation (Triangulation)

POMS Classification	Response to Question About "Acceptance"	Response to Question About Maintaining Positive Outlook
High		
Mother	"I guess you never really accept it."	"I just keep telling myself as long she eats the way she does and takes her insulin and checks her blood, she'll be normal."
Father	"There's nothing we can do about it."	"I try to always think in my head that they're going to figure it out soon, but I have the feeling they're not."
Low		
Mother	"We've accepted it from the beginning."	"We eat a much better diet, and it's not like we're losing anything that we need to sustain a normal life."
Father	"I think we pretty well accept it. It's a fact of life."	"[If we feel down], we just talk it out."

SOURCE: Adapted and excerpted from Breitmayer, Ayres, and Knafl (1993, p. 241). Used by permission of the authors and Sigma Theta Tau International.

qualitative research is often simplistically defined solely by the absence and/or critique of numbers, while quantitative research is simplistically defined solely by the presence of numbers.

In quantitative research, the appeal to numbers gives studies their rhetorical power. Statistics, especially inferential statistics, are a naturalized and rule-governed means of producing what is perceived to be the most conclusive knowledge about a target phenomenon (John, 1992). Inferential statistics authorize studies as scientific and contribute to the "fixation of belief" whereby readers accept findings as facts and not artifacts (Amann & Knorr-Cetina, 1988, p. 85). They are a display of evidence in the "artful literary display" (Gephart, 1988, p. 63) we know as the scientific report, and they are a means to create meaning. Indeed, quantitative significance is arguably less found than created, as writers rhetorically enlist readers, with the use of words such as *high* and *substantial,* to accept their findings as significant (Gephart, 1986). Statistical meaning is not "inherent in numbers" but rather "accomplished by terms used to describe and interpret numbers" (Gephart, 1988, p. 60).

By contrast, in qualitative research, numbers are looked on with some suspicion as overly simplifying the complex. Indeed, qualitative researchers are often antagonistic toward numbers, referring to the use of numbers as number crunching and to those who use them as number crunchers and ranking numbers low in their "hierarchy of credibility" (Becker, 1967, p. 241). Wanting to move "beyond numbers" (Greenhalgh & Taylor, 1997), and committed to sampling information-rich cases, thick description and fully rounded and grounded understanding, qualitative researchers often eschew numbers as a violation of the knowledge and ethical imperatives of qualitative research. Numbers also present a representational problem to qualitative researchers who want to satisfy both scientific and humanistic/artistic criteria in their write-ups. While quantitative researchers prize figures, qualitative researchers prize figures of speech. In short, while numbers are seen to confer epistemic authority in quantitative inquiry, they may also be seen to undermine the authority, authenticity, and artfulness of qualitative work.

Qualitative researchers are especially concerned about the "dubious use" of numbers (Stern, 1989, p. 139) to authorize and legitimize qualitative work. For example, one dubious use of numbers occurs when writers become so preoccupied with providing exact numbers that they end up overcounting or counting things that cannot be counted (Sandelowski, 2001). Overcounting will seriously detract from an aesthetic presentation of findings and, even more important, can easily divert researchers away from the qualitative mandate to develop and present a fully rounded interpretation of things. An example is when researchers emphasize the numbers of respondents falling into categories instead of detailing the qualitative nature of the categories themselves.

Another example of the dubious use of numbers is acontextual counting, whereby writers draw unsubstantiated inferences from numbers or offer no other information about participants or an event except numbers (Sandelowski, 2001). One example is when researchers offer no relevant descriptive material to contextualize a number. They might say that 40% of the children they observed were angry but offer no other information about these children. A second example is when researchers count up the number of times persons referred to a certain event and then conclude that this event was the most important event in the lives of those persons who referred to it the most. Or, researchers might count up the number of times participants used the word *angry* and conclude that people who used it more frequently were angrier than those who used it less frequently. Without some narrative or other theoretical formulation concerning talk or the salience of life events that would allow researchers to draw such conclusions, the conclusions remain theoretically invalid.

Yet, in their efforts to move beyond numbers and to avoid their dubious use, qualitative researchers might not recognize how integral numbers are in the qualitative analysis process, especially for the recognition of patterns in data and deviations from those patterns and for generalizing from data. Pattern recognition implies seeing something over and over again in one case or across a selection of cases. Finding that a *few, some,* or *many* participants showed a certain pattern, or that a pattern was *common* or *unusual* in a group of participants, implies something about the frequency, typicality, or even intensity of an event. Anytime qualitative researchers place raw data into categories or discover themes to which they attach codes, they are drawing from the numbered nature of phenomena for their analysis. Numbers are a powerful way to generate meaning from qualitative data; to document, verify, and test interpretations or conclusions; and to represent target events and experiences.

Moreover, numbers are powerful devices to show the complexity and labor of qualitative work. Qualitative writers too often apologize for their *small* sample sizes. Yet instead of showing contrition, they might show the *large* numbers of which such ostensibly small samples are often actually composed. A recently completed 17-month ethnographic study of the implementation of a computerized patient record system on a hospital unit included interviews with 20 informants totaling 325 pages of text, 124 observations of events captured in 1,162 pages of fieldnotes, and the review of documents totaling 820 pages of text (Bailey, 2000). A study of 10 participants, interviewed only once, can yield 250 pages of raw data alone. Writers of qualitative research can take advantage of the prevailing cultural belief that more is better by playing the numbers game. If this rhetorical game is played well, then there will be no doubt of the true sample size, amount of data produced from, and labor involved in even $N = 1$ studies.

The Borkan et al. (1991) report of their mixed methods study includes two effective examples of the use of numbers to document procedural and analytical moves. Figure 12.2 is intended to convey the systematic procedure used to ensure interrater reliability. Figure 12.3 is intended to convey the distribution and interpretation of data from which the predictor variables *organic narrative* and *mechanistic narrative* were created. By counting the numbers of persons responding in each category, the researchers showed that they accounted for all of their data, did not discount any data, and noticed when they had no data. Both of these figures serve to convince readers of the tight and mindful link between the first and qualitative portion of the study and the second and quantitative portion of the study.

Quotes

While numbers play a starring role in quantitative write-ups, quotes (from interviews and participant observations with participants) play a starring role

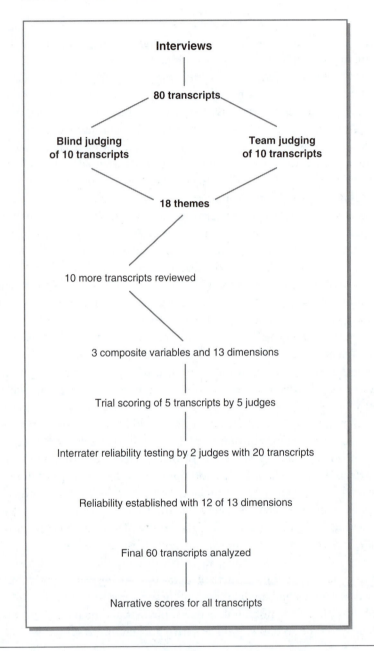

Figure 12.2   Numerical Display to Document Procedural Moves

SOURCE: Morgan, D. L. (1998). Practical strategies for combining qualitative and quantitative methods: Applications to health research. *Qualitative Health Research, 8,* 362–376. Reprinted by permission of Elsevier Science.

Poles: Organic		1–3	4	5–7	Mechanistic
Name					
	Disease				Fracture
		1%	15%	49%	
Illustrative quotes:					
"sickness"					"broken hip"
"osteoporosis"					"shattered bone"
Pathophysiology					
	Broke and fell				Fell and broke
		10%	14%	64%	
Illustrative quotes:					
"I think you break your hip before you go down."					"I landed on my hip and knew it was broke."
Prognosis					
	Total impairment				Complete recovery
		14%	10%	70%	
Illustrative quotes:					
"I might have to go to a nursing home."					"I'm going to recover fully."

Figure 12.3   Numerical Display to Document Analytical Moves

SOURCE: Adapted from Borkan, Quirk, and Sullivan (1991, p. 950).

in qualitative write-ups. The quote is arguably the analog to the number, as they are both rhetorical devices used to appeal to readers to accept findings as scientifically and/or ethnographically valid. Quotes authenticate qualitative write-ups in that they demonstrate to readers that the writer has been "there" in the field (Geertz, 1988, chap. 1), the closeness of the writer to the data and to the persons providing them (Richards, 1998), and the writer's attention to the "particularit[ies] of everyday life" (Golden-Biddle & Locke, 1993, p. 601). Whereas numbers are used in quantitative research write-ups primarily for their evidentiary power, quotes are used in qualitative research write-ups for their evidentiary power and their aesthetic value. While numbers emphasize generality, quotes "privilege" individuality and "model . . . the diversity within generality" (Richardson, 1990, p. 40) that are hallmarks of qualitative research.

Quotes are used in qualitative research write-ups to validate findings and to vitalize the presentation of those findings (Sandelowski, 1994b). The function of quoting here is to offer evidence for a conclusion or claim; to illustrate an interpretive point; to represent, and facilitate understanding of, the thoughts and feelings of the persons studied; to foster in readers an identification between them and the persons quoted; to evoke certain feelings in readers; and/or to provoke action from readers (Howarth, 1990; Weiss, 1994). Like statistics and the work of statistics, quotes are rhetorical devices intended to persuade readers of the trustworthiness of a study, and quoting is a highly skilled craft that entails aesthetic and even moral choices. Writers must decide whether to quote at all; authenticity may be at stake if there are no quotes, while anonymity may be at stake if there are too many or too revealing quotes. Writers must then decide what, how, when, where, and why to quote. Such decisions include what segments of talk to quote, how to edit the "messiness" of human talk (DeVault, 1990, p. 109) so that it speaks to the reader and for the participant, how to stage (i.e., introduce and leave) quotes, where to use quotes (e.g., interspersed throughout the text, in sets in confined sections of the text, in tabular displays), and why to use quotes (e.g., to convey the informational content or evoke the feeling tone of an experience). In short, quoting and doing statistics both entail complex efforts to persuade, but they exert their influence in different ways.

Tables 12.2 and 12.3 illustrate the use of quotes to flesh out instrument scores. The quotes are used here to link key constructs (mood, perception of effect of child's illness on family relationships, acceptance of child's illness, and strategies to maintain positive outlook) and to show their hypothesized relationship to each other.

Crafting Convincing Mixed Methods Studies Texts

In conclusion, writing mixed methods studies entails both "craft and responsibility" (Schwalbe, 1995, p. 394). Writers of mixed methods studies must have the skill and motivation to permit both qualitative and quantitative readers "access" (p. 396) to their work. Writing mixed methods studies requires an understanding of differences, of how aesthetic considerations enter into the creation of convincing write-ups of both qualitative and quantitative research, and of whether and how diverse aesthetic sensibilities can be brought together. Mixed methods studies are themselves "mixed metaphors" (Wallace & Van Fleet, 1998) in that qualitative research and quantitative research are viewed as standing for different approaches to inquiry. Although there is no inherent incompatibility between numbers and words that precludes their being used together to represent the findings of a study, there is an inherent clash between, for example, the use of language and formatting styles to convey facts and express meanings or to establish a personal presence and discount one. And these differences in the look and feel of studies reflect differences between qualitative and quantitative research that cannot be overlooked. Although the emphasis on the compatibility of qualitative and quantitative research is intended to be reconciliatory and to move beyond pointless paradigm wars, it makes no sense to minimize differences that clearly exist on the "shop floor" of research (Becker, 1996, p. 60). There may very well be some overall similarities between doing statistics and doing phenomenology (cf. Dzurec & Abraham, 1986), but on the shop floor of research, they are nothing like each other. Moreover, such depictions of identity can paradoxically undermine the claim to mixed methods studies; if phenomenology and statistics are like each other, then arguably nothing has been mixed in studies using both of these modes of inquiry.

Accordingly, the question is how best to accommodate the mixes in mixed methods studies. Writers of mixed methods studies must find a "shared grammar" (Stevenson & Beech, 1998, p. 795) by which to communicate with and thereby create one community from the diverse communities reading mixed methods studies. They must "get the words right" for the purposes that they use them. As Bazerman (1988) summarized it,

> Getting the words right is more than a fine tuning of grace and clarity; it is defining the entire enterprise. And getting the words right depends not just on an individual's choice. The words are shaped by the discipline—in its communally developed linguistic resources and expectations; in its stylized identification and structuring of realities to be discussed; in its literature; in its active procedures of reading, evaluating, and using texts; in its structured interactions between writer and reader. The words arise out of the activity, procedures, and relationships within the community. (p. 47)

Crafting convincing mixed methods studies texts requires using words— especially the epistemologically and emotionally loaded terms *qualitative* and *quantitative*—in ways that will be accessible and appealing to the mixed audiences for mixed methods studies and respectful of the highly diverse communities participating in the creation of and served by mixed methods studies. Respectful use means, for example, not defining or depicting qualitative research as a nonentity (i.e., nonquantitative) and not depicting quantitative research as number crunching.

Crafting convincing mixed methods studies entails making the right appeals. There is nothing inherently more appealing about large statistically representative samples, from which nomothetic generalizations can be drawn, than smaller informationally representative samples, from which idiographic generalizations can be drawn. Rather, the one will be more appealing to the other in different writing-reading contexts. Qualitative research becomes more convincing when it is combined with quantitative research only in interpretive communities more convinced by quantitative rhetoric than by qualitative rhetoric. In short, writers of mixed methods studies must carefully consider what appeals to make and must avoid making appeals based on misunderstandings of what validity and generalizability mean in qualitative versus quantitative research. But like the failed effort to mix paradigms, the effort to mix incompatible appeals will undermine the power of any text to convince because they will cancel each other out. A writer cannot simultaneously appeal to extensive engagement with participants and controlled relations with participants to convince readers of the validity of findings.

Finally, writers and readers of mixed methods studies must develop a "rhetorical self-consciousness" (Bazerman, 1988, p. 320). They need to know how language affects us and "how we play along" (Schwalbe, 1995, p. 401). Writers and readers need to "know what each other is doing" (p. 402). Whether drawing from the power of the number or the word, from the figure or the figure of speech, or from the table or the tableaux, writers and readers must understand and play them as the "power games" (Stevenson & Beech, 1998) they are.

Notes

1. I consider here only researchers and not other readers such as research participants, policy makers, and other audiences for research reports.

2. Publishers may also determine the kinds of displays that will appear in research reports, but they, like writers, are influenced by prevailing conventions for how and what to display. Ironically, although so much of human knowledge is composed of the visual, publishers of science and ethnographic texts often prevail on writers to limit their displays, either for reasons of cost or because such displays may be considered more cosmetic—a "pretty picture"—than functionally necessary to show a finding. The literary title, composed of an artful phrase intended to capture the essence of a set of findings, followed by a colon and then a phrase signifying the contents of the article in more prosaic terms, often suffers the same fate in self-consciously scientific publication venues. The "flowery" title is viewed as a "frill" and a deterrent to database classification and retrieval (Levinson, 1990. p. 159).

3. Explicitly visual fields such as visual anthropology and visual sociology emphasize photographs, which constitute a complex domain of visual display not addressed here.

4. Although mathematics is an artful science (King, 1992), statistics are not deliberately and self-consciously used in quantitative research for their aesthetic qualities.

References

Amann, K., & Knorr-Cetina, K. (1988). The fixation of visual evidence. In M. Lynch & S. Woolgar (Eds.), *Representation in scientific practice* (pp. 85–121). New York: Kluwer Academic.

American Psychological Association. (1994). *Publication manual of the American Psychological Association.* Washington, DC: Author.

Annells, M. (1996). Grounded theory method: Philosophical perspectives, paradigm of inquiry, and postmodernism. *Qualitative Health Research, 6,* 379–393.

Aronson, N. (1984). Science as a claims making activity: Implications for social problems research. In J. W. Schneider & J. Kitsuse (Eds.), *Studies in the sociology of social problems* (pp. 1–30). Norwood, NJ: Ablex.

Atkinson, P., & Silverman, D. (1997). Kundera's *Immortality:* The interview society and the invention of the self. *Qualitative Inquiry, 3,* 304–325.

Bailey, D. (2000). *Nurse work and the computerized patient record.* Unpublished doctoral dissertation. University of North Carolina at Chapel Hill.

Bazerman, C. (1988). *Shaping written knowledge: The genre and activity of the experimental article in science.* Madison: University of Wisconsin Press.

Beach, R. (1993). *A teacher's introduction to reader-response theories.* Urbana, IL: National Council of Teachers of English.

Becker, H. S. (1967). Whose side are we on? *Social Problems, 14,* 239–247.

Becker, H. S. (1996). The epistemology of qualitative research. In R. Jessor, A. Colby, & R. A. Shweder (Eds.), *Ethnography and human development: Context and meaning in social inquiry* (pp. 53–71). Chicago: University of Chicago Press.

Blaikie, N. W. (1991). A critique of the use of triangulation in social research. *Quality & Quantity, 25,* 115–136.

Blumenthal, D. (1999). Representing the divided self. *Qualitative Inquiry, 5,* 377–392.

Borkan, J. M., Quirk, M., & Sullivan, M. (1991). Finding meaning after the fall: Injury narratives from elderly hip fracture patients. *Social Science & Medicine, 33,* 947–957.

Boyatzis, R. E. (1998). *Transforming qualitative information: Thematic analysis and code development.* Thousand Oaks, CA: Sage.

Breitmayer, B. J., Ayres, L., & Knafl, K. A. (1993). Triangulation in qualitative research: Evaluation of completeness and confirmation purposes. *Image: Journal of Nursing Scholarship, 25,* 237–243.

Cartwright, L. (1998). A cultural anatomy of the Visible Human Project. In P. A. Treichler, L. Cartwright, & C. Penley (Eds.), *The visible woman: Imaging technologies, gender, and science* (pp. 21–43). New York: New York University Press.

Charmaz, K. (2000). Grounded theory: Objectivist and constructivist methods. In N. K. Denzin & Y. S. Lincoln (Eds.), *Handbook of qualitative research* (2nd ed., pp. 509–535). Thousand Oaks, CA: Sage.

Chibnik, M. (1999). Quantification and statistics in six anthropology journals. *Field Methods, 11,* 146–157.

Clifford, J., & Marcus, G. E. (Ed.). (1986). *Writing culture: The poetics and politics of ethnography.* Berkeley: University of California Press.

Cohen, M. Z., Tripp-Reimer, T., Smith, C., Sorofman, B., & Lively, S. (1994). Explanatory models of diabetes: Patient practitioner variation. *Social Science & Medicine, 38,* 59–66.

Denzin, N. K., & Lincoln, Y. S. (2000). Introduction: The discipline and practice of qualitative research. In N. K. Denzin & Y. S. Lincoln (Eds.), *Handbook of qualitative research* (2nd ed., pp. 1–28). Thousand Oaks, CA: Sage.

DeVault, M. L. (1990). Talking and listening from women's standpoint: Feminist strategies for interviewing and analysis. *Social Problems 37,* 96–116.

Dey, I. (1993). *Qualitative data analysis: A user-friendly guide for social scientists.* London: Routledge.

Dzurec, L. C., & Abraham, I. L. (1986). Analogy between phenomenology and multivariate statistical analysis. In P. L. Chinn (Ed.), *Nursing research methodology: Issues and implementation* (pp. 55–66). Rockville, MD: Aspen.

Eisner, E. (1981). On the differences between scientific and artistic approaches to qualitative research. *Educational Researcher 10,* 5–9.

Eisner, E. (1985). Aesthetic modes of knowing. In E. Eisner (Ed.), *Learning and teaching the ways of knowing: Eighty-fourth yearbook of the National Society for the Study of Education, Part II* (pp. 23–36). Chicago: National Society of the Study of Education.

Eisner, E. (1991). *The enlightened eye: Qualitative inquiry and the enhancement of educational practice.* New York: Macmillan.

Fish, S. (1980). *Is there a text in this class? The authority of interpretive communities.* Cambridge, MA: Harvard University Press.

Geertz, C. (1988). *Works and lives: The anthropologist as author.* Stanford, CA: Stanford University Press.

Gephart, R. P. (1986). Deconstructing the defense for quantification in social science: A content analysis of journal articles on the parametric strategy. *Qualitative Sociology, 9,* 126–144.

Gephart, R. P. (1988). *Ethnostatistics: Qualitative foundations for quantitative research.* Beverly Hills, CA: Sage.

Gergen, M. M., & Gergen, K. J. (2000). Qualitative inquiry: Tensions and transformations. In N. K. Denzin & Y. S. Lincoln (Eds.), *Handbook of qualitative research* (2nd ed., pp. 1025–1046). Thousand Oaks, CA: Sage.

Gifford-Gonzalez, D. (1993), You can hide, but you can't run: Representation of women's work in illustrations of paleolithic life. *Visual Anthropology Review, 9,* 23–41.

Golden-Biddle, K., & Locke, K. (1993). Appealing work: An investigation of how ethnographic texts convince. *Organization Science, 4,* 595–616.

Goody, J. (1977). *The domestication of the savage mind.* Cambridge, UK: Cambridge University Press.

Greenhalgh, T., & Taylor, R. (1997). How to read a paper: Papers that go beyond numbers (qualitative research). *British Medical Journal, 315,* 740–743.

Gusfield, J. (1976). The literary rhetoric of science: Comedy and pathos in drinking driver research. *American Sociological Review, 41,* 16–34.

Heron, J., & Reason, P. (1997). A participatory inquiry paradigm. *Qualitative Inquiry, 3,* 274–294.

Howarth, W. (1990). Oliver Sacks: The ecology of writing science. *Modern Language Studies, 20,* 103–120.

John, I. D. (1992). Statistics as rhetoric in psychology. *Australian Psychologist, 27,* 144–149.

King, J. P. (1992). *The art of mathematics.* New York: Fawcett Columbine.

Krieger, S. (1983). *The mirror dance: Identity in a women's community.* Philadelphia: Temple University Press.

Krieger, S. (1991). *Social science and the self: Personal essays on an art form.* New Brunswick, NJ: Rutgers University Press.

Latour, B. (1988). Drawing things together. In M. Lynch & S. Woolgar (Eds.), *Representation in scientific practice* (pp. 19–68). New York: Kluwer Academic.

Latour, B., & Woolgar, S. (1986). *Laboratory life: The construction of scientific facts.* Princeton, NJ: Princeton University Press.

Law, J., & Lynch, M. (1988). Lists, field guides, and the descriptive organization of seeing: Birdwatching as an exemplary observational activity. In M. Lynch & S. Woolgar (Eds.). *Representation in scientific practice* (pp. 267–299). New York: Kluwer Academic.

Law, J., & Whittaker, J. (1988). On the art of representation: Notes on the politics of visualization. In G. Fyfe & J. Law (Eds.), *Picturing power: Visual depiction and social relations* (pp. 160–183). London: Routledge.

Levinson, J. (1990). *Music, art, and metaphysics: Essays in philosophical aesthetics.* Ithaca, NY: Cornell University Press.

Linnekin, J. (1987). Categorize, cannibalize? Humanistic quantification in anthropological research. *American Anthropologist, 89,* 920–926.

Lynch, M. (1985). Discipline and the material form of images: An analysis of scientific visibility. *Social Studies of Science, 15,* 37–66.

Lynch, M., & Edgerton, S. Y. (1988). Aesthetics and digital image processing: Representational craft in contemporary astronomy. In G. Fyfe & J. Law (Eds.), *Picturing power: Visual depiction and social relations* (pp. 184–220). London: Routledge.

McGill, L. T. (1990). Doing science by the numbers: The role of tables and other representational conventions in scientific journal articles. In A. Hunter (Ed.), *The rhetoric of social research: Understood and believed* (pp. 129–141). New Brunswick, NJ: Rutgers University Press.

Miles, M. B., & Huberman, A. M. (1994). *Qualitative data analysis: An expanded sourcebook* (2nd ed.). Thousand Oaks, CA: Sage.

Moore, L. J., & Clarke, A. E. (1995). Clitoral conventions and transgressions: Graphic representations in anatomy texts, 1900–1991. *Feminist Studies, 21,* 255–301.

Nisbet, R. (1976). *Sociology as an art form.* New York: Oxford University Press.

Norris, J. R. (1997). Meaning through form: Alternative modes of knowledge representation. In J. M. Morse (Ed.), *Completing a qualitative project: Details and dialogue* (pp. 87–115). Thousand Oaks, CA: Sage.

Radley, A., & Billig, M. (1996). Accounts of health and illness: Dilemmas and representations. *Sociology of Health & Illness, 18,* 220–240.

Richards, L. (1998). Closeness to data: Goals of qualitative data handling. *Qualitative Health Research, 8,* 319–328.

Richardson, L. (1990). *Writing strategies: Reaching diverse audiences.* Newbury Park, CA: Sage.

Richardson, L. (2000). Writing: A method of inquiry. In N. K. Denzin & Y. S. Lincoln (Eds.), *Handbook of qualitative research* (2nd ed., pp. 923–948). Thousand Oaks, CA: Sage.

Riessman, C. K. (1990). Strategic uses of narrative in the presentation of self and illness: A research note. *Social Science & Medicine, 30,* 1195–1200.

Root-Bernstein, R. S. (1984). On paradigms and revolutions in science and art: The challenge of interpretation. *Art Journal, 44,* 109–118.

Rothert, M., Rovner, D., Holmes, M., Schmitt, N., Talarczyk, G., Kroll, J., & Gogate, J. (1990). Women's use of information regarding hormone replacement therapy. *Research in Nursing & Health, 13,* 355–366.

Sandelowski, M. (1994a). The proof is in the pottery: Toward a poetic for qualitative inquiry. In J. Morse (Ed.), *Critical issues in qualitative research methods* (pp. 46–63). Thousand Oaks, CA: Sage.

Sandelowski, M. (1994b). The use of quotes in qualitative research. *Research in Nursing & Health, 17,* 479–482.

Sandelowski, M. (1995a). On the aesthetics of qualitative research. *Image: Journal of Nursing Scholarship, 27,* 205–209.

Sandeloswski, M. (1995b). Triangles and crystals: On the geometry of qualitative research. *Research in Nursing & Health, 18,* 569–574.

Sandelowski, M. (1998). Writing a good read: Strategies for re-presenting qualitative data. *Research in Nursing & Health, 21,* 375–382.

Sandelowski, M. (2001). Real qualitative researchers don't count: The use of numbers in qualitative research. *Research in Nursing & Health, 24,* 230–240.

Sandelowski, M., Harris, B. G., & Holditch-Davis, D. (1991). Amniocentesis in the context of infertility. *Health Care for Women International, 12,* 167–178.

Sandelowski, M., Holditch-Davis, D., & Harris, B. G. (1992). Using qualitative and quantitative methods: The transition to parenthood of infertile couples. In J. F. Gilgun, K. Daly, & G. Handel (Eds.), *Qualitative methods in family research* (pp. 301–322). Newbury Park, CA: Sage.

Sapir, E. (1951). Culture, genuine and spurious. In D. G. Mandelbaum (Ed.), *Selected writings of Edward Sapir in language, culture, and personality* (pp. 308–331). Berkeley: University of California Press.

Saukko, P. (2000). Between voice and discourse: Quilting interviews on anorexia. *Qualitative Inquiry, 6,* 299–317.

Schattschneider D. (1994, November). Escher's metaphors, *Scientific American,* pp. 66–71.

Schwalbe, M. (1995). The responsibilities of sociological poets. *Qualitative Sociology, 18,* 393–413.

Schwandt, T A. (2000). Three epistemological stances for qualitative inquiry: Interpretivism, hermeneutics, and social constructionism. In N. K. Denzin & Y. S. Lincoln (Eds.), *Handbook of qualitative research* (2nd ed., pp. 189–213). Thousand Oaks, CA: Sage.

Shapin, S. (1984). Pump and circumstance: Robert Boyle's literary technology. *Social Studies of Science, 14,* 481–520.

Silverman, D. (2000). Analyzing talk and text. In N. K. Denzin & Y. S. Lincoln (Eds.), *Handbook of qualitative research* (2nd ed., pp. 821–834). Thousand Oaks, CA: Sage.

Skrtic, T. M. (1990). Social accommodation: Toward a dialogical discourse in educational inquiry. In E. G. Guba (Ed.), *The paradigm dialog* (pp. 125–135). Newbury Park, CA: Sage.

Stafford, B. M. (1991). *Body criticism: Imaging the unseen in enlightenment art and medicine.* Cambridge, MA: MIT Press.

Stafford, B. M. (1994). *Artful science: Enlightenment entertainment and the eclipse of visual education.* Cambridge, MA: MIT Press.

Star, S. L. (1983). Simplification in scientific work: An example from neuroscience research. *Social Studies of Science, 13,* 205–228.

Stern, P. N. (1989). Are counting and coding a cappella appropriate in qualitative research? In J. M. Morse (Ed.), *Qualitative nursing research: A contemporary dialogue* (pp. 135–148). Rockville, MD: Aspen.

Stevenson, C., & Beech, I. (1998). Playing the power game for qualitative researchers: The possibility of a postmodern approach. *Journal of Advanced Nursing, 27,* 790–797.

Tashakkori, A., & Teddlie, C. (1998). *Mixed methodology: Combining qualitative and quantitative approaches* (Applied Social Research Methods, No. 46). Thousand Oaks, CA: Sage.

Theoretical coding families. (1998). [Online]. Available: www.geocities.com/research triangle/lab/1491/gtm-i-families.html

Thorne, S. (1997). The art (and science) of critiquing qualitative research. In J. M. Morse (Ed.), *Completing a qualitative project: Details and dialogue* (pp. 117–132). Thousand Oaks, CA: Sage.

Tierney, W. C. (1995). (Re) Presentation and voice. *Qualitative Inquiry, 1,* 379–390.

Tyler. S. A. (1986). Postmodern ethnography: From document of the occult to occult document. In J. Clifford & G. E. Marcus (Eds.), *Writing culture: The poetics and politics of ethnography* (pp. 122–140). Berkeley: University of California Press.

Van Maanen, J. (1988). *Tales of the field: On writing ethnography.* Chicago: University of Chicago Press.

Van Maanen, J. (1995). An end to innocence: The ethnography of ethnography. In J. Van Maanen (Ed.), *Representation in ethnography* (pp. 1–35). Thousand Oaks, CA: Sage.

Waldby, C. (2000). Virtual anatomy: From the body in the text to the body on the screen. *Journal of Medical Humanities, 21,* 85–107.

Wallace, D. P., & Van Fleet, C. (1998). Qualitative research and the editorial tradition: A mixed metaphor. *Library Trends. 46,* 752–769.

Weiss, R. S. (1994). *Learning from strangers: The art and method of qualitative interview studies.* New York: Free Press.

West, P. (1990). The status and validity of accounts obtained at interview: A contrast between two studies of families with a disabled child. *Social Science & Medicine, 30,* 1229–1239.

Wolcott, H. F (1990). *Writing up qualitative research.* Newbury Park, CA: Sage.

Wolfer, J. (1993). Aspects of "reality" and ways of knowing in nursing: In search of an integrating paradigm. *Image: Journal of Nursing Scholarship, 25,* 141–146.

Margarete Sandelowski is Professor and Director of the Annual Summer Institutes in Qualitative Research in the School of Nursing at the University of North Carolina at Chapel Hill. She is the author of more than 100 publications in the areas of infertility and childbearing, gender and technology, and qualitative methodology, including the award-winning book *With Child in Mind: Studies of the Personal Encounter With Infertility* (1993). Her most recent book is *Devices and Desires: Gender, Technology, and American Nursing* (2000). She is currently principal investigator of a 5-year study, funded by the National Institute of Nursing Research, National Institutes of Health, to develop the analytical and interpretive techniques to conduct qualitative meta-syntheses.

13

An Improved Role for Qualitative Research in Mixed Methods

Selection: Howe, K. R. (2004). A critique of experimentalism. *Qualitative Inquiry,* *10,* 42–61.

Editors' Introduction

Kenneth Howe specializes in the philosophy of education and has written widely about research from philosophical and qualitative perspectives. His 2004 article represents a critique of mixed methods research. He approaches the discussion of mixed methods from the perspective of an individual who is concerned about the direction of educational research resulting from the United States' No Child Left Behind Act of 2001 and the National Research Council's 2002 report on scientific research in education. Both of these initiatives, Howe believes, elevate the importance of experimental research and place qualitative research in a secondary, supportive role.

Howe critiques two types of experimental research: neoclassical experimentalism and mixed methods experimentalism. The former, which emphasizes the importance of experimental research, oversells randomization, downplays external validity for internal validity, overstates the importance of causality, and misappropriates ideas of research from medical science. Mixed methods experimentalism, on the other hand, stresses quantitative approaches and portrays an ambiguous position for qualitative methods in experiments. As an alternative to both approaches, Howe suggests the use of mixed methods interpretivism, in which qualitative methods hold the primary role in experiments. The mixed methods interpretive researcher would focus on the role of inclusion by giving access to participants' voices and engaging participants in dialogue. This article represents an important challenge to mixed methods research in which the author contends that qualitative, participant-based approaches are not currently given an important role but also suggests that researchers need to use an interpretive-qualitative approach in mixed methods studies.

Discussion Questions and Applications

1. In your reading of mixed methods studies, do you think that Howe's central argument that qualitative research is of secondary interest in mixed methods research holds true?

2. Locate a mixed methods study. Is the interpretive approach used? Are participants' perspectives included and is there a dialogue with them for the qualitative strand?

3. Consider how you would plan a mixed methods experimental study to include qualitative research. What are some approaches for incorporating qualitative research into an experiment so that it has a primary role?

Related References That Extend the Topic

Examine the following references to read more concerns about the use of qualitative research in mixed methods studies:

Denzin, N. K., & Lincoln, Y.S. (2005). Introduction: The discipline and practice of qualitative research. In N. K. Denzin & Y. S. Lincoln (Eds.), *The SAGE handbook of qualitative research* (3rd ed., pp. 1–32). Thousand Oaks, CA: Sage.

Giddings, L. S. (2006). Mixed-methods research: Positivism in drag? *Journal of Research in Nursing, 11*(3), 195–203.

A Critique of Experimentalism

Kenneth R. Howe
University of Colorado at Boulder

The concept of scientifically based research occupies a central place in the thinking of the newly formed Institute of Education Sciences and seems well on its way to becoming the dominant paradigm in educational research more generally. What interpretation becomes recognized as the correct one thus has important implications. This article identifies two versions of experimentalism that have emerged: neoclassical and mixed methods. Both versions of experimentalism are judged to be methodologically retrograde. Neoclassical experimentalism is little more than a throwback to the Campbell-Stanley era and its dogmatic adherence to an exclusive reliance on quantitative methods. Mixed-methods experimentalism, although incorporating an auxiliary role for qualitative methods, fails to understand the deeper epistemological roots of qualitative methods. The article briefly sketches the alternative of mixed-methods interprevitism, which elevates the voice of research participants to a primary position and thereby reverses the epistemological ordering of quantitative-experimental and quantitative intepretivist methods.

Keywords: scientifically based research; quantitative methods; qualitative methods; experimentalism; interpretivism

The concept of scientific research[1] occupies a central place in the No Child Left Behind Act of 2001, as well as in the newly formed Institute of Education Sciences. It appears to be well on its way to becoming the dominant standard for designing and evaluating educational research more generally. Thus, how it is interpreted has potentially huge implications for the future course of educational research.

SOURCE: This article is reprinted from *Qualitative Inquiry*, Vol. 10, Issue 1, pp. 42–61, 2004. Reprinted with permission of Sage Publications, Inc.

In this article I critically examine the meaning of scientific research for the two methodological frameworks that are currently ascendant: *neoclassical experimentalism* and *mixed-methods experimentalism*. Both place experimental-quantitative research methods first among scientific methods and relegate qualitative methods to an auxiliary role. They differ with regard to how significant this auxiliary role is. I then briefly describe an alternative: *mixed-methods interpretivism,* a view that reverses the epistemological primacy of quantitative-experimental and qualitative-interpretivist methods. I argue that both forms of experimentalism are retrograde, whereas mixed-methods interpretivism has moved forward with the evolution of social science methodology during the past quarter century.

Neoclassical Experimentalism

Classical experimentalism is a term that may be applied to the approach to educational research articulated by Campbell and Stanley (1963) in their seminal monograph *Experimental and Quasi-Experimental Designs for Research.* There they lauded the experiment as

> the *only* means for settling disputes regarding educational practice, as the *only* way of verifying educational improvements, and as the *only* way of establishing a cumulative tradition. (p. 2, italics added)

When conceived as the comprehensive, one best methodology for educational research, classical experimentalism had all but disappeared. But it has recently made a comeback in the context of the debate about what constitutes scientific research. This *neo*classical experimentalism, as I shall call it, fits squarely within the Campbell-Stanley (1963) framework. Both emphasize investigating causal relationships as the means by which to build a repertoire of "what works," and both rely almost exclusively on quantitative methods.

Neoclassical experimentalism differs from classical experimentalism in two minor but nonetheless noteworthy ways. First, neoclassical experimentalism is even more restrictive in terms of the designs and analysis techniques it endorses than is classical experimentalism. Campbell and Stanley (1963) generally construed the "true," randomized experiment as the methodological gold standard, like the neoclassical experimentalists. However, although Campbell and Stanley believed that "quasi experiments" are often quite defensible, neoclassical experimentalists are highly critical of these designs, to the point where it is not clear if they endorse using them at all (e.g., Coalition for Evidence-Based Policy, 2002; Whitehurst, 2003). Second, neoclassical experimentalism exploits the perceived role of randomized experiments in medical research to support the contention that educational research should recommit itself to an emphasis on randomized experiments (e.g., Boruch, 2002; Coalition for Evidence-Based Policy, 2002).

Neoclassical experimentalism is retrograde. It ignores the evolution in social science research methodology regarding the value of qualitative methods and their status with respect to quantitative methods. And it provides no fresh answers to long-standing criticisms of classical experimentalism's penchant to trade external for internal validity, to oversell randomization, and to oversell the ability of randomized experiments to provide causal explanations.

Ignoring the Evolution of Thought on Social Research Methodology

Neoclassical experimentalists would do well to pay close attention to how Campbell changed his views in the decade following publication of the Campbell-Stanley (1963) monograph. For he "recanted" his dismissive attitude toward qualitative methods, partly in response to growing disappointment with experimentalist research and partly in response to developments in the philosophy of science. Here is what he had to say in "Qualitative Knowing in Action Research":

> The polarity of quantitative-experimental versus qualitative approaches to research on social action remains unresolved, if resolution were to mean a predominant justification of one over the other. . . . Each pole is at its best in its criticisms of the other, not in invulnerability of its own claims to descriptive knowledge. . . . If we are to be truly scientific, we must reestablish the qualitative grounding of the quantitative. (Campbell, 1974, pp. 29–30)

In this, his more mature view, Campbell eschewed the single-minded pursuit of quantitative-experimental methods as the road to scientific research. In this view, quantitative and qualitative methods do not exclude one another and neither occupies a position of ultimate authority. Instead, quantitative and qualitative methods of knowing cross-check one another.

Campbell (1974) unpacked his general conception of the relationship between quantitative and qualitative methods of knowing in terms of what he called the "presumptive" nature of knowledge. The basic idea here is that the only way to test a given claim within a given theory or conceptual scheme is to presume the truth of the vast majority of other claims within that theory or scheme. For Campbell, a large number, perhaps most, of the claims that are presumed are qualitative and, thus, so are many of the judgments that have to be made in the course of conducting research. When quantitative experimental research is detached from its qualitative grounding, the result is an "unhealthy division of labor" (Campbell, 1974, p. 13).

Campbell was not alone among prominent quantitative researchers in jettisoning classical experimentalisrn and the rigid quantitative/qualitative divide along with it. Lee Cronbach became one of experimentalism's most comprehensive and effective critics. Cronbach (1975) began his assault with his celebrated "Beyond the Two Disciplines of Scientific Psychology."[2] He cast considerable doubt on the idea that social science could be modeled on natural science, particularly regarding the possibility of accumulating robust generalizations about human behavior. Cronbach (1980, 1982) subsequently elaborated his criticisms of classical experimeritalism in two volumes on evaluation research. Several of these criticisms are taken up below.

Trading External Validity for Internal Validity

Among the major drawbacks of randomized experiments are problems with external validity, including inconsistency in implementing interventions across contexts ("dispensing a curriculum" is not quite the same as "dispensing a pill"). There is a trade-off between internal and external validity: The more investigators restrict the population and the treatment to achieve internal validity, the less external validity the study will have.

External validity should take greater priority than internal validity, at least in practical fields such as education. Ironically, despite their emphasis on "what works," this is not the ordering that experimentalists embrace. Thomas Cook (2002), for example, who adopts randomized experiments as the generally preferred methodology for education research, said, "randomized experiments are best when a causal question is simple, sharply focused and easily justified" (p. 179). Cook goes on to say that when applied to schools, among the things that make random assignment "most feasible" are treatments that are short and that require no teacher training (p. 184).

This is the research-methodology tail wagging the educational-practice dog. Putting a premium on internal validity encourages educational researchers to focus on easy-to-manipulate, simplistic interventions and to avoid questions about existing policy and practice that for one reason or another, are not suited to being investigated via randomized experiments. Consider important policy questions of the day such as the effects of standards-based accountability and public school choice, both features of the No Child Left Behind Act of 2001. Randomized experiments can be conducted only at the margins of these policies. Thus, however internally valid such experiments may be, they are only marginally relevant to determining the effectiveness of the educational policies and practices currently of greatest concern.

More concretely, consider the celebrated experiment on New York's school voucher program (Myers, Peterson, Mayer, Chou, & Howell, 2000). Students were randomly assigned to receive vouchers for private schools from a pool of applicants larger than the number of vouchers available. The study thus controlled for an important source of selection bias, namely, that those applying for vouchers are likely to be more motivated, and so on, than the general population. The subsequent analysis compared those who had applied and received the vouchers with those who applied but did not receive vouchers. The researchers concluded that the vouchers resulted in some modest gains in achievement for African American students.

Whatever the internal validity of this research (which is threatened by the differential drop-out problem discussed below), its external validity is quite limited. Even if there were evidence of modest achievement gains (the finding of any achievement gains whatever is disputed[3]), it would only show that voucher students outperform would-be voucher students. This would not come close to establishing that vouchers are an educational reform that will improve achievement overall (as its proponents so often claim). Students left behind would also need to improve (or at least not be hurt) by the departure of voucher students, a question the study did not address. Furthermore, the experiment failed to rule out several competing hypotheses for why voucher students might show improved achievement. One alternative hypothesis is that improved achievement (were it to be documented) could be the general effect of school choice, which could be just as powerful in public school choice system as in a voucher system. Another alternative is that, independent of choice, improved achievement could be produced by providing students with better *public* schools!

Overselling Randomization

Randomization is touted as if it were some magic bullet for what allegedly ails educational research (e.g., Boruch, 2002; Coalition for Evidence-Based Policy, 2002; Cook, 2002). To be sure, all other things being equal, randomization effectively reduces bias in estimating effects compared to other methods of control. But all other things rarely are equal.

First, social researchers typically must forgo random *selection* and make do with random *assignment*. The resulting estimates, however unbiased, are thus restricted to a population of volunteers. This does not always create a significant problem. But where the population of volunteers is likely to be substantially different from the target population, whatever reduction in bias is achieved by randomization may be outweighed by the need to generalize to that target population. Imagine using only volunteers to investigate the effectiveness of a program designed to reduce school violence.

Second, randomization provides no defense against the bias that often results from differential drop-out rates between treatment and control groups. In the case of school vouchers, for example, those who drop out of the treatment are likely to be unhappy with it, be seeing no benefit, and so on. No similar kind of systematic reasons apply to dropouts from the control group(s). Statistical adjustments maybe employed to help equalize treatment and control groups, but this is one of the very things that neoclassical experimentalists want to avoid by employing true rather than quasi experiments.

Third, more often than not, researchers cannot employ random assignment; at least they cannot and also investigate the most important questions in educational policy and practice. Random assignment is often ruled out on political/legal grounds. For example, in states with charter schools on the books, neither students nor larger units of analysis may be randomly assigned to participate. Yet, the effects charter schools are producing is an extremely important policy question that clearly ought to be, and is being, investigated. Credible nonexperimental results are being produced (e.g., as summarized by Gill, Timpane, Ross, & Brewer, 2001) that only the most hidebound experimentalist could ignore.

Overselling Experiments as Establishing Cause

The randomized experiment is frequently touted as the surest, if not *only*, way to make a causal inference in social research.[4] This is sheer dogma. The technique of the randomized experiment is neither sufficient nor necessary for establishing causation.

Randomized experiments are not sufficient to establish causal relationships because the inferences drawn from them so often involve only a very "gappy," black box account of relationships such that the precise cause(s) of the effect(s) cannot be identified (Cronbach, 1982). Acquiring a better understanding of causal mechanisms requires substantive knowledge of the contents and workings of the black box, something that cannot be obtained merely by employing the formal device of the randomized experiment.

Randomized experiments are not necessary to establish causal relationships because in cases where substantive background knowledge is available, robust causal relationships (at least in the statistical sense) can be established without randomized experiments. "Cigarette smoking causes cancer" is a good example. The gappy, black box correlation has been filled in with animal studies on the effects of exposure to tar, examinations of smoker's lungs, analyses of the chemical contents of cigarette smoke, studies that correlate the duration of cigarette smoking with the likelihood of developing lung cancer, and so on. There probably are not any causal relationships in education that are as firmly established as the link between cigarette smoking and lung cancer, but the principle is the same. For example, there have been no randomized experiments to show that race and parental income are causally related to academic performance, but the persistence of the associations makes it hard to deny that such causal relationships exist. Furthermore, various gap-filling explanations for low performance have been proffered, including lack of resources and experiences in the home, students being called on to care for siblings, peer pressure to avoid "acting White," and so on.

Misappropriating Medical Research

In addition to the general failure to acknowledge and entertain the methodological pitfalls described above, neoclassical experimentalism misappropriates medical research. Neoclassical experimentalists (e.g., the Coalition for Evidence-Based Policy) heavily tout medical research as the model for educational research, particularly the random clinical trial. But the analogy is seriously flawed: It submerges important differences between medical and educational research as well as important similarities.

An important difference between the fields of medical research and educational research is that it is typically much easier to zero in on the treatment and to maintain its consistent administration in clinical medicine than in education. Compare the treatment defined as "x mgs. of compound y each morning" to the treatment defined as "instruction in connected math 5 hours per week." The context of the administration of the treatment is much less of a complicating factor in clinical medicine than in education. As indicated above, "dispensing curriculum" is quite different from "dispensing a pill." Finally, the precision with which outcomes can be measured varies considerably. Compare "a 10-point reduction in diastolic blood pressure" with "a 10-month growth in mathematics understanding."

An important similarity between the fields of medical research and educational research is that nonrandomized clinical trials are quite common in medical research, particularly outside of pharmaceutical research.[5] (Randomized clinical trials are most common in pharmaceutical research because, as the above illustration suggests, it is relatively easy to enforce the experimental conditions, including maintaining the standardization of the treatment.) Clinical medical research is divided into four phases, ranging from Phase 1, exploratory research on safety and side effects, to Phase 4, tracking the effects of a treatment after it has been put into general use. (Phase 4 pertains to medical research's "external validity" question.) Randomized clinical trials typically are employed in Phase 3 trials but they are not required in any phase.

Another important similarity between the fields of medical research and educational research is that the knowledge that has been accumulated through randomized clinical trials is not the only or even the most important factor in improved public health. Improved hygienic conditions and better nutrition, followed next by the (nonexperimental) development of immunizations and antibiotics, are credited with being, by far, the most important measures historically (e.g., Schneiderman & Speers, 2001). In a related vein, the effectiveness of medical care for given groups interacts with their socioeconomic status. Just as socioeconomic status is highly correlated with school performance, it is also highly correlated with health status. (According to one commentator, "low socioeconomic position is as strong a risk factor for poor health outcomes as smoking," Lynch, 2001, p. 52). And just as there is a persistent gap in school performance associated with socioeconomic status, there is a persistent gap in health status. Thus, if contributing to closing the achievement gap is one of the overriding goals of educational research, then medical research is not a model to be emulated.[6]

Conclusion

Boruch (2002)—in the vanguard of neoclassical experimentalism—warned that the educational research community may well resist embracing randomized experiments as the methodological ideal because of the "ideological posturing that so often substitutes for evidence in the education world" (p. 11). This remark is not only gratuitous; it gets the shoe on the wrong foot. Neoclassical experimentalism's attempted appropriation of medical research is patently selective. And it otherwise ignores the criticisms initiated by Campbell and Cronbach in the mid-1970s that were subsequently taken up and extended by a number of thinkers from the mid-1980s on.[7]

Mixed-Methods Experimentalism

Mixed-methods experimentalism is the view exemplified in the National Research Council (2002) report *Scientific Research in Education* (SRE). SRE assigns a significant role to qualitative methods. And they may be employed either singly or in combination with quantitative methods. In this respect, mixed-methods experimentalism is an advance over neoclassical experimentalism.

On the other hand, like neoclassical experimentalism, mixed-methods experimentalism places quantitative-experimental research methods and determining "what works" at the center of education science. Also like neoclassical experimentalism, mixed-methods experimentalism calls for a greater emphasis on randomized experiments without providing any real defense of why and without responding to the criticisms regarding the overselling of experimentalism.[8] In this and several other ways to be discussed below, mixed-methods experimentalism is not that distant from neoclassical experimentalism. It, too, is retrograde.

An Essentialist Conception of Science

The strategy in SRE was to set down the general features of science and then to determine what forms of educational scholarship fit. The committee seemed to assume that various sciences have a shared essence that it was their task to *discover*. SRE says things such as "At its core, scientific inquiry is the same in all fields" (National Research Council, 2002, p. 2) and the "accumulation of knowledge is the ultimate goal of [all] research" (National Research Council, 2002, p. 24). Although the committee did some hand waiving about how scientific progress is disjointed and is characterized by uncertainty and by fits and starts, they eventually identified the general aims of scientific educational research as "theory building" and "rigorous studies of interventions" (National Research Council, 2002, p. 126).

The project of articulating a general conception of science was largely abandoned in the wake of positivism, particularly a general conception that would include both the natural and social sciences (e.g., Chalmers, 1999). This does not mean that nothing hangs on the question of what qualifies as science, such that reasoned argument about it would be out of place. (Consider, for example, the question of whether "creation science" really qualifies as science.) The approach of SRE just is not very helpful.

The answer to the question of whether a certain inquiry approach is to be called "science" or "scientific" cannot be provided by *inspection* to determine whether that approach fits a set of predetermined categories. In addition to the inherent vagueness found at the edges of any concept, the terms "science" and "scientific" have a clear evaluative dimension (e.g., Chalmers, 1999). When the question of whether to apply these terms to a given activity is contested, we have to *decide* whether the activity counts as science or as scientific. Such a decision unavoidably turns on what values will be promoted or blunted.

An Outmoded Philosophy of Social Science

Related to its essentialism, SRE implicitly assumes some version of the principle of the "unity of science," in which social science (if it is to be science) must mimic the natural sciences. In this view, social science and natural science exhibit only a *difference of degree* such that social science is simply more complex than natural science in virtue of involving many more relevant variables over which investigators have little or no control.

Against this kind of view, Anthony Giddens (1976) has remarked, "Those who still wait for a Newton of social science are not only waiting for a train that won't arrive, they're in the wrong station altogether" (p. 13). The kind of *interpretivist* philosophy of social science[9] Giddens's remark exemplifies embraces a *difference of kind* between social science and natural science such that human behavior, unlike atoms and molecules, can be fully understood only from the insiders' perspective, in terms of the interpretation of meanings that actors employ. SRE does little more than waive at this alternative.[10] Human agency—a fundamental feature of social life bound up with the fact that humans are pervasive interpreters of others as well as themselves (Taylor, 1987)—is treated as little more than a factor that complicates social research by making humans less well behaved than billiard balls.[11]

The failure of SRE to give more serious attention to the interpretivist perspective is a significant lacuna. Interprevitism's influence is strongly felt in the philosophy of social science, and its various variants are embraced by a significant proportion of educational researchers (see Howe, 2003). Moreover the interpretivist perspective challenges several prominent features of SRE's characterization of scientific educational research.

The question of demarcation. SRE asserts that scientific educational research is "empirical," to be cleanly distinguished from other kinds of education scholarship, the humanities in particular.[12] But the line between empirical social research and the humanities cannot be drawn very distinctly, if at all, given interpretivist methodology, in which the aims, requisite skills, and vocabularies of social science and the humanities significantly overlap (e.g., Cronbach, 1975; Taylor, 1987). It may be worth drawing such a line nonetheless, but SRE makes no convincing case for doing so. The committee seemed to just go with their intuitions and customary usage and to presuppose that the matter is unproblematic. But the matter is not unproblematic to the extent that it encourages the belief that empirical questions can be emptied of conceptual and value content and once emptied, may serve as the pristine foundation of *truly* empirical science. The project of demarcating science in this way—and thereby rendering it: uncontaminated by metaphysics and values—was (is) the pipe dream of positivist social science.[13]

Education science as cumulative. As indicated previously, SRE holds that "the accumulation of knowledge is the ultimate goal of [all] research"

(National Research Council, 2002, p. 24). But the idea that social science proceeds by piling up more and more on truths that survive testing is by no means unproblematic.[14] As Cronhach (1975) observed, "generalizations decay"; what at one time describes the social situation well might later be "valid only as history" (pp. 122–123). The point is not that generalizations are fallible and that mistaken ones may need to be subsequently corrected. (This would apply to the belief that bleeding patients is an effective medical treatment, for example. Bleeding is not now effective and never was.) The point is that what may be correctly generalized about human institutions and practices changes over time. A generalization that is now false could have been true at an earlier time and place. (Women compose a distinct minority of students enrolled in medical schools, for example.)

Giddens (1976) added a twist to Cronbach's (1975) observation: The practice of social research itself can be a factor in hastening the decay of generalizations, as a consequence of the "double hermeneutic." Social researchers engage in various interpretive (hermeneutical) acts in the process of coming to an understanding of the group they are studying. When researchers subsequently disseminate their findings to a public audience, members of this audience engage in (or at least may engage in) their own interpretive (hermeneutical) acts. This constitutes the "double" part of the double hermeneutic, and it has the potential to stimulate behavior on the part of the public that results in the decay of generalizations about social life. For "critical" researchers, *making* generalizations decay— generalizations documenting oppressive relationships, in particular—is an explicit goal of social research (e.g., Fay, 1975, 1987).

My aim in this section has not been to jettison the idea of the accumulation of knowledge in education science wholesale, but to point to limitations in SRE's characterization. There are two. First, research does not have to be cumulative in the sense of building on what research has shown is true of social life; it may aim to demolish such truths. Second, even when the aim is accumulating knowledge in the straightforward sense of building on to what is true, such truths are subject to decay.

Causal relationships and causal mechanisms. SRE endorses a variety of research questions and a variety of research methods. In chapter 5, "Designs for the Conduct of Scientific Research in Education," it specifies how the two should be fitted together. At the most rudimentary level are descriptive questions: "What is happening?" These fit with quantitative methods such as surveys and qualitative methods such as ethnographies. At the next level are causal questions: "Is there a systematic effect?" These fit with quantitative methods, particularly the "ideal" of the randomized experiment. Qualitative methods are a source of causal hypotheses and may be used to "strengthen" causal inferences by helping eliminate alternative hypotheses. At the final level are causal mechanism questions: "Why or how is it happening?" These fit with a wide variety of quantitative and qualitative methods.

Quantitative and qualitative methods, then, cut across the three types of questions (i.e., both kinds of methods can he appropriately employed with respect to each type of question). Beyond this, SRE is rather vague on how things fit together, particularly regarding causation. Randomized experiments are singled out as the "ideal" for investigating the "causal relationships" type questions. As indicated above, qualitative methods are a source of causal hypotheses and may play the auxiliary role of helping "strengthen" inferences about causal relationships by eliminating alternative hypotheses. Qualitative methods do not otherwise play a role in inferring causal relationships.[15] The status of qualitative methods is less clear when it comes to investigating "causal mechanisms." Here it seems that qualitative methods may play a central (as opposed to auxiliary) role in the logic of causal inference. In particular, they may be used to help get beyond the black box, "gappy" understanding of causal mechanisms to which randomized experiments are often limited.

There is a tension, if not incoherence, in SRE's position on the role of qualitative methods in making causal inferences. In particular, it is difficult to see any real difference between "causal mechanisms" and "causal relationships." Questions about the causal mechanism that results in some effect, E, are more refined and precise than the questions about the causal relationship that results in E. This is a relative and rather arbitrary difference. It is not at all clear why, given SRE's position on investigating causal relationships, investigating causal mechanisms should not proceed in the same experimentalist way. Causal mechanisms seem to be nothing other than more fine-grained causal relationships within the black box.

There is an important distinction to be made within social science regarding causation, but it is different from SRE's distinction between causal relationships and causal mechanisms. In particular, it is the distinction between the *regularity* and *intentional* conceptions of causation. The regularity conception construes causation in terms of relationships among *descriptive* variables grounded in the *outsider's perspective*. The intentional conception construes causation in terms of relationships among *intentional states* and *actions* grounded in the *insider's perspective*.[16]

According to John Searle (1984, 1995), human behavior must be understood against a complex background of "intentionality" that defines norm-regulated practices. Documented regularities among descriptive variables do not constitute causal explanations of human behavior; they call for them (Searle, 1984). Searle turned the typical, experimentalist construal on its head: Quantitative findings documenting regularities constitute the auxiliary, discovery work; filling in the black box requires investigating matters best handled with qualitative methods. Take the following example. We begin with the observed regularity that African American students living in "Trackton" exhibit low academic achievernent.[17] This regularity in and of itself is not a causal explanation of anything. To provide such an explanation, we conduct an ethnographic study that gets at the perceptions and practices of the actors involved. We conclude that the differences among the linguistic practices of African American students and their White teachers cause distorted communication between them that in turn, causes lower academic performance on the part of the students.

Intentional causation is a central element of the interpretivist perspective, but there are no good reasons not to also employ the regularity sense of causation in social and educational research as appropriate (e.g., Fay 1975, 1996; Giddens, 1976; Howe, 2003). For example, "Poverty causes low performance in school" is "gappy" to be sure, and fails to speak to intentions, but it is an informative and coherent claim that does no violence to the concept of causation. Social and educational research can make fruitful use of such causal claims about complex social mechanisms over which people may have little control or awareness.

Conclusion

Mixed-methods experimentalism is a direct descendant of classical experimentalism and is less congenial to qualitative methods than it might first appear. It elevates quantitative-experimental methods to the top of the methodological hierarchy and constrains qualitative methods to a largely auxiliary role in pursuit of the *technocratic* aim of accumulating knowledge of "what works." It is not that qualitative methods can never be fruitfully and appropriately used in this way, but their natural home is within an interpretivist framework with the *democratic* aim of seeking to understand and give voice to the insider's perspective regarding various educational policies and practices. This feature of qualitative-interpretivist methodology—associated with fundamental developments in the philosophy of social science during approximately the past quarter century—is scarcely even acknowledged in SRE.

Mixed-methods experimentalism gives primacy to quantitative-experimental methods over qualitative-interpretive methods to determine "what works," as if determining "what works" were somehow the self-certifying aim of educational research. "What works" is not an innocent notion. Concrete instances of the claim "Intervention *I* works" are elliptical for instances of the claim "Intervention *I* works to accomplish outcome *O*." The desired outcomes are embraced (if only tacitly) as more valuable than other possible outcomes, and the question of their value is off the table for anyone except policy makers and researchers. In this way the aim of determining "what works" is *technocratic:* it focuses on the question of whether interventions are effective in achieving *given* outcomes.

An Alternative: Mixed-Methods Interpretivism

What I call "mixed-methods interpretivism" reverses the primacy of quantitative-experimental and qualitative-interpretive methods such that quantitative methods play an auxiliary role in an overarching interpretivist-qualitative framework (Howe, 2003). The question of "what works" is construed much more expansively: The question of the value of the desired outcomes remains on the table to be assessed by various stakeholders.

Mixed-methods interpretivism actively engages stakeholder participation through the principles of *inclusion* and *dialogue*.[18] Inclusion is a general methodological principle that serves to control bias by ensuring the representativeness of samples. But it also has (or can have) a democratic dimension: ensuring that all relevant voices are heard.

The principle of dialogue adds an interpretivist dimension to inclusion and thickens its democratic dimension. Interpretivism emphasizes understanding people in their own terms, in their own social settings. Engaging them in dialogue is the most effective means of achieving this aim. As in the case of inclusion, there are both methodological and democratic justifications for employing dialogue: The deeper and more genuine expressions of beliefs and values that emerge through dialogue both foster a more accurate description of views held and *un*distort democratic deliberation.

Qualitative research methods such as participant observation, interviews, focus groups, and the like are well suited for promoting dialogue. Each technique involves some form of interaction between researchers and research participants that permits researchers to get below surface appearances to obtain a richer and more nuanced understanding of social life. There is a tension here, of course. Research participants can be mistaken or misinformed about the harms and benefits of various educational policies and practices, including to themselves. They typically also lack background knowledge and technical expertise. Thus, when researchers enter into dialogue with research participants, simply elucidating how participants think things work, and ought to work, can be no more than one element of full-blown—or *critical*—dialogue. Critical dialogue includes bringing expert knowledge to bear and subjecting the views and self-understandings of research participants to rational scrutiny.

Because mixed-methods interpretivism is, indeed, a mixed methods approach, it cannot be distinguished from mixed-methods experimentalism simply in terms of the methods employed. How the role of participants is construed—democratic versus technocratic—is the determining factor. Below are three examples that help illuminate the differences between mixed-methods experimentalism and mixed-methods interpretivism.[19]

Example 1: School choice policy. The question of whether a school choice policy is a good one is not the same as the question of whether it works in the sense of attaining the goals policy makers and theoreticians have for it. Judgments about the worth of program goals themselves, about competing goals, about unintended consequences, and about how to balance these are all relevant to the question of whether a school choice policy is a good one. These are the kinds of things many stakeholders know about and that in the name of democracy, ought to have an effective say about. Having an effective say requires that stakeholders be included in genuine dialogue.

Qualitative methods are best suited for fostering dialogue, though as indicated above, they also may be used instrumentally to determine "what works," with no real commitment to the democratic dimension of dialogue. On the other hand, although quantitative methods are best suited for situations in which the variable and outcomes of interest are settled on ahead of time, they maybe employed within an overarching democratic framework in which the effects of given polices are crucial to deliberation. For example, whether school choice policies cause increased segregation is critical in the current policy debate. Once again, the crucial difference between mixed-methods experimentalism and mixed-methods interpretivism is how the role of participants is construed.

Example 2: Research on the "hidden curriculum." Research on the "hidden curriculum" and related features of schools fit naturally with the dialogical approach associated with mixed-methods interpretivism. Lois Weis and Michelle Fine (1993) wrote in the introduction to *Beyond Silenced Voices,* there is "a *discursive underground* of students and adults that flourish within the margins of our public schools. These voices need to be heard . . . if we are serious about schools as a democratic public sphere" (p. 2). How femininity, masculinity, race, and beliefs and attitudes about sexual orientation are shaped and reinforced by school cultures and curricula are among the issues with which students and teachers are engaged in dialogue by educational researchers. Among the more specific questions addressed are how certain voices are missing from the culture and curricula, what the consequences might be, and what measures might be taken in response.

Perhaps there is a randomized experiment lurking here somewhere, but it is difficult to see how an emphasis on experimentation would significantly advance this general area of research. On the contrary, such an emphasis would hamper it.

Example 3: Research on teaching and learning. Mixed-methods interpretivism applies least obviously and straightforwardly to research on teaching and learning, and this is where experimentalism applies best. Because there is often considerable agreement on explicit goals and outcomes in this arena, dialogue is rendered less necessary and researchers are relatively safe to proceed with ascertaining "what works."

But they are not *completely* safe, for educational research can never be free of value commitments. Here, it will be helpful to distinguish between *value neutrality* and *value freedom* (Howe, 2003). Educational research can be value neutral in the sense of being *neutral among* different moral-political stances. This is not to say that educational research can ever be value free, however. For example, research on the acquisition of basic computation skills is a good candidate for the kind of investigation that can quite plausibly be characterized as value neutral. But it is important to note that to the extent that the acquisition of computation skills may be correctly characterized as value neutral, *neutrality does not go all the way down.* Broader questions about values are lurking, even in a relatively uncontroversial area such as math education. For example, what approaches to math curricula and instruction best prepare students to become competent democratic citizens? What approaches to math curricula and instruction are least likely to be exclusionary of certain kinds of students? What approaches to math curricula and instruction are most likely to make students critical mathematical thinkers and to foster a healthy skepticism of mathematics as an all-purpose intellectual tool? What trade-offs are to be made among mathematics and other subjects? And so on. These are not technical "what works" questions.[20]

Concluding Remarks

The contrast between the technocratic thrust of experimentalism and the democratic thrust of interpretivism gets at the political dimensions of educational research. Although it is clearly an important part of the academic debate, there is a political dimension that is considerably less high flown. In these concluding remarks, I speculate about what besides academic debate is driving the demand to define standards for scientific educational research and about what some of the consequences are likely to be.

First, the imposition of external standards is something that K–12 has been enduring for some time. Standards have recently arrived at the academy: first in teacher education and now in research. Arguably, the standards-setting movement in education is inherently about power and control, under the banner of protecting the public from incompetent or misguided practitioners.[21] Groups like the committee that worked diligently to prepare SRE have scrambled to show how what they do qualifies as science to regain some of their power to influence policy makers. But they may very well have been diverted onto the trail of a red herring. Organizations such as the Fordham Foundation, the Manhattan Institute, and the Heritage Foundation, for example, have considerable influence on policy makers, and it is doubtful that this is because the product they produce measures up to high scientific standards. More likely, it is because their product is sensitive to the ideological predilections and agendas of the current powers that be and that it is conceived and marketed accordingly (Howe, 2002).

Second, the strong endorsement of randomized trials as the "gold standard" (by the neoclassical experimentalists) and the "ideal" (by the mixed-methods experimentalists) creates the imperative to anticipate and vigorously control all the variables that are predetermined to be relevant vis-à-vis "what works." This puts blinders on researchers and drives educational research in a certain political direction: away from raising critical questions about the social and institutional context of schooling and toward various interventions that "work" given the status quo. Researchers who persist in the social critique of educational practice are liable to be written off for their alleged "ideological posturing."

Finally, it is not just the "methodological fundamentalists"[22] who have bought into the "what works" approach. A sizable number of rather influential and otherwise sensible educational researchers—several on the National Research Council committee, for example—have also signed on. This might be a compromise in response to the current political climate; it might be a backlash against the perceived excesses of postmodernism; it might be both. It is an ominous development, whatever the explanation.

Notes

1. I include cognates such as "scientifically based" and "evidence based" as part of the general territory.

2. Interestingly, Cronbach presented this paper at the same 1974 meeting of the American Psychological Association as the Campbell paper described above. Cronbach (1982) noted the similar turns their thinking had taken in these papers.

3. See Winerip (2003) for a summary.

4. The concept of cause is particularly nettlesome in social research. It can assume two different meanings. One is the "intentional" meaning of cause, in which casual explanations are *teleological* (i.e., appeal to agents' purposes and interpretations of meanings). This meaning is rarely (if ever) considered in the context of experimentalism. (Intentional causation is discussed in greater detail in the section herein on mixed-methods experimentalism.) The second is the more familiar "regularity" meaning of cause, where causal explanations are *descriptive* (i.e., appeal only to observed regularities). The regularity sense is seen as particularly problematic in social research because the putative causal relationships are statistical, not deterministic ones (Cronbach, 1982).

5. I recently did a study, "unscientific" to be sure, but revealing nonetheless. I went to the Medline Web site and looked under "coronary disease"—the treatment of which has got to be considered one of modern medicine's success stories. As I expected, I found that the majority of the clinical studies described there were not randomized experiments. Indeed, I found one study comparing medical and surgical treatments of coronary ischemia in which the researchers claimed that their nonrandomized study was actually methodologically *superior* to a randomized clinical trial because it included a much more representative sample of the population of interest than would be possible with a sample of patients willing to volunteer for a randomized study.

6. Of course, it is highly dubious that better research methodology will solve the problem in either case. We already have pretty good understandings of the direction of causation between socioeconomic status on one hand and school performance and health status on the other hand, however "gappy" they may be.

7. A lot more could be said about the quantitative/qualitative debate—a debate that neoclassical experimentalists have conveniently avoided participating in. But that is a discussion for another place. See Howe (2003) for a comprehensive treatment of the issues.

8. Here is what the National Research Council (2002) had to say on the issue:

> In estimating the effects of programs, we urge the expanded use of random assignment. Randomized experiments are not perfect. Indeed, the merits of their use in education have been seriously questioned. . . . For instance, they typically cannot test complex causal hypotheses, they may lack generalizability to other settings, and can be expensive. However, we believe that these and other issues do not generate a compelling rationale against their use in education research and that issues related to ethical concerns, political obstacles, and other potential barriers often can he resolved. . . . Establishing cause is often exceedingly important—for example, in large-scale deployment of interventions—and the ambiguity correlational of quasi-experiments can be undesirable for practical purposes. (p. 125)

9. I use "interpretivism" in an expansive way to include a variety of post-positivist views that insist social research must include a special "intentionalist" vocabulary and an associated array of "qualitative" methods. Many such interpretivist

views, including Giddens's (1976) and my own pragmatic view (Howe, 2003), advocate mixed methods, not an exclusive reliance on an intentionalist vocabulary and qualitative methods.

10. This is about all the National Research Council (2002) had to say on the topic:

> Differences in the phenomena typically under investigation do distinguish the research conducted by physical and social scientists. . . . Unlike atoms or molecules, people grow up and change over time. The social, cultural, and economic conditions they experience evolve with history. The abstract concepts and ideas that are meaningful to them vary across time, space, and cultural tradition. *These circumstances have led some social science and education researchers to investigate approaches that look distinctly different from those of physical researchers* [italics added], while still aligning with the guiding principles outlined [in this volume]. (p. 81)

11. See especially *Scientific Research in Education* subsection "Human Volition," (National Research Council, 2002, beginning on p. 86).

12. Interestingly, philosophy and history, both humanities disciplines, fit the general characterization of science provided early in *Scientific Research in Education*: "a continuous process of rigorous reasoning supported by a dynamic interplay among methods, theories, and findings" (National Research Council, 2002, p. 2).

13. One of positivism's basic tenets was that science is the paragon of knowledge, the only *real* kind of knowledge (save logic and math). One of its ambitions was to *demarcate* science from pretenders to knowledge, such as metaphysics, ethics, and aesthetics. The project failed, and one of the primary reasons was that Quine, Kuhn, and others convincingly undermined the notion that you could cleanly isolate the empirical contents of science from its conceptual (or theoretical) content. So, there are relatively fundamental philosophical reasons to be suspicious of the assumption that "scientifically based" research can be isolated on the basis of its "empirical" content.

14. This conception of scientific progress has been seriously challenged even in physical sciences, most famously by Thomas Kuhn (1962).

15. This division of labor between qualitative and quantitative methods was typical in the early days of the quantitative/qualitative debate. It maps, à la positivism, qualitative methods on to the "context of discovery" and quantitative methods on to the "context of justification."

16. The idea of "intentional" has a much broader meaning in philosophy than in ordinary usage. It has to do with the "aboutness" that characterizes concepts crucial to understanding human behavior, such as knowledge, belief, doubt, and so on. Knowledge, belief, and doubt are each about the planets, algebra, politics, and so on. Concepts in the physical sciences and "behaviorese" do not have this "aboutness" feature and are thus not intentional.

17. The example is based on Heath (1983).

18. Here I collapse three principles first articulated in House and Howe (1999)—inclusion, dialogue, and deliberation—into two.

19. These examples are adapted from Howe (2003).

20. Examples like this make me less than sanguine about following the authors of *Scientific Research in Education* (National Research Council, 2002) in drawing a sharp line between science and philosophy—as if we can avoid doing (or presupposing) something *philosophical* as we engage in empirical research.

21. The American Educational Research Association membership got a bit of a scolding from Russ Whitehurst in this vein at the 2003 convention (Whitehurst, 2003).

22. This term is borrowed from House (2003).

References

Boruch, R. (2002). The virtues of randomness. *Education Next, 2*(3), 36–42. Retrieved from http://www.educationnext.org/20023/36.html

Campbell, D. (1974, September). *Qualitative knowing in action research.* Kurt Lewin Award Address, Society for the Psychological Study of Social Issues, presented at the meeting of the American Psychological Association, New Orleans, LA.

Campbell, D., & Stanley, J. (1963). *Experimental and quasi-experimental designs for research.* Chicago: Rand McNally.

Chalmers, A. (1999). *What is this thing called science?* (3rd ed.). Indianapolis, IN: Hackett.

Coalition for Evidence-Based Policy (2002). *Bringing evidence-driven progress to education: A recommended strategy for the U.S. Department of Education.* Author. Available from http://www.excelgov.org/displayContent.asp?NewsItemID=4541& Keyword=prppcEvidence

Cook, T. (2002). Randomized experiments in educational policy research: A critical examination of the reasons the educational evaluation community has offered for not doing them. *Education Evaluation and Policy Analysis, 24*(3), 175–199.

Cronbach, L. (1975). Beyond the two disciplines of scientific psychology. *American Psychologist, 30,* 116–127.

Cronbach, L. (1982). *Designing evaluations of educational and social programs.* San Francisco: Jossey-Bass.

Cronbach, L., Ambron, S. R., Dornbusch, S. M., Hess, R. D., Hornick, R. C., Phillips, D. C., et al. (1980). *Toward reform of program evaluation: Aims, methods, and institutional arrangements.* San Francisco: Jossey-Bass.

Fay, B. (1975). *Social theory and political practice.* Birkenhead, UK: Allen and Unwin.

Fay, B. (1987). *Critical social science.* Ithaca, NY: Cornell University Press.

Fay, B. (1996). *Contemporary philosophy of social science.* Malden, MA: Blackwell.

Giddens, A. (1976). *New rules of sociological method.* New York: Basic Books.

Gill, B., Timpane, M., Ross, K., & Brewer, D. (2001). *Rhetoric versus reality: What we know and what we need to know about vouchers and charter schools.* Santa Monica, CA: RAND.

Heath, S. (1983). *Ways with words: Language, life, and work in communities and classrooms.* New York: Cambridge University Press.

House, E. (2003). Bush's neo-fundamentalism and the new politics of evaluation. *Studies in Education Policy and Educational Philosophy, 2.* Available from www.upi.artisan.se

House, E., & Howe, K. (1999). *Values in evaluation and social research.* Thousand Oaks, CA: Sage.

Howe, K. (2002, April 10). Free market free for all, *Education Week, 21*(30), 32, 34–35.

Howe, K. (2003). *Closing methodological divides: Toward democratic educational research.* Dordrecht, the Netherlands: Kluwer.

Kuhn, T. (1962). *The structure of scientific revolutions.* Chicago: University of Chicago Press.

Lynch, J. (2001). Socioeconomic factors in the behavioral and psychosocial epidemiology of cardiovascular disease. In N. Schneiderman, M. Spears, J. Silva, H. Tames, & J. Gentry (Eds.), *Integrating behavioral and social sciences with public health* (pp. 51–72). Washington, DC: American Psychological Association.

Myers, D., Peterson, P., Mayer, D., Chou, J., & Howell, W. (2000). *School choice in New York City after two years: An evaluation of the school choice scholarship program.* Washington, DC: Mathematica Policy Research.

National Research Council. (2002). *Scientific research in education.* Washington, DC: National Academy Press.

No Child Left Behind Act of 2001, Pub. L. No. 107–110, 115 Stat. 1425 (2002).

Schneiderman, N., & Speers, N. (2001). Behavioral science, social science, and public health in the 21st century. In N. Schneiderman, M. Spears, J. Silva, H. Tames, & J. Gentry (Eds.), *Integrating behavioral and social sciences with public health* (pp. 3–30). Washington, DC: American Psychological Association.

Searle, J. (1984). *Minds, brains, and science.* Cambridge, MA: Harvard University Press.

Searle, J. (1995). *The construction of social reality.* New York: Free Press.

Taylor, C. (1987). Interpretation and the sciences of man. In P. Rabinow & W. Sullivan (Eds.), *Interpretive social science: A second look* (pp. 33–81). Los Angeles: University of California Press.

Weis, L., & Fine, M. (1993). Introduction. In L. Weis & M. Fine (Eds.), *Beyond silenced voices: Class, race, and gender in United States schools* (pp. 1–8). Albany, NY: State University of New York Press.

Whitehurst, G. (2003, April). *The Institute of Education Sciences: New wine and new bottles.* Presentation at the annual meeting of the American Educational Research Association, Chicago, IL.

Winerip, M. (2003, May 7). What some much-noted data really showed about vouchers. *New York Times.* Available from http://www.nytimes.com/2003/05/07/education/07EDUC.html?pagewanted=print&position=

Kenneth R. Howe is professor in the Educational Foundations, Policy, and Practice Program area, director of the Education and the Public Interest Center, and associate dean of Graduate Studies, University of Colorado at Boulder. He specializes in education policy, professional ethics, and philosophy of education. He has conducted research on a variety of topics, ranging from the quantitative/qualitative debate to a philosophical examination of constructivism to a defense of multicultural education. His books include the *Ethics of Special Education* (with Ofelia Miramontes), *Understanding Equal Education Opportunity: Social Justice, Democracy and Schooling, Values in Evaluation and Social Research* (with Earnest House), and *Closing Methodological Divides: Toward Democratic Educational Research*. He teaches courses in the social foundations of education, the philosophy of education, and philosophical issues in educational research.

14

An Alternative to Reconciling the Different Realities of Qualitative and Quantitative Research

Selection: Sale, J. E., Lohfeld, L. H., & Brazil, K. (2002). Revisiting the quantitative-qualitative debate: Implications for mixed-methods research. *Quality & Quantity, 36,* 43–53.

Editors' Introduction

Three Canadian researchers in the health sciences—Joanna Sale, Lynne Lohfeld, and Kevin Brazil—revisit the debate between quantitative and qualitative research with specific implications for mixed methods research. Through their discussion we turn full circle back to the earlier debates that were described by Tashakkori and Teddlie in Chapter 1 of this volume. This article adds to the philosophical discussion by linking the paradigm debate question directly into the design discussion of mixed methods research.

In this 2002 article, Sale et al. start by noting that combined quantitative and qualitative methods are becoming widely practiced and accepted in health care research. However, many researchers adopt mixed methods uncritically, without considering the underlying assumptions behind the qualitative-quantitative debate. Their core assumption is that quantitative and qualitative researchers view reality differently (the former believes in an external reality; the latter, a reality shaped by individuals) as well as reporting research in different journals, drawing from different sources of funding, and having different expertise, methods, and terms. Although the authors see a compatibility between quantitative and qualitative paradigms, bridging across quantitative and qualitative research is difficult (or incommensurate) because both forms of inquiry draw on different types of reality. However, the authors propose an alternative that would not violate the philosophical assumptions of either quantitative or qualitative research: if the qualitative and quantitative research is viewed as independent and additive (such as where one method builds on the other), then it is possible to do mixed methods research.

Discussion Questions and Applications

1. The authors make the assumption that the qualitative and quantitative paradigm perspectives hold opposite views toward the nature of reality. Do you agree?

2. As you look through the research designs presented earlier (Chapters 4–7), do you think that Sale et al. have eliminated the possibility of triangulated designs?

3. The authors discuss how the qualitative and quantitative approaches have a different view of the phenomenon under study. Do you think that the difference is the view of the phenomenon, the research questions, or how a phenomenon is studied (through methods and procedures)?

Related References That Extend the Topic

Further discussions about the incompatibility of quantitative and qualitative research include:

Howe, K. R. (1988). Against the quantitative-qualitative incompatibility thesis or dogmas die hard. *Educational Researcher, 17,* 10–16.
Smith, J. K., & Heshusius, L. (1986). Closing down the conversation: The end of the quantitative-qualitative debate among educational inquiries. *Educational Researcher, 15,* 4–12.

Revisiting the Quantitative-Qualitative Debate

Implications for Mixed-Methods Research

Joanna E. M. Sale

Institute for Work & Health; Health Research
Methodology Program, Department of Clinical
Epidemiology & Biostatistics, McMaster University

Lynne H. Lohfeld

St. Joseph's Hospital and Home; Department of
Clinical Epidemiology & Biostatistics, McMaster University

Kevin Brazil

St. Joseph's Health Care System Research Network,
St. Joseph's Community Health Centre; Department of
Clinical Epidemiology & Biostatistics, McMaster University

ABSTRACT: *Health care research includes many studies that combine quantitative and qualitative methods. In this paper, we revisit the quantitative-qualitative debate and review the arguments for and against using mixed-methods.*

SOURCE: Sale, J. E., Lohfeld, L. H., & Brazil, K. (2002). Revisiting the quantitative-qualitative debate: Implications for mixed-methods research. *Quality & Quantity, 36*, 43–53. Reprinted with permission of Springer.

Corresponding author: Joanna E. M. Sale, Institute for Work & Health, 481 University Ave., Suite 800, Toronto, ON, Canada M5G 2E9. E-mail: jsale@interlog.com

In addition, we discuss the implications stemming from our view, that the paradigms upon which the methods are based have a different view of reality and therefore a different view of the phenomenon under study. Because the two paradigms do not study the same phenomena, quantitative and qualitative methods cannot be combined for cross-validation or triangulation purposes. However, they can be combined for complementary purposes. Future standards for mixed-methods research should clearly reflect this recommendation.

Keywords: mixed-methodology, quantitative-qualitative debate, qualitative methods, quantitative methods, scientific paradigms

1. Introduction

Health care research includes many studies that combine quantitative and qualitative methods, as seen in numerous articles and books published in the last decade (Caracelli and Greene, 1993; Caracelli and Riggin, 1994; Casebeer and Verhoef, 1997; Datta, 1997; Droitcour, 1997; Greene and Caracelli, 1997; House, 1994; Morgan, 1998; Morse, 1991; Tashakkori and Teddlie, 1998). As many critics have noted, this is not without its problems. In this paper, we revisit the quantitative-qualitative debate which flourished in the 1970s and 1980s and review the arguments for and against using mixed-methods. In addition, we present what we believe to be a fundamental point in this debate.

Some people would say that we are beyond the debate and can now freely use mixed-method designs to carry out relevant and valuable research. According to Carey (1993), quantitative and qualitative techniques are merely tools; integrating them allows us to answer questions of substantial importance. However, just because they are often combined does not mean that it is always appropriate to do so.

We believe that mixed-methods research is now being adopted uncritically by a new generation of researchers who have overlooked the underlying assumptions behind the qualitative-quantitative debate. In short, the philosophical distinctions between them have become so blurred that researchers are left with the impression that the differences between the two are merely technical (Smith and Heshius, 1986).

Objective

Combining qualitative and quantitative methods in a single study is widely practiced and accepted in many areas of health care research. Despite the arguments presented for integrating methods, we will demonstrate that each of these methods is based on a particular paradigm, a patterned set of assumptions concerning reality (ontology), knowledge of that reality (epistemology), and the particular ways of knowing that reality (methodology) (Guba, 1990). In fact, based on their paradigmatic assumptions, the two methods do not study the same phenomena. Evidence of this is reflected by the notion that quantitative methods cannot access some of the phenomena that health researchers are interested in, such as lived experiences as a patient, social interactions, and the patients' perspective of doctor-patient interactions. The information presented in this paper is not new in the sense that we are making a "new" case for or against the debate. Rather, based on the paradigmatic differences concerning the phenomenon under study, we propose a "new" solution for using mixed-methods in research that we believe is both methodologically and philosophically sound.

2. The Two Paradigms

The quantitative paradigm is based on positivism. Science is characterized by empirical research; all phenomena can be reduced to empirical indicators which represent the truth. The ontological position of the quantitative paradigm is that there is only one truth, an objective reality that exists independent of human perception. Epistemologically, the investigator and investigated are independent entities. Therefore, the investigator is capable of studying a phenomenon without influencing it or being influenced by it; "inquiry takes place as through a one way mirror" (Guba and Lincoln, 1994: 110). The goal is to measure and analyze causal relationships between variables within a value-free framework (Denzin and Lincoln, 1994). Techniques to ensure this include randomization, blinding, highly structured protocols, and written or orally administered questionnaires with a limited range of predetermined responses. Sample sizes are much larger than those used in qualitative research so that statistical methods to ensure that samples are representative can be used (Carey, 1993).

In contrast, the qualitative paradigm is based on interpretivism (Altheide and Johnson, 1994; Kuzel and Like, 1991; Secker et al., 1995) and constructivism (Guba and Lincoln, 1994). Ontologically speaking, there are multiple realities or multiple truths based on one's construction of reality. Reality is socially constructed (Berger and Luckmann, 1966) and so is constantly changing. On an epistemological level, there is no access to reality independent of our minds, no external referent by which to compare claims of truth (Smith, 1983). The investigator and the object of study are interactively linked so that findings are mutually created within the context of the situation which shapes the inquiry (Guba and Lincoln, 1994; Denzin and Lincoln, 1994). This suggests that reality has no existence prior to the activity of investigation, and reality ceases to exist when we no longer focus on it (Smith, 1983). The emphasis of qualitative research is on process and meanings.

Techniques used in qualitative studies include in-depth and focus group interviews and participant observation. Samples are not meant to represent large populations. Rather, small, purposeful samples of articulate respondents are used because they can provide important information, not because they are representative of a larger group (Reid, 1996).

The underlying assumptions of the quantitative and qualitative paradigms result in differences which extend beyond philosophical and methodological debates. The two paradigms have given rise to different journals, different sources of funding, different expertise, and different methods. There are even differences in scientific language used to describe them. For example, the term "observational work" may refer to case control studies for a quantitative researcher, but to a qualitative researcher it would refer to ethnographic immersion in a culture. "Validity" to a quantitative researcher would mean that results correspond to how things really are out there in the world, whereas to a qualitative researcher "valid" is a label applied to an interpretation or description with which one agrees (Smith and Heshusius, 1986). Similarly, the phrase "research has shown . . ." or "the results of research indicate . . ." refers to an accurate reflection of reality to the quantitative researcher, but to a qualitative researcher it announces an interpretation that itself becomes reality (Smith and Heshusius, 1986).

The different assumptions of the quantitative and qualitative paradigms originated in the positivism-idealism debate of the late 19th century (Smith, 1983). The inherent differences rarely are discussed or acknowledged by those using mixed-method designs. The reasons why may be because the positivist paradigm has become the predominant frame of reference in the physical and social sciences. In addition, research methods are presented as not belonging to or reflecting paradigms. Caracelli and Greene (1993) refer to mixed-method designs as those where neither type of method is inherently linked to a particular inquiry paradigm or philosophy. Guba and Lincoln (1989) claim that questions of method are secondary to questions of paradigms. We argue that methods are shaped by and represent paradigms that reflect a particular belief about reality. We also maintain that the assumptions of the qualitative paradigm are based on a worldview *not* represented by the quantitative paradigm.

3. Arguments Presented for Mixed-Method Research

Having discussed some of the basic philosophical assumptions of the two paradigms, we are better able to address the arguments given for combining quantitative and qualitative methods in a single study. There are several viewpoints as to why qualitative and quantitative methods can be combined.

First, the two approaches can be combined because they share the goal of understanding the world in which we live (Haase and Myers, 1988). King et al. (1994) claim that both qualitative and quantitative research share a unified logic, and that the same rules of inference apply to both.

Second, the two paradigms are thought to be compatible because they share the tenets of theory-ladenness of facts, fallibility of knowledge, indetermination of theory by fact, and a value-ladened inquiry process. They are also united by a shared commitment to understanding and improving the human condition, a common goal of disseminating knowledge for practical use, and a shared commitment for rigor, conscientiousness, and critique in the research process (Reichardt and Rallis, 1994). In fact, Casebeer and Verhoef (1997) argue we should view qualitative and quantitative methods as part of a continuum of research with specific techniques selected based on the research objective.

Third, as noted by Clarke and Yaros (1988), combining research methods is useful in some areas of research, such as nursing, because the complexity of phenomena requires data from a large number of perspectives. Similarly, some researchers have argued that the complexities of most public health problems (Baum, 1995) or social interventions, such as health education and health promotion programs (Steckler et al., 1992), require the use of a broad spectrum of qualitative and quantitative methods.

Fourth, others claim that researchers should not be preoccupied with the quantitative-qualitative debate because it will not be resolved in the near future, and that epistemological purity does not get research done (Miles and Huberman, 1984).

None of these arguments adequately addresses the underlying assumptions behind the paradigmatic differences between qualitative and quantitative research. However, Reichardt and Rallis (1994) acknowledge the possibility of contention between the two paradigms concerning the nature of reality by conceding that the two paradigms are incompatible if the qualitative paradigm assumes that there are no external referents for understanding reality. We have argued that the qualitative paradigm does assume that there are no external referents for understanding reality. Therefore, we propose that in addressing this fundamental assumption, Reichardt and Rallis dismiss their own claim of compatibility between methodological camps.

An interesting argument has been made by Howe (1988) who suggests that researchers should forge ahead with what works. Truth, he states, is a normative concept, like good. Truth is what works. This appears to be the prevalent attitude in mixed-methods research. Howe's argument seems to suggest that only pragmatists, or those not wedded to either paradigm, would attempt to combine research methods across paradigms. But this does not address the issue of differing ontological assumptions of the two paradigms.

A more interesting and complicated issue is the explanation of results from studies using qualitative and quantitative methods which appear to agree. How can the results be similar if the two paradigms are supposedly looking at different phenomena? Achieving similar results may be merely a matter of perception. In order to synthesize results obtained via multiple methods research, people often simplify the situation under study, highlighting and packaging results to reflect what they think is happening. The truth is we rarely know the extent of disagreement between qualitative and quantitative results because that is often not reported. Another possibility which may account for seemingly concordant results could be that both are, in fact, quantitative. Conducting a frequency count on responses to open-ended questions is not qualitative research. Given the overwhelming predominance of the positivist worldview in health care research, this is not surprising. This often translates to the misapplication of the canons of good "science" (quantitative research) to qualitative studies (see Sandelowski, 1986).

Perhaps the only convincing argument for mixing qualitative and quantitative research methods in a single study would be to challenge the underlying assumptions of the two paradigms themselves. A sound argument would be that both qualitative and quantitative paradigms are based on the tenets of positivism, not constructivism or interpretivism. Howe (1992) gives the impression of making this argument by denying there is an "either-or" choice to be made. Rather, he claims, both quantitative and qualitative researchers should embrace positivism coloured by a certain degree of interpretivism, an adjustment which he proposes is made possible by the critical social research model (or the critical educational research model) which eschews the positivist-interpretivist split in favour of compatibility.

A legitimate argument would have been for Howe and others who appear to be leaning toward this position (e.g. Reichardt and Rallis, 1994) to claim that the paradigmatic debate was oversimplified by a positivism-interpretivism split, and that the qualitative paradigm actually espoused positivism. If we take the position that qualitative researchers operate within a positivist world, we could argue that such a position actually negates or undermines the quantitative-qualitative debate in the first place because it does away with the beliefs about reality from which qualitative research arose. We believe, however, that one cannot be both a positivist and an interpretivist or constructivist.

Closely tied to the arguments for integrating qualitative and quantitative approaches are the reasons given for legitimately combining them. Two reasons for this are prevalent in the literature. The first is to achieve cross-validation or triangulation—combining two or more theories or sources of data to study the same phenomenon in order to gain a more complete understanding of it (Denzin, 1970). The second is to achieve complementary results by using the strengths of one method to enhance the other (Morgan, 1998). The former position maintains that research methods are interdependent (combinant); the latter, that they are independent (additive). Although these two reasons are often used interchangeably in the literature, it is important to make a distinction between them.

4. The Phenomenon of Study

It is probably safe to say that certain phenomena lend themselves to quantitative as opposed to qualitative inquiry and vice versa in other instances. Both quantitative and qualitative researchers often appear to study the same phenomena. However, these researchers' definition of what the phenomena are and how they can best be described or known differ. Both paradigms may label phenomena identically, but in keeping with their paradigmatic assumptions, these labels refer to different things.

For the quantitative researcher, a label refers to an external referent; to a qualitative researcher, a label refers to a personal interpretation or meaning attached to phenomena. For example, a quantitative researcher might use a factory record as if it were representative of what actually happens in the workplace, whereas a qualitative researcher might interpret it as one of the ways that people in a factory view their work environment (Needleman and Needleman, 1996). Because there is no external referent with which to gauge what the truth is, there is no interest in assessing the record as representative of the one and only reality in the workplace. Rather, the ways people use and describe it are expected to vary due to people's differing realities based on such characteristics as gender, age, or role (e.g., employer, manager, worker). Another example is surgical waiting lists. To a quantitative researcher, the list is like a bus queue; patients are taken off the list based on the urgency of need for surgery or some other factors. To a qualitative researcher, the key to understanding the meaning of the list rests with determining how it is organized, managed and used by the people who actively create and maintain it (Pope and Mays, 1993).

These two examples demonstrate that although qualitative and quantitative paradigms may use common labels to refer to phenomena, what the labels refer to is not the same. There are differences of phenomena *within* each paradigm as well. However, the differences in phenomena between the two paradigms are philosophical differences, whereas the difference in phenomena within each paradigm are not. Within the quantitative paradigm, we may compare the results of a magnetic resonance imaging (MRI) scan to those of a computed tomography (CT) scan. Although they may appear to reveal different realities, the use of the scans assumes that there is something to measure that exists independent of our minds. Both scans are trying to approximate or capture the one reality which correlates with the phenomenon of interest. Within the qualitative paradigm, one may compare the results of a phenomenological study to those of a grounded theory study on how nurses cope with the deaths of their patients. These two types of qualitative studies do not assume that external referents for coping skills exist independent of our minds.

Having taken the position that the quantitative and qualitative paradigms do not study the same phenomena, it follows that combining the two methods for cross-validation/triangulation purposes is not a viable option. (Cross validation refers to combining the two approaches to study the same phenomenon.) Ironically, in a comprehensive review of mixed-method evaluation studies, Greene and Caracelli (1989) found that methodological triangulation was actually quite rare in mixed-method research, used by only 3 of 57 studies. Combining the two approaches in a complementary fashion is also not advisable if the ultimate goal is to study different aspects of the same phenomenon because, as we argue, mixed-methods research cannot claim to enrich the same phenomenon under study. The phenomenon under study is not the same across methods. Not only does cross-validation and complementarity in the above context violate paradigmatic assumptions, but it also misrepresents data. Loss of information is a particular risk when attempts are made to unite results from the two paradigms because it often promotes the selective search for similarities in data.

5. Further Considerations in Mixed-Method Research Designs

The most frequently used mixed-method designs start with a qualitative pilot study followed by quantitative research (Morgan, 1998). This promotes the misperception that qualitative research is only exploratory, cannot stand on its own, and must be validated by quantitative work because the latter is "scientific" and studies truth. In response, qualitative researchers have increasingly tried to defend their work using quantitative criteria, such as validity and reliability, as defined in quantitative studies. They also increasingly use computer programs specifically designed for analysing qualitative data, such as NUD.IST or Ethnograph, in quantitative (counting) ways. These practices seriously violate the assumptions of the qualitative paradigm(s). For research to be valid or reliable in the narrow (quantitative) sense requires that what is studied be independent of the inquirer and be described without distortion by her interests, values, or purposes (Smith and Heshusius, 1986). This is not how qualitative studies unfold. They are based on the minimum distance between the investigator and the investigated, and seek multiple definitions of reality embedded in various respondents' experiences. Therefore, it is more appropriate for qualitative researchers to apply parallel but distinct canons of rigor appropriate to qualitative studies (Strauss and Corbin, 1990).

It is difficult to say whether the growing trend of quantifying qualitative research is a direct result of mixing quantitative and qualitative approaches. It does seem to be a result of researchers from the two paradigms attempting to work together, or the desire for qualitative research to be "taken seriously" in the world of positivist research, such as is commonly found in medicine. In our opinion, mixing research methods across paradigms, as is currently practiced, often diminishes the value of both methods. Pressure is being exerted from the quantitative camp for qualitative research to "measure up" to its standards without understanding the basic premises of qualitative investigations. Proponents of the qualitative paradigm need to address this pressure, but "without slipping on the mantle of quantitative inquiry" (Smith and Heshusius, 1986: 10). This pressure will no doubt continue to escalate as combined methods research becomes more common.

6. Our Solution

The key issues in the quantitative-qualitative debate are ontological and epistemological. Quantitative researchers perceive truth as something which describes an objective reality, separate from the observer and waiting to be discovered. Qualitative researchers are concerned with the changing nature of reality created through people's experiences—an evolving reality in which the researcher and researched are mutually interactive and inseparable (Phillips, 1988b). Because quantitative and qualitative methods represent two different paradigms, they are incommensurate. As Guba states, "the one [paradigm] precludes the other just as surely belief in a round world precludes belief in a flat one" (1987: 31). Fundamental to this viewpoint is that qualitative and quantitative researchers do *not*, in fact, study the same phenomena.

We propose a solution to mixed-methods research and the quantitative-qualitative debate. Qualitative and quantitative research methods have grown out of, and still represent, different paradigms. However, the fact that the approaches are incommensurate does not mean that multiple methods cannot be combined in a single study if it is done for complementary purposes. Each method studies different phenomena. The distinction of phenomena in mixed-methods research is crucial and can be clarified by labelling the phenomenon examined by each method. For example, a mixed-methods study to develop a measure of burnout experienced by nurses could be described as a qualitative study of the lived experience of burnout to inform a quantitative measure of burnout. Although the phenomenon 'burnout' may appear the same across methods, the distinction between "lived experience" and "measure" reconciles the phenomenon to its respective method and paradigm.

This solution differs from that of merely using the strengths of each method to bolster the weaknesses of the other(s), or capturing various aspects of the same phenomena. This implies an additive outcome for mutual research partners. Based on this assertion, qualitative and quantitative work can be carried out simultaneously or sequentially in a single study or series of investigations.

7. Implications

Given that we have returned to debate in a no-debate world, what is the outlook for mixed-paradigm research? As Phillips (1988a) points out, it may be that quantitative and qualitative approaches are inadequate to the task of understanding the emerging science of wholeness because they give an incomplete view of people in their environments. Perhaps in a "Kuhnian" sense, a new paradigm is in order, one with a new ontology, epistemology, and methodology. Alternatively, we have proposed seeking complementarity which we believe is both philosophically and practically sound. This solution lends itself to new standards for mixed-paradigm research. We hope that future guidelines which assess the quality of such research consider this recommendation.

References

Altheide, D. L., & Johnson, J. M. (1994). Criteria for assessing interpretive validity in qualitative research. In: N. K. Denzin, & Y. S. Lincoln (eds.), *Handbook of Qualitative Research*. Thousand Oaks, CA: Sage Publications, pp. 485–499.

Baum, F. (1995). Researching public health: Behind the qualitative-quantitative methodological debate. *Social Science and Medicine* 40: 459–468.

Berger, P. L., & Luckmann, T. (1966). *The Social Construction of Reality: A Treatise in the Sociology of Knowledge*. Garden City, NY: Doubleday.

Caracelli, V. J., & Greene, J. C. (1993). Data analysis strategies for mixed-method evaluation designs. *Educational Evaluation and Policy Analysis* 15: 195–207.

Caracelli, V. J., & Riggin, L. J. C. (1994). Mixed-method evaluation: Developing quality criteria through concept mapping. *Evaluation Practice* 15: 139–152.

Carey, J. W. (1993). Linking qualitative and quantitative methods: Integrating cultural factors into public health. *Qualitative Health Research* 3: 298–318.

Casebeer, A. L., & Verhoef, M. J. (1997). Combining qualitative and quantitative research methods: Considering the possibilities for enhancing the study of chronic diseases. *Chronic Diseases in Canada* 18: 130–135.

Clarke, P. N., & Yaros, P. S. (1988). Research blenders: Commentary and response. *Nursing Science Quarterly* 1: 147–149.

Creswell, J. W. (1998). *Qualitative Inquiry and Research Design: Choosing Among Five Traditions.* Thousand Oaks, CA: Sage Publications.

Datta, L. (1997). Multimethod evaluations: Using case studies together with other methods. In: E. Chelimsky & W. R. Shadish (eds.), *Evaluation for the 21st Century: A Handbook.* Thousand Oaks, CA: Sage Publications, pp. 344–359.

Denzin, N. K. (1970). *The Research Act in Sociology.* London: Butterworth.

Denzin, N. K., & Lincoln, Y. S. (1994). Introduction: Entering the field of qualitative research. In: N. K. Denzin & Y. S. Lincoln (eds.), *Handbook of Qualitative Research.* Thousand Oaks, CA: Sage, pp. 1–17.

Droitcour, J. A. (1997). Cross design synthesis: Concept and application. In: E. Chelimsky, & Shadish, W. R. (eds.), *Evaluation for the 21st Century: A Handbook.* Thousand Oaks, CA: Sage Publications, pp. 360–372.

Greene, J. C., & Caracelli, V. J. (eds.) (1997). *Advances in Mixed-Method Evaluation: The Challenges and Benefits of Integrating Diverse Paradigms.* San Francisco: Jossey-Bass Publishers.

Greene, J. C., Caracelli, V. J. & Graham, W. F. (1989). Toward a conceptual framework for mixed-method evaluation designs. *Educational Evaluation and Policy Analysis* 11: 255–274.

Guba, E. (1987). What have we learned about naturalistic evaluation? *Evaluation Practice* 8: 23–43.

Guba, E. G. (1990). The alternative paradigm dialog. In: E. G. Guba (ed.), *The Paradigm Dialog.* Newbury Park, CA: Sage, pp. 17–30.

Guba, E. G., & Lincoln, Y. S. (1989). *Fourth Generation Evaluation.* Newbury Park, CA: Sage Publications.

Guba, E. G., & Lincoln, Y. S. (1994). Competing paradigms in qualitative research. In: N. K. Denzin & Y. S. Lincoln (eds.), *Handbook of Qualitative Research.* Thousand Oaks, CA: Sage, pp. 105–117.

Haase, J. E., & Myers, S. T. (1988). Reconciling paradigm assumptions of qualitative and quantitative research. *Western Journal of Nursing Research* 10: 128–137.

House, E. R. (1994). Integrating the quantitative and qualitative. In: C. S. Reichardt & S. F. Rallis (eds.), *The Qualitative-Quantitative Debate: New Perspectives.* San Francisco: Jossey-Bass, pp. 13–22.

Howe, K. R. (1988). Against the quantitative-qualitative incompatibility thesis or dogmas die hard. *Educational Researcher* 17: 10–16.

Howe, K. R. (1992). Getting over the quantitative-qualitative debate. *American Journal of Education* 100: 236–257.

King, G., Keohane, R. O., & Verba, S. (1994). *Designing Social Inquiry: Scientific Inference in Qualitative Research.* Princeton: Princeton University Press.

Kuzel, A. J., & Like, R. C. (1991). Standards of trustworthiness for qualitative studies in primary care. In: P. G. Norton, M. Steward, F. Tudiver, M. J. Bass, & E. V. Dunn (eds.), *Primary Care Research*. Newbury Park, CA: Sage Publications, pp. 138–158.

Miles, M., & Huberman, A. (1984). Drawing valid meaning from qualitative data: Toward a shared craft. *Educational Researcher* 13: 20–30.

Morgan, D. L. (1998). Practical strategies for combining qualitative and quantitative methods: Applications to health research. *Qualitative Health Research* 8: 362–376.

Morse, J. M. (1991). Approaches to qualitative-quantitative methodological triangulation. *Nursing Research* 40: 120–123.

Needleman, C., & Needleman, M. L. (1996). Qualitative methods for intervention research. *American Journal of Industrial Medicine* 29: 329–337.

Phillips, J. R. (1988a). Diggers of deeper holes. *Nursing Science Quarterly* 1: 149–151.

Phillips, J. R. (1988b). Research blenders. *Nursing Science Quarterly* 1: 4–5.

Pope, C., & Mays, N. (1993). Opening the black box: An encounter in the corridors of health sciences research. *British Medical Journal* 306: 315–318.

Reichardt, C. S., & Rallis, S.F. (1994). Qualitative and quantitative inquiries are not incompatible: A call for a new partnership. *New Directions for Program Evaluation* 61: 85–91.

Reid, A. J. (1996). What we want: Qualitative research. *Canadian Family Physician* 42: 387–389.

Sandelowski, M. (1986). The problem of rigour in qualitative research. *Advances in Nursing Science* 8: 27–37.

Secker, J., Wimbush, E., Watson, J., & Milburn, K. (1995). Qualitative methods in health promotion research: Some criteria for quality. *Health Education Journal* 54: 74–87.

Smith, J. K. (1983). Quantitative versus qualitative research: An attempt to clarify the issue. *Educational Researcher* 12: 6–13.

Smith, J. K., & Heshusius, L. (1986). Closing down the conversation: The end of the quantitative-qualitative debate among educational inquiries. *Educational Researcher* 15: 4–12.

Steckler, A., McLeroy, K. R., Goodman, R. M., Bird, S. T., & McCormick, L. (1992). Toward integrating qualitative and quantitative methods: An introduction. *Health Education Quarterly* 19: 1–8.

Strauss, A., & Corbin, J. (1990). Chapter 1: Introduction. *Basics of Qualitative Research: Grounded Theory Procedures and Techniques*. Newbury Park, CA: Sage Publications, pp. 23–32.

Tashakkori, A., & Teddlie, C. (1998). *Mixed Methodology: Combining Qualitative and Quantitative Approaches*. Thousand Oaks, CA: Sage Publications.

PART II

Exemplar Research Studies

R esearchers and methodologists interested in mixed methods research need to consider how mixed methods approaches are conducted and reported in practice in addition to understanding important methodological issues associated with this research approach. Therefore, scholars can benefit by examining mixed methods research studies as complements to methodological discussions. Part II includes a collection of original research articles drawn from the social and health sciences in which authors use mixed methods to study topics in their fields. That is, in the studies that follow, the researchers use both quantitative and qualitative approaches and integrate these approaches to address their studies' purposes and questions.

Why should mixed methods researchers read exemplar studies? Researchers can examine how methodological concepts are applied in practice. Published studies illustrate the different types of mixed methods designs as well as the decisions and procedures that accompany these designs. They also provide models for how mixed methods studies can be successfully written for publication. In addition, they can be used to inform others (advisors, committee members, reviewers) about how mixed methods studies are conducted and reported. Graduate students proposing mixed methods projects can educate committee members about this approach by sharing a published example that used a similar design. Researchers developing proposals for funding might reference published studies using the proposed approach to inform reviewers who may not be familiar with mixed methods designs.

We have selected nine mixed methods research studies to serve as examples and applications of the concepts discussed in Part I. These studies are only a few of the countless published mixed methods studies available across the social and health sciences. In making our selections we looked for studies that reflect the different types of mixed methods designs and integration strategies used by researchers. In addition, we wanted the studies to address a variety of topics and be spread across different disciplines, and thus we include examples representing education, family science, psychology, sociology, program evaluation, and the health sciences.

We have organized the exemplar research studies by mixed methods design type. As introduced in Part I, there are numerous typologies for classifying mixed methods designs, such as those by Greene, Caracelli, and Graham (Chapter 5), Morse (Chapter 6), and Creswell, Plano Clark, Gutmann, and Hanson (Chapter 7). Creswell and Plano Clark (2007) reviewed 12 different mixed methods design typologies found in the literature and concluded that there are four major types of mixed methods designs being used by researchers: concurrent/triangulation, embedded, sequential explanatory, and sequential exploratory. These designs are suited to address different research objectives (Plano Clark, Creswell, Green, & Shope, in press) and are differentiated by the timing of the quantitative and qualitative methods (concurrent or sequential) and how the quantitative and qualitative methods are mixed or integrated (merged together, embedded one within the other, or connected from one to the other). The designs also can differ in terms of the relative priority of the methods (equal, quantitative, or qualitative) for addressing the study's objectives.

The *concurrent/triangulation design* involves collecting and analyzing quantitative and qualitative data concurrently, merging the two sets of data, and using the combination to best understand a research problem. We include two concurrent/triangulation examples that illustrate different ways to merge data sets. In Chapter 15, Luzzo (1995) merges his results in a discussion to better understand gender differences in college students' career development. Idler, Hudson, and Leventhal (1999) merge their two data sets during data analysis using data transformation in their study of African American elders' self-ratings of health in Chapter 16.

The *embedded design* consists of embedding one method (qualitative or quantitative) within a larger study guided by the other method (quantitative or qualitative), having the secondary method address a different question, and using the secondary method to enhance the implementation and/or interpretation of the primary method. Examples of this design in the literature most often embed a qualitative component within a quantitative experimental study. As an example, Donovan et al. (2002) embed a qualitative study before their intervention to improve their recruitment procedures for a randomized control trial of prostate cancer treatments in Chapter 17. Victor, Ross, and Axford (2004) embed a qualitative component during their intervention study of the use of group sessions for patients with osteoarthritis of the knee in Chapter 18. In Chapter 19, Messer, Steckler, and Dignan (1999) conduct a qualitative study as a follow-up after their experimental evaluation of a program to promote cervical cancer screening.

The *sequential explanatory design* involves implementing the methods in two distinct phases, starting with quantitative data collection and analysis, connecting from the quantitative results to a qualitative phase, and using the qualitative data collection and results to follow up or explain the initial quantitative results. In Chapter 20, Way, Stauber, Nakkula, and London (1994) implement a qualitative phase as a follow-up to explain an unexpected quantitative result in their study of adolescent depression and substance use. Thøgersen-Ntoumani and Fox (2005) identify four types of individuals based on quantitative data about physical activity and mental well-being and then explore these types by selecting individuals representing each group for qualitative study in Chapter 21.

Finally, the *sequential exploratory design* also consists of two phases, but begins with the collection and analysis of qualitative data, builds from the qualitative results to a quantitative phase, and is used when a topic needs to be explored qualitatively before it can be measured or tested quantitatively. In Chapter 22, Milton, Watkins, Studdard, and Burch (2003) need qualitative results to guide the development of an instrument to study the factors that predict changes in the size of adult education programs. Richter (1997) generates a model from her qualitative study of Thai women's child care decision making and then quantitatively tests the model with a representative sample in Chapter 23.

We provide a brief introduction to each research study. These introductions highlight our assessments of the studies' topics, mixed methods approaches, and significant features. In addition, using Morse's (1991) notation (presented in Chapter 6 of this volume) and Ivankova, Creswell, and Stick's (2006) guidelines for drawing visual diagrams for mixed methods designs, we developed a visual diagram for each study that attempts to convey its overall design, procedures, and products. The authors of the articles *did not* provide diagrams of their procedures in their published articles. Thus, we hope that these visual diagrams will help readers see the big picture of the studies' designs. Additionally, readers should note the different styles of the diagrams (such as using vertical and horizontal layouts) as possible options for depicting their own studies.

Like all research, each of these studies has its own strengths and weaknesses. Therefore, these selections are not meant to be viewed as perfect templates of mixed methods research, but as sound applications of how researchers use mixed methods approaches to address real research problems and questions. Readers should consider what they can learn from each study as well as their ideas for how it could have been made stronger, particularly in light of the issues addressed in Part I. The following list of discussion questions should encourage readers to apply the methodological selections and to critically examine how mixed methods research was applied and reported within these research studies.

Discussion Questions for Exemplar Research Studies

1. What philosophical perspective appears to provide the foundation for the study? How might the study have been different if a different perspective had been used? (See Chapters 1–3.)

2. How were the mixed methods design characteristics of timing (simultaneous or sequential), priority (equal, quantitative, or qualitative), and integration (how the quantitative and qualitative methods were mixed) implemented? (See Chapters 4–7.)

3. Classify the study's mixed methods design. Which typology did you use and why? (See Chapters 4–7.)

4. What mixed methods sampling strategies did the authors report? (See Chapter 8.)

5. How did the authors collect and analyze their quantitative and qualitative data? Did they use a mixed methods data analysis strategy? (See Chapter 9.)

6. What was the authors' reason(s) for integrating quantitative and qualitative research? Was it implied or stated explicitly? (See Chapter 10.)

7. How did the researchers validate their findings? (See Chapter 11.)

8. Describe the overall writing structure used and the specific rhetorical devices that linked the quantitative and qualitative aspects of the study. (See Chapter 12.)

9. How does this study respond to critiques about mixed methods research? Did it place qualitative research in a primary or secondary role? Were the quantitative and qualitative methods used to examine the same phenomenon or different phenomena? (See Chapters 13–14.)

15

A Concurrent/Triangulation Mixed Methods Design With Merged Results

Selection: Luzzo, D. A. (1995). Gender differences in college students' career maturity and perceived barriers in career development. *Journal of Counseling & Development, 73*, 319–322.

Editors' Introduction

Luzzo examined gender differences in college students' career development and maturity in his 1995 study. The purpose of this investigation was to quantitatively measure and qualitatively describe the differences. As illustrated in Figure 15.0, he collected and analyzed quantitative data using well-established measures and, during the same time frame, he conducted and analyzed interviews about participants' career development with a subset of the quantitative sample. The two datasets were analyzed and reported independently and then the results were merged into a larger understanding in the final discussion (depicted at the bottom of Figure 15.0). This study is an example of a concurrent/triangulation design in which the researcher implemented the quantitative and qualitative methods simultaneously, appeared to give them equal priority, and merged them during the interpretation. Noteworthy features of this study include using the same individuals in the two samples to make the two sets of results more readily comparable, counterbalancing the order participants completed the quantitative and qualitative data collection as a means to reduce the influence of one method on the other, and reporting the study in a concise manner.

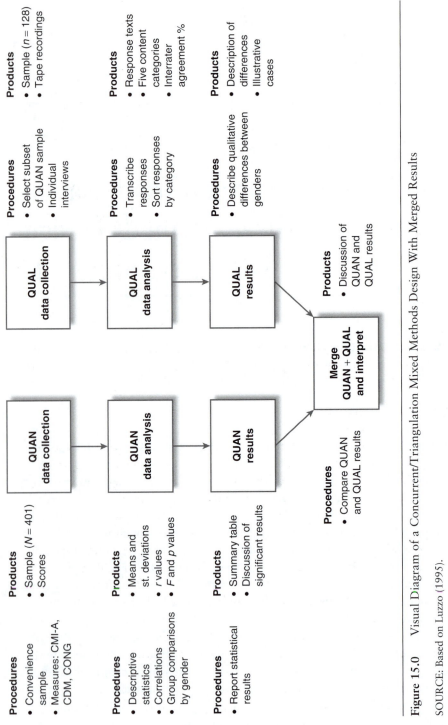

Figure 15.0 Visual Diagram of a Concurrent/Triangulation Mixed Methods Design With Merged Results

SOURCE: Based on Luzzo (1995).

NOTE: CMI-A indicates Career Maturity Inventory-Attitude Scale; CDM, Career Decision Making Skills; CONG, Vocational Congruence.

Gender Differences in College Students' Career Maturity and Perceived Barriers in Career Development

Darrell Anthony Luzzo
Johnson County Community College

Gender differences in 401 college students' career maturity were investigated. Quantitative measures included career-mature attitudes, career decision-making skills, and vocational congruence. Analyses revealed that female students scored significantly higher than did male students on each of the career maturity measures (p <.005). Nearly one third of the students (n = 128) were also interviewed. Qualitative analyses of the interviews revealed that the perception of barriers may serve as a motivating force in many students' career development. Findings suggest that current theories of career development may be lacking in their application to many of today's college students. Ideas for future research on the perception of barriers to career attainment are discussed.

Little doubt exists that gender is an important moderating variable in college students' career development. Early investigations searching for simple gender differences in career development were extremely limited (see Hackett,

SOURCE: This article is reprinted from Luzzo, D. A., Gender differences in college students' career maturity and perceived barriers in career development, in *Journal of Counseling & Development*, 73, 319–322. © 1995, The American Counseling Association. Reprinted with permission. No further reproduction authorized without written permission from the American Counseling Association.

Lent, & Greenhaus, 1991). Furthermore, as many career developmentalists agree (e.g., Diamond, 1987; Osipow, 1983), current vocational theories do not adequately explain the developmental process and occupational choice systems for women. Diamond (1987) recently summarized this theoretical dilemma:

> Traditional career development theory was based almost exclusively on studies of male subjects and gave little attention to the fact that for women the developmental process over the life span was different from that of men and far more complex. . . . Although several promising attempts have been made to provide one, little exists today in the way of a fully developed theory of women's career development (p. 15).

An example of one particularly noteworthy attempt to provide a comprehensive theory of women's career development is Astin's (1984) sociopsychological model, which focuses on early socialization experiences and structural opportunity differences between women and men. Although Astin's perspective has been important in opening up new theoretical aspects for consideration, her model of women's career development, like others recently proposed (e.g., Betz & Fitzgerald, 1987; Gottfredson, 1981; Hackett & Betz, 1981; Harmon, 1978), has not gone uncriticized. Criticisms of these models include poorly defined constructs and an overemphasis on the role of personal factors on the circumscription of women's career choices (see Betz & Fitzgerald, 1987; Gilbert, 1984; Gutek & Larwood, 1987).

One of the more established gender differences in career development was discussed by Farmer (1985) in the presentation of her career and achievement motivation model. According to Farmer, women's career motivation is much more vulnerable to competing role priorities and environmental demands than men's career motivation. In other words, women are much more likely than men to experience the effects of increased role confusion and environmental stressors in the career development process. "Many women find themselves in a role expansion mode in which they not only work full time but also hold primary responsibility for child rearing and maintaining the home and family life while their husband's roles remain relatively unchanged" (Gilbert, Dancer, Rossman, & Thorn, 1991, pp. 107–108). Fitzgerald and Betz (1983) agreed that the most salient issue in the career development of women seems to be the role conflict and confusion experienced between the roles of mother and that of worker. As London and Greller (1991) recently summarized, work-family conflict is a salient issue given the increased numbers of women in the workforce.

Swanson and Tokar's (1991) recent investigation of college students' perceptions of barriers to career attainment opens up an important new domain in the attempt to develop a comprehensive theory of career development. Although they assessed a relatively small sample of students, Swanson and Tokar discovered that college students perceive a variety of career-related barriers. Using a free-response method in their investigation, Swanson and Tokar offered students "the opportunity to generate their own lists of perceived barriers across a range of career-related topics" (p. 102). These open-ended responses were then coded across several topic areas. Analyses revealed that all of the responses dealing with sacrificing career for children, child-care concerns, and role conflict were provided by women. Men were more likely to indicate financial issues as barriers to career goal attainment.

Swanson and Tokar (1991) raised several interesting questions regarding the role of career-related barriers in women's and men's career development: "The present results suggest that individuals do recognize attitudinal or self-concept factors as well as environmental constraints to their career aspirations; however . . . we know little about what compromises individuals face as a result of confronting barriers, and how they cope with such compromises" (p. 104). They called for future research to analyze how perception of barriers affect career-related behavior and other career development variables, such as decision-making skills.

The current investigation sought, first, to establish quantitative gender differences in college students' career maturity. Next, interviews were conducted with approximately one third of the participants to provide information about qualitative career development differences. Qualitative analyses allowed for an exploration of the role conflicts and perceived barrier differences between women and men and the impact of such differences in the career development process.

Method

Participants

The students included in the investigation of quantitative gender differences in career maturity consisted of 401 undergraduates (250 female, 151 male) attending a large state university in Southern California. About 75% of the participants were 20 years of age or younger, $M= 19.86$, $SD = 1.53$. The majority of the participants were White American (52%); the remainder were African American (7%), Hispanic (12%), Asian American (15%), and Filipino (10%). Nearly two thirds of the participants were freshmen and sophomores. A total of 128 of the participants (78 women, 50 men) in the quantitative portion of the study were also interviewed by the researcher for the qualitative portion. All students participated in the study as part of an introductory psychology course requirement.

Quantitative Measures

Career-mature attitudes were assessed by the 50-item Career Maturity Inventory-Attitude Scale (CMI-A; Crites, 1978). The CMI-A was selected on the basis of its widespread use as a measure of career development. According to Crites, the CMI-A elicits the feelings, subjective reactions, and dispositions that an individual has toward making a career choice and entering the world of work.

Crites (1978) reported internal consistency coefficients for each of the five subscales of the CMI-A ranging from .50 to .72. Dunn and Veltman (1989) reported test-retest reliability for the CMI-A of .71. Furthermore, numerous reviews (e.g., Westbrook, 1984) have established firm evidence of criterion-related validity for the CMI-A, noting expected relationships between the measure and such variables as realism of occupational aspirations, goal orientation, career decisiveness, and commitment to career choice. On the basis of their review of several studies using the CMI-A, Wallbrown, Silling, and Crites (1986) contended that the measure represents a relatively clear, stable, cohesive dimension of individual differences that conceptualizes the affective career maturity of students.

Career decision-making skills were assessed by the Decision-Making Scale of the Career Development Inventory's University and College Form (CDM; Super, Thompson, Lindeman, Jordaan, & Myers, 1981). The CDM measures an individual's competence in resolving 20 different simulated career problems. Scores on this scale moderately relate to several other measures of career decision-making ability and knowledge (Jepsen & Prediger, 1981). The manual reports alpha coefficients for college men and women ranging from .60 to .82. Clear evidence of the criterion validity of this measure has been supported by various studies (e.g., Jordaan & Heyde, 1979).

Vocational congruence was determined by comparing a student's inventoried measure of vocational interests (Vocational Preference Inventory [VPI]; Holland, 1978) with her or his stated career aspiration. As Holland stated in the VPI manual, the instrument has moderate to high reliability, with test-retest reliability ranging from .54 to .80, with a median of .71. Participants' career aspirations were coded using the *Dictionary of Holland Occupational Codes* (Gottfredson, Holland, & Ogawa, 1982). This method of measuring the work environment is commonly used in studies of vocational congruence (see Spokane, 1985).

The actual calculation of vocational congruence followed Iachan's (1984) recommended scoring procedure, a method for which Holland (1987) has provided considerable support. Iachan's calculation takes into account the increasing importance of agreement in positions corresponding to the highest ranks. Using the three-letter code for the person and the environment (provided by the VPI and the participants' stated career aspiration, respectively), there are 29 possible levels of congruence, ranging from 0–28. Higher scores indicate greater vocational congruence.

Qualitative Measures

Individual interviews were conducted with participants by the researcher. The interviews lasted approximately 15–20 minutes and were tape-recorded for coding and analysis. Interviews began with an opportunity for participants to summarize their own personal career development, a free-response method similar to the process used by Swanson and Tokar (1991). Following these opening remarks, the researcher asked participants to provide further information about any of the specific career-related issues mentioned in their original statements. The main purpose of these interactions with participants was to provide additional, open-ended information about some of the gender differences in college students' career maturity. This information lent itself well to an analysis of role conflicts and perceived barrier differences between women and men.

The results of the interviews were coded by both the researcher and a research assistant. Participants' responses were written on 4 × 6-inch cards, with participants' gender written on the back of each card. Next, each index card was sorted into one of five content categories: family-related barriers, study skill barriers, gender-related barriers, ethnic identity barriers, and financial barriers. These categories were selected on the basis of related investigations (see Nieva & Gutek, 1981; Swanson & Tokar, 1991) and the specific purposes of this study. The percentage of agreement between the two coders was over 90% for all categories. Disagreements were discussed by the two coders until a consensus decision was reached regarding their placement.

Procedure

Each student completed a 15-page packet of materials, which included a demographics questionnaire (gender, age, ethnicity, year in college, current grade point average, career aspiration, parents' occupations, and parents' levels of completed education) and the various measures. All students completed the packets within 50 minutes. The students included in the qualitative analysis were interviewed by the researcher within 2 weeks of completing the packet. The order in which these students completed the packet and participated in the interview was counterbalanced.

Results

Quantitative Analyses

The means and standard deviations for women and men on each of the quantitative measures of career maturity are shown in Table 15.1. Correlations between each of the career maturity measures were as follows: CMI-A and CDM, $r = .195$; CMI-A and congruence, $r = .305$; CDM and congruence, $r = .128$. A MANOVA using students' age, grade point average (GPA), and years in college as covariates revealed a significant effect for gender, multivariate $F(1, 338) = 9.556$, $p < .001$. Follow-up univariate ANOVAs revealed that female students ($M = 37.49$) scored significantly higher on the CMI-A than did male students ($M = 35.75$), $F(1, 338) = 7.989$, $p < .005$. Female students ($M = 13.36$) displayed significantly greater decision-making skills than did male students ($M = 12.40$), $F(1, 338) = 17.183$, $p < .001$. Finally, female students ($M = 20.52$) showed greater congruence than did male students ($M = 18.23$), $F(1, 338) = 11.552$, $p < .001$.

Qualitative Analysis

The clearest gender difference in students' discussions of career development was in their approach to career planning and decision making. When asked to recount their process of career development over the past few years, women routinely revealed a well-planned process in everything—the decision to go to college, the choice of a major, and the choice of a career aspiration. Male students,

Table 15.1   Means and Standard Deviations for Women and Men on Each of the Career Maturity Measures

Gender		CMI-A	CDM	CONG
Sample[a]	M	36.84	13.00	19.67
	SD	5.07	2.46	7.54
Women[b]	M	37.49	13.36	20.52
	SD	4.94	2.06	7.03
Men[c]	M	35.75	12.40	18.23
	SD	5.14	2.92	8.17

NOTE: CMI-A = Career Maturity Inventory-Attitude Scale. CDM = Career Decision Making Skills. CONG = Vocational Congruence. Possible scale ranges for each measure are as follows: CMI-A (0-50), CDM (0-20), and CONG (0-28).

[a]$N = 401$.

[b]$n = 250$.

[c]$n = 151$.

on the other hand, generally reported rather sporadic and unplanned career decisions. The dialogues of two 19-year-old sophomores illustrate the differences.

When asked to describe the last few years of her career development, the female participant explained the following:

> Well . . . around my junior year of high school I decided that I was going to go to college. My parents thought I was crazy. It's not that I was stupid or anything, but they just expected me to work and save up some money for later. They said that they'd believe it when they saw it. Well, here I am a few years later! All during my junior and senior years [of high school] I took a lot of R.O.P. classes to learn about different jobs, and I decided that the area of social work was the best. I knew that a major in social work would probably prepare me best for a graduate program, which is my ultimate goal. So, after my first semester here I entered the major. Connections got me a part-time job, and now I know more than ever that I want to get my M.S.W. and keep going in social work.

When asked to explain his career development, the male participant, typical of many of the male students with whom the researcher interacted, described the following:

> Well . . . it was always understood that I would go to college. It was just a matter of where and to major in what. I decided that I wanted to stick around here since I have a girlfriend who lives in Redondo Beach, and Long Beach State is a good college. I still really haven't decided what I want to do. I'm a business major. What really matters to me is that I get a degree that will get me a job after graduation, but I haven't really liked classes too much so far. I don't know. I'll get a bachelor's degree in something, probably do well in interviews and then I'll get a job.

Another common trend was revealed in students' responses to their perception of future career challenges. Both female and male students often indicated financial concerns. Beyond that similarity, however, the responses were dramatically different. Of the 78 females who participated in the interviews, 48 (over 60%) indicated that either deciding when to have children, juggling work and family responsibilities, or making sacrifices to have children were primary concerns. Of the 50 men who participated in the interview, only 3 (6%) reported similar concerns.

Discussion

As revealed by quantitative analyses, the female students who participated in this investigation scored significantly higher than the male students on all three of the inventoried measures of career maturity (career-mature attitudes, career decision-making skills, and vocational congruence). Even so, qualitative analyses revealed that women were much more likely than men to mention role conflicts and barriers that they perceive as stumbling blocks along the career development pathway.

Swanson and Tokar (1991) previously suggested that college students recognize various environmental constraints to their career aspirations. The results of this investigation provide further support for that notion. In addition, the results of this study begin to address the impact of perceiving barriers to career attainment and how college students react to such perceptions.

Commonly cited concerns of the women who were interviewed included finding adequate day care for their children, being able to find a college that provided adequate flexibility to work around their children's needs, and so forth. Only three of the men who were interviewed mentioned similar barriers. These results support the idea that today's middle- and late-adolescent women are much more likely to consider the integration of occupational and family roles in adulthood than are adolescent men. As Farmer (1985) theorized, women's career development is significantly affected by competing role priorities and environmental influences. This investigation supports Farmer's claim and raises new questions about the impact of role priorities and environmental barriers in the career development process.

As surfaced during the interviews (and consistent with the quantitative data), undergraduate women seem to be much more planned in the career decision making process than undergraduate men. One reason for the difference might be women's perception of the need to overcome the variety of other life-role obstacles they face. In the case of perceived barriers, some women seem to have found ways to use such obstacles to their benefit. In other words, the perception of barriers may serve as a motivating force for careful career planning and exploration. It may be that without the perception of such barriers many of the men lack a realization of the utility of planning. They do not seem to make the conscious effort to design intermediate and long-range career goals. The result of this lack of awareness may help explain the dilemma that many graduating men experience—the realization that they have no idea what comes next. It is then, much later than advised, that these students seek career counseling that could (and should) have been sought long before (Jordaan & Heyde, 1979).

Alternative explanations for the results of this investigation include the possibility that women participants in the study may not actually be more planful than men in making career decisions; instead, women may simply have increased skills in articulating and describing their plans. Although quantitative analyses indicated women's significantly greater skill at career decision making, the degree to which performance on the assessment instrument used in this investigation predicts actual career decisions is not entirely clear.

Another competing explanation for the findings of this study might be the claim that young men and women attending this particular institution of higher education are significantly different from those attending other institutions across the country. This question of generalizability of the findings is an important one. Despite the representation of various ethnic groups in the investigation, there is no question that additional research is necessary before these findings may be regarded as broadly applicable.

Despite these lingering questions, the results emphasize some important career development concepts. Whereas perceived barriers to career attainment might initially be viewed as problematic, the results of this investigation support the identification and clarification of such barriers. Counselors and clients are encouraged to develop strategies for using the perception of barriers as motivating forces in career maturity. Developing these strategies might be helpful in increasing clients' planfulness and exploration in the career decision-making process.

References

Astin, H. S. (1984). The meaning of work in women's lives: A sociopsychological model of career choice and work behavior. *The Counseling Psychologist, 12,* 117–126.

Betz, N., & Fitzgerald, L. (1987). *The career psychology of women.* Orlando, FL: Academic.

Crites, J. O. (1978). *The Career Maturity Inventory.* Monterey, CA: McGrawHill/CTB.

Diamond, E. E. (1987). Theories of career development and the reality of women at work. In B. A. Gutek & L. Larwood (Eds.), *Women's career development.* Newbury Park, CA: Sage.

Dunn, C. W., & Veltman, G. C. (1989). Addressing the restrictive career maturity patterns of minority youth: A program evaluation. *Journal of Multicultural Counseling and Development, 17,* 156–164.

Farmer, H. S. (1985). Model of career and achievement motivation for women and men. *Journal of Counseling Psychology, 32,* 363–390.

Fitzgerald, L. F., & Betz, N. E. (1983). Issues in vocational psychology of women. In W. B. Walsh & S. H. Osipow (Eds.), *Handbook of vocational psychology* (Vol. 1, pp. 83–144). Hillsdale, NJ: Erlbaum.

Gilbert, L. A. (1984). Comments on the meaning of work in women's lives. *The Counseling Psychologist, 12,* 129–130.

Gilbert, L. A., Dancer, L. S., Rossman, K. M., & Thorn, B. L. (1991). Assessing perceptions of occupational-family integration. *Sex Roles, 24,* 107–119.

Gottfredson, L. S. (1981). Circumscription and compromise: A developmental theory of occupational aspirations. *Journal of Counseling Psychology, 28,* 545–579.

Gottfredson, G. D., Holland, J. L., & Ogawa, D. K. (1982). *Dictionary of Holland occupational codes.* Palo Alto, CA: Consulting Psychologist's Press.

Gutek, B. A., & Larwood, L. (1987). Introduction: Women's careers are important and different. In B. A. Gutek & L. Larwood (Eds.), *Women's career development*. Newbury Park, CA: Sage.

Hackett, G., & Betz, N. E. (1981). A self-efficacy approach to the career development of women. *Journal of Vocational Behavior, 18*, 326–339.

Hackett, G., Lent, R. W., & Greenhaus, J. H. (1991). Advances in vocational theory and research: A 20-year retrospective. *Journal of Vocational Behavior, 38*, 3–38.

Harmon, L. (1978). Career counseling for women. In L. S. Hansen & R. S. Rapoza (Eds.), *Career development and counseling of women*. Springfield, IL: Thomas.

Holland, J. L. (1978). *The Vocational Preference Inventory*. Palo Alto, CA: Consulting Psychologist's Press.

Holland, J. L. (1987). Some speculation about the investigation of person-environment transactions. *Journal of Vocational Behavior, 31*, 337–340.

Iachan, R. (1984). A measure of agreement for use with the Holland classification systems. *Journal of Vocational Behavior, 24*, 133–141.

Jepsen, D. A., & Prediger, D. J. (1981). Dimensions of adolescent career development. A multi-instrument analysis. *Journal of Vocational Behavior, 19*, 350–368.

Jordaan, J. P., & Heyde, M. B. (1979). *Vocational maturity during the high school years*. New York: Teacher's College.

London, M., & Greller, M. M. (1991). Demographic trends and vocational behavior: A twenty year retrospective and agenda for the 1990s. *Journal of Vocational Behavior, 38*, 125–164.

Nieva, V. F., & Gutek, B. A. (1981). *Woman and work: A psychological perspective*. New York: Praeger.

Osipow, S. H. (1983). *Theories of career development* (3rd ed.). Englewood Cliffs, NJ: Prentice-Hall.

Spokane, A. R. (1985). A review of research on person-environment congruence in Holland's theory of careers. *Journal of Vocational Behavior, 26*, 306–343.

Super, D. E., Thompson, A. E., Lindeman, R. H., Jordaan, J. P., & Myers, R. A. (1981). *Career Development Inventory* (College and University Form). Palo Alto, CA: Consulting Psychologist's Press.

Swanson, J. L., & Tokar, D. M. (1991). College students' perceptions of barriers to career development. *Journal of Vocational Behavior, 38*, 92–106.

Wallbrown, F. H., Silling, S. M., & Crites, J. O. (1986). Testing Crites' model of career maturity: A hierarchical strategy. *Journal of Vocational Behavior, 28*, 183–190.

Westbrook, B. W. (1984). Career maturity: The concept, the instruments, and the research. In W. B. Walsh & S. H. Osipow (Eds.), *Handbook of vocational psychology* (Vol. 1, pp. 263–303). Hillsdale, NJ: Erlbaum.

Darrell Anthony Luzzo is a professor of psychology in the Division of Humanities and Social Sciences at Johnson County Community College. Correspondence regarding this article should be addressed to Darrell Anthony Luzzo, 12345 College at Quivira, Overland Park, KS 66210.

16

A Concurrent/Triangulation Mixed Methods Design With Data Transformation

Selection: Idler, E. L., Hudson, S. V., & Leventhal, H. (1999). The meanings of self-ratings of health: A qualitative and quantitative approach. *Research on Aging,* *21*(3), 458–476.

Editors' Introduction

Idler, Hudson, and Leventhal (1999) used quantitative and qualitative data to investigate how African American elders' quantitative ratings of their health and qualitative descriptions of their ratings relate to their biomedical conditions. The authors collected quantitative measures of participants' health ratings, demographics, and medical history and conducted qualitative interviews about the meanings of their ratings (see left side of Figure 16.0). They initially analyzed the two data sets separately, but after coding the qualitative responses, the authors applied procedures for transforming the qualitative codes into quantitative scores. Next, they statistically analyzed the quantified qualitative results with the quantitative data to determine if the qualitative responses were related to the quantitative ratings (see right side of Figure 16.0). Therefore, Idler et al. implemented the two methods simultaneously in a concurrent/triangulation design and merged the data sets during data analysis using data transformation. This study highlights important considerations related to transforming data, including software issues, needing an adequate qualitative sample size, and how to use a theory to quantify complex qualitative responses.

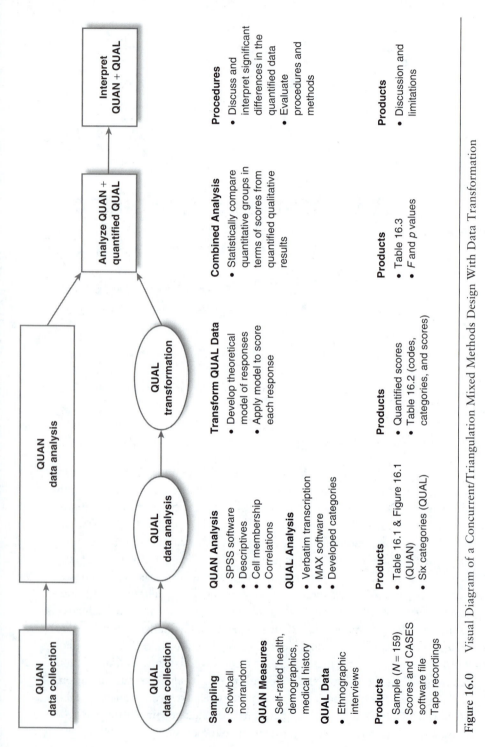

Figure 16.0 Visual Diagram of a Concurrent/Triangulation Mixed Methods Design With Data Transformation

SOURCE: Based on Idler, Hudson, and Leventhal (1999).

The Meanings of Self-Ratings of Health

A Qualitative and Quantitative Approach

Ellen L. Idler
Rutgers, The State University of New Jersey

Shawna V. Hudson
Rutgers, The State University of New Jersey

Howard Leventhal
Rutgers, The State University of New Jersey

Self-ratings of health are central measures of health status that predict outcomes such as mortality and declines in functional ability. Qualitative and quantitative data are used to test the hypothesis that definitions of health that are narrowly biomedical are associated with underestimates of self-ratings relative to respondents' medical histories, while definitions that are broad and

SOURCE: This article is reprinted from *Research on Aging*, Vol. 21, Issue 3, pp. 458–476, 1999. Reprinted with permission of Sage Publications, Inc.

Authors' Note: This research was conducted with the support of the Center for the Health Promotion of Elderly Minorities (P20 AG12072, Howard Leventhal, principal investigator), a project of the National Institute on Aging. The authors would like to thank the staff of the Rutgers University Center for Research on Health and Behavior and the participants in the survey.

inclusive are related to relatively better self-ratings. A sample of 159 elderly African Americans rates their health and reports "what went through your mind." Analysis of variance shows that respondents who overestimate their health are more likely to report ratings based on social activities and relationships, or psychological, emotional, or spiritual characteristics, rather than biomedical criteria. The authors conclude that inclusive definitions of health facilitate more positive self-ratings of health, given a fixed health status; methodologically, they conclude that this is a promising method for exploring self-ratings of health.

*S*elf-ratings of health have become an increasingly important topic of study, particularly for elderly populations. For one thing, their ability to predict mortality in long-term follow-up studies has been demonstrated so repeatedly now that it is almost becoming a cliché (Idler and Benyamini 1997). Even when more objective measures of health status are included in the study, simple, global self-ratings predict survival during short follow-up periods of just 2 years (Ho 1991; Rakowski, Mor, and Hiris 1991) and long periods of up to 13 years (Krzyanowski and Wysocki 1986; Chipperfield 1993). These studies have come from representative probability samples from all over the globe; the four just named come from, respectively, Hong Kong, the United States (national sample), Poland, and Canada. Other studies with similar findings have been reported from Israel (Kaplan, Barell, and Lusky 1988), Wales (Shahtahmasebi, Davies, and Wenger 1992), the Netherlands (Pijls, Feskens, and Kromhout 1993), Lithuania (Appels et al. 1996), and numerous sites around the United States. All in all, the powerful predictive effect of this variable has been shown in many languages and cultures.

And yet, the proliferation of epidemiological studies with large, representative samples and increasingly sophisticated measures of physical health status has not produced a significant amount of progress in understanding the mechanism by which this simple self-categorization should be so strongly related to subsequent events. What is it that people are saying when they rate their health? What do they mean?

Traditionally, qualitative approaches in the social sciences are used when an area of research is being mapped out for the first time (Creswell 1994). The virtues of qualitative approaches, their engagement with typical life situations, their naturalism, their sensitivity to the vernacular participants use, and their ability to capture the perceptions of respondents "from the inside" make them especially suitable for describing unknown terrain (Miles and Huberman 1994). Such studies are usually thought of as preceding more structured quantitative studies; for example, insights gained from open-ended interviews could be used to develop scales for new constructs. In our case, however, we are initiating a qualitative study following publication of a large number of quantitative studies, as these latter studies leave us with unanswered questions about the meaning of self-ratings of health.

Qualitative studies of the meaning of self-ratings of health are rare. Groves, Fultz, and Martin (1992) analyzed pretest data from the General Social Survey in which respondents *(N = 100)* were asked to give self-ratings of health and then to elaborate on them ("When you answered the last question about your health, what did you think of?"). Their coding of responses yielded 10 categories, of which the absence or presence of illness was the most frequently mentioned (31%). Other categories included health behaviors (14%), physical performance or ability (7%), and health service use (6%). The analysis presents results only of first responses, and no details of transcription or coding procedures are given. Krause and Jay (1994) present data from interviews with 158 respondents, in which the self-rated health question was followed by "Tell me why you say that." Responses were taped and transcribed closely, but not verbatim. Coding produced 91 categories that were collapsed eventually to 4, including (in order of frequency) health problems, physical functioning, health behavior, and health comparisons. Data were analyzed primarily by first-mentioned responses but also by multiple mentions; results showed that there were age differences but no sex, race, or education differences in the referents used and that those who compared their health to others were especially likely to rate their own health as excellent. A shortcoming of both of these studies is that neither included an assessment of the respondent's health other than the self-rating, thus neither can provide much insight into the question of whether such meanings are related to differences between self-ratings and physical status.

One qualitative study did address this issue with a sample of elderly Floridians (Borawski, Kinney, and Kahana 1996) *(N = 885)* who were asked to rate their health (very healthy, healthy, fairly healthy, and sick or very sick) and then were asked, "Could you tell us why you feel this way?" Responses were recorded verbatim (on paper). Coding categories were developed from a sample of 50 responses, and two judges coded the remaining responses, with interrater reliability of 98.5%. Five global categories emerged for first-mentioned responses (in order of frequency): physical health focused, attitudinal/behavioral, health transcendence, externally focused, and nonreflective. The respondents' health status was assessed by counting the number of significant health problems, including severe conditions, intense pain, five or more prescription medications, or frequent shortness of breath. Self-ratings of health (dichotomized) and none versus one or more serious health problems were cross classified to produce four groups, two with congruent and two with noncongruent health appraisals. Health "optimists" were significantly more likely to use attitudinal/behavioral criteria for their ratings and were more likely to give answers reflecting a transcendence of physical health. The study also found that "poor health realists" and those respondents who gave nonreflective answers had higher risks of mortality. This study comes closest to the present study in the question it addresses, as it considers the respondent's actual physical health status when evaluating the meanings of self-ratings. The Borawski et al. (1996) study shares one problem, however, with other studies of this type, and that is the problem of handling multiple responses. Borawski et al.'s (1996) solution, as in Krause and Jay (1994), was to create combinatorial codes, which produced very small frequencies and limited analytic power.

Despite the methodological issues, a substantive finding that emerges from all of these studies, and that is actually underscored by the problem of multiple mentions, is that the criteria respondents use in rating their health are complex and multilayered. This means that, while a majority of respondents use physical health criteria in evaluating their health, many respondents also discuss health in terms that focus more on what the body can do, on social role activities they are or are not capable of, or on even more expansive criteria such as their emotional or spiritual well-being. These are not generally thought of in connection with the biomedical model of physical health. Anthropological and qualitative sociological studies of definitions of health commonly conclude that health is not a unitary concept (Blaxter 1985), that perceptions of health are determined by many factors other than the absence or presence of disease (Litva and Eyles 1994), and that commonly held views of the meaning of health are far more inclusive than those held by health care practitioners (Fylkesnes and Førde 1991; Idler 1979). It bears repeating that the respondents in these studies, and in the large number of mortality studies, are, after all, being asked to rate their *health*, not their disease burden or their medical history.

The present study attempts to build on existing qualitative studies by employing qualitative and quantitative methods in the analysis of data that include both detailed measures of physical health status and open-ended data on the meanings of self-rated health, and by coding the qualitative data in a way that both preserves the detail of the original responses and handles the problem of multiple mentions. We construct a coding scheme that captures the criteria for self-ratings of health ranging from the most restrictive and biomedical to the most "wholistic" and inclusive and test it to see if that scheme differentiates respondents who have overestimated and underestimated their health, given their self-ratings and medical history. The coding scheme organizes the open-ended responses into six categories that range from answers that (1) reflect narrowly biomedical criteria, to those that (2) include functioning, to those that (3) add health behaviors, then to those that (4) use ability to engage in social activities, to those that (5) discuss social relationships, and finally to those that (6) employ psychological, emotional, or spiritual criteria for describing health. The hypothesis to be tested is that respondents who use more expansive, wholistic criteria in rating their health will be more likely to overestimate their health relative to their medical history; those who use more restrictive criteria will more likely underestimate their health.

Method

Data Collection

The data used in this analysis were gathered as part of the Rutgers University Center for Health Promotion in Elderly African-Americans. The Center, one of six exploratory centers funded by the National Institute on Aging (NIA), has four primary projects: a medical history interview, an ethnographic interview, an immune study, and a hypertension study. The data described in this article were gathered in the medical history and ethnographic interviews.

A snowball sample of participants was recruited from the local area using several starting points, including health screenings sponsored by the center and the county Office on Aging, local churches, senior citizen centers, senior housing complexes, local community organizations, and an urban health clinic. Nine African American interviewers interviewed participants in the location of their choice, including homes, churches, and senior centers. Interviews lasted from 45 minutes to 2 hours and were entered directly into laptop computers using Computer Assisted Survey Execution System (CASES). Ethnographic interviewers taped the interviews for subsequent transcription. A total of 212 participants completed either the medical history or the ethnographic interview, 187 and 189, respectively. The number of participants completing both is 163; missing data on the open-ended question reduces the effective sample size to 159.

Recorded ethnographic interviews were transcribed verbatim by another interviewer back into space left for them in the CASES file for each interview. This novel use of the CASES program allowed us to maximize the relationship between the qualitative and quantitative data in the project; CASES allows for export of data as ASCII text files as well as files that can be read into SPSS for quantitative analysis. We set a transcription limit of 7 lines of 70 characters per answer in CASES with an extra 15 lines added at the end of the transcribing file for responses that were more than 7 lines. Once transcribed, the qualitative data were imported into MAX (Kuckartz 1993), a program for the coding and analysis of qualitative data.

Measures

Self-rated health. Participants in the ethnographic interview were asked, "In general, would you say your health is: excellent, very good, good, fair, or poor? Could you tell me what goes through your mind when you say that?" This question was asked at the beginning of the interview to avoid influence from the health-related content of the interview.

Sociodemographic factors. Age, sex, and level of education were recorded.

Medical history. The respondent's medical history was assessed by a detailed review of approximately 64 diseases from 13 illness categories, with open-ended probes for additional illnesses in each category. A panel of six internists rated every disease in the list for its expected severity of impact on life expectancy (reliability of the six ratings was $\alpha = .97$). The score for each respondent sums all illnesses reported and weights them by severity as determined by the physician panel. Thus, this measure is not adjusted for the personal severity of each illness but only for "usual" severity and therefore is not as sensitive as a medical history elicited by a physician. However, the medical history interview is unusually extensive compared with other self-report surveys, and the physician-derived weighting is a further refinement.

Analysis

Two undergraduate students were trained and supervised by the authors to code the interview transcripts; weekly meetings were held to resolve discrepancies and add new codes. Initial coding focused on preserving as much detail as possible; multiple codes were assigned to each response, as many as were necessary. Intercoder reliability for the self-rated health question was .85 (number of agreements/(number of agreements + number of disagreements)) (Miles and Huberman 1994). Using MAX, the large number of initial codes that had been assigned could be grouped into fewer categories, namely, the six categories mentioned above, for disease, functioning, health practices, social activities, social relationships, and psychological/spiritual criteria. We then took each individual's response and coded it just once for the most inclusive category into which any of its codes fell. This procedure eliminated the analytic problem of multiple mentions, because each individuals response was coded only once; the unit of analysis could remain the individual, but the assignment to a single category of inclusiveness implies the potential existence of less inclusive codes in the same response. Statistical analysis was performed with SPSS.

Results

Our elderly sample had an average age of 74.2 (see Table 16.1). Seventy-five percent were female, and more than half completed high school. Only 28% were married at the time of the interview. The samples distribution on the self-rated health variable showed that 65% rated their health as good or better; this differs slightly from National Health Interview Survey data from 1994, in which 60% of Blacks aged 65 to 74, and 53% of Blacks aged 75 years and older gave good or better self-ratings (U.S. Department of Health and Human Services 1996). The ratings of our sample are almost identical to those given by the sample of elderly Whites in the Borawski et al. (1996) study. The medical history scores for the sample average 265.4; the median score is 238.0.

Table 16.2 shows the coding, frequencies, and categorization for the open-ended responses to the self-rated health question. The middle column of Table 16.2 shows the complete list of initial codes assigned. The left-hand column shows how many respondents gave a reply with that code. So, for example, the following response was given three initial codes; one for "serious medical condition," although several conditions were mentioned; one for "have symptoms," since pain is mentioned; and one for "the doctor says":

> Eleven years ago I had a mastectomy. I've had a very bad case of high blood pressure for many years. For 15 years, I've had diabetes. I have a sciatic nerve problem,

Table 16.1   Descriptive Statistics for Quantitative Data, Health of Elderly Minorities Project, N = 159

Variable	Mean/Percentage	SD	Range
Sex (male)	25.2%		
Age	74.2	7.36	58–95
Education (high school)	54.7%		
Marital status (married)	28.3%		
Self-rated health			
Excellent	6.3%		
Very good	24.5%		
Good	34.6%		
Fair	24.5%		
Poor	10.1%		
Medical history score	265.4	157.79	0–989

which causes my legs to hurt when I walk. The last doctor I went to wanted to do surgery to remove the nerves around my spine. I refused and said I'd come back when I couldn't walk at all. He said if I didn't want surgery, he couldn't help me.

This woman's response is also an example of a response that belongs in the first grouped coding category, because it contains only the purely biomedical criteria of physical health, diagnoses, and symptoms. Her reasons for rating her health are restricted to diagnosed illnesses and symptoms and to what her doctor says about them; she also rated her health as poor. More than a third (37%) of the sample falls in this narrowly defined biomedical category.

The next set of codes adds physical functioning criteria to the range of considerations people report. The following response combines both symptoms and functioning criteria: "With the things I have I would say it's just fair. I can't walk any distance. I would say fair. I tire very easily. I'm pushing myself all the time now." This respondent uses information not only from symptoms (tiredness, having to push herself) but also from what she finds she can or cannot do in daily life (walk any distance). Her response is assigned a group code for the highest level initial code within it, a 2 for physical functioning. The physical functioning group code was assigned to 13.8% of the sample.

The next category adds health risk behaviors to the criteria considered by the respondent. This category is more inclusive because it reveals the respondents' perception that they are in some way responsible for their health in that they attribute their present state of health to actions that they have or have not taken. Although some of the behaviors that were mentioned, such as avoiding fatty meats or losing weight, may have been the result of medical advice, other self-care activities, such as taking garlic or cod liver oil, were probably self-initiated. Here is an example of such a response:

Right now I have diabetes and that's something you know about. I have to work with it. Most of my problems is cause by what I did in the past. I am taking my medicine and staying away from the sweets.

This respondent rated her health as fair. She includes a diagnosis in her reflections, but also shows an understanding of the causes of the disease, a result of her past habits, and a responsibility for "working with" the disease in the present. Overall, 10.1% of the responses fell into this category.

The fourth category expands the concept of health further by including responses that mention social role responsibilities beyond basic functioning. Codes in this group include activities mentioned by respondents that are of the "want to do" rather than the "need to do" type. People mentioning work, shopping, or helping others are referring to meeting (or no longer being able to meet) the normative obligations that come with the social roles of employee, spouse, or friend. For example,

Table 16.2   Frequencies for Qualitative Data on Reasons for Self-Rated Health, Health of Elderly Minorities Project

N Mentioning[a]	Initial Code Description	Group Coding Category (%)[b]
		1. Physical health, diagnoses, Symptoms (37.1)
79	Do have serious medical condition.	
38	Doctor says . . .	
31	Have symptoms, that is, pain, tiredness.	
18	Have good physical feelings (i.e., energy).	
18	Do not have symptoms.	
18	Do not have serious medical conditions.	
6	Comparison to self in the past when health was better.	
6	Comparison to self in the past when health was worse.	
3	Do not have good physical feelings (i.e., energy).	
		2. Physical functioning (13.8)
16	Can get around.	
15	Can take care of myself.	
9	Cannot get around.	
7	Can eat without assistance.	
2	Cannot eat without assistance.	
3	Cannot take care of myself.	
2	Can think for myself.	
1	Can speak and hear well.	
1	Cannot speak or hear well.	
		3. Health risk behaviors (10.1)
12	I take care of myself.	
10	I see the doctor when I need to.	
4	I eat a good diet.	
3	I should lose some weight.	
2	I eat a poor diet.	
2	I exercise.	
2	My cholesterol is bad.	
2	I do not take care of myself.	
1	I rest.	
1	I am active.	
1	My cholesterol is good.	

(Continued)

Table 16.2 (Continued)

N Mentioning[a]	Initial Code Description	Group Coding Category (%)[b]
		4. Social role activities beyond Basic functioning (8.8)
8	Can do what I want to do.	
5	Can still work.	
4	Can no longer do what I want to do.	
3	Can help others.	
2	Cannot work any more.	
1	Can attend social events.	
1	Can do my own shopping.	
		5. Social relationships (6.9)
10	Compared to others, my health is better.	
2	Compared to others, my health is worse.	
2	Having a good marriage, happy family.	
2	Tension in family.	
1	My good health keeps my children happy.	
		6. Psychological, spiritual, emotional (23.3)
16	Some days are good, some are bad.	
13	I try to keep my mind off my body.	
12	God blesses me.	
9	Aches and pains are normal for my age.	
9	I feel happy, satisfied with my life.	
5	I keep a positive attitude.	
3	I feel unhappy.	
2	I keep my mind alert, busy.	
2	I do not feel unhappy.	
1	I am lucky.	
1	I do not feel happy.	
Total 427		100

NOTE: Table refers to responses to question "What went through your mind (when you rated your health as excellent, very good, good, fair, or poor)?"

a. All reasons coded; multiple instances of same code within response counted only once.

b. Proportion or sample when each individual's whole response is categorized only once, by highest level code within it.

> I can go to a lot of organizations. On Monday I go to exercise, on Tuesday I go to embroidery, and on Wednesday I go to Senior Citizens. On Thursday I go back to embroidery and on Friday, wherever anyone needs me I go. Then I go to [inaudible] twice a month.

This respondent rated her health as good. Her reflection on her health status is made up entirely of the roles she plays in various community organizations; she mentions no other criteria at all in deciding on her rating. In all, 8.8% of respondents fell into this category.

The next most inclusive level consists of responses that dwell on the relationship of the respondent with others. Social relationships are the basis for ratings when respondents say they arrive at a sense of their own health by comparing it with that of others that they know or by attributing their health to a happy marriage or a strong family. The use of social comparisons in perceptual processes has a long and distinguished tradition of research in social psychology (Suls and Wills 1991). Studies of patients have usually found that individuals who make comparisons of their own health with others often choose as their object of comparison others who are doing more poorly than themselves, thereby enhancing their own feelings of well-being. Our small data set supports this finding, in that 10 respondents felt their own health to be better than others, and only 2 perceived it to be worse. This man rated his health as very good:

> I look at others who are less fortunate. They don't have the ability to go around and do their work, wait on other people to do the things that they would like. Having to wait on somebody to come in and do for them. And I feel very thankful.

This is a more inclusive category than the others because it implies that the standards by which respondents are measuring their health are malleable, that the meaning of aches and pains, or the inability to walk a mile, or the fact that one cannot work at a job any longer are relative and can shift according to the social context in which they are judged. This category also includes the criteria that quality and supportiveness of social relationships are critical to health. In all, 6.9% of our respondents fell into this category.

The final category in our restrictiveness-inclusiveness scheme is for respondents who used psychological, emotional, or spiritual criteria for their health ratings. These respondents were all in some way asserting the importance of their emotional well-being, or their faith in God, as the reason for their rating. Frequently, the respondent also mentioned a set of physical health problems or limitations that they then discounted by saying, "but you have to keep a positive attitude." The most frequently cited code in this category is for people who report the relativizing perception that although they have bad days, those days are followed by good days, an interpretation other researchers have noted in studies of the chronically ill (Charmaz 1991). The power of positive thinking is exemplified by the following respondent:

> My mind is uplifted. I just have that mind, and when I said my health is very good, it helps to say it because you got to look up. It's your thinking . . . so many times we just think and look down but we have to think positive. We have to think and then it makes you feel good. Because if you down in the dumps and you think you down there and so many people complain and its no need. I'm just grateful I think positive.

Other respondents gave explicitly religious reasons for their ratings, including the nicely put. "I am a Christian and he made me very good." A key characteristic of this category, and the reason we placed it at the top of the hierarchy, is that the assertion of the importance of the non-physical criteria of attitudes, emotions, or religious belief nearly always takes place in the context of already-mentioned health problems; virtually all of the responses in this category also had a code for physical health or for functioning. So these responses not only included other criteria beyond the biomedical but they were also, usually explicitly, actually denying the importance of the body in determining one's state of health. Nearly a quarter (23.3%) of the respondents fell in this category.

Figure 16.1 shows how we constructed the relationship between the excellent, very good, good, fair, and poor ratings respondents gave themselves and their more objective physical health as it was determined by their score on the medical history. We divided the distribution for the medical history score to match the distribution of the respondents on self-rated health. Thus, for example, we match the best 6.3% of the medical history scores with the "excellent" health group because 6.3% of our respondents said their health was excellent. The "very good" group was 25.2% of the sample, so we take the next 25.2% of the medical history scores to match it, and so on. In the figure, we show the cross classification of these two sets of categories. Respondents whose medical history ranking matches their self-rating will fall on or near the diagonal. The figure shows that while there is some relationship between the self-ratings and medical history, it is only moderately strong. The Pearson r for the two variables is .28 ($p < .001$), a figure similar to that found in other studies. We created four categories from the figure, two for respondents whose ratings were as expected (good health and poor health realists); one for those whose "excellent," "very good," or "good" ratings were paired with a high medical history score (overestimators); and one whose "good," "fair," or "poor" ratings did not match their quite low medical history scores (underestimators). According to these criteria, almost half of the sample (42.9%) give themselves good or better self-ratings and have

| Self-rated health | Medical history[2] | | | | Serious illnesses |
	No illness 6.3%	30.8%	65.4%	89.9%	100%
Excellent 6.3%	R+ 1 (10.0%)	R+ 4 (10.3%)	O 3 (5.5%)	O 2 (5.3%)	O 0 (0%)
Very good 30.8%	R+ 4 (40.0%)	R+ 11 (28.2%)	R+ 13 (23.6%)	O 7 (18.4%)	O 4 (23.5%)
Good 65.4%	U 4 (40.0%)	R+ 17 (43.6%)	R+ 18 (32.7%)	O 12 (31.6%)	O 4 (23.5%)
Fair 89.9%	U 1 (10.0%)	U 6 (15.4%)	U 16 (29.1%)	R– 12 (31.6%)	R– 4 (23.5%)
Poor 100%	U 0 (0%)	U 1 (2.6%)	U 5 (9.1%)	R– 5 (13.2%)	R– 5 (29.4%)

O	Health overestimators	(N = 33)	20.2%
R+	Good health realists	(N = 70)	42.9%
R–	Poor health realists	(N = 27)	16.6%
U	Health underestimators	(N = 33)	20.2%

Figure 16.1   Construction of Categories for Health Overestimation/Underestimation by Cross Classification of Self-Rated Health and Medical History, Health of Elderly Minorities Sample[1]

1. Pearson r for these two variables is .28 ($p < $ .001). χ^2 test of significance not valid because of the large number of cells with small (< 5) expected values.

2. Cutoffs for medical history categories match distribution for self-rated health categories; see Table 16.1.

medical history scores to match (good health realists), 20.2% overestimate their health, 20.2% underestimate their health, and 16.6% are realistic about their poor health. This distribution is similar to that reported in the Borawski et al. (1996) study in which, with a less detailed measure of physical health status, 52.4% were good health realists. 14.1% are termed health optimists, 12.8% were health pessimists, and 20.7% were poor health realists.

Table 16.3 addresses the research question, "Are the criteria used to evaluate health, as given by these open-ended responses, related to the ratings individuals give their health, once those ratings have been adjusted for medical history?" In the last column, we see mean scores for the six-level grouped codes. If more expansive, wholistic definitions of health are associated with better relative self-ratings, then those who overestimate their health should have the highest averages, reflecting the most inclusive definitions, and those who underestimate their health should have the lowest, reflecting the most restrictive. The data support this expectation. Health overestimators have the highest scores, with poor health realists and health underestimators virtually the same with the lowest. The differences are statistically significant ($p = .024$) overall; post hoc tests show that overestimators have significantly more inclusive definitions of health than underestimators.

Table 16.3 also shows that the tendency to underestimate or overestimate health is not related to age; while poor health realists tend to be younger than the other groups, one-way analysis of variance shows no significant differences in the mean ages of the four groups. Likewise, there are no differences in the gender distributions of the four groups. There are differences by education. The overall F test for the variable is significant, with health overestimators and good health realists having higher levels of education than poor health realists and health underestimators, although post hoc tests showed no significant differences within any pair. The direction of the differences is suggestive, however. Given the known association of education with better health status and lower mortality the good health realists should be expected to have the highest scores, and they do; that the health overestimators also score this high is interesting, since this group has relatively poor physical health.

Discussion

The importance of this study rests at least as much on its development of a methodological approach to the study of a well-known problem in the research literature as it does on its findings; we enthusiastically endorse the usefulness of combining quantitative and qualitative approaches to the same data. First, we believe that it is essential to preserve the complexity and detail of respondents' answers. To this end, we (1) tape recorded and transcribed

Table 16.3   Analysis of Variance for Characteristics of Health Overestimators, Underestimators, and Realists

	Age	Education	Sex	Grouped Code
Health overestimators	73.4	2.67	0.66	3.84*
Good health realists	75.4	2.87	0.78	3.13
Poor health realists	71.6	2.15	0.81	2.46
Health underestimators	74.5	2.21	0.73	2.55*
F value	1.88	2.87	0.78	3.22
df	3	3	3	3
p value	.135	.038	.509	.025

*Post hoc tests show that the indicated mean scores are significantly different from each other at the $p < .05$ level.

interviews rather than relying on interview notes and (2) coded every reason given within a response. Although this approach produces a large number of coding categories, it permits the combining and recombining of these categories to test different ideas. Second, the linking of quantitative and qualitative data deepened our understanding of the processes underlying self-assessments of health. What good would it do us to know how a person reasoned about their self-rating without knowing what that self-rating was or how it compared with a more objective measure of their health status? The reasoning behind self-assessments of health is useful only if we know something about the state of health the respondent is reacting to.

The limitations of the study are significant and must be acknowledged. The sample is a nonrandom sample of elderly African Americans, and generalization to samples from other populations requires empirical testing. Although this and other related projects were motivated by an interest in minority health, our respondents made little or no reference to their minority status. Thus, it is difficult to say if their responses are distinctive in any way. The distribution in the sample of self-ratings of health and the correlation between the ratings and the medical history scores are quite similar to those reported in other studies. In addition, the relatively higher levels of participation in religious activities in the African American community and in the participants in our study may have influenced the prevalence of religiously related meanings of health. Moreover, some interviews were conducted inside church buildings, creating a source of potential bias in this area. Replication of the qualitative data collection and coding on more diverse and representative samples is needed.

Our study findings emerged only after we resolved the problem of multiple mentions by organizing the responses into groups defined by a theoretical model of how individuals interpret their health status. This model of restrictiveness-inclusiveness allowed us to represent each respondent's answer just once, at their high point of inclusiveness, but in a way that captured other responses they may have given. We did not arbitrarily choose one of several codes to represent a respondent's multiple answers, nor did we create cumbersome combination categories that could not be analyzed. The usefulness of our scheme lay in its ability to discriminate among self-ratings for so-called health optimists, health pessimists, and realists, which it did. This finding suggests that broader and more inclusive definitions of what "health" is allow respondents to be more versatile in their depiction of their own health; expansive definitions allow individuals to take more things into account when considering their well-being. The implication of the direction of the finding is that when individuals do this, they draw on social, psychological, and even spiritual resources that moderate the impact of poor physical health on self-ratings.

Indeed, throughout the quotations presented here, even in those in which respondents demonstrate relatively restricted definitions of health, we see evidence of active selves creating meaning, choosing points of view and rejecting others. The woman who rejected her doctor's advice about back surgery, or the diabetic who was "working with it," or the woman who criticized those who allow themselves to be "down in the dumps"—all of these respondents demonstrate the plasticity of conceptions of health. Our study supports other findings that show that respondents pick and choose their frames of reference and sources of comparison with respect to health and that they tend to do this in patterned, predictable ways (VanderZee, Buunk, and Sanderman 1995; Suls, Marco, and Tobin 1991).

We believe we have presented a testable model for the investigation of the meaning of self-ratings of health and provided preliminary empirical support. Our study also makes clear the feasibility of obtaining detailed qualitative data in community samples that are of sufficient size for statistical analysis. The techniques used for data collection, direct transcription into CASES, transformation of free response data from CASES into MAX to assess the frequency of responses for specific code categories, and conversion of the data to SPSS files for statistical analysis merit wider use for getting at the raw data of health perceptions. We urge other researchers to "take the plunge" and explore the intersection of these methods.

References

Appels, A., H. Bosma. V Grabauskas, A. Gostautas, and F. Sturmans. 1996. "Self-Rated Health and Mortality in a Lithuanian and a Dutch Population." *Social Science and Medicine* 42 (5): 681–89.

Blaxter, Mildred. 1985. "Self-Definition of Health Status and Consulting Rates in Primary Care." *The Quarterly Journal of Social Affairs* 1(2): 131–71.

Borawski, Elaine, Jennifer Kinney, and Eva Kahana. 1996. "The Meaning of Older Adults' Health Appraisals: Congruence With Health Status and Determinant of Mortality." *Journal of Gerontology: Social Sciences* 51B (3): S157–70.

Charmaz, Kathy. 1991. *Good Days Bad Days: The Self in Chronic Illness.* New Brunswick, NJ: Rutgers University Press.

Chipperfield, Judith. 1993. "Incongruence Between Health Perceptions and Health Problems." *Journal of Aging and Health* 5 (4): 475–96.

Creswell, John. 1994. *Research Design: Qualitative & Quantitative Approaches.* Thousand Oaks, CA: Sage.

Fylkesnes, Knut and Olav Førde. 1991. "The Tromsø Study: Predictors of Self-Evaluated Health—Has Society Adopted the Expanded Health Concept?" *Social Science and Medicine* 32 (2): 141–46.

Groves, Robert, Nancy Fultz, and Elizabeth Martin. 1992. "Direct Questioning About Comprehension in a Survey Setting." Pp. 49–64 in *Questions About Questions: Inquiries Into the Cognitive Bases of Surveys,* edited by Judith M. Tanur. New York: Russell Sage.

Ho, Suzanne. 1991. "Health and Social Predictors of Mortality in an Elderly Chinese Cohort." *American Journal of Epidemiology* 133: 907–21.

Idler, Ellen. 1979. 'Definitions of Health and Illness and Medical Sociology." *Social Science and Medicine* 13A: 732–31.

Idler, Ellen and Yael Benyamini. 1997. "Self-Rated Health and Mortality: A Review of Twenty-Seven Community Studies." *Journal of Health and Social Behavior* 38: 21–37.

Kaplan, Giora, Vita Barell, and Ayala Lusky. 1988. "Subjective State of Health and Survival in Elderly Adults." *Journal of Gerontology: Social Sciences* 43 (4): S114–20.

Krause, Neal and Gina Jay. 1994. "What Do Global Self-Rated Health Items Measure?" *Medical Care* 32(9): 930–42.

Krzyzanowski, Michal and Miroslaw Wysocki. 1986. "The Relation of Thirteen-Year Mortality to Ventilatory Impairment and Other Respiratory Symptoms: The Cracow Study." *International Journal of Epidemiology* 15: 56–64.

Kuckartz, Udo. 1993. *MAX User's Manual.* English version—introduction, translation, and design by Renata Tesch. Desert Hot Springs, CA: Qualitative Research Management.

Litva, Andrea and John Eyles. 1994. "Health or Healthy: Why People Are Not Sick in a Southern Ontarian Town." *Social Science and Medicine* 39 (8): 1083–1091.

Miles, Matthew and A. Michael Huberman. 1994. *Qualitative Data Analysis: An Expanded Sourcebook.* Thousand Oaks, CA: Sage.

Pijls, Loek, Edith Feskens, and Daan Kromhout. 1993. "Self-Rated Health, Mortality, and Chronic Diseases in Elderly Men: The Zutphen Study, 1985–1990." *American Journal of Epidemiology* 138 (10): 840–48.

Rakowski, William, Vincent, Mor, and Jeffrey Hiris. 1991. "The Association of Self-Rated Health With Two-Year Mortality in a Sample of Well Elderly." *Journal of Aging and Health* 3: 527–45.

Shahtahmasebi, Said, Richard Davies, and G. Clare Wenger. 1992. "A Longitudinal Analysis of Factors Related to Survival in Old Age." *The Gerontologist* 32 (3): 404–13.

Suls, Jerry, Christine A. Marco, and Sheldon Tobin. 1991. "The Role of Temporal Comparison, Social Comparison, and Direct Appraisal in the Elderly's Self-Evaluation of Health." *Journal of Applied Social Psychology* 21: 1125–44.

Suls, Jerry, and Thomas A. Wills, eds. 1991. *Social Comparison: Contemporary Theory and Research*. Hillsdale, NJ: Lawrence Erlbaum.

U.S. Department of Health and Human Services. 1996. *Health: United States, 1995*. Hyattsville, MD: U.S. Public Health Service.

VanderZee, Karen I., Bram P. Buunk, and Robert Sanderman. 1995. "Social Comparison as a Mediator Between Health Problems and Subjective Health Evaluations." *British Journal of Social Psychology* 34: 53–65.

Ellen L. Idler, Ph.D., is a professor of sociology in the Department of Sociology and the Institute for Health, Health Care Policy, and Aging Research at Rutgers University. She studies psychosocial factors in the health of elderly people. Her current projects include a study of religion and spirituality in adaptation to open-heart surgery, the development of screening instruments for geriatric depression in primary care, the impact of self-rated health on different causes of death in Danish elderly, and religion and spirituality as predictors of the quality of life in the last year of life of community-dwelling elderly.

Shawna V. Hudson is a doctoral candidate in sociology at Rutgers University and recipient of a Social Science Research Council Sexuality Research Dissertation Fellowship. Her research interests include qualitative methodology, social gerontology, sexuality, and culture; her dissertation examines the content and context of sexual imagery on U.S. network television. She received support for her work on the current article from a research supplement for graduate assistants from the National Institute of Aging.

Howard Leventhal, Ph.D., is Board of Governors professor of health psychology at the Institute for Health, Health Care Policy, and Aging Research, and the Department of Psychology at Rutgers University. His research interests include the role of threat and action plans on attitudes and behavior, cognitive and emotional factors involved in people's common-sense representation of symptoms, chronic illness and medical treatments, and factors affecting engaging in and preventing behaviors that pose risks to health.

17

An Embedded Experimental Before-Intervention Mixed Methods Design

Selection: Donovan, J., Mills, N., Smith, M., Brindle, L., Jacoby, A., Peters, T., Frankel, S., Neal, D., & Hamdy, F. (2002). Improving design and conduct of randomized trials by embedding them in qualitative research: ProtecT (prostate testing for cancer and treatment) study. *British Medical Journal, 325,* 766–769.

Editors' Introduction

The ProtecT Study Group designed a randomized control trial to test the effectiveness of three different treatments for prostate cancer, but they found they were having only limited success at recruiting individuals to participate. Donovan et al. (2002) therefore conducted a qualitative study of their recruitment process before the intervention (see Figure 17.0). Their qualitative data sources included interviews with men who had received the recruitment information, audiotapes of recruitment sessions, and interviews with men and recruiters to elaborate on some of the audiotaped sessions. The authors thematically analyzed the data and identified issues with the language and organization used to present the information during recruitment appointments. Using this information, the recruitment procedures were modified. These changes resulted in a significant increase in the rate of consent and thereby improved the effectiveness and efficiency of the subsequent quantitative trial. Thus, this study is an example of embedding a qualitative study before an experiment in order to design and/or improve the experimental procedures.

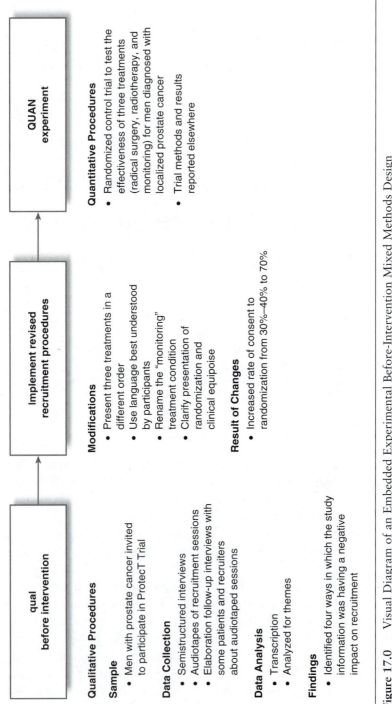

Qualitative Procedures

Sample

- Men with prostate cancer invited to participate in ProtecT Trial

Data Collection

- Semistructured interviews
- Audiotapes of recruitment sessions
- Elaboration follow-up interviews with some patients and recruiters about audiotaped sessions

Data Analysis

- Transcription
- Analyzed for themes

Findings

- Identified four ways in which the study information was having a negative impact on recruitment

Modifications

- Present three treatments in a different order
- Use language best understood by participants
- Rename the "monitoring" treatment condition
- Clarify presentation of randomization and clinical equipoise

Result of Changes

- Increased rate of consent to randomization from 30%–40% to 70%

Quantitative Procedures

- Randomized control trial to test the effectiveness of three treatments (radical surgery, radiotherapy, and monitoring) for men diagnosed with localized prostate cancer
- Trial methods and results reported elsewhere

qual before intervention → Implement revised recruitment procedures → QUAN experiment

Figure 17.0 Visual Diagram of an Embedded Experimental Before-Intervention Mixed Methods Design

SOURCE: Based on Donovan et al. (2002).

Improving Design and Conduct of Randomised Trails by Embedding Them in Qualitative Research

ProtecT (Prostate Testing for Cancer and Treatment) Study

Jenny Donovan, Nicola Mills,
Monica Smith, Lucy Brindle,
Ann Jacoby, Tim Peters,
Stephen Frankel, David Neal,
and Freddie Hamdy
for the ProtecT Study Group

ABSTRACT: **Problem** *Recruitment to randomised trials is often difficult, and many important trials are not mounted because recruitment is thought to be "impossible."*

SOURCE: Donovan, J., Mills, N., Smith, M., Brindle, L., Jacoby, A., Peters, T., Frankel, S., Neal, D., & Hamdy, F. (2002). Improving design and conduct of randomized trials by embedding them in qualitative research: ProtecT (prostate testing for cancer and treatment) study. *British Medical Journal, 325,* 766–769. Reprinted with permission of British Medical Journal Publishing Group Ltd.

Design Controversial ProtecT (prostate testing for cancer and treatment) trial embedded within qualitative research.

Background and setting Screening for prostate cancer is hotly debated, and evidence from trials about the effectiveness of treatments (surgery, radiotherapy and monitoring) is lacking. Mounting a treatment trial is controversial because of past failures and concerns that differences in complications of treatment but not survival make randomisation unacceptable to patients and clinicians, particularly for a trial including monitoring.

Strategy for change In-depth interviews explored interpretation of study information. Audiotape recordings of recruitment appointments enabled scrutiny of content and presentation of study information by recruiters. Initial qualitative findings showed that recruiters had difficulty discussing equipoise and presenting treatment equally; they unknowingly used terminology that was misinterpreted by participants. Findings were used to determine changes to content and presentation of information.

Effects of change Changes to the order of presenting treatments encouraged emphasis on equivalence, misinterpreted terms were avoided, the non-radical arm was redefined, and randomisation and clinical equipoise were presented more convincingly. The randomisation rate increased from 40% to 70%, all treatments became acceptable, and the three arm trial became the preferred design.

Lessons learnt Changes to information and presentation resulted in efficient recruitment acceptable to patients and clinicians. Embedding this controversial trial within qualitative research improved recruitment. Such methods probably have wider applicability and may enable even the most difficult evaluative questions to be tackled.

Background

The randomised controlled trial is the widely acknowledge design of choice for evaluating the effectiveness of medical and surgical interventions,[1] but recruitment is often much lower than anticipated.[2–4] Methodological literature is almost exclusively statistical and epidemiological, and very little of it is concerned with conduct or the particular demands that trials put on trialists and participants. Problems with mounting surgical trials are well known,[5] and systematic reviews have identified a range of barriers for clinicians and patients.[2 6] Nested studies within ongoing trials could help to elucidate recruitment difficulties.[6]

The ProtecT (prostate testing for cancer and treatment) feasibility study provided such an opportunity. The study was controversial; although consensus existed that a trial of treatment was urgently needed, intense debate continued about whether it could be mounted. This was because of the differences in complications of treatment (but not in survival) between radical surgery, radiotherapy, and monitoring and the evidence from previous failures, including a Medical Research Council trial (PR06) and small scale attempts to randomise.[7 8]

In the ProtecT study, men aged 50–69 were invited to a nurse led clinic in general practice, where they were given detailed information about the implications of testing for prostate specific antigen, uncertainties about treatments, and the need for a treatment trial. If the men consented, blood was taken for prostate specific antigen testing. Participants with abnormal results were invited to undergo further diagnostic testing. Men diagnosed with localised prostate cancer were randomised in a nested trial of recruitment strategies to see a nurse or urologist for an "information" appointment. The men were given details about the treatments and the need for a randomised trial and were asked to consent to randomisation to either a three arm (surgery, radiotherapy, monitoring) or a two arm (surgery, radiotherapy) trial. If they refused randomisation, a patient led preference for treatment was agreed. A multicentre research ethics committee gave ethical approval.

Strategy for change

We used qualitative research methods to investigate the process of recruitment:

• In-depth interviews with men after receipt of prostate specific antigen results and diagnosis—to elicit interpretations of study information and experiences of the study, including treatment preferences (LB with JD)

• Detailed examination of pairs of audiotaped recruitment ("information") appointments and follow up interviews to examine the delivery of information by recruiters and its interpretation by patients (NM, MS, JD, AJ)

• Detailed examination of other information appointments (all were routinely audiotaped) to investigate reasons for different levels of recruitment between centres and over time (JD).

All interviews were semistructured and carried out by using a checklist of topics to ensure that the same areas were covered but allowing issues to emerge that were of importance to the men themselves. Interviews and information

Table 17.1   Consent to randominsation to ProtecT study over time

Consent to randominsation to ProtecT study over time (patients with data available on final treatment decision). Values are numbers (percentages)

Date	Eligible	Consent to randomisation	Accept allocation*
October 1999 to May 2000	30	30–40%	60–70%

Document 1† circulated (changes to order of presentation; avoidance of "trial," "watchful waiting"; positive presentation of "monitoring" as involving regular tests; re-emphasis that patients eligible for all treatments; presentation of randomisation as reasonable way to reach treatment decision)

August 2000	45	23 (51)	18 (78)

Document 2† circulated (re-emphasis of monitoring as regular testing and review with possibility of radical treatment if disease localised; importance of eliciting and challenging patients' views if at odds with evidence; re-emphasis of no compulsion to accept allocation)

November 2000	67	39 (58)	30 (77)

Document 3† circulated ("good" and "not so good" examples of presentation of information to facilitate equal presentation of treatments)

January 2001	83	51 (61)	38 (75)

Intensive training programme (re-emphasis and role playing for centres 2 and 3 about equal presentation of treatments, challenging patients' views, need for randomised trial, and randomisation as reasonable method of treatment choice; non-radical arm named "active monitoring")

May 2001	155	108(70)‡	76(70)

*Denominator is men consenting to randomisation.

†Documents available from authors.

‡95% confidence interval 62% to 77% with exact binomial method.

appointments were audiotaped and fully transcribed. We analysed the data by using the methods of "constant comparison," in which transcripts are scrutinised for similar themes and then examined in detail within themes.[9][10]

We used early findings to devise presentation strategies, which were implemented initially in one centre. We reproduced the findings and recommendations for changes to the content and presentation of information in three documents and circulated them to recruiters in June, October, and November 2000, and we developed a training programme and delivered it to recruiters. JD evaluated the impact of the documents and training by listening to subsequent information appointments. Recruitment (consent to randomisation and acceptance of allocation) was calculated regularly.

Effects of change

The rate of consent to randomisation changed over time as the findings from the qualitative research were introduced through the circulation of documents and delivery of training (Table 17.1), increasing from 30–40% in May 2000 to 70% by May 2001. The findings from the qualitative research had an impact on the conduct of the trial in four major ways.

(1) Organisation of study information

Study information was based on the results of the team's systematic review of the literature,[11] and treatments were presented in a standard order: surgery, then radiotherapy, and finally monitoring. Recordings of information appointments and patient interviews in the early part of the study showed clearly that the treatments were not presented or interpreted equally. Surgery and radiotherapy were portrayed in detail as aggressive, curative treatments, and monitoring was portrayed briefly as "watchful waiting" (box 17.1). Recruiters were asked to present the treatments in a different order: (1) monitoring, (2) surgery, and (3) radiotherapy and to describe their advantages and disadvantages in equivalent detail.

Box 17.1   How treatments were presented

a) Early presentation of treatments

Clinician 1: "We believe that you are suitable for any of these three treatments . . . The first is radical prostatectomy. Probably the simplest answer is to remove the prostate gland completely—that gives you the opportunity of removing the whole of the cancer in its entirety. The problem is that radical prostatectomy is a major operation and there are risks . . . [26 lines follow]

"The second method is radiotherapy—you are trying to destroy the cancer cells by means of x rays without removing the gland . . . [30 lines follow]

"The final treatment is what we call watchful waiting. The basis of this is that we don't know whether your tumour is going to progress or not, and we can simply just watch it carefully . . . [10 lines follow]

"We can do [randomisation] for the three treatments—that is, surgery, radiotherapy, or watchful waiting—or if you didn't want to consider watchful waiting, just to compare two treatments which actually try to cure the disease, either surgery or radiotherapy"

(Continued)

(Continued)

b) Presentation and interpretation of "watchful waiting"

Clinician 2: "Watching it and treating—it's not treatment immediately, it's a different form of management: you're managing the disease rather than treating immediately, you're monitoring it and treating it if [it] shows signs of progression . . . if it does start to progress and cause problems you deal with them usually with hormone treatment"

Patient: "Well I suppose it's better for me to say now that I feel I would rather have something done about it at this stage"

Clinician 3: "Monitoring—obviously older people often choose that because they feel, you know, if they may not be around in 10 years time and it may be a good bet to take"

Patient: "Hmm"

(2) Terminology used in study information

Patients may interpret trial and clinical terminology differently than intended. [12][13] For example, "trial" was sometimes interpreted as monitoring ("try and see"), and recruiters sometimes assumed that patients had refused randomisation when they were really questioning monitoring. Also, the phrase intended to reflect evidence of good 10 year survival ("the majority of men with prostate cancer will be alive 10 years later") was interpreted as an (unexpected) suggestion that some might be dead in 10 years. Recruiters were thus asked to replace "trial" with "study" and to present survival in terms of "most men with prostate cancer live long lives even with the disease."

(3) Specification and presentation of the non-radical arm

It was quickly apparent that the non-radical treatment option caused difficulties for patients and recruiters. "Conservative monitoring" was meant to emphasise regular review and lack of radical intervention. Recruiters often called it "watchful waiting," but patients interpreted this as "no treatment," as if clinicians would "watch while I die" (Box 17.1a).

In June 2000 (document 1) the non-radical arm was renamed "monitoring" and redefined to involve three monthly or six monthly prostate specific antigen tests, with intervention if required or requested. Recruiters emphasised the slow growing nature of most prostate cancers and presented monitoring first. Men were clearly informed that the risk with monitoring was that future radical treatment might not be possible if the tumour progressed or the patient was no longer fit enough for it. An immediate impact was seen as some patients accepted monitoring, but scrutiny of information appointments showed that some recruiters continued to express it as "inactive" compared with radical treatments (Box 17.1b).

Documents 2 and 3 included examples of "good" and "not so good" presentation of information and renamed the non-radical arm "active monitoring," emphasising scrutiny of regular prostate specific antigen results so that radical treatments could remain an option for men who wanted them if the cancer progressed. Recruiting staff were then able to express confidence in this treatment option (Box 17.2).

Box 17.2   Presentation of "active monitoring"

Clinician 4: "The first one would be to be monitored very closely and not to receive any active intervention, and that would be by watching you every three months certainly for the first year—we'll bring you back, we'll do the blood test we check the prostate, and if the disease remains stable then obviously you know everybody's happy. If the blood test starts to change, it is extremely sensitive and it would give us an indication that there may be more activity there, so then all the options are discussed again"

---

(4) Presentation of randomisation and clinical equipoise

Recruiters and patients also had difficulty with randomisation and clinical equipoise. Each document contained guidance on this. We found it necessary to emphasise that recruiters must be genuinely uncertain about the best treatment, believe the patient to be suitable for all three treatments, and be confident in these beliefs. Patients commonly expressed lay views that cancer should be removed, told stories of friends or relatives who had died of advanced disease, or brought media information that was often biased in favour of radical treatments. Recruiters were encouraged to elicit these views and then discuss differences with ProtecT study information, explain that randomisation offered a way of resolving the dilemma of treatment choice, attempt randomisation before the end of the information appointment, and inform patients that they could have time to consider whether the allocated treatment was acceptable.

Lessons learnt

Qualitative research methods are increasingly included in health services research, conventionally to help in the interpretation of quantitative results or understanding of trials.[12] [14] [15] In the ProtecT feasibility study we inverted the normal relations between these methods and embedded the randomised trial within the qualitative study. We showed that the integration of qualitative research methods allowed us to understand the recruitment process and elucidate the changes necessary to the content and delivery of information to maximise recruitment and ensure effective and efficient conduct of the trial. The routine recording of information appointments was crucial: the content and method of delivery of the information provided the context within which the men's interpretations of the information could be set.

The qualitative research illuminated four ways in which study information was having a negative impact on the study. Some of the issues raised were simple, such as reordering the presentation of treatments and avoiding terms that had particular and unanticipated meanings for patients. These "simple" issues would probably not have become apparent without the qualitative research. "Watchful waiting," for example, is commonly used to describe a non-interventionist treatment. In lay terms, this conveys an impression of willful neglect, in which the disease is watched and everyone waits for an event—death. It was only when the non-radical arm was redefined as "active monitoring" that patients and clinicians gained confidence in it as a legitimate option. Whether the term is more acceptable in other countries, such as the United States, needs investigation.

Other issues that emerged were more complex. It has been shown elsewhere that patients have difficulty with randomisation.[15-17] In this study most men could recall and understand randomisation, but they often found it difficult to accept. Equipoise was particularly difficult but has received remarkably little examination in the literature. We found it essential that recruiting staff were able to express confidently that men were eligible for all three treatments, that the most effective treatment was unknown, that a trial was urgently needed, and that randomisation could provide a plausible way of reaching a decision. If recruiters gave any indication that they were not completely committed to these aspects, patients would question randomisation, often using subtle and sophisticated reasoning that surprised some recruiters.

Although our intention was to maximise both recruitment and informed consent, changes to the content and delivery of information could potentially be used to coerce patients and artificially inflate randomisation rates. One outcome might then be to increase dropouts, but, as the table shows, the proportion who accepted the treatment allocation remained similar throughout the study. We are currently exploring reasons for rejection of allocation. The process of verbally presenting study information and obtaining written consent is not usually tape recorded or available for later scrutiny as they were here. Recruitment and informed consent in other trials may not have been maximised, because of different interpretations by patients and researchers. Although these methods carry a danger of coercion, our findings indicate that we ensured that the study became more ethical over time as participants received unambiguous information that allowed them to make an accurately informed decision about whether to accept randomisation. Many men rejecting randomisation early on had received unbalanced information open to misinterpretation.

The controversial nature of the study and the extreme differences between the treatment arms might limit the generalisability of the findings to other randomised trials. However, controversial trials attempting to tackle difficult or "impossible" questions could be the very studies that need to benefit from the qualitative evaluation used here. Indeed, the extreme nature of the treatment choices illuminated issues that were very difficult and encouraged patients to be explicit about their interpretations. The plausibility of these findings suggests that these methods could have a role in improving the efficiency and conduct of trials in general.

The findings also support the contention that the conduct of trials is not straightforward. The concepts inherent in trials, particularly randomisation and equipoise, are complex and difficult and place particular demands on participants and recruiters. Better training and information for these groups may help, but this study suggests that qualitative methods need to be used in feasibility phases in order to understand recruitment to particular trials.

Health services research is a developing tradition, in which different disciplines and paradigms are brought together to tackle health related questions. Combining different approaches can be difficult, but the ProtecT study brought together the qualitative traditions of sociology and anthropology, epidemiological and statistical disciplines informing randomised trial design, and academic urology and nursing. The method of the study contravened conventional approaches by being driven not by the randomised trial design but by the qualitative research. Effectively, the ProtecT feasibility study embedded the randomised trial within the qualitative research and followed a sociological iterative approach. Thus qualitative research methods applied in combination with open minded clinicians and flexible or innovative trial designs may enable even the most difficult evaluative questions to be tackled and have substantial impacts even on apparently routine and uncontroversial trials.

Key learning points

Recruitment to randomised controlled trials is often problematic, potentially threatening the power and external validity of trials and wasting resources

Embedding the controversial ProtecT randomised trial within qualitative research allowed detailed investigation of the presentation of study information by recruiters and its interpretation by participants

Changes to the content and delivery of study information increased recruitment rates from 40% to 70%

The embedding of randomised controlled trials in qualitative research may enable even the most difficult evaluative questions to be tackled and could have substantial impacts on recruitment to apparently routine trails

Reference Notes

1. Altman DG. Better reporting of randomised controlled trials: the CONSORT statement. *BMJ* 1996; 313: 570–1.
2. Lovato L, Hill K, Hertert S, Hunninghake D, Probstfield J. Recruitment for controlled clinical trials: literature summary and annotated bibliography. *Control Clin Trials* 1997; l8: 328–57.
3. Tognoni G, Alli C, Avanzini F, Bettelli G, Colombo F, Corso R, et al. Randomised clinical trials in general practice: lessons from a failure. *BMJ* 1991; 303: 969–71.

4. Pringle M, Churchill R. Randomised controlled trials in general practice: gold standard or fool's gold? *BMJ* 1995; 311: 1382–3.

5. Baum M. Reflections on randomised controlled trials in surgery. *Lancet* 1999; 353: 6–8.

6. Ross S, Grant A, Counsell C, Gillespie W, Russell L, Prescott R. Barriers to participation in randomised controlled trials: a systematic review. *J Clin Epidemiol* 1999; 52: 1143–56.

7. O'Reilly P, Martin L, Collins G. Few patients with prostate cancer are willing to be randomised to treatment [letter]. *BMJ* 1999; 318: 1556.

8. Livesey J, Cowan R, Brown C, Clarke. N, Logue P, Lyons J, et al. Trial of randomisation between radical prostatectomy and radiotherapy in early prostate cancer. *Clin Oncol* 2000; 12: 63.

9. Glaser B, Strauss A. *The discovery of grounded theory*. Chicago: Aldine, 1967.

10. Ritchie J, Spencer L. Qualitative data analysis for applied policy research. In: Brynman A, Burgess R, eds. *Analysing qualitative data*. London: Routledge, 1994.

11. Selley S, Donovan JL, Faulkner A, Coast J, Gillatt D. Diagnosis, management and screening of early localised prostate cancer a systematic review. *Health Technol Assess* 1997; 1(2): 1–96.

12. Featherstone K, Donovan J. Random allocation or allocation at random? Patients' perspectives of participation in a randomised controlled trial. *BMJ* 1999; 317: 1177–80.

13. Donovan JL, Blake D. "Just a touch of arthritis, doctor? Qualitative. study of interpretation of reassurance among patients attending rheumatology clinics. *BMJ* 2000; 320: 541–4.

14. Mays N, Pope C. *Qualitative research is health care*. London: BMJ, 1996.

15. Snowdon C, Garcia J, Elbourne D. Making sense of randomisation: responses of parents of critically ill babies to random allocation of treatment in a clinical trial. *Soc Sci Med* 1997; 45: 1337–55.

16. Roberson N. Clinical trial participation. Viewpoints from racial/ethnic groups. *Cancer* 1994; 74: 2687–91.

17. Featherstone K, Donovan JL. "Why don't they just tell me straight, why allocate it?" The struggle to make sense of participating in a randomised controlled trial. *Soc Sci Med* 2002; 55: 709–19.

Department of Social Medicine, University of Bristol, Bristol BS8 2PR

Jenny Donovan
professor of social medicine

Nicola Mills
research associate

Lucy Brindle
research associate

Stephen Frankel
professor of epidemiology and public health

Centre for Health Services Research, University of Newcastle upon Tyne, Newcastle upon Tyne NE2 4AA

Monica Smith
research associate

Department of Primary Care, University of Liverpool, Liverpool L69 3BX

Ann Jacoby
professor of medical sociology

Division of Primary Health Care, University of Bristol, Bristol BS6 6JL

Tim Peters
professor of primary care health services research

School of Surgical Sciences, University of Newcastle upon Tyne, Newcastle upon Tyne NE2 4HH

David Neal
professor of surgery

Division of Clinical Sciences, University of Sheffield, Sheffield S5 7AU

Freddie Hamdy
professor of urology

Correspondence to: J Donovan jenny.donovan@bris.ac.uk

Members of the ProtecT Study Group are John Anderson, Miranda Benney, Sally Burton, Daniel Dedman, Ingrid Emmerson, David Gillatt, John Goepel, Louise Goodwin, John Graham, David Gunnell, Helen Harris, Barbara Hattrick, Peter Holding, David Jewell, Clare Kennedy, Sue Kilner, Peter Kirkbride, J Athene Lane, Hing Leung, Teresa Mewes, Steven Oliver, Jon Oxley, Ian Pedley, Philip Powell, Mary Robinson, Liz Salter, Mark Sidaway, Carol Torrington, Lyn Wilkinson, and Andrea Wilson.

Contributors: JD, FCH DEN, and TP designed the ProtecT feasibility study. JD, NM, MS, LB, AJ, and SF analysed the qualitative data, and FH, JD, and DN integrated the findings into the ProtecT study. All authors contributed to the writing of the paper. JD, FH, and DN are the guarantors.

Funding: The research was funded jointly by the UK NHS research and development health technology assessment programme and the MRC health services research collaboration. Support for the ProtecT study also came from the South West NHS research and development directorate. The department of social medicine of the University of Bristol is the lead centre of the MRC health services research collaboration.

Competing interests: None declared.

18

An Embedded Experimental During-Intervention Mixed Methods Design

Selection: Victor, C. R., Ross, F., & Axford, J. (2004). Capturing lay perspectives in a randomized control trial of a health promotion intervention for people with osteoarthritis of the knee. *Journal of Evaluation in Clinical Practice, 10*(1), 63–70.

Editors' Introduction

Victor, Ross, and Axford (2004) conducted an experiment to test the benefits of health promotion group sessions for patients with osteoarthritis of the knee. They implemented typical experimental procedures of having a control and intervention group and collecting quantitative outcome measures before and after the intervention in order to statistically compare the groups (see the "Quantitative Experiment" box in Figure 18.0). These researchers also conducted a qualitative study during the experiment (see the "Qualitative Study" box in Figure 18.0). They collected open-ended responses on the baseline survey, and during the intervention they also collected patient diaries and tape recordings of the treatment sessions for the intervention group. While the authors report finding no significant clinical benefits from the intervention, they compared and contrasted their quantitative and qualitative information to develop a better understanding of patient experiences and meaning of arthritis embedded within the context of the overall experiment. This study illustrates the use of unobtrusive data collection methods embedded during an intervention to qualitatively study the intervention process of an experiment.

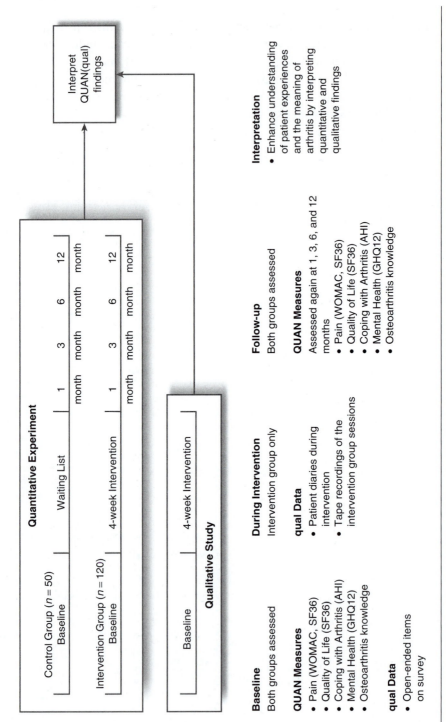

Figure 18.0 Visual Diagram of an Embedded Experimental During-Intervention Mixed Methods Design

SOURCE: Based on Victor, Ross, and Axford (2004).

Capturing Lay Perspectives in a Randomized Control Trial of a Health Promotion Intervention for People With Osteoarthritis of the Knee

Christina R. Victor BA MPhil PhD Hon MFPHM
Professor of Social Gerontology, Department of Public
Health Sciences, St. George's Hospital Medical School, London, UK

Fiona Ross BSc PhD RGN DN
Professor of Primary Care Nursing, Faculty of
Health and Social Care Sciences, St George's Hospital
Medical School/Kingston University, London, UK

John Axford BSc MD FRCP
Consultant and Reader in Rheumatology,
Academic Unit of Musculoskeletal Disease,
St George's Hospital Medical School, London, UK

ABSTRACT: *Osteoarthritis (OA) is a common and often disabling condition that predominately affects older adults. It is the commonest cause of locomotor disability and forms a major element of the workload in primary*

SOURCE: This article is reprinted from Victor, C. R., Ross, F., & Axford, J. Capturing lay perspectives in a randomized control trial of a health promotion intervention for people with osteoarthritis of the knee. *Journal of Evaluation in Clinical Practice*, Vol. 10, Issue 1, pp. 63–70, 2004. Reprinted with permission of Blackwell Publishing.

care. Previous studies suggest that there are both deficits in the knowledge patients have about their disease and extensive 'unmet' information needs. This paper explores the patients' perspective on the meaning and significance of living with arthritis, identified through quantitative and qualitative approaches undertaken during a trial that evaluated the effectiveness of a primary care-based patient education programme. This paper draws on qualitative and quantitative data from: the baseline interview (knowledge of arthritis, satisfaction with services and support received in primary care); patient diaries (individual goals and reflections on treatment); and group teaching sessions (themes describing the patient's experience). The different data sources were interrogated for common and divergent themes. One hundred and ninety-four participants were identified and 170 completed baseline interviews. Participants were predominantly female (73%), with a mean age of 63 and arthritis of long-standing; 55% reported that they had had it for 5 years or more. Use of primary care services was high, with 41% consulting their GP in the 2 weeks before interview. Levels of information were low, with less than 25% receiving support/advice about the disease, pain management or its impact upon daily life. Set against negative perceptions of the quality of services, patients' personal priorities were for improved pain management and enhanced mobility/functional ability. The combined quantitative and qualitative data provide insight into the patients' perspective on the causes and impact of knee OA, individual goals desired from treatment and the quality of care. There is consistent evidence of unmet needs for information and support and the priority placed by patients on finding strategies to cope with OA and maintaining independence. Even within a tightly defined study sample participating in the intervention, a diversity of experience and goals were revealed, which highlights the importance of taking account of contextual factors and individual differences when evaluating complex interventions.

Keywords: lay perspectives, osteoarthritis, patient observation

Introduction

Osteoarthritis (OA) is a chronic degenerative disease that predominantly, but not exclusively, affects older adults. Estimating the prevalence of OA within the general population is problematic because of diagnostic uncertainties. However, OA probably affects 10% of the adult population and is the commonest cause of locomotor disease amongst adults in Great Britain (Martin *et al.* 1988; Steven 1992). Although the prevalence of OA increases with age, half of all those with OA are aged under 65 years (Scott *et al.* 1998). There is a marked gender imbalance, with, at all ages, prevalence rates 40% higher in women as compared with men (McCormick *et al.* 1995). The incidence to prevalence ratio of approximately 70% indicates that this is a chronic long-term condition (McCormick *et al.* 1995). In the UK, treatment of musculo-skeletal disorders accounts for 6% of hospital expenditure and 15% of primary care expenditure. The cost of treating OA represents 4% of the total UK National Health Service budget (Steven 1992). In a 'typical' general practice of 10 000 adults there would be approximately 1000 people with OA, which would generate two arthritis-related consultations per person; 2000 consultations per annum (McCormick *et al.* 1995).

The broad aim of treatment is to relieve symptoms and to maintain independence, promote physical and mental health and quality of life and to enable sufferers to 'cope' with their disease (British Society for Rheumatology 1993). There is no single course of treatment for OA as there are a variety of potential interventions, including surgery and use of medications, both prescribed and non-prescribed, as well as complementary therapies. One approach to achieving the major treatment objectives in OA is the use of self-management and patient education programmes. Such interventions as developing educational packages and providing teaching and support programmes have demonstrated potential benefits for both patients (improvements in knowledge, and physical and mental well-being) and providers of health care (reductions in service use) (Balint & Szebenyi 1997; Hawley 1995; Barlow & Barefoot 1996; Holman & Lorig 1997; Barlow *et al.* 1997). These interventions are based upon the premise that people with OA lack knowledge both about the causes of the disease and the appropriate management of their condition to enable them to manage daily activities and maintain their independence. The contradictory and ambivalent nature of health promotion interventions has been recognized by Lorig *et al.* (1987) and Hirano *et al.* (1994), but there is a need to undertake further work in defining the parameters of complex interventions through exploratory qualitative work. This paper sets out to explore more fully the meaning and significance of arthritis for those patients who took part in a trial of a health promotion intervention by interrogating both the quantitative and qualitative data collected during the trial for converging themes.

Method

Context

Twenty-two south-west London general practices referring patients to the Rheumatology Department at St. George's Hospital were randomized to intervention or waiting-list control group. Patients aged 45+ with knee OA (radiologically confirmed) were recruited to participate in the trial between November 1995 and May 1997. Prior to the start of the trial a research interviewer 'blind' to their status interviewed all patients. The nurse-led health promotion intervention was delivered through four, 1-hour group sessions (six to eight participants) in the primary care setting. The sessions covered information (about the disease, medication and other treatments), activities (exercise and relaxation) and skills (strategies for pain management and joint protection). Outcome measures for pain (WOMAC and SF 36), health-related quality of life (SF 36), coping with arthritis (AHI), mental health (GHQ 12) and OA knowledge were assessed at baseline, and 1, 3, 6 and 12 months. Overall our findings indicate there were no clinically significant benefits from the intervention, further information about the trial and the methods can be found elsewhere (Ross *et al.* 1998; Triggs *et al.* 2000). However, the design of the study took account of the complex intervention being evaluated and incorporated a qualitative strand. This has enabled us to interrogate the outcomes derived from the baseline data identified through the structured interview and to enhance our understanding of the patient's experience of living with arthritis and goals for care supplemented by diary data and the tape-recorded intervention education sessions.

Sources of data

Three data sources were used in this paper: baseline interview, patient diaries and transcribed group discourse from the health promotion sessions.

Structured baseline interview

In addition to the outcome measures described above, participants were asked about their knowledge of arthritis (via an 'open question' and a 10-item knowledge scale), the information received from their general practitioner (GP), improvements in health, and their satisfaction with services and patient perceptions of quality of services.

Diaries

Participants in the intervention group received a diary at a home visit from the research nurse facilitating the health promotion group, prior to the start of the intervention. The prime function of the diaries was to support the educational intervention by inviting participants to review their symptoms and use of medication and other therapeutic strategies for the duration of the intervention (4 weeks) and to identify goals (or outcomes) they hoped to achieve during the intervention. Diaries are a useful social research tool (Elliot 1997) as they provide an opportunity to compare the outcomes desired from treatment, as articulated by participants, with the validated measures used to evaluate the outcomes of treatment, such as WOMAC and SF-36. Overall 94/120 intervention group participants completed some/all of the diary and 73 specified a goal, which they hoped to achieve from the intervention and treatment. Content analysis generated themes and categories emerging from identified goals and the participants' experience of symptoms.

Patient education sessions

A standardized approach was facilitated by one of two research nurses that, as noted above, covered information about OA, and approaches towards the management of pain and other symptoms within the context of enhancing participants' ability to manage their daily activities. All the group teaching sessions were tape recorded and a representative sample of eight complete groups (32 sessions) were transcribed verbatim and major themes were identified using content analysis, and validated in a process of peer review.

Results

The results reported here integrate the quantitative and qualitative data in relation to: characteristics of participants; knowledge about OA and its management; outcomes desired from treatment; and quality of services.

Characteristics of participants

Of the 194 participants originally identified, 170 were included in the baseline interview. Of the 24 who did not participate; four were excluded at X-ray, 11 refused and nine were not contactable. The study population was predominantly female (73%) and the mean age was 63 (range 45–90) (Table 18.1). One-third of participants lived alone and 41% came from ethnic minority groups. At least half of the participants (55%) had their OA for at least 3 years and 60% had it in both knees and 60% in other joints. Underlying this quantified and arguably simplistic categorization of the participants' OA status and history are stories of their experience (recounted in the groups), which illustrate greater complexity and the variable and intermittent nature of symptoms:

Well, I have it in my left knee but it's rather new. I have a lot of bits of arthritis all over the place and they seem to come and go . . . (F58)

I have OA in my left knee and sometimes my shoulders . . . it comes and goes . . . I've had it for quite a few years. I get quite a lot of pain . . . (F56)

For nearly half the participants, arthritis presented a significant challenge and had a major impact on their daily lives. This was supported by data from the baseline interview, where it was reported by 46% that arthritis limited their daily activities and 45% that pain from OA had, in the past month, stopped them from doing something that they had wanted to do. One-third (37%) reported that the pain from their knee OA had been severe in the previous week and 36% had a maximum walking distance of less than half a mile. Hence for this group arthritis not only significantly limited their daily activities, but threatened their independence, as these comments illustrate:

Actually I started with this arthritis in my ankles. My ankles swelled up, this was in 1980 and I could barely walk . . . (F57)

I've got it in both knees and in the left foot and it's like a gnawing pain all the time . . . (F59)

Table 18.1   Patient Characteristics and Comparison With General Population

Variable	Oak sample (n = 170)
Socio-demographic	
Age: mean (range)	63 (45–90)
Female	73%
Married	52%
Living alone	33%
Non-white ethnic group	41%
Home owners	66%
Higher education	34%
Employed	28%
Professional or managerial	33%
Morbidity	
OA in both knees	59%
Knee OA for more than 3 years	55%
OA in other joints	64%
Limiting long term illness	25%
Health service use for knee OA	
Inpatient stay in last year	11%
Day case treatment in last year	9%
Outpatient visit in last 3 months	41%

Knowledge about arthritis and its management

The 10-item knowledge instrument, devised specifically for this study, assessed levels of knowledge of arthritis. Overall participants had a mean score of 15 (range 0–20) (Table 18.2). Examination of responses to the individual items demonstrates that a significant number of participants were unsure as to the physiology of OA, were uncertain how to manage an acute episode and unclear as to the likely 'end point' of the disease (ending up in a wheelchair). As part of this, participants were asked to describe, in their own words, what they thought caused arthritis. Overall 33% had no idea, or did not know what caused OA (Table 18.3). Typical of these answers were comments such as 'Goodness knows' or 'I haven't a clue?' (Table 18.4). Accidents/injuries (26%) and occupational factors (16%) were the most frequently cited causes and included comments upon the hazards of falls, fishing and cricket (Table 18.4). Old age, weight and climatic factors were reported causes of arthritis (Table 18.2):

I adore the sun, as you can see [but] it kills me . . . I get more pain. (F54)

This patchy knowledge about OA is interesting in the light of patient perceptions of access to information and use of services. Although the level of use of secondary services by participants approximates to the national norm, they were heavy and regular users of primary care services (Table 18.1). In the 2 weeks prior to interview 41% had consulted their GP, which is twice the national norm of 21%. However, despite these apparently high levels of contact, prior to participating in the study, participants reported that they had received little information and support about arthritis from their GP (or other member of the primary care team). Only 16% reported that their GP had given

Table 18.2   Knowledge About Arthritis (%) (*n* = 168)

	True	False	Don't know
Strong thigh muscles help to hold the knees in place	59	14	27
Most people with osteoarthritis end up in a wheelchair	27	49	24
Pain in the knee is something you should just put up with	32	65	3
If your knee feels hot you should go for a walk	22	49	27
People with osteoarthritis should rest as much as possible	34	60	6
Being overweight does not affect the knees	18	79	3
Leg exercises are good for the knee	88	5	7
Only old people get osteoarthritis	5	92	3
Osteoarthritis is very common	83	5	12
In osteoarthritis, the cartilage gets thinner	50	7	42

Table 18.3   What Do You Think Causes Arthritis? ($n = 168$)

Cause	% n
No idea/don't know	33 (56)
Accident/injury	26 (43)
Occupation/activity	16 (27)
Old age	12 (20)
Weather	5 (9)
Weight	4 (7)
Other	4 (6)

Table 18.4   What Causes Arthritis?

No idea/don't know	'I don't know. No history in our family' 'Goodness knows' 'I haven't a clue'
Accident/injury	'I would think falls' 'Accident at work 5 years ago' 'Motorcycle accident'
Occupation/activity	'Years ago I did a lot of fishing' 'Kneeling down' 'I played a lot of cricket'
Old age	'I believe it's an ageing effect' 'Old age' 'I think it's just old age. That's what the GPs in the family have told me'
Weather	'Dampness, coldness' 'Standing in snow' 'Cold weather' 'Standing in the heat'
Weight	'Overweight' 'I've been overweight for years'

them information about OA of the knee; 27% reported being given advice about managing pain and 12% advice about 'coping' with daily activities.

The paucity of information recall from health care professionals about OA of the knee is reinforced by the qualitative data. Analysis of the group discourse during the intervention demonstrated many instances of difficulties in communicating with doctors and the very real lack of information participants felt that they had been given about their condition:

Things like this are hard to come by–information . . . they are on arthritis. (F54)

For some participants the information gap was perceived in terms of being marginalized:

I know I asked about it when I had the operation and he [doctor] said 'Oh no there is nothing I can do about it'. (F9)
    They don't tell you anything like that at the hospital . . . the doctor said if 'I was as good as you at 83 I wouldn't mind at all'. (F12)

Outcomes desired from treatment

Participants' preferences for treatment were measured in two ways: via the baseline survey and through qualitative analysis of entries in the diaries completed by the intervention group. Table 18.5 summarizes findings from the baseline interview, which shows that pain management and improvements in mobility/functional ability were the areas of health where respondents prioritized improvements. Confirmation of the primacy of functional ability in maintaining an independent life in the community is supported by the qualitative diary data. Seventy-three participants completed the section on goals in their diaries, which were classified into three main themes: functional ability (41), 'looking after yourself' (35) and quality of life (8).

The predominance of mobility concerns within the theme of functional activity is evident, with participants looking for improvements in this area (Table 18.6). More surprising were the aspirations to achieve better health through taking exercise and losing weight. Although, as noted earlier, the experience of pain is a major concern, the participants stated goals in terms of maximizing and increasing their daily activity as a strategy to manage their pain, rather than identifying 'pain control' itself as an major or single issue. Twenty-one participants stated no goal.

Table 18.5   The Three Areas of Health in Which Respondents Would Most Like to See Improvements

	%
Pain	27
Walking/bending	25
General mobility	15
Self-care	9
Household tasks	9
Family/social	5
Work	5
Mental health	4

In combination these two data sets demonstrate the overriding concern of participants with enhancing their ability to cope with activities of daily living, which reinforces the concerns expressed during the groups:

> And you think, what are you going to be like. Are you going to be able to do for yourself? . . . It's not being able to do what you normally do indoors, like cleaning windows and stuff like that. (F51)
>
> You get exasperated. You know you should be doing those things you were doing 20 years ago, and know you can't get on a step ladder and get your curtains down. (F12)

Satisfaction with quality of services

Two questions designed to assess the quality of service provision were included in the baseline interview. Almost half (49%) of participants reported that they were very satisfied with the care they received from their GP and 38% were somewhat satisfied; only 3.5% were very dissatisfied. Participants were also asked if they would recommend their GP to a friend or relative with OA knee. Again levels of satisfaction were high, with half (49%) reporting

Table 18.6   Type of Goal Recorded by Participants

	Responses
Functional ability	
Walk faster/farther	9
Walk without pain	9
Kneel to garden	4
Perform daily activities better/without pain	9
Manage stairs	8
Improve knee	2
Look after yourself	
Exercise	6
Recreational exercise	16
Lose weight	8
Eat healthily	1
Quality of life	
To be more healthy	2
Help/teach others	3
Look forward to future	1
Enjoy family activities	1
Have a better quality of life	1
Other	21
No goal	21

Sum greater than 94 as some participants had more than one goal.

they would definitely recommend their GP and 22% that they would probably recommend them and only 6% reporting that they definitely would not recommend their GP. These findings are in stark contrast to some of the views expressed during the group sessions, which indicate that some patients were extremely dissatisfied with the service they had received:

> What I find in this country are that the doctors treat you like you are the last thing around in the world . . . Anything that I have with the doctor, I never have an explanation. Whereas the sessions were helpful as: 'you are explaining what is going on in your body'. (F13)
>   . . . I was under the . . . hospital for a long time with it [OA] and in the end they gave up and [said it was] wear and tear.

The diversity of views identified through analysis of both the quantitative and qualitative sources of data reflects the individual needs of the respondents and the range of relationships with health care services. It also may call into question methods of investigating satisfaction with services and in particular the rather insensitive nature of 'closed' type questions in elucidating responses to the quality of health care.

Discussion

The evidence for the effectiveness of self-management and patient education programmes in osteoarthritis is contested. The majority of work has been carried out in the United States of America and there are doubts concerning the robustness of the evidence because of small sample sizes, failure to use control groups and the inclusion of 'volunteer' patient groups and those using specialist/ self-help services. However, all the studies do seem to demonstrate that people with OA present significant information deficits in terms of their understanding of the disease, its management and how the disease may progress.

Our study was undertaken with a clinically defined group of people with established OA who were in frequent contact with the primary care team. Although the study population presented a homogeneous group in terms of their major socio-demographic characteristics, severity of disease and duration, the views given by participants when describing their disease serve to highlight the diverse ways in which OA of the knee is understood, the variation in the patient experience and different priorities placed on personal goals. These patient factors are rarely taken into account in designing clinical trials of complex interventions and go some way to challenge reductionist assumptions that attempt to define patient samples using narrow criteria.

Levels of knowledge and information concerning the causes of OA were low. Only a minority of the participants in this study could recall having been given information about OA and ways of managing it from their GP (or other member of the primary care team). If patients are not well informed, this reduces the potential for participation and positive approaches to self-care and creates opportunities for misunderstanding and mismanagement. Patient perceptions that OA is viewed as an inevitable part of ageing and is thus marginalized by health care professionals, was a cross-cutting theme in the data that emerged from views related to information received and the quality of services. The comments of our participants suggest that there are considerable opportunities for primary care-based interventions to promote independence, activities of daily living and physical and mental well-being.

There was also a lack of clarity as to the likely progression of the disease, with approximately one-half of patients unclear as to whether the 'end stage' of OA would result in wheelchair use. The emphasis upon mobility and functional ability-related outcomes, in both the qualitative and quantitative parts of the study reinforces the impact that OA has upon activities of daily living and the ability to live independently in the community. This emphasis upon mobility offers some validation for the focus on mobility/functional ability demonstrated by many arthritis-specific health outcome measures such as the WOMAC or AIMS. However, our participants also sought improvement in broader health-related domains such as weight loss. It is these more 'patient-centred' outcomes that may offer a useful complement to the routinely used functionalist outcome indicators.

Our study suggests that patients with OA currently lack support and information about the disease and its management in primary care. The combined quantitative and qualitative data provide insight into the patients' perspective on the causes and impact of knee OA, individual goals desired from treatment and the quality of care. Even within a tightly defined study sample participating in the intervention, a diversity of experiences and goals was revealed, which highlights the importance of taking account of contextual factors and individual differences when evaluating complex interventions.

Acknowledgements

Arthritis and Rheumatism Council for funding. Jeremy Shindler (for advice on general practice), Heather Cadbury and Lesley Murdoch (research nurses responsible for the intervention), Eric Triggs and Susan Vernon (research assistants).

References

Balint, G., & Szebenyi, B. (1997). Non-pharmacological therapies in osteoarthritis. *Balliere's Clinical Rheumatology*, 11(4), 795–815.

Barlow, J. H., & Barefoot, J. (1996). Group education for people with arthritis. *Patient Education and Counselling*, 27, 257–267.

Barlow, J. H., Williams, B., & Wright, C. (1997). Improving arthritis self-management among older adults; 'Just what the doctor didn't order'. *British Journal of Health Psychology, 2*, 175–186.

British Society for Rheumatology/Royal College of Physicians (1993). *Guidelines for the Diagnosis, Investigation and Management of Osteoarthritis of the Hip and Knee*. Royal College of Physicians, London.

Elliott, H. (1997). *The use of diaries in sociological research on health experience Sociological research online*. [WWW document]. URL http://www.socres online.org.uk/socresonline/2/2/7.html

Hawley, D. J. (1995). Psychosocial interventions in the treatment of arthritis. *Bailliere's Clinical Rheumatology*, (4), 802–823.

Hirano, P. C., Laurent, D. D., & Lorig, K. (1994). Arthritis patient education studies, 1987–91. *Patient Education and Counselling, 24*, 9–54.

Holman, H. R., & Lorig, K. R. (1997). Overcoming barriers to successful ageing: self-management of osteoarthritis. *Western Journal of Medicine, 167*(4), 265–268.

Lorig, K., Kankol, L., & Gonzalez, V. (1987). Arthritis patient education: a review of the literature. *Patient Education and Counselling, 10*, 207–252.

Martin, J., Meltzer, H., & Elliot, D. (1988). *The Prevalence of Disability Amongst Adults, OPCS Surveys of Disability in Great Britain*. Report number 1. HMSO, London.

McCormick, A., Fleming, D., & Charlton, J. (1995). *Morbidity Statistics from General Practice: Fourth Nation Study*. Series MB5, No. 3. HMSO, London.

Ross, F., Triggs, E., Cadbury, H., Axford, J., & Victor, C. R. (1998). Evaluation of education for people with osteoarthritis of the knee: recruitment and retention issues in study design. *Nurse Researcher, 6* (1), 49–59.

Scott, D. L., Shipley, M., Dawson, A., Edwards, S., Symons, D. P. M., & Wolf, A. D. (1998). The clinical management of rheumatoid and osteoarthritis: strategies for improving clinical effectiveness. *British Journal of Rheumatology, 37*, 3546–3547.

Steven, M. M. (1992). Prevalence of chronic arthritis in four geographical areas of the Scottish Highlands. *Annals of Rheumatic Disease, 51*, 186–194.

Triggs, E., Victor, C. R., Ross, F., & Axford, J. (2000). Subject to approval: recruiting the sample for a primary care based evaluation of patient education. *Methods of Information in Medicine, 39*, 241–245.

Correspondence

Professor Christina R. Victor

Department of Public Health Sciences

St. George's Hospital Medical School

London SW17 0RE

UK

19

An Embedded Experimental After-Intervention Mixed Methods Design

Selection: Messer, L., Steckler, A., & Dignan, M. (1999). Early detection of cervical cancer among Native American women: A qualitative supplement to a quantitative study. *Health Education & Behavior, 8*(26), 547–562.

Editors' Introduction

Messer, Steckler, and Dignan (1999) evaluated a program aimed at reducing the rates of mortality from cervical cancer among Native American women in the Cherokee and Lumbee tribes of North Carolina. As depicted in the "QUAN" box in Figure 19.0, their study began with a rigorous experimental design using procedures such as random assignment, pre- and posttests, and attempting to control for confounding factors. After analyzing the results of the experiment, the authors were surprised to find a disparity in the program's effects between the two communities. Therefore, they added a qualitative evaluation to enhance their understanding of the factors related to the program's effectiveness (see the "qual" box in Figure 19.0). This study is an example of an embedded design with a qualitative "supplement" occurring after the completion of the main quantitative experiment. This study provides a model for reporting rigorous descriptions of both the quantitative and qualitative procedures in one article as well as articulating the need for a retrospective qualitative study after an intervention.

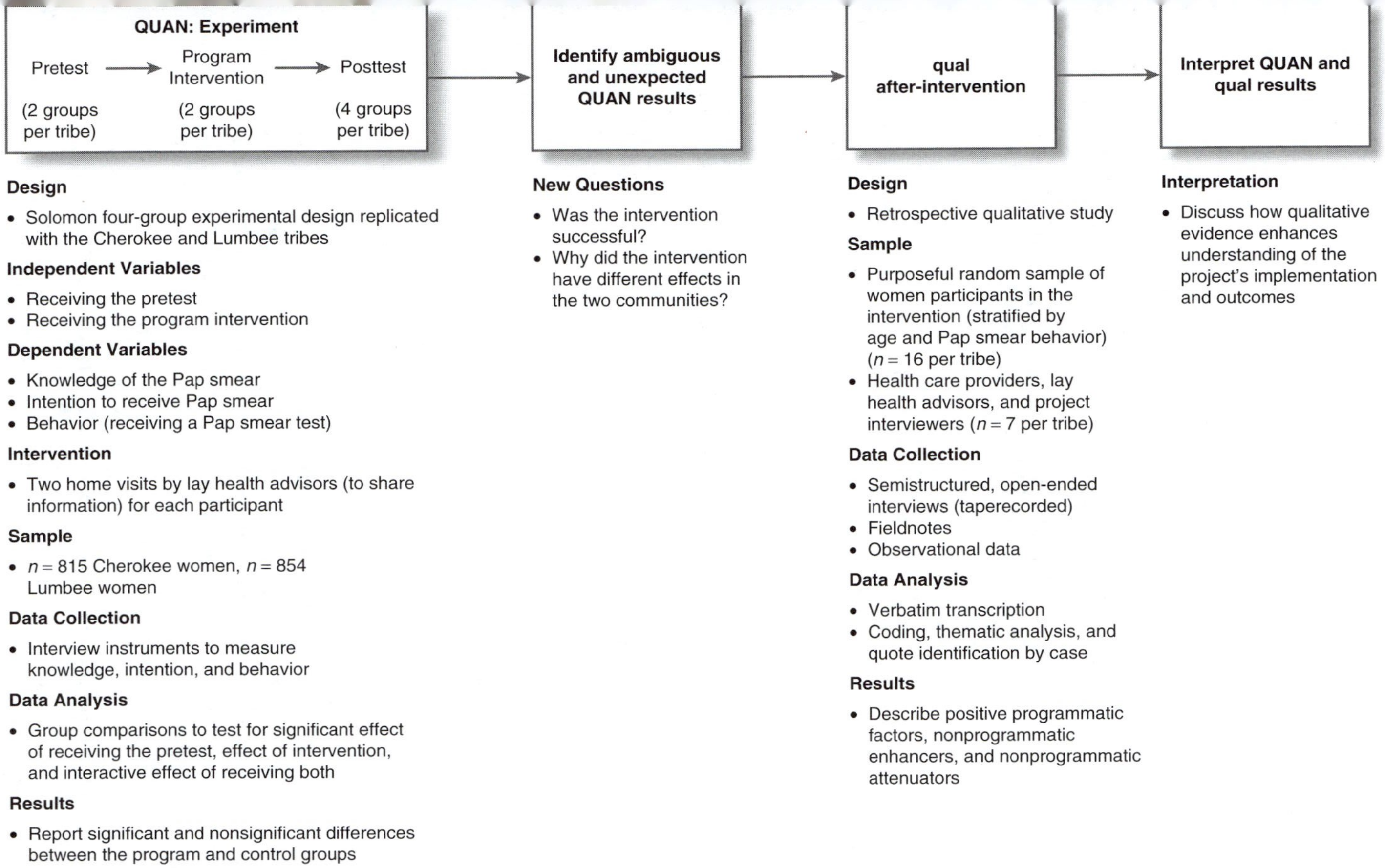

QUAN: Experiment

Pretest → Program Intervention → Posttest

(2 groups per tribe) (2 groups per tribe) (4 groups per tribe)

Design
- Solomon four-group experimental design replicated with the Cherokee and Lumbee tribes

Independent Variables
- Receiving the pretest
- Receiving the program intervention

Dependent Variables
- Knowledge of the Pap smear
- Intention to receive Pap smear
- Behavior (receiving a Pap smear test)

Intervention
- Two home visits by lay health advisors (to share information) for each participant

Sample
- $n = 815$ Cherokee women, $n = 854$ Lumbee women

Data Collection
- Interview instruments to measure knowledge, intention, and behavior

Data Analysis
- Group comparisons to test for significant effect of receiving the pretest, effect of intervention, and interactive effect of receiving both

Results
- Report significant and nonsignificant differences between the program and control groups

---

Identify ambiguous and unexpected QUAN results

New Questions
- Was the intervention successful?
- Why did the intervention have different effects in the two communities?

---

qual after-intervention

Design
- Retrospective qualitative study

Sample
- Purposeful random sample of women participants in the intervention (stratified by age and Pap smear behavior) ($n = 16$ per tribe)
- Health care providers, lay health advisors, and project interviewers ($n = 7$ per tribe)

Data Collection
- Semistructured, open-ended interviews (taperecorded)
- Fieldnotes
- Observational data

Data Analysis
- Verbatim transcription
- Coding, thematic analysis, and quote identification by case

Results
- Describe positive programmatic factors, nonprogrammatic enhancers, and nonprogrammatic attenuators

---

Interpret QUAN and qual results

Interpretation
- Discuss how qualitative evidence enhances understanding of the project's implementation and outcomes

Figure 19.0 Visual Diagram of an Embedded Experimental After-Intervention Mixed Methods Design

SOURCE: Based on Messer, Steckler, and Dignan (1999).

Early Detection of Cervical Cancer Among Native American Women

A Qualitative Supplement to a Quantitative Study

Lynne Messer, MPH
University of North Carolina at Chapel Hill

Allan Steckler, DrPH
University of North Carolina at Chapel Hill

Mark Dignan, PhD
AMC Cancer Research Institute, Denver, Colorado

The North Carolina Native American Cervical Cancer Prevention Project was a 5-year (1989–1995) National Cancer Institute-funded, community-based, early detection of cervical cancer intervention implemented among two Native American tribes in North Carolina: the eastern band of the Cherokee Indians and the Lumbee. The initial quantitative analysis of the intervention showed modest effects and found that the intervention had different effects in the two communities. Due to the equivocal findings, a retrospective qualitative study was conducted. The qualitative study found that two types of factors influenced

SOURCE: This article is reprinted from *Health Education & Behavior*, Vol. 8, Issue 26, pp. 547–562, 1999. Reprinted with permission of Sage Publications, Inc.

the intervention's results. The first were project and intervention characteristics, and the second were community and cultural factors over which the project had no control. The community and cultural factors took two forms: enhancers, which contributed to greater intervention effect, and attenuators, which created barriers to success. Examples of each factor are presented, and implications for cervical cancer detection among Native American women are discussed.

In the early 1980s, when the study reported in this article was planned, cancer rates among Native American populations were generally lower than those of other Americans, yet the pattern of cancer occurrence was distinctive. For Native American women, cancer was the second leading cause of death (with diseases of the heart being first) in 1981.[1,2] Furthermore, Native American women experienced cervical cancer mortality at more than twice the rate of all other women in the United States. The Native American age-adjusted mortality rate for cervical cancer between 1984 and 1988 was 7.6 per 100,000, compared to 3.1 per (100,000 for all U.S. women).[3] Native American cervical cancer mortality rates for women living in the southeastern United States (based on data from the Nashville Indian Health Service) was 11.6 per 100,000 for the same 1984-to-1988 time period. This mortality rate was nearly four times the rate for all females in the United States.[3] This excess mortality from cervical cancer among Native American women was especially troubling because cervical cancer can almost always be effectively treated if detected at an early stage.[2]

By the early 1990s, the age-adjusted cervical cancer mortality rates for Native American women had improved. In the 1989-to-1993 period, the total U.S. rate was 3.0 per 100,000, the overall Indian Health Service rate was 5.8 per 100,000, and the Nashville Indian Health Services rate (all Native American women living in the southeastern United States) was 3.1 per 100,000.[4]

This article reports the results of a qualitative study that was designed to supplement the quantitative evaluation of a health education program for early cervical cancer detection among women in two Native American communities in North Carolina. The study reported in this article was supported by the National Cancer Institute and was based on mortality data available when the project was initially planned, that is, in the early 1980s.

Overview of the North Carolina Native American Cervical Cancer Prevention Project

The overall purpose of the North Carolina Native American Cervical Cancer Prevention Project (NCP) was the reduction of mortality from cervical cancer among Native American women in the Lumbee and Cherokee tribes of North Carolina. The intervention for the NCP was a community-based, individualized health education program. The intervention was based on social learning theory[5,6] and self-efficacy theory.[7,8] It also employed the minority health communication model;[9] the predisposing, reinforcing, and enabling causes in educational diagnosis and evaluation model;[10] and the communication-behavior change framework.[11,12] These social science theories and models were used to help develop the cancer detection and control messages delivered by lay health advisors to Native American women in the two communities.[13,14]

The target population for the NCP was women 18 years of age and older who were enrolled members of the Cherokee and Lumbee tribes of North Carolina. The goals of the program were to increase the proportion of the target population who (1) obtained Pap smears on a regular basis and (2) followed recommendations for follow-up diagnosis and treatment after an abnormal Pap smear.

The Two Study Communities

While both sites are home to Native American populations, the Cherokee and Lumbee tribes live in distinct areas geographically, physically, economically, and culturally. The Cherokees are a cohesive population with long-standing tribal traditions, while the Lumbees are somewhat less cohesive and are not formally recognized by the federal government. The Cherokee population is much smaller than the Lumbee, with approximately 1,400 women in the target population; it is geographically confined both by tribal land boundaries and mountain topography. The Lumbee tribe is much larger (with roughly 10,400 women eligible for the project) and is geographically dispersed over one of the largest counties in North Carolina.

Economically, the communities are different as well. Cherokee residents are employed primarily in seasonal work and tourism in souvenir shops, restaurants, and more recently, casinos. The Lumbee tribe members are more likely to be employed in year-round shift work or in agriculture.

Culturally, there is a pronounced contrast between the two communities. The Cherokee is a much more tribal and traditional culture. Almost exclusively Native American, the Indian presence is central to the community's existence. The community of Cherokee is the traditional home of the eastern band of the Cherokee Nation, with both historical and cultural implications. Native American spirituality and healing arts are practiced in Cherokee. In contrast, the town of Lumberton, the geographical focal point for the Lumbee tribe, is far more urban and nonnative. Robeson County, which contains Lumberton, is approximately one-third Caucasian, one-third African American, and one-third

Native American. Because the area is the transplanted home of a collection of tribes now known as the Lumbee, there is little historical significance, and the Native American presence is not a central focus of the area. Little Native American spirituality or healing is acknowledged or practiced, and the primary religion among tribal members is Christianity.

In terms of familial relationships, Cherokee is a matriarchal society, while the Lumbee's is a patriarchal one. Among the Cherokee, families tend to remain on the tribal lands, and those who leave often return. Lumbee families, in contrast, are much more dispersed geographically, with relatives reuniting for family gatherings and special occasions.

These community and cultural factors suggested to the NCP researchers that a culturally sensitive and community-oriented intervention model was necessary to conduct the educational program they were planning. The lay health advisor model, described below, was therefore selected as the main educational method to be used in the NCP.

The Use of Lay Health Advisors

The lay health advisor model employs social networks to encourage behavioral and social change. It attempts to do so by working with the natural social networks of a community, by strengthening already existing network ties, and by enhancing the total network through natural helpers.[13–16]

The lay health advisor approach has been used in a variety of church- and community-based programs to address numerous health concerns.[17–24] It aspires to empower lay persons by offering training, counseling techniques, professional knowledge, and support.[25,26] It is a cultural model that builds on the strengths within the community and considers the influence of naturally existing sources of social and community support.

Numerous steps were taken by the NCP's developers to make the project culturally appropriate and sensitive.[27] Employing lay health advisors to deliver the project's educational messages to Native American women was one such attempt.[28] Furthermore, the educational interventions were designed to address the specific differences between the Lumbee and Cherokee tribes. For example, it became apparent that religion and active church participation was an important element in the Lumbee population; churches were community resources commonly relied upon to help address barriers to health care, such as transportation and child care. Thus, the Lumbee lay health advisors inquired about church membership during the intervention and referred women to this source to address barriers to obtaining screening. In the Cherokee population, extended family was found to play a role similar to the church among the Lumbee. Accordingly, the Cherokee lay health advisors inquired about the family as a source of assistance for women with specific barriers to obtaining screening.

The project intervention involved two home visits to each participant by lay health advisors, called *project guides*. The project guides were local Native American women chosen because of their familiarity with the local communities and their acceptance within their communities as reliable sources of information.[29] The face-to-face, individual visits were conducted in each woman's home. At the initial NCP visit, the woman completed a computerized Health Risk Appraisal (HRA) adapted for Native Americans. Following the completion of the HRA, the project guide determined the woman's perceived barriers to obtaining a Pap smear. After barriers were determined, the participant watched a videotape discussing cervical cancer and Pap smears. The project guide then reviewed the tape with the woman. The first session ended with each woman being given a personalized folder with educational materials, a refrigerator magnet, and an appointment for a follow-up meeting with the project guide. At the second appointment, the project guide reviewed the HRA results, answered any questions the participant had about the educational material that had been left, and asked closure questions regarding the woman's plans for making or keeping an appointment for a Pap smear or follow-up care. The initial visit lasted approximately 45 minutes, and the second visit lasted about 20 minutes.[29]

The Quantitative Study

Study Design

The NCP study employed a Solomon four-group design with a total of 1,000 women per tribe participating in the project.[30] Participants were randomly assigned to one of four groups, each to contain 250 women. This research design was replicated in the Cherokee and Lumbee tribes (see Table 19.1).

As Table 19.1 shows, in each tribe 500 women were to receive the pretest, 500 women were to receive the intervention, and all 1,000 women were to receive the posttest. All three project components, the pretest, intervention, and posttest, involved individual, face-to-face interviews with participants conducted by Native American interviewers. The actual number of participants in each group completing the study is also shown in Table 19.1.

Among the Cherokee, 540 women completed the pretest interview, 481 women participated in the two-visit intervention, and 815 completed the posttest. There were 478 Lumbee women who completed the pretest, 431 who

Table 19.1   Study Design and Number of Participants

	Design			Number of Participants		
Group	Pretest	Intervention	Posttest	Desired Number	Actual Cherokee Number	Actual Lumbee Number
1	O	X	O	250	210	211
2		X	O	250	238	216
3	O		O	250	175	220
4			O	250	192	207

NOTE: X indicates received intervention; O indicates completed pre- or posttest.

participated in the program, and 854 who completed the posttest. Of Lumbee women, 11.8% refused to participate in the project; 20.3% of Cherokee women refused to participate. Project outcomes determined the differences between the case group and control group on three factors: knowledge, attitudes, and behaviors with regard to cervical cancer and early detection.

Study Results

The primary outcome measures used to evaluate the effectiveness of the NCP included knowledge of the Pap smear, reports of intentions to obtain a Pap smear within the next year, and self-reports of having had a Pap smear within the past year. As mentioned, the Solomon four-group design structured both the intervention and evaluation of the project in the Cherokee and Lumbee communities. This design was chosen to determine the extent to which the pretest interview influenced the effectiveness of the program. It was reasoned that discussing cervical cancer with women, even in the context of a pretest interview, could be associated with changes in knowledge, intentions, or even behavior. Analyses of the posttest data focused on testing the effect of receiving the pretest interview, the intervention, and the interactive effect of receiving both pretest interview and the program. Results from the data analyses are summarized in Tables 19.2 and 19.3.

Table 19.2 shows the results for the Cherokee population. As Table 19.2 indicates, among women who received the pretest interview, there were no significant differences in knowledge or intention between the groups that did and did not receive the program. For behavior, however, women who received the pretest interview and the program were more likely to report having Pap smears in the past year than were women who received the pretest interview but did not receive the program. For the groups that did

Table 19.2   Effects of the North Carolina Native American Cervical Cancer Prevention Project Intervention Among the Cherokee

	Pretest		No Pretest	
Dependent Variables	Control	Program	Control	Program
Knowledge (% correct on knowledge test)	76.1	76.7	76.0	86.9[a]
Intention (% of women indicating intent to obtain a Pap test)	47.9	45.7	48.4	48.0
Behavior (% of women who received a Pap test)	65.1	71.0[a]	62.5	76.0[a]

a. Indicates a significant difference between the program and control.

Table 19.3   Effects of the North Carolina Native American Cervical Cancer Prevention Project Intervention Among the Lumbee

	Pretest		No Pretest	
Dependent Variables	Control	Program	Control	Program
Knowledge (% of correct on knowledge test)	76.4	81.5	81.2	84.6[a]
Intention (% of women indicating intent to obtain a Pap test)	33.2	44.9[a]	53.9	46.1
Behavior (% of women who received a Pap test)	69.1	74.6[a]	66.8	74.0

a. Indicates a significant difference between the program and control.

not receive the pretest interview, significant differences in knowledge and behavior were found among women who received the program.

Table 19.3 shows the results for the Lumbee population. Significant differences in intention to obtain a Pap smear in the next year and in behavior (i.e., obtained a Pap smear in the past year) were found among women who received the pretest interview and the program. Among Lumbee women who did not receive the pretest interview, knowledge was greater for those who received the program.

The results shown in Tables 19.2 and 19.3 suggest that effects of the pretest interview and program were not entirely consistent in the two target populations. Significant differences between the program and control groups were found for one outcome, behavior (Pap smear in the past year), regardless of the pretest in the Cherokee population. In the Lumbee population, a significant behavior effect was found only among women who received the pretest and the program. Findings for knowledge and intention also differed in the two populations.

The disparity in effects between the two tribes was not anticipated by the project's developers. The quantitative evaluation techniques employed by the project provided little information that could explain the differences in how the intervention operated in the two communities. The need to understand both if the intervention was successful and why the intervention had different effects among the two groups led to the qualitative evaluation described below.

The Qualitative Study

The qualitative evaluation reported here helped compensate for the limitations of the larger quantitative study by providing additional information in the following areas: (1) it provided information from the project participants as to why and how the intervention may or may not have worked, (2) it helped identify causes or determinants of the program outcomes, and (3) it provided context sensitivity by placing evaluation findings in their social, cultural, historical, and temporal contexts.[31]

Study Design

The qualitative evaluation study was summative and retrospective. It took place after the intervention and quantitative data collection were completed and required the participants to reflect upon experiences in the project. Two types of qualitative data were collected: observational data and in-depth interview data. The observational data consisted of observations of the women participants' contexts. It did not include observations of the interventions.

Sample

Interviews with health care providers, project guides, project interviewers, and project participants were conducted for the qualitative evaluation. In Cherokee, interviews were conducted with 4 health care providers, 1 project guide, 2 interviewers, and 16 women participants. In the Lumbee tribe, 6 health care providers, 1 project guide, and 16 women participants were interviewed.

Within each community, a purposeful random sample of women who had participated in the intervention was drawn. Evaluators suspected that within the target population, subsets of women would provide different perspectives on the project: (1) women older and younger than 50 years of age and (2) women who did and did not receive a Pap smear during the course of the project. The age stratification was an attempt to illuminate the potential differences in effect. Additionally, the perspective of women who were not convinced to obtain Pap smears was hypothesized to differ from that of women who were compelled to obtain Pap smears. The purposeful random sample was an attempt to capture these differences.

To identify women to be interviewed, a random sample of 20 women was drawn from the participant list for each tribe. Of the 20, 10 women were over 50 years of age, and 10 were 50 years of age or younger. Then, within each age group, 5 women were chosen who reported getting cervical cancer smears during the course of the project, and 5 women were chosen who reported not getting Pap smears. Twice as many women were drawn in each condition as were desired to ensure 20 women would be interviewed. Of the 20 who consented to be interviewed, a total of 16 interviews were eventually completed—4 women in each condition in each community. Fully half the requested women declined to participate in the evaluation. The reason cited was feeling they had given enough time to the project already.

Data Collection Procedures

A semistructured, open-ended interview format was used in all the interviews. The interviews were conducted in a sequential fashion. The initial meeting with the principal investigator and project manager informed the creation of the interview questions to be used with project guides, project interviewers, and the health care providers. The interviews with the guides, interviewers, and providers then influenced the development of the interview questions used with the Native American women.

Observational data were collected in a variety of settings including individual homes, local establishments, places of work, and health care facilities and were recorded three times per day during data collection. In addition, extensive field notes were made immediately following each interview.

All interviews were tape-recorded. Each interviewee was informed prior to taping that the interview would be transcribed, his or her name would not be associated with anything he or she said, and if at any time he or she wished the recorder to be turned off, it would be. Interviews with project guides and project interviewers lasted approximately 1 hour. They were asked about their duties, how they felt about their job, what they perceived women got out of the project, and about perceived reasons for and barriers to the project's success.

Health care providers were interviewed next. A health care provider was a physician or nurse representing a health care facility that performs Pap smears on Native American women in each study community. The providers interviewed were the individuals who performed cancer screens on the Native American project participants. Interviews took place at each provider's health care facility. Provider interviews lasted approximately 1 hour and asked about provider awareness of the project, perceived reasons for and barriers to the project's success, changes in levels of service, and typical Pap smear appointment procedures.

Native American women who had participated in the project were the last group to be interviewed. The majority of the interviews occurred in the participants' homes. The interviews lasted approximately 35 minutes and asked about participants' general impressions of the project, the aspects of the program that encouraged them to follow the NCP cervical cancer screen guidelines, those elements of the NCP that were less compelling in their Pap smear decision making, and important lessons they learned from the project.

Data Analysis

All interviews were transcribed verbatim; they were then reviewed for accuracy and to allow the addition of evaluator comment lines. Comment lines are evaluator notes that indicate the speaker's feelings and pertinent reflections from the conversation. While the project staff, provider, and participant data were analyzed separately, the data analysis process was the same for each.

The evaluation plan was to conduct cross-case content analysis. For cross-case analysis, answers from different participants were grouped by topics within the interview guide. An example of a topic would be "feelings about the project" This process allowed the interview questions to constitute a descriptive analytical framework for data analysis. The cases were separated by condition. For instance, one condition was "Lumbee women over 50 years of age, no Pap smear." The responses to a particular question given by the four Lumbee women in this condition were considered a case. The Lumbee case could then be compared with the Cherokee case of the same condition, or it could be compared with another Lumbee case of a different condition (i.e., Lumbee women 50 years of age or younger, with Pap smear).

"Content analysis is the process of identifying, coding, and categorizing the primary patterns in the data. This means analyzing the content of interviews and observations."[32] The content within each case was coded, and themes were generated for each topic of the interview guide. Quotations were identified from the transcripts, which characterized each theme, and cross-classification matrices were generated to summarize the case analyses.

Strategies employed to enhance the integrity of the data and the evaluation included testing of rival hypotheses, comparing different kinds of cases, testing negative cases, and triangulation of sources.[32] In considering rival hypotheses, the researcher tries to find alternative ways of organizing or explaining the data. If on comparing different kinds of cases, an evaluator gets similar responses to questions, the researcher can feel fairly secure the response is somewhat universal (to the population under investigation). In testing negative cases, the researcher's understanding of patterns and trends is increased by considering the instances and cases that do not fit the pattern. Finally, triangulation of sources involves checking the consistency of different data sources within the same method.[32] Each of these methods was employed to validate the results and enhance the credibility of the qualitative findings.

Results

As described above, the qualitative data were originally stratified and analyzed by age and Pap smear condition because the research team expected to find differences among these groups. However, these differences did not emerge. Participants responded similarly regardless of their age or whether they had obtained Pap smears. For that reason, the results presented below are in the aggregate rather than by stratified group.

The qualitative data analysis found several elements of the program that all participants responded to positively. These programmatic components help explain the beneficial effects of the program. The qualitative study also found several nonprogrammatic factors that affected the project outcomes. These nonprogrammatic factors are reported below as *program enhancers* and *program attenuators*.

Programmatic Factors

Three programmatic elements were identified as having positive effects in both the Cherokee and Lumbee communities. The first was that the participants in both communities generally liked the project and the project guides. They enjoyed having their awareness levels increased, feeling cared about, feeling encouraged to take better care of themselves, and feeling that they were helping others at the same time they were helping themselves. Women also liked the home visits and having misinformation corrected. The fact the project was designed for Native American women specifically made participants feel important. The guides were almost uniformly perceived to be competent, nice, respectful, informed, caring, and to genuinely enjoy their work. The participants' positive feelings about the project may help explain the NCP's positive effect in the two communities.

I thought it was great. . . . Indian women are more focused on their own children as opposed to focused on their own health. And this just lets someone be aware of their self for just a few minutes of the interview. (Cherokee woman, 50 years of age or younger, with Pap smear)

I was glad it was aimed at Indian women to make them more aware of what they need to take care of their bodies. . . . Sometimes you read all this stuff in magazines and so forth and you don't really feel like it has much to do with Indian women. (Cherokee woman, over 50 years of age, with Pap smear)

She [the project guide] was very thorough. . . . I thought she was real good and explained whatever I needed to know. And made sure I understood everything. (Lumbee woman, over 50 years of age, no Pap smear)

The second programmatic factor was that some women in both the Cherokee and Lumbee communities indicated they had already formed the habit of getting a yearly Pap smear and would have continued to do so independently of their project experience. Said one woman, "I always get a Pap smear every year. . . . Sometimes it might go 14 months, but every year" (Lumbee woman, 50 years of age or younger, with Pap smear). Another woman said, "I think it [the project] was just more of a reminder to me since I already affiliated it [the cervical cancer screen] with the same routine I go through every year when I get my physical" (Lumbee woman, Over 50 years of age, no Pap smear). For these women, therefore, the project served as a reminder about information they already knew and as a reminder to get their annual Pap tests.

The third programmatic factor found to explain the project's success relates to the salience of the cancer detection and control messages to the Native American women. The most common messages were (1) it is important to get regular Pap smears, (2) early detection of cervical cancer results in early treatment and better long-term health outcomes, and (3) women need to take care of themselves if they are to be able to take care of the loved ones that depend on them. Women also reported learning more about cancer generally. These messages seemed to hit home with Native American women. "It made me think more about making sure I get a checkup . . . how necessary it really is" (Cherokee woman, 50 years of age or younger, with Pap smear). "If you go get the Pap smears, and the cancer, it's caught in the early stages, there's help for you" (Cherokee woman, over 50 years of age, with Pap smear). "Somebody's depending on you, you know what I'm saying? . . . Got to take care of yourself so you can take care of them" (Lumbee woman, 50 years of age or younger, no Pap smear).

The qualitative evaluation found supplementary reasons for the project's success in the Cherokee community which relate to the community's close-knit nature. Interviewees reported the NCP was successful in the Cherokee community because project personnel were perceived to have spent time "laying groundwork," were knowledgeable about the community and were genuinely trying to return power to the women of the tribe. Tribal government and service providers were aware and supportive of the project, and women participants knew other women in the community who were also participating in the project and could discuss their experience. "He [the principal investigator] spent time laying the groundwork. He met with our tribal council, met with our doctors, and really seemed to know and respect the population he was working with" (Cherokee health care provider). By contrast, the Lumbee tribe is still striving for federal recognition and therefore has a less powerful tribal system and is much more diverse geographically and ethnically. Lumbee interviewees did not report appreciating the groundwork project personnel put into the community prior to the NCP's implementation. One service provider echoed a common sentiment when he said, "I remember one proposal, but I didn't know it had occurred; I don't recall awareness of this project going on" (Lumbee health care provider).

Nonprogrammatic Factors

In both the Cherokee and Lumbee communities, there were concurrent, nonprogrammatic factors that affected the results of the NCP. These factors can be characterized as program enhancers and program attenuators.

Program Enhancers

Enhancers Occurring Among the Cherokee

Among the Cherokee, three additional program enhancers were detected. During the course of the NCP project, a Women's Evening Clinic was initiated by the Indian Health Service hospital located in the community. The Women's Evening Clinic was a full service, after-hours, monthly clinic exclusively utilizing women practitioners. It provided child care, refreshments, and was eagerly supported by Cherokee project guides. The clinic served to increase access, provided a woman-friendly environment, and addressed some of the most common barriers cited by the Cherokee women for not getting cervical cancer screening. Many NCP participants stated that they would not have received a Pap test had it not been for the Women's Evening Clinic. "I don't know I would have gotten one [a Pap smear] without the Women's Clinic. . . . It certainly made it a lot easier" (Cherokee woman over 50 years of age, no Pap smear).

The second non programmatic enhancer was the existence and use of the Cherokee Hospital Diabetes Clinic. Because diabetes is so prevalent among Native Americans, a number of women reported attending the diabetes clinic every few months to be checked and have their medication refilled. The doctors working in the diabetes clinic encouraged women to keep up with their annual exams, among them cervical cancer screens, and would often ensure a woman received a cancer screen the same day as her visit to the diabetes clinic. One woman reported, "Usually I'm there [at the diabetes clinic] and they just do it right then. They're not gonna stop and say, 'Did you have an appointment for this today'" (Cherokee woman, 50 years of age or younger, with Pap smear). The Cherokee women's reports are in contrast to other studies that have found diabetic women were no more likely to have obtained cervical cancer screens than nondiabetic women.[33-35]

Third, within the Cherokee community, there were several deaths due to cancer during the course of the NCP. Because Cherokee is such a close-knit and interrelated community, these cancer deaths caused general cancer awareness to be raised considerably. "Especially in this community here where ya know everybody and are sort of interrelated and everyone knows aunt, uncles, cousins, whatever who just died from cancer . . . it makes you aware of it" (Cherokee woman over 50 years of age, no Pap smear). NCP participants reported being powerfully affected by the cancer deaths in their community and pursuing cervical cancer screens as a result.

Enhancers Occurring Among the Lumbee

In Robeson County, home of the Lumbee Indians, the Robeson County Health Department (RCHD) conducted a breast and cervical cancer project that also employed an outreach worker. The project began shortly after the commencement of the NCP. The RCHD project was designed to encourage women to receive yearly exams; project employees stated they saw a large percentage of Native American women. The second nonprogrammatic enhancer involves strict quality control measures instituted in all health care settings during the NCP's tenure in the community. The rigorous quality control measures were designed to ensure all health care clients received their yearly exams, including cervical cancer screens. To do so, the health care providers within Robeson County actively encouraged women to take detective measures and were held accountable for doing so.

All providers are constantly reminded every time they open up a record that a Pap needs to be given. And we review records every month. If a woman needed a Pap, came in, and didn't get one, the provider is out of compliance and in big trouble. I'd say we've done more Paps based on this peer review every month than anything. (Lumbee health care provider)

It would be difficult to separate the effects of the NCP from the effects of these other efforts.

Program Attenuators

Attenuators Occurring in Both Communities

Community elements also served to attenuate the effects of the NCP. Three attenuating factors were reported by both Cherokee and Lumbee project participants. First, the project was perceived by some women as an invasion of their privacy. This perception persisted despite the fact that all women consented to participate in the project. One woman reported,

> They just got too personal with their questions . . . like which kind of social groups I belonged to and some of the details of your sex life. I didn't feel like that related to any of the Indian health. I guess I'm a private person so some of them I answered and some I didn't. (Cherokee woman, 50 years of age or younger, no Pap smear)

As a result, some women refused to cooperate with the interviews and the overall project.

The second common attenuator was the reported cultural belief that one does not go to the doctor unless one is sick. This belief conflicted directly with the NCP's instructions to get a yearly cervical cancer screen. A project participant said, "Well, you just don't go to the doctor unless you're sick. . . . If things are going okay, you just don't question it" (Lumbee woman, over 50 years of age, no Pap smear). Another explained it this way: "We're very passive about things, certainly about personal health problems that you need to aggressively attack, may be . . . Indians have survived so much and it seems our instinct is that if you are passive enough you can survive anything" (Cherokee woman, over 50 years of age, with Pap smear).

The third nonprogrammatic attenuator involves the behavior of physicians in both the Cherokee and Lumbee communities. Women consistently reported that their physicians told them they no longer needed cervical cancer screening if they were over a certain age (i.e., 50 years of age), had experienced menopause, or had undergone a partial or complete hysterectomy.

> No, I haven't had one [a cervical cancer screen] in a lot of years. I had different doctors tell me that I didn't need it. Some said after 15 years they didn't give Pap smears. See, I had a complete hysterectomy and they said that was why. The doctor explained it all to me. (Cherokee woman, over 50 years of age, no Pap smear)

Furthermore, the women reported believing their physicians' advice over that of the NCP. Physicians providing women with inaccurate information regarding the need for cervical cancer screens would directly decrease the effect of the NCP.

Attenuators Occurring Among the Cherokee

The Cherokee program participants reported two additional attenuating factors. The first is due to the fact that Cherokee is a primarily tourism-based economy, with the summer season providing the bulk of each family's yearly income. The NCP took place over several years, with some components transpiring during the summer. Cherokee women reported annoyance that the project took place during the summer season, thereby taking up some of their valuable income earning time. "Well, the summertime is hard. . . . Most women are working two jobs plus trying to keep their kids out of trouble. . . . No one had time to sit and talk about cancer and got mad when you pushed a little" (Cherokee project guide). The second nonprogrammatic attenuator has to do with the Cherokee people's relationship with and feelings about the health care available to them. While they were appreciative of free medical care, they identified certain practices of the local Indian Health Service hospital as barriers to getting the medical care they needed. Women and health care providers reported it generally took several months to get an appointment for a nonacute condition; even with an appointment, there is often a waiting time of several hours; when a woman walks in without an appointment, she will often have to wait all day to see a doctor; the hospital's hours are Monday through Friday, 8 a.m. to 5 p.m., thereby requiring a patient to take time off work; and patient information at the hospital is not perceived to be confidential. "A lot of people can't afford to go anywhere but up here at the hospital to get their Pap smears and they're not real comfortable with the facilities. That's the biggest problem nobody talks about" (Cherokee woman, 50 years of age or younger, with Pap smear). Because the hospital is the only tribal health care provider, the participants' negative feelings toward the hospital attenuated the effects of the NCP because the primary behavioral message of the project was that women should get annual Pap tests by their regular health care providers.

Attenuators Occurring Among the Lumbee

The Lumbee participants also reported their relationship with the local hospital as a program attenuator. Because the Lumbee are not a federally recognized tribe, they are ineligible for Indian Health Services. There is no hospital exclusively serving the Native American community. The public, not-for-profit, local hospital is the only one in Robeson County; the next closest hospitals are located 30 minutes north and south of Lumberton. Several interviewees commented on rumors that the local hospital treats its Native American clients poorly. While no woman could say she had experienced this effect directly, there was an overall negative perception of the hospital within the community. This perception affected project outcomes because women were reticent to visit a hospital they perceived to be discriminatory.

> Course, no one will say it directly, but just the other day a woman was telling me that for generations, the Indian population has had a problem with the health department. And everyone knows they've had a long-standing problem with the hospital. . . . There used to be a double standard at the hospital [for Whites and Native Americans]. I think it's a carryover from that. (Lumbee health care provider)

Discussion

The qualitative study, launched as a result of ambiguous quantitative results, found two types of factors that influenced the projects results. The first was characteristics of the project and the intervention itself. The second was community and cultural factors over which the project did not have control. There were two categories of such community and cultural factors: enhancers, which contributed to greater intervention effect, and attenuators, which created barriers to success.

Project factors that contributed to intervention effectiveness were that Native American women in both communities liked the project, the guides, and the notion of contributing to their larger communities. The guides were perceived to be competent, effective, and to care about their communities. Also, the project's messages about the importance of regular medical checkups, including Pap tests, were highly salient to the Native American women. The project reinforced many participants' commitment to annual Pap smears. Among the Cherokee, the project was seen as helping empower the community due to its linkage to and support by the tribal government.

Despite careful attention to randomization and the prevention of contamination between the case and control groups, community and cultural factors beyond the researchers' control profoundly affected the project's implementation and outcomes. Factors that enhanced the effect of the intervention in the Cherokee community were the initiation of a women's clinic, the prevalence of women using the diabetes clinic, and increased awareness of cancer due to several deaths in the community. Among the Lumbee, the initiation of a breast and cervical cancer outreach program by the RCHD and local service providers' rigorous quality control efforts enhanced program effects. Factors that tended to attenuate the intervention's effect were some women's perception that the project was an invasion of privacy; the cultural belief that one does not go to the doctor unless sick; some doctors' inaccurate information about the need for Pap tests; the project's timing during an economically important season, thus reducing some women's willingness to participate; and perceived lack of confidentiality and discrimination by health care providers in both communities. These findings are significant because they point to the importance of community and cultural factors on target populations.

Both the quantitative and qualitative evaluation indicated that the Cherokee community should have been successful at getting women in for cervical cancer screens. Some of the factors thought to predispose the Cherokee women to success include the close-knit nature of the community, the presence of family nearby to help provide transportation and child care, the provision of free health care at the tribal hospital, and the timely initiation of the Women's Evening Clinic. The quantitative evaluation indicated that the Cherokee experienced only mild change in attitudes, behaviors, and intentions with regard to getting cervical cancer screens. The qualitative evaluation demonstrated that were it not for the Women's Evening Clinic, women would have pursued even fewer Pap-smear appointments than they did. Contrary to expectation, women reported the local, free health care provider to be one barrier to not getting Pap smears. These data encourage community interventionists to objectively assess community resources. Resources may exist that are not well utilized for compelling reasons. Community members themselves are the only reliable information source regarding what works and what does not work in their communities.

Of additional interest was how well the lay health advisor model worked among the Cherokee and Lumbee. The literature suggests that community acceptance in Native American communities is crucial. The use of lay health advisor project guides was invaluable to the project's success. Given the delicate nature of the material the guides were discussing with participants, to have attempted the intervention with anyone other than locally known, liked, and respected women would have significantly reduced the projects success.

Study Limitations

The qualitative study was done after the quantitative study was completed and was added onto the project to help explain the equivocal quantitative findings. The retrospective nature of the evaluation potentially contributed to inaccurate recall of project activities, individual behavior, and immediate perceptions of the project. Retrospective limitations could affect the accuracy of the qualitative evaluation's findings. Finally, due to a limited budget, the qualitative study was done on a very small scale: one researcher conducted all interviews in both communities in 2 months, transcribed and analyzed the data, and produced the report.

Implications for Practice

1. *The combination of qualitative and quantitative methodologies proved useful.* The qualitative study produced information that was able to help explain and interpret the equivocal quantitative findings. The qualitative study could have been even more useful if it had been planned for and carried out throughout the project, including an initial community assessment planning phase.

2. *Cultural and community factors both enhanced and attenuated the intervention's effect, thus contributing to the ambiguous quantitative results.* Assessment of community and culture are necessary before beginning and then during a project such as the NCP. Examples of using qualitative methods to conduct community assessments prior to beginning a public health intervention exist in the literature.[31]

3. *Despite the mixed quantitative results, the lay health advisor approach was successful.* Clearly, the project guides were a strength of the intervention method. The moderate success of the project should not be considered an indictment of the efficacy of the lay health advisor approach. Rather, Native American women reported the guides to be one of the most compelling elements of the project.

4. *Project participants in one community reported feeling empowered by the intervention.* While this was not an explicit goal of the project, the women indicated that their increased sense of power contributed to their decision to seek cervical cancer screens. This finding suggests the empowerment of project participants to be a worthwhile goal.

5. *Awareness of the economic and cultural cycles of a community can be important to an intervention's outcome.* These cycles affect both the participant's ability and desire to complete a project.

References

1. U.S. Congress, OTA: *Indian Health Care* (OTA-H-290). Washington, DC, U.S. Government Printing Office, 1996.

2. Dignan, M., Michielutte, R., Blinson, K., Sharp, P., Wells, H.B., Sands, E: Cervical cancer prevention: An individualized approach. *Alaska Med 35*(4): 279–284, 1993.

3. Valway, S. (ed.): *Cancer Mortality Among Native Americans in the United States: Regional Differences in Indian Health 1984–1988 & Trends Over Time, 1968–1987.* USDHHS, PHS, IHS.

4. Cobb, N., Paisano, R. E: *Cancer Mortality Among American Indians and Alaska Natives in the United States: Regional Differences in Indian Health. 1989–1993.* Rockville, MD, Indian Health Service, 1997. (IHS Pub. No. 97-615-23)

5. Bandura, A: *Social Learning Theory.* Englewood Cliffs, NJ, Prentice Hill, 1977.

6. Glanz, K., Lewis, F., Rimer, B: *Health Behavior and Health Education: Theory, Research, and Practice.* San Francisco, Jossey-Bass, 1997.

7. Strecher, V., DeVellis, B. M., Becker, M. H., Rosenstock, I. M: The role of self-efficacy in achieving health behavior change. *Health Education Quarterly* 8: 209–260, 1986.

8. Bandura, A: *Self Efficacy Changing Societies.* New York, Cambridge University Press, 1995.

9. Alcalay, R: *Rationale and Guidelines for Developing a Minority Health Communication Model.* Unpublished manuscript, 1980.

10. Green, L. W., Kreuter, M. W: *Health Promotion Planning An Educational and Environmental Approach.* Mountain View, CA, Mayfield, 1991.

11. McGuire, W. J: Public communication as a strategy for inducing health-promoting behavior change. *Prev Med* 13:229–319, 1984.

12. Green, L. W., McAlister, A. L: Macro-intervention to support health behavior: Some theoretical perspectives and practical reflections. *Health Education Quarterly* 11: 322–339, 1984.

13. Beam, N., Tessaro, I: The lay health advisor model in theory and practice: An example of an agency-based program. *Family and Community Health* 17(3): 70–79, 1984.

14. Collins, A. H., Pancoast, D. L: *Natural Helping Networks.* Washington, DC, National Association of Social Workers, 1976.

15. Israel, B. A: Community-based social network interventions: Meeting the needs of the elderly. *Dan Med Bull* 6: 36–44, 1988.

16. Israel, B. A: Social networks and social support: Implications for natural helper and community level interventions. *Health Education Quarterly* 12(1): 65–80, 1985.

17. Eng, E., Hatch, J. W: Networking between agencies and black churches: The lay health advisor model. *J Prev Hum Serv* 10(1): 123–146, 1991.

18. Earp, J., Viadro, C., Vincus, A., Altpeter, M., Flax, V., Mayne, L., Eng, E: Lay health advisors: A strategy for getting the word out about breast cancer. *Health Educ Behav* 24(4): 432–451, 1997.

19. Eng, E: The Save Our Sisters Project: A social network strategy for reaching rural Black women. *Cancer* 72: 1071–1077, 1993.

20. Eng, E., Smith, J: Natural helping functions of lay health advisors in breast cancer education. *Breast Cancer Res Treat* 35: 23–29, 1995.

21. Watkins, E.L., Harlan, C., Eng, E., Gansky, S.A., Gehan, D., Larson, K: Assessing the effectiveness of lay health advisors with migrant farmworkers. *Family and Community Health* 16: 72–87, 1994.

22. Booker, V., Grube, J., Kay, B., Gutierrez-Najera, L., Stewart, G: Changes in empowerment: Effects of participation in a lay health promotion program. *Health Educ Behav* 24(4): 452–464, 1997.

23. Schulz, A., Israel, B., Becker, A., Hollis, R: "It's a 24-hour thing . . . A living-for-each-other concept": Identity, networks, and community in an urban village health worker project. *Health Educ Behav* 24(4): 465–480, 1997.

24. Baker, E., Bouldin, N., Durham, M., Lowell, M., Gonzalez, M., Jodaitis, N., Cruz, L., Torres, I., Torres, M., Adams, S: The Latino health advocacy program: A collaborative lay health advisor approach. *Health Educ Behav* 24(4): 495–509, 1997.

25. Eng, E., Young, R: Lay health advisors as community change agents. *Family and Community Health* 15(1): 24–40, 1992.

26. Service, C., Sabler, E. J. (eds.): *Community Health Education: The Lay Health Advisor Approach*. Durham, NC, Health Care Systems, 1979.

27. Michielutte, R., Sharp, P. C., Dignan, M. B., Blinson, K: Cultural issues in the development of cancer control programs for American Indian populations. *J Health Care Poor Underserved* 5(4): 280–296, 1994.

28. Sharp, P. C., Dignan, M. B., Blinson, K., Konen, J.C., McQuellon, R., Michielutte, R., Cummings, L., Hinojosa, L., Ledford, V: Working with lay health educators in a rural cancer-prevention program. *American Journal of Health Behavior* 22(1): 18–27, 1998.

29. Dignan, M., Sharp, P., Blinson, K., Michielutte, R., Konen, J., Bell, R., Lane, C: Development of a cervical cancer education program for Native American women in North Carolina. *J Cancer Educ* 9: 235–242, 1994.

30. Campbell, D. T., Stanley, J. C: *Experimental and Quasi-Experimental Designs for Research*. Chicago, Rand McNally, 1963.

31. Gittelsohn, J., Harris, S. B., Burris, K. L., Kakegamic, L., Landman, L.T., Sharma, A., Wolever, T. M. S., Logan, A., Barnie, A: Use of ethnographic methods for applied research on diabetes among the Ojibway-Cree in Northern Ontario. *Health Education Quarterly* 23(3): 365–382, 1996.

32. Patton, M. Q: *Qualitative Evaluation and Research Methods* (2nd ed.). Newbury Park, CA, Sage, 1990.

33. Howard, B. V., Cowan, L. D., Go, O., Welty, T. K., Robbins, D. C., Lee, E. T: Adverse effects of diabetes on multiple cardiovascular disease risk factors in women: The Strong Heart Study. *Diabetes Care* 21(8): 1258–1265, 1998.

34. Welty, T. K., Lee, E. T., Yeh, J., Cowan, L. D., Fabsitz, R. R., Le, N. A., Robbins, D. C., Oopik, A. J., Howard, B. V: Cardiovascular disease risk factors among American Indians: The Strong Heart Study. *Am J Epidemiol* 142(3): 269–287, 1995.

35. Howard, B. V., Lee, E. T., Cowan, L. D., Fabsitz, R. R., Howard, W. J., Oopik, A. J., Robbins, D. C., Savage, P. J., Yeh, J. L., Welty, T. K: Coronary heart disease prevalence and its relation to risk factors in American Indians: The Strong Heart Study. *Am J Epidemiol* 142(3): 254–268, 1995.

Lynne Messer is in the Department of Health Behavior and Health Education, School of Public Health, University of North Carolina at Chapel Hill. **Allan Steckler** is in the Department of Health Behavior and Health Education, School of Public Health, University of North Carolina at Chapel Hill. **Mark Dignan** is at the AMC Cancer Research Institute, Denver, Colorado.

Address reprint requests to Lynne Messer, MPH, Department of Health Behavior and Health Education, School of Public Health, University of North Carolina, Chapel Hill, NC 27599-7400; phone: (919) 563-2547; fax: (919) 966-2921: e-mail: lmesser@sph.unc.edu.

20

A Sequential Explanatory Mixed Methods Design to Explain Findings

Selection: Way, N., Stauber, H. Y., Nakkula, M. J., & London, P. (1994). Depression and substance use in two divergent high school cultures: A quantitative and qualitative analysis. *Journal of Youth and Adolescence, 23*(3), 331–357.

Editors' Introduction

Way, Stauber, Nakkula, and London (1994) investigated the relationship between depression and substance use for suburban and urban youth. Their study began with the collection of measures of depression and substance use from samples at two high schools ("QUAN" boxes in Figure 20.0). From the analysis, the authors identified a finding that needed further explanation: substance use was a significant predictor of depression at one school but not the other. In order to explain this difference, the authors thematically analyzed qualitative interview data from participants who had high depression scores to describe the different meanings of substance use across the two schools ("qual" boxes in Figure 20.0). This is an example of a sequential explanatory design to explain initial quantitative results with a follow-up qualitative phase. Highlights of this study include reporting the quantitative and qualitative strands in separate sections so that the reader can easily see the steps in the process, using quantitative results to select the best participants for the qualitative phase, and discussing how the qualitative results provide an explanation for the quantitative results in the discussion.

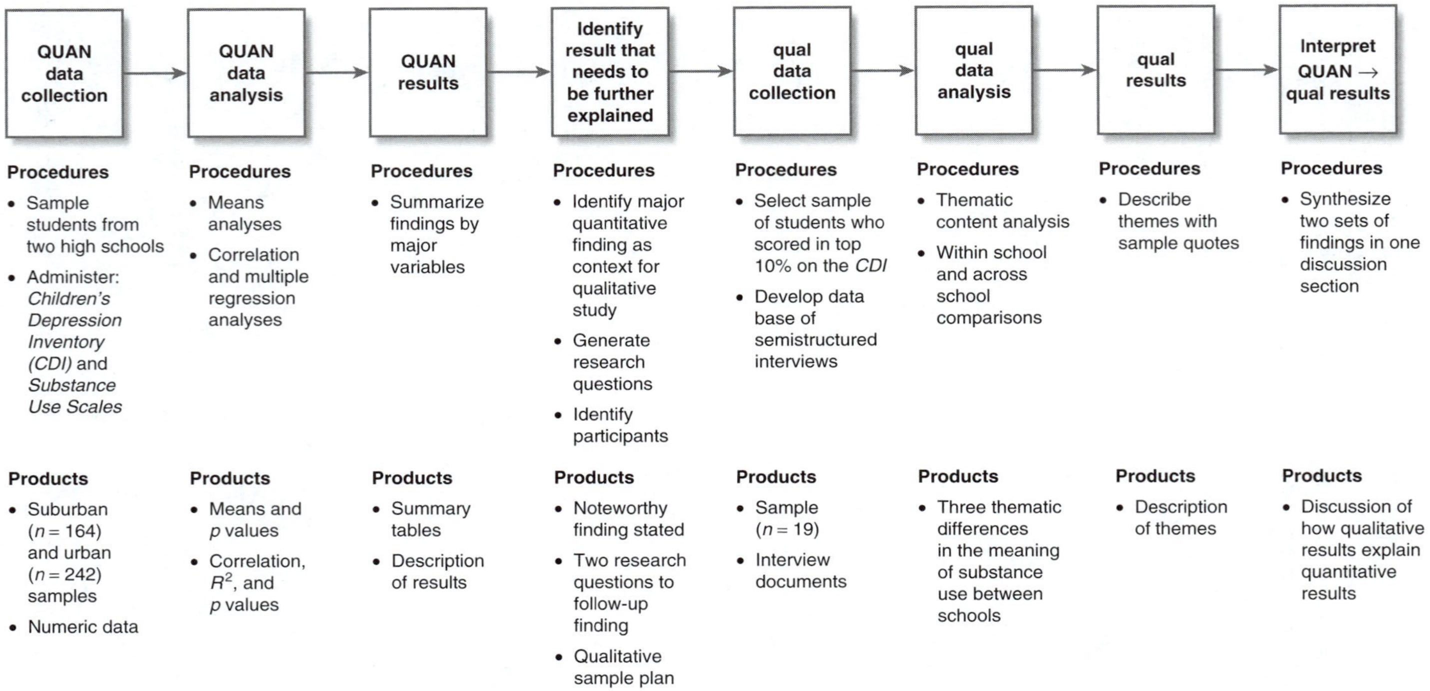

Figure 20.0 Visual Diagram of a Sequential Explanatory Mixed Methods Design to Explain Findings

SOURCE: Based on Way, Stauber, Nakkula, and London (1994).

Depression and Substance Use in Two Divergent High School Cultures

A Quantitative and Qualitative Analysis

Niobe Way[1]
Yale University

Helena Y. Stauber[2]
Harvard University

Michael J. Nakkula[3]
Harvard University

Perry London[4]
Rutgers University

Received September 24, 1992; accepted September 4, 1993

Research has generally concluded that adolescent depression and substance use are strongly interrelated, but has rarely considered how this relationship may

SOURCE: This article is reprinted from Way, N., Stauber, H. Y., Nakkula, M. J., & London, P. (1994). Depression and substance use in two divergent high school cultures: A quantitative and qualitative analysis. *Journal of Youth and Adolescence, 23*(3), 331–357. Reprinted with permission.

The research was funded by the National Institute of Drug Abuse (NIDA), Grant No. 1 R01 DA-06844, Perry London, principal investigator. The views, opinions, and findings contained in their article are not to be construed as NIDA's position or policy.

vary across diverse populations. In this study, we used quantitative and qualitative methods to explore the relationships among depression and cigarette, alcohol, marijuana, and harder drug use across two culturally disparate environments: a suburban and an inner-city high school. Our sample included 164 suburban and 242 inner-city high school students. The students completed Kovacs' Children's Depression Inventory of 1985 and substance use measures derived from various sources. In-depth semistructured interviews were conducted with subjects who scored in the top 10% of the CDI (N = 19) from both schools. Our quantitative findings indicated a positive association between depression and cigarette, marijuana, and harder drug use among the suburban students, and no association between depression and the use of any substances for the urban students. There were no significant differences in levels of reported depression across samples. However, with the exception of marijuana use, suburban students reported greater involvement in substance use than urban students. Our qualitative analyses suggest that across-school differences in the relationships among depression and substance use may be related to the varied meanings of depression and substance use that are informed by cultural context.

Introduction

Over the past 30 years an abundance of research on adolescents and young adults has investigated the relationships among depression and substance use. The results of these studies suggest that adolescents or young adults who are heavy cigarette, drug, or alcohol users are more likely to show signs of depression than light or nonusers (Aneshensel and Huba, 1983; Braucht et al., 1973; Kaminer, 1991; Kaplan et al., 1980; Kaplan et al., 1984; Kennedy et al., 1987; Paton et al., 1977; Reinherz et al., 1991; Robins and Przybeck, 1985; Shiffman and Wills, 1985; Simons et al., 1991). Researchers and practitioners have typically concluded that there is a strong association between depression and substance use among adolescents (Blau et al., 1988; Kaplan et al., 1984; Reinherz et al., 1991; Simons et al., 1988).

There has been little research, however, that has explored the effects of gender, ethnicity, social class, or environment (e.g., urban vs. suburban) on the relationships among depression and substance use. The few studies that have examined such sociodemographic differences have concluded that this type of investigation is critical (Dembo et al., 1979; Paton and Kandel, 1978; Prendergast, 1974; Siegel and Ehrlich, 1989). Paton and Kandel (1978) report widely disparate relationships between depression and substance use among different ethnic groups, and between males and females within selected ethnic groups. They found no relationship between depression and drug use among either black or Puerto Rican adolescents; however, this relationship was highly significant for white adolescents, with higher levels of depression associated with higher levels of drug use. Furthermore, the relationship between depression and drug use was significantly stronger for the white girls in the sample than for the white boys.

Siegel and Ehrlich (1989) report socioeconomic status (SES) differences in levels of depression among adolescent substance abusers. The high SES, white adolescent substance abusers scored significantly higher on the depression scale (The Children's Depression Inventory) than the low SES, white adolescent substance abusers. Their findings suggest that the relationships among depression and substance use may vary across social class. Siegel and Ehrlich (1989) state that the low success rates among treatment programs for drug-abusing adolescents may be related to a failure to "take into account the possibility that adolescents from different ethnic or socio-economic backgrounds may take drugs (and alcohol) for different reasons" (p. 925). Drug and alcohol use may not be related to depression for lower SES adolescents as it is for higher SES adolescents.

While researchers have examined gender, ethnic, social class, or environmental (e.g., rural vs. urban) differences in levels of drug use (Kaplan *et al.*, 1984; Kaplan *et al.*, 1984; Siegel and Ehrlich, 1989), type of drug use (Hager *et al.*, 1971; Harris, 1971; Siegel and Ehrlich, 1989; Smart and Fejer, 1969), and levels of depression (Baron and Perron, 1986; Doerfler *et al.*, 1988; Kaplan *et al.*, 1980; Siegel and Ehrlich, 1989), they rarely have looked for such sociodemographic differences in the *relationships* among depression and substance use.

In the present study we used both quantitative and qualitative methods to explore the relationships among depression and cigarette, alcohol, marijuana, and harder drug use in two culturally divergent school environments: an inner-city public high school and a suburban public high school. The inner-city school and the suburban school are characterized by differences in racial and ethnic composition, social class, geographic location, and educational and community resources. We assume that differences we may find between the two schools reflect a complex combination of these social class, racial, ethnic, and environmental factors. Rather than attempting to tease out the differential effects of such factors, as was done in the previously cited studies (e.g., Paton and Kandel, 1978), our analyses are conducted at a more macro level where individual contributions coalesce to form the distinct community of the school culture.

We conducted an integrative analysis of quantitative and qualitative data in which quantitative results were used to select participants, generate questions, and provide a context for the qualitative analysis. Therefore, the paper is divided into two methods and results sections, one for the quantitative analysis and one for the contingent qualitative analysis. The two sets of findings are synthesized through a single discussion section.

Quantitative Analysis

Method

Subjects

The sample included 164 students from a suburban high school (grades nine [$N = 44$], ten [$N = 36$], eleven [$N = 35$], and twelve [$N = 49$], 75 boys, 89 girls) and 242 students from an inner-city high school (grades nine [$N = 45$], ten [$N = 33$], eleven [$N = 68$], and twelve [$N = 96$], 108 boys and 134 girls). Both schools were located in the Greater Boston area. The students from the suburban high school primarily described themselves as Irish-American (26%), Italian-American (11%), Irish and Italian-American (5%), or white with no ethnicity specified (45%). The students from the inner-city high school primarily described themselves as African-American (35%), Puerto Rican or Dominican (31%), Haitian (12%), white (7%), or American Indian (4%).

The suburban students came from predominantly middle- or working-class families, while the urban students came from predominantly working-class or poor families. These variations in social class were inferred from the parents' educational backgrounds, their current occupations, the families' housing situations, and the percentage of students who receive subsidized lunches (see Table 20.1).

In addition to social class differences, the schools had substantially different dropout rates: It is projected that 32% of the freshman students in the urban school vs. 4% in the suburban school will not graduate. Due to this important distinction, our study does not attempt a broad description of the comparative experiences of inner-city and suburban youth. However, while the elevated dropout rate in the urban school restricts the generalizability of our findings, our inclusion of students from the four high school grade levels makes it possible to capture the experiences of numerous inner-city students who are potential dropouts. As such, while this study does not reflect the behavioral and emotional characteristics of students who have dropped out, neither does it provide a uniform picture of inner-city students who have fully circumvented risk for dropping out.

In both schools, students were recruited for the study through presentations made to their classrooms by members of our research team. In the suburban school where tracking exists, equal numbers of required courses were targeted for presentation within each academic track, allowing us to reach a sample of students that was representative of the whole school population. In the urban school there is no tracking, but large numbers of students receive special education services. As such, we targeted proportional numbers of

Table 20.1   Student Reports of Parent Job-Type, Parent Education Levels, Family Housing, and School-Reported Percentages of Subsidized Lunches

	Parents' jobs			
	Suburban school		Urban school	
	Mothers	Fathers	Mothers	Fathers
"Professional"	21%	40%	4%	4%
"Semiprofessional"	16	10	9	6
Business person	6	9	8	8
Own business	1	8	5	6
Blue-collar job	12	19	25	39
Office-clerical	22	3	4	0
Other	5	4	5	5
Unemployed	16	4	39	20
Don't know	0	1	4	13

	Parents' education			
	Suburban school		Urban school	
	Mothers	Fathers	Mothers	Fathers
Graduate school	11%	16%	2%	2%
College grads	23	35	7	7
Some college	18	14	9	9
High school grads	25	12	21	16
Trade school	14	13	7	7
Less than twelfth grade	5	5	33	23
Don't know	4	5	23	35

	Housing	
	Suburban school	Urban school
Project housing	0%	19%
Two- or three-family homes	12	36
Apartments	4	28
Single-family homes	84	15
Rent home	12	71
Own home	82	27

	Students eligible for subsidized lunches	
	Suburban school	Urban school
	3%	80%

mainstream vs. special education classrooms for our presentations. Across all of the classrooms from which we recruited in both schools, 80–90% of the students agreed to participate. Of those students who agreed to participate, 98% in both schools agreed to *both* the questionnaire and the interview. Participants were paid five dollars for completing the questionnaire measures and five dollars to participate in a follow-up interview.

Questionnaires

Children's Depression Inventory (CDI). All students completed the CDI (Kovacs, 1985), a 27-item questionnaire designed to assess the severity of depressive symptoms from mid-childhood through late adolescence. The scale, based on the BDI for adults, measures symptoms such as disturbances in mood, eating behaviors, self-esteem, and interpersonal behavior. For each item, students are asked to check one of three descriptions that best apply to them during the last 2 weeks (e.g., "I am sad all the time," "I am sad many times," "I am sad once in a while"). Responses to each item are scored on a 0–2 scale (from *least depressed* to *most depressed*). A total score of 19 or above, out of a maximum of 54 points, is considered a strong indicator of depression (Kovacs, 1982). According to Kovacs (1983), the CDI's "readability" is at the first grade level, thus increasing its accessibility to students in a high school population at various levels of literacy. The CDI has been used with urban and suburban samples and has typically indicated minor or no significant differences by grade, sex or race (Doerfler *et al.*, 1988; Finch *et al.*, 1985; Kovacs, 1980–1981). The CDI has shown high internal consistency ranging from .71 to .86, and test-retest reliability ranging from .38 to .87, depending on the length of time between tests and the population studied (Kovacs, 1983; Saylor *et al.*, 1984). It has also been reported to be strongly related to other self-report measures of constructs associated with depression (e.g., self-concept, hopelessness, and anxiety; Doerfler *et al.*, 1988; Kovacs, 1982; Way *et al.*, 1990). In the present study, inter-item reliability, using Chronbach's α, was .80 for the urban school and .88 for the suburban school.

Substance Use Scales. Our substance use scales were derived from the Institute of Behavioral Science's Health Questionnaire (Donovan *et al.*, 1985) and the California Substance Use Survey (Skager and Firth, 1988). Additional questions were developed in consultation with students from each school who advised us on the use of appropriate and accessible language for their age group and cultures.[5] Separate measures for cigarettes, alcohol, marijuana, and harder drugs (e.g., cocaine and LSD) employed Likert-type scales to assess the age at which the student started using the particular substance, the frequency of use, the amount of use at any one time, and when, where, and with whom the use typically occurs. Total scores for each measure included age of initiation, frequency, amount, and patterns of use.

The alcohol use measure, for example, was comprised of 9 equally weighted questions: 1 for age of initiation ("How old were you when you had your first whole drink?"), 2 for frequency of use (e.g., "How often do you drink alcohol?"), 2 for amount of use at any one time (e.g., "When you drink, how many whole drinks do you usually have at a time?"), and 4 for patterns of use (i.e., "When do you usually drink alcohol?" "What kind of alcohol do you drink most often?" "Have you even gotten drunk during school?" "In the past year, have you ever been too drunk or hung over to stay at school?"). An overall alcohol score, is the summed total of the individual responses to each of these nine equally weighted questions. Rather than simply assessing frequency of use, the alcohol scale taps into other factors that contribute to the severity of alcohol-use problems. As a case in point, a student who reports drinking on average three beers at a time every week during the weekends, and has occasionally gotten drunk during school would receive a higher score on the alcohol measure than a peer who reports drinking a six pack of beer at a time about once a month during the weekends, and has never gotten drunk during school. However, if this latter student has occasionally gotten drunk during school, then he or she would receive the same score as the former student. Scaling and scoring procedures were similar for each of the substance use measures.[6]

For the urban school, inter-item reliability for cigarettes was .82, for alcohol .86, for marijuana .78, and for harder drugs .73. For the suburban school, inter-item reliability for cigarettes was .86, for alcohol .84, for marijuana .82, and for harder drugs .92.

Procedure

Parental consent forms were distributed and collected prior to questionnaire administration. Consent forms provided a brief description of the study and emphasized the confidentiality of student responses. In addition, prior to completing the questionnaires, all students were verbally assured of full confidentiality. Questionnaires were identified by number codes rather than student names. The researchers maintained a list with participants' names and corresponding code numbers for the purpose of identifying students for follow-up interviews.

All 406 participants completed the questionnaires during one class period. To maximize the comfort of participants and the likelihood of honest responses, teachers were asked to leave the classroom during questionnaire administration. At least two research team members were present throughout the administrations to distribute and collect questionnaires, monitor student contact, and respond to students' questions and concerns. The use of simple language made the questionnaires accessible to most students. However, in a small number of cases ($N = 8$) where reading deficiencies were profound, a team member read the questions aloud to students in a private setting.

Results

Comparisons Across Schools

Means Analysis. The mean scores and standard deviations for depression and substance use, and a comparison of means across schools are shown in Table 20.2. Levels of reported depression did not differ significantly across schools. The mean depression score (9.2) and the range of scores (0–31) in the suburban school were very similar to the mean depression score (9.4) and range (0–29) in the urban school. There were significant differences between schools, however, in reported prevalence of students' drug and alcohol use. Suburban students reported using significantly more cigarettes, alcohol, and harder drugs than the urban students.[7] The average score for marijuana use was similar across schools (see Table 20.2).

Correlation and Multiple Regression Analyses. The results of analyses of correlation among depression and different substances are shown in Table 20.3. In both schools, all forms of substance use were highly intercorrelated. Depression scores among the students in the suburban sample were positively correlated with cigarette use ($r = .33$, $p < .0001$), with marijuana use ($r = .24$, $p < .0021$), and with harder drug use ($r = .22$, $p < .0037$). Depression and alcohol use was not significantly correlated ($r = .14$, $p < .074$); however, the nonsignificant correlation went in the same direction as the other significant correlations. A multiple regression analysis showed that substance use

Table 20.2   Mean Scores, Standard Deviations, and Comparisons of Means Across Schools[a]

	Suburban school	Urban school	p Value
Depression	9.2 (7.1)	9.4 (5.9)	NS
Cigarette smoking	5.5 (5.9)	3.7 (4.9)	.001
Alcohol use	16.8 (10.1)	11.7 (8.4)	.0001
Marijuana use	6.8 (6.7)	6.4 (5.9)	NS
Harder drug use	24.0 (6.0)	22.2 (1.1)	.001

[a]Standard deviations are in parentheses.

(the combined effect of cigarettes, alcohol, marijuana, and harder drugs) explained 16% of the variability ($p < .001$) in depression for the suburban sample. Depression, however, was not significantly correlated with *any* of these substances in the urban sample.

Comparisons Within Schools

Gender Differences

Means Analyses. Means and standard deviations for depression and each substance, for boys and girls across both schools, are shown in Table 20.4. In the urban sample, males and females did not have significantly different depression scores, yet the girls were overrepresented in the top 10% of the sample, with 19 of the 24 highest depression scores.[8] The findings were similar for our suburban sample: males and females did not have significantly different depression scores, but again, the girls were overrepresented in the top 10% of the sample with 11 of the 16 highest depression scores.

Table 20.3   Correlations Among Depression and Substance Use

| | Suburban school | | | | |
	Depression	Cigarette smoking	Alcohol use	Marijuana use	Harder drug use
Depression	–	$.33^a$	.14	$.24^b$	$.22^b$
Cigarette smoking		–	$.58^a$	$.65^a$	$.41^a$
Alcohol use			–	$.57^a$	$.39^a$
Marijuana use				–	$.72^a$
Harder drug use					–
	Urban school				
	Depression	Cigarette smoking	Alcohol use	Marijuana use	Harder drug use
Depression	–	.06	−.04	−.06	.07
Cigarette smoking		–	$.53^a$	$.42^a$	$.22^a$
Alcohol use			–	$.54^a$	$.23^a$
Marijuana use				–	$.26^a$
Harder drug use					–

$^a p < .0001.$

$^b p < .01.$

Females in the suburban sample used significantly less alcohol, marijuana, and harder drugs than males (see Table 20.4). There was no gender difference for cigarette use. Urban girls' scores on cigarettes, alcohol, marijuana, and harder drugs were not significantly different from boys' scores. However, when we looked at differences between girls and boys within the dominant ethnic groups in the urban school (African-American, Puerto Rican, and Haitian), we found that African-American girls, on average, scored significantly lower on the marijuana scale than African-American boys (means = 6.6 and 10.3, respectively, $p < .03$). No other statistically significant gender differences in substance use were found within or across ethnic groups.

Correlation and Multiple Regression Analyses. The results of the correlation analyses for the depression and substance use scores for girls and boys can be seen in Table 20.5. Similar to the findings for the entire urban sample, data from urban girls alone and from urban boys alone revealed no significant correlation between depression and substance use of any kind.

For the girls in the suburban sample, depression was correlated with the use of cigarettes ($r = .40, p < .0001$), alcohol ($r = .21, p < .05$), marijuana ($r = .36, p < .0006$), and harder drugs ($r = .36, p < .0006$). For the boys in the suburban sample, there were significant correlations between depression and the use of cigarettes ($r = .24, p < .03$), marijuana ($r = .22, p < .05$), and harder drugs ($r = .25, p < .03$), but not between depression and alcohol use.

These correlational findings suggest that the relationship between depression and substance use may be stronger for girls than for boys in the suburban sample. To test this possibility, multiple regression models were created using interaction effects of gender and each of the substances (separately) in

Table 20.4   Means and Standard Deviations Across Gender Within Each School[a]

	Suburban school			Urban school		
	Girls	Boys	pValue	Girls	Boys	pValue
Depression	9.8 (7.7)	8.5 (6.4)	NS	10.1 (6.1)	8.6 (5.5)	NS
Cigarette smoking[b]	5.2 (6.0)	5.8 (5.8)	NS	4.2 (5.2)	3.1 (4.5)	NS
Alcohol use	14.5 (9.6)	19.4 (10.1)	.002	11.0 (8.2)	12.5 (8.8)	NS
Marijuana use	5.3 (4.6)	8.6 (8.3)	.004	5.9 (5.2)	7.1 (6.6)	NS
Harder drug use	22.8 (3.3)	25.4 (9.2)	.03	22.1 (1.1)	22.2 (1.2)	NS

[a]Standard deviations are in parentheses.

[b]Standard deviations are high relative to the means for cigarette smoking because the analyses include nonsmokers, which lowers the means. This results in a wide range of variation above each mean for smokers.

Table 20.5   Pearson Correlations Between Depression and Substance Use Across Gender Within Each School

| | Urban | | Suburban | |
	Females Depression	Males Depression	Females Depression	Males Depression
Cigarette smoking	.07	.07	.40[a]	.24[b]
Alcohol use	.01	−.10	.21[b]	.10
Marijuana use	−.04	−.05	.35[a]	.23[b]
Harder drug use	.07	.08	.36[a]	.26[b]

[a]p < .001.

[b]p < .05.

the prediction of depression. These multiple regression models revealed that gender interacted significantly with marijuana and with harder drugs in the prediction of depression. Marijuana alone accounted for 5% of the variance in depression in the suburban school ($p < .002$). Although the main effect of gender ($p < .07$) did not significantly enhance the prediction of depression ($R^2 = .07$), the addition of the interaction variable for marijuana and gender ($p < .03$) to the model containing both main effects did significantly enhance the explained variance in depression ($R^2 = .10$). The picture was similar for harder drug use and gender. Harder drug use alone accounted for 5% of the variance in depression in the suburban school ($p < .003$). The addition of gender ($p < .09$) to the model was not significant ($R^2 = .06$); however, the addition of the interaction variable for harder drug use and gender ($p < .007$) to the model significantly enhanced the explained variance in depression ($R^2 = .11$). Gender did not interact significantly with alcohol or cigarettes in the prediction of depression.

These multiple regression findings indicate that, as suggested by the correlational findings, there are significant gender differences in the relationship between depression and marijuana use, and between depression and harder drug use within the suburban sample. However, there are no significant gender differences in the relationship between depression and alcohol use or depression and cigarette use.

Grade Differences

Analysis of Variance. The grade differences in reported levels of depression and cigarette, alcohol, marijuana, and harder drug use within the two schools are shown in Table 20.6. Within the suburban school, there were significant differences between grades in levels of cigarette ($p < .0005$), alcohol ($p < .0001$), and marijuana use ($p < .0001$). Students in the eleventh and twelfth grades reported greater alcohol use than did the ninth- and tenth-grade students, and greater cigarette use than the tenth-grade students. The twelfth graders also reported heavier patterns of marijuana use than the ninth and tenth graders, while the eleventh graders reported a heavier pattern of marijuana use than did the ninth graders. Within the urban school, grade differences were found only for alcohol use ($p < .01$). Eleventh graders reported greater alcohol use than did twelfth graders. No other grade differences were found in patterns of substance use in the urban school (see Table 20.6).

Multiple Regression Analyses. Interactions between grade level and substance use were examined to determine whether they predicted depression. No significant interaction effects were found in either school. For each grade, the relationships between depression and substance use of each type were similar to the overall relations (i.e., across all grades) between these variables in each school.

Table 20.6   Mean Differences Across Grade for Depression and Substance Use

	Suburban school						
	Grades						
	9	10	11	12	F value	Scheffé contrasts	N
Depression	9.9	7.5	9.2	9.8	.93	NS	163
Cigarette smoking	4.6	2.7	7.6	7.2	6.26[a]	10 < 11 and 12	160
Alcohol use	10.8	13.5	20.4	21.8	14.80[a]	9 and 10 < 11 and 12	162
Marijuana use	4.1	4.5	8.7	9.5	8.05[a]	9 and 10 < 12, 9 < 11	160
Hard drug use	22.4	22.2	25.2	25.9	3.29	NS	157

	Urban school						
	Grades						
	9	10	11	12	F value	Scheffé Contrasts	N
Depression	7.8	8.8	8.9	10.8	3.08	NS	231
Cigarette smoking	4.6	4.0	4.4	3.1	1.41	NS	230
Alcohol use	11.4	14.5	13.6	9.6	4.02[b]	12 < 11	224
Marijuana use	5.8	8.4	6.9	5.8	1.74	NS	225
Hard drug use	22.0	22.0	22.3	22.3	.87	NS	222

[a] $p < .001$.
[b] $p < .01$.

Qualitative Analysis

Method

Perhaps our most noteworthy quantitative finding was the distinction between the two schools in patterns of substance use as predictors of depression. Depression was significantly correlated with cigarette, marijuana, and harder drug use in the suburban school, whereas in the urban school, depression was not significantly correlated with any type of substance use. As an initial step in exploring possible explanations for this finding, we analyzed interviews from the most depressed students (according to the CDI) in both schools.

Our analyses focused on the following questions: (a) How might students with similarly high depression levels across the two schools differ in their perspectives on substance use? (b) How might these possible differences in perspectives begin to explain why depression and substance use are differentially related across the schools?

Subjects

Our qualitative analyses were conducted on interview data from the 19 students across both schools who scored in the top 10% of our sample on the CDI, with depression scores ranging from 19 to 30. This range is consistent with the top 10% of scores reported by Kovacs (1985) in her large normative sample for the CDI. The 19 students comprise all of the subjects in the top 10% of the CDI scores who were interviewed.[9]

The suburban sample included 10 students: four boys (1 ninth grader, 1 tenth grader, 1 eleventh grader, and 1 twelfth grader) and 6 girls (3 ninth graders, 1 tenth grader, 1 eleventh grader, and 1 twelfth grader). Nine of the students were white and one was African-American. Our urban sample included 9 students; 2 boys (a ninth grader and a twelfth grader) and seven girls (1 ninth grader, 2 tenth graders, 2 eleventh graders, and 2 twelfth graders). Of the 2 boys, 1 was Haitian and the other Puerto Rican; of the 7 girls, 3 were African-American, 2 were Puerto Rican, 1 was Haitian, and 1 was white.

The Interview

The interview is semi-structured, and designed to explore the extent, nature, and quality of the participants' thoughts and feelings about a range of personal, interpersonal, and behavioral phenomena. The interview process is guided by open-ended questions that lead into topical areas including substance use. Initial responses to interview questions (such as "How often do you drink?" "What is it that you like about drinking?" "Why don't you drink more than you do?") were probed by the interviewer to invite increasingly detailed and thoughtful reports of students' self-perspectives on their substance use or nonuse. These kinds of questions were asked for each substance (e.g., "Why do you think you haven't tried marijuana?" "Why do you smoke cigarettes?" etc.). The goal of the interview is to explore the meaning and attributions that the students assign to their behavior.

Procedure

Interviews were conducted by advanced doctoral students in counseling or developmental psychology. Participants were interviewed in one-on-one meetings held in private rooms at the respective school sites. We assured all participating students of full confidentiality.

Our interview analyses consisted of detailed readings of students' perspectives on substance use and their reasons for choosing to use or abstain from use. Typical of many qualitative approaches, our method involved a content analysis in which interview data were partitioned into content domains for the comparison of themes across individual cases (Strauss, 1987). Three trained readers independently read for common themes in students' descriptions of their substance use patterns. Themes were identified and compared within and across schools. Only those themes that were identified by all three readers *independently* were considered common themes in the interviews. The following results section describes the common themes detected from the interviews of the urban and suburban depressed sample by the three data analysts.

Results

Differences in Substance Use

The interviews indicated that substance use was more pervasive among the depressed students in the suburban sample than among those in the inner-city sample. Seven of the 10 students in the suburban sample reported active substance use. Among the 7 current substance users, all reported smoking cigarettes, 6 reported drinking alcohol, 2 reported smoking marijuana, and 1 reported using harder drugs. In contrast to the students at the suburban school, only 3 of the 9 depressed inner-city teens reported active substance use. Of those 3, 2 claimed to smoke cigarettes and drink alcohol, and the third claimed only to drink alcohol. None of the depressed students in the inner-city sample reported current use of marijuana or experimentation (current or past) with drugs harder than marijuana.

Differences in Meaning

The readers independently identified three common differences across the two schools in the ways that these depressed youth spoke about substance use.

Substance Use: Escape from Problems or Cause of Problems? Five of the 10 depressed students at the suburban school spoke about cigarettes, alcohol, marijuana, and harder drugs as a way to "escape" problems or "relax," while only 1 out of 9 depressed students in the inner-city drew an association between substance use and "escaping" or "relaxing." Among most of the depressed urban youth (8 out of 9), substance use was described as a cause of stress, rather than as an escape from it. In contrast, in the suburban school, only 4 out of 10 depressed students mentioned problems that have resulted or could result from using substances. While both ways of describing substance use (an escape from problems and a source of problems or stress) were almost equally evident (5 vs. 4) in the suburban school, in the urban school, the view that substance use causes problems was clearly predominant among the depressed students.

Included among students' responses from the suburban school is that of Millie, a tenth grader with a history of "off-again-on-again" cigarette and marijuana use, who reports resuming smoking cigarettes after a breakup with her boyfriend: "I got mad and started smoking [cigarettes] again [and] I was smoking weed all the time because I wanted to escape." Janice, a ninth grader at the same high school, smokes about eight cigarettes a day and claims that "something about it relaxes me—if I had to quit now I'd probably get real tense." She also views alcohol as a way to relax, even though "it makes you tired afterwards." Nicole, another ninth grader who smokes about a pack of cigarettes a day, says "I just like the way it makes me feel—it relaxes me sometimes." Drinking for Nicole is one way to "laugh a lot and forget about my problems." Alex, a junior at the suburban high school who has been heavily involved in drugs for many years, claims that while he does not necessarily use drugs to "run away," he views them as "a good way to get away." He also states that he uses LSD and other drugs "not *just* as an escape but because I like it."

In contrast, Roxie, a sophomore from the urban sample who occasionally drinks alcohol "but only a little bit," states that she sees no benefit to using, only costs:

Smoke, I think it smells. . . . Why, why should you risk the point of drinking, you know? I see it as pointless, I guess, to get drunk and have a hangover the next morning. . . . I don't see what's the point in doing those things. It'll mess your head up.

Glen, a freshman at the inner-city school, who occasionally drinks alcohol, says he does not want to drink more than he does because he see the bad health effects drinking has had on his father. He also says he does not want to use marijuana because he watches his friends smoke and realizes that it leads only to problems. When asked by the interviewer why he stays away from marijuana, he says:

> Just, you cut school, people use it in school, my friends, before school starts and they all be dazed and they got a headache and stuff like that. I don't want to get that.

Vera, a sophomore at the inner-city school who occasionally smokes ciga-rettes and drinks "sips" of alcohol claims that she controls her use of these substances because she thinks using them often is "stupid" and pointless. She has decided to stop using marijuana because she had a bad experience with it and believes that using drugs just leads to trouble:

> Because to me I think that cigarettes are just like weed. Because I'm like, none of them. Cigarettes always gave me nothing. All weed gave me was that [a "bad trip" on marijuana]. You know, I could have died. . . . It was so scary. . . . So it's like dumb you know, why people do it. Now I think why do they do it? I mean they could die.

Mara, a senior, who does not use any substances, claims that she does not drink because:

> Sometimes when you get drunk you might react improperly, and then you might hit someone and hurt someone that you—that's close to you. So I don't want it to affect anyone.

With regard to drugs, she claims the following:

> Drugs can make people very, very, very—not unattractive, but they might look like someone who is sick and I don't want to look like someone—when people's on the diet and they never eat—they become skinny, skinny and you see bones only. . . . They look like that when they do drugs all the time and never stop.

Yolanda, a freshman in the urban school, claims that she does not use drugs because "I just hear too many people dying . . . of overdose . . . I don't want to be one of them."

In short, substance use was depicted primarily as a cause of problems by the depressed students in the inner-city sample. In the depressed suburban sample, by contrast, substance use was described both as an escape and as a potential problem. It is important to note that the depressed students from each school who depicted substance use as a cause of problems included both substance users and nonusers.

Interpersonal Relationships and Substance Use. Students from both the urban and suburban samples discussed the connection between substance use and relationships with family and friends. However, there were differences between the two samples in the way that relationships were reported to affect their substance use decisions. Six out of 10 of the depressed students from the suburban sample emphasized the fear of disappointing or angering someone important to them as a primary inhibitor of substance use, while only 1 out of 9 inner-city students mentioned these factors as reasons not to use. On the other hand, most of the depressed inner-city students (7 out of 9) cited examples of the negative impact drugs or alcohol has had on someone close to them and on people in the community, and stated that this influenced their decisions to abstain or use at low levels. Only 3 out of 10 depressed students from the suburban sample mentioned seeing the negative effects on others as a reason to abstain or modulate use.

Alisann, a senior at the suburban school, stopped using LSD and cocaine because of disapproval from friends. Gaby, a junior at the suburban school, has decided not to drink more than two bottles of beer at a time "because like my parents, they're trusting me tonight, and look what I'm doing, they'll never be able to trust me again and I wouldn't drink that much, you know." And Terence, a suburban freshman, told the interviewer how he could possibly lose friends if he used drugs, and "I don't think my mother would like it either."

Unlike these suburban teens, stories from the depressed, inner-city teens speak poignantly of the negative impact of substance use on people close to them. For example, Tara, a senior at the inner-city school, talks about earlier childhood memories of her mother's heavy use of marijuana and alcohol, recalling that "when she was high or drunk she was the meanest person in the world." Such memories, Tara says, make her want to prevent similar experiences for her own children:

> The reason why I don't do it [drugs], because my mother used to do it, and now because I got two kids. So I said I'm not even gonna—I mean, I don't want them to grow up the way I grew up. So I'm not even gonna do it.

Glen, an urban freshman, says he does not want to drink because he sees the effects on his alcoholic father:

> I don't want to be like him, I don't want to drink that much. Because I think some-
> times he's going to pass away because of his liver—because he drinks too much.

In addition, he says he does not use marijuana or cocaine because he has
watched his ex-best friend and his uncle become heavily involved in drugs
and destroy their lives. Similarly, Elena, an urban junior, has decided not to
drink anymore because she has seen the negative impact of alcohol on a boy
whom she liked.

Relationships are mentioned among both the suburban and urban students
as influencing their decision to abstain or modulate their use of substances.
However, the specific effects of their relationships differed: At the suburban
school, the majority of students cited a reluctance to disappoint others, whereas
in the urban school, almost all of the teenagers stated that seeing the negative
impact on others was one of their main reasons to modulate or abstain from use.

Peer Pressure and Substance Use. Six of the 10 depressed students in the suburban sample reported succumbing to peer pressure to use substances, while
none of the depressed students in the urban sample reported being influenced
by peer pressure to use or not to use substances. Five of these urban students
explicitly stated that they have avoided peer pressure, while none of the
depressed suburban students spoke about avoiding peer pressure.

A suburban sophomore, Millie, provided this telling account of peer pressure:

> I don't like drinking, I don't enjoy it, but everyone else was partying so what
> else is there to do. . . . I don't want to drink but I want to have a good time
> with everybody so I do.

Millie adds that when she is at a party drinking she is afraid that she would
accept harder drugs if someone were to ask her. Blane, a suburban senior,
says he has recently stopped drinking, and that doing so required his complete disassociation from all of his friends who drink. He said the pressure
to drink when he was with them would have prevented his efforts toward
abstinence. Terence, a suburban freshman, says that while he has not yet
experienced pressure to use substances, he can imagine drinking to fit
in at a party "but that hasn't happened yet." Alisann, a suburban senior,
openly acknowledges that she began to smoke and drink because her friends
were doing it. However, she said she eventually stopped because she
switched friends and her current friends disapprove of her drinking and
using drugs. MaryAnn, a suburban freshman, says that she has increased the
number of cigarettes she smokes a day "not because of any reason—just
because of the kids I've been hanging around with increased, so I've just
increased and there's no reason why I have."

In contrast, Elena a junior at the inner-city school, stresses her independent stance with her friends:

> If my friends choose to do it, they do it. But they know me. They know me, I don't do it [use substances]. If I wanted to do it, I'd do it, but they have [no] control over me. . . . They know that I'll do what I want to do when I want to do it, and they can't tell me.

Mara, an inner-city senior, matter-of-factly states "I don't do drugs just because I don't want to do it." Glen, a freshman, claims that there is peer pressure to use marijuana but that he "just stays out of that." But, he adds, he feels pressure from his father to drink and he finds that kind of pressure harder to resist. Yolanda and Roxy, a freshman and sophomore, respectively, say that they are aware of peer pressure to use substances but that they have never felt it personally. Yolanda says the pressure has not affected her because nobody in her family or among her friends drinks or uses drugs. In sum, the suburban depressed students report being more influenced by peer pressure to use substances than their counterparts in the urban sample.

Summary and Discussion

This comparative study of urban and suburban high school students found between-school similarities in levels of reported depression, differences in levels of reported substance use, and most importantly, differences in the *relationships* among depression and substance use. In addition, our qualitative analyses provide possible explanations for the quantitative differences revealed in the relationships among depression and substance use across the two schools.

It is noteworthy, in our quantitative findings, that levels of depression were similar across the urban and suburban school samples. This finding stands in contrast to what one might expect given the relatively more stressful environment of the inner-city. It is possible that inner-city adolescents may develop psychological and emotional resilience in response to the extraordinary stresses of their social environment, resulting in levels of depression that do not exceed what might be expected in other populations of adolescents.

While there were no significant gender differences in the mean level of depression within each school, girls were overrepresented in the top 10% of depression scores in both schools, suggesting gender differences in the severity, if not the overall prevalence, of depression. The lack of significant gender differences in mean depression scores on the CDI is consistent with previous findings in other large scale studies (Doerfler *et al.*, 1988; Green, 1980; Kovacs, 1983; Weissman *et al.*, 1980). However, similar to our findings, studies that have looked beyond the mean scores on the depression scale have found, typically, that more girls score in the higher range of depression scores on the CDI than boys (McCauley et al., 1988; Reinherz et al., 1991; Worchel et al., 1987).

Our failure to find grade differences in levels of depression within either school is consistent with previous findings on the relationship between age and depression among adolescents (Doerfler et al., 1988; Green, 1980; Kovacs, 1983; Weissman et al., 1980). The CDI has been administered to children and adolescents from varying backgrounds and has consistently revealed no significant relationship between the age of the respondent and the severity of self-rated depressive symptomatology (Doerfler et al., 1988; Weissman et al., 1980).

The suburban school students in our study reported higher levels of cigarette, alcohol, and harder drug use than the inner-city school students, while there were equal levels of reported marijuana use in both schools. These findings are similar to related research that has found a lower rate of reported drug use among African-American youth when compared with other ethnic groups such as European-Americans (Darling and Brown, 1992; McCord, 1990). When interpreting our findings, however, one must consider the drop-out rates of public education. The inner-city school, which is quite typical of urban public schools, has a drop-out rate approximately eight times higher than that of the suburban school (32% vs. 4% respectively). Our school-based study, therefore, excludes those adolescents who have left school, perhaps as a result of substance use problems or other high-risk behaviors. It is important to remember, however, that not only were there equal levels of reported marijuana use across the two schools, but the distribution of cigarette, marijuana, and alcohol use was normal in both schools. Therefore, the exclusion of many of the urban dropouts did not lead to the exclusion of urban alcohol and drug users.[10]

Levels of reported substance use differed by gender and by grade in the suburban school; in the urban school, alcohol use varied by grade, and marijuana use differed only by gender for the African-American youth. These findings are somewhat similar to those of other studies, which have found age and gender differences in levels of substance use among adolescents; younger adolescents and girls have reported less substance use than older adolescents and boys respectively (Andrews et al., 1992). However, contrary to findings in previous studies, our data from the urban school indicate that younger adolescents were not less likely to use cigarettes, marijuana, or harder drugs than older adolescents, and with the exception of marijuana use among African-American youth, girls were not less likely to use substances than boys. The finding that African-American girls used significantly less marijuana than African-American boys is similar to the finding among Caucasian youth in the suburban school.

A possible explanation for this lack of grade differences in the level of substance use in the urban sample is that drugs may be more accessible to adolescents not yet in high school in the inner-city than they are for their peers in the suburbs. Therefore, urban adolescents who decide to experiment with substances may begin at an earlier age (e.g., seventh or eighth grade) than their peers in the suburbs. Thus, when the relationship between age and substance use is examined in a high school population, transitions from not using to experimentation, or from experimentation to regular or heavy substance use, are not as readily apparent among inner-city students as among suburban students. Another equally plausible explanation for the lack of grade differences in substance use in the urban school is that the urban students who increase their use of substances during high school may be more likely to drop out than their peers in the suburban school. Therefore, the expected relationships among grade and substance use are not apparent in the urban sample because the older adolescents who may use more substances than the younger adolescents simply are not in school anymore.

Our findings indicated gender and school differences in the relationships among substance use and depression. In the suburban sample, gender differences were detected specifically in the relationships between depression and marijuana use, and between depression and harder drug use. The relationships between depression and these substances, respectively, was greater for suburban girls than for suburban boys. This finding replicates previous findings regarding the differences between white girls and boys in the relationships among depression and substance use (Paton and Kandel, 1978; Reinhertz et al., 1991). If suburban girls are more likely to be socially stigmatized for using drugs, such as marijuana or harder drugs, than suburban boys (in middle class communities, at least, there may be more pressures for girls not to use drugs than boys), then perhaps the suburban girls who decide to engage in drug use (ignoring the social consequences) may be more likely to experience or be experiencing psychological difficulties (i.e., feeling depressed) than the suburban boys who engage in drug use. For suburban boys, drug use may be more commonly sanctioned and, therefore, suburban male substance users may be more psychologically or socially heterogeneous than their female counterparts (i.e., it may not only be the boys who are feeling depressed who choose to use drugs). Suburban boys may be also less likely to become depressed after using drugs because they may not be as socially stigmatized for using drugs as are suburban girls. Because of the possible social stigmatization for suburban girls who use drugs, those who decide to use drugs may be more likely to be on the "fringe" of their female peers. Those on the "fringe" may more likely be depressed or become depressed as a result of the social stigmatization of either using drugs or simply being on the "fringe."

There were no gender differences, however, in the urban school with respect to the relationships among depression and substance use. There were no relationships among depression and substance use for either the boys or the girls. Given these findings, it is difficult to explain the apparent absence of gender differences in these relationships. It appears that the phenomena of substance use and depression are different among the urban students from those among the suburban students. These phenomena for urban adolescents must be explored further before hypotheses can be made concerning the lack of gender differences between depression and each of the substances.

With regard to school differences, depression in the suburban school was positively correlated with the use of cigarettes, marijuana, and harder drugs, while in the urban school, depression was not correlated with the use of any substances. This finding lends support to Siegel and Ehrlich's (1989) and Paton and Kandel's (1978) contention that "adolescents from different ethnic [and] or socio-economic backgrounds may take drugs for different reasons" (Siegel and Ehrlich, 1989, p. 925). This finding also suggests that depression may be associated with different behaviors depending on the social context. Darling and Brown (1992) recently found that delinquency, including heavy drug use, and academic disengagement were related among adolescents in rural and suburban areas, but not in urban areas. They assert, along with Sutherland and Cressey (1978), that problem behaviors may cluster differently depending on the social context in which the child lives. With respect to the current study, depression may simply be a different type of phenomenon for urban youth than for suburban youth.

However, it is important to remember that *both* schools revealed no significant correlations between alcohol use and depression (although the relationship was significant for suburban girls, there were no gender differences found in the interactional analyses). Given the prevalence and social acceptability of alcohol use among many high school students, one of the reasons for this finding may be that those students who do use alcohol to deal with their depression or become depressed after using alcohol may be outnumbered by those who use alcohol to have "fun" or "relax" with their peers in a socially acceptable way. This type of phenomenon could explain the nonsignificant correlation between depression and alcohol use in both schools.

The qualitative analyses described in this paper focused on one major finding of this study, namely, the differential relationship between depression and substance use across the suburban and inner-city school samples. Analyses of interview data from the most depressed students in each school elucidated possible reasons for this dissimilar relationship. First, the view that substance use is a vehicle for relaxation or "escape" may be a perspective unique to individuals living in relatively sheltered environments. Our interview data suggest that depressed children in the inner-city sample are markedly more in touch with the deleterious effects of substance use than are depressed students from the suburban school. The urban students commonly gave examples of the negative effects of drug and alcohol use on close family members or friends. The suburban depressed students rarely gave such responses; when they did speak about the negative aspects of substance use, these students primarily focused on their fears of disappointing others if they engaged in substance use. Since the urban students seem to be more acutely aware of the potential negative effects of substance use itself, perhaps these students may be less likely than the suburban students to use substances to cope with depression.

Varying perspectives on depression may further explain school differences in the relationships among depression and substance use. For example, the belief that depressed or painful feelings are "treatable" (e.g., through the use of substances) may be more common among people living in relative privilege than among people for whom depression associated with life's difficulties may seem as endemic as the difficulties themselves.

The aforementioned interpretations, however, assume depression to be a cause, rather than a consequence, of substance use. Given that our quantitative analyses highlight associations rather than directionality between the variables, no conclusions are being drawn about cause and effect between depression and substance use.[11] However, if substance use is causing depression rather than vice versa, perhaps the social stigmatization that suburban substance users may feel leads them to become increasingly depressed. Social stigmatization may occur for suburban boys who are *heavily* involved with substances as opposed to suburban girls for whom it may occur at all levels of involvement with substances. There were stories in the interviews among the nondepressed girls and some of the nondepressed boys that conveyed a sense of disgust at their peers, girls or boys, whom they thought were heavily involved in drugs.

Finally, depressed students in the inner-city who are reporting less susceptibility to peer pressure and reporting a perspective that substance use augurs trouble rather than relief may be describing aspects of a need to preserve a measure of personal security that the urban environment cannot consistently provide for them. A commitment to avoid drugs in the interest of maintaining personal safety may prevail especially in the face of depression or despair when life may feel particularly out of one's control. In contrast, children raised in the suburbs may feel a greater personal freedom to take certain risks when they are feeling depressed, or to consciously experience depression when they are using substances, believing that the fundamental securities of their environment will nonetheless remain intact.

Our qualitative study of depressed students' beliefs and attitudes about substance use suggests that depressed urban and suburban students may differ in their views about substance use. These different attitudes and beliefs may be centrally important to understanding why depression and substance use are differently related across schools. However, in future studies it would be important to examine beliefs and attitudes concerning substance use held by a broader population of students, including those reporting no, low, or moderate levels of depression. Such an examination could help determine whether the attitudes and beliefs revealed in our qualitative analyses are unique to depressed students (and somehow related to "being depressed") or whether these beliefs are typical of the larger student body in each school.

Implications

Our finding concerning urban and suburban school differences in the relationship between substance use and depression has implications for future research, and potentially, for the goals of adolescent substance use treatment programs. First, subsequent research is needed to determine whether the apparent relationship between depression and substance use for suburban students, and the apparent absence of this relationship for urban students, is representative of the experiences of urban and suburban adolescents in other geographical areas. If, as suggested by our study and by previous research, the psychological correlates of substance use typically vary across urban and suburban populations of adolescents, than the effective treatment of adolescent substance use and abuse will necessarily rest upon a consideration and incorporation of these differences. Effective treatment for suburban adolescents, for example, should include a concurrent focus on the depression that may both motivate and ensue from substance use, particularly for adolescent girls. In addition, further research on the psychological correlates of urban adolescents' substance use is needed to enhance the efficacy of treatment programs for this population. Increasing evidence that the psychological diversity of adolescent substance users is informed by factors such as gender, ethnicity, and environmental context argues strongly for prevention and intervention efforts that are sensitive to the role of these differences in the etiology and psychological consequences of substance use.

Notes

1. Post-Doctoral Fellow, Psychology Department, Yale University. B.A. from University of California, Berkeley, and Ed.D. from the Graduate School of Education, Harvard University. Research interests include the phenomenology of high-risk

behavior and social development among urban adolescents. To whom reprint requests should be addressed at Department of Psychology, Yale University, Box 208205, New Haven, Connecticut 06520.

2. Doctoral student in Counseling and Consulting Psychology, Graduate School of Education, Harvard University. B.A. from Mount Holyoke College and Ed.M. from the Graduate School of Education, Harvard University. Research interests include the relationships among high-risk behavior, personality variables, and cultural context.

3. Instructor in Human Development and Psychology, Graduate School of Education, Harvard University. B.A. from Michigan State University, M.A. from University of Minnesota-Duluth, and Ed.D. from Harvard Graduate School of Education. Research interests include integrating quantitative and qualitative methods in social science research and the phenomenology of high-risk behavior.

4. Formerly Dean of the Graduate School of Applied and Professional Psychology, Rutgers University, and Professor of Education, Graduate School of Education, Harvard University. B.A. Yeshiva University, M.A. and Ph.D. Teachers College, Columbia University. Research interests included adolescent high-risk behavior and ethnic and religious identity development. Deceased June 1992.

5. These consultations with students, some with reading disabilities, allowed us to create measures that are accessible to students with diverse reading skills.

6. Throughout this paper, the phrases "levels of substance use" or "levels of cigarette, alcohol, marijuana use or harder drug" are intended to describe patterns of use inclusive of but not limited to frequency of use.

7. For the urban students, relatively little harder drug use was reported, resulting in a non-normal distribution for this variable. However, harder drug use was normally distributed in the suburban sample. This discrepancy should be kept in mind when examining the results regarding harder drug use.

8. Six of these 19 were Haitian girls, revealing that a highly disproportionate percentage of very depressed girls were Haitian (only 12% of our sample were Haitian). The mean depression score for Haitian girls was 14.8, by far the highest mean in our sample.

9. From the total sample in each school, interviews were conducted with 90 students in the suburban school and 85 students in the urban school. These students were randomly selected from each school sample (only 2 or 3 students in each school refused to be interviewed). The 19 students whose interviews were used for this qualitative analysis were all the students whose CDI scores were in the top 10% in the sample, and who were randomly selected to be interviewed from the total sample.

10. This may not be the case for harder drug users. Since few students in the urban school reported using harder drugs, we believe the high dropout rate in the inner-city may have led to a very negatively skewed distribution of harder drug use in the urban school. Mensch and Kandel (1988) concluded, in their research on dropouts, that there is a strong positive association between heavy drug use and dropping out of school.

11. Given that our study assesses one point in time and does not include a control group, we were not able to determine causality among the variables.

References

Andrews, J. A., Hops, H., Duncan, S. C., Tildesley, E., Ary, D., and Smolkowksi, K. (1992, March). Long-term consequences of level of substance use in adolescence. Paper presented at the fourth biennial meetings of the Society for Research on Adolescence, Washington, DC.

Aneshensel, C. S., and Huba, G. J. (1983). Depression, alcohol use, and smoking over one year: A four wave longitudinal causal model. *J. Abnorm. Psychol.* 92: 134–150.

Blau, G., Gillespie, J., Felner, R. D., and Evans, E. G. (1988). Predisposition to drug use in rural adolescents: Preliminary relationships and methodological considerations. *J. Drug Educat.* 18: 13–22.

Braucht, G. N., Brakarsch, D., Follingstad, D., and Berry, K. L. (1973). Deviant drugs use in adolescence: A review of psychological correlates. *Psychol. Bull.* 79: 92–106.

Darling, N., and Brown, B. B. (1992, March) Patterning of academic performance and deviance among African-American and European-American youths in three communities. Paper presented at the biennial meetings of the Society for Research on Adolescence, Washington, DC.

Dembo, R., Burgos, W., Des Jarlais, D., and Schmeidler, J. (1979). Ethnicity and drug use among urban junior high school youths. *Intl. J. Addict.* 14: 557–568.

Doerfler, L., Felner, R., Rowlison, R., Raley, P., & Evans, E. (1988). Depression in children and adolescents: A comparative analysis of the utility and construct validity of two assessment measures. *J. Consult. Clin. Psychol.* 56: 769–772.

Donovan, J., Costa, F., and Jessor, R. (1985). *Health Questionnaire.* University of Colorado, Institute of Behavioral Science.

Finch, A. J., Saylor, C. F., and Edwards, (1985). Children's Depression Inventory: Sex and grade norms for normal children. *J. Consult. Clin. Psychol.* 53: 424–425.

Green, B. J. (1980). Depression in early adolescence: An exploratory investigation of its frequency, intensity, and correlates (Doctoral dissertation, Pennsylvania State University). *Dissert. Abst. Int.* 41: 3890B.

Hager, D. L., Verner, A. M., & Stewart, C. S. (1971). Patterns of adolescent drug use in middle America. *J. Counsel. Psychol.* 18: 292–297.

Harris, E. M. (1971). Measurement of alienation of college students: Marijuana users and nonusers. *J. School Health* 41: 130–133.

Kaminer, Y. (1991). The magnitude of concurrent psychiatric disorders in hospitalized substance abusing adolescents. *Child Psychiat. Human Develop.* 22: 89–95.

Kaplan, S. L., Nussbaum, M., Skomorowsky, P., Shenker, R., and Ramsey, P. (1980). Health habits and depression in adolescence. *J. Youth Adolesc.* 9: 299–304.

Kaplan, S. L., Landa, B., Weinhold, C., and Shenker, R. (1984). Adverse health behaviors and depressive symptomatology in adolescents. *J. Am. Acad. Child Psychiat.* 23: 595–601.

Kennedy, B., Konstantareas, M., and Homatidis, S. (1987). A behavior profile of polydrug abusers. *J. Youth Adolesc.* 16: 115–117.

Kovacs, M. (1980–1981). Rating scales to assess depression in school-aged children. *Acta Paedopsychiat.* 46: 305–315.

Kovacs, M. (1982). The Children's Depression Inventory: A self-rated depression scale for school-aged youngsters. Unpublished manuscript, University of Pittsburgh.

Kovacs, M. (1983). Definition and assessment of childhood depressions. In Ricks, D. F., and Dohrenwend, B. S. (eds.), *Origins of Psychopathology: Problems in Research and Public Policy*. Cambridge University Press, New York.

Kovacs, M. (1985). The Children's Depression Inventory. *Psychol. Bull.* 21: 995–998.

Mensch, B. S., and Kandel, D. B. (1988). Dropping out of high school and drug involvement. *Sociol. Educat.* 61: 95–113.

McCauley, E., Burke, P., Mitchell, J., and Moss, S. (1988). Cognitive attributes of depression in children and adolescents. *J. Consult. Clin. Psychol.* 56: 903–908.

McCord, J. (1990). Problems behaviors. In Feldman, S. S., and Elliot, G. R. (eds.), *At the Threshold: The Developing Adolescent*. Harvard University Press, Cambridge, MA.

Paton, S., and Kandel, D. B. (1978). Psychological factors and adolescent illicit drugs use: Ethnicity and sex differences. *Adolescence* 13: 187–199.

Paton, S., Kessler, R., and Kandel, D. (1977). Depressive mood and adolescent illicit drug use: A longitudinal analysis. *J. Genet. Psychol.* 131: 267–289.

Prendergast, T. J. (1974). Family characteristics associated with marijuana use among adolescents. *Int. J. Addict.* 12: 625–632.

Reinherz, H. Z., Frost, A. K., and Pakiz, B. (1991). Changing faces: Correlates of depressive symptoms in late adolescence. *Family Commun. Health* 14: 52–63.

Robins, L. N., & Przybeck, T. R. (1985). Age of onset of drug use as a factor in drug and other disorders. In Jones, C. L., and Battjes, R. J. (eds.), *Etiology of Drug Abuse: Implication for Prevention*. National Institute of Drug Abuse, Rockville, MD.

Saylor, C. F., Finch, A. J., Spirito, A., and Bennett, B. (1984). The Children's Depression Inventory: A systematic evaluation of psychometric properties. *J. Consult. Clin. Psychol.* 52: 955–967.

Shiffman, S., and Wills, T. A. (1985). *Coping and Substance Use*. Free Press, New York.

Siegel, R. A., and Ehrlich, A. (1989). A comparison of personality characteristics, family relationships, and drug-taking behavior in low and high socioeconomic status adolescents who are drug abusers. *Adolescence* 24: 925–936.

Simons, R. L., Whitbeck, L. B., Conger, R. D., and Melby, J. N. (1991). The effects of social skills, values, peers, and depression on adolescent substance use. *J. Early Adoles.* 11: 466–481.

Simons, R., Conger, R. D., and Whitbeck, L. B. (1988). A multistage social learning model of the influences of family and peers upon adolescent substance abuse. *J. Drug Issues* 18: 293–315.

Skager, R., and Firth, S. L. (1988). *Identifying High Risk Substance Users in Grades 9 and 11: A Report Based on the 1987/1988 California Substance Abuse Survey*. Crime Prevention Center, Office of the Attorney General, Sacramento, CA.

Strauss, A. (1987), *Qualitative Analysis for Social Scientists*. Cambridge University Press, New York.

Smart, R. G., and Fejer, D. (1969). Illicit drug users: Their social backgrounds, drug use and psychopathology. *J. Health Social. Behav.* 10: 297–308.

Sutherland, E. W., and Cressey, D. R. (1978). *Criminology* (10th ed.). Lippincott, Philadelphia, PA.

Way, N., Stauber, H., and Nakkula, M. (1990). Hopelessness, depression, and substance use in two divergent cultures. Paper presented at the Society for Research on Child Development in Seattle, WA.

Weissman, M. M., Orvaschel, H., and Padian, N. (1980). Children's symptom and social functioning self-report scales: Comparison of mothers' and children's reports. *J. Nervous and Mental Dis.* 168: 736–740.

Worchel, F., Nolan, B., and Wilson, V. (1987). New perspectives on child and adolescent depression. *J. School Psychol.* 25: 411–414.

21

A Sequential Explanatory Mixed Methods Design With Participant Selection

Selection: Thøgersen-Ntoumani, C., & Fox, K. R. (2005). Physical activity and mental well-being typologies in corporate employees: A mixed methods approach. *Work & Stress, 19*(1), 50–67.

Editors' Introduction

Thøgersen-Ntoumani and Fox (2005) used a sequential mixed methods approach to identify and describe a typology of physical activity and mental well-being for adults at one organization. They collected quantitative measures with an online survey and used cluster analysis techniques to identify four distinct categories of physical activity and mental well-being: self-assured, unhappy, exercising happy, and physically unhappy employees. Next, the authors selected and interviewed participants representing each cluster to qualitatively describe what it means to be a cluster member and to validate the identified clusters. Thus, the authors used sequential timing, starting with a quantitative phase that led to a qualitative phase (Figure 21.0). This study was driven by the quantitative development of the four categories, and thus it appears to prioritize the quantitative phase. Note how the authors connected the phases by selecting cases for qualitative exploration that represented each of the quantitatively derived categories. They also used the qualitative results to describe a profile for and confirm the distinctiveness of each of the four clusters identified in the typology.

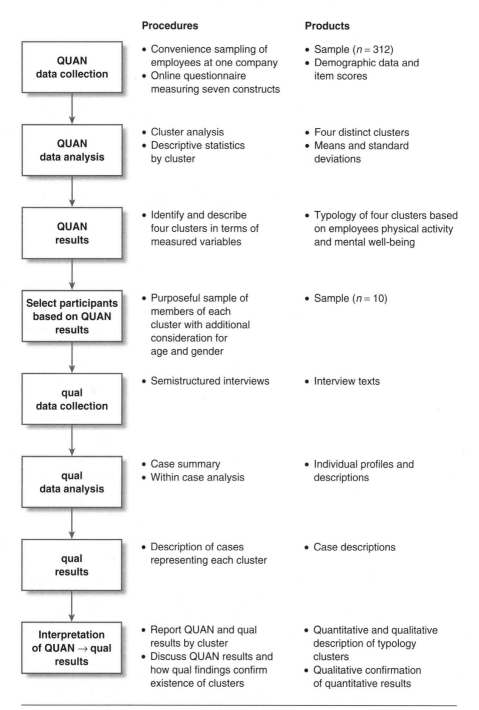

Figure 21.0   Visual Diagram of a Sequential Explanatory Mixed Methods Design
With Participant Selection

SOURCE: Based on Thøgersen-Ntoumani and Fox (2005).

Physical Activity and Mental Well-Being Typologies in Corporate Employees

A Mixed Methods Approach

Cecilie Thøgersen-Ntoumani[1]
University of Wolverhampton

Kenneth R. Fox[2]
University of Bristol

ABSTRACT: *There is now a body of evidence suggesting that physical activity contributes to physical and mental well-being. The aim of the study was to identify physical activity and mental well-being typologies in corporate employees, using both quantitative and qualitative research methods. This method of identification of at-risk groups may inform efforts to design and deliver more cost-effective wellness interventions in the workplace. In the quantitative phase, participants were 312 corporate employees (n = 204 males and n = 108 females), representing various job roles in a multi-national IT company. The mean age of the participants was 34.1 (SD = 8.1). Questionnaires were administered through the*

SOURCE: This article is reprinted from Physical activity and mental well-being typologies in corporate employees: A mixed methods approach. Thøgersen-Ntoumani, C., & Fox, K. R. *Work & Stress*, 19(1), 2005, Taylor and Francis, Ltd. Reprinted with permission of the publisher (Taylor & Francis Ltd, http://www.informaworld.com).

internet to measure physical activity and indicators of global, work-related, and physical well-being. A hierarchical cluster analysis examined the number of physical activity and well-being clusters. Four distinct clusters were identified, and validated statistically by means of a MANOVA test on mental well-being indicators not used in the clustering. Furthermore, ten semi-structured interviews were conducted with 5 male and 5 female participants, representing cases from each of the cluster groups. This was to determine the degree of fit between the cluster description and the individual interview accounts, and to provide a richer source of information regarding the underpinnings of the clusters. The results demonstrate the value and efficacy of using a multi-method approach to identify potential target populations for further study and for targeted interventions.

Keywords: Mixed methods, typologies, mental well-being, corporate employees, exercise, physical activity

Introduction

International organizations and governmental institutions alike now recognize that the workplace is a key venue for improving public health (Department of Health, 1999; US Department of Health and Human Services, 1996). As a consequence and as stated by Taylor (2000), the Confederation of British Industry, the UK Health and Safety Executive, and the Department of Health (1999) are anxious to persuade senior managers in organizations to implement work-site programmes and activities to enhance health and well-being. Employers are also interested in implementing programmes, as they recognize that the health of their employees is linked to absenteeism and productivity at work (O'Donnell, 2000).

Recently, occupational health research has also directed more attention to the role of employee well-being in individual and organizational outcomes. For example, evidence is now accumulating to show links between positive affect while at work, job satisfaction (Fisher, 2000; Judge, Locke, Durham, & Kluger, 1998) and work performance (Cote, 1999). Furthermore, job satisfaction itself appears to be important to the maintenance of health and the prevention of illness (Romney & Evans, 1996), as well as to job performance (Judge, Thoresen, Bono, & Patton, 2001). It has also been suggested that perceptions of job competence may enhance individual performance in the work setting (Markus, Cross, & Wurf, 1990). Despite this emerging evidence linking mental well-being and key individual and organizational outcomes, little research attention has been directed towards factors that may promote positive well-being in the workplace. In the context of the present study, it is suggested that physical activity and weight-related issues are worthy of consideration.

Role of Physical Activity in Employee Well-Being

The recent Chief Medical Officer's report 'At least five a week' (Department of Health, 2004) along with the report of the Surgeon General (US Department of Health and Human Services, 1996) and the World Health Organization (2003) clearly establish the preventive and therapeutic effects of regular physical activity for a range of physical diseases. A strong case is also made that physical activity helps with recovery from depression and can enhance psychological well-being in the general population (Department of Health, 2004). For example, research suggests that physical activity is positively associated with self-esteem (Fox, 2000), subjective well-being and mood (Biddle, 2000) and health-related quality of life (Rejeski, Brawley, & Schumaker, 1996).

Research examining the relationship between physical activity and mental well-being in employees has not been extensive but has generally produced positive associations (Daley & Parfitt, 1996; Kirkcaldy, Cooper, Shephard, & Brown, 1994; Siu, Cooper, & Leung, 2000), although there are exceptions (Altchiler & Motta, 1994; Shephard, 1996). A recent study by Thøgersen-Ntoumani, Fox, and Ntoumanis (in press) modelled the interrelationships between exercise participation and several well-being components. This work indicated that exercise was significantly related to higher levels of physical self-perception and physical satisfaction, and higher job satisfaction which was mediated by greater enthusiasm at work. These specific components of well-being were positively related to the more global indicators of life satisfaction and self-esteem. In view of the above, physical activity may have an important role to play in the generation of employee well-being.

Targeting Groups at-Risk and in High Need

A useful approach for wellness interventions would be to identify groups of employees who have different ways of dealing with themselves and the challenges that they face in their lives and in their work roles. The needs of such groups could then be documented and better accommodated through tailored interventions in the workplace. Such an approach might be considered a type of social marketing. Indeed, the main aim of social marketing is to design programmes for specific groups of people, with a view to maximizing engagement and enhancing cost-effectiveness. One step of the social marketing process is 'consumer analysis', which works to divide the 'market' into sub-groups that are homogeneous on certain variables, for example on lifestyle and levels of wellness. This process of market segmentation (Donovan & Owen, 1994) is central to the purpose of the present study.

Self-selection to physical activity programmes in the workplace seems to be problematic. Shephard (1999) reported that those employees who tend to participate in work place exercise programmes are the health-conscious minority who may already be participating in community fitness programmes. As a result, these employees have less scope for development in terms of health and well-being benefits. In contrast, those with low levels of well-being have more room for improvement. However, current programmes are often unattractive to the higher risk, poorly motivated and inactive employee, possibly because existing programmes are not designed around their needs. The main purpose of the present study is therefore to explore the feasibility of creating physical activity and well-being typologies of employees as a method of targeting groups for tailored exercise and wellness interventions.

A Mixed Methods Approach to the Study of Typologies

In order to target employees at risk, it is necessary to identify these groups or types based on the variables of interest. A typology is considered a classification of individuals which is based on theory (Hair, Anderson, Tatham, & Black, 1998). In the present paper, the typologies that were identified were based on components of mental well-being, levels of physical activity participation, and the demographic variables of age and BMI. This is an extension of the modelling work previously described by Thøgersen-Ntoumani et al. (in press).

Mixed methods approaches combining quantitative and qualitative data, providing complementary perspectives on the research problem (Sparkes, 1992), are increasingly advocated in health-service-related research (Morse, Swanson, & Kuzel, 2001) as they provide information on both outcomes and processes. Cluster analysis is the standard quantitative tool for identifying typologies (Hair et al., 1998). The cluster analytic method serves as a means of categorizing individuals into groups based on a profile of variables. Grouping is usually achieved by allocating individuals to their 'nearest neighbour' based on profile scores. The number of groups selected is dependent on the needs of parsimony, maximizing homogeneity within groups, discrimination between groups, and minimizing misclassification error. There is a play off between these parameters for the most practically useful solution.

By its nature, cluster analysis produces little information about intra-group variation. Furthermore, other than the characteristic profile of the group, no detailed information is provided about the meaning of such a profile to the lifestyle or well-being of the group member. Qualitative techniques such as interview content analysis could be used to accompany cluster analysis in order to provide a richer source of data on group membership. This may help to capture the meaning of group membership at the individual level (Sofaer, 1999). It also utilizes the principle of triangulation (Morse, 1994) and may provide some confirmation or disconfirmation of the validity of the clustering procedure. Consequently, in the present study, a mixed methods approach was used featuring cluster analysis and follow-up semi-structured interviews with some cluster members.

Purposes of the Present Studies

Owing to the nature and novelty of the research design, and limited existing evidence in this area of work, no direct hypotheses were stated. However, the purpose of the present study was two-fold. The first was to identify typologies of employees based on demographic variables, physical activity levels and indicators of mental well-being relating to the working-and non-working lives of employees. The identified clusters were also tested for their validity using statistical comparison procedures. The second was to explore, using semi-structured interviews, the meaning of membership of a cluster at the level of the individual.

Methods

Participants and Procedures

A questionnaire pack was transferred to the internet, and an e-mail invitation to complete was sent to all employees at one large multi-national IT company located in the south-west of England ($N = 1529$). Participants in the quantitative phase of the study ($N = 312$) consisted of male ($n = 204$), and female ($n = 108$) corporate employees. Overall, they represented a 33.2% response rate to the initial e-mail invitation. The mean age of the participants was 34.1 years ($SD = 8.1$). A range of employees with different job descriptions at the site participated. These included managers/supervisors (13.1%), engineers (28.2%), specialists and analysts (17.6%), production/technical staff (6.1%), clerical workers (10.6%), and others (23.7%). Age and job roles of participants were representative of the total workforce at that location.

At the end of each questionnaire, the participants were asked to supply a contact point should they be interested in being interviewed as a follow-up to the questionnaire study. After a cluster analysis, a purposeful sample of ten participants with at least two from each of the clusters was selected to provide a range of potentially enlightening cases (Bernard, 1994). Age and gender issues were considered in this selection. This resulted in five female (aged between 31 and 37 years old) and five male (aged between 31 and 54 years old) employees from the company being interviewed.

Instruments

In the quantitative part of the study, several instruments were used to measure physical activity and mental well-being.

Life satisfaction. Global life satisfaction was measured using the Satisfaction With Life Scale (SWLS; Diener, Emmons, Larsen, & Griffin, 1985). This scale consists of five items measured on a 7-point Likert scale ranging from 1 = Strongly disagree to 7 = Strongly agree. An example item is 'In most ways, my life is close to my ideal', and several studies have reported adequate validity and reliability results for the scale (Diener et al., 1985; Pavot, Diener, Colvin, & Sandvik, 1991).

Self-esteem. Messer and Harter's (1986) Adult Self-Perception Profile (ASPP) was used to measure the subscales of global self-worth (6 items) and perceptions of job competence (4 items). The items are presented in a structured alternative format with 'sort of true for me' and 'really true for me' options. This has been shown to minimize the tendency of socially desirable responding (Messer & Harter, 1986). Each item is scored from 1 to 4, where 1 represents the least adequate self-judgement, and 4 indicating the most favourable self-judgement. Half of the items in each sub-scale are reverse scored. The authors of this scale found support for adequate levels of validity and reliability (Messer & Harter, 1986).

Job-related perceptions. Perceived job competence was assessed using the appropriate subscale from Messer and Harter's Adult Self-Perception Profile (1986). A shortened version of Brayfield and Rothe's (1951) Job Satisfaction questionnaire by Judge et al. (1998) was used to measure global job satisfaction. It consists of five items, where the response category ranges from 0 = Strongly disagree to 10 = Strongly agree. An example item is 'I feel fairly well satisfied with my present job'. The authors reported high levels of reliability and validity for this version of the scale (Judge et al., 1998).

Job affect. Job affect within the past week was measured using the Job Affect Scale (JAS) (Brief, Burke, George, Robinson, & Webster, 1988). The scale is based on Watson and Tellegen's (1985) bi-polar model of mood (positive and negative affect), and consists of 20 items. (The variables from the Job Affect Scale [Brief et al., 1988], which measured negative states at work were not included in the cluster analysis, as the focus of the study was on the presence of positive psychological states. However, these two variables were used to statistically validate the clusters.) A confirmatory factor analysis of the JAS revealed that the scale should be conceptualized as four unipolar factors rather than as a bi-polar structure of mood (Burke, George, Brief, Roberson, & Webster, 1989). They labelled the four factors nervousness, relaxation, enthusiasm and fatigue at work. Participants were asked to indicate on a Likert-type scale ranging from 1 = Very slightly or not at all to 5 = Very much, how much they felt each of the mood descriptors at work during the past week. Brief et al. (1988) did not examine the internal reliability coefficient of this scale, but another study found an internal reliability above .7 for this scale (Thøgersen-Ntoumani et al., in press).

Physical self-perceptions. There is increasing evidence that physical self-perceptions, or the view that we have of our body and its capabilities, provide an important link between physical activity and mental benefits (Fox, 2000) and may provide important indications of well-being. This may be explained by the physical self-functioning as the 'public' or 'outer' self (Harter, 1990), and therefore it may have important implications for social interaction and well-being in the workplace. Furthermore, research has identified that physical self-worth, a domain of self-esteem, is significantly associated with positive emotional health regardless of the mediating role of self-esteem (Sonstroem & Potts, 1996). The six-item physical self-worth subscale from the Physical Self-Perception Profile (PSPP; Fox, 1990) was used to represent physical self-perception. This is a 6-item scale designed to estimate global judgements of the worth of the body, its qualities and capabilities. It is set in a similar format to Harter's scales and has received strong support for its validity and reliability across a variety of populations (Byrne, 1996).

Additionally, as a sub-element of life satisfaction, physical satisfaction was measured using a 4-item scale designed to assess a cognitive dimension of physical well-being (Thøgersen, Fox, & Ntoumanis, 2002). Using a Likert-type scale ranging from 1 = Completely dissatisfied to 5 = Completely satisfied, this scale measures degree of satisfaction with health, weight, shape and appearance. A previous study (Thøgersen et al., 2002) extracted one factor from the scale, which explained 60.4% of the variance.

Physical activity. Self-reported level of physical activity was measured using Baecke's Habitual Physical Activity Questionnaire (Baecke, Burema, & Frijters, 1982). This questionnaire not only calculates a total index of physical activity, but also measures physical activity in three different domains: occupational; exercise and sport; and leisure-time. In this study, respondents were allowed to record up to four different sport and exercise activities (as in Sternfeld, Ainsworth, & Quesenberry, 1999). The overall exercise and sport index is calculated by coding the intensity of the different exercises or sports, and then multiplying them by hours and months. Each individual index of physical activity was used in order to discriminate between different domains of physical activity. Evidence for the questionnaire's reliability and validity has been provided in several studies (Baecke et al., 1982; Jacobs, Ainsworth, Hartman, & Leon, 1993).

Weight status. This was assessed using body mass index (wt in kg/ht in m^2) derived from self-reported height and weight. This has been linked to mental well-being variables such as life satisfaction (Greeno, Jackson, Williams, & Fortmann, 1998).

Analyses

Quantitative phase. A cluster analysis was performed to examine the physical activity, demographic and positive well-being profiles of the employees. The cluster analysis consists of groups that share within-cluster homogeneity and between-cluster heterogeneity on the variables entered. Therefore, individuals within clusters are similar in some way and unlike those individuals from other clusters (Aldenderfer & Blashfield, 1984). All variables were first converted into standardized Z scores. The Ward hierarchical method was chosen to minimize the within-cluster differences and avoid problems with 'chaining' of observations found in the single linkage method (Hair et al., 1998). To determine the number of clusters, the agglomeration schedule coefficients were inspected. According to Norusis (1992), small coefficients indicate that fairly homogeneous clusters are being merged. In contrast, large coefficients indicate that clusters that contain quite dissimilar members are being combined. Degree of increment in the coefficients (in percentage) was examined when comparing different cluster solutions (for more information, see Hair et al., 1998).

Qualitative phase. The interviews followed a semi-structured format. The unit of analysis was the individual cluster member, and the analysis of the interviews followed a case-specific, rather than a thematic, approach. The advantage of a case-specific approach is that it provides greater opportunity to understand the complexity of an individual's experience (Stake, 1994). In addition, an 'interpretive-descriptive' approach to analysis was taken (Maykut & Morehouse, 1994), where the main focus is to reconstruct a 'recognizable reality' for the participants (Strauss & Corbin, 1990).

The actions of the researcher include recording, constructing, and producing an individual profile, and construing, clarifying, and producing meanings of the experience (Zucker, 2001). In addition, as suggested by Miles and Huberman (1994), after each interview, a short summary of the case was written to facilitate analysis. Simple maps of experience were produced for each individual as a data management tool. Research rigour is important regardless of the research methodology. The principles of trustworthiness, credibility, dependability, and confirmability of research, which are the qualitative parallels to the conventional criteria of internal and external validity and reliability used in quantitative studies (Denzin & Lincoln, 2000) were considered throughout.

Results

The agglomeration schedule revealed that there was a large percentage increase in the coefficients from a four-cluster to a three-cluster solution. It was therefore concluded that the best summary of the data was found with four distinct clusters (Figure 21.1). With the exception of age, all variables contributed significantly to the cluster solution.

Clusters: Quantitative and Qualitative Findings

Cluster 1. The first cluster was subjectively labelled *The self-assured employee* ($n = 87$; 29.6%) because relative to the other clusters, individuals in this cluster reported high levels of self-esteem and life satisfaction, as well as being very satisfied with the physical aspects of themselves (i.e. health, weight, shape and appearance). In addition, their mean scores on physical activity were moderate. Compared to normative data using the Satisfaction With Life Scale (SWLS), the mean level of life satisfaction ($M = 27.1$; Table 21.1) was considered in the range 'satisfied' (Range = 26–30; Pavot & Diener, 1993). Mean levels of self-esteem ($M = 20.1$) were similar to norms produced by Messer and Harter (1986) based on full-time working women ($M = 19.9$–20.4). However, perceptions of job competence (as a domain of self-esteem) were notably lower ($M = 12.6$) than the norms (Messer & Harter, 1986; $M = 14.2$–14.4) but this was derived from a US population. However, mean levels of job satisfaction ($M = 36.0$) were higher than two ($M = 34.5$ and $M = 35.0$) out of three ($M = 37.7$) different samples of employees using the modified job satisfaction inventory by Judge et al. (1998). Furthermore, levels of enthusiasm ($M = 16.4$) and relaxation at work ($M = 11.3$) were above the mid-point of their respective scales. This cluster's mean level of physical self-worth ($M = 16.4$) was comparable to the mean level of males in a student population ($M = 16.7$–17.4; Fox, 1990) and a general adult population ($M = 16.9$; Sonstroem, Speliotis, & Fava, 1992), and substantially larger than the mean of physical self-worth for obese males and females ($M = 10.6$–13.4; Fox, 1990). In addition, levels of physical satisfaction were high, with a mean of 21.7 out of a maximum of 30. It was

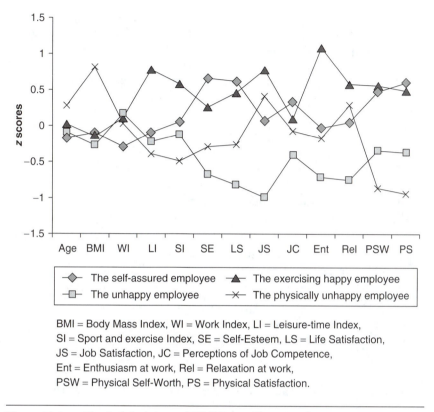

BMI = Body Mass Index, WI = Work Index, LI = Leisure-time Index,
SI = Sport and exercise Index, SE = Self-Esteem, LS = Life Satisfaction,
JS = Job Satisfaction, JC = Perceptions of Job Competence,
Ent = Enthusiasm at work, Rel = Relaxation at work,
PSW = Physical Self-Worth, PS = Physical Satisfaction.

Figure 21.1   Physical Activity and Well-Being Clusters (all scores are standardized)

interesting to note that, although this cluster could be described as moderate on physical activity indices compared to the other cluster groups, it is clear from normative data by Baecke et al. (1982; Work: $M = 2.6–2.9$; Sport/Exercise: $M = 2.4–2.8$; Leisure-time: $M = 2.8–3.1$), that this cluster's level of participation in sport and exercise activities ($M = 3.1$) was high, although this is in comparison to samples derived in the USA.

When they were interviewed, the selected cases ($n = 4$) from 'The self-assured employees' cluster clearly projected high levels of life satisfaction. They reported employing strategies to maintain high levels of work and life satisfaction. For example, one of the participants described how he used emotion-focused coping (Lazarus, 2000) in dealing with stressful circumstances that had taken place in the company over the previous few months:

I think I've become more detached. So when there were a lot of these recent . . . organizational changes, I was taking things really personally, things going wrong, and I was kind of taking it all on myself, things I had done or whatever . . . More recently, I think I had a realisation that . . . though I am contributing to try and change the organisation and make things better, there's so many things going wrong . . . I cannot actually control everything, and so I've just had this realisation . . . I have become more detached from myself. And that way I deal with it better (Allan, pseudonym, 31 years old).

Three of the participants in cluster 1 could be described as having a stable or true sense of self, as their self-esteem levels did not fluctuate as a result of stressful periods at work. They seemed to be able to segregate their working lives from their private worlds. However, there was an exception. It was notable that one of the interviewees ('Lucy', 33 years old) characterized her level of self-esteem as comparatively low, which she attributed to her work experiences. It became clear that Lucy was relatively dependent on her job to feel good about herself. Accordingly, it seemed that her levels of self-esteem were contingent upon her successes as well as interpersonal relationships.

The high level of physical satisfaction that the members of cluster 1 reported was important, given the role that it seemed to play in well-being at work. It was common for all of the cluster members that physical-and work-related well-being were associated. For example, one female interviewee stated that

Table 21.1   Means *(M)* and Standard Deviations *(SD)* of the Variables Used for Each Cluster

	(1) The self-assured employee (n = 87)	*(2) The unhappy employee (n = 86)*	*(3) The exercising happy employee (n = 66)*	*(4) The physically unhappy employee (n = 55)*
All variables (score ranges)	*M (SD)*	*M (SD)*	*M (SD)*	*M (SD)*
Age	32.8 (6.7)	33.4 (8.5)	34.3 (8.0)	36.4 (8.5)
BMI	24.1 (2.9)	23.4 (2.9)	23.9 (2.8)	27.7 (5.9)
Work index	2.2 (0.2)	2.3 (0.3)	2.3 (0.3)	2.3 (0.3)
Leisure-time index	2.8 (0.6)	2.7 (0.6)	3.4 (0.8)	2.6 (0.6)
Exercise and sport index	3.1 (0.5)	3.0 (0.7)	3.4 (0.5)	2.7 (0.5)
Self-esteem (1–24)	20.1 (2.6)	15.3 (3.1)	18.6 (2.9)	16.6 (4.0)
Life satisfaction (1–35)	27.1 (4.0)	17.7 (5.5)	26.0 (4.8)	21.4 (5.9)
Job satisfaction (1–50)	36.0 (7.9)	26.6 (7.8)	42.5 (4.8)	39.2 (5.3)
Perceptions of job competence (1–16)	12.6 (2.2)	10.7 (2.8)	12.1 (2.2)	11.6 (2.7)
Enthusiasm at work (1–30)	16.4 (3.4)	13.3 (3.6)	21.2 (3.3)	15.6 (3.2)
Relaxation at work (1–20)	11.3 (2.7)	8.8 (2.7)	12.9 (2.6)	12.0 (2.8)
Physical self-worth (1–24)	16.4 (1.9)	14.3 (2.1)	16.6 (2.0)	13.1 (2.1)
Physical satisfaction (1–30)	21.7 (3.1)	17.3 (3.6)	21.3 (3.7)	14.8 (4.1)

And you do have more energy, don't you? And so, if you've got more energy, you're gonna be better at your job as well . . . you're definitely more on the ball when you do exercise (Kate, 32 years old).

Furthermore, the experience of feeling physically fit, one manifestation of physical well-being, seemed to enhance coping capacity:

> If I am reasonably fit then I'm better able to cope with problems that hit me, whether they're personal or whether they're at work (Allan, 31 years old).

Cluster 2. The second cluster was labelled *The unhappy employee* ($n = 86$; 29.3%) as members of this group were very dissatisfied with their lives and had low levels of self-worth. This unhappiness also extended into the work context, as they reported very low levels of satisfaction with their jobs and had low levels of positive affect at work. Their means scores revealed that this group could be categorized as being 'slightly dissatisfied' with life ($M = 17.7$) according to Pavot and Diener (Range = 15–19; 1993). Their levels of self-esteem ($M = 15.3$) were much lower, approximately by one point less on the scale, than norms produced by Messer and Harter (1986), as were their perceptions of job competence ($M = 10.7$). This cluster's level of job satisfaction was substantially lower ($M = 26.6$) than three other samples of employees assessed by the modified version of the job satisfaction scale (Judge et al., 1998). Their levels of enthusiasm and relaxation at work during the week were also less than 50% of the maximum of the scale. According to physical self-worth norms produced by Fox (1990), this cluster's level ($M = 14.3$) was lower than most normative student samples, except for one female sample ($M = 13.6$). Finally, levels of physical activity were more or less similar to norms produced by Baecke et al. (1982), except that, on average, they engaged in slightly more sport and exercise activities ($M = 3.0$).

The interviews with members from cluster 2 ($n = 2$) indicated that the unhappiness they were experiencing seemed to derive from different sources. For the female cluster member, the lack of professional confidence and perceived lack of job competence seemed to be the cause of the major part of her stress, which contributed to low levels of self-esteem:

> I think, I'm personally finding it difficult when I'm not fully confident in the area that I'm in . . . so . . . I don't feel that my background, technical knowledge . . . or business knowledge is as good as I would hope it was. Yeah, so that puts added pressure on me, I think, because I'm not feeling that I'm particularly up to the job (Lisa, 37 years old).

The male employee from this cluster group was also very unhappy due to his work situation. However, whereas Lisa's stress stemmed from her own perception of lack of job competence, this employee had just received a negative performance ranking by the management of the company: he believed that the negative performance appraisal affected his job performance, due to the lack of control he felt as a result of it, which subsequently made him feel less positive about himself as a person:

> I think the . . . ranking thing affects your productivity, because at times you just, you wonder why you're doing some of this stuff, because you don't know whether you're going to be thrown out in six months, you don't know whether your ranking is gonna go up (Simon, 54 years old).

Compared to normative data, this cluster's level of physical well-being was low. Both interviewees highlighted the relationship between physical well-being and unhappiness at work and Lisa explained how these were related for her:

> I guess worries about the job . . . means that I don't sleep as well at night. I haven't slept well for quite a few years really, but I've been particularly bad on occasions and I put that down to either because I've been, you know, not feeling very well or because of my job's been particularly bad and I'm worrying about it at the time.

Both Simon and Lisa acknowledged the role of exercise to physical health, but both reported that they exercised irregularly. Further, neither of them described any well-being benefits of exercise. In fact, Lisa stated:

> When I play squash, I always lose. So frankly, it doesn't necessarily make me feel any better. I don't particularly enjoy sport though.

The results of the interviews revealed that the two cluster members were not adopting effective segmentation or compensatory strategies in order to enhance or protect their levels of well-being. Segmentation strategies work to prevent spill-over of stress from one area of life to another, whereas compensatory strategies refer to engaging in other pleasant activities in a different domain of life to compensate for dissatisfaction in another (Sirgy, Efraty, Siegel, & Lee, 2001).

Cluster 3. The third cluster was named *The exercising happy employee* ($n = 66$; 22.5%). Indeed, it is clear based on normative data that this cluster was very physically active, being much higher than norms published by Baecke et al. (1982). With a mean level of 26.0 on life satisfaction, this group could also be considered to be 'satisfied' with their lives according to Pavot and Diener's (1993) criteria. In contrast, their levels of self-esteem ($M = 18.6$)

were, perhaps surprisingly, lower than norms based on both female and male samples of full-time employees as were their perceptions of job competence ($M = 12.1$) (Messer & Harter, 1986). However, levels of job satisfaction ($M = 42.5$) were very high, compared to results by Judge et al. (1998). Perhaps as a result, levels of enthusiasm ($M = 21.2$) and relaxation at work ($M = 12.9$) were several points above the mid-line of both scales. The cluster's level of physical self-worth ($M = 16.6$) was nearly identical to a normative sample of male college students ($M = 16.7$; Fox, 1990) and an adult sample ($M = 16.9$; Sonstroem et al., 1992).

The interview accounts confirmed that work-related well-being was high in both of the selected cluster members. For both of the participants in this cluster, the level of job satisfaction was seen to impact on the way they evaluated satisfaction with their lives more generally. For example, one of the cluster members stated:

> I think there are definite relationships. I spend eight hours, and actually more, inside [name of company], so if you're not happy with that, then it does have a huge impact on your life, because it's very difficult to be unhappy eight hours per day, and then sort of happy (Alice, 36 years old).

The interview analysis revealed the extent to which exercise was a central part of their lives and to their well-being in general. For example, when describing the main contributions to her level of life satisfaction, one of the participants (Rebecca, 31 years old) stated that 'if I was to split between job, relationships and exercise . . . there'd almost be a one-third split'.

Alice also expressed how exercise related to life satisfaction:

> So for me it's things around . . . health and fitness. I put quite a lot of emphasis on that . . . feelings that outside of work, I'm achieving goals as well. So for me, in the past it's been a lot around travelling and that kind of thing, but always . . . deciding what it is that when you're eighty and sitting in your rocking chair, looking back at life and thinking, oh I wish I'd, you know, done that . . . I think it's always additional stimulation, constant learning that I'm looking for . . . to have new experiences outside of work.

Exercising was thus seen as one way of retaining high levels of well-being. Similarly, the degree to which the effects of exercise generalized to feelings at work was illustrated by Rebecca:

> [it] makes me feel better, so therefore it makes everything more productive, and in a better mood, you know, because you're doing what you really want to do and you're satisfied that you're feeling healthy and that you can go and do

these things . . . If I can have activity in the morning I will feel in a better mood than if I haven't done it . . . exercise clears your mind.

The centrality of exercise in the lives of these two participants was clear. For example, as a result of being pregnant, Alice was not able to sustain her previously very high levels of exercise participation, and this had a negative effect on her life satisfaction: 'when I can't [exercise], there's a sense of being a little bit out of control'. Indeed, this could pose a threat to well-being, as maintaining perceptions of control facilitate well-being (Peterson, 1999). Similarly, Rebecca had turned down the offer of a new, exciting job because accepting the job was associated with less opportunity to engage in exercise. Therefore, both participants felt that levels of overall well-being were somewhat contingent upon exercise participation.

Cluster 4. The employees in the fourth cluster, called *The physically unhappy employee* ($n = 55$; 18.7%) were relatively overweight and, perhaps as a result, had a low level of physical self-worth and physical satisfaction compared to the other groups. These employees were also the least physically active. Physical activity levels in this group may be considered to be lower on work index ($M = 2.3$) and leisure-time index ($M = 2.6$), and their sport/exercise index was the lowest among this sample ($M = 2.7$). The mean BMI ($M = 27.7$) is classed as moderately overweight. An inspection of the mean of this cluster ($M = 21.4$) shows that this group could be considered 'slightly satisfied' with life (Pavot & Diener, 1993). Levels of self-esteem ($M = 16.6$) and perceptions of job competence ($M = 11.6$) were substantially lower than norms produced by Messer and Harter (1986). In contrast, the mean level of job satisfaction in this group ($M = 39.2$) was larger than results from the samples described by Judge et al. (1998). In addition, enthusiasm ($M = 15.6$) and relaxation ($M = 12.0$) at work were above the mid-point of the scale. Finally, physical self-worth ($M = 13.1$) was lower in absolute terms compared to normal-weight normative samples of males and females ($M = 15.8$; Van de Vliet et al., 2002), and was comparable to the norms of an obese male population (Fox, 1990; $M = 13.4$). As expected, therefore, mean levels of physical satisfaction were also below the mid-point of the scale ($M = 14.8$). This group therefore represented overweight, relatively inactive people with a not very positive view of themselves.

With regard to the two participants in cluster 4 who were interviewed, one of their most evident characteristics was their relatively low levels of self-esteem. Clearly, for both interviewees in this cluster, levels of self-esteem and life satisfaction were contingent upon performance appraisals and reactions from other people at work. This was represented very well in a statement by Kyle (43 years old):

what people think about me is important, and how you're ranked and paid. That's the company's way of telling people how valuable you are to them . . . [that affects] satisfaction at work. If you're not being valued, then what's the point? . . . If the manager doesn't appreciate what I'm doing, that's a very key to satisfaction or enjoyment in life . . . I think they [life satisfaction and job satisfaction] are very closely linked . . . I think it's one of those male things, where I find a lot of my status comes from my job.

Likewise, Vernon (39 years old) stated that the reason why he was relatively dependent on his job to feel good about himself was because 'it's an area where you tend to be more specifically judged than you might be in other ways'. According to Campbell (1999), people with low levels of self-esteem have great enhancement needs, and as a consequence they are more vulnerable to negative feedback from other people. Therefore, there seems to be a great deal of negative spill-over between life at work, and general well-being.

There were differences within this group in the importance that they afforded to health and fitness as a determinant of life satisfaction. Whereas health was the most important determinant for Kyle, Vernon did not place great weight on levels of health:

I think as I've become a more sort of social person and social groups that I tend to sort of be part of are not very health-orientated in themselves . . . then my sort of whole life satisfaction which is a lot better than it was really stands from an improvement in my sort of social satisfaction, even though my actual physical health might have diminished. Whatever it was that my health allowed me to do wasn't particularly driving any great . . . life satisfaction *per se* (Vernon).

Both Kyle and Vernon reported engaging in occasional exercise, either as a way of keeping healthy (Kyle) or as a means of 'feeling better' (Vernon). In contrast to a lot of the other interviewees who recognized the importance of exercise to their well-being at work, Kyle and Vernon did not perceive any positive spill-over between participation in exercise, and their level of well-being at work.

I see exercise as a way of achieving health rather than for life satisfaction. I mean there is satisfaction of achieving a journey, but that's not my main concern, my main concern is to get amazingly healthy . . . but I find that certainly a lot more satisfaction at work has to do with the actual work itself (Kyle).

Cluster Solution Validation

Some validation has been provided by the logical pattern of cluster means in comparison to available published norms on key variables used to determine the clusters. Aldenderfer and Blashfield (1984) suggested that an appropriate validation technique is to compare the clusters on variables *not* used to create the cluster solution. This external validation procedure selects variables of theoretical and practical importance and uses them as a benchmark for validating the cluster solution. Two such variables were selected in this study: nervousness and fatigue at work during the past week.

A one-way MANOVA test was carried out with the four cluster groups serving as the grouping variable and the two validation variables serving as the dependent variables.

The MANOVA was significant: Pillai's trace = .196, F (6, 580) = 10.52, $p < .001$. The univariate tests showed that both validation variables differed significantly between the clusters. *Post-hoc* tests with Bonferroni adjustment revealed significant differences among the groups. Specifically, participants in 'The unhappy employee' cluster were significantly more nervous and fatigued at work compared to the other groups (Table 21.2). The means showed that 'The exercising happy employee' group had the most favourable scores on the negative job affect variables. Those employees who were the happiest were more likely to be the least likely to experience high levels of negative affect. In conclusion, then, the above pattern of differences provides some further initial validation of the typologies.

Table 21.2   Means (*M*) and Standard Deviations (*SD*) of Negative Affect at Work for Each Cluster

Affect at work (score ranges)	(1) The self-assured employee	(2) The unhappy employee	(3) The exercising happy employee	(4) The physically unhappy employee
	M (SD)	M (SD)	M (SD)	M (SD)
Nervousness at work (1–30)	9.7$_a$ (3.2)	13.3$_b$ (5.1)	9.6$_a$ (3.9)	9.8$_a$ (3.6)
Fatigue at work (1–20)	8.4$_a$ (2.6)	10.7$_b$ (3.9)	7.6$_a$ (2.7)	8.8$_a$ (3.0)

Clusters with the same subscripts in the same row do not differ significantly at $p < .05$.

Discussion

The purpose of the present study was to examine the number and structure of typologies based on mental well-being, physical activity and weight status variables in a sample of corporate employees. A mixed-method approach, combining quantitative and qualitative data, has supported the existence of four distinct and meaningful typologies. The first cluster was labelled 'The self-assured employee', because members of this cluster constituted a group of employees who were functioning well in life, with generally high levels of self-esteem, life satisfaction, and satisfaction with their physical selves. The relatively large percentage of employees in this cluster (29.6%) was encouraging given the high levels of well-being displayed by its members. For this group of employees, well-being in different domains tended to cluster together. Furthermore, they seemed to stand independently of relatively low levels of perceived job competence suggesting that they were derived from elements of life outside work. One of these areas may be exercise and sport participation which in this cluster were high and which were accompanied by high levels of physical satisfaction. This suggestion of a causal influence was supported by interview data.

Cluster group 2, 'The unhappy employee', could be considered to be the most maladaptive in terms of well-being. The low levels of well-being that members exhibited generalized across global, work-related- and physical well-being. Specifically, compared to established norms, this cluster group was slightly dissatisfied with life, had low levels of self-esteem, low perceptions of competence at work and low levels of job satisfaction and less positive affective states at work. Literature has previously established an average correlation between job satisfaction and life satisfaction of $r = .35$ (Tait, Padgett, & Baldwin, 1989), although the dominant direction of causality is not clear.

The qualitative analysis confirmed this profile and the possible spill-over among areas of well-being and life. Both interviewees from this cluster believed that a lack of satisfaction and negative feelings at work adversely affected not only their perceived job performance, but also their levels of physical well-being to the extent that they believed it produced extensive somatic problems. Indeed, previous research has shown that negative affective states and low levels of global well-being are associated with a range of physical illnesses and ailments (Ryff & Singer, 1998; Salovey et al., 2000). Taking into consideration the potential maladaptive consequences of low levels of well-being in 'the unhappy' employees, it was worrying to discover the relatively high percentage of employees in this cluster group (29.3%). Clearly, an important target group for consideration for intervention has been identified.

Members of 'The exercising happy employee' cluster engaged in a high amount of both leisure-time and sport and exercise activities when compared to the other clusters and to norms. The concurrent high levels of work-related well-being, life satisfaction and physical well-being (i.e. physical self-worth and physical satisfaction) support a positive relationship between physical activity and mental well-being previously documented in research with employee populations (Thøgersen-Ntoumani et al., in press) and the general population (Biddle, Fox, & Boutcher, 2000). The qualitative analysis revealed the extent to which the interviewees from this cluster believed that exercising had positive effects not only on physical well-being, but also on global and work-related well-being. Specifically, the interview participants from this cluster group described how exercise had mood-regulating properties in the workplace and how it served to enhance perceptions of work performance. Indeed, several of the interviewees described the importance of feeling physically capable and productive within the job.

The least physically active group in the present study was 'The physically unhappy employee'. Possibly the combined effects of low levels of physical activity and being overweight, contributed to the very low levels of physical well-being in this group. Indeed, previous research has found that perceptions of the physical self are highly associated with, and often an outcome of, exercise participation (Fox, 2000). Also confirmed in the interviews were the low levels of self-esteem and its links with perceptions of job competence in this group. This may be an effect of negative spill-over between stressful working situations and self-perceptions. In support of this argument, the plasticity hypothesis proposed by Brockner (1988) suggests that people with low self-esteem are more affected by events in their environment than their high self-esteem counterparts. Members of this group are less likely to be attracted to strategies such as exercise, especially when overweight, to counteract these effects.

Given the apparently complex interaction between physical activity and elements of mental well-being in these employees, efforts to examine the characteristics that determine who may derive benefits from physical activity participation and who might not should be a priority of future research. In the context of the present study, it is possible that the type of motivation underlying exercise behaviour played a role in the potential well-being benefits that could be derived from its participation. The qualitative data suggested that one of the factors that discriminated between members of the different clusters was the degree to which the physical activity behaviour had been internalized. Whereas some of the participants engaged in physical activity out of guilt (e.g. 'Lisa'), others saw exercising as an integral part of who they were and enjoyed both the process and outcomes associated with exercising ('Rebecca' and 'Alice'). Self-Determination Theory suggested by Deci and Ryan (1985) may be useful to explain the differential nature of the relationship between exercise and well-being between members of the different cluster groups. Specifically, Deci and Ryan (1985) suggested that motivation towards a behaviour, such as exercise, can be self-determined (autonomous), extrinsic or amotivated. Whereas self-determined motivation signifies behaviours that are engaged in out of pleasure or due to the perceived benefits that the behaviour brings, extrinsic motivation is characterized when people either feel that they are being controlled by other people or external events or because they feel some internal pressure to participate, such as feeling guilty when one does not exercise. According to Vallerand (1997), self-determined types of motivation are associated with more positive affective outcomes compared to behaviours that are either under external or internal control. This is because behaviours that are self-determined are characterized by a higher degree of volition or free will. In the case of the participants from the present study, 'Lisa's' motivation to participate in exercise could be characterized as extrinsic, whereas 'Rebecca' and 'Alice's' motivations were clearly more self-determined. Future longitudinal experimental research should examine more closely the processes by which physical activity becomes more self-determined so that programmes can be designed to help employees reach this motivational state.

While the present study represented an initial effort to combine quantitative and qualitative approaches to data collection and analysis, it none the less carried with it some limitations that should be considered in future research. First of all, the cluster solution included two demographic variables (age and BMI), one of which (i.e. age) did not work well to discriminate between the clusters. This may be explained in part by the relatively restricted age range in the sample.

Second, a case study approach was adopted in the qualitative phase of the analysis. However, time and accessibility factors restricted the degree to which the individual case could be studied over time. Ideally, the qualitative phase of the study would include numerous interviews over a fixed amount of time and, if possible, could be supplemented with observations. This was not possible in the present study, but larger-scale studies could aim to explore this in future research.

Third, it is not possible to infer causal links between physical activity and mental well-being as a cross-sectional design was adopted. It is possible that the relationship between physical activity and well-being was bi-directional. The triangulated approach used in this study, however, did provide some support for causal links. The qualitative phase of this study allowed us to examine the processes by which physical activity related to different elements of well-being. Indeed, the examination of processes in qualitative research may be one way of supporting causal links between constructs (for a detailed discussion of using qualitative methods for causal explanations, see Maxwell, 2004). It is, however, also important to emphasize that qualitative research does not attempt to construct general laws of causality, but emphasizes contextualized causality (Miles & Huberman, 1994).

In conclusion, this study has provided some preliminary evidence for the feasibility and value of using a multi-method approach to the identification of typologies of employees. Distinct groups were located and described by a profile of mental well-being, weight status and physical activity variables. These groups were confirmed by follow-up interviews on a small sample of cluster members. Importantly, this study identified a cluster of employees with very low levels of well-being which generalized across the different domains of life. Another cluster of employees displayed low levels of physical well-being and self-esteem, which also appeared to have some implications for how they felt at work. These two cluster groups are important to target for interventions in the workplace. In view of the results suggesting that low levels of well-being in one life domain spill over into other domains, strategies that can effectively improve well-being pertaining to one specific life domain, such as the physical self are worthwhile. It is suggested that perhaps facilitating the self-development of self-determined motivation for physical activity could be an important strategy in enhancing well-being.

The qualitative element added further value by providing important insight into the interaction among the profile variables and the explanations and meaning described by some of its members. There is scope to extend this multimethod approach further. Once identified and confirmed, a more comprehensive needs analysis of the clusters can be undertaken with regard to the health behaviour of interest, which is in this case physical activity participation. Intervention programmes can then be designed, piloted and subsequently refined, and their effectiveness assessed through an experimental investigation.

Note

The first author was formerly with the University of Wales, Aberystwyth, UK.

References

Aldenderfer, M. S., & Blashfield, R. K. (1984). *Cluster analysis.* Beverly Hills, CA: Sage Publications.

Altchiler, L., & Motta, R. (1994). Effects of aerobic and nonaerobic exercise on anxiety, absenteeism, and job satisfaction. *Journal of Clinical Psychology, 50,* 829–840.

Baecke, J.A. H., Burema, J., & Frijters, J. E. R. (1982). A short questionnaire for the measurement of habitual physical activity in epidemiological studies. *The American Journal of Clinical Nutrition, 36,* 936–942.

Bernard, H. R. (1994). *Research methods in anthropology: Qualitative and quantitative approaches.* Thousand Oaks, CA: Sage Publications.

Biddle, S. J. H. (2000). Emotion, mood and physical activity. In S. J. H. Biddle, K. R. Fox, & S. H. Boutcher (Eds.), *Physical activity and psychological well-being* (pp. 63–87). London: Routledge.

Biddle, S. J. H., Fox, K. R., & Boutcher, S. H. (Eds.) (2000). *Physical activity and psychological well-being*. London: Routledge.

Brayfield, A. H., & Rothe, H. F. (1951). An index of job satisfaction. *Journal of Applied Psychology, 35*, 307–311.

Brief, A. P., Burke, M. J., George, J. M., Robinson, B. S., & Webster, J. (1988). Should negative affectivity remain an unmeasured variable in the study of job stress? *Journal of Applied Psychology, 73*, 193–198.

Brockner, J. (1988). *Self-esteem at work*. Lexington, MA: Lexington Books.

Burke, M. J., George, J. M., Brief, A. P., Roberson, L., & Webster, J. (1989). Measuring affect at work: Confirmatory analyses of competing mood structures with conceptual linkage to cortical regulatory systems. *Journal of Personality and Social Psychology, 57*, 1091–1102.

Byrne, B. M. (1996). *Measuring self-concept across the life span: Issues and instrumentation*. Washington, DC: American Psychological Association.

Campbell, J. D. (1999). Self-esteem and clarity of the self-concept. In R. F. Baumeister (Ed.), *The self in social psychology* (pp. 223–239). Philadelphia, PA: Psychology Press.

Cote, S. (1999). Affect and performance in organizational settings. *Current Directions in Psychological Science, 8*, 65–68.

Daley, A. J., & Parfitt, G. (1996). Good health—Is it worth it? Mood states, physical well-being, job satisfaction and absenteeism in members and non-members of a British corporate health and fitness club. *Journal of Occupational and Organizational Psychology, 69*, 121–134.

Deci, E. L., & Ryan, R. M. (1985). *Intrinsic motivation and self-determination in human behavior*. New York: Plenum Press.

Denzin, N. K., & Lincoln, Y. S. (2000). *The handbook of qualitative research*. Thousand Oaks, CA: Sage Publications.

Department of Health (1999). White paper. In *Saving lives: Our healthier nation*. London: HMSO.

Department of Health (2004). *At least five a week. Evidence on the impact of physical activity and its relationship to health*. A report from the Chief Medical Officer. London: Department of Health.

Diener, E., Emmons, R. A., Larsen, R. J., & Griffin, S. (1985). The Satisfaction With Life Scale. *Journal of Personality Assessment, 49*, 71–75.

Donovan, R. J., & Owen, N. (1994). Social marketing and population interventions. In R. K. Dishman (Ed.), *Advances in exercise adherence* (pp. 249–290). Champaign, IL: Human Kinetics.

Fisher, C. D. (2000). Mood and emotions while working: Missing pieces of job satisfaction? *Journal of Organizational Behavior, 21*, 185–202.

Fox, K. R. (1990). *The physical self-perception profile manual*. DeKalb: Office for Health Promotion, Northern Illinois University.

Fox, K. R. (2000). The effects of exercise on self-perceptions and self-esteem. In S. J. H. Biddle, K. R. Fox, & S. H. Boutcher (Eds.), *Physical activity and psychological well-being* (pp. 88–117). London: Routledge.

Greeno, C. G., Jackson, C., Williams, E. L., & Fortmann, S. P. (1998). The effect of perceived control over eating on the life satisfaction of women and men: Results from a community sample. *International Journal of Eating Disorders, 24*, 415–419.

Hair, J. F., Anderson, R. E., Tatham, R. L., & Black, W. C. (1998). *Multivariate data analysis* (5th ed.). Upper Saddle River, NJ: Prentice Hall.

Harter, S. (1990). Causes, correlates, and the functional role of global self-worth: A life-span perspective. In R. J. Sternberg, & J. Kolligian, Jr. (Eds.), *Competence considered* (pp. 67–97). New Haven, CT: Yale University Press.

Jacobs, D. R., Ainsworth, B. E., Hartman, T. J., & Leon, A. S. (1993). A simultaneous evaluation of 10 commonly used physical activity questionnaires. *Medicine and Science in Sports and Exercise, 25*, 81–91.

Judge, T. A., Locke, E. A., Durham, C. C., & Kluger, A. K. (1998). Dispositional effects on job and life satisfaction: The role of core evaluations. *Journal of Applied Psychology, 83*, 17–34.

Judge, T. A., Thoresen, C. J., Bono, J. E., & Patton, G. K. (2001). The job satisfaction-job performance relationship: A qualitative and quantitative review. *Psychological Bulletin, 127*, 376–407.

Kirkcaldy, B. D., Cooper, C. L., Shephard, R. J., & Brown, J. S. (1994). Exercise, job satisfaction and well-being among superintendent police officers. *European Review of Applied Psychology, 44*, 117–123.

Lazarus, R. S. (2000). Toward better research on stress and coping. *American Psychologist, 55*, 665–673.

Markus, H., Cross, S., & Wurf, E. (1990). The role of the self-system in competence. In R. J. Sternberg & J. Kolligian, Jr. (Eds.), *Competence considered* (pp. 205–225). New Haven, CT: Yale University Press.

Maxwell, J. A. (2004). Using qualitative methods for causal explanation. *Field Methods, 16*, 243–264.

Maykut, P., & Morehouse, R. (1994). *Beginning qualitative research: A philosophic and practical guide.* London: The Falmer Press.

Messer, B., & Harter, S. (1986). *Manual for the adult self-perception profile.* Denver, CO: University of Denver.

Miles, M. B., & Huberman, A. M. (1994). *Qualitative data analysis: An expanded sourcebook.* Thousand Oaks, CA: Sage Publications.

Morse, J. M. (1994). 'Emerging from the data': The cognitive processes of analysis in qualitative inquiry. In J. M. Morse (Ed.), *Critical issues in qualitative research methods* (pp. 23–43). Thousand Oaks, CA: Sage Publications.

Morse, J. M., Swanson, J., & Kuzel, A. J. (Eds.) (2001). *The nature of qualitative evidence.* Thousand Oaks, CA: Sage Publications.

Norusis, M. J. (1992). *SPSS/PC+ Professional statistics, version 5.0.* Chicago, IL: SPSS.

O'Donnell, M. P. (2000). Health and productivity management: The concept, impact, and opportunity: Commentary to Goetzel and Ozminkowski. *American Journal of Health Promotion, 14*, 215–217.

Pavot, W., & Diener, E. (1993). Review of the Satisfaction With Life Scale. *Psychological Assessment, 5*, 164–172.

Pavot, W., Diener, E., Colvin, C. R., & Sandvik, E. (1991). Further validation of the Satisfaction With Life Scale: Evidence for the cross-method convergence of well-being measures. *Journal of Personality Assessment, 57*, 149–161.

Peterson, C. (1999). Personal control and well-being. In D. Kalmeman, E. Diener, & N. Schwarz (Eds.), *Well-being: The foundations of hedonic psychology* (pp. 288–301). New York: Russell Sage Foundation.

Rejeski, W. J., Brawley, L. R., & Schumaker, S. A. (1996). Physical activity and health-related quality of life. *Exercise and Sport Sciences Reviews, 24*, 71–108.

Romney, D. M., & Evans, D. R. (1996). Toward a general model of health-related quality of life. *Quality of Life Research, 5*, 235–241.

Ryff, C. D., & Singer, B. (1998). The contours of positive human health. *Psychological Inquiry, 9*, 1–28.

Salovey, P., Rothman, A. J., Detweiler, J. B., & Steward, W. T. (2000). Emotional states and physical health. *American Psychologist, 55*, 110–121.

Shephard, R. J. (1996). Worksite fitness and exercise programs: A review of methodology and health impact. *American Journal of Health Promotion, 10*, 436–445.

Shephard, R. J. (1999). Do work-site exercise and health programs work? *The Physician and Sportsmedicine Online* (February 1999). Retrieved February 17, 2002, from http://www.physsportsmed.com/issues/1999/02_99/shepherd.htm

Sirgy, M. J., Efraty, D., Siegel, P., & Lee, D.-J. (2001). A new measure of quality of work life (QWL) based on need satisfaction and spillover theories. *Social Indicators Research, 55*, 241–302.

Siu, O. L., Cooper, C. L., & Leung, T. W. (2000). Three-wave trend study of managerial stress in Hong Kong: The role of Type A behaviour and exercise. *International Journal of Stress Management, 7*, 153–157.

Sofaer, S. (1999). Qualitative methods: What are they and why use them? *Health Services Research*. Retrieved January 26, 2001, from the World Wide Web: http://www.findarticles.com/sofaer.html

Sonstroem, R. J., & Potts, S. A. (1996). Life adjustment correlates of physical self-concepts. *Medicine & Science in Sports and Exercise, 28*, 619–625.

Sonstroem, R. J., Speliotis, E. D., & Fava, J. L. (1992). Perceived physical competence in adults: An examination of the Physical Self-Perception Scale. *Journal of Sport and Exercise Psychology, 10*, 207–221.

Sparkes, A. C. (1992). The paradigm debate: An extended review and a celebration of difference. In A. C. Sparkes (Ed.), *Research in physical education and sport: Exploring alternative visions* (pp. 9–60). London: The Falmer Press.

Stake, R. E. (1994). Case studies. In N. K. Denzin, & Y. S. Lincoln (Eds.), *Handbook of qualitative research* (pp. 236–247). Thousand Oaks, CA: Sage Publications.

Sternfeld, B., Ainsworth, B. E., & Quesenberry, C. P. (1999). Physical activity patterns in a diverse population of women. *Preventive Medicine, 28*, 313–323.

Strauss, A., & Corbin, J. (1990). *Basics of qualitative research: Grounded theory procedure and techniques*. Newbury Park, CA: Sage Publications.

Tait, M., Padgett, M. Y., & Baldwin, T. T. (1989). Job and life satisfaction: A re-evaluation of the strength of the relationship and gender effects as a function of the date of the study. *Journal of Applied Psychology, 74*, 502–507.

Taylor, H. (2000). Differences between exercisers and non-exercisers on work-related variables. *International Journal of Stress Management, 7,* 307–309.

Thøgersen, C., Fox, K. R., & Ntoumanis, N. (2002). Testing the mediating role of physical acceptance in the relationship between physical activity and self-esteem: An empirical study with Danish public servants. *European Journal of Sports Science, 2,* 1–13.

Thøgersen-Ntoumani, C., Fox, K. R., & Ntoumanis, N. (in press). Relationships between exercise and three components of mental well-being in corporate employees. *Psychology of Sport and Exercise.*

US Department of Health and Human Services (1996). *Physical activity and health: A report of the Surgeon General.* Atlanta, GA: US Department of Health and Human Services, Centers for Disease Control and Prevention, and the National Center for Chronic Disease Prevention.

Vallerand, R. J. (1997). Toward a hierarchical model of intrinsic and extrinsic motivation. In M. P. Zanna (Ed.), *Advances in experimental social psychology* (vol. 29, pp. 271–360). New York: Academic Press.

Van de Vliet, P, Knapen, J., Onghena, P., Fox, K. R., Van Coppenolle, H., & Pieters, D. A. (2002). Assessment of physical self-perceptions in normal Flemish adults versus depressed psychiatric patients. *Personality and Individual Differences, 32,* 855–863.

Watson, D., & Tellegen, A. (1985). Toward a consensual structure of mood. *Psychological Bulletin, 98,* 219–235.

World Health Organization (2003). Diet and physical activity: A public health priority. Retrieved November 09, 2003, from: http://www.who.int/dietphysical activity/en/

Zucker, D. M. (2001). Using case study methodology in nursing research. *The Qualitative Report, 6.* Retrieved May 17, 2002, from: http://www.nova.edu/ssss/QR/QR6-2/zucker.html

---

[1]*Research Institute in Healthcare Science, University of Wolverhampton, UK;*
[2]*Centre for Sport, Exercise and Health, Department of Exercise & Health Sciences, University of Bristol, Tyndall Avenue, Bristol, UK.*

Correspondence: Cecilie Thøgersen-Ntoumani, Research Institute in Healthcare Science, School of Sport, Reforming Art and Leisure, University of Wolverhampton, Walsall Campus, Gorway Road, Walsall, WS1 3BD, UK. E-mail: ect@aber. ac.uk (until July 2005).

22

A Sequential Exploratory Mixed Methods Design With Instrument Development

Selection: Milton, J., Watkins, K. E., Studdard, S. S., & Burch, M. (2003). The ever widening gyre: Factors affecting change in adult education graduate programs in the United States. *Adult Education Quarterly, 54*(1), 23–41.

Editors' Introduction

Higher education researchers Milton, Watkins, Studdard, and Burch (2003) studied changes in the size of adult education programs in the United States by identifying important factors and measuring the extent to which they predict change. As summarized in Figure 22.0, their resulting design was a sequential exploratory mixed methods approach that began with a qualitative phase, moved to instrument development, and concluded with a primarily quantitative phase. This study highlights how rigorous instrument development procedures can be used to connect qualitative results to quantitative data collection. The authors identified three themes (program integration, responsiveness to change, and leadership) from their qualitative analysis. They used these themes as scales and wrote items for each scale supported by quotes from the interviews. The instrument development was also informed by the literature, refined during pilot testing, and tested for high internal consistency. This quantitative instrument was administered in the final phase of the study to determine the relationship among the variables, and the authors reflected on what was learned from both the qualitative and quantitative findings during the interpretation.

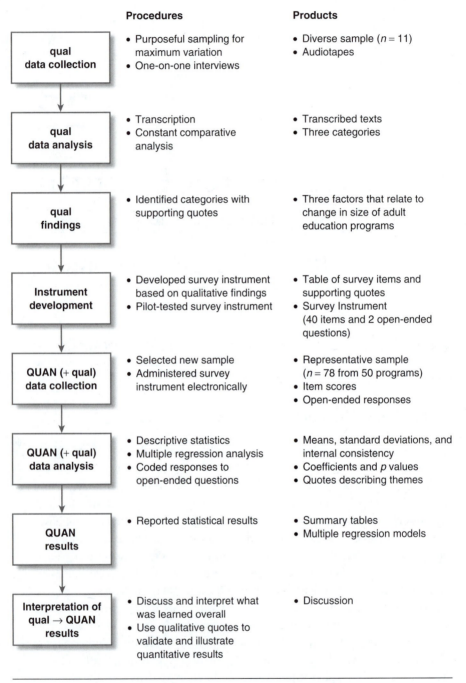

Procedures

Products

qual data collection
- Purposeful sampling for maximum variation
- One-on-one interviews

- Diverse sample ($n = 11$)
- Audiotapes

qual data analysis
- Transcription
- Constant comparative analysis

- Transcribed texts
- Three categories

qual findings
- Identified categories with supporting quotes

- Three factors that relate to change in size of adult education programs

Instrument development
- Developed survey instrument based on qualitative findings
- Pilot-tested survey instrument

- Table of survey items and supporting quotes
- Survey Instrument (40 items and 2 open-ended questions)

QUAN (+ qual) data collection
- Selected new sample
- Administered survey instrument electronically

- Representative sample ($n = 78$ from 50 programs)
- Item scores
- Open-ended responses

QUAN (+ qual) data analysis
- Descriptive statistics
- Multiple regression analysis
- Coded responses to open-ended questions

- Means, standard deviations, and internal consistency
- Coefficients and p values
- Quotes describing themes

QUAN results
- Reported statistical results

- Summary tables
- Multiple regression models

Interpretation of qual → QUAN results
- Discuss and interpret what was learned overall
- Use qualitative quotes to validate and illustrate quantitative results

- Discussion

Figure 22.0   Visual Diagram of a Sequential Exploratory Mixed Methods Design With Instrument Development

SOURCE: Based on Milton, Watkins, Studdard, and Burch (2003).

The Ever Widening Gyre

Factors Affecting Change in Adult Education Graduate Programs in the United States

Judy Milton
University of Georgia

Karen E. Watkins
University of Georgia

Scarlette Spears Studdard
University of Georgia

Michele Burch
University of Georgia

The purpose of this study was to develop an understanding of recent changes that have occurred in the size of adult education graduate programs. Three factors (program integration, responsiveness to change, and leadership) that

SOURCE: This article is reprinted from *Adult Education Quarterly*, Vol. 54, Issue 1, pp. 23–41, 2003. Reprinted with permission of Sage Publications, Inc.

The authors wish to thank the students in our EADU 9600 seminar at the University of Georgia for contributions to the initial pilot study on which this research was based, Dr. Tom Valentine for assistance with the statistical analyses, the anonymous *AEQ* reviewers for their comments and suggestions, and Mr. Peter Delaney, graduate project manager at Peterson's, for archival data on graduate school programs.

*contributed to changes in the number of students and faculty in graduate pro-
grams were identified and measured through a mixed-method study incorporating both qualitative interview and survey data analyses. The findings
indicate that program integration has a significant effect on change in student
enrollment, whereas program integration, innovation, and leadership together
significantly predict variance in faculty growth. Implications for adult education graduate programs and directions for further research are discussed.*

   Keywords: *adult education; graduate programs; higher education
administration*

D uring the 1990s, a number of adult education graduate programs
closed or merged with other programs. These changes point to a possible loss of vitality in the field of study. On the other hand, programs have
always closed at the same time that other programs grew or new ones
opened. This is evident in increased student enrollment and added faculty
positions in some programs during this same period. In addition, various
areas of adult education practice, such as human resource development
(HRD), have never been stronger. Understanding the organizational factors
related to these changes in the number and size of academic programs may
help faculty and administrators better prepare to counteract negative trends
and to support continued growth.

Historical Perspective

Adult education as a field of study emerged in the first quarter of the 20th century to meet the needs of teachers and administrators engaged in vocational
education for industry, agriculture, and home economics. From an historical
perspective, three overlapping periods in the development of adult education
programs in higher education were identified, with each period focusing on a
different aspect of development. The first period, from the first quarter of the
20th century through the 1980s, focused on the creation of courses and programs for practitioners and the establishment of graduate programs. The second period, primarily from the 1960s through the 1980s, began to conceptualize
a framework and establish a curriculum for graduate programs to train professional adult educators (Jensen, Liveright, & Hallenbeck, 1964). The third
period, beginning in the late 1980s, has attempted to understand the organizational issues that affect adult education graduate programs. This section offers
a brief overview of each of these periods.

   Courses dealing with the methodology of adult education were being
taught at Columbia University by 1918, and the term *adult education* first

appeared in the title of a course at the same university in 1922. The number of graduate-level courses in adult education increased from that time, with the exception of a small decline during World War II, and the number of institutions offering these courses also continued to grow. Teachers' College at Columbia University established the first Department of Adult Education in 1930, followed by Ohio State University in 1931 and the University of Chicago in 1935 (Houle, 1964). By 1962, 15 universities in the United States had graduate programs leading to master's and doctoral degrees in adult education (Houle, 1964). This number increased dramatically in the 1960s and 1970s, due in large part to federal funding for new educational programs in literacy and adult basic education (Peters & Kreitlow, 1991), and this growth continued into the 1980s.

In the 1960s, scholars in adult education began to focus on the "conceptual foundations of adult education as a university discipline" (Jensen et al., 1964, p. xiii) to design programs of graduate study to prepare professional leaders for the field of practice. Contributing to this effort, Knowles (1962) began to elaborate a theory to support graduate degree programs. In 1964, Jensen et al. edited the volume *Adult Education: Outlines of an Emerging Field of University Study*. This book brought together ideas from other disciplines and provided guidelines for a graduate program of study in adult education, including criteria for program development (Dickerman, 1964) and graduate curricula (Liveright, 1964). The curriculum framework suggested by Liveright (1964) focused on developing program content to provide graduates with (a) competence to practice the profession of adult education, (b) an understanding of the social context of the practice, (c) philosophy and values for effective practice, (d) zest for continued study and lifelong learning, and (e) competence in conducting and interpreting research. In 1986, the Commission of Professors of Adult Education (CPAE) adopted the *Standards for Graduate Programs in Adult Education* (n.d.) that embodied the elements of this framework (Peters & Kreitlow, 1991).

By 1990, there were 43 doctoral and 104 master's degrees in adult, continuing, and extension education offered by 105 institutions in the United States (*Peterson's Guide*, 1990). Although the number of institutions offering degrees had continued to increase since the 1960–1970s, other changes were beginning to take place. During the 1990s, new degree programs continued to be established, including the master's degree at the University of Alaska, Anchorage and Cleveland State University and doctoral degrees at Fordham University and the University of Idaho. Other programs, such as North Carolina State University, Northern Illinois University, and the University of Georgia, continued to grow. At the same time, some large programs, such as Syracuse University, Ohio State University, and Boston University, closed.

Other programs reorganized with faculty dispersed into other departments, some of which no longer offered a degree in adult education. At the time of this study in 2000, 74 institutions in the United States offered 38 doctoral and 72 master's degrees in adult, continuing, and community education (*Peterson's Graduate and Professional Programs,* 2000). These numbers indicated approximately a 25% decrease in the number of adult education graduate degrees being offered and a 29% decline in the number of institutions that offered these degrees.

These changes in the number and size of graduate programs have occurred against the backdrop of continuing conversations among adult education graduate faculty about the nature of the field of study. These discussions have been documented beginning with Jensen et al. (1964) and continuing with Merriam and Cunningham (1989); Peters, Jarvis, and Associates (1991); and Wilson and Hayes (2000) as well as with reports in the proceedings from the Commission of Professors of Adult Education (particularly Greenland, 1993; Polson & Schied, 1994).

In a 1988 CPAE study, Kreitlow identified the following nine danger signals for graduate programs: (a) isolation from other disciplines, (b) lack of commitment to the department with which the program is affiliated, (c) acceptance of educators not trained in adult education, (d) homogeneous age range of faculty members, (e) lack of internal communication, (f) decline in funded research, (g) limited publication record, (h) decline in image within the college, and (i) concerns by graduate students about the status of the program.

> Politics, changing social conditions, the loss of strong faculty members, changing institutional priorities, hard economic times, lethargy—any of these can account for a decline in graduate programs . . . time spent studying what it takes for a program to grow would be time well spent. (Peters & Kreitlow, 1991, p. 168)

In the early 1990s, an ad hoc committee of the CPAE conducted a qualitative study, "Strengthening University Support for Adult Education Graduate Programs" (Knox, Caffarella, Courtenay, Deshler, & Ross-Gordon, 1993). This research identified the following five areas of "program strength or vulnerability" (p. 70): faculty, students, image, resources, and administrative relations. Leadership, program quality, cooperation with and from stakeholders, and congruence with institutional values were strategies suggested for increasing long-term support. However, beyond these two CPAE reports, research has focused primarily on the content context, and delivery of graduate education with few published efforts (curriculum: Harrison, 1995; the professoriate: Peterson & Provo, 1998) to systematically study the factors that have influenced continuing changes in adult education graduate programs.

Purpose of the Study

Compelled by concerns similar to the nine danger signals expressed by Kreitlow (1988) and the findings of the CPAE report (Knox et al., 1993), this study was conducted to determine key organizational factors that have influenced recent changes in the size of adult education graduate programs in the United States and the implications these factors suggest for the development of robust programs.

Two research questions guided this study:

1. *Research Question 1:* What factors have had an effect on changes in adult education graduate programs during the past 5 years?

2. *Research Question 2:* To what extent did these factors predict change in size of adult education programs over the past 5 years?

Research Context

This research was undertaken as a collaborative effort with 11 students in a doctoral research seminar in adult education. The professor and graduate assistant developed the research design and guided all phases of this project. The initial research was accomplished working both in small groups and as a whole group using face-to-face meetings and Web-based conferencing. The Facilitate.com conferencing site enabled the researchers to maintain a record of the work in the small groups and provided an audit trail during data analysis.

The first phase (conducting interviews and initial qualitative analysis) and the second phase (development of items and piloting of the survey) of the study included all members of the seminar. Based on the results of the pilot survey, a smaller group from the original class consisting of the professor and 3 doctoral students continued the research with two additional phases (reanalysis of the interview data and revision and administration of the survey). The reanalysis of the qualitative data and refinement of the survey items and format were used to increase the reliability and validity of this study.

Methodology

To answer the research questions, this study used a mixed-method research design to examine programs offering graduate degrees in adult education. First, qualitative analysis of interview data was used to identify and define factors related to recent changes in programs and to generate survey items. Survey methodology was then used to measure faculty and administrators' perceptions of these factors' influence on changes in the size of graduate programs in terms of an increase or decrease in the number of faculty and the number of students.

Qualitative Interviews

Qualitative data were collected through 11 semistructured interviews conducted with a purposeful sample (Patton, 2002) of adult education faculty and administrators. Participants were selected to represent diverse adult education programs based on program size, geographic regions of the United States, and responsibilities of the individuals within programs (full–time faculty and those with administrative responsibilities). Of the interviews, 9 were conducted by telephone, and 2 were conducted in person, with the length of interviews averaging 45 to 60 minutes. The open-ended questions included general questions about the state of the field and more specific questions about the respondent's own adult education program.

Constant comparative analysis (Merriam, 1998; Strauss & Corbin, 1990) was used to develop descriptive codes (Miles & Huberman, 1994) from the transcribed interview data. The first interview was coded collectively by the large group to establish a common understanding of the data. The remaining interviews were coded by the interviewer based on this collective insight. Small groups of three or four students then worked together to complete two additional rounds of coding. First, each group refined codes across three to four interviews. The groups then compared the codes that had emerged across all interviews and identified three categories that were congruent, mutually exclusive and exhaustive. These categories were named *program integration, responsiveness to change,* and *leadership* to reflect the purpose of the research (Merriam, 1998). Second, new small groups made up of one student from each of the previous groups analyzed all the interviews for a specific category to validate its use as a factor that had affected changes in adult education graduate programs during the past 5 years. Interview data supporting each factor were posted in the Web conference as a method for both peer review (Lincoln & Guba, 1985) and data management.

Survey Instrumentation

The instrument was designed using the categories identified in the qualitative data. Program integration, responsiveness to change, and leadership were the three independent variables selected to measure the dependent variable of change in size of adult education graduate programs. As indicators of the overall health of the adult education graduate programs, change in the size of the student enrollment (master's and/or doctoral students) and change in the number of full-time equivalent (FTE) faculty were selected to operationalize the dependent variable of change in program size.

A pool of survey items was developed for each category based on the interview data and informed by the literature (Fowler, 1993). The pilot survey, consisting of 52 Likert scale questions and two open-ended questions in a Web-based format, was completed by one individual in each of 13 adult education programs selected to represent a range of demographic and programmatic factors. All items on the pilot survey were tested for alpha reliability, and low-performing items (correlation < .5) were revised, replaced, or eliminated.

Development of the final survey items drew on the findings from the qualitative analysis of the interviews, the results of the pilot survey, and a review of relevant literature. For this study, the three independent variables were defined as follows: *Program integration* is the identity, image, and value given to the program by others in both the college and the institution. *Responsiveness to change* is program and curriculum innovations, focused on three areas (use of technology, inclusion of international global issues, and development of new curricula and teaching practices). *Leadership* is the direction provided within the program, including establishment of liaisons outside of the program, procurement of institutional resources, and negotiation of change. The dependent variable *change in program size* is change in student enrollment and change in FTE faculty. Table 22.1 gives selected items developed to measure each variable with representative quotations from the qualitative data supporting each one. The final survey instrument incorporated technical suggestions offered by respondents to the pilot instrument and an expert on survey design.

The 40 items in the final survey were primarily Likert-type questions. The scales for program integration, responsiveness to change, and leadership used a 6-point response scale from *strongly disagree* to *strongly agree*. The 3 items for change in program size used a 5-point response scale from *decreased a lot* to *increased a lot*. Other questions about changes in programs had a yes or no response choice. All items were stated in the positive. Section 1 consisted of 12 items relating to the integration of the program into the college as well as the institution. Section 2 consisted of 8 items regarding the perception of change or innovations in individual programs. Section 3 consisted of 8 items relating to issues of internal leadership in the program. Section 4 contained 3 questions designed to elicit information about the actual changes in size of the program in terms of any increase or decrease in number of FTE faculty and any increase or decrease in the number of students between 1994 and 1999 as well as 6 questions about other changes that may have occurred. The final section asked 2 demographic questions and 1 to solicit additional comments.

Table 22.1 Definitions of Variables and Development of Survey Items

Item	Supporting Qualitative Data
Program integration[a]	
Faculty members outside of our program view the adult education program as a specific discipline with clear boundaries.	"There is the perception that adult education has melted into other curriculums instead of standing alone as a discipline."
Our adult education program has a strong connection to other departments in the college.	"We've had the demise of a number of programs . . . because of lack of coupling . . . within a given institution. Didn't make friends. Didn't cross department lines. . . . We've tried to do that very strongly."
There is agreement among our faculty on what our adult education program should be.	"We had a chair . . . and one of the reasons he liked adult education was because he saw it as anything . . . and he didn't want it to be narrowed down. . . . [This] has helped us to create our image problem."
Most of our colleagues in other departments value the curriculum in the adult education program.	"You know that some of my colleagues do not understand what adult education is all about. I have a difficult time explaining it to them. Now if they don't understand it, how can you expect the general public to understand our mission?"
Responsiveness to change[b]	
Our adult education faculty have integrated the use of new technologies into our teaching.	"If we truly emsbrace technology as an integral part of our teaching methods, we will see a change in both how we teach and especially in terms of regular face-to face student-to-student and faculty-to-student interactions."
The curriculum of our adult education program has changed significantly in the past 5 years.	"There is almost nothing in our current inventory of courses in our department that has remained unchanged or was there 6 years ago. We are on the cutting edge."
Faculty in our adult education program are increasingly collaborating with international colleagues.	"We're thinking globally, and so we try to encourage our faculty to go to international conferences and find out what's going on in the world and have international colleagues."
The curriculum of our adult education program reflects changes in society, including issues of race, ethnicity, and gender.	"Yet, in our changing world, we in higher education need 'to look' more like that world. We also need to acknowledge that if we embrace diversity as a value then what and how we teach will change."

Item	Supporting Qualitative Data
Leadership[c]	
The leadership of our adult education program is efficient at gaining resources within the institution.	"It was very disorganized; the person who was professor in charge was battling wars constantly with the department head; he was losing resources."
Leaders outside of our adult education program make key decisions about our program.	"There was no negotiation. We went into a meeting and when we came out we were handed a booklet that told us where [we would be]."
The leadership of our adult education program is aware of the broader policy issues of the college and the institution.	"I'm optimistic about our program. But it's not the best of times politically for all of higher education or our program. . . . Many adult education administrators have not learned to play the political game well."
Change in program size[d]	
Between 1994 and 1999 the number of tenure track faculty who taught in the program has [changed].	"That's a sore point because in the past several years we have not gotten approval to replace as we encounter retirement."
Between 1994 and 1999 the number of students enrolled in [master's or Ph.D. and Ed.D.] programs has [changed].	"The students are still coming and are eager to learn." "And so we were losing students . . . It was just a mess."

a. The identity, image, and value given to the program by others in both the college and the institution

b. Program and curriculum innovations focused on three areas—use of technology, inclusion of international global issues, and development of new curricula and teaching practices

c. Providing direction within the program, including establishment of liaisons outside of the program procurement of institutional resources, and negotiation of change

d. Change in student enrollment and change in full-time equivalent faculty

Analysis of the survey data established the reliability of the scales used to measure the independent variables. The scales were treated as additive and tested for internal consistency using Cronbach's alpha (Nunnally, 1994). All scales were reliable with coefficients of .9099 (program integration), .7678 (responsiveness to change), and .8560 (leadership).

Sample

Adult education graduate programs were the unit of analysis in this study. Selection of programs for the sample began by using the *CPAE Directory*

Part I, compiled by Dr. Lee Pierce (1998), to identify adult education programs in the United States. Programs outside of the United States were not included because differences in higher education systems may have confounded the results. Individuals in these programs were then identified from the *CPAE Directory of Professional Colleagues* (Pierce, 1999). Individuals who were listed as adjunct or who did not list an e-mail address were not included. Two faculty members with national knowledge of adult education graduate programs reviewed the list, suggested appropriate changes to update it, and verified the finalist.

Individuals who met the sample criteria were e-mailed a cover letter requesting their participation in the study and providing the address and password for the Web site to complete the survey. A copy of the survey was also attached to the e-mail message. Respondents were given the option of completing the survey on the Web, returning it as an e-mail attachment, or faxing the completed survey. Most responded to the survey on the Web.

A total of 12 people who were asked to participate either had permanent fatal flaws with their e-mail address or replied that they did not want to participate. In addition, 1 individual was added to the sample when she was asked by a member of her university to complete the survey. Also, 1 individual had moved to a different location and responded based on his new institution, adding another program to the sample. The resulting sample was composed of 131 individuals representing 71 adult education programs.

Several strategies were used to improve response rates (Dillman, 2000). These included individual cover letters sent out via e-mail that assured the individual the responses to the survey and program identity would he confidential and stressed the importance of the recipient's participation. The letter was sent on the faculty member's e-mail account and contained her signature. Follow-up consisted of a second e-mail message to everyone in the sample as a reminder and thank you. The final response rate consisted of 78 individuals representing 50 programs or an adjusted response rate of 60% of individuals and 70% of adult education programs. The responses represented programs in both public and private institutions located in all regions of the country. Programs varied in size from 1 to more than 10 faculty.

Data Analysis and Results

Descriptive results of the survey questions are presented in Tables 22.2 and 22.3. All analyses were conducted at the program level, the unit of interest in this study. To accomplish this, multiple responses from the same program were collapsed into one case representing the mean of responses from that program.

Table 22.2   Descriptive Statistics of Items for Independent Variables (N = 50)

Item	M	SD
Program integration		
Our adult education program is generally respected throughout the college.	4.4	1.4
Most of our colleagues in other departments value the curriculum in the adult education program.	4.1	1.3
Our adult education program effectively markets itself within the college.	3.4	1.5
Our adult education program receives a fair allocation of available funds from the college.	3.5	1.5
Morale among our adult education program faculty is generally high.	4.3	1.5
Our college has a broader vision of education than only K–12.	3.8	1.6
Our adult education program fits well in its current location in the institution.	4.0	1.7
Faculty members outside of our program view the adult education program as a specific discipline with clear boundaries.	3.1	1.4
Our adult education program has a strong connection to the other departments in the college.	3.7	1.3
The survival of our adult education program has not been threatened.	3.6	1.8
There is agreement among our faculty on what our adult education program should be.	3.9	1.7
The dean views our adult education program as integral to the purposes/goals of the college.	3.9	1.6
Responsiveness to change		
Our adult education program offers courses through a variety of distance learning formats.	3.5	1.7
Our adult education faculty have integrated the use of new technologies into our teaching.	4.0	1.4
Our adult education program has integrated global issues and readings into the curriculum.	4.2	1.4
Our adult education program has integrated global experiences for students into the curriculum.	3.4	1.6
Faculty in our adult education program are increasingly collaborating with international colleagues.	3.7	1.7
The curriculum of our adult education program reflects changes in society, including issues of race, ethnicity, and gender.	5.0	1.3
Teaching practices in our adult education program have changed significantly in the past 5 years.	4.2	1.3
The curriculum of our adult education program has changed significantly in the past 5 years.	4.2	1.4

(Continued)

Table 22.2 (Continued)

Item	M	SD
Leadership		
The leadership of our adult education program maintains a positive relationship with the administrators of our college.	4.9	1.4
The leadership of our adult education program effectively negotiates issues affecting this program.	4.5	1.5
The leadership of our adult education program is efficient at gaining resources within the institution.	4.0	1.4
The leadership of our adult education program is aware of the broader policy issues of the college and the institution.	5.1	1.1
The leadership of our adult education program fosters the commitment of the faculty in the program.	4.6	1.4
The leadership of our adult education program facilitates change to meet the needs of the institution.	4.4	1.4
Leaders outside of our adult education program make key decisions about our program.[a]	3.3	1.7
The leadership of our adult education program thinks and plans strategically.	4.4	1.4

NOTE: Mean and standard deviation measured on 6-point response scale (1= *strongly disagree*, 6 *strongly agree*).

a. Reverse-scored item.

Table 22.3   Descriptive Statistics of Items for Dependent Variables ($N = 50$)

Changes in Your Adult Education Program	M	SD
In the past 5 years the number of tenure track faculty who taught in the program has [indicate change].	3.0	1.2
In the past 5 years the number of students enrolled in Ph.D. and Ed.D. programs has [indicate change].	3.7	1.2
In the past 5 years the number of students enrolled in the master's program has [indicate change].	3.4	1.2

NOTE: Mean and standard deviation measured on 5-point response scale (1= *decreased a lot*, 5 = *increased a lot*).

The relationships among the three independent variables were determined using multiple regression analyses. Table 22.4 depicts the Pearson correlation coefficients and coefficients of determination of the independent variables. As can be seen, one pair, program integration and leadership, show high intercorrelation, sharing 69% of observed variance, but not shared identity, as this does not account for 31% of the variance. Responsiveness to change is only moderately correlated with the other two measures, with 17% and 21% shared variance. Although the three independent variables are related, they are conceptually distinct and statistically distinguishable.

Initial analysis of items used to measure the dependent variable found that change in faculty FTE and change in student enrollment were two distinct methods of growth and could not be collapsed into one construct (not significant at $p \le .05$). Therefore, change in student enrollment (consisting of two items, one regarding master's enrollment and one regarding doctoral enrollment) was treated as one dependent variable and change in the number of FTE faculty was maintained as a separate dependent variable.

Figure 22.1 depicts the final multiple regression analysis of the independent variables related to change in graduate student enrollments. Program integration was significantly related to an increase in student enrollments, although it accounted for only 16% of the variance. When responsiveness to change and leadership were added to the multiple regression model, the three variables accounted for only 26% of the variance and this result was not significant.

Figure 22.2 indicates that 32% of the variance in FTE faculty growth was explained with a multiple regression model of the three independent variables and that this relationship was highly significant. In addition, appropriate program integration within the university and strong internal leadership were significant as individual factors in change in faculty size. Although responsiveness to change was also important in predicting change in faculty size as part of the model, it was not significant as an individual factor.

Additional factors indicating recent changes in programs were examined using frequency analysis. Programs were asked to indicate whether they had experienced changes in leadership, organizational location, or identity in the past years. Table 22.5 presents these results.

Table 22.4   Intercorrelations of the Three Independent Variables

	Responsiveness to Change		Leadership	
Factor	r	r^2	r	r^2
Program integration	.46**	.21	.83**	.69
Leadership	.42**	.17		

$**p \le .01.$

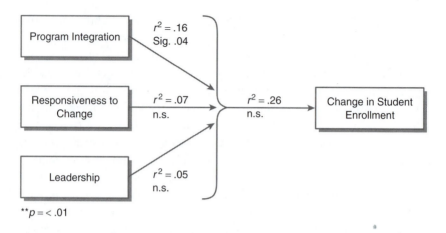

Figure 22.1   Multiple Regression Model for Changes in Student Enrollment

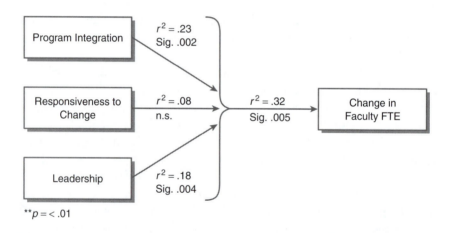

Figure 22.2   Multiple Regression Model for Changes in Faculty Full Time Equivalent

Table 22.5   Percentage of Program Reporting Changes in the Past 5 Years

Item	Percentage Yes
Change in leadership	63
Change in program name	28
Program merged with other programs	33
Change in location within the college	31
Change in location within the institution	9

Discussion

This research was undertaken to help understand organizational factors related to the changes in size that have occurred in graduate programs of adult education. The discussion in this section addresses the findings related to each of the factors.

On one level, this study documented the changes in graduate programs that were already becoming quite visible, such as the reconfiguration and renaming of graduate adult education departments. Almost two thirds of the respondents reported changes in leadership in their programs over the past 5 years. A number of respondents also noted that there was no longer an adult education program per se, just adult education faculty ("who were 5 years closer to retirement!") and that the program name was now educational leadership, HRD, higher education, or instructional technology.

On another level, this study sought to identify factors that are necessary for a program to thrive. Program integration, responsiveness to change, and leadership were three critical organizational factors that emerged from the qualitative interviews with faculty and administrators in adult education programs and were measured through the survey results. The same themes discovered in the interview data appeared again in the responses to two open-ended questions included in the survey. "Please explain any other changes that have occurred" and "We would appreciate any additional comments you would like to offer." The respondents' comments offered additional insight into the factors measured by the survey and are used to illustrate the issues currently being faced in adult education graduate programs.

Change in Size

Change in student enrollment and change in the number of full-time faculty were the yardsticks used for measurement in this study. The only strong correlate of change in student enrollment was program integration. This is not altogether surprising because the identity and value of the program within the institution would be of interest to students deciding to enroll in a particular program. Information about leadership and curriculum changes would not be as apparent to students before they enroll in a program, though it may be important for student retention.

However, it did not necessarily follow that more students enrolled in a program led to hiring more faculty for the program. In fact, only about one quarter of the programs (26%) reported an increase in faculty although almost half (46%) reported increases in master's and doctoral students. Approximately 40% of the programs maintained a status quo in the number of students (36%) and number of FTE faculty (39%). One third of the programs

(35%) reported a decrease in FTE faculty, whereas only 18% of the programs reported a decrease in the number of students.

The three factors of program integration, responsiveness to change, and leadership together had a significant relationship to the change in the number of FTE facility, and program integration and leadership were significant as individual factors. If attention to program identity, establishing ties within the institution, and managing change have a positive relationship with gaining additional faculty, then it would appear that practices such as a shared vision for the program, attention to the institutions policy issues and goals, and effective negotiation strategies are vital to a program's growth.

Program Integration

Program integration was viewed as a double-edged sword. Establishing well-defined boundaries for a graduate program of adult education has long been a goal as a means of defining the discipline (Knowles, 1962). The majority of programs included in this study were located in the college of education, and the respondents made it clear with comments such as "Our dean seems to have a pretty narrow worldview—and it is teacher education" that this is the primary focus of colleges of education at this time. Within this environment, creating boundaries may increase the possibility of marginalizing adult education programs. At the same time, respondents were concerned that expanding programs across departments or disciplines poses the risk of dilution and absorption into broader educational missions. However, as one of the survey participants wrote, "the most important change in adult education programs could be the integration of adult education into the main focus of education."

Not only do faculty need to understand the politics of their own particular institution, they need to be actively involved in changing and reinforcing perceptions. Many are already doing this, as evidenced by one faculty member who wrote:

> The university has been very supportive, especially my division and dean. Many of the other graduate school of education faculty do not understand adult education, but are increasingly gaining respect for the program as they see the high quality of the work, research and teaching.

And another respondent wrote:

> We are constantly aware of the need to be visible and our long term survival depends on our ability to find ways to be integrated with teacher ed[ucation]. It also helps us that there are now other non-teacher ed[ucation] master's programs (i.e., ed[ucational] technology).

Programs that are not able to achieve this balance may face the same dilemma as this respondent: "This survey was difficult to complete since there is only one coordinator/faculty AND the program is being eliminated."

Responsiveness to Change

Adult educators are aware of the social and economic issues driving current changes within our broader society. Some have resisted these forces judging by this statement, "Little change has occurred since the faculty has little interest in change." Comments such as "We have split into two strong, even contested, orientations—HRD and social change/social action" increase the possibility of dissension and the potential loss of confidence by administrators as well as students. The particular focus of a program, whether one of social action, HRD, or some combination, was an issue raised by a few participants in this survey and may warrant further study. A more consistent theme in their comments was a concern about their ability to adapt and change in response to students' needs. One participant expressed the frustration of responding to change in this way:

> The entire enterprise of academe has changed drastically in the past five years. We have gone from the academy to the business . . . students are routinely viewed as customers. Research has been emphasized above all else. However, the most disappointing aspect of being a faculty member . . . has been the inability for people and programs to change.

Leadership

Internal leadership was identified as one of the significant factors affecting adult education graduate programs. The necessity for exercising these skills is more crucial now than ever for forging a strong identity, winning friends, and securing resources for a program, as advocated by this respondent: "Deans do not support what they don't understand. By engaging in more articulation with education in general, programs probably would come out better financially and in the selection of new resources and faculty." All too often though, it was the perceived lack of leadership that appeared to be more obvious, as noted in a number of statements such as "A lack of leadership is abundant!!!!"

One very poignant quote that surfaced in this study seemed to sum up many of the frustrations and challenges that are currently facing graduate programs:

> The current surviving adult ed[ucation] program is now charged with justifying its existence within a college that focuses almost exclusively on K–12 . . . . Keeping an adult ed[ucation] program going at this university, in spite of

support from the top of the university, is an exhausting and time consuming endeavor. It steals time from scholarship and fragments focus. . . . In addition, being in a program that everyone seems to like, but is not central to anyone's main purpose (in leadership positions, that is) means that we are in line for very few resources and little support. . . . It's frustrating and discouraging to be a scholar in this field. . . . I am an adult educator, but in order to be so at this institution, I find I must spend at least half of my time, if not more, networking, advocating, marketing, etc. etc., at an institutional and college level in order to keep it alive.

Implications and Conclusion

What is clear from these data, particularly the comments from the faculty, is that graduate programs in adult education are facing divergent, and sometime divisive, views of the field of study, giving them reason to be concerned. With W. B. Yeats (1921/1996, p. 187), we see the field of study:

> Turning and turning in the widening gyre
>
> The falcon cannot hear the falconer;
>
> Things fall apart; the centre cannot hold

Clearly, enrolling more students was not sufficient to ensure an increase in faculty, as the decline in the number of faculty and the reconfiguration of existing adult education programs indicate. Program integration, although strongly correlated with changes in size in this study, was also mentioned as raising the potential to diffuse or dilute the strengths of the program. In addition, as some of our respondents suggested, the goal of lifelong learning may have been so successfully promoted that programs throughout colleges of education now embrace this mission, making programs in adult education only one voice among many as champions of that mission.

The findings from this research also suggest that there may be other perspectives to consider in developing effective programs. With budget cuts and changing national priorities, changes in size of student enrollment and the total number of faculty may no longer be good indicators of the overall health of a graduate program. In fact, it may not be the number of students or faculty who are in a program but rather the extent to which the mission of that program is considered essential to the mission of the institution. The significance of program integration, responsiveness to change and leadership accounted for only a third of the variance in change in FTE faculty in graduate programs. Identifying and defining other measures, such as political considerations, resource constraints, or competing providers of higher education, can provide additional insight into understanding the changes that are taking place.

Adult education graduate programs in the United States have developed within a model of graduate education that has changed little in the past century. At a time when many disciplines and institutions of higher education are reconceptualizing themselves, two basic premises of this study can be questioned. First, the focus on adult education graduate programs implies the existence of boundaries—departmental structures, programs of study, degrees offered, and even the traditions of graduate study—that have been defined by the structure of the traditional university. These limitations are being challenged by an increasing diversity of participants in and providers of higher education. Second, the idea that growth is a positive indicator of a program's well-being may ignore other characteristics of graduate education. Are these premises, in fact, representative of the status quo? Usher, Bryant, and Johnston (1997) suggested that "educational forms, including those of adult education, are increasingly becoming more diverse in terms of goals, processes, and organizational structures, curricula, and pedagogy" (p. 23).

As the boundaries between different disciplines of education and between education and other fields of practice are being challenged, transformed, and reinvented, the findings from this study may offer some thoughts for generating new understandings of adult education graduate programs. It also leaves questions to answer. Further research is needed to identify and measure additional variables that can help adult educators understand the full picture of effective graduate programs and to compare the changes in adult education graduate programs with changes in other graduate programs. It is equally important to create and test new models for graduate education programs that address the changing needs of adults. Systems of higher education, and adult education programs in particular, in other countries are also experiencing change. Additional studies in these other locations may provide new insights and perspectives that would be useful for adult educators in the United States.

The findings of this study related to program integration, responsiveness to change, and leadership offer compelling implications and potential guidance for scholars who would design, develop, and administer graduate programs in adult education. Viable programs have strong leadership, are well integrated into the university, and are responsive to change both within the institution and in society. Although these characteristics may have always distinguished effective programs, it now appears that they are necessary for a program to survive. In this time of change in higher education, it is also hoped that these findings will serve as a basis for continued discussion about the *what* and *how* of graduate education to address the challenges facing adult education programs, provide opportunities for critique and innovation, and open the possibilities for adult educators to reconceptualize graduate study in adult education in the 21st century.

References

Dickerman. W. (1964). Implications for programs of graduate study in adult education. In G. Jensen, A. A. Liveright, & W. C. Hallenbeck (Eds.), *Adult education: Outlines of an emerging field of study* (pp. 307–326). Washington, DC: Adult Education Association of the United States.

Dillman, D. (2000). *Mail and internet survey: The tailored design method* (2nd ed.). New York: John Wiley.

Fowler. F. J., Jr. (1993). *Survey research methods* (2nd ed.). Newbury Park, CA: Sage.

Greenland, A. (Ed.). (1993). *Visions and revisions for the 21st century. Proceedings of the Annual Conference of the Commission of Professors of Adult Education.* Dallas, TX: Commission of Professors of Adult Education.

Harrison, C. (1995). A survey of graduate adult education programs and the adult learning and development curriculum. *Adult Education Quarterly 45*, 197–212.

Houle, C. O. (1964). The emergence of graduate studying adult education. In G. Jensen, A. A. Liveright, & W. C. Hallenbeck (Eds.), *Adult education: Outlines of an emerging field of study* (pp. 69–83). Washington, DC: Adult Education Association of the United States.

Jensen, G., Liveright, A. A., & Hallenbeck, W. C. (Eds.). (1964). *Adult education: Outlines of an emerging field of study.* Washington, DC: Adult Education Association of the United States.

Knowles, M. S. (1962). A general theory of the doctorate in education. *Adult Education, 12*, 136–141.

Knox, A. B., Caffarella, R., Courtenay, B., Deshler, D., & Ross-Gordon, J. (1993). Strengthening university support for adult education graduate programs. In A. Greenland (Ed.), *Visions and revisions for the 21st century. Proceedings of the Annual Conference of the Commission of Professors of Adult Education* (pp. 69–75). Dallas, TX: Commission of Professors of Adult Education.

Kreitlow, B.W. (1988). Danger signals: Trouble brewing for graduate programs in adult education. In C. R. Oaklief & B. Zelenak (Eds.), *Proceedings of the 1988 Commission of Professors of Adult Education Annual Conference* (pp. 55–58). Tulsa, OK: Commission of Professors of Adult Education. (ERIC Document Reproduction Service No. ED361510)

Lincoln, Y. S., & Guba, E.G. (1985). *Naturalistic inquiry.* Beverly Hills, CA: Sage.

Liveright. A. A. (1964). The nature and aims of adult education as a field of graduate study. In G. Jensen, A. A. Liveright, & W. C. Hallenbeck (Eds.), *Adult education: Outlines of an emerging field of study* (pp. 85–101). Washington, DC: Adult Education Association of the United States.

Merriam, S. B. (1998). *Qualitative research and case study applications in education* (2nd ed.). San Francisco: Jossey-Bass.

Merriam, S. B., & Cunningham, P. M. (Eds.). (1989). *Handbook of adult and continuing education*. San Francisco: Jossey-Bass.

Miles, M. B., & Huberman, A. M. (1994). *Qualitative data analysis: An expanded sourcebook* (2nd ed.). Thousand Oaks. CA: Sage.

Nunnally, J. C. (1994). *Psychometric theory* (3rd ed.). New York: McGraw-Hill.

Patton, M. Q. (2002). *Qualitative evaluation and research methods* (3rd ed.). Thousand Oaks, CA: Sage.

Peters, J. M., Jarvis, P., & Associates. (Eds.). (1991). *Adult education: Evolution and achievements in a developing field of study*. San Francisco: Jossey-Bass.

Peters, J. M., & Kreitlow, B. W. (1991). Growth and future of graduate programs. In J. M. Peters. P. Jarvis, & Associates (Eds.), *Adult education: Evolution and achievements in a developing field of study* (pp. 145–183). San Francisco: Jossey-Bass.

Peterson, S. L., & Provo, J. (1998). Profile of the adult education and human resource development professoriate: Characteristics and personal fulfillment. *Adult Education Quarterly 48*, 199–215.

Peterson's graduate and professional programs: An overview 2000. (2000). Lawrenceville, NJ: Peterson's.

Peterson's guide to graduate and professional programs: An overview 1990. (1990). Lawrenceville, NJ: Peterson's.

Pierce, W. L. (1998). *Directory of adult education graduate program in North America part I: Program contact information*. Hattiesburg, MS: Commission of Professors of Adult Education.

Pierce, W. L. (1999). *CPAE directory of professional colleagues*. Hattiesburg, MS: Commission of Professors of Adult Education.

Polson, C. J., & Schied, F. M. (Eds.). (1994). *Challenge and change Proceedings of the Annual Conference of the Commission of Professors of Adult Education*. Nashville, TN: Commission of Professors of Adult Education. (ERIC Document Reproduction Service No. ED427180)

Standards for graduate programs in adult education. (n.d.). Lanham, MD: American Association for Adult and Continuing Education.

Strauss, A., & Corbin, J. (1990). *Basics of qualitative research: Grounded theory procedures and techniques*. Newbury Park, CA: Sage.

Usher, R., Bryant, I., & Johnston, R. (1997). *Adult education and the postmodern challenge: Learning beyond the limits*. New York: Routledge.

Wilson, A. L., & Hayes, E. R. (Eds.). (2000). *Handbook of adult and continuing education* (New ed.). San Francisco: Jossey-Bass.

Yeats,W. B. (1996).The second coming. In R. J. Finneran (Ed.), *The collected poems of W.B. Yeats* (Rev. 2nd ed., p. 187). New York: Scribner Paperback Poetry. (Original work published 1921)

Judy Milton is a doctoral student in the Department of Adult Education at the University of Georgia.

Karen E. Watkins is a Professor of Adult Education and Interim Associate Dean of Research and External Affairs in the College of Education at the University of Georgia.

Scarlette Spears Studdard is an adjunct assistant professor at the University of Georgia in the Department of Adult Education and the Women's Studies Program.

Michele Burch is a doctoral student in the Department of Adult Education at the University of Georgia.

23

A Sequential Exploratory Mixed Methods Design to Generate and Test a Model

Selection: Richter, K. (1997). Child care choice in urban Thailand: Qualitative and quantitative evidence of the decision-making process. *Journal of Family Issues, 18*(2), 174–204.

Editors' Introduction

Richter (1997) used two extensive qualitative and quantitative data sets to generate and test a model of child care decision making grounded in the perspectives of urban Thai women. The focus of the study's first phase was on analyzing qualitative focus group and one-on-one interviews to develop a model of the preferences considered when urban Thai women make decisions about child care (presented as a figure in the form of a prism). Using this conceptual model, the author hypothesized specific relationships among factors, and these relationships were quantitatively tested using a survey of a representative sample. Therefore, as depicted in Figure 23.0, this sequential exploratory mixed methods study used and interpreted the data sets in two phases and seemed to give priority to the initial qualitative phase. This study is an example of how an in-depth qualitative study can be followed by a quantitative phase, where the two phases are connected by generating hypotheses based on qualitative results and using the quantitative data to test the extent to which the qualitative results generalize to a larger sample.

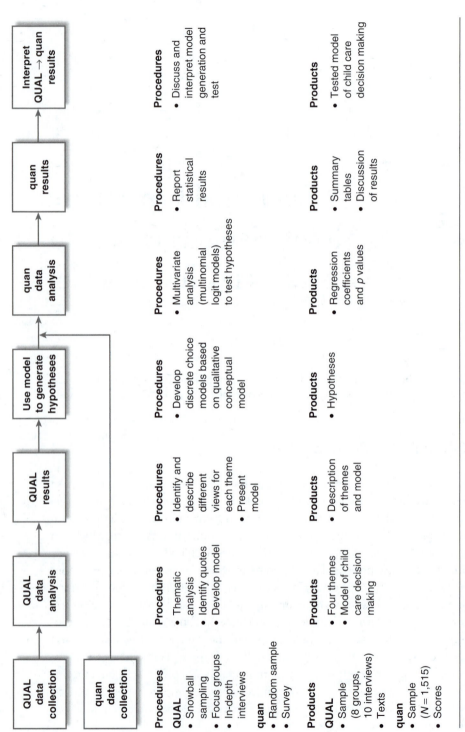

Figure 23.0   Visual Diagram of a Sequential Exploratory Mixed Methods Design to Generate and Test a Conceptual Model

SOURCE: Based on Richter (1997).

Child Care Choice
in Urban Thailand

Qualitative and Quantitative Evidence
of the Decision-Making Process

Kerry Richter
Child Trends, Inc.

This article uses qualitative and quantitative evidence to examine child care decision making in Bangkok, Thailand. The preference model developed from qualitative data predicts a strong preference for care by a relative, even if the child has to live separately from his/her mother, and distrust of nonrelative and formal care. Overall about three quarters of children in the sample were cared for by their mother (some of whom were combining work with child care) or

SOURCE: This article is reprinted from *Journal of Family Issues*, Vol. 18, Issue 2, pp. 174–204, 1997. Reprinted with permission of Sage Publications, Inc.

Author's Note: This article results from a project on child care in urban Thailand conducted at the Institute for Population and Social Research, Mahidol University, Salaya, Thailand. The project was funded under the Rockefeller Foundation Program on Women's Status and Fertility. Coinvestigators for the project were Chai Podhisita, Kusol Soonthorndhada, and Aphichat Chamratrithirong. This article was completed with support from grants from the Mellon Foundation and from the National Institute for Child Health and Human Development (NICHD, Grant No. 1-HD28263) to the Population Research Institute, The Pennsylvania State University. The author is indebted to Clifford Clogg for his help with the analysis, and to three anonymous reviewers for their comments.

another relative when they were age 2. Although the degree to which mothers were working in a formal setting was the strongest predictor of being in non-maternal care, children of higher socioeconomic status were also found more likely to be in nonmaternal care and less likely to be in a relative's care. The results are discussed in light of changing roles for women in a society undergoing rapid socioeconomic change.

The shift from an agricultural and rural society to an urbanized industrial economy has a profound effect on family life. Both the function of the family and the roles of those within the family are transformed, and particularly for women the centrality of family concerns to individual identity and livelihood may be diminished. Child care becomes increasingly complex when the mother's role must be balanced with work outside the home. In the rural household, extended family members were often on hand to help care for young children, and agricultural work could easily be combined with child care. But the demands of the formal labor market in an urban setting mean that mothers must leave their children in the care of others when they are working, and this often means paying a nonrelative for child care if family members are not available (Masini & Stratigos, 1991; Oppong & Abu, 1985; Standing, 1983).

The relatively high status of women in Thailand, combined with a flexible social structure and rapid socioeconomic development, indicates that needs for child care are changing dramatically. Women in present-day Bangkok face an entirely different set of decisions regarding work, fertility, and child care than their mothers did. Labor force participation for women in the childbearing years has increased rapidly: In Bangkok, 58% of women aged 20 through 49 were in the labor force in 1972 versus 82% in 1992, whereas the proportion of employed women who worked in agriculture for the country as a whole dropped from 74% to 64% during the same period. This has occurred in the context of high, out-migration from rural areas: Bangkok's population increased from about 3 million in 1971 to about 8 million in 1993. Migration is concentrated in the young adult age groups, and a recent survey found that although women were equally likely as men to migrate to Bangkok, they were more likely to make long-term moves. At the same time, Thailand's total fertility rate (TFR) dropped to near replacement level in a generation; the TFR dropped from 6.3 in 1965 to 2.4 in 1989, and the contraceptive prevalence rate is currently over 70% (Chamratrithirong et al., 1995; Institute for Population and Social Research, 1987; Knodel, Chamratrithirong, & Debavalya, 1987; National Statistical Office, 1972, 1992; Yoddumnern-Attig, Richter, Soonthorndhada, Sethaput, & Pramualratana, 1992).

These economic and social changes have been accompanied by an increase in the availability of child care choices, including new forms of care that are unfamiliar to Bangkok parents. The number of nurseries and preschools has grown rapidly in recent years; in 1982 there were 1,037 officially registered preschools, and this figure had risen to 1,611 by 1992. However, many small neighborhood centers are operated informally and it is impossible to count the number of children in unregistered facilities. In addition to conventional day-care centers, some nurseries that have opened feature 24-hour care, so that parents may take their children home on weekends or only visit them for a few hours a week. There are agencies that train young women to be "nannies" (live-in babysitters) and place them in private homes (Ministry of Education, 1992; Wongboonsin, Mason, & Choe, 1991).

Thus there are indications that Thai women are less able to combine their roles as workers and mothers, that coresidence with extended family members is less frequent, and that there is increased reliance on new forms of child care. At the same time, the variation in Bangkok women's circumstances in terms of socioeconomic status, educational attainment, degree of labor-market participation, and occupational type leads to great diversity in child care needs and constraints. Although some women may choose to care for their children themselves because the family can afford to give up their income, others may not have the skills that would allow them to make enough income to afford paid child care. Women working in the informal sector may be able to take their children along to work, whereas office or factory workers must pay a nonrelative or rely on a day-care facility. Additionally, the large number of in-migrants to Bangkok includes many women who migrate without their children, leaving them in the care of grandparents in rural areas. Other working women in Bangkok, even those whose children are born in the city, send them to their families in their rural hometowns if they are unable to find care for them. Each of these situations requires a different decision-making process as women attempt to balance the constraints of time and money with their personal goals and preferences. As Thailand undergoes rapid industrialization, these issues will become increasingly prominent, and the situation of women in Bangkok reveals much about directions for change throughout the developing world.

The purpose of the article is to develop a model of child care decision making by integrating qualitative and quantitative data on attitudes, values, and expectations regarding child care choice. It explores how women (and their families) are resolving their child care needs and ideals, and how they make decisions about child care in the face of constraints. From these findings, a model of child care decision making is developed. This model is tested using multivariate analysis of data from a representative sample of Bangkok women. The results are discussed in light of how child care needs and preferences are being met in a rapidly industrializing urban setting, and how both economic and noneconomic factors contribute to child care choice.

Data and Methods

This article uses both qualitative and quantitative data to investigate these issues. Qualitative methods are increasingly being used in demography to ground demographic issues in the context of the cultural setting being examined. They are particularly useful for gaining an understanding of the cultural basis for social change by aiding in the definition of social norms and values, which are the basis for individual decision making (Axinn, Fricke, & Thornton, 1991; Caldwell, Hill, & Hull, 1988; Folch-Lyon, de la Macorra, & Schearer, 1981; Knodel et al., 1987). For this study, qualitative methods are included because they are most appropriate for developing a model of child care decision making—which involves attitudes, ideals, and cultural norms.

Qualitative data were drawn from in-depth interviews and focus group sessions. Participants were selected from three different types of employment: white collar, who worked at a formal job in an office or institutional setting and held at least a bachelor's degree; blue collar, who did skilled or unskilled labor in a formal setting and may have had some secondary education; and the informal sector, who worked on their own account or in a family business.[1] Several nonworking women were interviewed as well. Guidelines for both the in-depth interviews and focus groups were similar; experiences and attitudes about child care situations of different types, and opinions about quality and sources of conflict were probed in both settings. In the in-depth interviews, respondents were also asked to relate their life history, with special attention to decision making about work and child care. In both settings, hypothetical situations were presented of women facing certain child care and/or economic constraints. By asking opinions on the best solution to the situation, this method deliberately removed respondents from their own experience and thus revealed a great deal about social norms and values. In interpreting the data, special attention was paid to differences in attitudes by socioeconomic class and personal experience. Where appropriate, direct quotes from the respondents are used to illustrate the points discussed.

The quantitative phase of the project consisted of a household survey of a representative sample of 1,515 ever-married women in the Bangkok metropolitan area.[2] The survey collected life history information from each respondent concerning her work, husband's work, migration, marriage, fertility, and household coresidence with family members and others after marriage.

Detailed child care histories were obtained for the first, second, and youngest child of each respondent. This included information on type of child care, selection of care, and quality of care for the entire period of time when the child was under the age of 5. Respondents were also asked about ideal forms of care for children at various ages. This data set thus contains a remarkably rich set of information to explore the interrelationships among work, child care, and family.

Previous Research on Child Care Choice

Much of the U.S. literature on child care choice is concerned with how economics, government policy, and situational factors affect women's labor-force participation and type of child care (Floge, 1989; Folk & Beller, 1993; Hofferth & Wissoker, 1992; Lehrer, 1983, 1989; Leibowitz, Klerman, & Waite, 1992; Mason & Kuhlthau, 1992). Only a few studies have examined child care preferences or the decision-making process that families make in selecting child care. Criticism has arisen of the focus on cost without a consideration of preferences, particularly in light of the fact that a high proportion of parents in the United States rely on unpaid care by relatives (Hofferth, 1991; Sonenstein, 1991). Mason and Kuhlthau (1989) found that ideals about child care were influenced by opinions about gender equality and women's roles, and that these ideals have an effect on child care choice whereas women's income and wages do not (Kuhlthau & Mason, 1990). Johansen, Leibowitz, and Waite (1994) also found that many situational factors lessened in importance when measures of the value parents place on various characteristics of care were included in the model. In a review article, Mason and Duberstein (1992) called for further research on the decision-making process in women's choice between work and child care, and the stress that such considerations may invoke.

An increasing number of studies set in developing countries examine child care, with special attention to recent changes in women's labor force participation, child care arrangements, and the division of household labor. Oppong and Abu (1985) found that urban women in Ghana experienced the greatest conflict between their maternal and occupational roles when they worked far from home, worked long hours, and worked in the modern sector. DaVanzo and Lee (1983) had similar results in Malaysia, where women's wages and hours worked were positively related to the likelihood that persons other than the parents were taking care of children. In Brazil, Connelly, DeGraff, and Levison (1996) found that the decision to work and the choice of child care were jointly determined: The presence of young children and the availability of alternative care had a strong effect on women's employment, whereas such employment had a strong affect on the likelihood of nonparental care. In urban Mexico, Wong and Levine (1992) found that the availability of low-cost child care, such as residence in an extended household, had a significant effect on mother's labor-force participation.

Child care has received increasing notice from Thai researchers, with particular attention to the situation for women working in the formal sector. One survey found a considerable increase in the percentage of children in nonmaternal care in Bangkok in recent years, which was attributable to the rise in women's educational levels and decline in fertility (Wongboonsin et al., 1991). Other small-scale studies found that the majority of working women depend on their relatives and servants for child care; only a very few employed a trained nurse to care for their children at home or sent them to a nursery due to the high cost. Working women who lived in a nuclear family often had problems with finding a trusted person to care for their children and expressed distrust of the nonrelatives they hired to care for their children (Bunyanupongsa, 1987; Jaroensuk, 1981).

Thus, though a number of researchers in the U.S. have examined the determinants of child care type and its relationship with women's employment, few have explored the decision-making process that families go through to make this choice. Research on child care in developing countries has begun to raise some of the issues that families face as women enter the formal labor market in large numbers; but in Thailand, such research has been mainly limited to small-scale studies.

Child Care Ideals and Preferences

Opinions on the best form of care for children of various ages were discussed in the in-depth interviews and focus group discussions, as well as the household survey. Respondents were asked who they thought was the best person to care for a child of various ages; if the mother was chosen, they were asked what was the second best choice if the mother had to work or was not available for another reason. Results from the household survey are shown in Table 23.1.

Care by the Mother

The majority of respondents in the household survey said that the mother is the first choice for care of children up to age 3, with a few (less than 4%) saying that both parents should care for the child. Most respondents in the in-depth interviews and focus group discussions also voiced a preference for mothers caring for their own babies and young children. They said that the mother understands her children best, makes sure that they eat properly, and is the best person to care for them in time of illness.

When, then, does the need or desire of the mother to work outside the home overtake her preference to care for her child herself? Many in the focus group discussions and in-depth interviews said that it is a necessity of modern life for mothers to work due to the rise in the cost of living, both for general expenses and child rearing specifically. Others gave noneconomic reasons for mothers to work. To elicit opinions about the choice between working and caring for a child when the mother's income is not necessary to support the family and child care alternatives are available, a hypothetical situation about a high-status woman was presented. Respondents were asked whether a woman with a good job, whose husband also had a well-paying job and who lived in an extended-family household with servants, should quit her job when her first child was born. Respondents were divided on this issue, with

Table 23.1   Opinions About Ideal Care for a Child of Various Ages, Asked of Ever-Married Women Age 15 Through 44 in Bangkok Metropolitan Area (in Percentages) (N = 1,515)

	Age of Child			
	Birth to 6 months	6 months to 1 year	1 to 3 years	3 to 5 years
First choice				
Mother	94.6	85.5	62.8	29.7
Both parents	3.8	3.5	2.4	1.4
Maternal grandparents	0.6	3.6	5.0	3.0
Paternal grandparents	0.3	0.7	0.9	0.4
Other/any relative	0.3	2.6	4.0	2.5
Nonrelative/others[a]	0.3	3.4	6.1	2.2
Nursery/school	0.1	0.7	18.9	60.8
Total	100.0	100.0	100.0	100.0
If mother is not available				
Father	13.7	11.3	8.8	5.5
Maternal grandmother	38.9	33.3	24.2	9.6
Paternal grandmother	9.4	8.4	6.9	3.0
Other/any relative	24.0	24.1	15.8	6.3
Nonrelative/others[a]	11.6	11.0	7.7	2.2
Nursery/school	0.7	1.0	1.7	4.4
Mother not chosen first	1.6	11.0	34.9	68.9
Total	100.0	100.0	100.0	100.0

a. Includes answers "anyone available," "older people in the neighborhood," and so on.

those working at informal or blue-collar jobs more likely to say that the woman should quit her job. Some felt that mothers should only work if they are forced to for economic reasons.

> I think she should quit her job to take care of the child because her husband has a good income, he has good status. Anyway, getting close to your children is better [than working]; having other people take care [of the child] is not as good as the mother. Because their status is good and they're not in trouble. (Informal sector worker with young children)

Others felt that there was no reason for the woman to quit, because relatives and servants were available to care for the child. Some high-status women mentioned the reasons that women may work even when the income is not badly needed by the family.

> She should work because not working will make you feel not valuable, worthless. If she is living with her husband's family, it will make her more independent if she goes out and works, and has freedom. (White-collar worker with older children.)

In the informal sector women's focus group, there was a great deal of discussion on this issue:

P1:   It's better to be with the child because her husband makes enough money.

P2:   I think she should keep the job because at home they have enough servants.

P3:   Yes, but who will raise the baby better than its own mother? We love our baby; the work shouldn't come first.

P2:   We have to make a foundation for our children, not just give them [money] day by day, that's all. The more, the better so that our children won't have to work so hard like us. If you're afraid that the baby won't be warm or secure, she can come back in the evening and play with the kid, and plus she has holidays where she can give time to her child; then during the week she has good servants to take care of the baby.

Moderator: But over here you think the mother should leave the job; why?

P3:   Because we're tired from work. We would rather stop and take care of the baby.

P1:   Yes, the new mother is excited about the baby.

P2:   Yes, that's true. Imagine you're breastfeeding the baby, can you leave the baby then? And some children won't drink milk from the bottle. (Informal sector focus group)

This discussion clearly shows the conflicts that women face between providing their children with the high-quality care and security that they feel only the mother can provide, and planning for the child's economic future by continuing to work. Although some women of lower educational attainment were willing to quit working if their husband has a well-paying job, others are insecure about their economic future if they do so. Blue- and white-collar women tended to see the value of working for the woman's individual development and autonomy, with some citing independence from the extended family specifically. But most made these statements in the context that good quality child care was available as an alternative.

Another alternative that some respondents cited was for mothers to combine work and child care by working in the informal sector, whether in their home or nearby. Those working in a formal setting also often took their child to work as a back-up form of care, such as when the regular caretaker was unavailable or the pre-school was closed for a holiday. Although few respondents suggested that taking a child to work is an ideal solution, many mentioned it as a way of continuing to earn income in the face of economic necessity when there were no acceptable child care alternatives.

It should be noted that a substantial minority of respondents in the household survey chose a relative or others as the first choice to care for a child over 6 months, presumably because it is better for the mother to work. This may be because it is seen as a logical division of labor within the household:

> At first I thought that I would take care of my baby myself, and my mother sold fruit here, but then she started staying home and I came to work. Mom is older so it's better for her to stay at home (to care for the child) and let me sell things. (Informal sector worker with young children)

Care by Relatives

Relatives, and particularly the grandmother, were the clear second choice to the mother to care for young children. The preference for relatives' care if the mother is not available is apparent in the bottom half of Table 23.1, with nearly 50% choosing the grandmother as the second best choice for a young baby and another 24% choosing another (or any) relative. Over and over again, respondents said that they can trust their own relatives; as mentioned above, the grandmother was sometimes thought to be a better choice for child care than the mother if the mother could bring in a good income herself. Often they said "They raise them like their own children"; "They take care of her better than me"; "They won't even let me discipline my child."

The preference for relatives' care expressed by respondents reflects the traditional prevalence of extended-family residence in Thailand. Preference for maternal relatives was stated by many respondents; in the household survey, 39% chose the maternal grandmother as a second best choice for young babies versus 9% for the paternal grandmother. This follows the customary pattern of postmarital residence in north and northeast Thailand, where the preference is for the husband to move in with the wife's parents for at least a short period of time (Potter, 1976; Thorbek, 1987). In fact, most reports of conflict with relatives over child care in the in-depth interviews were with those from the paternal side and most reports of high-quality care were from the maternal side. The continuing theme in reports of conflict, however, was that mothers cannot complain to their relatives directly. This is mainly due to the Thai tradition of respect to older relatives and the desire to avoid conflict, particularly with in-laws. But respondents also stated that they cannot complain, because they depend on their relatives for child care.

P1:   Sometimes they [paternal relatives] let my baby play alone, they don't follow him around. I am not very happy about it.

Moderator: And what do you do?

P1:   I don't do anything. I just get frustrated and ask my older kids to take care of him.

Moderator: If you see your mother or your mother-in-law treat your children some way you don't like, what would you do, would you take the children back (home)?

P1:   We can't do that.

P2:   The grandmother would cry, they won't like it. (Informal sector focus group)

For this reason, some high-status respondents preferred having a non-relative care for the children.

> If we leave it to the grandmothers [to care for the child] when they do something that we don't approve of, we cannot tell them, even though we know in theory how a child should be raised. So, we can tell the babysitter to do what we want her to do. The babysitter won't let the child have its own way too much. (White-collar focus group)

But many respondents continued to express a preference for relatives' care even in situations with conflict, and the network of obligations among extended families is still strong.

> Even if you had a conflict [in the past], you're still related. You can trust your own relatives. (Informal sector focus group)

The choice of child care becomes more difficult when no close relatives are living nearby. Living separately from young children is not uncommon for Bangkok women (Richter, 1996). The most typical pattern is for children to be sent to the maternal relatives (usually the grandparents) in the mother's rural hometown. However, there is a great deal of variation in the situations, with some children living with paternal relatives and some remaining behind when the mother migrated to Bangkok alone. Those who consider having their child live apart from them must weigh the costs and benefits. This usually involves choosing between care by a relative versus a nonrelative; having the child live in Bangkok versus a rural area; and of course, living with the mother versus seeing her only when she is able to visit. Many of those in the in-depth interviews and focus group discussions who lived apart from their child were forced to do so by economic circumstances. Others, including some high-status women, chose to have their children cared for by relatives, even if they had to live apart, rather than having to hire a nonrelative in Bangkok.

> It would be better for the child's mental health [to live separately]. Whether you have a chance to talk to your child or not, the relatives will surely love the child and would give the best to him. (White-collar focus group)

Living separately from young children appears to be another effect of the massive rural-to-urban migration of recent years, as well as an example of the flexibility of the Thai family structure that has been described by other research (Chamratrithirong, Morgan, & Rindfuss, 1988; Chamratrithirong et al., 1995; Keyes, 1977).

Care by Nonrelatives

Though relatives are preferred, many of the respondents had relied on a nonrelative for child care at some point. A substantial minority (about 11%) said that a nonrelative was the second best choice to the mother for a child under 1 year old (Table 23.1). Clear status differences emerged in the type of babysitter preferred by the respondents in the qualitative phase of the study. Those of higher status preferred a live-in servant or a babysitter who came to their home every day, whereas blue-collar or informal-sector women often took their child to a neighbor. This was partly due to the higher cost of a live-in nanny or in-home babysitter, but other issues were raised as well, as discussed below. Across status groups, a caretaker known to the parents directly or through a relative, friend, or neighborhood contact was preferred.

In the in-depth interviews and focus group discussions, respondents were asked the qualities they would look for if they must find a nonrelative to care for their child. Women working in informal-sector jobs tended to live in neighborhoods where people were known to each other and found a babysitter through informal networks of friends, neighbors, and relatives. They also counted on this network to report on how well the babysitters cared for their child.

Moderator: How do you know if the person loves children?

P1:   It has to be someone we can trust.

P2:   Usually people tell you. We have to take the kid first and then wait to have the people around the house tell us how the babysitter treats our baby.

P1:   And if she doesn't do a good job, we can bring the baby back. (Informal sector focus group)

Women of higher status also relied on networks of relatives and friends, particularly in finding a live-in servant from up-country. In the past, it was easy to find young women from up-country to provide this kind of care, but with changes in the Thai economy, it has become very difficult.

P1: In the past it was very easy [to find a babysitter] and they didn't even demand a salary, they were happy with what they could get [room and board only].

P2: Now it's very difficult. They usually want a place where they can just do housework. If the job involves taking care of a baby, they don't want it.

P3: Yes, most girls now want to go to work in a factory. If the salary is about the same, they would choose the factory and if the child is very active and they have to work hard, they won't come at all. (White-collar worker focus group)

Some higher status respondents had very high qualifications for a babysitter, expressing a preference for a "nanny" trained by an agency or more formal types of care if they were unable to find a live-in servant through personal contacts. These alternatives are much more expensive than those found informally.

Although some respondents reported that they had found high quality and trusted babysitters for their children, the household survey found that reports of conflict with nonrelatives were higher than for all other types. A general feeling of mistrust was present in discussions of finding a non-relative to care for young children. This was expressed both in actual experiences of neglect and abuse by babysitters and in "horror stories" heard from others.

> These young girls, we can't trust them because they could drop our baby and we wouldn't know. We worry about our baby's brains because we've heard about a case where the baby was dropped and the child became retarded. (White-collar worker focus group)

Formal Care

Nearly one fifth (19%) of the respondents in the household survey said that a child should enter a preschool or nursery by age 1 to 3, and the majority (61%) said that a child should enter school at age 3 to 5 (see Table 23.1).[3] In the focus group discussions and in-depth interviews, several higher status women stated that nurseries provided a better quality of care than in-home or outside babysitters. This is both because the people who worked there were trained and because they had better facilities, such as screens on the windows and sometimes even doctors available. But women working in the informal sector said that they preferred the flexibility of a babysitter over the more formal and expensive care provided at a nursery.

Although most respondents thought that children should enter preschool by about age 3, a general dislike was expressed among women at all socioeconomic levels for bringing younger children to a formal setting. Parents were concerned about having no control over what the children ate and whether they ate, and disliked the fact that the children had to sleep at the same time. This viewpoint came from a belief that young children need more individual care, as well as from rumors and direct experience with poor-quality nurseries.

> I took my oldest daughter to a nursery when she was 2 1/2 years old so that she would learn something. The neighbor said that they saw the teacher whip my child with a belt. So I brought my baby home after only 1 day. I paid already too. (Factory worker focus group)

> P1: I once sent my child to a nursery, a legal, registered nursery. . . . I was expecting that they would know what kind of food to give to babies according to their level of development but they did not really do it that way. They just did what was convenient for them.

P2: I have seen a nursery feeding five to six kids with one spoon, one plate.

P3: The children that are sent to a nursery usually get sick, prone to colds. Some nurseries try to tempt the parents by installing air conditioners. I think that is not very good for the children because usually children get chronic colds and they lose their appetite. (White-collar worker focus group)

Formal care available in Bangkok varies a great deal both in cost and quality. It may be that the quality of the facilities that are affordable for women working in the informal sector is unacceptable to them. Yet the discussion indicates that high fees do not guarantee good quality care, and facilities are poorly regulated (Richter, Podhisita, Chamratrithirong, & Soonthorndhada, 1992). Formal care is a recent phenomenon in Bangkok, and unfamiliarity as well as bad experiences and word of mouth has led to the general mistrust expressed by many respondents as a child care choice for the youngest children.

A Model of Child Care Decision Making

Although there is some degree of consensus among parents about the ideal form of care, particularly for the youngest children, there are many considerations that dictate the actual form of care chosen. The qualitative phase of the research clearly showed that the priority for parents is to have someone they trust to care for their children, if not a relative then someone recommended by a relative or otherwise known to them. The availability of an acceptable child care provider, as well as economic need and/or the desire for individual actualization and autonomy, also contributes to the mother's decision to work. Determinants of the form of care chosen thus include not only the economic status of the family, but also the availability of relatives and the informal networks of nonrelatives available as babysitters. Though we had assumed that living apart from young children was a last resort dictated by economic necessity, we found that even some high-status women chose to send their child to relatives up-country if they did not have a trusted babysitter in Bangkok. Thus the rapidity of socioeconomic change has resulted not only in new choices but in unfamiliar challenges for parents.

For these reasons, the model of child care decision making that we have developed (see Figure 23.1) is in the form of a prism. As women move farther away from their first choice of child care, they are faced both with more choices and more factors to consider. A mother must weigh her need or desire to work with the availability of acceptable child care alternatives and/or her ability to combine work and child care. Costs mainly become a

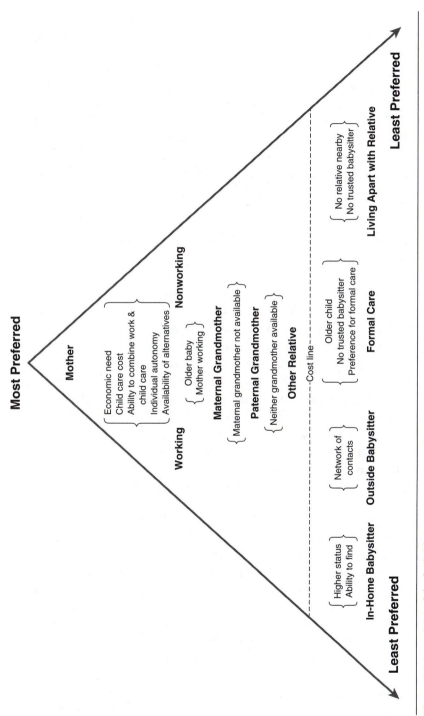

Figure 23.1   A Model of Child Care Decision Making

factor if no relative is available to care for the child, though there may be opportunity costs or emotional costs associated with care by the mother or a nonpreferred relative.

Thus, although some of the factors (shown in brackets in Figure 23.1) that women must consider in their decision making are based on economic status and costs, others are based more on personal preference or situational factors. The child's age, for example, is an important consideration for entry into formal care. And as the choice of child care moves further away from the apex of the prism, the clarity of the choice becomes more fuzzy and the decision-making process less defined. This model forms the background of the quantitative findings presented below.

Determinants of Labor Force Participation and Child Care Choice

Results from the household survey on whether the mother worked and, if so, the type of child care chosen, are presented for children at age 2. This is a particularly active age when it is difficult for women to combine work and child care, but when most feel children are too young to enter preschool. Information about mother's work status and children's child care arrangements were derived from the work and child care histories (for details on how variables were operationalized, see the Appendix). From the sample of 1,515 women, child care information was obtained for 1,562 children who had reached the age of 2 by the time of the survey.[4]

Table 23.2 shows the distribution of children by mother's work status and child care type at this age. Overall, about one third of children (33%) were cared for by a nonworking mother and another quarter (23%) by a mother who combined work with child care. One fifth (20%) were cared for by a relative, so that about three quarters of children at this age were in a preferred situation as defined by the model outlined above. Another 7% were cared for by a nonrelative in the home (a babysitter or live-in servant). Of those who were not cared for by a relative or a nonrelative at home (a total of 18%), more than half (10%) lived separately from their mothers. In other words, if a working mother did not have a relative or babysitter in the home to care for her child, she was as likely to live separately from the child as to find another child care arrangement outside the home. These findings provide further evidence for the preference model outlined above: A large percentage of mothers managed to care for their child themselves, even if they worked, and care by a relative was preferred to care by a nonrelative outside the home, even if the child had to live separately from the mother.

Table 23.2 Child Care at Age 2 by Various Characteristics (in percentages)

| | Working Mother/Nonmaternal Care | | | | | | | | |
	Nonworking Mother	Care by Mother	Relative	Nonrelative at Home	Nonrelative Outside	Nursery/ Center	Living Separately	Total	N
Total	34	23	20	7	4	4	10	100	(1,562)
Child's birth cohort									
Before 1977	40	22	21	5	2	2	10	100	(140)
1977 through 1982	31	24	19	6	5	2	13	100	(243)
1982 through 1986	35	22	19	9	3	5	9	100	(346)
1987 through 1991	30	25	21	5	5	6	8	100	(216)
Number of siblings									
Only child	28	19	25	7	5	5	12	100	(644)
One sibling	33	24	18	8	3	4	10	100	(624)
Two or more siblings	47	31	12	3	3	1	4	100	(294)
Mother's age at birth									
Under 20	33	23	23	2	2	1	16	100	(180)
20 through 24	39	22	17	3	4	3	12	100	(553)
25 through 29	31	20	25	8	4	4	8	100	(527)
30 and over	27	30	16	14	4	5	5	100	(302)
Mother's education									
Less than primary graduate	38	32	16	0	1	4	9	100	(100)
Primary graduate	39	29	14	3	3	3	9	100	(950)
Secondary	43	16	18	5	5	3	11	100	(219)
University	9	6	40	23	5	8	10	100	(293)

(Continued)

Table 23.2 (Continued)

		Working Mother/Nonmaternal Care							
	Nonworking Mother	Care by Mother	Relative	Nonrelative at Home	Nonrelative Outside	Nursery/ Center	Living Separately	Total	N
Mother's migrant status									
Nonmigrant	31	24	24	7	4	4	8	100	(996)
Migrant	39	22	13	7	4	3	13	100	(566)
Mother's workplace									
Home	–	82	8	2	1	3	4	100	(319)
Market/other informal	–	36	30	5	7	2	21	100	(154)
Factory	–	2	43	4	13	2	37	100	(103)
Office/school/institution	–	1	49	22	9	7	13	100	(365)
Mother's ideal child care response									
Mother	34	24	17	7	4	3	11	100	(1,051)
Relative	23	34	28	2	4	0	9	100	(94)
Nonrelative	29	17	28	10	3	4	9	100	(127)
Formal care	34	18	23	7	3	8	7	100	(290)
Ideal care if mother working									
Relative	32	25	20	5	4	3	12	100	(671)
Nonrelative	41	22	13	9	4	3	9	100	(352)
Formal care	18	32	5	18	14	5	9	100	(22)

| | Nonworking Mother | Working Mother/Nonmaternal Care | | | | | | | |
		Care by Mother	Relative	Nonrelative at Home	Nonrelative Outside	Nursery/ Center	Living Separately	Total	N
Father's occupation									
Professional/technical	16	10	30	25	3	8	8	100	(158)
Clerical	27	11	28	13	11	4	6	100	(137)
Trade	35	31	15	7	0	4	9	100	(245)
Services	31	25	17	3	5	4	14	100	(155)
Manufacturing	46	7	17	3	7	1	18	100	(123)
Construction	47	19	23	1	1	1	9	100	(56)
Labor	38	28	18	3	2	5	7	100	(439)
Father's presence in household									
Present	34	23	20	7	3	3	9	100	(1,484)
Absent	23	17	22	5	9	0	24	100	(78)
Presence of household members									
Maternal grandmother	27	21	37	5	2	5	2	100	(285)
Paternal grandmother	35	28	25	3	2	2	5	100	(302)
Other adult female relatives	33	23	27	7	2	3	6	100	(515)

The determinants of child care choice to be examined are shown in Table 23.2, with further details in the Appendix. The variable measuring child's birth cohort serves as an indicator of trends in type of care. Number of siblings provides a measure of other demands on the mother's time, as well as of economies of scale that may be relevant for child care decisions. Mother's age at child's birth serves as a proxy for her years of labor-market experience, as well as for the likelihood that the grandmother is available for care. Educational attainment is a measure of her human capital as well as an indicator of the child care ideals discussed earlier. The mother's migrant status measures the likely availability of extended family members for child care. Because the mother's work status, workplace, and occupation are strongly correlated, only her workplace is examined; this gives a direct measure of the flexibility of the mother's job with regard to working hours, the formality of the setting, and so on. Socioeconomic status is measured by the father's occupation; though women make substantial contributions to household income in Thailand, the husband's earning status is a significant determinant of the ability of a mother to forgo working to care for the child or, conversely, to pay for alternative child care if she wishes to work (Richter & Havanon, 1994). The presence of family members in the household who may be available to provide child care, including the grandmother and other adult females, is also examined. Mother's child care preferences are included to examine whether they have an additional effect on child care choice when other factors are controlled.

Although Table 23.2 shows sharp differences by socioeconomic status and household coresidence variables, multivariate analysis is needed to disentangle these effects, particularly in regard to the balance between preferences, the ability to afford paid care, and the availability of relatives. Following the conceptual model of child care decision making developed above, a series of discrete choice models were estimated using the continuation-ratio logit approach (Fienberg, 1980; Agresti, 1984). Thus child care choice was examined as a sequence of decisions, and different factors may be more or less important at different stages of decision making. The first decision examined is whether the mother worked when the child was age 2. This decision depends on the mother's desire and ability to care for the child herself, household economic need, and the availability of alternate forms of care. If the mother does work, parents are seen to follow a system of preferences by which they ultimately choose a form of child care. As more preferred choices of care are eliminated, they turn to the next most acceptable type. In the binary choice between nonmaternal care and maternal care for working mothers, we expect that the ability to combine work and child care depends both on the mother's job characteristics and on the family's ability to pay for child care. Next to be examined are the factors differentiating whether a child is cared for by a relative or a nonrelative, given that they are not cared for by their mother. The preference model developed from the qualitative data predicts that this most preferred choice of nonmaternal care cuts across occupational and socioeconomic class lines, and is mainly determined by the availability of relatives. However, some high-status respondents expressed the desire for independence from relatives if they could afford paid child care. Finally, a multinomial logit model is estimated to explore the determinants of whether a child is cared for by a nonrelative in the home, by a nonrelative outside the home, is in formal care, or is living separately from the mother—given that the child is not cared for by the mother or another relative. As cost becomes a factor in child care decision making, the "next best" choice of care may differ by family resources, the mother's job flexibility and the preferences discussed above.

Results for the three binary choice models are shown in Table 23.3. Model 1 shows no increasing trend to mothers working when other factors are controlled, confirming the results of Wongboonsin et al. (1991). The expected relationship between employment and fertility is found, with children in larger families less likely to have a working mother. Two economic indicators—mother's secondary education and father's employment in manufacturing—have a negative effect on whether the mother is working. These groups may be seen as having midlevel socioeconomic status, where it makes more sense economically for the mother to care for children herself than to pay for care; or alternatively, that the family can afford for the mother to take time away from the labor market while children are small, as expressed by several blue-collar women in the qualitative data. Children of mothers with a university education are particularly likely to have a working mother at this age, even with other factors controlled. Migrant women are less likely to work, which has been a consistent finding in research on migration and the labor market in Bangkok (Richter & Ogena, 1995). If the father is absent from the household, the mother is more likely to work, probably as a result of economic need. And as expected, with other factors controlled, those who state a preference for relative care and who live with the maternal grandmother are more likely to work.

Model 2 explores the factors determining whether the child is in nonmaternal care given that the mother is working. The mother's workplace, measuring the flexibility of her job, has the strongest effect on whether the child is cared for by the mother; her age or education or the number of children in the family are not significant factors, and there does not appear to be a trend. The ability to pay for child care also has an effect on whether the mother cares for the child herself, as those whose fathers worked in professional or clerical jobs or in manufacturing were more likely to be in nonmaternal care.

Table 23.3   Logistic Regression Models for 2-Year-Old Children

	Mother Working		Nonmaternal Care		Relative Care	
	Beta	SE	Beta	SE	Beta	SE
Intercept	0.74	0.24	−1.53	0.44	−0.10	0.48
Child's birth cohort (Before 1977)						
1977 through 1981	0.28	0.18	0.12	0.34	−0.44	0.31
1982 through 1986	0.05	0.18	−0.21	0.35	−0.32	0.30
1987 through 1989	0.20	0.20	−0.37	0.39	−0.27	0.33
Child's number of siblings (Only child)						
One sibling	−0.31**	0.14	−0.13	0.25	−0.17	0.20
Two or more siblings	−0.97***	0.18	−0.12	0.35	0.33	0.34
Mother's age at child's birth (Under 20)						
20 through 24	−0.33*	0.20	0.11	0.35	−0.22	0.34
25 through 29	−0.04	0.21	−0.16	0.38	0.25	0.36
30 and over	0.33	0.25	−0.51	0.45	−0.17	0.42
Mother's education (Primary)						
Secondary	−0.42**	0.17	−0.30	0.42	−0.35	0.32
University	1.65***	0.25	−0.15	0.50	−0.44	0.29
Mother's migrant status (Nonmigrant)						
Migrant	−0.24*	0.13	0.14	0.25	−0.48**	0.21
Mother's workplace (Home)						
Market/informal			2.24***	0.25	−0.06	0.38
Factory			5.27***	0.75	0.29	0.40
Office/institution			6.10***	0.61	0.60*	0.36
Father's occupation (Labor/construction)						
Professional	0.29	0.28	1.31**	0.60	−0.69**	0.31
Clerical	0.09	0.24	1.07**	0.48	−0.78**	0.32
Trade	0.02	0.17	0.08	0.31	−0.28	0.32
Services	0.22	0.21	−0.54	0.38	−0.76**	0.34
Manufacturing	−0.59***	0.22	1.15*	0.60	−0.71*	0.40
Father's presence in the household (Present)						
Absent	0.52*	0.31	0.80	0.52	−0.91**	0.39

	Mother Working		Nonmaternal Care		Relative Care	
	Beta	SE	Beta	SE	Beta	SE
Presence of household members						
Maternal grandmother	0.40**	0.18	−0.02	0.34	1.60***	0.25
Paternal grandmother	−0.18	0.16	0.08	0.30	1.47***	0.27
Other adult female relative	−0.15	0.14	0.15	0.27	0.42**	0.20
Mother's child care preference[a] (Mother)						
Relative	0.77***	0.27	−0.43	0.42		
Nonrelative	0.30	0.22	0.37	0.42	−0.35	0.22
Formal care	−0.21	0.16	0.17	0.33	−0.28	0.24
−2 Log likelihood	1696.4		537.0		717.2	
N	1562		941		619	

NOTE: Models estimate whether the mother is working, whether the child is in nonmaternal care versus maternal care given that the mother is working, and relative versus nonrelative care given that care is not by the mother (omitted variable in parentheses).

[a]For Models 1 & 2, first choice of care; for Model 3, preference if mother must work. "Relative" is the omitted category for Model 3.

$*p < .10; **p < .05; ***p < .01.$

Though qualitative evidence showed that women may be more likely to place children in another's care when a close relative is available, the presence of extended family members in the household did not significantly affect whether the children were cared for by their mother. It should be remembered however that effect occurs when controlling for mother's workplace; in other words, given that the mother's job allows it, mothers may also be better able to combine work and child care when family members are available to help. Finally, the preference for alternate forms of care does not play a significant role when other factors are controlled.

Model 3 shows the factors affecting whether a child is cared for by a relative given that they are not cared for by their mother. As predicted, variables measuring the presence of potential caregivers within or outside the household are significant. These include the mother's migrant status (an indicator of potential relatives outside the household but within Bangkok) and the presence of the maternal or paternal grandmother and other adult females in the household. The father's absence is also significant, even when migrant status is taken into account; though very few fathers were listed as primary caregivers in the sample, they may provide backup or secondary care (Richter et al., 1992). Those of higher socioeconomic status, as measured by the father's occupation, are less likely to be in a relative's care. In other words, there is an indication that higher income families are more likely to use paid child care, further evidence of the desire expressed earlier for separation from extended families. This relationship holds even though the mother's stated preference for nonrelative care does not.

Table 23.4 shows the results of the multinomial logit model of factors differentiating type of care when the child is not cared for by the mother or another relative.[5] The contrast is shown between choosing (a) a nonrelative in the home versus outside the home; (b) a nonrelative in the home versus formal care; (c) a nonrelative outside the home versus formal care; and (d) a nonrelative outside the home versus living separately. The model reveals that although recent birth cohorts appear to have experienced a decline in in-home babysitters, this corresponds with a rise in the use of nonrelatives outside the home when other factors are controlled; recent cohorts are also more likely to be in this arrangement than to live separately. Larger families tend to have an in-home babysitter rather than care by an outside babysitter or formal care, probably due to the economies of scale offered by having one sitter care for two or more children. Children with older mothers are less likely to live separately than to be cared for by a nonrelative outside the home, indicating in part the greater likelihood of available grandparents for younger mothers. Those whose mother has a university education are more likely to be cared for by a nonrelative in the home than by one outside the home, as predicted; but they are also more likely to live separately than to be cared for by a nonrelative outside the home. The same is true for children of migrants, as expected. Those whose mother works at home are more likely to have an in-home than an outside babysitter, presumably because the mother can provide supervision. They are also more likely to be in formal care, as are children living with a maternal grandmother. In other words, the small group of children whose mother and/or maternal grandmother are available for care, yet are not cared for by them, are likely to be in formal care. The presence of other female relatives besides the grandmother also appears to enable the use of an in-home sitter, likely for supervision. Father's occupation, as a measure of socioeconomic status, does not significantly predict the type of nonrelative care chosen, given that children are in nonrelative care, except that those with a professional/clerical father are more likely to have an outside babysitter than to live separately. Nor does the mother's preference for a relative or for formal care seem to affect whether the child lives separately or is in formal care, likely because such preferences are closely associated with other factors.

Table 23.4   Multinomial Logit Model Contrasting Various Types of Nonrelative Care

	Nonrelative at Home versus Outside Home		Nonrelative at Home versus Formal Care		Nonrelative Outside Home versus Separately		Nonrelative Outside Home versus Formal Care	
	Beta	SE	Beta	SE	Beta	SE	Beta	SE
Intercept	1.67	1.46	–0.59	1.45	–4.17	1.25	–2.26	1.64
Child's birth cohort								
(Before 1977)								
1977 through 1981	–1.23*	0.74	1.37	0.99	0.96	0.64	2.60	1.06
1982 through 1986	–0.24	0.74	–0.03	0.81	0.41	0.67	0.20	0.92
1987 through 1989	–1.84**	0.81	–1.16	0.87	1.33*	0.71	0.68	0.96
Child's number of siblings								
(Only child)								
One sibling	0.86*	0.44	1.06**	0.49	–0.42	0.40	0.21	0.55
Two or more siblings	–0.19	0.70	1.60	1.01	0.32	0.66	1.79*	1.06
Mother's age at child's birth								
(Under 20)								
20 through 24	–1.00	0.97	0.18	1.15	1.26*	0.73	1.17	1.16
25 through 29	–0.64	0.99	–0.36	1.14	1.68**	0.79	–0.28	1.15
30+	–0.32	1.06	–0.27	1.21	2.22**	0.89	0.05	1.25
Mother's education								
(Primary)								
Secondary	0.12	0.65	1.15	0.95	–0.52	0.56	1.03	0.97
University	1.93***	0.60	0.76	0.69	–1.67***	0.59	–1.18	0.73
Mother's migrant status								
(Nonmigrant)								
Migrant	0.67	0.44	–0.07	0.50	–0.81**	0.40	–0.74	0.56
Mother's workplace								
(Home)								
Market/informal	–2.17**	1.04	1.33	0.97	1.75*	0.93	3.51***	1.18
Factory	–2.38**	1.08	1.19	1.12	1.47	0.90	3.57***	1.23
Office/institution	–1.96	0.98	1.11	0.80	2.23**	0.92	3.07	1.05

(Continued)

Table 23.4 (Continued)

	Nonrelative at Home versus Outside Home		Nonrelative at Home versus Formal Care		Nonrelative Outside Home versus Separately		Nonrelative Outside Home versus Formal Care	
	Beta	SE	Beta	SE	Beta	SE	Beta	SE
Father's occupation								
(Labor/construction/ manufacturing)								
Professional/clerical	0.48	0.51	0.90	0.58	0.80*	0.48	0.42	0.64
Trade/services	0.65	0.60	−0.13	0.62	−0.53	0.53	−0.78	0.70
Presence of household members								
Maternal grandmother	−0.13	0.66	−1.57*	0.62	1.10	0.74	−1.44*	0.74
Paternal grandmother	−0.18	0.70	−0.90	0.70	0.36	0.64	−0.72	0.81
Other adult female relative	1.11**	0.51	−0.12	0.50	−0.58	0.50	−0.99	0.62
Mother's child care preference								
(Relative)								
Nonrelative	0.62	0.46	0.05	0.55	0.34	0.42	−0.56	0.60
Formal care	0.11	0.52	−0.71	0.57	0.81	0.50	−0.82	0.64
-2 log likelihood	626.1							
N	324							

NOTE: Care is not by the mother or another relative (omitted variable in parentheses).
$*p < .10; **p < .05; ***p < .01.$

Discussion

The goal of this article has been to construct a model of child care decision making, with particular attention to preferences and how they are balanced with economic factors. The setting for the study is one where rapid socioeconomic development has created new roles for women, as evidenced by higher educational attainment, lower fertility, greater proportions working in a formal setting, urban migration creating distance from extended family, and a lessened ability to combine work and child care. Given this setting, the preference model developed from the qualitative data predicted a strong preference for care by a relative, even if the child had to live separately from their mother. Respondents expressed distrust of nonrelative care and of placing children in a formal setting at a young age. Those who needed to rely on a nonrelative preferred someone known to them; higher-status women tended to rely on a network of relatives and friends to find an in-home servant or babysitter, whereas those working in an informal setting tended to rely on neighbors.

The quantitative analysis of actual child care arrangements taken from a representative sample of Bangkok women tested both to what extent the preference model accurately predicts child care choice and whether the preferences expressed by working mothers are being met in reality. Overall, about three quarters of children were cared for by their mother or another relative when they were age 2. The mother's work status at this age was related to situational factors (the number of children in the family, presence of the maternal grandmother), the mother's educational status, and her preferences. Economic factors as measured by the father's occupation were less important, though there is some indication that mothers who preferred to care for their child themselves and could afford to forgo working were doing so. Though the degree to which mothers were working in a formal setting was the strongest predictor of being in nonmaternal care (given that she worked), we also found evidence that children of higher socioeconomic status were more likely to be in nonmaternal care. And though the availability of relatives was the strongest predictor of being in a relative's care (given that the child is in nonmaternal care), those of higher socioeconomic status were also found to be less likely to be in a relative's care. Focusing on children cared for by nonrelatives, the quantitative model confirmed that more educated mothers tended to choose a nonrelative in the home over one outside the home, and would choose living separately from the child over this arrangement as well. The decline in care by in-home babysitters for recent cohorts seems to have led to increased use of outside babysitters rather than formal care.

What do these findings reveal about how social changes affect women's roles within the family? In this urban setting, there is emerging evidence for a greater diversity in child care choices, and this diversity implies increasing separation from the extended family. Families with greater economic resources and where the mother is working in the modern sector appear to be choosing paid care over that by a relative. It is important not to overstate the evidence for this trend: Care by the mother or a relative remains both the predominant ideal and the major form of care for young children. Several key factors in child care choice are unmeasured by the model, such as whether the grandmother is still living and/or healthy enough to care for a young child, and families who can afford it may prefer to hire a babysitter only given that the grandmother is on the scene to supervise. Still, respondents in the qualitative phase of the research raised issues of independence from the family when secure child care could be found.

In several ways we have found similarities to the U.S. situation, such as higher-status families having a greater tendency to use nonrelative paid care and using more formal types of care. Important differences remain, such as the greater ability of women to combine work and child care, and the continued greater preference for relative care even if the child must live separately. These findings help to confirm results from small-scale studies in Thailand (Bunyanupongsa, 1987; Jaroensuk, 1981; & Wongboonsin et al., 1991) and Latin America (Connelly et al., 1996; Wong & Levine, 1992) on the relationship between child care and women's entry into the modern labor market. They also confirm that child care preferences have an effect on child care choice even when controlling for economic and situational factors (Johansen et al., 1994; Kuhlthau & Mason, 1990). Finally, by presenting qualitative evidence on child care decision making and on the values and social norms underlying these decisions, we are able to see the reasoning behind complex decision-making patterns that has been absent from previous research. It also enables the analysis to go beyond post facto evidence on economic determinants of child care type by allowing us to order decision making in the sequence that such choices are usually made. The model presented here should be tested by research in other contexts to provide further insight into this process.

APPENDIX   Variable Definitions and Construction

Variable	Source	Definition
Child care type	Child care histories	Child care at age 2
Child's birth cohort	Fertility history	Grouped from year of child's birth
Number of siblings	Fertility history	Number of older and younger children when child was age 2
Mother's age at child's birth	Fertility history	Grouped from mother's age at child's birth
Mother's education	Survey question	Grouped from years of education
Mother's migrant status	Migration history	Whether mother born in Bangkok
Mother's workplace	Work history	Workplace when child was age 2
Mother's ideal child care	Survey question	Grouped (see Table 23.1)

Variable	Source	Definition
Father's occupation	Father's work history	Father's occupation when child was age 2
Father present	Household coresidence history	Presence when child was age 2
Maternal grandmother present	Household coresidence history	Presence when child was age 2
Paternal grandmother present	Household coresidence history	Presence when child was age 2
Other female relatives present	Household coresidence history	Presence when child was age 2

Notes

1. Four focus groups were held for participants who had children under age 10: three for women in each of the occupational sectors and one for men in the blue-collar sector. Approximately 7 to 9 participants took part in each focus group. Ten in-depth interviews were held for women with children of various ages and in various work statuses and occupations, including nonworking women. Participants were identified by personal contacts with businesses in the area and "snowball sampling" techniques (Yoddumnern-Attig, Pituckmahaket, & Kanungsukkasem, 1993).

2. The sample was obtained by selecting 60 blocks at random using detailed maps of the city prepared by the National Statistical Office (NSO). Within each block, 25 cases were selected using target guidelines for three major work status groups—housewives, informal status workers, and workers outside the home. These guidelines were established to assure that a sufficient proportion of women working outside the home were obtained, because they tended to be much less accessible in the field than housewives and women working in the informal sector. The target guidelines were set according to data from the 1987 Labor Force Survey performed by the NSO (1987). The completed sample was found to conform to other comparable surveys and census data in regard to the women's age, fertility, and labor force participation. Further details on the qualitative and quantitative data may be found in Richter et al. (1992).

3. The quantitative survey revealed that 4% of children were in a formal setting at age 2 (see Table 23.2), 10% by age 3, and 39% by age 4 (Richter et al., 1992). Respondents often did not make a clear distinction among the various types of formal care, likely because such facilities are such a recent phenomenon in Bangkok. Even children as young as 18 months were described as going to "school" whereas some as old as age 4 were reported as attending a "nursery." For this reason, these statistics combine the various types of formal care.

4. A few cases ($n = 10$) were eliminated because the children were living separately from their mother with a nonrelative, sometimes in an institutional setting. Because the circumstances of these children is so different from those living with a relative, they are not included in the bivariate or multivariate analysis. See Richter (1996) for further details on children living separately from their mother.

5. Due to the small number of cases, some variables have been eliminated and categories combined for the final model.

References

Agresti, A. (1984). *Analysis of ordinal categorical data*. New York: John Wiley.

Axinn, W. G., Fricke, T. E., & Thornton, A. (1991). The microdemographic community-study approach: Improving survey data by integrating the ethnographic method. *Sociological Methods and Research, 20*(2), 187–217.

Bunyanupongsa, K. (1987). Problems of child-rearing for working women in Muang district of Chiang Mai (in Thai). Social Science Institute, Chiang Mai University.

Caldwell, J. C., Hill, A. G., & Hull, V. J. (Eds.). (1988). *Microapproaches to demographic research*. London: Kegan Paul International.

Chamratrithirong, A., Morgan, S. P., & Rindfuss, R. R. (1988, June). Living arrangements and family formation. *Social Forces, 66,* 926–950.

Chamratrithirong, A., Archavanitkul, K., Richter, K., Guest, P., Thongthai, V., Boonchalaksi, W., Piriyathamwong, N., & Vong-Ek, P. (1995). *National migration survey of Thailand*. Institute for Population and Social Research, Publication No. 188.

Connelly, R., DeGraff, D. S., & Levison, D. (1996). Women's employment and child care in Brazil. *Economic Development and Cultural Change, 44*(3), 619.

DaVanzo, J., & Poh Lee, D. L. (1983). The compatibility of child care with market and non-market activities: Preliminary evidence from Malaysia. In M. Buvinic, M. A. Lycette, & W. P. McGreevey (Eds.), *Women and poverty in the Third World* (pp. 62–91). Baltimore: Johns Hopkins University Press.

Fienberg, S. E. (1980). *The analysis of cross-classified categorical data: Second edition*. Cambridge: MIT Press.

Floge, L. (1989). Changing household structure, child-care availability, and employment among mothers of preschool children. *Journal of Marriage and the Family, 51*(1), 51–63.

Folch-Lyon, E., de la Macorra, L., Schearer, S. B. (1981). Focus group and survey research on family planning in Mexico. *Studies in Family Planning, 12*(12), 409–432.

Folk, K. F., & Beller, A. H. (1993). Part-time work and child care choices for mothers of preschool children. *Journal of Marriage and the Family, 55*(1), 146–157.

Hofferth, S. L. (1991). Comments on *The importance of child care costs to women's decision making*. In D. M. Blau (Ed.), *The economics of child care* (pp. 119–125). New York: Russell Sage Foundation.

Hofferth, S. L., & Wissoker, D. A. (1992). Price, quality and income in child care choice. *Journal of Human Resources, XXVII*(1), 70–111.

Institute for Population and Social Research (1987). Contraceptive use prevalence survey. Salaya: Mahidol University.

Jaroensuk, S. (1981). Survey of child-rearing of working mothers. Unpublished master's thesis (in Thai). Bangkok: Ramkhamhaeng University, Faculty of Education.

Johansen, A. S., Leibowitz, A., & Waite, L. J. 1994. Parents' demand for child care. Rand Labor and Population Program Working Paper series 94–13.

Keyes, C. F. 1977. *The golden peninsula: Culture and adaptation in mainland Southeast Asia.* New York: Macmillan.

Knodel, J., Chamratrithirong, A., & Debavalya, N. (1987). *Thailand's reproductive revolution: Rapid fertility decline in a Third World setting.* Madison: University of Wisconsin Press.

Kuhlthau, K., & Mason, K. O. (1990). Type of child care: Determinants of use in a metropolitan area. Presented at the annual meeting of the Population Association of America, Toronto.

Lehrer, E. L. (1983). Determinants of child care mode choice: An economic perspective. *Social Science Research, 12*(1), 69–80.

Lehrer, E. L. (1989). Preschoolers with working mothers: An analysis of the determinants of child care arrangements. *Journal of Population Economics, 1*(2), 251–268.

Leibowitz, A., Klerman, J. A., & Waite, L. J. (1992). Employment of New Mothers and Child Care Choice: Differences by Children's Age. *Journal of Human Resources, XXVII*(1), 112–133.

Masini, E., & Stratigos, S. (Eds.). (1991). *Women, households and change.* Tokyo: United Nations University Press.

Mason, K. O., & Duberstein, L. (1992). Consequences of child care for parents' well-being. In A. Booth (Ed.), *Child care in the 1990's: Trends and consequences.* Hillsdale, N.J.: Lawrence Erlbaum.

Mason, K. O., & Kuhlthau, K. (1989). Determinants of child care ideals among mothers of pre-school aged children. *Journal of Marriage and the Family, 51*(3), 593–603.

Mason, K. O., & Kuhlthau, K. (1992). The perceived impact of child care costs on women's labor supply and fertility. *Demography, 29*(4), 523–44.

Ministry of Education. (1992). Personal communication.

National Statistical Office. (1972). *Report of the labor force survey.* Bangkok: Office of the Prime Minister.

National Statistical Office. (1987). *Report of the labor force survey.* Bangkok: Office of the Prime Minister.

National Statistical Office. (1992). *Report of the labor force survey.* Bangkok: Office of the Prime Minister.

Oppong, C., & Abu, K. (1985). *Seven roles of women: The impact of education, migration and employment on Ghanian mothers.* Women, Work and Development Series. Geneva: International Labor Office.

Potter, J. M. (1976). *Thai Peasant Social Structure*. Chicago: University of Chicago Press.

Richter, K. (1996). Living separately as a child care strategy: Implications for women's work and family in urban Thailand. *Journal of Marriage and the Family, 58*(2), 327–39.

Richter, K., Podhisita, C., Chamratrithirong, A., & Soonthorndhada, K. (1992). *Child care in urban Thailand: Choice and constraint in a changing society*. Institute for Population and Social Research Publication No. 163.

Richter, K., Podhisita, C., Chamratrithirong, A., Soonthorndhada, K., &Havanon, N. (1994). *Women's economic contribution to households in Thailand: A re-definition*. Population Council/International Center for Research on Women Working Paper.

Richter, K., Podhisita, C., Chamratrithirong, A., Soonthorndhada, K., Havanon, N., & Ogena, N. (1995). The effect of gender, migration and family formation on employment transitions in Bangkok. Presented at the annual meetings of the Population Association of America, San Francisco.

Sonenstein, F. L. (1991). The child care preferences of parents with young children: How little is known. In J. Hyde & M. Essex (Eds.), *Parental leave and child care: Setting a research and policy agenda* (pp. 337–353). Philadelphia: Temple University Press.

Standing, G. (1983). Women's work activity and fertility. In R. A. Bulatao & R. D. Lee, et al. (Eds.), *Determinants of fertility in developing countries* (pp. 416–438). Washington, DC: National Academy Press.

Thorbek, S. (1987). *Voices from the city: Women of bangkok*. London: Zed Books.

Wong, R., & Levine, R. E. (1992). The effect of household structure on women's economic activity and fertility: Evidence from recent mothers in urban Mexico. *Economic Development and Cultural Change, 41*(1), 89–102.

Wongboonsin, K., Mason, K. O., & Choe, M. K. (1991). Child care in Thailand: Determinants and health consequences for preschool-aged children. Presented at the annual meeting of the American Sociological Association, Cincinnati.

Yoddumnern-Attig, B., Richter, K., Soonthorndhada, A., Sethaput, C., & Pramualratana, A. (1992). *Changing roles and statuses of women in Thailand: A documentary assessment*. Institute for Population and Social Research Publication No. 161.

Yoddumnern-Attig, B., Pituckmahaket, O., & Kanungsukkasem, U. (1993). The main types and steps of sampling. In B. Yoddumnern-Attig, G. A. Attig, W. Boonchalaksi, K. Richter, & W. Boonchalaksi (Eds.), *Qualitative research in a developing world: An introduction to studying populations and health* (chapter 13). Mahidol University. Institute for Population and Social Research Publication No. 172.

References Cited in the Editors' Introductions

Bishop, V. (2006). Mixed methodologies [Special Issue]. *Journal of Research in Nursing, 11*(3).

Brewer, J., & Hunter, A. (2005). *Foundations of multimethod research: Synthesizing styles* (2nd ed.). Thousand Oaks, CA: Sage.

Bryman, A. (2006). Integrating quantitative and qualitative research: How is it done? *Qualitative Research, 6*(1), 97–113.

Bryman, A. (2007). Barriers to integrating quantitative and qualitative research. *Journal of Mixed Methods Research, 1*(1), 8–22.

Caracelli, V. J., & Greene, J. C. (1993). Data analysis strategies for mixed-method evaluation designs. *Educational Evaluation and Policy Analysis, 15*(2), 195–207.

Caracelli, V. J., & Greene, J. C. (1997). Crafting mixed-method evaluation designs. In J. C. Greene & V. J. Caracelli (Eds.), *Advances in mixed-method evaluation: The challenges and benefits of integrating diverse paradigms* (pp. 19–32). San Francisco: Jossey-Bass.

Creswell, J. W., & Plano Clark, V. L. (2007). *Designing and conducting mixed methods research*. Thousand Oaks, CA: Sage.

Creswell, J. W., Plano Clark, V. L., Gutmann, M. L., & Hanson, W. E. (2003). Advanced mixed methods research designs. In A. Tashakkori & C. Teddlie (Eds.), *Handbook of mixed methods in social and behavioral research* (pp. 209–240). Thousand Oaks, CA: Sage.

Creswell, J. W., & Tashakkori, A. (2007). Developing publishable mixed methods manuscripts [Editorial]. *Journal of Mixed Methods Research, 1*(2), 107–111.

Creswell, J. W., Tashakkori, A., Jensen, K. D., & Shapley, K. L. (2003). Teaching mixed methods research: Practices, dilemmas, and challenges. In A. Tashakkori & C. Teddlie (Eds.), *Handbook of mixed methods in social and behavioral research* (pp. 619–637). Thousand Oaks, CA: Sage.

Donovan, J., Mills, N., Smith, M., Brindle, L., Jacoby, A., Peters, T., et al. (2002). Improving design and conduct of randomised trials by embedding them in qualitative research: ProtecT (prostate testing for cancer and treatment) study. *British Medical Journal, 325*, 766–769.

Greene, J. C. (2006). Toward a methodology of mixed methods social inquiry. *Research in the Schools, 13*(1), 93–98.

Greene, J. C., & Caracelli, V. J. (Eds.). (1997). *Advances in mixed-method evaluation: The challenges and benefits of integrating diverse paradigms.* New Directions for Evaluation, no. 74. San Francisco: Jossey-Bass.

Greene, J. C., & Caracelli, V. J. (2003). Making paradigmatic sense of mixed methods practice. In A. Tashakkori & C. Teddlie (Eds.), *Handbook of mixed methods in social and behavioral research* (pp. 91–110). Thousand Oaks, CA: Sage.

Greene, J. C., Caracelli, V. J., & Graham, W. F. (1989). Toward a conceptual framework for mixed-method evaluation designs. *Educational Evaluation and Policy Analysis, 11*(3), 255–274.

Howe, K. R. (2004) A critique of experimentalism. *Qualitative Inquiry, 10*(1), 42–61.

Idler, E. L., Hudson, S. V., & Leventhal, H. (1999). The meanings of self-ratings of health: A qualitative and quantitative approach. *Research on Aging, 21*(3), 458–476.

Ivankova, N. V., Creswell, J. W., & Stick, S. (2006). Using mixed methods sequential explanatory design: From theory to practice. *Field Methods, 18*(1), 3–20.

Jick, T. D. (1979). Mixing qualitative and quantitative methods: Triangulation in action. *Administrative Science Quarterly, 24,* 602–611.

Johnson, R. B. (2006). New directions in mixed methods research [Special Issue]. *Research in the Schools, 13*(1).

Johnson, R. B., & Onwuegbuzie, A. J. (2004). Mixed methods research: A research paradigm whose time has come. *Educational Researcher, 33*(7), 14–26.

Johnson, R. B., Onwuegbuzie, A. J., & Turner, L. A. (2007). Toward a definition of mixed methods research. *Journal of Mixed Methods Research, 1*(2), 112–133.

Luzzo, D. A. (1995). Gender differences in college students' career maturity and perceived barriers in career development. *Journal of Counseling & Development, 73,* 319–322.

Mertens, D. M. (2003). Mixed methods and the politics of human research: The transformative-emancipatory perspective. In A. Tashakkori & C. Teddlie (Eds.), *Handbook of mixed methods in social and behavioral research* (pp. 135–164). Thousand Oaks, CA: Sage.

Messer, L., Steckler, A., & Dignan, M. (1999). Early detection of cervical cancer among Native American women: A qualitative supplement to a quantitative study. *Health Education & Behavior, 26*(4), 547–562.

Milton, J., Watkins, K. E., Studdard, S. S., & Burch, M. (2003). The ever widening gyre: Factors affecting change in adult education graduate programs in the United States. *Adult Education Quarterly, 54*(1), 23–41.

Morgan, D. L. (2007). Paradigms lost and pragmatism regained: Methodological implications of combining qualitative and quantitative methods. *Journal of Mixed Methods Research, 1*(1), 48–76.

Morse, J. M. (1991). Approaches to qualitative-quantitative methodological triangulation. *Nursing Research, 40,* 120–123.

National Research Council. (2002). *Scientific research in education.* Washington, DC: National Academy Press.

Onwuegbuzie, A. J., & Johnson, R. B. (2006). The validity issue in mixed research. *Research in the Schools, 13*(1), 48–63.

Plano Clark, V. L., Creswell, J. W., Green, D. O., & Shope, R. J. (In press). Mixing quantitative and qualitative approaches: An introduction to emergent mixed methods research. In S. Hesse-Biber (Ed.), *The handbook of emergent methods.* New York: Guilford Press.

Richter, K. (1997). Child care choice in urban Thailand: Qualitative and quantitative evidence of the decision-making process. *Journal of Family Issues, 18*(2), 174–204.

Sale, J. E., Lohfeld, L. H., & Brazil, K. (2002). Revisiting the quantitative-qualitative debate: Implications for mixed-methods research. *Quality & Quantity, 36,* 43–53.

Sandelowski, M. (2003). Tables or tableaux? The challenges of writing and reading mixed methods studies. In A. Tashakkori & C. Teddlie (Eds.), *Handbook of mixed methods in social and behavioral research* (pp. 321–350). Thousand Oaks, CA: Sage.

Stange, K. C. (2004). Multimethod research. *Annals of Family Medicine, 2*(1).

Tashakkori, A., & Creswell, J. W. (2007). The new era of mixed methods [Editorial]. *Journal of Mixed Methods Research, 1*(1), 3–7.

Tashakkori, A., & Teddlie, C. (1998). *Mixed methodology: Combining qualitative and quantitative approaches.* Thousand Oaks, CA: Sage.

Tashakkori, A., & Teddlie, C. (Eds.). (2003a). *Handbook of mixed methods in social and behavioral research.* Thousand Oaks, CA: Sage.

Tashakkori, A., & Teddlie, C. (2003b). The past and future of mixed methods research: From data triangulation to mixed model designs. In A. Tashakkori & C. Teddlie (Eds.), *Handbook of mixed methods in social and behavioral research* (pp. 671–701). Thousand Oaks, CA: Sage.

Teddlie, C., & Yu, F. (2007). Mixed methods sampling: A typology with examples. *Journal of Mixed Methods Research, 1*(1), 77–100.

Thøgersen-Ntoumani, C., & Fox, K. R. (2005). Physical activity and mental well-being typologies in corporate employees: A mixed methods approach. *Work & Stress, 19*(1), 50–67.

Victor, C. R., Ross, F., & Axford, J. (2004). Capturing lay perspectives in a randomized control trial of a health promotion intervention for people with osteoarthritis of the knee. *Journal of Evaluation in Clinical Practice, 10*(1), 63–70.

Way, N., Stauber, H. Y., Nakkula, M. J., & London, P. (1994). Depression and substance use in two divergent high school cultures: A quantitative and qualitative analysis. *Journal of Youth and Adolescence, 23*(3), 331–357.

Author Index

Subject Index

About the Editors

Vicki L. Plano Clark is codirector of the Office of Qualitative and Mixed Methods Research, a service and research unit that provides methodological support for proposal development and funded projects at the University of Nebraska–Lincoln (UNL). She is also a research assistant professor in the Quantitative, Qualitative, and Psychometric Methods program housed in UNL's Department of Educational Psychology. She teaches research methods courses, including foundations of educational research and mixed methods research, and serves as managing editor for the *Journal of Mixed Methods Research*. She specializes in mixed methods research designs and qualitative research and her research interests include the procedural issues that arise when implementing different designs as well as disciplinary contexts for conducting research. She has authored and coauthored more than 25 articles, chapters, and student manuals, including the book *Designing and Conducting Mixed Methods Research* (Sage, 2007, with John W. Creswell). Her writings include methodological discussions as well as empirical studies in the areas of science education, family research, counseling psychology, and family medicine. She served as laboratory manager in UNL's Department of Physics and Astronomy for 12 years, working with the Research in Physics Education Group, and has been a principal investigator on three National Science Foundation projects.

John W. Creswell is the Clifton Institute Endowed Professor at the University of Nebraska–Lincoln, and in this capacity he directs a mixed methods research project studying human resource development within the undergraduate leadership program in education. He is also a professor of Educational Psychology and teaches courses and writes about qualitative methodology and mixed methods research. He has been at the University of Nebraska–Lincoln for 30 years and has authored ten books, many of which focus on research design, qualitative research, and mixed methods research. In addition, he codirects the Office of Qualitative and Mixed Methods Research that provides campus support for scholars incorporating qualitative and mixed methods research into projects for extramural funding. He serves as the coeditor for the new Sage journal, *Journal of Mixed Methods Research*, and he has been an adjunct professor of Family Medicine at the University of Michigan and assisted faculty on topics related to research methodology in the health sciences. He has recently been selected to be a Senior Fulbright Scholar and will be working internationally to encourage social and human science researchers to use mixed methods research. He plays the piano, writes poetry, and actively engages in sports.